# AMERICAN CONSERVATISM

# AMERICAN
# CONSERVATISM

## Reclaiming *an* Intellectual Tradition

### ANDREW J. BACEVICH, EDITOR

THE LIBRARY OF AMERICA

# Contents

*Introduction* by Andrew J. Bacevich          xiii

## FIRST PRINCIPLES: THREE RESPONSES

RUSSELL KIRK
Conservatism Defined        5

WILLIAM F. BUCKLEY, JR.
Notes Toward an Empirical Definition of Conservatism     12

FRANK S. MEYER
The Recrudescent American Conservatism     28

## THE FUNDAMENTALS: TRADITION, RELIGION, MORALITY, AND THE INDIVIDUAL

HENRY ADAMS
The Dynamo and the Virgin (1900)     47

WALTER LIPPMANN
FROM "Journalism and the Higher Law"     57

GEORGE SANTAYANA
Materialism and Idealism in American Life     62

HERBERT HOOVER
FROM *American Individualism*     75

ZORA NEALE HURSTON
How It Feels To Be Colored Me     84

IRVING BABBITT
What I Believe: Rousseau and Religion     89

WILLIAM HENRY CHAMBERLIN
The Choice Before Civilization   104

WHITTAKER CHAMBERS
Foreword in the Form of a Letter to My Children   119

FRANK CHODOROV
The Most Precious Heirloom   140

JOHN COURTNEY MURRAY
E Pluribus Unum: The American Consensus   148

WILLMOORE KENDALL
FROM *The Conservative Affirmation*   163

HARRY V. JAFFA
On the Nature of Civil and Religious Liberty: Reflections
on the Centennial of the Gettysburg Address   188

JOAN DIDION
The Women's Movement   205

ALLAN BLOOM
Our Ignorance   213

ANDREW SULLIVAN
Here Comes the Groom: A (Conservative) Case For Gay
Marriage   228

SHELBY STEELE
Affirmative Action: The Price of Preference   233

RICHARD JOHN NEUHAUS
Can Atheists Be Good Citizens?   244

MICHAEL NOVAK
FROM *The Catholic Ethic and the Spirit of Capitalism*   256

CHRISTOPHER LASCH
The Soul of Man under Secularism   278

GLENN LOURY
Leadership Failure and the Loyalty Trap   291

ANTONIN SCALIA
Dissent in *Obergefell v. Hodges*                                      303

## LIBERTY AND POWER: THE STATE AND THE FREE MARKET

RANDOLPH BOURNE
FROM *The State*                                                      313

ALBERT JAY NOCK
FROM *Our Enemy, The State*                                           337

RICHARD WEAVER
The Great Stereopticon                                               347

JOHN T. FLYNN
FROM *The Road Ahead*                                                364

MILTON FRIEDMAN
Capitalism and Freedom                                               369

IRVING KRISTOL
"When Virtue Loses All Her Loveliness": Some Reflections
    on Capitalism and "the Free Society"                             383

MURRAY ROTHBARD
FROM *For a New Liberty*                                             397

PATRICK DENEEN
Unsustainable Liberalism                                             415

## THE TIES THAT BIND: THE LOCAL AND FAMILIAR

JOHN CROWE RANSOM
Reconstructed but Unregenerate                                       431

ROBERT NISBET
The Loss of Community                                                450

EUGENE GENOVESE
FROM *The Southern Tradition*                                        468

WENDELL BERRY
Local Knowledge in the Age of Information                            481

## THE EXCEPTIONAL NATION: AMERICA AND THE WORLD

THEODORE ROOSEVELT
The Strenuous Life                                              495

HENRY CABOT LODGE
Speech in the U.S. Senate on the League of Nations              506

CHARLES BEARD
Giddy Minds and Foreign Quarrels: An Estimate of
American Foreign Policy                                     534

JAMES BURNHAM
FROM *The Struggle for the World*                               558

ROBERT A. TAFT
FROM *A Foreign Policy for Americans*                           574

REINHOLD NIEBUHR
FROM *The Irony of American History*                            584

RONALD REAGAN
Address to Members of Parliament                               590

WILLIAM PFAFF
FROM *The Irony of Manifest Destiny*                            602

*Sources and Acknowledgments*                                  613
*Index*                                                        617

# Introduction

## By Andrew J. Bacevich

THE MODERN American conservative tradition—roughly dating from the dawn of the twentieth century—emerged in reaction to modernity itself. Modernity meant machines, speed, and radical change—taboos lifted, bonds loosened, and, according to Max Weber, "the disenchantment of the world." It induced, and perhaps required, centralization. States accrued power. Bureaucracies thickened. Banks, corporations, rail systems, and industrial enterprises grew to mammoth proportions. War became more destructive.

Modernity promised liberation and for many did improve the quality of everyday life. Yet it also subjected individuals to immense and only dimly comprehended forces. In exchange for choice, it demanded conformity. Modernity demolished tradition or rendered it irrelevant. What remained of the past might retain interest as artifact but was drained of substantive relevance.

Liberals, progressives, leftists—choose what label you will—have tended to embrace modernity, seeing it, on balance, as a positive force. By comparison, conservatives have typically viewed modernity as a threat, responding to it with a mixture of apprehension, alarm, and horror. This anthology collects in a single volume noteworthy examples of the American conservative critique prompted by the encroachments of modernity.

That said, I am not suggesting that in the long, contentious, at times bitter debate about America's purpose and destiny, proponents of conservatism have necessarily gotten things right. The issues being contested are too complex to allow for reductive judgments of right or wrong, good or bad. Yet in the crisis that has enveloped twenty-first-century America—a crisis made starkly manifest by Donald Trump's election as U.S. president in 2016—conservative principles deserve a second look, even, or especially, from those who bridle at the very use of the term.

Skeptics might respond that Americans today already have more than ample exposure to conservative perspectives, whether coming directly from Trump's White House, from megaphone-wielding House and Senate Republicans, or from outlets such as FoxNews, AM talk radio, and right-wing websites. Yet all of these qualify as conservative only in the sense that blue-chip recruits at a football factory qualify as "student-athletes." Any resemblance to the real article is superficial and manufactured.

Donald Trump is not a conservative. Nor are the leaders of the Republican Party over which Trump presides. Prominent GOP figures such as Kentucky senator Mitch McConnell seem to adhere to no worldview worthy of the name. As for the provocateurs who inhabit the sprawling universe of rightwing media, their principal motive is not to promote genuine conservative values but to rabble-rouse and line their own pockets. Indeed, allowing Trump, McConnell, Sean Hannity, Laura Ingraham, Rush Limbaugh et al. to present themselves as exemplary conservatives testifies to the pervasive corruption of contemporary American political discourse.

So except among the multitudes who sport MAGA hats and look to the likes of Sean, Laura, and Rush for instruction, the conservative brand has of late been badly tarnished and even degraded. As a result, conservatism today has become synonymous with meanness, bigotry, and retrograde attitudes. The contents of this book suggest that this condescending characterization is wildly off the mark.

How did the American conservative tradition acquire a reputation as both noxious and intellectually disreputable? Trumpism provides a convenient but utterly inadequate answer to that question. More important are two related factors that long precede Trump. The first factor is history—or at least the myth-history to which Americans choose to attribute abiding significance. The second is the anti-conservative progressive tradition, whose adherents long ago seized the high ground in American intellectual life and have successfully defended it ever since.

Of course, it is progressives who curate that myth-history and thereby determine the hierarchy of truths that it purportedly yields. Preeminent in determining that hierarchy were two specific events, the one related to politics and the other to America's role in the world. The first was the Great Depression. Then hard on its heels—as much sequel as distinct episode—came World War II.

Broadly speaking, in each case, the analysis and prescriptions offered by leading conservatives proved at least inadequate, where not downright misguided. On the Great Depression, fearing an irreversible expansion of state power, conservatives resisted the conclusion that restoring economic health was going to require large-scale and protracted federal intervention. On World War II, until the attack on Pearl Harbor, many influential conservatives strenuously opposed U.S. entry into the conflict that Nazi Germany had begun and appeared to be winning, fearing a recurrence of the disillusionment that occurred just two decades earlier when the United States, discarding all past precedent, had raised an army to fight in Europe.

Conservatives can no more escape these twin failures of judgment—for so they have been judged ever since—than the ghost of Jacob Marley can shed his chains. Yet concluding that on the two pivotal episodes of the twentieth century the left was right and the right was wrong soon enough gave rise to its own misimpressions and mistakes.

Crediting the New Deal with restoring American prosperity has turned out to be a vast oversimplification, impeding our understanding of the factors that finally brought the Great Depression to an end. In that regard, the global conflagration of another war rather than an array of well-intentioned but sometimes contradictory domestic reforms proved decisive. Worse still, identifying "isolationism" as an abiding temptation to which Americans were susceptible imparted an interventionist tilt in postwar U.S. policy, contributing appreciably to catastrophes such as Vietnam and the 2003 invasion of Iraq. Intent on inoculating the United States from so-called isolationism, the foreign policy establishment fell prey to militarism and ultimately preventive war. Throughout, dissent voiced by conservative intellectuals went largely unheeded.

In the aftermath of World War II, with the liberal ascendency in politics now at its height, liberal thinkers and activists denied even the existence of an intellectually coherent and morally acceptable alternative to their own beliefs. Liberals occupied, indeed owned, the "vital center" of American politics, as the historian and Harvard product Arthur Schlesinger Jr. put it, thereby consigning all others to the ignominious fringes.[1] To the left of this vital center were communists, to the right conservatives. In Schlesinger's construct, both were enemies of freedom: American communists as lackeys of the Soviet Union, conservatives as willing pawns of Big Business.

To the literary critic Lionel Trilling, writing in 1950, the facts of the case were likewise plain to see. Liberalism, he wrote, was "not only the dominant but even the sole intellectual tradition" present on the American scene. Try as he might, Trilling could discern "no conservative or reactionary ideas in general circulation," merely "irritable mental gestures which seem to resemble ideas."[2]

Other members of the eastern academic elite concurred. In an influential book that appeared in 1953, Harvard professor Louis Hartz ruled that "the American community is a liberal community." Conservatism, largely confined to the antebellum South, was beset by "fantastic contradictions" that made it "an alien child in a liberal family, tortured and confused" and doomed to destruction.[3] American politics did not allow for an alternative to liberalism.

The prize-winning historian Richard Hofstadter, who like Trilling taught at Columbia, indicted what he called "the far right wing" for "a categorical folkish dislike of the educated classes and of anything respectable, established, pedigreed, or cultivated."[4] Thus did conservative inclinations invite lampooning.

According to Schlesinger, Trilling, Hartz, Hofstadter, and other members of their exalted but thoroughly unrepresentative community, sincere seekers after enlightenment necessarily look left. As a

---

[1] Arthur M. Schlesinger, Jr., *The Vital Center: The Politics of Freedom* (Boston: Houghton Mifflin, 1949).

[2] Lionel Trilling, *The Liberal Imagination* (New York: Viking, 1950), xv.

[3] Louis Hartz, *The Liberal Tradition in America* (New York: Harcourt, Brace, 1955), 3, 8.

[4] Richard Hofstadter, *Anti-Intellectualism in American Life* (New York: Alfred A. Knopf, 1963), 12, 39.

class, therefore, intellectuals have tended to embrace a progressive outlook, taking for granted the correlation between a liberal orientation and wise, farsighted, or providentially foreordained outcomes. By extension, serious conservative thinkers have tended to languish outside of the mainstream, talking to one another without reaching a larger audience. Indeed, in some quarters, even today, the very phrase "conservative intellectual tradition" carries with it oxymoronic connotations.

Handed down as if from the atop Mount Olympus, or at least from Morningside Heights and Harvard Yard, this verdict seemed incontrovertible—at least it did until Vietnam rolled around and the hegemony of postwar liberalism crumbled with astonishing suddenness. A New Left rose up to deflate Cold War liberalism's pretensions to inevitability and presented conservative intellectuals an unforeseen opportunity to be heard. Yet even before Vietnam and the upheaval of the 1960s, they had begun to challenge their marginalization, if not effectively, at least noisily.

Launching his conservative journal of opinion in 1955, the young journalist William F. Buckley declared that *National Review* "stands athwart history, yelling Stop."[5] As a branding ploy, it was a clever formulation. Yet it was also a bit of journalistic flimflam. The purpose of Buckley's magazine was not to stop history, but to nudge it in a positive direction. Much the same can be said about conservatism itself. Yet such nudging presumes a capacity to distinguish between truth and folly.

Unfortunately, postwar movement conservatives, many of them rallying around Buckley and his upstart magazine, struggled to make that distinction. What little most Americans today know about conservatives after World War II does not make for a flattering or reassuring record. For example, many (including Buckley himself) supported Wisconsin senator Joseph McCarthy in his reckless crusade to purge the U.S. government of communists and fellow travelers.[6] When revolutionaries led by Mao Zedong seized power in Beijing, they insisted

---

[5] William F. Buckley, Jr., "Our Mission Statement," *National Review*, November 19, 1955.
[6] William F. Buckley, Jr., and L. Brent Bozell, *McCarthy and His Enemies* (Chicago: Henry Regnery, 1954).

that the defeated Nationalists, now sequestered on the island of Taiwan, continued to represent the "real" China. Perhaps most egregious were conservative attitudes regarding civil rights, the great moral issue of the day. Sympathizing with white southerners who were resisting efforts to dismantle segregation, many conservatives attributed greater importance to preserving the social status quo than to confronting racial injustice. In all of this, postwar conservatives managed to convey the impression of being ill-tempered, small-minded, devoid of both judgment and compassion, and given on occasion to views that were at least disquieting, if not altogether repellent.

Yet let me suggest that what we have here are examples of self-described conservatives violating genuine conservative precepts. Reprehensible? Yes. Unforgivable? Well, only if promoting eugenics, enacting racist immigration laws, and criminalizing the possession and consumption of alcoholic beverages, as progressives did after World War I, invalidates the basic principles that progressives and liberals hold dear.[7]

To his followers, Jesus had commanded: love God and love your neighbor. Over the course of two millennia, Christians acting in his name proceeded to commit numberless crimes up to and including genocide. Do these crimes nullify Christ's teachings? No, they merely testify to the abiding sinfulness of humankind. So too with American conservatism: it deserves to be judged by the core principles that conservatives have articulated, not by the occasions when those principles have been trampled upon.

The essays that follow explore those principles. Taken collectively, these essays do not comprise anything approximating a seamless whole. Conservatism is more akin to an ethos or a disposition than to a fixed ideology. So the thinkers featured in these pages frequently disagree with one another—much as do progressives, not to mention Marxists, socialists, fascists, anarchists, libertarians, and distributists. Intellectuals tend to be a quarrelsome lot.

Yet their intramural quarrels notwithstanding, most American conservatives, most of the time, subscribe to a common set of propositions

---

[7] Thomas C. Leonard, "Eugenics and Economics in the Progressive Era," *Journal of Economic Perspectives* 19 (Fall 2005): 207–224.

from which to fashion a critique of American politics, policies, and culture and to proffer alternatives. Those propositions have evolved over time—conservatism is anything but static. Yet in the first quarter of the twenty-first century, they have come to center on the following:

- a commitment to individual liberty, tempered by the conviction that true freedom entails more than simply an absence of restraint;
- a belief in limited government, fiscal responsibility, and the rule of law;
- veneration for our cultural inheritance combined with a sense of stewardship for Creation;
- a reluctance to discard or tamper with traditional social arrangements;
- respect for the market as the generator of wealth combined with a wariness of the market's corrosive impact on human values;
- a deep suspicion of utopian promises, rooted in an appreciation of the recalcitrance of history and humankind's recurring susceptibility to hubris.

No doubt my own prejudices inform this brief rendering of conservative tenets. Much the same can be said about the materials included in this anthology. Many readers familiar with what conservatives consider their intellectual canon might have chosen otherwise. So allow me to offer several brief observations regarding the overall scope and contents of the volume.

First, *American Conservatism: Reclaiming an Intellectual Tradition* does not claim to provide a fully comprehensive record of that tradition. Any such attempt would result in a book that would be unwieldy, uneconomical, and probably unreadable. So the selections that follow are just that: selective.

Second, in choosing texts for inclusion, my aim has been to assemble a representative sample of the best American conservative thought drawn from across the modern era, defined as dating from the turn of the twentieth century. I have attempted in particular to recognize once prominent writers, among them Irving Babbitt, Albert Jay Nock, Richard Weaver, who in recent decades may have suffered from neglect. Yet I have also singled out figures such as Patrick Deneen and Andrew Sullivan, who are still in the process of making their contribution to the American conservative tradition.

Third, I have prioritized quality of thought over name recognition. This has resulted in the exclusion of figures who may have figured prominently in the contemporary conservative movement, but who were not original thinkers. Hence, the absence of Phyllis Shlafly, Barry Goldwater, and Patrick Buchanan, among others. Their absence from this volume does not imply disrespect. In political histories of modern American conservatism, each will have an important place. But when it comes to deepening our understanding of the American conservative intellectual tradition, writers such as Whittaker Chambers, Russell Kirk, and Murray Rothbard have left far more important legacies.

Fourth, I have excluded altogether anyone associated with what in the last quarter of the twentieth century became known as neoconservatism. My reasoning is quite simple: While neoconservatives for a time made a considerable impact on the national conversation and even arguably on U.S. foreign policy, they were never genuinely conservative. Neoconservatism is a heresy akin to antinomianism, its adherents declaring themselves unbound by the constraints to which others are obliged to attend. In a volume on American exceptionalism or on the various manifestations of American radicalism, neoconservatives will deserve a place, but not here.

Fifth, and very much in contrast, this anthology includes contributions from individuals who may not have identified themselves as conservatives, but whose work makes them de facto fellow travelers. Whatever the banner under which they marched, they articulated truths that resonate with the American conservative tradition. Charles Beard, Randolph Bourne, Wendell Berry, Christopher Lasch, and Reinhold Niebuhr are examples.

Finally, I ought to acknowledge up front that women and people of color are underrepresented in the table of contents. Joan Didion, Zora Neale Hurston, Glenn Loury, and Shelby Steele are all here. Yet the fact is that until relatively recently, major contributors to American conservative thought have tended to be male and white. To pretend otherwise is to falsify history.

The essays I have collected here may not convert nonbelievers. That is not my purpose. Yet the United States today finds itself at a crossroads. We confront perplexing problems to which there are no glib answers or easy solutions. The questions we face are fundamental: What is the common good? What is the meaning of freedom? What are the responsibilities of citizenship? What is America's proper role in the world?

Most fundamentally, on each of these, we wonder where to look for guidance. My firm conviction is this: to understand how the United States arrived at its present confused and divided straits—and perhaps even to begin navigating back toward less troubled waters—the American conservative tradition offers insights worth considering. I invite readers of this volume to consider that proposition.

*Andrew J. Bacevich*
*Walpole, Massachusetts*
*April 2019*

# AMERICAN CONSERVATISM

# FIRST PRINCIPLES

*Three Responses*

# RUSSELL KIRK

Keeping his distance from the centers of American intellectual life, Russell Amos Kirk (1898–1994) fashioned a multifaceted career as a moral philosopher, social critic, editor, and prolific writer of both fiction and nonfiction. Kirk shared and expounded on the outlook of Edmund Burke, the eighteenth-century Anglo-Irish statesman and political philosopher. Here Kirk, in reflections taken from his introduction to the *Portable Conservative Reader* (1982), offers his version of the principles that define conservatism.

———

## Conservatism Defined

### SUCCINCT DESCRIPTION

"WHAT IS CONSERVATISM?" Abraham Lincoln inquired rhetorically, as he campaigned for the presidency of the United States. "Is it not adherence to the old and tried, against the new and untried?" By that test, the candidate told his audience, Abraham Lincoln was a conservative.

Other definitions have been offered. In Ambrose Bierce's *Devil's Dictionary* one encounters this: "Conservative, *n*. A statesman who is enamored of existing evils, as distinguished from the Liberal, who wishes to replace them with others."

Definition of these words "conservative" and "conservatism" is not easily accomplished. In this anthology we examine a body of opinions, or a set of general political principles, which were enunciated during the French Revolution. These views of society have been more fully developed during the past two centuries; they have exerted a strong influence upon the practical politics and the political speculation of Europe and the Americas.

As a coherent body of political thought, what we call conservatism is a modern development. It is approximately as old as the different body of opinions called liberalism, and some decades older than the ideologies called socialism, communism, and anarchism. The roots of conservative thought, for all that, extend deep into the history of ideas and of social institutions.

In various medieval cities, particularly in Italy, the title of "conservator" was given to guardians of the laws. English justices of the peace originally were styled *custodes pacis*—conservators of the peace. Chaucer, in "The House of Fame," uses the word "conservatif" in its sense of protection and preservation. Jeremy Taylor, in the seventeenth century, wrote that "the Holy Spirit is the great conservative of the new life." The word, in short, implied security—a commendatory word. But not until the third decade of the nineteenth century was the word incorporated into the English lexicon of political controversy.

True, one might trace a continuity of conservative political thought (though not of the word itself) back into the seventeenth century. Lord Falkland, during the English Civil Wars, touched upon the essence of conservative convictions in declaring, "When it is not necessary to change, it is necessary not to change." A rudimentary conservatism may be discerned in colonial America, too, assuming definite form just after the American Revolution in the most successful conservative device, the Constitution of the United States.

For that matter, conservative impulses and interests have existed ever since a civil social order came into being. By analogy, it is possible to speak of Aristophanes as a conservative, or Plato, or Cicero. But in this present volume we have space for conservative beliefs and attitudes only in their modern context. Indeed, the looming bulk of able writing by eminent conservatives requires us to confine ourselves, in this collection, almost wholly to British and American literature.

So we commence with the age of Edmund Burke—the last quarter of the eighteenth century. Modern use of the word "conservatism" implies those principles of social thought and action that are set against radical innovation after the pattern of the French Revolution. Edmund Burke opposed his "moral imagination" to what has been called the "idyllic imagination" of Jean-Jacques Rousseau. From that contest arose what Walter Bagehot called "the conservatism of reflection." Almost by definition, ever since Burke published his *Reflections on the Revolution in France*, the principal conservatives in the Western world have been conscious or unconscious disciples of Burke.

Burke himself did not employ the word "conservative," speaking rather of "preservation"—as in his aphorism "Change is the means of our preservation," or his remark that the able statesman is one who combines with a disposition to preserve an ability to reform. During Burke's own lifetime there existed no sharp demarcation between the words "conservative" and "liberal."

As a term of politics, the word "conservative" arose in France during and just after the Napoleonic era. Philosophical statesmen as varied in opinion and faction as Guizot, Bonald, Maistre, Chateaubriand, and Tocqueville all were influenced by Burke's writings. Seeking for a word to describe a policy of moderation, intended to reconcile the best in the old order with the necessities of the nineteenth century, French political writers hit upon the concept of the *conservateur*, the guardian of the heritage of civilization and of the principles of justice.

From France, this concept passed into England. The editors of *The Quarterly Review*, in 1830, approved "conservative" over "Tory" to describe the British party of order. By the 1840s, the word "conservative" had attained popularity in the United States, being employed with approbation by John C. Calhoun, Daniel Webster, and Orestes Brownson.

Burke's political concepts spread rapidly across Europe, especially in the Germanys and the Austrian system. The European revolutionary movements of 1829–30 and of 1848 caused greater emphasis to be placed upon distinctions among conservatives, liberals, and radicals. Throughout Europe, conservatism came to mean hostility toward the principles of the French Revolution, with its violent leveling innovations; while liberalism increasingly signified sympathy with the revolutionary ideals of liberty, equality, fraternity, and material progress.

Conservatives, especially in Britain, soon found themselves opposing another radicalism than the theories of Rousseau: that is, the radical utilitarianism of Jeremy Bentham, called by John Stuart Mill "the great subversive." Thus the intellectual heirs of Burke, and the conservative interest generally, did battle on two fronts: against the successors of the Jacobins, with their "armed doctrine"; and against the economists of Manchester, with their reliance upon the nexus of cash payment.

Our first necessity here, then, is to endeavor to describe (rather than to define) the conservatives' understanding of society. In recent years the term "conservatism" often has been employed to mean "reactionary" or "obscurantist" or "oldfangled"; it has even been confounded with the economic dogmas of the Manchester School. What does the word really signify?

Strictly speaking, conservatism is not a political system, and certainly not an ideology. In the phrase of H. Stuart Hughes, "Conservatism is the negation of ideology." Instead, conservatism is a way of looking at the civil social order. Although certain general principles held by most conservatives may be described, there exists wide variety in application of these ideas from age to age and country to country. Thus conservative views and parties have existed under monarchical, aristocratic, despotic, and democratic regimes, and in a considerable range of economic systems. The conservatives of Peru, for instance, differ much from those of Australia, say; they may share a preference for the established order of society, these conservatives of the Spanish and of the English heritages; yet the institutions and customs which these conservative factions respectively wish to preserve are by no means identical.

Unlike socialism, anarchism, and even liberalism, then, conservatism offers no universal pattern of politics for adoption everywhere. On the contrary, conservatives reason that social institutions always must differ considerably from nation to nation, since any land's politics must be the product of that country's dominant religion, ancient customs, and historic experience.

Although it is no ideology, conservatism may be apprehended reasonably well by attention to what leading writers and politicians, generally called conservative, have said and done. So this anthology itself is a convenient means for ascertaining what a conservative is. "Conservatism," to put the matter another way, amounts to the consensus of the leading conservative thinkers and actors over the past two centuries. For our present purpose, however, we may set down below several general principles upon which most eminent conservatives in some degree may be said to have agreed implicitly. The following first principles are best discerned in the theoretical and practical politics of British and American conservatives.

First, conservatives generally believe that there exists a transcendent moral order, to which we ought to try to conform the ways of society. A divine tactic, however dimly descried, is at work in human society. Such convictions may take the form of belief in "natural law" or may assume some other expression; but with few exceptions conservatives recognize the need for enduring moral authority. This conviction contrasts strongly with the liberals' utilitarian view of the state (most consistently expressed by Bentham's disciples), and with the radicals' detestation of theological postulates.

Second, conservatives uphold the principle of social continuity. They prefer the devil they know to the devil they don't know. Order and justice and freedom, they believe, are the artificial products of a long and painful social experience, the results of centuries of trial and reflection and sacrifice. Thus the body social is a kind of spiritual corporation, comparable to the church; it may even be called a community of souls. Human society is no machine, to be treated mechanically. The continuity, the lifeblood, of a society must not be interrupted. Burke's reminder of the social necessity for prudent change is in the minds of conservatives. But necessary change, they argue, ought to be gradual and discriminatory, never "unfixing old interests at once." Revolution slices through the arteries of a culture, a cure that kills.

Third, conservatives believe in what may be called the principle of prescription. "The wisdom of our ancestors" is one of the more important phrases in the writings of Burke; presumably Burke derived it from Richard Hooker. Conservatives sense that modern men and women are dwarfs on the shoulders of giants, able to see farther than their ancestors only because of the great stature of those who have preceded us in time. Therefore conservatives very frequently emphasize the importance of "prescription"—that is, of things established by immemorial usage, so "that the mind of man runneth not to the contrary." There exist rights of which the chief sanction is their antiquity—including rights in property, often. Similarly, our morals are prescriptive in great part. Conservatives argue that we are unlikely, we moderns, to make any brave new discoveries in morals or politics or taste. It is perilous to weigh every passing issue on the basis of private judgment and private rationality. "The individual is foolish, but the species is wise," Burke declared. In politics we do well to abide by precedent and precept and even prejudice, for "the great mysterious incorporation of the human race" has acquired habits, customs, and conventions of remote origin which are woven into the fabric of our social being; the innovator, in Santayana's phrase, never knows how near to the taproot of the tree he is hacking.

Fourth, conservatives are guided by their principle of prudence. Burke agrees with Plato that in the statesman, prudence is chief among virtues. Any public measure ought to be judged by its probable long-run consequences, not merely by temporary advantage or popularity. Liberals and radicals, the conservative holds, are imprudent: for they dash at their objectives without giving much heed to the risk of new abuses worse than the evils they hope to sweep away. Human society being complex, remedies cannot be simple if they are to be effective. The conservative declares that he acts only after sufficient reflection, having weighed the consequences. Sudden and slashing reforms are perilous as sudden and slashing surgery. The march of providence is slow; it is the devil who always hurries.

Fifth, conservatives pay attention to the principle of variety. They feel affection for the proliferating intricacy of long-established social institutions and modes of life, as distinguished from the narrowing uniformity and deadening egalitarianism of radical systems. For the preservation of a healthy diversity in any civilization, there must survive orders and classes, differences in material condition, and many sorts of inequality. The only true forms of equality are equality in the Last Judgment and equality before a just court of law; all other attempts at leveling lead, at best, to social stagnation. Society longs for honest and able leadership; and if natural and institutional differences among people are destroyed, presently some tyrant or host of squalid oligarchs will create new forms of inequality. Similarly, conservatives uphold the institution of private property as productive of human variety: without private property, liberty is reduced and culture is impoverished.

Sixth, conservatives are chastened by their principle of imperfect-ibility. Human nature suffers irremediably from certain faults, the conservatives know. Man being imperfect, no perfect social order ever can be created. Because of human restlessness, mankind would grow rebellious under any utopian domination, and would break out once more in violent discontent—or else expire of boredom. To aim for utopia is to end in disaster, the conservative says: we are not made for perfect things. All that we reasonably can expect is a tolerably ordered, just, and free society, in which some evils, maladjustments, and suffering continue to lurk. By proper attention to prudent reform, we may preserve and improve this tolerable order. But if the old institutional and moral safeguards of a nation are forgotten, then the anarchic impulses in man break loose: "the ceremony of innocence is drowned."

Such are six of the major premises of what Walter Bagehot, a century ago, called "reflective conservatism." To have set down some principal convictions of conservative thinkers, in the fashion above, may be misleading: for conservative thought is not a body of immutable secular dogmas. Our purpose here has been broad description, not fixed definition. If one requires a single sentence—why, let it be said that for the conservative, politics is the art of the possible, not the art of the ideal.

Edmund Burke turned to first principles in politics only with reluctance, believing that "metaphysical" politicians let loose dreadful mischief by attempting to govern nations according to abstract notions. Conservatives have believed, following Burke, that general principles always must be tempered, in any particular circumstances, by what Burke called expedience, or prudence; for particular circumstances vary infinitely, and every nation must observe its traditions and historical experience—which should take precedence over universal notions drawn up in some quiet study. Yet Burke did not abjure general ideas; he distinguished between "abstraction" (or *a priori* notions divorced from a nation's history and necessities) and "principle" (or sound general ideas derived from a knowledge of human nature and of the past). Principles are necessary to a statesman, but they must be applied discreetly and with infinite caution to the workaday world. The preceding six conservative principles, therefore, are to be taken as a rough catalog of the general assumptions of conservatives, and not as a tidy system of doctrines for governing a state.

*1982*

# WILLIAM F. BUCKLEY, JR.

The best-known conservative in twentieth-century American public life, William F. Buckley, Jr. (1925–2008), forged an unmistakable persona out of his patrician upbringing, committed Catholicism, political savvy, and stylish wit to become a celebrated journalist. He founded and edited the journal *National Review*, wrote a widely read syndicated column, and for over three decades hosted the weekly program *Firing Line* on public television, dashing off best-selling novels as a sideline. In this essay, Buckley assesses the several strains of modern American conservatism.

———

## Notes Toward an Empirical Definition of Conservatism

I AM asked most frequently by members of the lecture audience two questions, to neither of which have I ever given a satisfactory answer. The first is asked by those who share my feelings that the world is in crisis and the nation imperiled: "What can I do?" I don't know, and I haven't the stomach to contrive an aphoristic answer. The second question, asked alike by friendly and hostile listeners, is "What is conservatism?" Sometimes the questioner, guarding against the windy evasiveness one comes to expect from lecturers, will add, "preferably in one sentence." On which occasions I have replied, "I could not give you a definition of Christianity in one sentence, but that does not mean that Christianity is undefinable." Usually that disposes of the hopes of those who wish a neatly packaged definition of conservatism which they can stow away in their mind alongside (or replacing?) the definitions of astrology, necrophilia, xenophobia, and philistinism. Those who are obstinate I punish by giving, with a straight face, Professor Richard Weaver's definition of conservatism as "a paradigm of essences towards which the phenomenology of the world is in continuing approximation"—as noble an effort as any I have ever read. The point is, of course, that we are at the stage dangerously close to mere verbal gambiting. I have never failed, I am saying, to dissatisfy an audience that asks the meaning of conservatism.

Yet I feel I know, if not what conservatism is, at least who a conservative is. I confess that I know who is a conservative less surely than I know who is a liberal. Blindfold me, spin me about like a top, and I will walk up to the single liberal in the room without zig or zag and find him even if he is hiding behind the flowerpot. I am tempted to try to develop an equally sure nose for the conservative, but I am deterred by the knowledge that conservatives, under the stress of our times, have had to invite all kinds of people into their ranks to help with the job at hand, and the natural courtesy of the conservative causes him to treat such people not as janissaries, but as equals; and so, empirically, it becomes difficult to see behind the khaki, to know surely whether that is a conservative over there doing what needs to be done, or a radical, or merely a noisemaker, or pyrotechnician, since our ragtag army sometimes moves together in surprising uniformity, and there are exhilarating moments when everyone's eye is right. I have, after all, sometimes wondered whether I am myself a true conservative. I feel I qualify spiritually and philosophically; but temperamentally I am not of the breed, and so I need to ask myself, among so many other things, how much it matters how one is temperamentally. There are other confusions.

Whittaker Chambers, for instance, distinguished sharply between a conservative and a "man of the Right." "You," he wrote me on resigning as an editor of *National Review*, "are a conservative, and I know no one with better title to the word. But I am not one, never was. I call myself, on those occasions when I cannot avoid answering the question, a man of the Right." I reflected on that letter, needless to say, as would you if you were the editor of a journal from which Whittaker Chambers had just withdrawn, and remarked an interesting thing: In the five-year history of the journal, Chambers was the only man to resign from its senior board of editors explicitly because he felt he could no longer move within its ideological compass; and yet he never wrote a piece for us (or in the last dozen years of his life, that I know of, for anyone else) that was out of harmony with the thrust of *National Review*'s position.

Oh, yes, people withdraw, and write and denounce you, and swear green grass will never grow over your grave on account of this or that offensive article or editorial or book review; but these losses are merely a part of the human attrition of outspoken journalism. They prove nothing, in our case, that has anything to do with ideological fecklessness. What I am saying is that notwithstanding the difficulty in formulating the conservative position, and the high degree of skepticism from our critics before *National Review* was launched, *National Review*'s position was, I believe, instantly intelligible, from the very first issue. *He would probably say that anyway* (the skeptic will charge), *it being in his and the journal's interest to say so*. But I make that statement on empirical grounds, as I propose to make others in this essay on the meaning of conservatism, which will reason a posteriori from the facts to the theory—and which will be based exclusively on my own experiences as editor of *National Review*. Since I shall not allude to it again, let me say so now unambiguously: This essay is about the experiences of *National Review* and their bearing, by the processes of exclusion, on a workable definition of contemporary conservatism. I do not by any means suggest that *National Review* is the only functioning alembic of modern conservatism, merely that it is the only one whose experiences I can relate with any authority, and that its experiences may be interesting enough to be worth telling.

Roughly the same group of men, representing the same vested interests in certain ideas and attitudes, continue to be the major participants in *National Review*. The magazine found instantly and expanded an audience which seemed intuitively to grant and to understand the happy eclecticism of the magazine's guiding ideas; whereas the critics, whose delighted line at the beginning was one or another variant on the theme: "This country needs a conservative magazine, and having read *National Review*, we *still* say what this country needs is a conservative magazine," finally, except for the bitter-enders, gave up, and began to refer to *National Review* as, plain and simple, a "conservative journal." Others, who, as I say, refuse to give up, will continue to refer to it only after a ritualistic pejorative: "the McCarthyite *National Review*," "the ultrarightist *National Review*," etc. But it being so that in language the governing law is usage, it is by now predictable that those who feel Peter Viereck or Clinton Rossiter or Walter Lippmann are the true architects of American conservatism are bound to enter the ranks of eccentricity, like the right-wing gentlemen who, because they continue to insist on referring to themselves as "liberals," have difficulty communicating with the rest of the world, which for two generations now has understood liberalism to mean something else, beginning, roughly, from the time Santayana observed that the only thing the modern liberal is concerned to liberate is man from his marriage contract.

Since this is to be an empirical probe, based, apologetically, on my personal experience as editor of *National Review*, I shall speak about people and ideas with which *National Review* has had trouble making common cause. In 1957, Whittaker Chambers reviewed *Atlas Shrugged*, the novel by Miss Ayn Rand wherein she explicates the philosophy of "Objectivism," which is what she has chosen to call her creed. Man of the right, or conservative, or whatever you wish to call him, Chambers did in fact read Miss Rand right out of the conservative movement. He did so by pointing out that her philosophy is in fact another kind of materialism—not the dialectical materialism of Marx, but the materialism of technocracy, of the relentless self-server, who lives for himself and for absolutely no one else, whose concern for others is explainable merely as an intellectualized recognition of the relationship between helping others and helping oneself. Religion is the first enemy of the Objectivist, and after religion, the state—respectively, the "mysticism of the mind," and "the mysticism of the muscle." "Randian Man," wrote Chambers, "like Marxian Man, is made the center of a godless world."

Her exclusion from the conservative community was, I am sure, in part the result of her desiccated philosophy's conclusive incompatibility with the conservative's emphasis on transcendence, intellectual and moral; but also there is the incongruity of tone, that hard, schematic, implacable, unyielding dogmatism that is in itself intrinsically objectionable, whether it comes from the mouth of Ehrenburg, or Savonarola, or Ayn Rand. Chambers knew that specific ideologies come and go, but that rhetorical totalism is always in the air, searching for the ideologue-on-the-make; and so he said things about Miss

Rand's tone of voice which, I would hazard the guess, if they were true of anyone else's voice, would tend to make it *eo ipso* unacceptable for the conservative. ". . . the book's [*Atlas Shrugged*'s] dictatorial tone . . . ," Chambers wrote, "is its most striking feature. Out of a lifetime of reading, I can recall no other book in which a tone of overriding arrogance was so implacably sustained. Its shrillness is without reprieve. Its dogmatism is without appeal . . . resistance to the Message cannot be tolerated because disagreement can never be merely honest, prudent, or just humanly fallible. Dissent from revelation so final can only be willfully wicked. There are ways of dealing with such wickedness, and, in fact, right reason itself enjoins them. From almost any page of *Atlas Shrugged*, a voice can be heard, from painful necessity, commanding: 'To a gas chamber—go!' The same inflexibly self-righteous stance results, too, in odd extravagances of inflection and gesture. . . . At first we try to tell ourselves that these are just lapses, that this mind has, somehow, mislaid the discriminating knack that most of us pray will warn us in time of the difference between what is effective and firm, and what is wildly grotesque and excessive. Soon we suspect something worse. We suspect that this mind finds, precisely in extravagance, some exalting merit; feels a surging release of power and passion precisely in smashing up the house."*

As if according to a script, Miss Rand's followers jumped *National Review* and Chambers in language that crossed the *i*'s and dotted the *t*'s of Mr. Chambers' point. (It is not fair to hold the leader responsible for the excesses of the disciples, but this reaction from Miss Rand's followers, never repudiated by Miss Rand, suggested that her own intolerance is easily communicable to other Objectivists.) One correspondent, denouncing him, referred to "Mr. Chambers's 'break' with Communism"; a lady confessed that on reading his review she thought she had "mistakenly picked up the *Daily Worker*"; another accused him of "lies, smears, and cowardly misrepresentations"; still another saw in him the "mind-blanking, life-hating, unreasoning, less-than-human being which Miss Rand proves undeniably is the cause of the tragic situation the world now faces. . . ."; and summing up, one Objectivist

---

* Several years later, a graduate student in philosophy, a disciple of Hayek, von Mises, and Friedman, analyzed the thought and rhetoric of Miss Rand and came to similar conclusions. Miss Rand, he wrote (*2*, References), is "hate blinded," "suffocating in her invective."

wrote that "Chambers the Christian communist is far more dangerous than Chambers the Russian spy."

What the experience proved, it seems to me, beyond the unacceptability of Miss Rand's ideas and rhetoric, is that no conservative cosmology whose every star and planet are given in a master book of coordinates is very likely to sweep American conservatives off their feet. They are enough conservative and anti-ideological to resist totally closed systems, those systems that do not provide for deep and continuing mysteries. They may be pro-ideology and unconservative enough to resist such asseverations as that conservatism is merely "an attitude of mind." But I predict on the basis of a long association with American conservatives that there isn't anybody around scribbling into his sacred book a series of all-fulfilling formulas which will serve the conservatives as an Apostles' Creed. Miss Rand tried it, and *because* she tried it, she compounded the failure of her ideas. She will have to go down as an Objectivist; my guess is she will go down as an entertaining novelist.

The conservative's distrust of the state, so richly earned by it, raises inevitably the question: How far can one go? This side, the answer is, of anarchism—that should be obvious enough. But one man's anarchism is another man's statism. *National Review*, while fully intending to save the nation, probably will never define to the majority's satisfaction what are the tolerable limits of the state's activity; and we never expected to do so. But we got into the problem, as so often is the case, not by going forward to meet it, but by backing up against it.

There exists a small breed of men whose passionate distrust for the state has developed into a theology of sorts, or at least into a demonology, to which they adhere as devotedly as any religious fanatic ever attempted to adhere to the will of the Lord. I do not feel contempt for the endeavor of either type. It is intellectually stimulating to discuss alternatives to municipalized streets, as it is to speculate on whether God's wishes would best be served if we ordered fried or scrambled eggs for breakfast on this particular morning. But conservatives must concern themselves not only with ideals, but with matters of public policy, and I mean by that something more than the commonplace that one must maneuver within the limits of conceivable action. We can read and take pleasure in the recluse's tortured deliberations on what will benefit his soul. Bernanos' *Diary of a Country Priest* was not only a masterpiece; it was also a best seller. And we can read with more than mere amusement Dr. Murray Rothbard's suggestion that lighthouses be sold to private tenants who will chase down the beam in speedboats and collect a dollar from the storm-tossed ship whose path it illuminates. Chesterton reminds us that many dogmas are liberating because, however much damage they do when abused, it cannot compare with the damage that might have been done had whole peoples not felt their inhibiting influence. If our society seriously wondered whether or not to denationalize the lighthouses, it would not wonder at all whether to nationalize the medical profession.

But Dr. Rothbard and his merry anarchists wish to *live* their fanatical antistatism, and the result is a collision between the basic policies they urge and those urged by conservatives who recognize that the state sometimes is, and is today as never before, the necessary instrument of our proximate deliverance. The defensive war in which we are engaged cannot be prosecuted by voluntary associations of soldiers and scientists and diplomats and strategists, and when this obtrusive fact enters into the reckonings of our state haters, the majority, sighing, yield to reality, whereas the small minority, obsessed by their antagonism to the state, would refuse to give it even the powers necessary to safeguard the community. Dr. Rothbard and a few others have spoken harshly of *National Review*'s complacency before the twentieth-century state in all matters that have to do with anti-Communism, reading their litanies about the necessity for refusing at any cost to countenance the growth of the state. Thus, for instance, Ronald Hamowy of the University of Chicago complained about *National Review* in 1961: ". . . the Conservative movement has been straying far under *National Review* guidance . . . leading true believers in freedom and individual liberty down a disastrous path . . . and that in so doing they are causing the Right increasingly to betray its own traditions and principles."*

---

* On behalf of the magazine I answered in part (*1*, References), "The American conservative needs to proceed within the knowledge of history and anthropology and psychology; we must live in our time. We must indeed continue to cherish our resentments against such institutionalized impositions upon our prerogatives as social security. But we must not, if we are to pass for sane in this tormented world, equate as problems of equal urgency, the repeal of the social security law, and the containment of the Soviet threat. The problems of assigning priorities to

And Henry Hazlitt (3, References), reviewing Dr. Rothbard's magnum opus, *Man, Economy, and State*, enthusiastically for *National Review*, paused to comment, sadly, on the author's "extreme apriorism," citing for instance, Dr. Rothbard's opinion that libel and slander ought not to be illegalized and that even blackmail, "'would not be illegal in the free society. For blackmail is the receipt of money in exchange for the service of not publicizing certain information about the other person. No violence or threat of violence to person or property is involved.' . . . when Rothbard wanders out of the strictly economic realm, in which his scholarship is so rich and his reasoning so rigorous, he is misled by his epistemological doctrine of 'extreme apriorism' into trying to substitute his own instant jurisprudence for the common law principles built up through generations of human experience."

"Extreme apriorism"—a generic bull's-eye. If *National Review*'s experience is central to the growth of contemporary conservatism, extreme apriorists will find it difficult to work with conservatives except as occasional volunteers helping to storm specific objectives. They will not be a part of the standing army, rejecting as they do the burden of reality in the name of a virginal antistatism. I repeat I do not deplore their influence intellectually, and tactically, I worry not at all. The succubi of Communism are quite numerous enough and eloquent enough to be counted upon to put their ghastly presences forward in effective protest against the marriage of any but the most incurable solipsist to a set of abstractionist doctrines the acceptance of which would mean the end of any human liberty. The virgins have wriggled themselves outside the mainstream of American conservatism. Mr. Hamowy, offering himself up grandly as a symbol of the undefiled conservative, has joined the Committee for a Sane Nuclear Policy.

We ran into the John Birch Society—or, more precisely, into Robert Welch. Mr. Welch's position is very well known. Scrubbed down, it is that one may reliably infer subjective motivation from objective result—*e.g.*, if the West loses as much ground as demonstrably it has lost during the past twenty years to the enemy, it can only be because

the two objectives is not merely a problem of intellectual discrimination, but of moral balance."

those who made policy for the West were the enemy's agents. The ultima ratio of this position was the public disclosure—any 300-page document sent to hundreds of people can only be called an act of public disclosure—that Dwight Eisenhower is a Communist. (To which the most perfect retort—was it Russell Kirk's?—was not so much analytical as artistic: "Eisenhower isn't a Communist—he is a golfer.")

In criticizing Mr. Welch, we did not move into a hard philosophical front, as for instance we did in our criticisms of Miss Rand or of the neoanarchists. Rather, we moved into an organizational axiom, the conservative equivalent of the leftists' *pas d'ennemi à gauche*. The position has not, however, been rigorously explicated or applied. Mr. Welch makes his own exclusions; for instance, Gerald L. K. Smith, who, although it is a fact that he favors a number of reforms in domestic and foreign policy which coincide with those favored by Mr. Welch (and by *National Review*), is dismissed as a man with an *idée fixe*, namely, the role of Perfidious Jew in modern society. Many right-wingers (and many liberals, and all Communists) believe in a *deus ex machina*. Only introduce the single tax, and our problems will wither away, say the followers of Henry George. . . . Only expose the Jew, and the international conspiracy will be broken, say others. . . . Only abolish the income tax, and all will be well. . . . Forget everything else, but restore the gold standard. . . . Abolish compulsory taxation, and we all shall be free. . . . They are called nostrum peddlers by some; certainly they are obsessed. Because whatever virtue there is in what they call for—and some of their proposals strike me as highly desirable, others as mischievous—no one of them can begin to do the whole job, which continues to wait on the successful completion of the objectives of the Committee to Abolish Original Sin. Many such persons, because inadequate emphasis is given to their pandemic insight, the linchpin of social reconstruction, are dissatisfied with *National Review*. Others react more vehemently; our failure to highlight *their* solution has the effect of distracting from its unique relevance and so works positively against the day when the great illumination will show us the only road forward. Accordingly, *National Review* is, in their eyes, worse than merely useless.

The defenders of Mr. Welch who are also severe critics of *National Review* are not by any means all of them addicts of the conspiracy school. They do belong, however inconsistently, to the school that says that we all must work together—as a general proposition, sound advice. Lenin distinguished between the sin of sectarianism, from which suffer all those who refuse to cooperate with anyone who does not share their entire position, right down to the dependent clauses, and the sin of opportunism, the weakness of those who are completely indiscriminate about their political associates.

The majority of those who broke with *National Review* as the result of our criticisms of Mr. Welch believe themselves to have done so in protest against *National Review*'s sectarianism. In fact, I believe their resentment was primarily personal. They were distressed by an attack on a man who had ingratiated himself with them and toward whom their loyalty hardened in proportion as he was attacked. So their bitterness ran over, and now it is widely whispered that *National Review* has been "infiltrated."

The questions we faced at *National Review* were two. The first, to which the answer was always plainly no, was whether Mr. Welch's views on public affairs were sound. The editors knew from empirical experience that they were not. Enough of us had recently been to college, or were in continuing touch with academic circles, to know that the approaches to the internal security and to foreign relations that have been practiced by successive administrations after the Second World War are endorsed by the overwhelming majority of the intellectuals of this country; therefore, any assumption that only a Communist (or a fool, as Mr. Welch allowed) could oppose the House Committee on Un-American Activities or favor aid to Poland and Yugoslavia must deductively mean that the nation's academies are staffed, primarily, by Communists (or fools). It is not merely common sense that rejects this assumption, but a familiarity with the intricate argumentation of almost the entire intellectual class (who, of course, are not fools, at least not in the sense in which Mr. Welch uses the word).

The second question then arose—whether it was necessary explicitly to reject Mr. Welch's position as an unrealistic mode of thought. And that had to be answered by asking whether at the margin it contributed or not to the enlightenment of right-wing thought. The answer was not as obvious as one might suppose. Ironically, the assumptions that reason will prevail and that logic and truth are self-evident—the constituent assumptions of those who believe that that syllogism is correct which says: "(a) We were all-powerful after World War II; (b)

Russia is now as powerful as we are; therefore, (c) we willed the enemy's ascendancy" (the essence of Mr. Welch's methodology)—argued in favor of leaving Mr. Welch alone. Thus might one reason if one believed that the truth will triumph: If Mr. Welch merely succeeds in drawing people's attention, which otherwise would not be drawn, to public events; if he scourges them to read about and think about public affairs, then those same people, though introduced to public concern by Mr. Welch, will by the power of reason reject, upon examination, Mr. Welch's specific counsels and graduate as informed members of the anti-Communist community.

But reason is *not* king (and many of those who have shrunk from Mr. Welch have done so less because on reflection they repudiate his analysis than because public scandal of a kind has in fact attached to discipleship in a movement dominated by a man with a very special set of views which reality rejects). And so it seemed necessary to say what one hoped would be obvious: that the Welch view is wrong, that it is wrong irrespective of the many personal virtues of Mr. Welch, and wrong irrespective of how many people who were otherwise politically lethargic are now, thanks to Mr. Welch, politically animated.

In consequence, *National Review* was widely criticized for "throwing mud" at Mr. Welch (a curious way to refer to the act of throwing at Mr. Welch his own statements!), and some battle lines (and some necks) were broken. Whom did we actually alienate? A body of people? A body of thought? I tend to think not, for the reasons I have suggested. If we alienated those who genuinely believe in *pas d'ennemi à droite*, why do these same people (a) applaud Mr. Welch's exclusion of Gerald L. K. Smith and (b) proceed to exclude us? It is no answer to the latter inconsistency that the penalty of turning against someone on your side excuses the turning away against the offender, and Mr. Welch, while failing to be consistent on point (a) above, *was* consistent in respect of (b). Aside from a few aggrieved references to *National Review*'s naïveté and to the Communists' need of conservative front men to implement the smear of the John Birch Society, he has not, as yet anyway, excluded us from the anti-Communist community.

For this reason I tend to put down our encounter with Mr. Welch as having no philosophical significance in an empirical probe of the contemporary locus of American conservatism—except to the extent it can be said that *National Review* rejects as out of this world what goes by the name of the conspiracy view of history. Most of the followers of Mr. Welch who broke with *National Review* on account of our criticisms of him showed themselves, by the inconsistency of their own position, to have acted primarily out of personal pique—to which, of course, they are entitled. But perhaps this brief analysis is relevant, if only because it explains why *National Review*'s noisiest collision did not serve any great purpose in the construction of an empirical definition of conservatism.

A few years ago, Max Eastman, the author and poet, wrote sadly that he must withdraw from the masthead of *National Review*:

> There are too many things in the magazine—and they go too deep—that directly attack or casually side-swipe my most earnest passions and convictions. It was an error in the first place to think that, because of political agreements, I could collaborate formally with a publication whose basic view of life and the universe I regard as primitive and superstitious. That cosmic, or chasmic, difference between us has always troubled me, as I've told you, but lately its political implications have been drawn in ways that I can't be tolerant of. Your own statement in the issue of October 11 (1958) that Father Halton labored "for the recognition of God's right to His place in Heaven" invited me into a world where neither my mind nor my imagination could find rest. That much I could take, although with a shudder, but when you added that "the struggle for the world is a struggle, essentially, by those who mean to unseat Him," you voiced a political opinion that I think is totally and dangerously wrong. . . .

Can you be a conservative and believe in God? Obviously. Can you be a conservative and not believe in God? This is an empirical essay, and so the answer is, as obviously, yes. Can you be a conservative and despise God and feel contempt for those who believe in Him? I would say no. True, Max Eastman is the only man who has left the masthead of *National Review* in protest against its proreligious sympathies, but it does not follow that this deed was eccentric; he, after all, was probably the only man on *National Review* with that old-time hostility to religion associated with evangelical atheism—with, *e.g.*, the names of Theodore Dreiser, Upton Sinclair, Henry Mencken, and Clarence

Darrow, old friends of Eastman. If one dismisses religion as intellectually contemptible, it becomes difficult to identify oneself wholly with a movement in which religion plays a vital role, and so the moment came when Max Eastman felt he had to go, even while finding it difficult to answer the concluding observation I made to him: "I continue to feel that you would be at a total loss as to what to criticize in the society the editors of *National Review* would, had they the influence, establish in America."

Mr. Eastman's resignation brought up an interesting point, to which I also addressed myself in my reply to my old friend:

> You require that I take your letter seriously, and having done so I must reproach myself rather than you. For if it is true that you cannot collaborate formally with me, then it must be true that I ought not to have collaborated formally with you; for I should hate for you to think that the distance between atheism and Christianity is any greater than the distance between Christianity and atheism. And so if you are correct, that our coadjutorship was incongruous, I as editor of *National Review* should have been the first to spot it and to act on it. All the more because my faith imposes upon me more rigorous standards of association than yours does.

I know now, several years after this exchange of letters, that my point here, that the reciprocal of the proposition that a God hater cannot associate fully with a Christian, is not in fact true—for reasons that are not easy to set down without running the risk of spiritual or philosophical condescension. But the risk must be taken, and I choose the Christian, rather than the secular, formulation because, although the latter can very handily be made—see, *e.g.*, Eric Voegelin's "On Readiness to Rational Discussion" (*4*, References)—it remains debatable in a way that the Christian formulation does not. The reason why Christian conservatives can associate with atheists is that we hold that, above all, faith is a gift and that, therefore, there is no accounting for the bad fortune that has beset those who do not believe or the good fortune that has befallen those who do. The proreligious conservative can therefore welcome the atheist as a full-fledged member of the conservative community even while feeling that at the very bottom the roots do not interlace, so that the sustenance that gives a special bloom to Christian conservatism fails to reach the purely secularist conservatism. Voegelin will argue on purely intellectual grounds, taking as his lesson the Socratic proposition that virtue can be taught, but only if virtue is defined as knowledge. Socrates defined knowledge, Voegelin reminds us, as transcendental cognition, as, in fact, requiring the ability to see far enough into the nature of things to recognize transcendence, a view he elaborated in *Protagoras*.

The God hater, as distinguished from the agnostic (who says merely that he doesn't know) or simply the habitual atheist (who knows there is no God, but doesn't much care about those who disagree), regards those who believe in or tolerate religion as afflicted with short-circuited vision. Their faith is the result of a combination of intellectual defectiveness and psychological immaturity, leading to the use of analysis and rhetoric which Max Eastman "can't be tolerant of."

The agnostic can shrug his shoulders about the whole thing, caring not whether, in his time, the conflict between the proreligious and antireligious elements within conservatism will be resolved. There are so many other things to do than think about God. "Are you anything?" a lady flightily addressed at her dinner table a scholarly gentleman and firebrand conservative who has always managed to nudge aside questions or deflect conversational trends that seemed to be moving into hard confrontations involving religion. He smiled. "Well, I guess I'm not *nothing*," and the conversation went on pleasantly. Max Eastman *is* nothing, and he can no more resist the opportunity to incant his nonbelief than the holy priest can resist the opportunity to proselyte—and so the tension.

Mr. Eastman, like many other programmatic conservatives, bases his defense of freedom primarily on pragmatic grounds. Erik von Kuehnelt-Leddihn once remarked that Friedrich Hayek's *Constitution of Liberty* seemed to be saying that if freedom were not pragmatically productive, there would be no *reason* for freedom. It appears to be the consensus of religious-minded conservatives that ordered freedom is desirable quite apart from its demonstrable usefulness as the basis for economic and political association. The research of the past ten years on Edmund Burke appears to have liberated him from the social pragmatists by whom he had been co-opted. Not to stray too far from the rules of this discussion, I cite a poll a few years ago which showed that the great majority of the readers of *National Review* think of themselves formally as religious people, suggesting that conservatism, of the kind I write about, is planted in a religious view of man.

Though as I say only a single resignation has been addressed to *National Review* in protest against the magazine's friendliness to religion, there is much latent discord, particularly in the academic world, centering on the question, not so much of whether God exists or doesn't (only a few continue to explore the question consciously, let alone conscientiously, and most of the latter are thought of as infra dig), but on the extent to which it is proper to show toward religion the intellectual disdain the God haters believe it deserves. Russell Kirk was not allowed inside the faculty of a major university in which, *mirabile dictu*, conservatives (specifically, libertarians) had control of the social science department—because of his "religiosity." The Mt. Pelerin Society, an organization of free-market economists and laymen, has recently trembled over inscrutable personal issues; but somewhere there, in the interstices of the strife, is a hardening of positions relating to religious differences, or differences over religion, which sometimes express themselves, loosely, in arguments between "traditionalist" and "libertarian" conservatism.

Though I say the antagonism is here and there seen to be hardening, I have grounds for optimism, based not merely on *National Review's* own amiable experiences with all but the most dedicated atheists, but on the conviction that the hideousness of a science-centered age has resulted in a stimulation of religious scholarship and of all of those other impulses, intellectual and spiritual, by which man is constantly confounding the most recent wave of neoterics who insist that man is merely a pandemoniac conjunction of ethereal gases. The atheists have not got around to answering Huxley's self-critical confession that neither he nor his followers had succeeded in showing how you can deduce Hamlet from the molecular structure of a mutton chop.

I repeat what is obvious: These are merely notes, though not I hope altogether desultory, suggesting where are some of the confines of contemporary conservatism, the walls it runs up against and bounces away from. The freeway remains large, large enough to accommodate very different players with highly different prejudices and techniques. The differences are now tonal, now substantive, but they do not appear to be choking each other off. The symbiosis may yet be a general consensus on the proper balance between freedom, order, and tradition.

## REFERENCES

1. Buckley, W. F., Jr., "'National Review': Criticism and Reply," *New Individualism Review*, 1961, *1* (No. 3), 3–11.
2. Goldberg, B., "Ayn Rand's 'For the New Intellectual,'" *New Individualism Review*, 1961, *1* (No. 3), 17–24.
3. Hazlitt, H. "The Economics of Freedom," *National Review*, 1962, *13*, 231–232.
4. Voegelin, E., "On Readiness to Rational Discussion," in A. Hunold (ed.), *Freedom and Serfdom: An Anthology of Western Thought* (Dordrecht, Holland), 1961, pp. 269–284.

*1963*

# FRANK S. MEYER

In the twentieth century, more than a few conservative American intellectuals underwent a conversion of sorts, beginning on the left, typically as committed Marxists, before moving sharply and irrevocably to the right. Frank Straus Meyer (1909–1972) was one such figure. A longtime contributor to *National Review*, Meyer is credited with developing the concept of "fusionism," an attempt to bridge the divide between conservatism's libertarian and traditionalist tendencies. For Meyer, the varieties of American conservatism possessed several core strands: a commitment to an objective moral order, an emphasis on the primacy of the individual, a hostility to utopianism, a conviction that state power should be limited, a devotion to the Constitution, and a belief in the superiority of Western civilization.

---

# The Recrudescent American
# Conservatism

TO DISCUSS conservatism in America today is to plunge at once into a tangle of semantic confusion. There have been over the past few years so many efforts, often contradictory, by scholars and journalists to extract its essence and define its limits that it is with some diffidence I begin with a rather broad and general description of it.

## WHAT IS CONSERVATISM?

This essay is concerned with conservatism as a political, social, and intellectual movement—not as a cast of mind or a temperamental inclination. Such a movement arises historically when the unity and balance of a civilization are riven by revolutionary transformations of previously accepted norms of polity, society, and thought. Conservatism comes into being at such times as a movement of consciousness and action directed to recovering the tradition of the civilization. This is the essence of conservatism in all the forms it has assumed in different civilizations and under differing circumstances. Sometimes such movements are successful, as was the return to the basic Egyptian tradition after Akhnaton's revolutionary changes. Sometimes they succeed for a time and modulate the later and further development of the revolutionary impulse, as did the Stuart restoration after the English Revolution or the European consolidation after the French Revolution and the reign of Napoleon. Sometimes they have little effect on contemporary events but make a tremendous impress on the consciousness of the future, as did the Platonic reaction to the destruction of the balance of civilization brought about by the overweening power drive of the Athenian *demos* and the arrogance of Sophistical thought. Sometimes they fail utterly and are lost to history.

In any era the problem of conservatism is to find the way to restore the tradition of the civilization and apply it in a new situation. But this means that conservatism is by its nature two-sided. It must at one and the same time be reactionary and presentist. It cannot content itself with appealing to the past. The very circumstances that call conscious conservatism into being create an irrevocable break with the past. The many complex aspects of the past had been held together in tension by the unity of the civilization, but that particular tension, that particular suspension in unity, can never be recreated after a revolutionary break. To attempt to recreate it would be pure unthinking reaction (what Toynbee calls "archaism") and would be bound to fail; nor could reaction truly restore the civilizational tradition to the recovery of which it was putatively directed. But while conservatism is not and cannot be naked reaction, neither can its concern with contemporary circumstances lead it, if it is to be true to itself, to be content with the status quo, with serving as a "moderating wing" within the existing situation. For that situation is the result of a revolutionary break with the tradition of the civilization, and to "conserve" it is to accept the radical break with tradition that conservatism exists to overcome.

Conservatism is neither reactionary yearning for an irremediably lost past, nor is it trimming acquiescence in the consolidation of revolution, just so long as the revolution does not go too fast. It is a vindication and renewal of the civilizational tradition as the fundament upon which reason must build to solve the problems of the present.

It is absurd, therefore, because one conservative voice in one period showed an underlying hostility to reason, to maintain, as is today so often done, that Edmund Burke's attitude to reason is an essential element of any definition of conservatism. True, no conservatism can accept utopian reliance upon the limited reason of one generation (or one school of thought within that generation), which ignores the tradition and builds upon arrogant confidence in its own experience and its own ratiocination. But conservatism is not antirational. It demands only that reason operate upon the foundation of the tradition of civilization, that is, upon the basis of the accumulated reason, experience, and wisdom of past generations.

From the point of view of contemporary "liberalism," it may indeed seem that any respect for tradition is *ipso facto* a repudiation of reason. This, together with the fact that Burke was to a rather strong degree critical of the claims of reason and that nineteenth-century conservatism often tended in this direction, may explain, although it does not excuse, the insistence of author after author in late years (most recently, Morton Auerbach in *The Conservative Illusion*) that no movement has a right to the name of conservatism if it does not fit the mould of an exaggerated representation of Burke's views on reason. Thus, the contemporary American conservative movement has consistently been denied its right to its self-chosen name by critics who refuse to think deeply and seriously about the phenomenon of conservatism, preferring instead facilely to derive their criteria from ephemeral characteristics of the conservatism of a single historical period.

It is easy to show that contemporary American conservatism is not a replica of nineteenth-century European conservatism; while it resembles it in some ways, it also resembles nineteenth-century European liberalism in its commitment to individual liberty and its corollary commitment to an economic system free of state control. But to show that, is to prove nothing of substance. The claim of the contemporary American conservative movement to the title conservative does not have to be based upon a surface resemblance to the conservative movement of another period. It is based upon its commitment to the recovery of a tradition, the tradition of Western civilization and the American republic, which has been subjected to a revolutionary attack in the years since 1932.

## THE CONTEMPORARY AMERICAN CONSERVATIVE MOVEMENT

The crystallization in the past dozen years or so of an American conservative movement is a delayed reaction to the revolutionary transformation of America that began with the election of Franklin Roosevelt in 1932. That revolution itself has been a gentler, more humane, bloodless expression in the United States of the revolutionary wave that has swept the globe in the twentieth century. Its grimmest, most total manifestations have been the phenomena of Communism and Nazism. In rather peculiar forms in late years it has expressed itself in the so-called nationalism typified by Nasser, Nkrumah, and Sukarno; in Western Europe it has taken the forms of the socialism of England or that of Scandinavia. Everywhere, however open or masked, it represents an aggrandizement of the power of the state over the lives of individual persons. Always that aggrandizement is cloaked in a rhetoric and a program putatively directed to and putatively concerned for "the masses."

The American form of that revolution differs little in its essentials from Western European democratic socialism. But, by an ironic twist of history, it has become known as "liberalism." (So far is it removed from the classical liberalism of the nineteenth century, with its overriding concern for individual liberty and the limitation of the state, that clear discourse requires some mode of differentiation; and I shall for that reason, through the rest of this essay, refer to this twentieth-century American development as Liberalism, with a capital L, reserving the lower case for classical liberalism.) Ushered in by the election of 1932, so thorough was the victory of Liberalism that for many years afterwards it met with no concerted resistance, in either the intellectual or political spheres. True, islands of resistance remained—in the Congress, in the academy among some economists and humanists, in the business community, in the endemic mass anti-Communist movement among some strata of the population. These were rear-guard actions; by and large, Liberalism dominated the scene, took over the academy and the organs of mass communication, controlled the Democratic Party, and slowly penetrated the Republican Party. Only in recent years has there emerged a consistent, cohesive conservative movement, based upon a broad consensus of principle, challenging Liberal assumptions and Liberal power all along the line.

In its origins intellectual, centered among a group of writers gathered around the old *Freeman*, *National Review*, and *Modern Age*, it early attracted a following and guided a movement in the universities, and gradually focused and channelized the energies of disparate tendencies opposed to Liberalism through all levels of society. During the past half dozen years its attitude began to be reflected among a group of young Congressmen, and it fully emerged on the national political arena with the nomination of Barry Goldwater at the Republican convention of 1964.

There are many strands in this movement, many trends in its thought. In particular there exists within it a continuing tension between an emphasis on tradition and virtue, on the one hand, and an emphasis on reason and freedom, on the other. I will return to this problem a little farther on; here I want only to say that these differences are but differences of emphasis, creating tensions within a common consensus, not sharply opposed points of view.

That common consensus of the contemporary American conservative movement is reflected, with different degrees of understanding and depth, at every level of the conservative movement. It underlies the principled positions of the consciously intellectual as it does the empirical positions and the instinctive attitudes of the political activists and the broad constituency of that movement. The clearest way, I think, to summarize this consensus is to contrast it with the beliefs and attitudes of the Liberal world outlook, which sets the prevailing tone of contemporary American society. I do not assert that every conservative accepts every one of the articles of belief I am positing or that every Liberal accepts each of the contrasted articles. But I would maintain that the attitudes adumbrated do reflect the overall opposition between the conservative and Liberal consensuses in America today.

*A.*   Conservatism assumes the existence of an objective moral order based upon ontological foundations. Whether or not individual conservatives hold theistic views—and a large majority of them do—this outlook is derived from a theistic tradition. The essential point, however, is that the conservative looks at political and social questions with the assumption that there are objective standards for human conduct and criteria for the judgment of theories and institutions, which it is the duty of human beings to understand as thoroughly as they are able and to which it is their duty to approximate their actions.

The Liberal position, in contrast, is essentially operational and instrumental. As the conservative's world is, in Richard Weaver's phrase, a world of essences to be approximated, the Liberal's world is a world of problems to be solved. Hence, the conservative's concern with such questions of essence as individual liberty and civilizational tradition. Hence, the Liberal's concern with modes and operations, such as democracy (a mode or means of government which implies that what is morally right is what fifty per cent plus one think is right), or progress (a concept that derives norms from the operation of historical events, establishing as the good the direction in which events have been moving and seem presently to be moving).

*B.*   Within the limits of an objective moral order, the primary reference of conservative political and social thought and action is to the individual person. There may be among some conservatives a greater emphasis upon freedom and rights, as among others a greater emphasis upon duties and responsibilities; but whichever the emphasis, conservative thought is shot through and through with concern for the person. It is deeply suspicious of theories and policies based upon the collectivities that are the political reference points of Liberalism— "minorities," "labor," "the people." There may be tension between those conservatives who stress individual freedom and those who stress community as a fabric of individual rights and responsibilities, but both reject the ideological hypostasization of associations of human beings into entities and the collectivist politics based upon it.

*C.*   The cast of American conservative thought is profoundly antiutopian. While it recognizes the continuing historical certainty of change and the necessity of basic principle being expressed under different circumstances in different ways, and while it strives always for the improvement of human institutions and the human condition, it rejects absolutely the idea that society or men generally are perfectible. In particular, it is perennially suspicious of the utopian approach that attempts to *design* society and the lives of human beings, whether in the light of abstract rationalist ideas or operational engineering concepts. It therefore rejects the entire Liberal *mystique* of "planning," which, no matter how humanitarian the motives of the planners, perforce treats human beings as faceless units to be arranged and disposed according to a design conceived by the planner. Rather, the conservative puts his confidence in the free functioning of the energies of free persons, individually and in voluntary cooperation.

*D.*   It is on the basis of these last two points—concern for the individual person and rejection of utopian design—that the contemporary American conservative attitude to the state arises. For the state, which has the ultimate power of enforcement of its dictates, is the necessary implement for successful Liberal planning and for effective control of the lives of individual human beings. Conservatives may vary on the degree to which the power of the state should be limited, but they are agreed upon the principle of limitation and upon the firmest opposition to the Liberal concept of the state as the engine for the fixing of ideological blueprints upon the citizenry. There is much difference among them on the manner and mode in which the state should be limited, but in opposition to the prevailing Liberal tendency to call upon it to act in every area of human life, from automation to social relations, they are firmly united upon the principle of limitation.

*E.*   Similarly, American conservatives are opposed to state control of the economy, in all its Liberal manifestations, whether direct or indirect. They stand for a free economic system, for two reasons. In the first place, they believe that the modern state is politically so strong, even without controls over the economy, that it concentrates power to a degree that is incompatible with the freedom of its citizens. When to that power is added control over the economy, such massive power is created that the last defenses against the state becoming a monstrous Leviathan begin to crack. Second—though this is subsidiary in the conservative outlook to the danger to freedom—conservatives in general believe, on the basis of classical and neoclassical economic theory, that a free economy is much more productive of material wealth than an economy controlled directly or indirectly by the state.

*F.*   American conservatism derives from these positions its firm support of the Constitution of the United States as originally conceived—to achieve the protection of individual liberty in an ordered society by limiting the power of government. Recognizing the many different partial outlooks that went into its inception, adoption, and execution, the conservative holds that the result was a constitutional structure concerned simultaneously with limiting the power of the individual states and of the federal government, and of the tripartite elements in both—through the careful construction of a tension of separate powers, in which ultimate sovereignty rested in no single part, but in the tension itself. Conservatives believe that this conception was the closest that human beings have come to establishing a polity which gives the possibility of maintaining at one and the same time individual liberty, underlying norms of law, and necessary public order. Against the Liberal endeavor to establish sovereignty, nominally in the democratic majority, actually in the executive branch of a national government, they strive to re-establish a federal system of strictly divided powers, so far as government itself is concerned, and to repulse the encroachment of government, federal or state, over the economy and the individual lives of citizens.

*G.*   In their devotion to Western civilization and their unashamed and unself-conscious American patriotism, conservatives see Communism as an armed and messianic threat to the very existence of Western civilization and the United States. They believe that our entire foreign and military policy must be based upon recognition of this reality. As opposed to the vague internationalism and the wishful thinking about Communist "mellowing" or the value of the United Nations that characterize Liberal thought and action, they see the defense of the West and the United States as the overriding imperative of public policy.

It is difficult to summarize in a short space the consensus of a variegated and living movement, especially when it is by its very nature opposed to ideology. I have attempted, however, to give here the best description of the contemporary American conservative movement that I have been able to derive from observation and experience. In confirmation of my summary, I would present from the actual political life of the conservative movement a statement which I think bears me out. It is the Statement of Principles of the American Conservative Union, founded in December, 1964, with the aim of coordinating and guiding American conservatism. I believe it states in brief compass the position I have been endeavoring to analyze, and as a practical political document shows the essential congruity of conservative thought with that analysis.

The American Conservative Union holds firm the truth that all men are endowed by their Creator with unalienable rights. To a world floundering in philosophical anarchy, we therefore commend a transcendent moral order against which all human institutions, in every commonwealth, may confidently be judged.

We believe that government is meant to serve men: by securing their rights under a rule of law that dispenses justice equally to all; and in times of danger by marshalling the might of the commonwealth against its enemies.

We remark the inherent tendency of government to tyranny. The prudent commonwealth will therefore labor tirelessly, by means agreeable to its peculiar genius and traditions, to limit and disperse the power of government. No task should be confided to a higher authority that can be performed at a subsidiary level; and whatever the people can do for themselves should not be confided to government at all.

We believe that the Constitution of the United States is the ideal charter for governing the American commonwealth. The checks and balances that distribute the power of our national authority, and the principle of federalism that reserves to the states or to the people all power not confided to the national authority, are the cornerstones of every freedom enjoyed in this commonwealth. To their integrity we pledge a jealous defense.

We have learned that man's liberty, no less than his material interests, is promoted by an economic system based on private property and directed by a free, competitive market. Such a system not only enlarges the scope of individual choice but by dispersing economic decisions provides a further bulwark against the concentration of political power. And no other system can assure comparable living standards and growth. As against the encroachments of the welfare state, we propose a state of welfare achieved by free, collaborative endeavor.

Today the American commonwealth, as well as the civilization that illuminated it, are mortally threatened by the global Communist revolution. We hold that permanent co-existence with Communism is neither honorable nor desirable nor possible. Communism would enslave the world by any means expedient to that end. We deem no sacrifice too great to avoid that fate. We would parry the enemy's thrusts—but more: by maintaining American military superiority and exerting relentless pressure against the Communist empire, we would advance the frontiers of freedom.

## TRADITIONALIST AND LIBERTARIAN EMPHASES WITHIN THE CONSERVATIVE MOVEMENT

There is, then, a consensus that gives the contemporary American conservative movement unity. As I argued at the beginning of this essay, it is a consensus that reflects a legitimate conservative outlook, in the sense that conservatism properly considered is not confined to the limited doctrines of the conservatism of any given historical period, but represents the effort to refresh and renew the tradition of a civilization and a nation in response to a radical challenge to that tradition. Nevertheless, although there is a conservative consensus today, there are stresses and strains within it, reflecting the differing emphases partially derived from variant strands of the tradition. Most of these stresses and strains within the conservative movement center around one fundamental clash of emphasis, that between what can be called the "traditionalist" and the "libertarian" elements within it.

The specifically American form of the Western tradition, which is the source and inspiration of contemporary American conservatism, is the consensus established by the Founding Fathers and incorporated in the constitutional settlement. While it is true that something of the tension between the traditionalist and libertarian emphases exists throughout the Western tradition and therefore exists within that consensual settlement, it had always been and remained at the time of the establishment of the Republic precisely that—a tension *within* a basic civilizational consensus. It is from that integrated foundation that the over-all consensus of the American conservatism of today is built. To some degree therefore the traditionalist-libertarian opposition within it is directly derived from its source. But many of the characteristics of that opposition, characteristics often threatening the maintenance of consensus, are derived from a very different source, from the naturalization in the United States, during this century and the last part of the nineteenth century, of the nineteenth-century conflict between European conservatism and European liberalism. This is historically ironic because that European conflict was the aftermath of the French Revolution, and neither that revolution nor the system which it overthrew had relevance for the American situation. By the same token, the positions of European liberalism and European conservatism of the nineteenth century are also irrelevant here.

The philosophical position upon which the American constitutional settlement was based had already brought into a common synthesis concepts which were placed in radical opposition by the European conservative-liberal struggle: a respect for the tradition together with a respect for reason, the acceptance of the authority of an organic moral order together with a fierce concern for the freedom of the individual person. That synthesis is neither liberal nor conservative in the nineteenth-century sense. Efforts of writers like Louis Hartz to maintain that it is essentially "liberal" either in the nineteenth-century European sense or the twentieth-century American sense are based on a misunderstanding of the Constitutional consensus—as well as being historically anachronistic; and this is also true of those who would equate that consensus with the point of view of nineteenth-century European conservatism.

Nineteenth-century conservatism defended values based upon a fundamental moral order and the authority of tradition, standing firmly against the corrosive attack of utilitarianism, positivism, and scientism. But it did not recognize as a truth corollary to its defense of moral values that acceptance by individual persons of the moral authority of objective standards of the good must be voluntary; when it is a mere surface acceptance imposed by external power, it is without meaning or content. Nineteenth-century conservatism was all too willing to substitute for the authority of the good the authoritarianism of human rulers, and to support an authoritarian political and social structure.

Nineteenth-century liberalism, on the other hand, stood firmly for the freedom of the individual person and, in defense of that freedom, developed the doctrine and practice of limited state power and the free economy. But as it did so, it corroded by its utilitarianism belief in an objective moral order as the foundation of respect for the value and integrity of the individual person and therefore the only firm foundation of individual freedom.

The traditionalist and the libertarian within the contemporary American conservative movement are not heirs of European conservatism and European liberalism because they draw from a common source in the American constitutional consensus. Their common effort to achieve a philosophical clarification of the consensus that underlies their actual empirical participation in the single movement is, however, impeded by the importation of the nineteenth-century European categories. As I have written elsewhere:

> The misunderstandings between libertarian and traditionalist are to a considerable degree the result of a failure to understand the differing levels on which classical liberal doctrines are valid and invalid. Although the classical liberal forgot—and the contemporary libertarian conservative sometimes tends to forget—that in the *moral* realm freedom is only a means whereby men can pursue their proper end, which is virtue, he did understand that in the *political* realm freedom is the primary end. If, with Acton, we "take the establishment of liberty for the realization of moral duties to be the end of civil society," the traditionalist conservative of today, living in an age when liberty is the last thought of our political mentors, has little cause to reject the contributions to the understanding of liberty of the classical liberals, however corrupted their understanding of the ends of liberty. Their error lay largely in the confusion of the temporal with the transcendent. They could not distinguish between the *authoritarianism* with which men and institutions suppress the freedom of men, and the *authority* of God and truth.[1]

The divergent emphases of traditionalist and libertarian are, however, gradually being resolved in the life of the American conservative movement. Several factors contribute to this resolution: common action in the political struggle against Liberalism; a conscious return to a study of the founding tradition of the Republic; and a deepening of contemporary conservative thought itself.

---

[1] "Freedom, Tradition, Conservatism" in *What Is Conservatism?*, ed. Frank S. Meyer (New York: Holt, Rinehart and Winston, Inc., 1964), pp. 15–16.

## PROBLEMS OF THE AMERICAN
## CONSERVATIVE MOVEMENT

The deepening of conservative thought, however, is only at its beginnings. This is understandable, because in the dozen years or so that
this conscious conservative movement has been in existence, its first
intellectual task has been to fight for recognition as a legitimate position in an intellectual climate of conformity to Liberal norms. A movement striving to gather its forces in a hostile environment will quite
naturally tend in the first instance to concentrate upon the simple
statement and restatement of its basic principles, and upon elaborating
those principles only insofar as it is necessary to sustain a critique of
the principles and practices against which the movement is arrayed.
When, following such a primary period of constitution, the intellectual sector of such a movement finds itself rather suddenly and
somewhat unexpectedly involved in a serious political development
like the Goldwater surge of 1960 to 1964, there arises an overwhelming
temptation to turn aside from further development of fundamental
thought and occupy itself with practical political questions of skills
and techniques. It is true that the skills and techniques of political
organization are essential to the success of a political movement, and
that conservatives have only recently begun to cultivate them; but
they are only auxiliaries for a movement which, by its nature, stands
for nothing less than a radical transformation of the consciousness of
an age.

This is what the contemporary American conservative movement
exists to do. It has no other excuse for being. Concentration on
method, without greater emphasis on transforming consciousness,
could lead only to practical political rivalry with Liberalism on its
own grounds. Such a development of conservatism would end by
making it a right-wing of the Liberal consensus, not a challenge to
its essence. The conservative movement in coming into being has set
itself a greater and much more difficult task: to appeal to the civilizational instincts and beliefs that it feels survive half-smothered in the
American people. But this cannot be done except upon the basis of
a broad and profound development of the conservative world view.

That task is complex. Although, simply stated, the world view of
conservatism is the world view of Western civilization, conservatism

in a revolutionary age cannot be content with pious repetition of a series of received opinions. Too much has been shattered for it to be possible ever merely to return to the forms and modes of the past. Conservatism needs to be more than preservative; its function is to restore, and to do so by creating new forms and modes to express, in contemporary circumstances, the essential content of Western civilization. To do this it cannot confine itself to a broad attack upon established Liberalism. It has to meet the pretensions of Liberalism area by area and point by point at the level that *conservative* pretensions to be the heirs of Western civilization demand. This requires nothing less than a critical appraisal of the corpus of the intellectual activity of the twentieth century, with the aim of applying ageless principles to it and thereby deepening those principles.

This is a task of which conservative scholars are becoming more and more aware. Nor would I want to give the impression that a good deal of work in this direction has not already been done. I emphasize the task, however, because upon a serious endeavor to fulfill it depends the growth to maturity of the American conservative movement.

Another problem corollary to this one, or more accurately derivative from it, confronts conservatism on a more immediate practical level. What I am referring to is the translation of conservative principles into specific alternatives to the accepted Liberal public policies. The weakness here is one of execution, a weakness which could be characteristic of any young and fresh movement and is not generically a conservative weakness. There is, however, a difficulty in overcoming it that derives from the underlying political stance of conservatism as compared with the stance of Liberalism, and from the tone of approach to social and political problems that prevails today because of the influence of Liberalism. Liberalism finds in every social situation problems to be collectively solved by planned action, usually action involving the use of the power of government. Conservatism considers some of these situations natural manifestations of the human spirit and not "problems" to be solved at all; others it recognizes as situations that can be improved, but only by time and the working of free human energies individually or in voluntary association; above all, it considers the greatest social and political problem the increasing provenance and power of the state and therefore considers a further increase of that provenance and power a greater evil than the specific evils against which the state is called into action.

Since regnant Liberalism creates an atmosphere in which positive solutions to every conceivable problem are demanded, to be "negative" is the greatest of sins. But if conservatism is to be true to its vision, a large portion of its program will be negative insofar as proposing governmental action to remedy social situations is concerned. It will propose the limitation of government in order to free the energies of citizens to go about remedying these situations in their several ways as they see best. In the Liberal atmosphere this can easily be made to sound callous, hard-hearted, uncaring. But to maintain that hardships, deprivations, social imbalances are not properly or effectively solved by state action is not to deny their existence. Rather it is to call upon the imaginative exercise of voluntary altruistic effort to restore a widespread sense of responsibility for social well-being and to guard against the moral degradation of citizens as direct clients of the state or as indirect petitioners for community largesse.

Some examples of what can be done may be seen in the recent work of the Foundation for Voluntary Welfare, headed by Richard C. Cornuelle. It has already brought to completion one project and begun another, each of which is directed to the remedy of social situations through voluntary effort. The United Student Aid Funds has already been established through the agency of the Foundation for Voluntary Welfare, with the assistance of bankers, businessmen, and administrators, to preempt a large part of the field of loans to students, which would otherwise have become an additional activity of expanding government. Mr. Cornuelle's next project is to take Marion County, Indiana, as a pilot community and there to enlist all available private resources in an all-out attempt to eliminate hard-core unemployment in that county.

This is conservative action of a kind which cannot be incorporated in a neat "positive program" for the political arena (similarly, the enormous constructive thrust of private industry, which we have come to take for granted, does not lend itself to neat political packaging). But such action could and would be multiplied a thousandfold if a conservatively directed citizenry ceased to look to government and if the corollary shrinkage of government left in the hands of the citizens resources now taxed from them to support government programs.

But even when the charge of callousness to human distress is countered, the charge of negativity still remains. The only answer conservatives can make to this charge, unless they wish to descend to unprincipled demagogy, is to show that a positive program for the preservation of freedom and the expansion of human energies requires a series of negative programs directed towards the dismantling of smothering governmental activities. Such a program can be effectively presented only if it analyzes compellingly and specifically the actuality of government activities area by area; otherwise, no matter how generally correct the criticism, it gives the impression of being merely destructive criticism. It is here that the conservative movement still lacks fully adequate programmatic development. It needs studies, such as those of Martin Anderson on urban renewal, of Arnold W. Green on governmental programs for the young, the old, for recreation, for automation, or of Roger A. Freeman on federal aid to education, in every field where Liberalism invokes state action. And further, it needs to develop means of effectively transmitting the conclusions of such studies to the electorate. Only in a few areas, such as national defense or the handling of crime, where government is the natural organ for positive action, can conservative programs be intrinsically "positive." Here, too, a great deal more development of general conservative positions is needed.

Such specification of a conservative program, negative or positive, is as necessary as the deepening and enriching of conservative thought on a higher level, which I discussed earlier. Until it is done, the statement of sharp conservative principle, which obviously demands deep-going change in the existing situation, can sound like irresponsible radicalism. If it is not backed up by a sober, specific, and conservatively restrained program of gradually phased transformation, the considered conservative position on limited government and resistance to Communism is in danger of being translated into such nightmares as the immediate cutting off of every Social Security check or the instigation of nuclear war against the Soviet Union.

Both in fundamental thought and in practical programmatics, the present need of the American conservative movement is to intensify its development. Its essential principles are clear; they constitute a doctrine that is truly conservative in that it is directed towards the recovery of the civilizational tradition. Its future depends upon its ability to deepen its understanding of those principles and achieve full maturity.

*1965*

# THE FUNDAMENTALS

*Tradition, Religion, Morality, and the Individual*

# HENRY ADAMS

The grandson and great-grandson of U.S. presidents, Henry Adams (1838–1918) found his vocation as a historian, novelist, and acute observer of the contemporary scene. In this essay, a chapter from his memoir *The Education of Henry Adams*, he contemplates the implications of technological progress.

———

## The Dynamo and the Virgin (1900)

UNTIL THE Great Exposition of 1900 closed its doors in November, Adams haunted it, aching to absorb knowledge, and helpless to find it. He would have liked to know how much of it could have been grasped by the best informed man in the world. While he was thus meditating chaos, Langley came by, and showed it to him. At Langley's behest, the Exhibition dropped its superfluous rags and stripped itself to the skin, for Langley knew what to study, and why, and how; while Adams might as well have stood outside in the night, staring at the Milky Way. Yet Langley said nothing new, and taught nothing that one might not have learned from Lord Bacon, three hundred years before; but though one should have known the Advancement of Science as well as one knew the Comedy of Errors, the literary knowledge counted for nothing until some teacher should show how to apply it. Bacon took a vast deal of trouble in teaching King James I and his subjects, American or other, towards the year 1620, that true science was the development or economy of forces; yet an elderly American in 1900 knew neither the formula nor the forces; or even so much as to say to himself that his historical business in the Exposition

47

concerned only the economies or developments of force since 1893, when he began the study at Chicago.

Nothing in education is so astonishing as the amount of ignorance it accumulates in the form of inert facts. Adams had looked at most of the accumulations of art in the storehouses called Art Museums; yet he did not know how to look at the art-exhibits of 1900. He had studied Karl Marx and his doctrines of history with profound attention, yet he could not apply them at Paris. Langley, with the ease of a great master of experiment, threw out of the field every exhibit that did not reveal a new application of force, and naturally threw out, to begin with, almost the whole art-exhibit. Equally, he ignored almost the whole industrial exhibit. He led his pupil directly to the forces. His chief interest was in new motors to make his air-ship feasible, and he taught Adams the astonishing complexities of the new Daimler motor, and of the automobile, which, since 1893, had become a night-mare at a hundred kilometres an hour, almost as destructive as the electric tram which was only ten years older; and threatening to become as terrible as the locomotive steam-engine itself, which was almost exactly Adams's own age.

Then he showed his scholar the great hall of dynamos, and explained how little he knew about electricity or force of any kind, even of his own special sun, which spouted heat in inconceivable volume, but which, as far as he knew, might spout less or more, at any time, for all the certainty he felt in it. To him, the dynamo itself was but an ingenious channel for conveying somewhere the heat latent in a few tons of poor coal hidden in a dirty engine-house carefully kept out of sight; but to Adams the dynamo became a symbol of infinity. As he grew accustomed to the great gallery of machines, he began to feel the forty-foot dynamos as a moral force, much as the early Christians felt the Cross. The planet itself seemed less impressive, in its old-fashioned, deliberate, annual or daily revolution, than this huge wheel, revolving within arm's-length at some vertiginous speed, and barely murmuring,—scarcely humming an audible warning to stand a hair's-breadth further for respect of power,—while it would not wake the baby lying close against its frame. Before the end, one began to pray to it; inherited instinct taught the natural expression of man before silent and infinite force. Among the thousand symbols of ultimate energy, the dynamo was not so human as some, but it was the most expressive.

Yet the dynamo, next to the steam-engine, was the most familiar of exhibits. For Adams's objects its value lay chiefly in its occult mechanism. Between the dynamo in the gallery of machines and the engine-house outside, the break of continuity amounted to abysmal fracture for a historian's objects. No more relation could he discover between the steam and the electric current than between the Cross and the cathedral. The forces were interchangeable if not reversible, but he could see only an absolute *fiat* in electricity as in faith. Langley could not help him. Indeed, Langley seemed to be worried by the same trouble, for he constantly repeated that the new forces were anarchical, and especially that he was not responsible for the new rays, that were little short of parricidal in their wicked spirit towards science. His own rays, with which he had doubled the solar spectrum, were altogether harmless and beneficent; but Radium denied its God,—or, what was to Langley the same thing, denied the truths of his Science. The force was wholly new.

A historian who asked only to learn enough to be as futile as Langley or Kelvin, made rapid progress under this teaching, and mixed himself up in the tangle of ideas until he achieved a sort of Paradise of ignorance vastly consoling to his fatigued senses. He wrapped himself in vibrations and rays which were new, and he would have hugged Marconi and Branly had he met them, as he hugged the dynamo; while he lost his arithmetic in trying to figure out the equation between the discoveries and the economies of force. The economies, like the discoveries, were absolute, supersensual, occult; incapable of expression in horse-power. What mathematical equivalent could he suggest as the value of a Branly coherer? Frozen air, or the electric furnace had some scale of measurement, no doubt, if somebody could invent a thermometer adequate to the purpose; but X-rays had played no part whatever in man's consciousness, and the atom itself had figured only as a fiction of thought. In these seven years man had translated himself into a new universe which had no common scale of measurement with the old. He had entered a supersensual world, in which he could measure nothing except by chance collisions of movements imperceptible to his senses, perhaps even imperceptible to his instruments, but perceptible to each other, and so to some known ray at the end of the scale. Langley seemed prepared for anything, even for an indeterminable number of universes interfused,—physics stark mad in metaphysics.

Historians undertake to arrange sequences,—called stories, or histories,—assuming in silence a relation of cause and effect. These assumptions, hidden in the depths of dusty libraries, have been astounding, but commonly unconscious and childlike; so much so, that if any captious critic were to drag them to light, historians would probably reply, with one voice, that they had never supposed themselves required to know what they were talking about. Adams, for one, had toiled in vain to find out what he meant. He had even published a dozen volumes of American history for no other purpose than to satisfy himself whether, by the severest process of stating, with the least possible comment, such facts as seemed sure, in such order as seemed rigorously consequent, he could fix for a familiar moment a necessary sequence of human movement. The result had satisfied him as little as at Harvard College. Where he saw sequence, other men saw something quite different, and no one saw the same unit of measure. He cared little about his experiments and less about his statesmen, who seemed to him quite as ignorant as himself and, as a rule, no more honest; but he insisted on a relation of sequence, and if he could not reach it by one method, he would try as many methods as science knew. Satisfied that the sequence of men led to nothing and that the sequence of their society could lead no further, while the mere sequence of time was artificial, and the sequence of thought was chaos, he turned at last to the sequence of force; and thus it happened that, after ten years' pursuit, he found himself lying in the Gallery of Machines at the Great Exposition of 1900, with his historical neck broken by the sudden irruption of force totally new.

Since no one else showed much concern, an elderly person without other cares, had no need to betray alarm. The year 1900 was not the first to upset schoolmasters. Copernicus and Galileo had broken many professorial necks about 1600; Columbus had stood the world on its head towards 1500; but the nearest approach to the revolution of 1900 was that of 310, when Constantine set up the Cross. The rays that Langley disowned, as well as those which he fathered, were occult, supersensual, irrational; they were a revelation of mysterious energy like that of the Cross; they were what, in terms of mediæval science, were called immediate modes of the divine substance.

The historian was thus reduced to his last resources. Clearly if he was bound to reduce all these forces to a common value, this common value could have no measure but that of their attraction on his own mind. He must treat them as they had been felt; as convertible, reversible, interchangeable attractions on thought. He made up his mind to venture it; he would risk translating rays into faith. Such a reversible process would vastly amuse a chemist, but the chemist could not deny that he, or some of his fellow physicists, could feel the force of both. When Adams was a boy in Boston, the best chemist in the place had probably never heard of Venus except by way of scandal, or of the Virgin except as idolatry; neither had he heard of dynamos or automobiles or radium; yet his mind was ready to feel the force of all, though the rays were unborn and the women were dead.

Here opened another totally new education, which promised to be by far the most hazardous of all. The knife-edge along which he must crawl, like Sir Lancelot in the twelfth century, divided two kingdoms of force which had nothing in common but attraction. They were as different as a magnet is from gravitation, supposing one knew what a magnet was, or gravitation, or love. The force of the Virgin was still felt at Lourdes, and seemed to be as potent as X-rays; but in America neither Venus nor Virgin ever had value as force;—at most as sentiment. No American had ever been truly afraid of either.

This problem in dynamics gravely perplexed an American historian. The Woman had once been supreme; in France she still seemed potent, not merely as a sentiment but as a force; why was she unknown in America? for evidently America was ashamed of her, and she was ashamed of herself, otherwise they would not have strewn fig-leaves so profusely all over her. When she was a true force, she was ignorant of fig-leaves, but the monthly-magazine-made American female had not a feature that would have been recognised by Adam. The trait was notorious, and often humorous, but anyone brought up among Puritans knew that sex was sin. In any previous age, sex was strength. Neither art nor beauty was needed. Everyone, even among Puritans, knew that neither Diana of the Ephesians nor any of the oriental Goddesses was worshipped for her beauty. She was Goddess because of her force; she was the animated dynamo; she was reproduction—the greatest and most mysterious of all energies; all she needed was to be fecund. Singularly enough, not one of Adams's many schools of education had ever drawn his attention to the opening lines of Lucretius, though they were perhaps the finest in all Latin literature, where the poet invoked Venus exactly as Dante invoked the Virgin:

> Quae quoniam rerum naturam *sola* gubernas.

The Venus of Epicurean philosophy survived in the Virgin of the Schools:—

> Donna, sei tanto grande, e tanto vali,
> Che qual vuol grazia, e a te non ricorre,
> Sua disianza vuol volar senz' ali.

All this was to American thought as though it had never existed. The true American knew something of the facts, but nothing of the feelings; he read the letter but he never felt the law. Before this historical chasm, a mind like that of Adams felt itself helpless; he turned from the Virgin to the Dynamo as though he were a Branly coherer. On one side, at the Louvre and at Chartres, as he knew by the record of work actually done and still before his eyes, was the highest energy ever known to man, the creator of four-fifths of his noblest art, exercising vastly more attraction over the human mind than all the steam-engines and dynamos ever dreamed of; and yet this energy was unknown to the American mind. An American Virgin would never dare command; an American Venus would never dare exist.

The question, which to any plain American of the nineteenth century seemed as remote as it did to Adams, drew him almost violently to study, once it was posed; and on this point Langleys were as useless as though they were Herbert Spencers or dynamos. The idea survived only as art. There one turned as naturally as though the artist were himself a woman. Adams began to ponder, asking himself whether he knew of any American artist who had ever insisted on the power of sex, as every classic had always done; but he could think only of Walt Whitman; Bret Harte, as far as the magazines would let him venture; and one or two painters, for the flesh-tones. All the rest had used sex for sentiment, never for force; to them, Eve was a tender flower, and Herodias an unfeminine horror. American art, like the American language and American education was as far as possible sexless. Society regarded this victory over sex as its greatest triumph, and the historian readily admitted it, since the moral issue, for the moment, did not concern one who was studying the relations of unmoral force. He cared nothing for the sex of the dynamo until he could measure its energy.

Vaguely seeking a clue, he wandered through the art-exhibit, and, in his stroll, stopped almost every day before St. Gaudens' General Sherman, which had been given the central post of honor. St. Gaudens himself was in Paris, putting on the work his usual interminable last touches, and listening to the usual contradictory suggestions of brother sculptors. Of all the American artists who gave to American art whatever life it breathed in the seventies, St. Gaudens was perhaps the most sympathetic, but certainly the most inarticulate. General Grant or Don Cameron had scarcely less instinct of rhetoric than he. All the others,—the Hunts, Richardson, John La Farge, Stanford White,—were exuberant; only St. Gaudens could never discuss or dilate on an emotion, or suggest artistic arguments for giving to his work the forms that he felt. He never laid down the law, or affected the despot, or became brutalised like Whistler by the brutalities of his world. He required no incense; he was no egoist; his simplicity of thought was excessive; he could not imitate, or give any form but his own to the creations of his hand. No one felt more strongly than he the strength of other men, but the idea that they could affect him never stirred an image in his mind.

This summer his health was poor and his spirits were low. For such a temper, Adams was not the best companion, since his own gaiety was not *folle*; but he risked going now and then to the studio on Mont Parnasse to draw him out for a stroll in the Bois de Boulogne, or dinner as pleased his moods, and in return St. Gaudens sometimes let Adams go about in his company.

Once St. Gaudens took him down to Amiens, with a party of Frenchmen, to see the Cathedral. Not until they found themselves actually studying the sculpture of the western portal, did it dawn on Adams's mind that, for his purposes, St. Gaudens on that spot had more interest to him than the cathedral itself. Great men before great monuments express great truths, provided they are not taken too solemnly. Adams never tired of quoting the supreme phrase of his idol Gibbon, before the Gothic Cathedrals:—"I darted a contemptuous look

on the stately monuments of superstition." Even in the footnotes of
his history, Gibbon had never inserted a bit of humor more human
than this, and one would have paid largely for a photograph of the fat
little historian, on the background of Notre Dame of Amiens, trying
to persuade his readers—perhaps himself,—that he was darting a contemptuous look on the stately monument, for which he felt in fact the
respect which every man of his vast study and active mind always feels
before objects worthy of it; but besides the humor, one felt also the
relation. Gibbon ignored the Virgin, because in 1789, religious monuments were out of fashion. In 1900 his remark sounded fresh and simple as the green fields to ears that had heard a hundred years of other
remarks, mostly no more fresh and certainly less simple. Without mal-
ice, one might find it more instructive than a whole lecture of Ruskin.
One sees what one brings, and at that moment Gibbon brought the
French Revolution. Ruskin brought reaction against the Revolution.
St. Gaudens had passed beyond all. He liked the stately monuments
much more than he liked Gibbon or Ruskin; he loved their dignity;
their unity; their scale; their lines; their lights and shadows; their decorative sculpture; but he was even less conscious than they of the force
that created it all,—the Virgin, the Woman,—by whose genius "the
stately monuments of superstition" were built, through which she was
expressed. He would have seen more meaning in Isis with the cow's
horns, at Edfoo, who expressed the same thought. The art remained,
but the energy was lost even upon the artist.

Yet in mind and person St. Gaudens was a survival of the 1500's; he
bore the stamp of the renaissance, and should have carried an image
of the Virgin round his neck, or stuck in his hat, like Louis XI. In mere
time he was a lost soul that had strayed by chance into the twentieth
century, and forgotten where it came from. He writhed and cursed
at his ignorance, much as Adams did at his own, but in the opposite
sense. St. Gaudens was a child of Benvenuto Cellini, smothered in an
American cradle. Adams was a quintessence of Boston, devoured by
curiosity to think like Benvenuto. St. Gaudens's art was starved from
birth, and Adams's instinct was blighted from babyhood. Each had but
half of a nature, and when they came together before the Virgin of
Amiens they ought both to have felt in her the force that made them
one; but it was not so. To Adams she became more than ever a channel of force; to St. Gaudens she remained as before a channel of taste.

For a symbol of power, St. Gaudens instinctively preferred the horse, as was plain in his horse and Victory of the Sherman monument. Doubtless Sherman also felt it so. The attitude was so American that, for at least forty years, Adams had never realised that any other could be in sound taste. How many years had he taken to admit a notion of what Michael Angelo and Rubens were driving at? He could not say; but he knew that only since 1895 had he begun to feel the Virgin or Venus as force, and not everywhere even so. At Chartres—perhaps at Lourdes,—possibly at Cnidos if one could still find there the divinely naked Aphrodite of Praxiteles,—but otherwise one must look for force to the Goddesses of Indian mythology. The idea died out long ago in the German and English stock. St. Gaudens at Amiens was hardly less sensitive to the force of the female energy than Matthew Arnold at the Grande Chartreuse. Neither of them felt Goddesses as power,—only as reflected emotion, human expression, beauty, purity, taste, scarcely even as sympathy. They felt a railway-train as power; yet they, and all other artists constantly complained that the power embodied in a railway-train could never be embodied in art. All the steam in the world could not, like the Virgin, build Chartres.

Yet in mechanics, whatever the mechanicians might think, both energies acted as interchangeable forces on man, and by action on man all known force may be measured. Indeed, few men of science measured force in any other way. After once admitting that a straight line was the shortest distance between two points, no serious mathematician cared to deny anything that suited his convenience, and rejected no symbol, unproved or unproveable, that helped him to accomplish work. The symbol was force, as a compass-needle or a triangle was force, as the mechanist might prove by losing it, and nothing could be gained by ignoring their value. Symbol or energy, the Virgin had acted as the greatest force the western world ever felt, and had drawn man's activities to herself more strongly than any other power, natural or supernatural, had ever done; the historian's business was to follow the track of the energy; to find where it came from and where it went to; its complex source and shifting channels; its values, equivalents, conversions. It could scarcely be more complex than radium; it could hardly be deflected, diverted, polarised, absorbed more perplexingly than other radiant matter. Adams knew nothing about any of them, but as a mathematical problem of influence on human progress, though all were occult, all reacted on his mind, and he rather inclined to think the Virgin easiest to handle.

The pursuit turned out to be long and tortuous, leading at last into the vast forests of scholastic science. From Zeno to Descartes, hand in hand with Thomas Aquinas, Montaigne and Pascal, one stumbled as stupidly as though one were still a German student of 1860. Only with the instinct of despair could one force oneself into this old thicket of ignorance after having been repulsed at a score of entrances more promising and more popular. Thus far, no path had led anywhere, unless perhaps to an exceedingly modest living. Forty-five years of study had proved to be quite futile for the pursuit of power; one controlled no more force in 1900 than in 1850, although the amount of force controlled by society had enormously increased. The secret of education still hid itself somewhere behind ignorance, and one fumbled over it as feebly as ever. In such labyrinths, the staff is a force almost more necessary than the legs; the pen becomes a sort of blind-man's dog, to keep him from falling into the gutters. The pen works for itself, and acts like a hand, modelling the plastic material over and over again to the form that suits it best. The form is never arbitrary, but is a sort of growth like crystallization, as any artist knows too well; for often the pencil or pen runs into side-paths and shapeless-ness, loses its relations, stops or is bogged. Then it has to return on its trail, and recover, if it can, its line of force. The result of a year's work depends more on what is struck out than on what is left in; on the sequence of the main lines of thought, than on their play or variety. Compelled once more to lean heavily on this support, Adams covered more thousands of pages with figures as formal as though they were algebra, laboriously striking out, altering, burning, experimenting, until the year had expired, the Exposition had long been closed, and winter drawing to its end, before he sailed from Cherbourg, on January 19, 1901, for home.

*1907*

# WALTER LIPPMANN

Throughout the middle third of the twentieth century, Walter Lippmann (1889–1974) commanded more respect and esteem than any other American journalist. A founding editor of *The New Republic*, he had as a young man shared that magazine's progressive perspective, which included support for the Wilsonian rationale for the U.S. entry into World War I. Chastened by the failure of Wilson's efforts to "make the world safe for democracy," Lippmann came to take more skeptical views of America's role in the world, of democratic politics, and of journalism itself.

## FROM "Journalism and the Higher Law"

VOLUME 1, Number 1, of the first American newspaper was published in Boston on September 25, 1690. It was called *Publick Occurrences*. The second issue did not appear because the Governor and Council suppressed it. They found that Benjamin Harris, the editor, had printed "reflections of a very high nature."[1] Even to-day some of his reflections seem very high indeed. In his prospectus he had written:

> That something may be done toward the Curing, or at least the Charming of that Spirit of Lying, which prevails amongst us, wherefore nothing shall be entered, but what we have reason to believe is true, repairing to the best fountains for our Information. And when there appears any material mistake in anything that is collected, it shall be corrected in the next. Moreover, the Publisher of these Occurrences is willing to engage, that whereas, there are many False Reports, maliciously made,

---

[1] "History of American Journalism," James Melvin Lee, Houghton Mifflin Co., 1917, p. 10.

and spread among us, if any well-minded person will be at the pains to trace any such false Report, so far as to find out and Convict the First Raiser of it, he will in this Paper (unless just Advice be given to the contrary) expose the Name of such Person, as A malicious Raiser of a false Report. It is suppos'd that none will dislike this Proposal, but such as intend to be guilty of so villainous a Crime.

Everywhere to-day men are conscious that somehow they must deal with questions more intricate than any that church or school had prepared them to understand. Increasingly they know that they cannot understand them if the facts are not quickly and steadily available. Increasingly they are baffled because the facts are not available; and they are wondering whether government by consent can survive in a time when the manufacture of consent is an unregulated private enterprise. For in an exact sense the present crisis of western democracy is a crisis in journalism.

I do not agree with those who think that the sole cause is corruption. There is plenty of corruption, to be sure, moneyed control, caste pressure, financial and social bribery, ribbons, dinner parties, clubs, petty politics. The speculators in Russian rubles who lied on the Paris Bourse about the capture of Petrograd are not the only example of their species. And yet corruption does not explain the condition of modern journalism.

Mr. Franklin P. Adams wrote recently: "Now there is much pettiness—and almost incredible stupidity and ignorance—in the so-called free press; but it is the pettiness, etc., common to the so-called human race—a pettiness found in musicians, steamfitters, landlords, poets, and waiters. And when Miss Lowell [who had made the usual aristocratic complaint] speaks of the incurable desire in all American newspapers to make fun of everything in season and out, we quarrel again. There is an incurable desire in American newspapers to take things much more seriously than they deserve. Does Miss Lowell read the ponderous news from Washington? Does she read the society news? Does she, we wonder, read the newspapers?"

Mr. Adams does read them, and when he writes that the newspapers take things much more seriously than they deserve, he has, as the mayor's wife remarked to the queen, said a mouthful. Since the war, especially, editors have come to believe that their highest duty is not to report but to instruct, not to print news but to save civilization, not to publish what Benjamin Harris calls "the Circumstances of Publique Affairs, both abroad and at home," but to keep the nation on the straight and narrow path. Like the Kings of England, they have elected themselves Defenders of the Faith. "For five years," says Mr. Cobb of the *New York World*, "there has been no free play of public opinion in the world. Confronted by the inexorable necessities of war, governments conscripted public opinion. . . . They goose-stepped it. They taught it to stand at attention and salute. . . . It sometimes seems that after the armistice was signed, millions of Americans must have taken a vow that they would never again do any thinking for themselves. They were willing to die for their country, but not willing to think for it." That minority, which is proudly prepared to think for it, and not only prepared, but cocksure that it alone knows how to think for it, has adopted the theory that the public should know what is good for it.

The work of reporters has thus become confused with the work of preachers, revivalists, prophets and agitators. The current theory of American newspaperdom is that an abstraction like the truth and a grace like fairness must be sacrificed whenever anyone thinks the necessities of civilization require the sacrifice. To Archbishop Whately's dictum that it matters greatly whether you put truth in the first place or the second, the candid expounder of modern journalism would reply that he put truth second to what he conceived to be the national interest. Judged simply by their product, men like Mr. Ochs or Viscount Northcliffe believe that their respective nations will perish and civilization decay unless their idea of what is patriotic is permitted to temper the curiosity of their readers.

They believe that edification is more important than veracity. They believe it profoundly, violently, relentlessly. They preen themselves upon it. To patriotism, as they define it from day to day, all other considerations must yield. That is their pride. And yet what is this but one more among myriad examples of the doctrine that the end justifies the means. A more insidiously misleading rule of conduct was, I believe, never devised among men. It was a plausible rule as long as men believed that an omniscient and benevolent Providence taught them what end to seek. But now that men are critically aware of how their purposes are special to their age, their locality, their interests, and their limited knowledge, it is blazing arrogance to sacrifice hard-won standards of credibility to some special purpose. It is nothing but the doctrine that I want what I want when I want it. Its monuments are the Inquisition and the invasion of Belgium. It is the reason given for almost every act of unreason, the law invoked whenever lawlessness justifies itself. At bottom it is nothing but the anarchical nature of man imperiously hacking its way through.

Just as the most poisonous form of disorder is the mob incited from high places the most immoral act the immorality of a government, so the most destructive form of untruth is sophistry and propaganda by those whose profession it is to report the news. The news columns are common carriers. When those who control them arrogate to themselves the right to determine by their own consciences what shall be reported and for what purpose, democracy is unworkable. Public opinion is blockaded. For when a people can no longer confidently repair 'to the best fountains for their information,' then anyone's guess and anyone's rumor, each man's hope and each man's whim becomes the basis of government. All that the sharpest critics of democracy have alleged is true, if there is no steady supply of trustworthy and relevant news. Incompetence and aimlessness, corruption and disloyalty, panic and ultimate disaster, must come to any people which is denied an assured access to the facts. No one can manage anything on pap. Neither can a people.

Statesmen may devise policies; they will end in futility, as so many have recently ended, if the propagandists and censors can put a painted screen where there should be a window to the world. Few episodes in recent history are more poignant than that of the British Prime Minister, sitting at the breakfast table with that morning's paper before him protesting that he cannot do the sensible thing in regard to Russia because a powerful newspaper proprietor has drugged the public. That incident is a photograph of the supreme danger which confronts popular government. All other dangers are contingent upon it, for the news is the chief source of the opinion by which government now proceeds. So long as there is interposed between the ordinary citizen and the facts a news organization determining by entirely private and unexamined standards, no matter how lofty, what he shall know, and hence what he shall believe, no one will be able to say that the substance of democratic government is secure. The theory of our constitution, says Mr. Justice Holmes, is that truth is the only ground upon which men's wishes safely can be carried out.[2] In so far as those who purvey the news make of their own beliefs a higher law than truth, they are attacking the foundations of our constitutional system. There can be no higher law in journalism than to tell the truth and shame the devil.

*1920*

---

[2] Supreme Court of the United States, No. 316, October term, 1919, Jacob Abrams et al., Plaintiffs in Error vs. the United States.

# GEORGE SANTAYANA

George Santayana (1863–1952) was a singular figure in American intellectual history. Born in Spain, Santayana grew up in Boston and was educated at Harvard, where he would achieve renown as a professor of philosophy. At the age of forty-eight, intent on escaping what he called the "thistles of trivial and narrow scholarship," he left both Harvard and the United States to spend the rest of his life in Europe. Santayana was the author of many books, including the novel *The Last Puritan* (1936), a devastating account of the spiritually enervating effects of privilege.

## Materialism and Idealism in American Life

THE LANGUAGE and traditions common to England and America are like other family bonds: they draw kindred together at the greater crises in life, but they also occasion at times a little friction and fault-finding. The groundwork of the two societies is so similar, that each nation, feeling almost at home with the other, and almost able to understand its speech, may instinctively resent what hinders it from feeling at home altogether. Differences will tend to seem anomalies that have slipped in by mistake and through somebody's fault. Each will judge the other by his own standards, not feeling, as in the presence of complete foreigners, that he must make an effort of imagination and put himself in another man's shoes.

In matters of morals, manners, and art, the danger of comparisons is not merely that they may prove invidious, by ranging qualities in an order of merit which might wound somebody's vanity; the danger is rather that comparisons may distort comprehension, because in

62

truth good qualities are all different in kind, and free lives are differ-ent in spirit. Comparison is the expedient of those who cannot reach the heart of the things compared; and no philosophy is more external and egotistical than that which places the essence of a thing in its relation to something else. In reality, at the centre of every natural being there is something individual and incommensurable, a seed with its native impulses and aspirations, shaping themselves as best they can in their given environment. Variation is a consequence of freedom, and the slight but radical diversity of souls in turn makes freedom requisite. Instead of instituting in his mind any comparisons between the United States and other nations, I would accordingly urge the reader to forget himself and, in so far as such a thing may be possible for him or for me, to transport himself ideally with me into the outer circumstances of American life, the better to feel its inner temper, and to see how inevitably the American shapes his feelings and judgements, honestly reporting all things as they appear from his new and unobstructed station.

I speak of the American in the singular, as if there were not millions of them, north and south, east and west, of both sexes, of all ages, and of various races, professions, and religions. Of course the one American I speak of is mythical; but to speak in parables is inevitable in such a subject, and it is perhaps as well to do so frankly. There is a sort of poetic ineptitude in all human discourse when it tries to deal with natural and existing things. Practical men may not notice it, but in fact human discourse is intrinsically addressed not to natural existing things but to ideal essences, poetic or logical terms which thought may define and play with. When fortune or necessity diverts our attention from this congenial ideal sport to crude facts and pressing issues, we turn our frail poetic ideas into symbols for those terrible irruptive things. In that paper money of our own stamping, the legal tender of the mind, we are obliged to reckon all the movements and values of the world. The universal American I speak of is one of these symbols; and I should be still speaking in symbols and creating moral units and a false simplicity, if I spoke of classes pedantically subdivided, or individuals ideally integrated and defined. As it happens, the sym-bolic American can be made largely adequate to the facts; because, if there are immense differences between individual Americans—for some Americans are black—yet there is a great uniformity in their environment, customs, temper, and thoughts. They have all been uprooted from their several soils and ancestries and plunged together into one vortex, whirling irresistibly in a space otherwise quite empty. To be an American is of itself almost a moral condition, an education, and a career. Hence a single ideal figment can cover a large part of what each American is in his character, and almost the whole of what most Americans are in their social outlook and political judgements.

The discovery of the new world exercised a sort of selection among the inhabitants of Europe. All the colonists, except the negroes, were voluntary exiles. The fortunate, the deeply rooted, and the lazy remained at home; the wilder instincts or dissatisfaction of others tempted them beyond the horizon. The American is accordingly the most adventurous, or the descendant of the most adventurous, of Europeans. It is in his blood to be socially a radical, though perhaps not intellectually. What has existed in the past, especially in the remote past, seems to him not only not authoritative, but irrelevant, inferior, and outworn. He finds it rather a sorry waste of time to think about the past at all. But his enthusiasm for the future is profound; he can conceive of no more decisive way of recommending an opinion or a practice than to say that it is what everybody is coming to adopt. This expectation of what he approves, or approval of what he expects, makes up his optimism. It is the necessary faith of the pioneer.

Such a temperament is, of course, not maintained in the nation merely by inheritance. Inheritance notoriously tends to restore the average of a race, and plays incidentally many a trick of atavism. What maintains this temperament and makes it national is social contagion or pressure—something immensely strong in democracies. The luckless American who is born a conservative, or who is drawn to poetic subtlety, pious retreats, or gay passions, nevertheless has the categorical excellence of work, growth, enterprise, reform, and prosperity dinned into his ears: every door is open in this direction and shut in the other; so that he either folds up his heart and withers in a corner—in remote places you sometimes find such a solitary gaunt idealist—or else he flies to Oxford or Florence or Montmartre to save his soul—or perhaps not to save it.

The optimism of the pioneer is not limited to his view of himself and his own future: it starts from that; but feeling assured, safe, and cheery within, he looks with smiling and most kindly eyes on everything and everybody about him. Individualism, roughness, and self-trust are supposed to go with selfishness and a cold heart; but I suspect that is a prejudice. It is rather dependence, insecurity, and mutual jostling that poison our placid gregarious brotherhood; and fanciful passionate demands upon people's affections, when they are disappointed, as they soon must be, breed ill-will and a final meanness. The milk of human kindness is less apt to turn sour if the vessel that holds it stands steady, cool, and separate, and is not too often uncorked. In his affections the American is seldom passionate, often deep, and always kindly. If it were given me to look into the depths of a man's heart, and I did not find goodwill at the bottom, I should say without any hesitation, You are not an American. But as the American is an individualist his goodwill is not officious. His instinct is to think well of everybody, and to wish everybody well, but in a spirit of rough comradeship, expecting every man to stand on his own legs and to be helpful in his turn. When he has given his neighbour a chance he thinks he has done enough for him; but he feels it is an absolute duty to do that. It will take some hammering to drive a coddling socialism into America.

As self-trust may pass into self-sufficiency, so optimism, kindness, and goodwill may grow into a habit of doting on everything. To the good American many subjects are sacred: sex is sacred, women are sacred, children are sacred, business is sacred, America is sacred, Masonic lodges and college clubs are sacred. This feeling grows out of the good opinion he wishes to have of these things, and serves to maintain it. If he did not regard all these things as sacred he might come to doubt sometimes if they were wholly good. Of this kind, too, is the idealism of single ladies in reduced circumstances who can see the soul of beauty in ugly things, and are perfectly happy because their old dog has such pathetic eyes, their minister is so eloquent, their garden with its three sunflowers is so pleasant, their dead friends were so devoted, and their distant relations are so rich.

Consider now the great emptiness of America: not merely the primitive physical emptiness, surviving in some regions, and the continental spacing of the chief natural features, but also the moral emptiness of a settlement where men and even houses are easily moved about, and no one, almost, lives where he was born or believes what he has been taught. Not that the American has jettisoned these impedimenta in anger; they have simply slipped from him as he moves. Great empty spaces bring a sort of freedom to both soul and body. You may pitch your tent where you will; or if ever you decide to build anything, it can be in a style of your own devising. You have room, fresh materials, few models, and no critics. You trust your own experience, not only because you must, but because you find you may do so safely and prosperously; the forces that determine fortune are not yet too complicated for one man to explore. Your detachable condition makes you lavish with money and cheerfully experimental; you lose little if you lose all, since you remain completely yourself. At the same time your absolute initiative gives you practice in coping with novel situations, and in being original; it teaches you shrewd management. Your life and mind will become dry and direct, with few decorative flourishes. In your works everything will be stark and pragmatic; you will not understand why anybody should make those little sacrifices to instinct or custom which we call grace. The fine arts will seem to you academic luxuries, fit to amuse the ladies, like Greek and Sanskrit; for while you will perfectly appreciate generosity in men's purposes, you will not admit that the execution of these purposes can be anything but business. Unfortunately the essence of the fine arts is that the execution should be generous too, and delightful in itself; therefore the fine arts will suffer, not so much in their express professional pursuit—for then they become practical tasks and a kind of business—as in that diffused charm which qualifies all human action when men are artists by nature. Elaboration, which is something to accomplish, will be preferred to simplicity, which is something to rest in; manners will suffer somewhat; speech will suffer horribly. For the American the urgency of his novel attack upon matter, his zeal in gathering its fruits, precludes meanderings in primrose paths; devices must be short cuts, and symbols must be mere symbols. If his wife wants luxuries, of course she may have them; and if he has vices, that can be provided for too; but they must all be set down under those headings in his ledgers.

At the same time, the American is imaginative; for where life is intense, imagination is intense also. Were he not imaginative he would not live so much in the future. But his imagination is practical, and the future it forecasts is immediate; it works with the clearest and least ambiguous terms known to his experience, in terms of number, measure, contrivance, economy, and speed. He is an idealist working on matter. Understanding as he does the material potentialities of things, he is successful in invention, conservative in reform, and quick in emergencies. All his life he jumps into the train after it has started and jumps out before it has stopped; and he never once gets left behind, or breaks a leg. There is an enthusiasm in his sympathetic handling of material forces which goes far to cancel the illiberal character which it might otherwise assume. The good workman hardly distinguishes his artistic intention from the potency in himself and in things which is about to realise that intention. Accordingly his ideals fall into the form of premonitions and prophecies; and his studious prophecies often come true. So do the happy workmanlike ideals of the American. When a poor boy, perhaps, he dreams of an education, and presently he gets an education, or at least a degree; he dreams of growing rich, and he grows rich—only more slowly and modestly, perhaps, than he expected; he dreams of marrying his Rebecca and, even if he marries a Leah instead, he ultimately finds in Leah his Rebecca after all. He dreams of helping to carry on and to accelerate the movement of a vast, seething, progressive society, and he actually does so. Ideals clinging so close to nature are almost sure of fulfilment; the American beams with a certain self-confidence and sense of mastery; he feels that God and nature are working with him.

Idealism in the American accordingly goes hand in hand with present contentment and with foresight of what the future very likely will actually bring. He is not a revolutionist; he believes he is already on the right track and moving towards an excellent destiny. In revolutionists, on the contrary, idealism is founded on dissatisfaction and expresses it. What exists seems to them an absurd jumble of irrational accidents and bad habits, and they want the future to be based on reason and to be the pellucid embodiment of all their maxims. All their zeal is for something radically different from the actual and (if they only knew it) from the possible; it is ideally simple, and they love it and believe in it because their nature craves it. They think life would be set free by the destruction of all its organs. They are therefore extreme idealists in the region of hope, but not at all, as poets and artists are, in the region of perception and memory. In the atmosphere of civilised life they miss all the refraction and all the fragrance; so that in their conception of actual things they are apt to be crude realists; and their ignorance and inexperience of the moral world, unless it comes of ill-luck, indicates their incapacity for education. Now incapacity for education, when united with great inner vitality, is one root of idealism. It is what condemns us all, in the region of sense, to substitute perpetually what we are capable of imagining for what things may be in themselves; it is what condemns us, wherever it extends, to think *a priori*; it is what keeps us bravely and incorrigibly pursuing what we call the good—that is, what would fulfil the demands of our nature—however little provision the fates may have made for it. But the want of insight on the part of revolutionists touching the past and the present infects in an important particular their idealism about the future; it renders their dreams of the future unrealisable. For in human beings—this may not be true of other animals, more perfectly preformed—experience is necessary to pertinent and concrete thinking; even our primitive instincts are blind until they stumble upon some occasion that solicits them; and they can be much transformed or deranged by their first partial satisfactions. Therefore a man who does not idealise his experience, but idealises *a priori*, is incapable of true prophecy; when he dreams he raves, and the more he criticises the less he helps. American idealism, on the contrary, is nothing if not helpful, nothing if not pertinent to practicable transformations; and when the American frets, it is because whatever is useless and impertinent, be it idealism or inertia, irritates him; for it frustrates the good results which he sees might so easily have been obtained.

The American is wonderfully alive; and his vitality, not having often found a suitable outlet, makes him appear agitated on the surface; he is always letting off an unnecessarily loud blast of incidental steam. Yet his vitality is not superficial; it is inwardly prompted, and as sensitive and quick as a magnetic needle. He is inquisitive, and ready with an answer to any question that he may put to himself of his own accord; but if you try to pour instruction into him, on matters that do not touch his own spontaneous life, he shows the most extraordinary powers of resistance and oblivescence; so that he often is remarkably expert in some directions and surprisingly obtuse in others. He seems to bear lightly the sorrowful burden of human knowledge. In a word, he is young.

What sense is there in this feeling, which we all have, that the American is young? His country is blessed with as many elderly people as any other, and his descent from Adam, or from the Darwinian rival of Adam, cannot be shorter than that of his European cousins. Nor are his ideas always very fresh. Trite and rigid bits of morality and religion, with much seemly and antique political lore, remain axiomatic in him, as in the mind of a child; he may carry all this about with an unquestioning familiarity which does not comport understanding. To keep traditional sentiments in this way insulated and uncriticised is itself a sign of youth. A good young man is naturally conservative and loyal on all those subjects which his experience has not brought to a test; advanced opinions on politics, marriage, or literature are comparatively rare in America; they are left for the ladies to discuss, and usually to condemn, while the men get on with their work. In spite of what is old-fashioned in his more general ideas, the American is unmistakably young; and this, I should say, for two reasons: one, that he is chiefly occupied with his immediate environment, and the other, that his reactions upon it are inwardly prompted, spontaneous, and full of vivacity and self-trust. His views are not yet lengthened; his will is not yet broken or transformed. The present moment, however, in this, as in other things, may mark a great change in him; he is perhaps now reaching his majority, and all I say may hardly apply to-day, and may not apply at all to-morrow. I speak of him as I have known him; and whatever moral strength may accrue to him later, I am not sorry to have known him in his youth. The charm of youth, even when it is a little boisterous, lies in nearness to the impulses of nature, in a quicker and more obvious obedience to that pure, seminal principle which, having formed the body and its organs, always directs their movements, unless it is forced by vice or necessity to make them crooked, or to suspend them. Even under the inevitable crust of age the soul remains young, and, wherever it is able to break through, sprouts into something green and tender. We are all as young at heart as the most youthful American, but the seed in his case has fallen upon virgin soil, where it may spring up more bravely and with less respect for the giants of the wood. Peoples seem older when their perennial natural youth is encumbered with more possessions and prepossessions, and they are mindful of the many things they have lost or missed. The American is not mindful of them.

In America there is a tacit optimistic assumption about existence, to the effect that the more existence the better. The soulless critic might urge that quantity is only a physical category, implying no excellence, but at best an abundance of opportunities both for good and for evil. Yet the young soul, being curious and hungry, views existence *a priori* under the form of the good; its instinct to live implies a faith that most things it can become or see or do will be worth while. Respect for quantity is accordingly something more than the childish joy and wonder at bigness; it is the fisherman's joy in a big haul, the good uses of which he can take for granted. Such optimism is amiable. Nature cannot afford that we should begin by being too calculating or wise, and she encourages us by the pleasure she attaches to our functions in advance of their fruits, and often in excess of them; as the angler enjoys catching his fish more than eating it, and often, waiting patiently for the fish to bite, misses his own supper. The pioneer must devote himself to preparations; he must work for the future, and it is healthy and dutiful of him to love his work for its own sake. At the same time, unless reference to an ultimate purpose is at least virtual in all his activities, he runs the danger of becoming a living automaton, vain and ignominious in its mechanical constancy. Idealism about work can hide an intense materialism about life. Man, if he is a rational being, cannot live by bread alone nor be a labourer merely; he must eat and work in view of an ideal harmony which overarches all his days, and which is realised in the way they hang together, or in some ideal issue which they have in common. Otherwise, though his technical philosophy may call itself idealism, he is a materialist in morals; he esteems things, and esteems himself, for mechanical uses and energies. Even sensualists, artists, and pleasure-lovers are wiser than that, for though their idealism may be desultory or corrupt, they attain something ideal, and prize things only for their living effects, moral though perhaps fugitive. Sensation, when we do not take it as a signal for action, but arrest and peruse what it positively brings before us, reveals something ideal—a colour, shape, or sound; and to dwell on these presences, with no thought of their material significance, is an æsthetic or dreamful idealism. To pass from this idealism to the knowledge of matter is a great intellectual advance, and goes with dominion over the world; for in the practical arts the mind is adjusted to a larger object, with more depth and potentiality in it; which is what makes people feel that the material world is real, as they call it, and that the ideal world is not. Certainly the material world is real; for the philosophers who deny the existence of matter are like the critics who deny the existence of Homer. If there was never any Homer, there must have been a lot of other poets no less Homeric than he; and if matter does not exist, a combination of other things exists which is just as material. But the intense reality of the material world would not prevent it from being a dreary waste in our eyes, or even an abyss of horror, if it brought forth no spiritual fruits. In fact, it does bring forth spiritual fruits, for otherwise we should not be here to find fault with it, and to set up our ideals over against it. Nature is material, but not materialistic; it issues in life, and breeds all sorts of warm passions and idle beauties. And just as sympathy with the mechanical travail and turmoil of nature, apart from its spiritual fruits, is moral materialism, so the continual perception and love of these fruits is moral idealism— happiness in the presence of immaterial objects and harmonies, such as we envisage in affection, speculation, religion, and all the forms of the beautiful.

The circumstances of his life hitherto have necessarily driven the American into moral materialism; for in his dealings with material things he can hardly stop to enjoy their sensible aspects, which are ideal, nor proceed at once to their ultimate uses, which are ideal too. He is practical as against the poet, and worldly as against the clear philosopher or the saint. The most striking expression of this material- ism is usually supposed to be his love of the almighty dollar; but that is a foreign and unintelligent view. The American talks about money, because that is the symbol and measure he has at hand for success, intelligence, and power; but as to money itself he makes, loses, spends, and gives it away with a very light heart. To my mind the most strik- ing expression of his materialism is his singular preoccupation with quantity. If, for instance, you visit Niagara Falls, you may expect to hear how many cubic feet or metric tons of water are precipitated per second over the cataract; how many cities and towns (with the number of their inhabitants) derive light and motive power from it; and the annual value of the further industries that might very well be carried on by the same means, without visibly depleting the world's greatest wonder or injuring the tourist trade. That is what I confidently expected to hear on arriving at the adjoining town of Buffalo; but I was deceived. The first thing I heard instead was that there are more miles of asphalt pavement in Buffalo than in any city in the world. Nor is this insistence on quantity confined to men of business. The President of Harvard College, seeing me once by chance soon after the beginning of a term, inquired how my classes were getting on; and when I replied that I thought they were getting on well, that my men seemed to be keen and intelligent, he stopped me as if I was about to waste his time. "I meant," said he, "*what is the number* of students in your classes."

Here I think we may perceive that this love of quantity often has a silent partner, which is diffidence as to quality. The democratic conscience recoils before anything that savours of privilege; and lest it should concede an unmerited privilege to any pursuit or person, it reduces all things as far as possible to the common denominator of quantity. Numbers cannot lie: but if it came to comparing the ideal beauties of philosophy with those of Anglo-Saxon, who should decide? All studies are good—why else have universities?—but those must be most encouraged which attract the greatest number of students. Hence the President's question. Democratic faith, in its diffidence about quality, throws the reins of education upon the pupil's neck, as Don Quixote threw the reins on the neck of Rocinante, and bids his divine instinct choose its own way.

The American has never yet had to face the trials of Job. Great crises, like the Civil War, he has known how to surmount victoriously; and now that he has surmounted a second great crisis victoriously, it is possible that he may relapse, as he did in the other case, into an apparently complete absorption in material enterprise and prosperity. But if serious and irremediable tribulation ever overtook him, what would his attitude be? It is then that we should be able to discover whether materialism or idealism lies at the base of his character. Meantime his working mind is not without its holiday. He spreads humour pretty thick and even over the surface of conversation, and humour is one form of moral emancipation. He loves landscape, he loves mankind, and he loves knowledge; and in music at least he finds an art which he unfeignedly enjoys. In music and landscape, in humour and kindness, he touches the ideal more truly, perhaps, than in his ponderous academic idealisms and busy religions; for it is astonishing how much even religion in America (can it possibly be so in England?) is a matter of meetings, building-funds, schools, charities, clubs, and picnics. To be poor in order to be simple, to produce less in order that the product may be more choice and beautiful, and may leave us less burdened with unnecessary duties and useless possessions—that is an ideal not articulate in the American mind; yet here and there I seem to have heard a sigh after it, a groan at the perpetual incubus of business and shrill society. Significant witness to such aspirations is borne by those new forms of popular religion, not mere variations on tradition, which have sprung up from the soil—revivalism, spiritualism, Christian Science, the New Thought. Whether or no we can tap, through these or other channels, some cosmic or inner energy not hitherto at the disposal of man (and there is nothing incredible in that), we certainly may try to remove friction and waste in the mere process of living; we may relax morbid strains, loosen suppressed instincts, iron out the creases of the soul, discipline ourselves into simplicity, sweetness, and peace. These religious movements are efforts toward such physi- ological economy and hygiene; and while they are thoroughly plebe- ian, with no great lights, and no idea of raising men from the most vulgar and humdrum worldly existence, yet they see the possibility of physical and moral health on that common plane, and pursue it. That is true morality. The dignities of various types of life or mind, like the gifts of various animals, are relative. The snob adores one type only, and the creatures supposed by him to illustrate it perfectly; or envies and hates them, which is just as snobbish. Veritable lovers of life, on the contrary, like Saint Francis or like Dickens, know that in every tenement of clay, with no matter what endowment or station, happiness and perfection are possible to the soul. There must be no brow-beating, with shouts of work or progress or revolution, any more than with threats of hell-fire. What does it profit a man to free the whole world if his soul is not free? Moral freedom is not an artificial condition, because the ideal is the mother tongue of both the heart and the senses. All that is requisite is that we should pause in living to enjoy life, and should lift up our hearts to things that are pure goods in themselves, so that once to have found and loved them, whatever else may betide, may remain a happiness that nothing can sully. This natural idealism does not imply that we are immaterial, but only that we are animate and truly alive. When the senses are sharp, as they are in the American, they are already half liberated, already a joy in themselves; and when the heart is warm, like his, and eager to be just, its ideal destiny can hardly be doubtful. It will not be always merely pumping and working; time and its own pulses will lend it wings.

*1921*

# HERBERT HOOVER

Were it not for his ineffectual response to the Great Depression while president, Herbert Hoover (1874–1964) might well be regarded as an American immortal, with his likeness carved into Mount Rushmore. Engineer, entrepreneur, humanitarian, philanthropist, and public servant: Hoover performed admirably in each of these roles. As shown here, he devoted considerable thought to plumbing the depths of the American character.

———————

## FROM *American Individualism*

### AMERICAN INDIVIDUALISM

WE HAVE witnessed in this last eight years the spread of revolution over one-third of the world. The causes of these explosions lie at far greater depths than the failure of governments in war. The war itself in its last stages was a conflict of social philosophies—but beyond this the causes of social explosion lay in the great inequalities and injustices of centuries flogged beyond endurance by the conflict and freed from restraint by the destruction of war. The urgent forces which drive human society have been plunged into a terrible furnace. Great theories spun by dreamers to remedy the pressing human ills have come to the front of men's minds. Great formulas came into life that promised to dissolve all trouble. Great masses of people have flocked to their banners in hopes born of misery and suffering. Nor has this great social ferment been confined to those nations that have burned with revolutions.

Now, as the storm of war, of revolution and of emotion subsides there is left even with us of the United States much unrest, much discontent with the surer forces of human advancement. To all of us, out of this crucible of actual, poignant, individual experience has come a deal of new understanding, and it is for all of us to ponder these new currents if we are to shape our future with intelligence.

Even those parts of the world that suffered less from the war have been partly infected by these ideas. Beyond this, however, many have had high hopes of civilization suddenly purified and ennobled by the sacrifices and services of the war; they had thought the fine unity of purpose gained in war would be carried into great unity of action in remedy of the faults of civilization in peace. But from concentration of every spiritual and material energy upon the single purpose of war the scene changed to the immense complexity and the many purposes of peace.

Thus there loom up certain definite underlying forces in our national life that need to be stripped of the imaginary—the transitory—and a definition should be given to the actual permanent and persistent motivation of our civilization. In contemplation of these questions we must go far deeper than the superficials of our political and economic structure, for these are but the products of our social philosophy—the machinery of our social system.

Nor is it ever amiss to review the political, economic, and spiritual principles through which our country has steadily grown in usefulness and greatness, not only to preserve them from being fouled by false notions, but more importantly that we may guide ourselves in the road of progress.

Five or six great social philosophies are at struggle in the world for ascendency. There is the Individualism of America. There is the Individualism of the more democratic states of Europe with its careful reservations of castes and classes. There are Communism, Socialism, Syndicalism, Capitalism, and finally there is Autocracy—whether by birth, by possessions, militarism, or divine right of kings. Even the Divine Right still lingers on although our lifetime has seen fully two-thirds of the earth's population, including Germany, Austria, Russia, and China, arrive at a state of angry disgust with this type of social motive power and throw it on the scrap heap.

All these thoughts are in ferment today in every country in the world. They fluctuate in ascendency with times and places. They compromise with each other in daily reaction on governments and peoples. Some of these ideas are perhaps more adapted to one race than another. Some are false, some are true. What we are interested in is their challenge to the physical and spiritual forces of America.

The partisans of some of these other brands of social schemes challenge us to comparison; and some of their partisans even among our own people are increasing in their agitation that we adopt one or another or parts of their devices in place of our tried individualism. They insist that our social foundations are exhausted, that like feudalism and autocracy America's plan has served its purpose—that it must be abandoned.

There are those who have been left in sober doubt of our institutions or are confounded by bewildering catchwords of vivid phrases. For in this welter of discussions there is much attempt to glorify or defame social and economic forces with phrases. Nor indeed should we disregard the potency of some of these phrases in their stir to action.—"The dictatorship of the Proletariat," "Capitalistic nations," "Germany over all," and a score of others. We need only to review those that have jumped to horseback during the last ten years in order that we may be properly awed by the great social and political havoc that can be worked where the bestial instincts of hate, murder, and destruction are clothed by the demagogue in the fine terms of political idealism.

For myself, let me say at the very outset that my faith in the essential truth, strength, and vitality of the developing creed by which we have hitherto lived in this country of ours has been confirmed and deepened by the searching experiences of seven years of service in the backwash and misery of war. Seven years of contending with economic degeneration, with social disintegration, with incessant political dislocation, with all of its seething and ferment of individual and class conflict, could but impress me with the primary motivation of social forces, and the necessity for broader thought upon their great issues to humanity. And from it all I emerge an individualist—an unashamed individualist. But let me say also that I am an American individualist.

For America has been steadily developing the ideals that constitute progressive individualism.

No doubt, individualism run riot, with no tempering principle, would provide a long category of inequalities, of tyrannies, dominations, and injustices. America, however, has tempered the whole conception of individualism by the injection of a definite principle, and from this principle it follows that attempts at domination, whether in government or in the processes of industry and commerce, are under an insistent curb. If we would have the values of individualism, their stimulation to initiative, to the development of hand and intellect, to the high development of thought and spirituality, they must be tempered with that firm and fixed ideal of American individualism—*an equality of opportunity*. If we would have these values we must soften its hardness and stimulate progress through that sense of service that lies in our people.

Therefore, it is not the individualism of other countries for which I would speak, but the individualism of America. Our individualism differs from all others because it embraces these great ideals: *that while we build our society upon the attainment of the individual, we shall safeguard to every individual an equality of opportunity to take that position in the community to which his intelligence, character, ability, and ambition entitle him; that we keep the social solution free from frozen strata of classes; that we shall stimulate effort of each individual to achievement; that through an enlarging sense of responsibility and understanding we shall assist him to this attainment; while he in turn must stand up to the emery wheel of competition.*

Individualism cannot be maintained as the foundation of a society if it looks to only legalistic justice based upon contracts, property, and political equality. Such legalistic safeguards are themselves not enough. In our individualism we have long since abandoned the laissez faire of the 18th Century—the notion that it is "every man for himself and the devil take the hindmost." We abandoned that when we adopted the ideal of equality of opportunity—the fair chance of Abraham Lincoln. We have confirmed its abandonment in terms of legislation, of social and economic justice,—in part because we have learned that it is the hindmost who throws the bricks at our social edifice, in part because we have learned that the foremost are not always the best nor the hindmost the worst—and in part because we have learned that social injustice is the destruction of justice itself. We have learned that the impulse to production can only be maintained at a high pitch if there is a fair division of the product. We have also learned that fair division can only be obtained by certain restrictions on the strong and the dominant. We have indeed gone even further in the 20th Century with the embracement of the necessity of a greater and broader sense of service and responsibility to others as a part of individualism.

Whatever may be the case with regard to Old World individualism (and we have given more back to Europe than we received from her) the truth that is important for us to grasp today is that there is a world of difference between the principles and spirit of Old World individualism and that which we have developed in our own country.

We have, in fact, a special social system of our own. We have made it ourselves from materials brought in revolt from conditions in Europe. We have lived it; we constantly improve it; we have seldom tried to define it. It abhors autocracy and does not argue with it, but fights it. It is not capitalism, or socialism, or syndicalism, nor a cross breed of them. Like most Americans, I refuse to be damned by anybody's word-classification of it, such as "capitalism," "plutocracy," "proletariat" or "middle class," or any other, or to any kind of compartment that is based on the assumption of some group dominating somebody else.

The social force in which I am interested is far higher and far more precious a thing than all these. It springs from something infinitely more enduring; it springs from the one source of human progress— that each individual shall be given the chance and stimulation for development of the best with which he has been endowed in heart and mind; it is the sole source of progress; it is American individualism.

The rightfulness of our individualism can rest either on philosophic, political, economic, or spiritual grounds. It can rest on the ground of being the only safe avenue to further human progress.

## PHILOSOPHIC GROUNDS

On the philosophic side we can agree at once that intelligence, character, courage, and the divine spark of the human soul are alone the property of individuals. These do not lie in agreements, in organizations, in institutions, in masses, or in groups. They abide alone in the individual mind and heart.

Production both of mind and hand rests upon impulses in each individual. These impulses are made of the varied forces of original instincts, motives, and acquired desires. Many of these are destructive and must be restrained through moral leadership and authority of the law and be eliminated finally by education. All are modified by a vast fund of experience and a vast plant and equipment of civilization which we pass on with increments to each succeeding generation.

The inherited instincts of self-preservation, acquisitiveness, fear, kindness, hate, curiosity, desire for self-expression, for power, for adulation, that we carry over from a thousand of generations must, for good or evil, be comprehended in a workable system embracing our accumulation of experiences and equipment. They may modify themselves with time—but in terms of generations. They differ in their urge upon different individuals. The dominant ones are selfish. But no civilization could be built or can endure solely upon the groundwork of unrestrained and unintelligent self-interest. The problem of the world is to restrain the destructive instincts while strengthening and enlarging those of altruistic character and constructive impulse—for thus we build for the future.

From the instincts of kindness, pity, fealty to family and race; the love of liberty; the mystical yearnings for spiritual things; the desire for fuller expression of the creative faculties; the impulses of service to community and nation, are moulded the ideals of our people. And the most potent force in society is its ideals. If one were to attempt to delimit the potency of instinct and ideals, it would be found that while instinct dominates in our preservation yet the great propelling force of progress is right ideals. It is true we do not realize the ideal; not even a single person personifies that realization. It is therefore not surprising that society, a collection of persons, a necessary maze of compromises, cannot realize it. But that it has ideals, that they revolve in a system that makes for steady advance of them is the first thing. Yet true as this is, the day has not arrived when any economic or social system will function and last if founded upon altruism alone.

With the growth of ideals through education, with the higher realization of freedom, of justice, of humanity, of service, the selfish impulses become less and less dominant, and if we ever reach the millennium, they will disappear in the aspirations and satisfactions of pure altruism. But for the next several generations we dare not abandon self-interest as a motive force to leadership and to production, lest we die.

The will-o'-the-wisp of all breeds of socialism is that they contemplate a motivation of human animals by altruism alone. It necessitates a bureaucracy of the entire population, in which, having obliterated the economic stimulation of each member, the fine gradations of character and ability are to be arranged in relative authority by ballot or more likely by a Tammany Hall or a Bolshevist party, or some other form of tyranny. The proof of the futility of these ideas as a stimulation to the development and activity of the individual does not lie alone in the ghastly failure of Russia, but it also lies in our own failure in attempts at nationalized industry.

Likewise the basic foundations of autocracy, whether it be class government or capitalism in the sense that a few men through unrestrained control of property determine the welfare of great numbers, is as far apart from the rightful expression of American individualism as the two poles. The will-o'-the-wisp of autocracy in any form is that it supposes that the good Lord endowed a special few with all the divine attributes. It contemplates one human animal dealing to the other human animals his just share of earth, of glory, and of immortality. The proof of the futility of these ideas in the development of the world does not lie alone in the grim failure of Germany, but it lies in the damage to our moral and social fabric from those who have sought economic domination in America, whether employer or employee.

We in America have had too much experience of life to fool ourselves into pretending that all men are equal in ability, in character, in intelligence, in ambition. That was part of the claptrap of the French Revolution. We have grown to understand that all we can hope to assure to the individual through government is liberty, justice, intellectual welfare, equality of opportunity, and stimulation to service.

It is in maintenance of a society fluid to these human qualities that our individualism departs from the individualism of Europe. There can be no rise for the individual through the frozen strata of classes, or of castes, and no stratification can take place in a mass livened by the free stir of its particles. This guarding of our individualism against stratification insists not only in preserving in the social solution an equal opportunity for the able and ambitious to rise from the bottom; it also insists that the sons of the successful shall not by any mere right of birth or favor continue to occupy their fathers' places of power against the rise of a new generation in process of coming up from the bottom. The pioneers of our American individualism had the good sense not to reward Washington and Jefferson and Hamilton with hereditary dukedoms and fixtures in landed estates, as Great Britain rewarded Marlborough and Nelson. Otherwise our American fields of opportunity would have been clogged with long generations inheriting their fathers' privileges without their fathers' capacity for service.

That our system has avoided the establishment and domination of class has a significant proof in the present Administration in Washington. Of the twelve men comprising the President, Vice-President, and Cabinet, nine have earned their own way in life without economic inheritance, and eight of them started with manual labor.

If we examine the impulses that carry us forward, none is so potent for progress as the yearning for individual self-expression, the desire for creation of something. Perhaps the greatest human happiness flows from personal achievement. Here lies the great urge of the constructive instinct of mankind. But it can only thrive in a society where the individual has liberty and stimulation to achievement. Nor does the community progress except through its participation in these multitudes of achievements.

Furthermore, the maintenance of productivity and the advancement of the things of the spirit depend upon the ever-renewed supply from the mass of those who can rise to leadership. Our social, economic, and intellectual progress is almost solely dependent upon the creative minds of those individuals with imaginative and administrative intelligence who create or who carry discoveries to widespread application. No race possesses more than a small percentage of these minds in a single generation. But little thought has ever been given to our racial dependency upon them. Nor that our progress is in so large a measure due to the fact that with our increased means of communication these rare individuals are today able to spread their influence over so enlarged a number of lesser capable minds as to have increased their potency a million-fold. In truth, the vastly greater productivity of the world with actually less physical labor is due to the wider spread of their influence through the discovery of these facilities. And they can arise solely through the selection that comes from the free-running mills of competition. They must be free to rise from the mass; they must be given the attraction of premiums to effort.

Leadership is a quality of the individual. It is the individual alone who can function in the world of intellect and in the field of leadership. If democracy is to secure its authorities in morals, religion, and statesmanship, it must stimulate leadership from its own mass. Human leadership cannot be replenished by selection like queen bees, by divine right or bureaucracies, but by the free rise of ability, character, and intelligence.

Even so, leadership cannot, no matter how brilliant, carry progress far ahead of the average of the mass of individual units. Progress of the nation is the sum of progress in its individuals. Acts and ideas that lead to progress are born out of the womb of the individual mind, not out of the mind of the crowd. The crowd only feels: it has no mind of its own which can plan. The crowd is credulous, it destroys, it consumes, it hates, and it dreams—but it never builds. It is one of the most profound and important of exact psychological truths that man in the mass does not think but only feels. The mob functions only in a world of emotion. The demagogue feeds on mob emotions and his leadership is the leadership of emotion, not the leadership of intellect and progress. Popular desires are no criteria to the real need; they can be determined only by deliberative consideration, by education, by constructive leadership.

*1922*

# ZORA NEALE HURSTON

A novelist and ethnographer of African American folk culture, Zora Neale Hurston (1891–1960) was a leading figure in the Harlem Renaissance. In time, she would become, according to the writer John McWhorter, "black people's favorite black conservative, quiet though her conservatism is kept." More precisely, she was an incorrigible dissenter. Hurston opposed the New Deal policies of Franklin D. Roosevelt, while sympathizing with the up-from-your-bootstraps philosophy of Booker T. Washington long after they had fallen out of favor. She condemned the bombing of Hiroshima, argued against U.S. interventionism abroad, and in 1952 supported Robert Taft's candidacy for president. She spoke out not only against segregation but also the use of state power to dismantle it. And she refused to be classified by race.

## How It Feels To Be Colored Me

I AM colored but I offer nothing in the way of extenuating circumstances except the fact that I am the only Negro in the United States whose grandfather on the mother's side was *not* an Indian chief.

I remember the very day that I became colored. Up to my thirteenth year I lived in the little Negro town of Eatonville, Florida. It is exclusively a colored town. The only white people I knew passed through the town going to or coming from Orlando. The native whites rode dusty horses, the Northern tourists chugged down the sandy village road in automobiles. The town knew the Southerners and never stopped cane chewing when they passed. But the Northerners were something else again. They were peered at cautiously from behind curtains by the timid. The more venturesome would come out on the porch to watch them go past and got just as much pleasure out of the tourists as the tourists got out of the village.

The front porch might seem a daring place for the rest of the town, but it was a gallery seat to me. My favorite place was atop the gate-post. Proscenium box for a born first-nighter. Not only did I enjoy the show, but I didn't mind the actors knowing that I liked it. I actually spoke to them in passing. I'd wave at them and when they returned my salute, I would say something like this: "Howdy-do-well-I-thank-you-where-you-goin'?" Usually automobile or the horse paused at this, and after a queer exchange of compliments, I would probably "go a piece of the way" with them, as we say in farthest Florida. If one of my family happened to come to the front in time to see me, of course negotiations would be rudely broken off. But even so, it is clear that I was the first "welcome-to-our-state" Floridian, and I hope the Miami Chamber of Commerce will please take notice.

During this period, white people differed from colored to me only in that they rode through town and never lived there. They liked to hear me "speak pieces" and sing and wanted to see me dance the parse-me-la, and gave me generously of their small silver for doing these things, which seemed strange to me for I wanted to do them so much that I needed bribing to stop. Only they didn't know it. The colored people gave no dimes. They deplored any joyful tendencies in me, but I was their Zora nevertheless. I belonged to them, to the nearby hotels, to the county—everybody's Zora.

But changes came in the family when I was thirteen, and I was sent to school in Jacksonville. I left Eatonville, the town of the oleanders, as Zora. When I disembarked from the riverboat at Jacksonville, she was no more. It seemed that I had suffered a sea change. I was not Zora of Orange County any more, I was now a little colored girl. I found it out in certain ways. In my heart as well as in the mirror, I became a fast brown—warranted not to rub nor run.

But I am not tragically colored. There is no great sorrow dammed up in my soul, nor lurking behind my eyes. I do not mind at all. I do not belong to the sobbing school of Negrohood who hold that nature somehow has given them a low-down dirty deal and whose feelings are all hurt about it. Even in the helter-skelter skirmish that is my life, I have seen that the world is to the strong regardless of a little pigmentation more or less. No, I do not weep at the world—I am too busy sharpening my oyster knife.

Someone is always at my elbow reminding me that I am the granddaughter of slaves. It fails to register depression with me. Slavery is sixty years in the past. The operation was successful and the patient is doing well, thank you. The terrible struggle that made me an American out of a potential slave said "On the line!" The Reconstruction said "Get set!"; and the generation before said "Go!" I am off to a flying start and I must not halt in the stretch to look behind and weep. Slavery is the price I paid for civilization, and the choice was not with me. It is a bully adventure and worth all that I have paid through my ancestors for it. No one on earth ever had a greater chance for glory. The world to be won and nothing to be lost. It is thrilling to think—to know that for any act of mine, I shall get twice as much praise or twice as much blame. It is quite exciting to hold the center of the national stage, with the spectators not knowing whether to laugh or to weep.

The position of my white neighbor is much more difficult. No brown specter pulls up a chair beside me when I sit down to eat. No dark ghost thrusts its leg against mine in bed. The game of keeping what one has is never so exciting as the game of getting.

I do not always feel colored. Even now I often achieve the unconscious Zora of Eatonville before the Hegira. I feel most colored when I am thrown against a sharp white background.

For instance at Barnard. "Beside the waters of the Hudson" I feel my race. Among the thousand white persons, I am a dark rock surged upon, overswept by a creamy sea. I am surged upon and overswept, but through it all, I remain myself. When covered by the waters, I am; and the ebb but reveals me again.

Sometimes it is the other way around. A white person is set down in our midst, but the contrast is just as sharp for me. For instance, when I sit in the drafty basement that is The New World Cabaret with a white person, my color comes. We enter chatting about any little nothing that we have in common and are seated by the jazz waiters. In the abrupt way that jazz orchestras have, this one plunges into a number. It loses no time in circumlocutions, but gets right down to business. It constricts the thorax and splits the heart with its tempo and narcotic harmonies. This orchestra grows rambunctious, rears on its hind legs and attacks the tonal veil with primitive fury, rending it, clawing it until it breaks through to the jungle beyond. I follow those heathen—follow them exultingly. I dance wildly inside myself; I yell within, I whoop; I shake my assegai above my head, I hurl it true to the mark *yeeeeooww!* I am in the jungle and living in the jungle way. My face is painted red and yellow, and my body is painted blue. My pulse is throbbing like a war drum. I want to slaughter something— give pain, give death to what, I do not know. But the piece ends. The men of the orchestra wipe their lips and rest their fingers. I creep back slowly to the veneer we call civilization with the last tone and find the white friend sitting motionless in his seat, smoking calmly.

"Good music they have here," he remarks, drumming the table with his fingertips.

Music! The great blobs of purple and red emotion have not touched him. He has only heard what I felt. He is far away and I see him but dimly across the ocean and the continent that have fallen between us. He is so pale with his whiteness then and I am *so* colored.

At certain times I have no race, I am *me*. When I set my hat at a certain angle and saunter down Seventh Avenue, Harlem City, feeling as snooty as the lions in front of the Forty-Second Street Library, for instance. So far as my feelings are concerned, Peggy Hopkins Joyce on the Boule Mich with her gorgeous raiment, stately carriage, knees knocking together in a most aristocratic manner, has nothing on me. The cosmic Zora emerges. I belong to no race nor time, I am the eternal feminine with its string of beads.

I have no separate feeling about being an American citizen and colored. I am merely a fragment of the Great Soul that surges within the boundaries. My country, right or wrong.

Sometimes, I feel discriminated against, but it does not make me angry. It merely astonishes me. How *can* any deny themselves the pleasure of my company! It's beyond me.

But in the main, I feel like a brown bag of miscellany propped against a wall. Against a wall in company with other bags, white, red and yellow. Pour out the contents, and there is discovered a jumble of small things priceless and worthless. A first-water diamond, an empty spool, bits of broken glass, lengths of string, a key to a door long since crumbled away, a rusty knife-blade, old shoes saved for a road that never was and never will be, a nail bent under the weight of things too heavy for any nail, a dried flower or two, still a little fragrant. In your hand is the brown bag. On the ground before you is the jumble it held—so much like the jumble in the bags, could they be emptied, that all might be dumped in a single heap and the bags refilled without altering the content of any greatly. A bit of colored glass more or less would not matter. Perhaps that is how the Great Stuffer of Bags filled them in the first place—who knows?

*1928*

# IRVING BABBITT

Irving Babbitt (1865–1933) was a proponent of the "New Humanism," which emphasized the importance of respecting tradition and abiding by limits. In this essay, dating from 1930, Babbitt denounces the sentimental utilitarianism whose origin he attributes to Jean-Jacques Rousseau, a source, in his view, of the moral confusion that pervaded American culture after World War I.

---

## What I Believe: Rousseau and Religion

### I

Rousseau is commonly accounted the most influential writer of the past two hundred years. Lord Acton, indeed, is reported to have said, with a touch of exaggeration, that "Rousseau produced more effect with his pen than Aristotle or Cicero or Saint Augustine or Saint Thomas Aquinas or any other man who ever lived." At all events this saying needs to be interpreted in the light of the saying of Madame de Staël that "Rousseau invented nothing but set everything on fire." His leading ideas were abundantly anticipated, especially in England. These ideas made their chief appeal to a middle class which, in the eighteenth century, was gaining rapidly in power and prestige, and has been dominant ever since.

The Rousseauistic outlook on life has also persisted, with many surface modifications, to be sure, but without any serious questioning on the part of most men of its underlying assumptions. To debate Rousseau is really to debate the main issues of our contemporary life in literature, politics, education, and above all, religion. It is not surprising, therefore, that his reputation and writings have from the outset to the present day been a sort of international battle ground. One cannot afford to be merely partisan in this strife, to be blind to Rousseau's numerous merits—for example, to all he did to quicken man's sense of the beauties of nature, especially wild nature. Neither should one forget that there is involved in all the strife a central issue toward which one must finally assume a clear-cut attitude.

Regarding this central issue—the source of the fundamental clash between Rousseauist and anti-Rousseauist—there has been and continues to be much confusion. A chief source of this confusion has been the fact that in Rousseau as in other great writers, and more than in most, there are elements that run counter to the main tendency. Rousseau has, for example, his rationalistic side. On the basis of this fact one professor of French[1] has just set out to prove that, instead of being the arch-sentimentalist he has usually been taken to be, "the real Rousseau is at bottom a rationalist in his ethics, politics, and theology."

Again, there are utterances in Rousseau quite in line with traditional morality. Another American scholar has therefore set out to show that it is a mistake to make Rousseau responsible for a revolution in ethics. Still another of our scholars has managed to convince himself on similar lines that Rousseau is not primarily a primitivist in his "Discourse on Inequality."

Most remarkable of all is a book that has just appeared,[2] the author of which covers with contumely practically all his predecessors in this field on the ground that they have been blinded by partisanship, and promises to give us at last the true meaning of Rousseau. Yet this writer does not even cite the passage that, as Rousseau himself correctly tells us, gives the key to his major writings. It is to this passage that every interpreter of Rousseau who is not academic in the bad sense will give prominence: for the thesis it sums up has actually wrought mightily upon the world. It has thus wrought because it has behind it an imaginative and emotional drive not found behind other passages of Rousseau that might in themselves have served to correct it.

---

[1] *La Pensée de Jean-Jacques Rousseau par Albert Schinz*; 2 vols., Smith College, 1929.
[2] *The Meaning of Rousseau*, Ernest Hunter Wright; Oxford University Press, 1929.

The passage to which I refer is one that occurs in Rousseau's account of the sudden vision that came to him by the roadside on a hot summer day in 1749 in the course of a walk from Paris to Vincennes. This vision has an importance for the main modern movement comparable to that of St. Paul's vision on the road to Damascus for the future development of Christianity. Among the multitude of "truths" that flashed upon Rousseau in the sort of trance into which he was rapt at this moment, the truth of overshadowing importance was, in his own words, that "man is naturally good and that it is by our institutions alone that men become wicked."

The consequences that have flowed from this new "myth" of man's natural goodness have been almost incommensurable. Its first effect was to discredit the theological view of human nature, with its insistence that man has fallen, not from nature as Rousseau asserts, but from God, and that the chief virtue it behooves man to cultivate in this fallen state is humility. According to the Christian, the true opposition between good and evil is in the heart of the individual: the law of the spirit can scarcely prevail, he holds, over the law of the members without a greater or lesser degree of succor in the form of divine grace. The new dualism which Rousseau sets up—that between man naturally good and his institutions—has tended not only to substitute sociology for theology, but to discredit the older dualism in any form whatsoever.

Practically, the warfare of the Rousseauistic crusader has been even less against institutions than against those who control and administer them—kings and priests in the earlier stages of the movement, capitalists in our own day. "We are approaching," Rousseau declared, "the era of crises, and the age of revolutions." He not only made the prophecy but did more than any other one man to insure its fulfillment. There are conservative and even timid elements in his writings; but as a result of the superior imaginative appeal of the new dualism based on the myth of man's natural goodness, the rôle he has actually played has been that of arch-radical. In one of the best balanced estimates that have appeared, the French critic, Gustave Lanson, after doing justice to the various minor trends in Rousseau's work, sums up accurately its major influence: "It exasperates and inspires revolt and fires enthusiasms and irritates hatreds; it is the mother of violence, the source of all that is uncompromising; it launches the simple souls who give themselves up to its strange virtue upon the desperate quest of the absolute, an absolute to be realized now by anarchy and now by social despotism."

I have said that there has been in connection with this Rousseauistic influence a steady yielding of the theological to the sociological or, as it may also be termed, the humanitarian view of life. One should add that there enters into the total philosophy of humanitarianism an ingredient that antedates Rousseau and that may be defined as utilitarian. Utilitarianism already had its prophet in Francis Bacon. Very diverse elements enter into the writings of Bacon as into those of Rousseau, but, like those of Rousseau, they have a central drive: they always have encouraged and, one may safely say, always will encourage the substitution of a kingdom of man for the traditional Kingdom of God—the exaltation of material over spiritual "comfort," the glorification of man's increasing control over the forces of nature under the name of progress.

Rousseauist and Baconian, though often superficially at odds with one another, have coöperated in undermining, not merely religious tradition, but another tradition which in the Occident goes back finally, not to Judæa, but to ancient Greece. This older tradition may be defined as humanistic. The goal of the humanist is poised and pro-portionate living. This he hopes to accomplish by observing the law of measure. Anyone who has bridged successfully the gap between this general precept and some specific emergency has to that extent achieved the fitting and the decorous. Decorum is supreme for the humanist even as humility takes precedence over all other virtues in the eyes of the Christian. Traditionally the idea of decorum has been associated, often with a considerable admixture of mere formalism, with the idea of the gentleman. Humanism and religion in their various forms have at times conflicted, but have more often been in alliance with one another. As Burke says in a well-known passage: "Nothing is more certain than that our manners, our civilisation, and all the good things that are connected with manners and with civilisation, have, in this European world of ours, depended for ages upon two principles; and were indeed the result of both combined; I mean the spirit of a gentleman and the spirit of religion."

## II

All the points of view I have been distinguishing—Baconian, Rousseauist, Christian, humanistic—often mingle confusedly. From all the confusion, however, there finally emerges a clear-cut issue—namely, whether humanitarianism, or, if one prefers, the utilitarian-sentimental movement, has supplied any effective equivalent for Burke's two principles. As for the "spirit of a gentleman," its decline is so obvious as scarcely to admit of argument. It has even been maintained that in America, the country in which the collapse of traditional standards has been most complete, the gentleman is at a positive disadvantage in the world of practical affairs; he is likely to get on more quickly if he assumes the "mucker pose."[3] According to William James, usually taken to be the representative American philosopher, the very idea of the gentleman has about it something slightly satanic. "The prince of darkness," says James, "may be a gentleman, as we are told he is, but, whatever the God of earth and heaven is, he can surely be no gentleman."

As to the spirit of religion, though its decline has in my opinion been at least as great as that of the spirit of a gentleman, it is far from being so obvious. In any case, everything in our modern substitutes for religion—whether Baconian or Rousseauistic—will be found to converge upon the idea of service. The crucial question is whether one is safe in assuming that the immense machinery of power that has resulted from activity of the utilitarian type can be made, on anything like present lines, to serve disinterested ends; whether it will not rather minister to the egoistic aims either of national groups or of individuals.

One's answer to this question will depend on one's view of the Rousseauistic theory of brotherhood. It is at this point, if anywhere, that the whole movement is pseudo-religious. I can give only in barest outline the reasons for my own conviction that it *is* pseudo-religious. It can be shown that the nature from which man has fallen, according to Rousseau, does not correspond to anything real, but is a projection of the idyllic imagination. To assert that man in a state of nature, or

---

[3] See "The Mucker Pose" by James Truslow Adams, *Harper's*, November, 1928.

some similar state thus projected, is good, is to discredit the traditional controls in the actual world. Humility, conversion, decorum—all go by the board in favor of free temperamental overflow. Does man thus emancipated exude spontaneously an affection for his fellows that will be an effective counterpoise to the sheer expansion of his egoistic impulses? If so, one may safely side with all the altruists from the Third Earl of Shaftesbury to John Dewey. One may then assume that there has been no vital omission in the passage from the service of God to the service of man, from salvation by divine grace to salvation by the grace of nature.

Unfortunately, the facts have persistently refused to conform to humanitarian theory. There has been an ever-growing body of evidence from the eighteenth century to the Great War that in the natural man, as he exists in the real world and not in some romantic dreamland, the will to power is, on the whole, more than a match for the will to service. To be sure, many remain unconvinced by this evidence. Stubborn facts, it has been rightly remarked, are as nothing compared with a stubborn theory. Altruistic theory is likely to prove peculiarly stubborn, because, probably more than any other theory ever conceived, it is flattering: it holds out the hope of the highest spiritual benefits—for example, peace and fraternal union—without any corresponding spiritual effort.

If we conclude that humanitarian service cannot take the place of the spirit of religion and that of a gentleman—Burke's "two principles"—what then? One should at least be able to understand the point of view of those who simply reject the modern movement and revert to a more or less purely traditionalist attitude. Dogmatic and revealed Christianity, they hold, has in it a supernatural element for which altruism is no equivalent. Religion of this type, they argue, alone availed to save the ancient world from a decadent naturalism; it alone can cope with a similar situation that confronts the world to-day.

But does it follow, because one's choice between the religious-humanistic and the utilitarian-sentimental view of life should, as I have said, be clear-cut, one is therefore forced to choose between being a pure traditionalist or a mere modernist? At bottom the issue involved is that of individualism. The Roman Catholic, the typical traditionalist, has in matters religious simply repudiated individualism. In this domain at least, he submits to an authority that is "anterior, superior, and exterior" to the individual. The opposite case is that of the man who has emancipated himself from outer authority in the name of the critical spirit (which will be found to be identical with the modern spirit), but has made use of his emancipation, not to work out standards, but to fall into sheer spiritual anarchy. Anyone, on the other hand, who worked out standards critically would be a sound individualist and at the same time a thoroughgoing modern. He would run the risk, to be sure, of antagonizing both traditionalists and modernists; of suffering, in short, the fate of Mr. Pickwick when he intervened between the two angry combatants. This hostility, at least so far as the traditionalist is concerned, would seem to be ill-advised. The true modern, as I am seeking to define him, is prepared to go no small distance with him in the defense of tradition.

At all events, anyone who seeks to deal in modern fashion—in other words, critically—with the religious problem, will be brought back at once to Rousseau. He will have to make his clear-cut choice, not between dogmatic and revealed religion, on the one hand, and mere modernism, on the other, but between a dualism that affirms a struggle between good and evil in the heart of the individual and a dualism which, like that of Rousseau, transfers the struggle to society.

Let us ask ourselves what it is the modern man has tended to lose with the decline of the older dualism. According to Mr. Walter Lippmann, the belief the modern man has lost is "that there is an immortal essence presiding like a king over his appetites." This immortal essence of which Mr. Lippmann speaks is, judged experimentally and by its fruits, a higher will. But why leave the affirmation of such a will to the pure traditionalist? Why not affirm it first of all as a psychological fact, one of the immediate data of consciousness, a perception so primordial that, compared with it, the denial of man's moral freedom by the determinist is only a metaphysical dream? The way would thus be open, as I pointed out in my FORUM review of *A Preface to Morals*, for a swift flanking movement on the behaviorists and other naturalistic psychologists, who are to be accounted at present among the chief enemies of human nature.

This transcendent quality of will—which is the source of humility and is, at the same time, immediate and intuitive—has often been associated traditionally with the operation of God's will in the form of grace. For this higher immediacy, Rousseau—at least the Rousseau who has influenced the world—tended to substitute the lower immediacy of feeling, thus setting up a sort of subrational parody of grace. In order to make this substitution plausible, he—and, in his wake, the sentimentalists—have resorted to the usual arts of the sophist, chief among which are a juggling with half truths and a tampering with general terms. For example, in their use of words like "virtue" and "conscience," they have eliminated more or less completely, in favor of vital impulse (*élan vital*), the equally vital principle of control (*frein vital*)—in short, the dualistic element that both religion and humanism require.

The half truth that has been used to compromise religion in particular is that, though religion is in itself something quite distinct from emotion, it is in its ordinary manifestations very much mixed up with emotion. I give an example of this error in its latest and fashionable form. In a very learned and, in some respects, able book,[4] the Reverend N. P. Williams seeks to show that St. Augustine's experience of grace or, what amounts to the same thing, his love of God, was only a "sublimation" of his "lust." St. Augustine was a very passionate man and his passionateness no doubt entered into his love of God. But if it could be shown that the love of God was in St. Augustine or any other of the major saints merely emotion, sublimated or unsublimated, religion would be only the "illusion" that Freud himself has declared it to be. The psychoanalytical divine, who is, I am told, a fairly frequent type in England, is about the worst *mélange des genres* that has appeared even in the present age of confusion.

Another example of prevailing misapprehensions in this field, and that not merely from the point of view of dogma but of keen psychological observation, is the standard treatment of Rousseau's religion by P. M. Masson, a work which has been almost universally acclaimed by scholars and which has, as a matter of fact, distinguished merits as a historical investigation. M. Masson admits that this religion is

---

[4] *The Ideas of the Fall and of Original Sin* (Bampton Lectures for 1924). See p. 331.

"without redemption or repentance or sense of sin," and then proceeds to speak of Rousseau's "profound Christianity"!

Religion has suffered not only from the Rousseauist but also from the pseudo-scientist. If the Rousseauist gives to emotion a primacy that does not belong to it, the pseudo-scientist claims for physical science a hegemony to which it is not entitled. A science that has thus aspired out of its due place runs the risk of becoming not only a "wild Pallas from the brain" but, in connection with its use in war, "procuress to the Lords of Hell." Mr. Walter Lippmann seeks to persuade us in his *Preface to Morals* that if one becomes "disinterested" after the fashion of the scientific investigator, one will have the equivalent not only of "humanism" but of "high religion." Certain scientific investigators are busy in their laboratories at this very moment devising poison gases of formidable potency. What proof is there that, so far as the scientific type of "disinterestedness" is concerned, these gases will not be pressed into the service of the will to power? In seeking to base ethics on monistic postulates, Mr. Lippmann has simply revived the error of Spinoza, who himself revived the error of the Stoics. This error becomes not less but more dangerous when associated with the methods of science. The question involved is at all events that of the will and finally of dualism. One cannot insist too often that "the immortal essence presiding like a king over man's appetites" is transcendent—in other words, set above "nature," not only in Rousseau's sense, but also in the sense that is given to the term by the man of science.

This higher will is felt in its relation to the impressions and impulses and expansive desires of the natural man as a will to refrain. In the great traditional religions, notably in Christianity and Buddhism, the will to refrain has been pushed to the point of renunciation. The modern movement, on the other hand, has been marked since the eighteenth century and in some respects since the Renaissance by a growing discredit of the will to refrain. The very word "renunciation" has been rarely pronounced by those who have entered into the movement. The chief exception that occurs to one is Goethe (echoed at times by Carlyle). Anyone who thinks of the series of Goethe's love affairs prolonged into the seventies is scarcely likely to maintain that his *Entsagung* was of a very austere character even for the man of the world, not to speak of the saint.

## III

One must admit that genuine renunciation was none too common even in the ages of faith. As for the typical modern, he is not only at an infinite remove from anything resembling renunciation, but is increasingly unable to accept the will to refrain or anything else on a basis of mere tradition and authority. Yet the failure to exercise the will to refrain in some form or degree means spiritual anarchy. A combination such as we are getting more and more at present of spiritual anarchy with an ever-increasing material efficiency—power without wisdom, as one is tempted to put it—is not likely to work either for the happiness of the individual or for the welfare of society. That the drift toward spiritual anarchy has been largely a result of the decline of dogmatic and revealed religion is scarcely open to question. It does not follow that the only hope of recovering spiritual discipline is in a return to this type of religion. Both naturalists and supernaturalists have been too prone to underestimate the value of the third possible attitude toward life which I have defined as the humanistic.

The humanist exercises the will to refrain, but the end that he has in view is not the renunciation of the expansive desires but the subduing of them to the law of measure. The humanistic virtues—moderation, common sense, and common decency—though much more accessible than those of the saint, still go against the grain of the natural man— terribly against the grain, one is forced to conclude from a cool survey of the facts of history. Such, indeed, is the difficulty of getting men to practice even humanistic control that one is led, not necessarily to revive the dogma of original sin, but to suspect that the humanitarians, both Baconian and Rousseauistic, are hopelessly superficial in their treatment of the problem of evil. The social dualism they have set up tends in its ultimate development to substitute the class war for what Diderot termed in his denunciation of the older dualism the "civil war in the cave."

One reason that Rousseau gave for his abandonment of his five children was that he had been robbed by the rich of the wherewithal to feed them. The ease with which multitudes have been persuaded to follow Rousseau in this evasion of moral responsibility puts one on the track of a human trait that one may actually observe in oneself and others, and that gives some positive justification to the theological

emphasis on the old Adam. This trait may be defined as spiritual indo-
lence, a disinclination to oppose to one's expansive desires any will to
refrain, and then to shift the blame on something or somebody else
for the unpleasant consequences.

It is evident that in the eyes of anyone who believes in the existence
in man of a higher will, with reference to which he may be a responsible moral agent, the characteristic modern malady is not plain and
unvarnished materialism but sham spirituality. The remedy would
seem to be in a reaffirmation in some form of the true dualism rather
than in the merely cynical and "hard-boiled" attitude so prevalent
nowadays among those who have become convinced of the final inan-
ity of the humanitarian type of idealism. Joubert wrote over a century
ago: "To all tender, ardent, and elevated natures, I say: Only Rousseau
can detach you from religion, and only true religion can cure you of
Rousseau." I have already made plain that in my judgment one may
not only oppose Rousseau on humanistic as well as religious grounds,
but that, while making abundant use of the wisdom of the past, one
may come at humanism itself in a more positive and critical fashion
than has been customary heretofore.


IV


I can scarcely hope, within the limits of an article, to make entirely
clear what I mean by a positive and critical humanism.[5] This, to judge
by certain current misunderstandings of my position, is a feat I have
been unable to accomplish in a series of volumes. I may, however,
touch briefly on a few of the main issues. A consideration of Rousseau
and his influence will be found to converge on two main problems—
the problem of the will, of which I have already spoken, and, of lesser
though still major importance, the problem of the intellect. That
Rousseau is at the headwaters of an anti-intellectualist trend extending down to James and Bergson and beyond is generally recognized.
This trend is prefigured in his saying that "the man who thinks is a

---

[5] The increasing use of this word of late has been accompanied by a growing confusion as to its meaning. I have attempted my own definition of the term and at the
same time set forth my views on the relation between humanism and religion in a
symposium on humanism to be issued shortly by Farrar and Rinehart.

depraved animal." At bottom the protest of this type of anti-intellectualist is against the mechanizing of the world by a scientific or pseudo-scientific rationalism. He seeks to escape from mechanism by the pathway of romantic spontaneity. This means practically that he is ready to surrender to the naturalistic flux in the hope of thus becoming "creative." Unfortunately this surrender involves a sacrifice of the standards and the conscious control that are needed to give to creation genuine human significance.

It is above all in dealing with the problems of the intellect and the will that I have sought to be positive and critical. As against the Rousseauistic emotionalist, it seems to me imperative to reëstablish the true dualism—that between vital impulse and vital control—and to this end to affirm the higher will first of all as a psychological fact. The individual needs, however, to go beyond this fact if he is to decide how far he is to exercise control in any particular instance with a primary view to his own happiness: in short, he needs standards. To secure standards, at least critically, he cannot afford, like the Rousseauist, to disparage the intellect. One needs to turn its keen power of analysis to an entirely different order of experience from that envisaged by physical science.

To have standards means practically to have some principle of unity with which to measure mere manifoldness and change. There is a power in man, often termed imagination, that reaches out and seizes likenesses and analogies and so tends to establish unity. The unity thus apprehended needs, however, to be tested from the point of view of its reality by the analytical intellect—the power that discriminates—working not abstractly but on the actual data of experience. The fraternal union that the Rousseauist would establish among men on the basis of expansive emotion is found, when tested in this way, to involve an imaginative flight from the reality of both the human and the natural order, and so to exist only in dreamland. An inspection of all the facts of human experience, past and present, would seem to show that what unity a man may achieve either within himself or with his fellow men must be based primarily, not upon feeling, but upon an exercise of the higher will.

One's conception of the constant and unifying factor in life will appear in one's use of general terms. It is plain that the humanist and the Rousseauist clash radically in their definitions. As a result of his elimination of the dualistic element, the Rousseauist has, as I have remarked, set up a "virtue" that, in the eyes of the humanist, is not true virtue; and so likewise for such terms as "justice" and "liberty," and above all (at least in its application to man) "nature." If there is to be a reintegration of the dualistic element into these words, there would seem to be needed an art of inductive defining somewhat similar to that which Socrates brought to bear upon the sophists. It is precisely at this point that the keen discrimination of which I have spoken would have its fullest play. At all events one may say that the standards that result from the coöperation of the imagination and the analytical intellect, and that are reflected in one's definitions, are finally pressed by the humanist into the service of the higher will with a view to imposing a right direction upon the impulses and expansive desires of the natural man.

The humanist is rather distrustful of sudden conversions and pistol-shot transformations of human nature. Hence his supreme emphasis on education. If the humanistic goal is to be attained, if the adult is to like and dislike the things he should—according to Plato, the ultimate aim of ethical endeavor—he must be trained in the appropriate habits almost from infancy. Occasional humanists may appear under present conditions, but if there is to be anything resembling a humanistic movement, the first stage would, as I have said, be that of Socratic definition; the second stage would be the coming together of a group of persons on the basis of this definition—the working out, in short, in the literal sense of that unjustly discredited word, of a convention; the third stage would almost inevitably be the attempt to make this convention effective through education.

V

The mention of education brings the whole discussion home to America. Our educators are more completely and more naïvely Rousseauistic than those of almost any other country. For example, there is an important survival of the religious-humanistic conception of education in France and Germany and, above all, England; whereas the assumption is all but universal among those who control our educational policies from the elementary grades to the university that anything that sets bounds to the free unfolding of the temperamental proclivities of the young, to their right to self-expression, as one may say, is outworn prejudice. Discipline, so far as it exists, is not of the humanistic or the religious type, but of the kind that one gets in training for a vocation or a specialty. The standards of a genuinely liberal education, as they have been understood, more or less from the time of Aristotle, are being progressively undermined by the utilitarians and the sentimentalists. If the Baconian-Rousseauistic formula is as unsound in certain of its postulates as I myself believe, we are in danger of witnessing in this country one of the great cultural tragedies of the ages.

Moreover Rousseauism not only dominates our education but has been eating into the very vitals of the Protestant religion. Practically, this means that Protestantism is ceasing to be a religion of the inner life and is becoming more and more a religion of "uplift." The result of the attempt to deal with evil socially rather than at its source in the individual, to substitute an outer for an inner control of appetite, has been a monstrous legalism, of which the Eighteenth Amendment is only the most notable example. Those Protestants who have allied themselves with an organization like the Anti-Saloon League have been violating one of the most necessary of Christian precepts—that which warns against confounding the things of God with the things of Caesar.

The multiplication of laws, attended by a growing lawlessness—the present situation in this country—is, as every student of history knows, a very sinister symptom. It may mean that our democratic experiment is, like similar experiments in the past, to end in a decadent imperialism. Nothing is farther from my thought than to suggest that we are on a fatal descending curve. I do not believe in any such fatality, and am in general skeptical of every possible philosophy of history—of the Spenglerian variety most of all. The all-important factor that the Spenglers are wont to overlook or deny in favor of collective tendencies is the moral choices of individuals. For example, the majority in the United States seems just now to be careless of the higher cultural values, to desire nothing better than a continuation of the present type of material prosperity based on the miracles of mass production. Individuals, however, are already standing aside from the majority and assuming a critical attitude toward its "ideals."

Whether this remnant will become sufficiently large to make itself felt in an important way, remains of course a question. At all events, there is an increasing number of persons in this country who can at least see the point of view of the rest of the world. This point of view may be defined as a curious blend of admiration for our efficiency and of disdain for our materialism. The foreigner is, however, far too prone to make America the universal scapegoat for the present domination of man by the machine.

Though the utilitarian-sentimental movement may have triumphed more completely in America than elsewhere, it has been extending its conquests over the whole of the Occident and is now invading the Orient. The issues it raises are, in short, international. That the peripheral merits of this movement are almost innumerable I should be the first to admit: indeed, almost everything in it seems plausible until one penetrates to its very center, and then one discovers an omission that unless corrected vitiates all the rest—the omission, namely, as I have been trying to show, of any reference to a higher will or power of control.

Without making any pretense to a prophetic rôle for which I am not qualified, I am yet willing to express the conviction that unless there is a recovery of the true dualism or, what amounts to the same thing, a reaffirmation of the truths of the inner life in some form—traditional or critical, religious or humanistic—civilization in any sense that has been attached to that term hitherto is threatened at its base. I speak of the interests of civilization, though my own prime objection to Rousseauism is that it is found finally not to make for the happiness of the individual.

*1930*

# WILLIAM HENRY CHAMBERLIN

William Henry Chamberlin (1897–1969) was another writer who made the journey from left to right, his transformation resulting from several years spent as a journalist covering the Soviet Union. His firsthand experience of Nazi Germany convinced him that collectivism in any form posed a proximate danger not only to the United States but to civilization itself.

———————

## The Choice Before Civilization

M R. JOHN STRACHEY, one of the ablest modern communist theoreticians, sees the world confronted by two alternatives: communism and barbarism. Were this diagnosis correct, the outlook for civilization would be dark indeed. A choice between communism and barbarism, a term which Mr. Strachey regards as identical with fascism, is no choice at all.

For everything barbarous that is associated with fascism can be duplicated, and often surpassed under communism. Call the dreary roll of fascist atrocities and name one that is not part of the stock-in-trade of the communist dictatorship in the Soviet Union. Killings of political opponents, wholesale consignment of "counter-revolutionaries" to concentration camps, extension of the number of offenses for which the death penalty is inflicted, punishment of innocent individuals for the offenses of relatives and friends, complete repression of freedom of press, speech, and assembly, regimentation of art and culture to serve the purposes of the ruling party: what item in this list is not just as characteristic of the Soviet Union as of Germany and Italy? And, if the race fanaticism which is peculiar to the German brand of fascism cannot be charged against the Soviet Union, the class fanaticism which prevails there has taken far more victims.

Fortunately there is a more real alternative to barbarism than communism. This alternative is liberty. Liberty or barbarism: this is indeed the choice before the civilization of the twentieth century.

The term "barbarism" in this connection requires some qualification. Neither Russia nor Germany nor Italy today can be accurately or reasonably compared with the broken fragments of the Roman Empire in the Dark Ages. There has been no such complete break-up of the elements of civilized life as history records after some sweeping incursions of nomadic barbarians. Under the dictatorships, as under the democracies, children go to school and adults read books and newspapers, visit art galleries, attend concerts.

Yet anyone who has lived for a long time in one of the collectivist dictatorships is likely to feel that some of the most precious aspects of civilization are irretrievably gone. I personally had this feeling very sharply on two occasions, once in Russia and once in Germany. In Russia it was the reaction to the death of some unknown peasant children; in Germany it was the result of an attempt on the life of a well-known political leader.

I was visiting the village of Zhuke, near Poltava in Ukraina, in the autumn of 1933, accompanied by the head of the local collective farm and a young agricultural expert, both Communists. They were assiduously guiding me to the houses of local Communists and of those peasants who held the posts of minor bosses in the collective farm. I finally decided to pick out a house at random; my companions showed little enthusiasm at my choice, but entered the whitewashed log cabin with me.

Crouched on a bench by the wall was a girl, perhaps twelve or thirteen years old, who looked dull and listless from undernourishment. Had she a father? Yes, he was working in the fields. A mother? No, the mother had died of hunger during the last winter. Brothers and sisters? Four, all dead of hunger. There was no declamation, no outburst of grief, just a stolid repetition of the story, which I had already heard in dozens of peasant houses in southern and southeastern Russia, of men, women, children dying in uncounted numbers because the Soviet government, believing that the peasants were sabotaging its programme of forced collectivization, had taken away the last reserves of food with its requisitions and then failed to supply any adequate relief when starvation came. That such avoidable human catastrophe could occur, and occur without one word of public protest or even comment in Russia, definitely seemed to me barbarous.

The circumstances of my German reaction were somewhat different. I learned on unimpeachable authority the amazing story of how a former Cabinet Minister, Treviranus, was playing tennis on his private court during the fateful days of the June 30th "purge," how a truckload of "SS men," Hitler's black-uniformed special guards, drove up determined to shoot him on the spot, and how Treviranus made a truly phenomenal escape by climbing over the garden wall, jumping into his automobile, which luckily stood outside, eluding his pursuers, and finally escaping to England when the situation became quieter.

Treviranus was not even a Social Democrat; he was a moderate German nationalist who for some reason was considered objectionable to the Nazi regime. It was decided to "bump him off" with no more ceremony than Scarface Al Capone's "mob" would have shown in getting rid of a competitor in the bootleg business. That such a thing could happen in placid, supremely orderly Berlin seemed not only barbarous but fantastic, grotesque.

I have never lived for any long period of time in Italy. But I can imagine that to many residents of Italy, both Italians and foreigners, the murder of Matteotti must have been the symbol of the death of some values of the mellow old Italian civilization which Mussolini could never replace, no matter how many soldiers he put into uniform, how many automobile roads he built or how fast and punctually the Italian trains ran under his guidance.

Regarded as isolated cases, of course, neither the deaths of the Ukrainian woman and her children nor the attack on Treviranus nor the murder of Matteotti could be regarded as of such transcendent importance. What lent focal, symbolic, universal significance to these individual tragedies was that they are so characteristic of the communist-fascist technique of government.

Collectivist dictatorship in any form means a kind of neo-medievalism in its contempt for the individual personality. It means an end of that respect for reason and for individual conscience that is a feature of a modern civilization with roots in the Renaissance, the Reformation, and the French Revolution. A German editor recently remarked to a foreign visitor:

> We have become a nation of mass meetings, mass theatres, mass celebrations, and mass elections.

This statement is true and is equally applicable to the Soviet Union and to Italy. In the collectivist state the individual is completely submerged in the mass. A trained psychologist could find in each of them a remarkable illustration of the powers of mass hypnotism. Get the average Russian, German, or Italian by himself, and the critical note is apt to be uppermost. But in the mass, fear and carefully stimulated enthusiasm operate much more effectively. This is why every modern-style dictatorship is so eager to line up the individual in its regimented mass organizations, to make him spend much of his time parading and shouting in unison, to leave as little scope as possible for solitary individual thought and reflection.

The collectivist state means the end of the individual personality. It has no tolerance for reason, if this contradicts the supposedly infallible pronouncements of the "leader"; it grants no right to the individual conscience, if this inspires protests against arbitrary arrests and executions in Russia or against Jew-baiting and militarization in Germany. So both the sincere Christian who feels that under certain circumstances he must obey God rather than man and the sceptical humanist who acknowledges no authority higher than that of his own reason must always be spiritual outlaws under the yoke of the collectivist dictatorship.

This yoke bears down especially hard on the creative artist in every field. The ideal of the humanistic civilization that the author, painter, musician should be the sole judge of the form and content of his work is indignantly and vigorously repudiated in all the collectivist states. The National Socialist Party organ *Völkischer Beobachter*, in its issue of May 21, 1934, served the following uncompromising notice on the German artist to get into uniform and march in step:

> So long as there remains in Germany any unpolitical, neutral, liberal or individualistic art, our task is not ended. There must no longer be a single artist who creates otherwise than nationally and with a national purpose. Every artist who withdraws from this preoccupation must be

hunted as an enemy of the nation until he gives up his intolerable resistance.

An admirable supplementary exhibit in the compulsory harnessing of art to the service of propaganda is to be found in the following definition of the aim of the Soviet writer, as set down in the constitution of the Soviet Writers' Union:[1]

> The creation of works of high artistic significance, saturated with the heroic struggle of the international proletariat, with the grandeur of the victory of socialism, and reflecting the great wisdom and heroism of the Communist Party . . . the creation of artistic works worthy of the great age of socialism.

Imagine how Shakespeare, Goethe, Tolstoy, Molière, or any other universal genius would fit into this artistic strait-jacket. The inevitable result of trying to turn literature, drama, and other forms of art into propaganda ballyhoo for an existing political and economic system is to make works of genuinely "high artistic significance" impossible. For the greatest creative geniuses have usually been neutral in relation to the political nostrums of their age. Some fine works have been inspired by protest against injustice and oppression. But the world's artistic heritage would scarcely be the poorer for the elimination of all the histories, poems, novels, and dramas that were deliberately written in glorification of the *status quo* of any period. One of Pushkin's most beautiful poems, his "Message to Siberia," was inspired by the courage and sufferings of the Decabristi, the aristocratic rebels against the autocracy in 1825, who were banished to hard labor in Siberia. It begins:

> Deep in the Siberian mine,
> Keep your patience proud;
> The bitter toil shall not be lost,
> The rebel thought unbowed,

and ends with the glowing lines:

---

[1] In the Soviet Union, as in Germany and Italy, all authors, in order to earn their living, must belong to a professional union.

The heavy-hanging chains will fall,
The walls will crumble at a word;
And Freedom greet you in the light
And brothers give you back your sword.


No doubt there were contemporaries of Pushkin who followed the rule, now prescribed for Soviet authors, of zealously praising the existing order. Court poets probably wrote odes about the "great wisdom and virtue" of Tsar Nicholas I and his chief Ministers. But, while Pushkin's generous praise of the proscribed Decabristi lives, the official eulogistic literature of the time is dead and forgotten; and it is not difficult to foresee that a similar fate will have overtaken the Soviet propaganda literature of the present age a century from now.

No art is safe from the meddling of dictatorships and dictators. Modern styles in architecture in Germany languish under Hitler's frown. The compositions of Dmitry Shostakovitch, one of the most brilliant and internationally well-known Soviet composers, have been completely banished from Soviet opera houses and concert halls because, according to reports from Moscow, Stalin attended a performance of Shostakovitch's opera, "Lady Macbeth of Mtzensk County," and expressed an unfavorable judgment on it. This suggests very vividly the appalling results that might follow from the accession to power some day of a dictator who was stone-deaf, or even tone-deaf.

Not content with giving their own artists the alternative of propaganda or silence, the collectivist dictatorships try to twist the creative thinkers of the past into propagandists for their pet theories. One of the most revealing and amusing products of Soviet scholarship is a recent book entitled "Shakespeare: A Marxist Interpretation," by A. A. Smirnov. No one would be more surprised than Shakespeare himself to find the ideas which have been discovered in his work by a Marxist investigator. Shakespeare, according to Mr. Smirnov, was "the humanist ideologist of the bourgeoisie of his time" who exposes "feudal knights and profit-knights of primary accumulation." Iago, in Mr. Smirnov's interpretation, becomes "the predatory cynical philistine merchant of the period of primary accumulation," while "Lear" is a criticism of the feudal aristocratic system. Caliban, for the first time in his life, becomes "a true revolutionary," and Shakespeare's tragedies and comedies are described as "militant revolutionary protests against feudal forms, conceptions, institutions," with their roots in "the revolutionary ideas and moods of the bourgeoisie."

Now under any system fools have written about geniuses. But Mr. Smirnov's brand of dogmatic absurdity is far more frequently encountered under dictatorship than under democracy; one can readily imagine a Nazi Goethe and a Fascist Dante that would be about as far removed from the original as this "Marxist" Shakespeare. And, what is still worse, any freak idea that adroitly flatters the ruling system may be made a compulsory article of faith, not open to criticism.

So it is evident that any spread of collectivist dictatorship, either in its fascist or in its communist form, will mean a further submergence of individual personality and a regimentation of thought and cultural life that is not only impossible, but almost unimaginable under free institutions. Belief that such a spread was inevitable has been general, especially during the darker period of the world crisis.

Yet it seems probable that dictatorship has now reached the limit of its conquests. It is noteworthy that these conquests have hitherto been achieved in lands where democracy was an alien and skin-deep conception of government, in Russia with its background of absolutism and popular ignorance, in Italy, where centuries of foreign misrule, poverty, and illiteracy blighted the effective working of a parliamentary system, in countries of Eastern and Southern Europe which lacked essential prerequisites for the successful functioning of democracy, such as general education, wide diffusion of private property, a sense, developed through centuries of struggle and experiment, of the importance of protecting the individual against the arbitrary violence of the state. Germany was culturally best suited for the introduction of a democratic system. But democracy there labored under the fatal handicap of being regarded as one of the terms of the hated Treaty of Versailles. Germany could no more be converted to a belief in the desirability of democracy by having it associated with all the material distress and psychological humiliation of a lost war than the southern states in America could be persuaded of the advantages of Negro suffrage by the methods which were employed during the Reconstruction era after the Civil War.

So up to the present time democracy has only lost ground that was never very securely held. In Spain, now given over to a devastating

civil war which seems bound to lead to dictatorship, the whole nineteenth century was filled with rebellions and civil disturbances. The
left-wing parties which were in control of the government at the time
of the outbreak of civil war in July, 1936, had themselves rebelled
against a conservative government, which possessed a parliamentary
majority, in 1934. There was not enough balancing moderate strength
in Spain to prevent the extremists of the left and the right from fighting their differences out on the battlefields of civil war, instead of
compromising and adjusting them in parliamentary debates.

The position of democracy is obviously vastly stronger in Great
Britain, France, and the United States. All these countries have passed
through revolutions undertaken to vindicate the right of the people
to govern themselves. America and Great Britain have no precedent
for army meddling in politics (a frequent cause of the downfall of
democratic experiments); and France has developed a tradition of
orderly republican government stretching back for sixty-five years.
The smaller countries that have preserved free institutions also possess
their historic backgrounds of freedom. Switzerland's early emergence
as a republic, Holland's heroic struggle against Spanish rule are not
without significance for the present day.

While there is of course freer expression of criticism and discontent
in the democracies than in the dictatorships, the margin of individual
well-being under the contrasted systems is so much in favor of the
free countries that they are in little danger of seeing their institutions
subverted by rebellion from within. War, of course, is an international
menace. But there seems to be at least a fair prospect that the area of
a future conflict may be largely confined to the dictatorships. In this
case the contrast in standards of living under the two systems will
become still greater.

One mildly disquieting symptom is the defeatist attitude toward
individual liberty and democratic methods of government that is prevalent in some circles of the left-wing intelligentsia in America and
Great Britain. Intellectual advocacy of fascism is still a rarity, although
fascism of some kind and not communism would certainly be the
result of a breakdown of free institutions in a country with a fairly
high material standard of living. But there is a pronounced tendency
among some liberals and radicals to create a curious double standard
of morals, in judging the Soviet Union and the rest of the world. The

standard applied to fascist and democratic regimes is hard and uncompromising. It suggests Jonathan Edwards, hell-fire and damnation of unbaptized infants. In the case of the Soviet government, however, no act of cruelty is too great to be forgiven, ignored, or praised with faint blame.

To get down to more concrete cases, one will find in liberal and radical journals many harrowing accounts of conditions in German and Italian concentration camps, but never a line of suggestion that the inmates of Soviet concentration camps are far more numerous and no better treated. One will look in vain in such journals for any severely critical comment on Soviet laws which would certainly have been denounced in the most vigorous terms if they had been promulgated by Hitler or Mussolini. Imagine the storm about the inherently barbarous character of fascism if Hitler should duplicate the Soviet law which prescribes death for theft of state property or Mussolini should take over the Soviet piece of legislation condemning to exile in Siberia innocent relatives of citizens who flee from the country without passports. And it is hard to understand by what peculiar logical processes individuals who are rightfully indignant over the execution of Sacco and Vanzetti and the imprisonment of Tom Mooney can simultaneously exalt or even condone a system that has slaughtered thousands of Russians on no more evidence than existed in the case of Sacco and Vanzetti, and has herded hundreds of thousands into concentration camps that are no more desirable places of residence than San Quentin Prison without any more reason than could be adduced for the imprisonment of Mooney.

This double standard of morals may be attributed partly to a lack of sense of proportion,[2] partly to profound ignorance of actual conditions under Soviet rule.[3] There is also a messianic faith in the redeeming vir-

---

[2] Every honest believer in democratic government must have resented the arrest of the Communist candidate for President, Mr. Earl Browder, by the Terre Haute police for the purpose of preventing him from exercising his constitutional right of free speech. But how lucky any anti-Stalinite speaker, Communist or non-Communist, would be in the Soviet Union if he could freely address large audiences in all the large cities of the country with no more serious penalty than a day in the lock-up of some Russian Terre Haute, such as Kursk or Kolomna!

[3] The index of Mr. John Strachey's book "The Nature of the Capitalist Crisis" reveals only one reference to the Soviet Union, a dogmatic statement, unsupported by any concrete evidence, that the dilemma of profits or plenty has been satisfactorily

tues of revolution. This faith is not disturbed by the obvious working out, in Russia at the present time, of what seems to be an unfailing law of historical development: that excesses of revolution lead to reaction just as unfailingly as excesses of reaction bring about revolution. This law has received striking fulfilment in the course of the two greatest social upheavals of modern times, the French and Russian revolutions. It is best depicted, in the case of France, not by any detailed history, but by Anatole France's vivid story, "The Gods Are Athirst." Here one sees revolutionary fanaticism, suffering, exaltation, terror reaching an apex and then, after the Ninth Thermidor and the execution of Robespierre and his leading associates, a new era setting in, milder as regards terror, also less idealistic, with everyone deciding to forget about impossible ideals, enjoy life, and get rich.

It is just such a Thermidorian stage that is now in progress in Russia. The Soviet bureaucracy is constantly improving its material position by comparison with the "proletariat," the theoretical sovereign of the country. Marriage and frequent childbearing are strongly recommended to the "emancipated" women. Army and navy officers receive old resounding titles instead of the simple "comrade commander" of revolutionary days. The manager in the factory, the parent in the home, the teacher in the school, all are being vigorously strengthened in authority. The dictatorship of the proletariat has never been anything but a play with words, an unreal and unrealizable conception; and now it becomes increasingly clear that the true beneficiary of the Russian Revolution is not the manual working class as a whole, still less the people as a whole, but the military, police, political, and economic bureaucracy that is firmly entrenched in the seats of power. Some of the members of this bureaucracy are ex-workers, and some are not. But none of them will ever work with their hands again so long as the present regime survives.

Revolutionary terrorism, if one may judge from the double experience of France and of the Soviet Union, passes through three stages, reflecting the changing psychology of the transition from the destruction of old inequalities to the consolidation of new ones. First there is

---

solved there. Such a root-and-branch critic of the capitalist system might, one would think, have profitably devoted a little more attention to the problems and defects which experience has indicated in the alternative communist system which he prefers.

mob violence, some of it sporadic and accidental, some of it directed against individuals who are personally unpopular. The victims of this stage are mostly members of classes prominently identified with the old regime.

The second stage is that of organized governmental mass terror, motivated partly by the determination to smash counter-revolution, partly by the necessity of suppressing very sternly the disillusionment that naturally makes itself felt among the masses when the revolution brings war and hunger, not the peace and plenty that have been promised.

And finally, when the new revolutionary order has become firmly established, when the new classes that have risen to power on the ruins of the old wish to insure and stabilize their position, a third phase of terror begins. The Revolution, in Taine's brilliant phrase, emulates the crocodile and begins to devour its young. When one sees the names of such prominent old Bolsheviks as Zinoviev and Kamenev, Smirnov and Yevdokimov in the list of sixteen who were shot for alleged conspiracy against Stalin, when such outstanding figures of the first years of the Revolution as Radek, Sokolnikov, Pyatikov, Bukharin, and Rykov are reported as arrested or suspected in connection with similar conspiracies, it is evident that the Thermidorian period of the Russian Bolshevik Revolution is here.

There is no new heaven and new earth at the end of the blood-soaked road of social revolution. There are only new individuals, new groups in power, shooting down their own more extreme former comrades as a means of keeping themselves there. Under circumstances of extreme oppression, where no other means of redress is left, revolution, like war, may be necessary and justifiable. But revolutions, like wars, tend to become more destructive with the passing of time. There is not the slightest justification for resorting to this uncommonly costly means of forcing political and economic change while the machinery of free institutions continues to function, most especially as the results of revolutions almost invariably fall so far short of the dreams of the fanatical idealists who are in the foreground during their early phases.

Viewed realistically from the standpoint of the common man, the collectivist utopias do not seem to deliver the goods. The abolition of normal safeguards of personal liberty, of security against arbitrary arrest and imprisonment opens the way to an amount of cruelty and injustice that must be seen to be adequately realized. Mr. Sinclair Lewis's picture of the prospective brutalities of a fascist regime in America is not in the least overdrawn. And, if the experience of Russia is any guide, these brutalities would only be greater, affecting more people, if communists rather than fascists were in supreme power. It is difficult to estimate the reserves of human bestiality and sadism that have been slowly, gradually, imperfectly bridled by the formation of democratic institutions and that immediately reappear in full force when the bars are let down under a dictatorship.

The causes of class antagonism are not removed in the collectivist states; only the symptoms are driven underground. People do not cease to suffer from poverty and want; they are only obliged to cease complaining. Not one of the present-day dictatorships gives its subjects a standard of living remotely comparable with that of the leading democratic countries.

Much of the inflated prestige of dictatorship, much of the impatient contempt for democracy that one encounters today is attributable to an exaggerated reaction against a misplaced emphasis in nineteenth century thought. Historical development at that time was interpreted too exclusively in political, legal, constitutional terms. Economic influences were apt to be neglected or pushed into the background.

Many political and economic publicists of the present time, I think, have erred in precisely the opposite direction. They have become so obsessed with a purely economic interpretation of history that they overrate the power of wealth and very much underrate the progressive significance of the curbs which the development of free institutions has placed on the arbitrary exercise of governmental power. They are altogether too ready to sacrifice liberty lightly on the altar of some doctrinaire blueprint of the perfect state, drawn up in accordance with fascist or communist specifications.

Now nothing could be more utopian in the worst sense of the word, more impracticable, more foredoomed to failure, than an attempt to solve the problem of wealth without considering the much more important problem of power. For one of the most serious and justified criticisms of large aggregations of wealth is the undue power and influence which they confer on their owners. This is a permanent menace in a democracy, a menace for which constant vigilance and a high sense of public spirit are the sole remedies.

But the power which wealth confers in a country that possesses freedom of speech, press, assembly, and voting is a very mild and tame thing compared with the absolute power that is vested in the rulers of the collectivist dictatorship. It is difficult to see how abuses arising from inequality of wealth will be cured by instituting a form of extreme inequality of power. The very concept of dictatorship implies that some people are dictating and others are being dictated to. In the light of all historical experience, it seems inevitable that the individuals and groups which are at the transitive end of the dictating process will build up not only a privileged status, but also a favored material position.

The idea, implicitly held by communists and uncritical admirers of the Soviet Union, that the remedy for the evils of private capitalism is to make the state the sole capitalist, simultaneously depriving the individual, under one-party dictatorship, of all effective safeguards against exploitation and oppression by the state, deserves more examination than it has received. Many of the most ruthless acts which can be laid to the account of private capitalism are attributable to the bigness and consequent sense of irresponsibility of some private corporations. But what corporation can be bigger, more irresponsible, more "soulless" than a state that operates everything from steel mills to barber shops, that sets the price which the peasant gets for his grain and the wage that is paid to the worker in mine or factory?

Such a state, even though its founders be the most high-minded idealists, is bound to turn into an extreme form of tyranny unless its enormous powers are somehow checked and controlled by counterbalancing forces from below. The most effective means of assuring "government of the people, by the people, for the people" are periodic free elections, with full liberty of speech and press and freedom of trade-union organization. All these checks are eliminated under both fascist and communist brands of collectivist utopia.

Mere reiteration of the principles of civil and political liberty is, of course, no adequate remedy for the maladjustments which have come to society with the machine age. Still less is salvation to be found in scrapping these liberties on the demonstrably illusory theory that economic welfare and security can be bought at the price of freedom.

For liberty is not a bare abstraction, an academic formula. It is a supremely important practical instrument for carrying on the organized life of society with much better material results and vastly less cruelty, oppression, and injustice than one must reckon with under any dictatorship. It should always be associated with progress, never with stagnation and the mere maintenance of the social and economic *status quo*. It will be a bad day for any country when the idea of liberty can be plausibly represented as a screen for wealth and special privilege. So far as there is definite human responsibility for the wasteful ferocity of violent revolution, it must lie mainly at the doors of those die-hard reactionary classes and groups that are too shortsightedly selfish to make the compromises, concessions, and adjustments that are necessary for orderly progress. A common bond of stiff-necked futility links the Roman Senator of the time of Sulla, the French aristocrat of the middle eighteenth century, the conservative Russian landlord or official of pre-war days.

The grip of the modern-style collectivist dictatorships is strong. They seem proof against anything but the unpredictable chances of unsuccessful war. Yet there is a fraudulent element in their claims of universal popular support that crops up again and again. It is a far more convincing achievement to win a 55 or 60 per cent majority in a free and honest election than to receive a unanimous vote of confidence (no other kind has been known for many years) at a Soviet Congress or a 99 per cent majority in a Hitler plebiscite.

John Milton's strong manly English style is old-fashioned. But the thought of the following quotation rings just as fresh and true today, with Western civilization facing the alternatives of democracy or dictatorship, as in Milton's time, when England had been the first large country to repudiate the divine rights of kings:[4]

> Certainly then that people must needs be mad or strangely infatuated, that build the chief hope of their common happiness or safety on a single person; who, if he happen to be good, can do no more than

---

[4] *Cf.* the essay on establishing a free commonwealth in "Areopagitica and Other Prose Works" (Everyman's Library ed.), p. 169.

another man; if to be bad, hath in his hands to do more evil without check than millions of other men. The happiness of a nation must needs be firmest and certainest in full and free council of their own electing, where no single person, but reason only, sways.

The struggle for liberty is unceasing, although the figures in the struggle change. In Voltaire's time kings and priests could fairly be regarded as outstanding enemies of human freedom. Now they have given place to communist and fascist dictators.

In an age of rapid social change and scientific advance it is certainly wrong to make a dogma and a fetish out of any detail of economic organization. It is not of vital importance whether railways and public utilities and similar enterprises are nationally or municipally or privately owned. Every country, provided it retains democratic self-government, can be depended on to work out the arrangement which is best suited to its needs.

But it is a matter of tremendous importance whether people can speak and write and vote freely, whether they can go to bed without fear of being dragged off to questioning, torture, exile, or execution by some irresponsible secret police, whether they can talk above a whisper about public affairs when there are unknown listeners. Once the juggernaut of collectivist dictatorship rolls over a country, irreparable damage is done to its standards of culture, to the quality of its human relations, to the most elementary canons of common decency. Freedom, once lost in a modern dictatorship, can be regained, if at all, only by a long and incredibly painful struggle. With the record of communism and fascism written large for all to read, the absolute and unconditional value of human liberty is no longer a theoretical or debatable proposition.

Patrick Henry's flaming phrase, liberty or death, is a sober statement of the alternative that confronts civilization in the twentieth century.

*1937*

# WHITTAKER CHAMBERS

No American conservative in the twentieth century elicited greater animus from some quarters and greater respect in others than Whittaker Chambers (1901–1961). While a Communist Party member in the 1920s, Chambers wrote for publications such as *The Daily Worker* and *The New Masses*. In the 1930s, he went underground, spying on behalf of the Soviet Union. In 1938, a disenchanted Chambers broke with the Party and returned to journalism, achieving success as an editor for *Time*. Subpoenaed a decade later by the House Un-American Activities Committee, Chambers offered testimony about others who had engaged in espionage for the Soviet Union. Among those he named was Alger Hiss, a highly respected figure in the foreign policy establishment. Called before a federal grand jury, Hiss denied under oath that he had betrayed his country. In the perjury trial that followed—with Chambers the prosecution's star witness—Hiss was convicted and served more than three years in prison. For decades the case remained highly divisive—proof to some that Communists had infiltrated the highest levels of the United States government, evidence to others of an anticommunist witch hunt. Chambers subsequently wrote a controversial memoir from which this excerpt is drawn.

# Foreword in the Form of a
# Letter to My Children

BELOVED CHILDREN,
I am sitting in the kitchen of the little house at Medfield, our second farm which is cut off by the ridge and a quarter-mile across the fields from our home place, where you are. I am writing a book. In it

I am speaking to you. But I am also speaking to the world. To both I owe an accounting.

It is a terrible book. It is terrible in what it tells about men. If anything, it is more terrible in what it tells about the world in which you live. It is about what the world calls the Hiss-Chambers Case, or even more simply, the Hiss Case. It is about a spy case. All the props of an espionage case are there—foreign agents, household traitors, stolen documents, microfilm, furtive meetings, secret hideaways, phony names, an informer, investigations, trials, official justice.

But if the Hiss Case were only this, it would not be worth my writing about or your reading about. It would be another fat folder in the sad files of the police, another crime drama in which the props would be mistaken for the play (as many people have consistently mistaken them). It would not be what alone gave it meaning, what the mass of men and women instinctively sensed it to be, often without quite knowing why. It would not be what, at the very beginning, I was moved to call it: "a tragedy of history."

For it was more than human tragedy. Much more than Alger Hiss or Whittaker Chambers was on trial in the trials of Alger Hiss. Two faiths were on trial. Human societies, like human beings, live by faith and die when faith dies. At issue in the Hiss Case was the question whether this sick society, which we call Western civilization, could in its extremity still cast up a man whose faith in it was so great that he would voluntarily abandon those things which men hold good, including life, to defend it. At issue was the question whether this man's faith could prevail against a man whose equal faith it was that this society is sick beyond saving, and that mercy itself pleads for its swift extinction and replacement by another. At issue was the question whether, in the desperately divided society, there still remained the will to recognize the issues in time to offset the immense rally of public power to distort and pervert the facts.

At heart, the Great Case was this critical conflict of faiths; that is why it was a great case. On a scale personal enough to be felt by all, but big enough to be symbolic, the two irreconcilable faiths of our time—Communism and Freedom—came to grips in the persons of two conscious and resolute men. Indeed, it would have been hard, in a world still only dimly aware of what the conflict is about, to find two other men who knew so clearly. Both had been schooled in the same view of history (the Marxist view). Both were trained by the same party in the same selfless, semisoldierly discipline. Neither would nor could yield without betraying, not himself, but his faith; and the different character of these faiths was shown by the different conduct of the two men toward each other throughout the struggle. For, with dark certitude, both knew, almost from the beginning, that the Great Case could end only in the destruction of one or both of the contending figures, just as the history of our times (both men had been taught) can end only in the destruction of one or both of the contending forces.

But this destruction is not the tragedy. The nature of tragedy is itself misunderstood. Part of the world supposes that the tragedy in the Hiss Case lies in the acts of disloyalty revealed. Part believes that the tragedy lies in the fact that an able, intelligent man, Alger Hiss, was cut short in the course of a brilliant public career. Some find it tragic that Whittaker Chambers, of his own will, gave up a $30,000-a-year job and a secure future to haunt for the rest of his days the ruins of his life. These are shocking facts, criminal facts, disturbing facts: they are not tragic.

Crime, violence, infamy are not tragedy. Tragedy occurs when a human soul awakes and seeks, in suffering and pain, to free itself from crime, violence, infamy, even at the cost of life. The struggle is the tragedy—not defeat or death. That is why the spectacle of tragedy has always filled men, not with despair, but with a sense of hope and exaltation. That is why this terrible book is also a book of hope. For it is about the struggle of the human soul—of more than one human soul. It is in this sense that the Hiss Case is a tragedy. This is its meaning beyond the headlines, the revelations, the shame and suffering of the people involved. But this tragedy will have been for nothing unless men understand it rightly, and from it the world takes hope and heart to begin its own tragic struggle with the evil that besets it from within and from without, unless it faces the fact that the world, the whole world, is sick unto death and that, among other things, this Case has turned a finger of fierce light into the suddenly opened and reeking body of our time.

My children, as long as you live, the shadow of the Hiss Case will brush you. In every pair of eyes that rests on you, you will see pass, like a

cloud passing behind a woods in winter, the memory of your father—
dissembled in friendly eyes, lurking in unfriendly eyes. Sometimes you
will wonder which is harder to bear: friendly forgiveness or forthright
hate. In time, therefore, when the sum of your experience of life gives
you authority, you will ask yourselves the question: What was my
father?

I will give you an answer: I was a witness. I do not mean a witness
for the Government or against Alger Hiss and the others. Nor do I
mean the short, squat, solitary figure, trudging through the impersonal
halls of public buildings to testify before Congressional committees,
grand juries, loyalty boards, courts of law. A man is not primarily a
witness *against* something. That is only incidental to the fact that he
is a witness *for* something. A witness, in the sense that I am using the
word, is a man whose life and faith are so completely one that when
the challenge comes to step out and testify for his faith, he does so,
disregarding all risks, accepting all consequences.

One day in the great jury room of the Grand Jury of the Southern
District of New York, a juror leaned forward slightly and asked me:
"Mr. Chambers, what does it mean to be a Communist?" I hesitated
for a moment, trying to find the simplest, most direct way to convey
the heart of this complex experience to men and women to whom
the very fact of the experience was all but incomprehensible. Then
I said:

> When I was a Communist, I had three heroes. One was a Russian. One
> was a Pole. One was a German Jew.
>
> The Pole was Felix Djerjinsky. He was ascetic, highly sensitive,
> intelligent. He was a Communist. After the Russian Revolution, he
> became head of the Tcheka and organizer of the Red Terror. As a young
> man, Djerjinsky had been a political prisoner in the Pawiak Prison
> in Warsaw. There he insisted on being given the task of cleaning the
> latrines of the other prisoners. For he held that the most developed
> member of any community must take upon himself the lowliest tasks
> as an example to those who are less developed. That is one thing that it
> meant to be a Communist.
>
> The German Jew was Eugen Leviné. He was a Communist. During
> the Bavarian Soviet Republic in 1919, Leviné was the organizer of the
> Workers' and Soldiers' Soviets. When the Bavarian Soviet Republic was
> crushed, Leviné was captured and court-martialed. The court-martial
> told him: "You are under sentence of death." Leviné answered: "We

Communists are always under sentence of death." That is another thing that it meant to be a Communist.

The Russian was not a Communist. He was a pre-Communist revolutionist named Kalyaev. (I should have said Sazonov.) He was arrested for a minor part in the assassination of the Tsarist prime minister, Von Plehve. He was sent into Siberian exile to one of the worst prison camps, where the political prisoners were flogged. Kalyaev sought some way to protest this outrage to the world. The means were few, but at last he found a way. In protest against the flogging of other men, Kalyaev drenched himself in kerosene, set himself on fire and burned himself to death. That also is what it meant to be a Communist.

That also is what it means to be a witness.

But a man may also be an involuntary witness. I do not know any way to explain why God's grace touches a man who seems unworthy of it. But neither do I know any other way to explain how a man like myself—tarnished by life, unprepossessing, not brave—could prevail so far against the powers of the world arrayed almost solidly against him, to destroy him and defeat his truth. In this sense, I am an involuntary witness to God's grace and to the fortifying power of faith.

It was my fate to be in turn a witness to each of the two great faiths of our time. And so we come to the terrible word, Communism. My very dear children, nothing in all these pages will be written so much for you, though it is so unlike anything you would want to read. In nothing shall I be so much a witness, in no way am I so much called upon to fulfill my task, as in trying to make clear to you (and to the world) the true nature of Communism and the source of its power, which was the cause of my ordeal as a man, and remains the historic ordeal of the world in the 20th century. For in this century, within the next decades, will be decided for generations whether all mankind is to become Communist, whether the whole world is to become free, or whether, in the struggle, civilization as we know it is to be completely destroyed or completely changed. It is our fate to live upon that turning point in history.

The world has reached that turning point by the steep stages of a crisis mounting for generations. The turning point is the next to the last step. It was reached in blood, sweat, tears, havoc and death in World War II. The chief fruit of the First World War was the Russian

Revolution and the rise of Communism as a national power. The chief fruit of the Second World War was our arrival at the next to the last step of the crisis with the rise of Communism as a world power. History is likely to say that these were the only decisive results of the world wars.

The last war simplified the balance of political forces in the world by reducing them to two. For the first time, it made the power of the Communist sector of mankind (embodied in the Soviet Union) roughly equal to the power of the free sector of mankind (embodied in the United States). It made the collision of these powers all but inevitable. For the world wars did not end the crisis. They raised its tensions to a new pitch. They raised the crisis to a new stage. All the politics of our time, including the politics of war, will be the politics of this crisis.

Few men are so dull that they do not know that the crisis exists and that it threatens their lives at every point. It is popular to call it a social crisis. It is in fact a total crisis—religious, moral, intellectual, social, political, economic. It is popular to call it a crisis of the Western world. It is in fact a crisis of the whole world. Communism, which claims to be a solution of the crisis, is itself a symptom and an irritant of the crisis.

In part, the crisis results from the impact of science and technology upon mankind which, neither socially nor morally, has caught up with the problems posed by that impact. In part, it is caused by men's efforts to solve those problems. World wars are the military expression of the crisis. World-wide depressions are its economic expression. Universal desperation is its spiritual climate. This is the climate of Communism. Communism in our time can no more be considered apart from the crisis than a fever can be acted upon apart from an infected body.

I see in Communism the focus of the concentrated evil of our time. You will ask: Why, then, do men become Communists? How did it happen that you, our gentle and loved father, were once a Communist? Were you simply stupid? No, I was not stupid. Were you morally depraved? No, I was not morally depraved. Indeed, educated men become Communists chiefly for moral reasons. Did you not know that the crimes and horrors of Communism are inherent in Communism? Yes, I knew that fact. Then why did you become a Communist? It would help more to ask: How did it happen that this movement, once a mere muttering of political outcasts, became this immense force that now contests the mastery of mankind? Even when all the chances and mistakes of history are allowed for, the answer must be: Communism makes some profound appeal to the human mind. You will not find out what it is by calling Communism names. That will not help much to explain why Communism whose horrors, on a scale unparalleled in history, are now public knowledge, still recruits its thousands and holds its millions—among them some of the best minds alive. Look at Klaus Fuchs, standing in the London dock, quiet, doomed, destroyed, and say whether it is possible to answer in that way the simple question: Why?

First, let me try to say what Communism is not. It is not simply a vicious plot hatched by wicked men in a sub-cellar. It is not just the writings of Marx and Lenin, dialectical materialism, the Politburo, the labor theory of value, the theory of the general strike, the Red Army, secret police, labor camps, underground conspiracy, the dictatorship of the proletariat, the technique of the coup d'état. It is not even those chanting, bannered millions that stream periodically, like disorganized armies, through the heart of the world's capitals: Moscow, New York, Tokyo, Paris, Rome. These are expressions of Communism, but they are not what Communism is about.

In the Hiss trials, where Communism was a haunting specter, but which did little or nothing to explain Communism, Communists were assumed to be criminals, pariahs, clandestine men who lead double lives under false names, travel on false passports, deny traditional religion, morality, the sanctity of oaths, preach violence and practice treason. These things are true about Communists, but they are not what Communism is about.

The revolutionary heart of Communism is not the theatrical appeal: "Workers of the world, unite. You have nothing to lose but your chains. You have a world to gain." It is a simple statement of Karl Marx, further simplified for handy use: "Philosophers have explained the world; it is necessary to change the world." Communists are bound together by no secret oath. The tie that binds them across the frontiers of nations, across barriers of language and differences of class and education, in defiance of religion, morality, truth, law, honor, the weaknesses of the body and the irresolutions of the mind, even unto death, is a simple conviction: It is necessary to change the world. Their power, whose nature baffles the rest of the world, because in a large measure the rest of the world has lost that power, is the power to hold convictions and to act on them. It is the same power that moves mountains; it is also an unfailing power to move men. Communists are that part of mankind which has recovered the power to live or die—to bear witness—for its faith. And it is a simple, rational faith that inspires men to live or die for it.

It is not new. It is, in fact, man's second oldest faith. Its promise was whispered in the first days of the Creation under the Tree of the Knowledge of Good and Evil: "Ye shall be as gods." It is the great alternative faith of mankind. Like all great faiths, its force derives from a simple vision. Other ages have had great visions. They have always been different versions of the same vision: the vision of God and man's relationship to God. The Communist vision is the vision of Man without God.

It is the vision of man's mind displacing God as the creative intelligence of the world. It is the vision of man's liberated mind, by the sole force of its rational intelligence, redirecting man's destiny and reorganizing man's life and the world. It is the vision of man, once more the central figure of the Creation, not because God made man in His image, but because man's mind makes him the most intelligent of the animals. Copernicus and his successors displaced man as the central fact of the universe by proving that the earth was not the central star of the universe. Communism restores man to his sovereignty by the simple method of denying God.

The vision is a challenge and implies a threat. It challenges man to prove by his acts that he is the masterwork of the Creation—by making thought and act one. It challenges him to prove it by using the force of his rational mind to end the bloody meaninglessness of man's history—by giving it purpose and a plan. It challenges him to prove it by reducing the meaningless chaos of nature, by imposing on it his rational will to order, abundance, security, peace. It is the vision of materialism. But it threatens, if man's mind is unequal to the problems of man's progress, that he will sink back into savagery (the A and the H bombs have raised the issue in explosive forms), until nature replaces him with a more intelligent form of life.

It is an intensely practical vision. The tools to turn it into reality are at hand—science and technology, whose traditional method, the rigorous exclusion of all supernatural factors in solving problems, has contributed to the intellectual climate in which the vision flourishes, just as they have contributed to the crisis in which Communism thrives. For the vision is shared by millions who are not Communists (they are part of Communism's secret strength). Its first commandment is found, not in the *Communist Manifesto*, but in the first sentence of the physics primer: "All of the progress of mankind to date results from the making of careful measurements." But Communism, for the first time in history, has made this vision the faith of a great modern political movement.

Hence the Communist Party is quite justified in calling itself the most revolutionary party in history. It has posed in practical form the most revolutionary question in history: God or Man? It has taken the logical next step which three hundred years of rationalism hesitated to take, and said what millions of modern minds think, but do not dare or care to say: If man's mind is the decisive force in the world, what need is there for God? Henceforth man's mind is man's fate.

This vision *is* the Communist revolution, which, like all great revolutions, occurs in man's mind before it takes form in man's acts. Insurrection and conspiracy are merely methods of realizing the vision; they are merely part of the politics of Communism. Without its vision, they, like Communism, would have no meaning and could not rally a parcel of pickpockets. Communism does not summon men to crime or to utopia, as its easy critics like to think. On the plane of faith, it summons mankind to turn its vision into practical reality. On the plane of action, it summons men to struggle against the inertia of the past which, embodied in social, political and economic forms, Communism claims, is blocking the will of mankind to make its next great forward stride. It summons men to overcome the crisis, which, Communism claims, is in effect a crisis of rending frustration, with the world, unable to stand still, but unwilling to go forward along the road that the logic of a technological civilization points out—Communism.

This is Communism's moral sanction, which is twofold. Its vision points the way to the future; its faith labors to turn the future into present reality. It says to every man who joins it: the vision is a practical problem of history; the way to achieve it is a practical problem of politics, which is the present tense of history. Have you the moral strength to take upon yourself the crimes of history so that man at last may close his chronicle of age-old, senseless suffering, and replace it with purpose and a plan? The answer a man makes to this question is the difference between the Communist and those miscellaneous socialists, liberals, fellow travelers, unclassified progressives and men of good will, all of whom share a similar vision, but do not share the faith because they will not take upon themselves the penalties of the faith. The answer is the root of that sense of moral superiority which makes Communists, though caught in crime, berate their opponents with withering self-righteousness.

The Communist vision has a mighty agitator and a mighty propagandist. They are the crisis. The agitator needs no soap box. It speaks insistently to the human mind at the point where desperation lurks. The propagandist writes no Communist gibberish. It speaks insistently to the human mind at the point where man's hope and man's energy fuse to fierceness.

The vision inspires. The crisis impels. The workingman is chiefly moved by the crisis. The educated man is chiefly moved by the vision. The workingman, living upon a mean margin of life, can afford few visions—even practical visions. An educated man, peering from the Harvard Yard, or any college campus, upon a world in chaos, finds in the vision the two certainties for which the mind of man tirelessly seeks: a reason to live and a reason to die. No other faith of our time presents them with the same practical intensity. That is why Communism is the central experience of the first half of the 20th century, and may be its final experience—will be, unless the free world, in the agony of its struggle with Communism, overcomes its crisis by discovering, in suffering and pain, a power of faith which will provide man's mind, at the same intensity, with the same two certainties: a reason to live and a reason to die. If it fails, this will be the century of the great social wars. If it succeeds, this will be the century of the great wars of faith.

You will ask: Why, then, do men cease to be Communists? One answer is: Very few do. Thirty years after the Russian Revolution, after the known atrocities, the purges, the revelations, the jolting zigzags of Communist politics, there is only a handful of ex-Communists in the whole world. By ex-Communists I do not mean those who break with Communism over differences of strategy and tactics (like Trotsky) or organization (like Tito). Those are merely quarrels over a road map by people all of whom are in a hurry to get to the same place.

Nor, by ex-Communists, do I mean those thousands who continually drift into the Communist Party and out again. The turnover is vast. These are the spiritual vagrants of our time whose traditional faith has been leached out in the bland climate of rationalism. They are looking for an intellectual night's lodging. They lack the character for Communist faith because they lack the character for any faith. So they drop away, though Communism keeps its hold on them.

By an ex-Communist, I mean a man who knew clearly why he became a Communist, who served Communism devotedly and knew why he served it, who broke with Communism unconditionally and knew why he broke with it. Of these there are very few—an index to the power of the vision and the power of the crisis.

History very largely fixes the patterns of force that make men Communists. Hence one Communist conversion sounds much like another—rather impersonal and repetitious, awesome and tiresome, like long lines of similar people all stolidly waiting to get in to see the same movie. A man's break with Communism is intensely personal. Hence the account of no two breaks is likely to be the same. The reasons that made one Communist break may seem without force to another ex-Communist.

It is a fact that a man can join the Communist Party, can be very active in it for years, without completely understanding the nature of Communism or the political methods that follow inevitably from its vision. One day such incomplete Communists discover that the Communist Party is not what they thought it was. They break with it and turn on it with the rage of an honest dupe, a dupe who has given a part of his life to a swindle. Often they forget that it takes two to make a swindle.

Others remain Communists for years, warmed by the light of its vision, firmly closing their eyes to the crimes and horrors inseparable from its practical politics. One day they have to face the facts. They are appalled at what they have abetted. They spend the rest of their days trying to explain, usually without great success, the dark clue to their complicity. As their understanding of Communism was incomplete and led them to a dead end, their understanding of breaking with it is incomplete and leads them to a dead end. It leads to less than Communism, which was a vision and a faith. The world outside Communism, the world in crisis, lacks a vision and a faith. There is before these ex-Communists absolutely nothing. Behind them is a threat. For they have, in fact, broken not with the vision, but with the politics of the vision. In the name of reason and intelligence, the vision keeps them firmly in its grip—self-divided, paralyzed, powerless to act against it.

Hence the most secret fold of their minds is haunted by a terrifying thought: What if we were wrong? What if our inconstancy is our guilt? That is the fate of those who break without knowing clearly that Communism is wrong because something else is right, because to the challenge: *God or Man?*, they continue to give the answer: *Man*. Their pathos is that not even the Communist ordeal could teach them that man without God is just what Communism said he was: the most intelligent of the animals, that man without God is a beast, never more beastly than when he is most intelligent about his beastliness. *"Er nennt's Vernunft,"* says the Devil in Goethe's *Faust, "und braucht's allein, nur tierischer als jedes Tier zu sein"*—Man calls it reason and uses it simply to be more beastly than any beast. Not grasping the source of the evil they sincerely hate, such ex-Communists in general make ineffectual witnesses against it. They are witnesses against something; they have ceased to be witnesses for anything.

Yet there is one experience which most sincere ex-Communists share, whether or not they go only part way to the end of the question it poses. The daughter of a former German diplomat in Moscow was trying to explain to me why her father, who, as an enlightened modern man, had been extremely pro-Communist, had become an implacable anti-Communist. It was hard for her because, as an enlightened modern girl, she shared the Communist vision without being a Communist. But she loved her father and the irrationality of his defection embarrassed her. "He was immensely pro-Soviet," she said, "and then—you will laugh at me—but you must not laugh at my father—and then—one night—in Moscow—he heard screams. That's all. Simply one night he heard screams."

A child of Reason and the 20th century, she knew that there is a logic of the mind. She did not know that the soul has a logic that may be more compelling than the mind's. She did not know at all that she had swept away the logic of the mind, the logic of history, the logic of politics, the myth of the 20th century, with five annihilating words: one night he heard screams.

What Communist has not heard those screams? They come from husbands torn forever from their wives in midnight arrests. They come, muffled, from the execution cellars of the secret police, from the torture chambers of the Lubianka, from all the citadels of terror now stretching from Berlin to Canton. They come from those freight cars loaded with men, women and children, the enemies of the Communist State, locked in, packed in, left on remote sidings to freeze to death at night in the Russian winter. They come from minds driven mad by the horrors of mass starvation ordered and enforced as a policy of the Communist State. They come from the starved skeletons, worked to death, or flogged to death (as an example to others) in the freezing filth of sub-arctic labor camps. They come from children whose parents are suddenly, inexplicably, taken away from them—parents they will never see again.

What Communist has not heard those screams? Execution, says the Communist code, is the highest measure of social protection. What man can call himself a Communist who has not accepted the fact that Terror is an instrument of policy, right if the vision is right, justified by history, enjoined by the balance of forces in the social wars of this century? Those screams have reached every Communist's mind. Usually they stop there. What judge willingly dwells upon the man the laws compel him to condemn to death—the laws of nations or the laws of history?

But one day the Communist really hears those screams. He is going about his routine party tasks. He is lifting a dripping reel of microfilm from a developing tank. He is justifying to a Communist fraction in a trade union an extremely unwelcome directive of the Central Committee. He is receiving from a trusted superior an order to go to another country and, in a designated hotel, at a designated hour, meet a man whose name he will never know, but who will give him a package whose contents he will never learn. Suddenly, there closes around that Communist a separating silence, and in that silence he hears screams. He hears them for the first time. For they do not merely reach his mind. They pierce beyond. They pierce to his soul. He says to himself: "Those are not the screams of man in agony. Those are the screams of a soul in agony." He hears them for the first time because a soul in extremity has communicated with that which alone can hear it—another human soul.

Why does the Communist ever hear them? Because in the end there persists in every man, however he may deny it, a scrap of soul. The Communist who suffers this singular experience then says to himself: "What is happening to me? I must be sick." If he does not instantly stifle that scrap of soul, he is lost. If he admits it for a moment, he has admitted that there is something greater than Reason, greater than the logic of mind, of politics, of history, of economics, which alone justifies the vision. If the party senses his weakness, and the party is peculiarly cunning at sensing such weakness, it will humiliate him, degrade him, condemn him, expel him. If it can, it will destroy him. And the party will be right. For he has betrayed that which alone justifies its faith—the vision of Almighty Man. He has brushed the only vision that has force against the vision of Almighty Mind. He stands before the fact of God.

The Communist Party is familiar with this experience to which its members are sometimes liable in prison, in illness, in indecision. It is recognized frankly as a sickness. There are ways of treating it—if it is confessed. It is when it is not confessed that the party, sensing a subtle crisis, turns upon it savagely. What ex-Communist has not suffered this experience in one form or another, to one degree or another? What he does about it depends on the individual man. That is why no ex-Communist dare answer for his sad fraternity the question: Why do men break with Communism? He can only answer the question: How did you break with Communism? My answer is: Slowly, reluctantly, in agony.

Yet my break began long before I heard those screams. Perhaps it does for everyone. I do not know how far back it began. Avalanches gather force and crash, unheard, in men as in the mountains. But I date my break from a very casual happening. I was sitting in our apartment on St. Paul Street in Baltimore. It was shortly before we moved to Alger Hiss's apartment in Washington. My daughter was in her high chair. I was watching her eat. She was the most miraculous thing that had ever happened in my life. I liked to watch her even when she smeared porridge on her face or dropped it meditatively on the floor. My eye came to rest on the delicate convolutions of her ear—those intricate, perfect ears. The thought passed through my mind: "No, those ears were not created by any chance coming together of atoms in nature (the Communist view). They could have been created only by immense design." The thought was involuntary and unwanted. I crowded it out of my mind. But I never wholly forgot it or the occasion. I had to crowd it out of my mind. If I had completed it, I should have had to say: Design presupposes God. I did not then know that, at that moment, the finger of God was first laid upon my forehead.

One thing most ex-Communists could agree upon: they broke because they wanted to be free. They do not all mean the same thing by "free." Freedom is a need of the soul, and nothing else. It is in striving toward God that the soul strives continually after a condition of freedom. God alone is the inciter and guarantor of freedom. He is the only guarantor. External freedom is only an aspect of interior freedom. Political freedom, as the Western world has known it, is only a political reading of the Bible. Religion and freedom are indivisible. Without freedom the soul dies. Without the soul there is no justification for freedom. Necessity is the only ultimate justification known to the mind. Hence every sincere break with Communism is a religious experience, though the Communist fail to identify its true nature, though he fail to go to the end of the experience. His break is the political expression of the perpetual need of the soul whose first faint stirring he has felt within him, years, months or days before he breaks. A Communist breaks because he must choose at last between irreconcilable opposites—God or Man, Soul or Mind, Freedom or Communism.

Communism is what happens when, in the name of Mind, men free themselves from God. But its view of God, its knowledge of God, its experience of God, is what alone gives character to a society or a nation, and meaning to its destiny. Its culture, the voice of this character, is merely that view, knowledge, experience, of God, fixed by its most intense spirits in terms intelligible to the mass of men. There has never been a society or a nation without God. But history is cluttered with the wreckage of nations that became indifferent to God, and died.

The crisis of Communism exists to the degree in which it has failed to free the peoples that it rules from God. Nobody knows this better than the Communist Party of the Soviet Union. The crisis of the Western world exists to the degree in which it is indifferent to God. It exists to the degree in which the Western world actually shares Communism's materialist vision, is so dazzled by the logic of the materialist interpretation of history, politics and economics, that it fails to grasp that, for it, the only possible answer to the Communist challenge: Faith in God or Faith in Man? is the challenge: Faith in God.

Economics is not the central problem of this century. It is a relative problem which can be solved in relative ways. Faith is the central problem of this age. The Western world does not know it, but it already possesses the answer to this problem—but only provided that its faith in God and the freedom He enjoins is as great as Communism's faith in Man.

My dear children, before I close this foreword, I want to recall to you briefly the life that we led in the ten years between the time when I broke with Communism and the time when I began to testify—the things we did, worked for, loved, believed in. For it was that happy life, which, on the human side, in part made it possible for me to do later on the things I had to do, or endure the things that happened to me.

Those were the days of the happy little worries, which then seemed so big. We know now that they were the golden days. They will not come again. In those days, our greatest worry was how to meet the payments on the mortgage, how to get the ploughing done in time, how to get health accreditation for our herd, how to get the hay in before the rain. I sometimes took my vacation in hay harvest so that I could help work the load. You two little children used to trample the load, drive the hay truck in the fields when you could barely reach the foot pedals, or drive the tractor that pulled up the loaded harpoons to the mow. At evening, you would break off to help Mother milk while I went on haying. For we came of age on the farm when we decided not to hire barn help, but to run the herd ourselves as a family.

Often the ovenlike heat in the comb of the barn and the sweet smell of alfalfa made us sick. Sometimes we fell asleep at the supper table from fatigue. But the hard work was good for us; and you knew only the peace of a home governed by a father and mother whose marriage the years (and an earlier suffering which you could not remember) had deepened into the perfect love that enveloped you.

Mother was a slight, overalled figure forever working for you in the house or beside you in the barns and gardens. Papa was a squat, overalled figure, fat but forceful, who taught John, at nine, the man-size glory of driving the tractor; or sat beside Ellen, at the wheel of the truck, an embodiment of security and power, as we drove loads of cattle through the night. On summer Sundays, you sat between Papa and Mama in the Quaker meeting house. Through the open doors, as you tried not to twist and turn in the long silence, you could see the far, blue Maryland hills and hear the redbirds and ground robins in the graveyard behind.

Only Ellen had a vague, troubled recollection of another time and another image of Papa. Then (it was during the years 1938 and 1939), if for any reason she pattered down the hall at night, she would find Papa, with the light on, writing, with a revolver on the table or a gun against the chair. She knew that there were people who wanted to kill Papa and who might try to kidnap her. But a wide sea of sunlight and of time lay between that puzzling recollection and the farm.

The farm was your kingdom, and the world lay far beyond the protecting walls thrown up by work and love. It is true that comic strips were not encouraged, comic books were banned, the radio could be turned on only by permission which was seldom given (or asked), and you saw few movies. But you grew in the presence of eternal wonders. There was the birth of lambs and calves. You remember how once, when I was away and the veterinarian could not come, you saw Mother reach in and turn the calf inside the cow so that it could be born. There was also the death of animals, sometimes violent, sometimes slow and painful—nothing is more constant on a farm than death.

Sometimes, of a spring evening, Papa would hear that distant honking that always makes his scalp tingle, and we would all rush out to see the wild geese, in lines of hundreds, steer up from the southwest, turn over the barn as over a landmark, and head into the north. Or on autumn nights of sudden cold that set the ewes breeding in the orchard, Papa would call you out of the house to stand with him in the now celebrated pumpkin patch and watch the northern lights flicker in electric clouds on the horizon, mount, die down, fade and mount again till they filled the whole northern sky with ghostly light in motion.

Thus, as children, you experienced two of the most important things men ever know—the wonder of life and the wonder of the universe, the wonder of life within the wonder of the universe. More important, you knew them not from books, not from lectures, but simply from living among them. Most important, you knew them with reverence and awe—that reverence and awe that has died out of the modern world and been replaced by man's monkeylike amazement at the cleverness of his own inventive brain.

I have watched greatness touch you in another way. I have seen you sit, uninvited and unforced, listening in complete silence to the third movement of the Ninth Symphony. I thought you understood, as much as children can, when I told you that that music was the moment at which Beethoven finally passed beyond the suffering of his life on earth and reached for the hand of God, as God reaches for the hand of Adam in Michelangelo's vision of the Creation.

And once, in place of a bedtime story, I was reading Shakespeare to John—at his own request, for I never forced such things on you. I came to that passage in which Macbeth, having murdered Duncan, realizes what he has done to his own soul, and asks if all the water in the world can ever wash the blood from his hand, or will it not rather

*The multitudinous seas incarnadine?*

At that line, John's whole body twitched. I gave great silent thanks to God. For I knew that if, as children, you could thus feel in your souls the reverence and awe for life and the world, which is the ultimate meaning of Beethoven and Shakespeare, as man and woman you could never be satisfied with less. I felt a great faith that sooner or later you would understand what I once told you, not because I expected you to understand it then, but because I hoped that you would remember it later: "True wisdom comes from the overcoming of suffering and sin. All true wisdom is therefore touched with sadness."

If all this sounds unduly solemn, you know that our lives were not; that all of us suffer from an incurable itch to puncture false solemnity. In our daily lives, we were fun-loving and gay. For those who have solemnity in their souls generally have enough of it there, and do not need to force it into their faces.

Then, on August 3, 1948, you learned for the first time that your father had once been a Communist, that he had worked in something called "the underground," that it was shameful, and that for some reason he was in Washington telling the world about it. While he was in the underground, he testified, he had worked with a number of other Communists. One of them was a man with the odd name of Alger Hiss. Later, Alger Hiss denied the allegation. Thus the Great Case began, and with it our lives were changed forever.

Dear children, one autumn twilight, when you were much smaller, I slipped away from you in play and stood for a moment alone in the apple orchard near the barn. Then I heard your two voices, piping together anxiously, calling to me: "Papa! Papa!" from the harvested cornfield. In the years when I was away five days a week in New York, working to pay for the farm, I used to think of you both before I fell asleep at night. And that is how you almost always came to me—voices of beloved children, calling to me from the gathered fields at dusk.

You called to me once again at night in the same orchard. That was a good many years later. A shadow deeper and more chilling than the autumn evening had closed upon us—I mean the Hiss Case. It was the first year of the Case. We had been doing the evening milking together. For us, one of the few happy results of the Case was that at last I could be home with you most of the time (in life these good things usually come too little or too late). I was washing and disinfecting the cows, and putting on and taking off the milkers. You were stripping after me.

In the quiet, there suddenly swept over my mind a clear realization of our true position—obscure, all but friendless people (some of my great friends had already taken refuge in aloofness; the others I had withdrawn from so as not to involve them in my affairs). Against me was an almost solid line-up of the most powerful groups and men in the country, the bitterly hostile reaction of much of the press, the smiling skepticism of much of the public, the venomous calumnies of the Hiss forces, the all but universal failure to understand the real meaning of the Case or my real purpose. A sense of the enormous futility of my effort, and my own inadequacy, drowned me. I felt a physical cold creep through me, settle around my heart and freeze any pulse of hope. The sight of you children, guiltless and defenseless, was more than I could bear. I was alone against the world; my longing was to be left completely alone, or not to be at all. It was that death of the will which Communism, with great cunning, always tries to induce in its victims.

I waited until the last cow was stripped and the last can lifted into the cooler. Then I stole into the upper barn and out into the apple orchard. It was a very dark night. The stars were large and cold. This cold was one with the coldness in myself. The lights of the barn, the house and the neighbors' houses were warm in the windows and on the ground; they were not for me. Then I heard Ellen call me in the barn and John called: "Papa!" Still calling, Ellen went down to the house to see if I were there. I heard John opening gates as he went to the calf barn, and he called me there. With all the longing of my love for you, I wanted to answer. But if I answered, I must come back to the living world. I could not do that.

John began to call me in the cow stable, in the milk house. He went into the dark side of the barn (I heard him slide the door back), into the upper barn, where at night he used to be afraid. He stepped outside in the dark, calling: "Papa! Papa!"—then, frantically, on the verge of tears: "Papa!" I walked over to him. I felt that I was making the most terrible surrender I should have to make on earth. "Papa," he cried and threw his arms around me, "don't ever go away." "No," I said, "no, I won't ever go away." Both of us knew that the words "go away" stood for something else, and that I had given him my promise not to kill myself. Later on, as you will see, I was tempted, in my wretchedness, to break that promise.

My children, when you were little, we used sometimes to go for walks in our pine woods. In the open fields, you would run along by yourselves. But you used instinctively to give me your hands as we entered those woods, where it was darker, lonelier, and in the stillness our voices sounded loud and frightening. In this book I am again giving you my hands. I am leading you, not through cool pine woods, but up and up a narrow defile between bare and steep rocks from which in shadow things uncoil and slither away. It will be dark. But, in the end, if I have led you aright, you will make out three crosses, from two of which hang thieves. I will have brought you to Golgotha—the place of skulls. This is the meaning of the journey. Before you understand, I may not be there, my hands may have slipped from yours. It will not matter. For when you understand what you see, you will no longer be children. You will know that life is pain, that each of us hangs always upon the cross of himself. And when you know that this is true of every man, woman and child on earth, you will be wise.

*Your Father*
*1952*

# FRANK CHODOROV

The son of Jewish immigrants, Frank Chodorov (1887–1966) was a native New Yorker who spent the entirety of his professional life in the city. A fierce opponent of the income tax, he was also an antiwar libertarian who lost his position as director of the Henry George School of Social Science for opposing U.S. participation in World War II even after Pearl Harbor. During the Cold War, he remained an implacable anti-interventionist.

## The Most Precious Heirloom

IS WESTERN civilization on the way out? Some of our more lugubrious prognosticators say so, declaring moreover that the passing has already begun; the *coup de grâce*, they insist, will be World War III. If that is so, then we of this era occupy a grandstand seat at an historical tragedy that will cause much puzzlement for the scholars to come. What data will they have to go by in trying to put together the plot of the long lost—our—civilization? Will they be able to reconstruct its main *motif*? This is a speculation that ought to interest us, not so much because of any interest in future scholarship, but because it might help us to explain ourselves to ourselves.

What is "western civilization"? To which question there is an antecedent: what is "civilization"? Much of the gloomy forebodings rests on the anticipated destruction by the atom bomb and other instruments of death, so that "the decline of western civilization" suggests a wiping out of all population. That is obviously an exaggeration born of fear. If the world is to be destroyed, if all life is to disappear, our age and all that preceded it will hardly be a matter of thought; it will never have been, and whatever succeeds us will have to be a new genesis.

But, it is more than likely that nature will defeat science, that despite the most thorough job of killing we might devise, at least one boy and one girl will escape, so that a new generation will arise to worry about what went on before they arrived.

When a civilization disappears all that is lost is an accumulation of knowledge; or, more exactly, the memory of that knowledge. A "lost" civilization is a body of ideas of which there is no record, or a frame of thought that once influenced the way people lived but has since been forgotten and has therefore lost significance. As with the impaired memory of senility, the past has no bearing on the present. Thus, as far as the Communists have been able to obliterate the knowledge and the values that obtained before their advent, the pre-1918 Russian civilization has been lost to Russia, even though records of it remain elsewhere.

No civilization is ever completely lost. Some trace of the accumulated knowledge of an age does seep through to its successors, if only through the artifacts it bequeaths, and no part of the world has ever been hermetically sealed off from the rest. Knowledge has a way of seeping through all barriers, of overcoming all exigencies. Though the debris of Rome buried the ancient civilization so deep as to bring on an apparently complete ignorance of it, known as the Dark Ages, some record of it found its way into the archives of the East, to facilitate the eventual reconstruction. And, above all, even on the dark continent of Europe some flickering torches were kept alive by intrepid monks, with a devotion that bespeaks an unquenchable faith in a renaissance. Now that a new "dark age" is being predicted, the story of these monks and their monasteries ought to be considered. Who will perform a similar office for the resurrection that must succeed the predicted decline?

Why do civilizations decline? Or, starting from the other end, how do they rise? The process of disintegration must be the reverse of the process of growth; hence, an understanding of the one is dependent on an understanding of the other.

If civilization is a body of ideas, it follows that it is the product of human thought, which in turn is stimulated by curiosity. A civilization comes because the reasoning animal puts his mind to the discovery of means for the improvement of his circumstances or the widening of his horizon. Since he is also endowed with the more significant characteristic of insatiability, he is never satisfied with one discovery but must go on seeking new gratifications for the ever-increasing number of desires his imagination conjures up. Out of the wheel came the cart; out of the cart came the railroad; out of the railroad came the automobile; out of the automobile came the airplane. On the spiritual side, which is another facet of desires, he invents an object of fear to worship, but soon finds that unsatisfying and comes up with the more solace-giving concept of a universal God of Love. When his primary desires are satisfied, his insatiable curiosity reaches out into what we call cultural fields, and he enriches his existence with music, art, literature, as well as with ideas that flatter his desire for self-identification, such as adornment and ostentation.

That's how civilizations arise. It is necessarily a graduated process. The will to exist precedes the will to live. Only after the problem of existence is pretty well solved does the human being discover in himself any interest in improvement; only then do the marginal satisfactions—baseball and Bach—lay claim to his thought. They are called marginal satisfactions because, if necessary, man can get along without them. Any old shelter will do for a castle in the beginning, but when his larder is full he starts hunting for such things as a rug, pictures, a clavichord—to say nothing of hot-and-cold running water—just to make the old place livable. A civilization flowers in proportion to the amount of thought and effort man can invest in the satisfaction of his marginal desires. It is an accumulatively productive enterprise. Obviously, any diversionary or destructive effort, like war, must interfere with the nurturing of a civilization; also, if the human being is insecure in the possession and enjoyment of his output, he loses interest in reaching out for new satisfactions and civilization is retarded. Peace and what we call property rights, which are in fact human rights, must obtain for a civilization to prosper.

Contrariwise, when living is difficult, when mere existence is the sum-total of satisfactions one can hope for, civilization hasn't a chance. And, whatever civilization has been built up will shrink as men have to give more and more thought to the primary problem of life. Men learn to get along without—without baseball and Bach—and in due time they forget that such things engaged the minds of their forebears. Long before the political entity of Rome collapsed, the number of Romans who took the slightest interest in the culture of the

Greeks, or who had any acquaintance with the learning of their own illustrious forefathers, had dwindled to a mere handful; the principal business of the mass was to keep alive, and that was so demanding that nothing else mattered. When the essential word of a language is "gimme," little value is put on the cadences of poetry. And, when that happens, civilization is on the toboggan.

That is the theory of the rise and fall of civilizations by which those who predict the fall of western civilization measure the current of events. For evidence, they point to Europe, where concentration on mere survival has crowded out the intense interest in cultural values that characterized its population during the nineteenth century. In America, they find a general deterioration of educational standards, even though there has been an increase in student attendance; the curricula of schools and colleges are loaded with functional, rather than self-improvement, courses, so that these institutions have become training centers for soldiers, farmers, clerks; they clinch their argument by pointing to the infantile literature which is popular in this country.

Those who have hope, have their rebuttals ready. But, there is one argument advanced by the pessimists that carries more weight than all the facts and figures they can corral. It is the fact that western man has given up on the underlying concept of his civilization: the primacy of the individual. Of that there can be no doubt. All that we call western civilization seminated in the idea that all things begin and end with the individual, that he is the be-all and end-all of life. "Nothing but the individual exists," wrote a nineteenth century philosopher, "and in the individual, nothing but the individual." This idea that the human soul is the only reality not only released the human being from fetishes but also placed on him the responsibility for his environment. Since in the eyes of God every man is king, it was up to him to prove himself.

Out of that tenet of faith came the philosophy of liberalism that is the mark of western civilization. In its political expression it lodged sovereignty in the individual and reduced government to the status of a maid-servant. In economics it gave rise to the doctrine of *laissez faire*. In social life it did away with the fictional castes. It stimulated man's spirit of adventure and he reached out into all fields, in the sciences and the arts, in industry and commerce, and the sum-total of his findings is western civilization. The whole came out of a philosophy, which in turn rested on a tenet of faith.

The evidence is all too strong that the philosophy is losing its hold on men. Among the erudite—always prone to clothe popular thought-trends with philosophic phraseology—the inclination is to sneer at the concept of "natural rights," traceable only to God; and the popular thought-trend, induced by the exigencies of life, is toward the idea that before the individual comes the group. Although it has not yet been phrased that way, the conviction is growing that God made Society, not man. For the habit of thinking, out of which comes the habit of living, is shaping itself around the axiom that Society (acting through the State) is an entity in itself, independent of and superior to its component parts; the individual is only a means, not an end. It is this all too obvious liquidation of the dignity of the individual that supports the contention that western civilization is on the way out.

A civilization dies hard. It is not a body of ideas acquired by a few inquisitive minds, but a way of thinking and living that has become habitual among men. Hence, a civilization does not pass out all at once on a given day; the process of deterioration is as tenuous as the process of gestation. The historian needs a date and a specific event to mark the passing of a civilization. The prognosticator suffers from the same conceit, and he picks on World War III as the finish-line of western civilization. The exigencies of that struggle, he argues, will require the abandonment of the individualistic premise on which western civilization is based; with that keystone gone, the entire superstructure must collapse.

It is generally agreed that the anticipated war will be fought along totalitarian lines. The battles will be between nations, not armies; all will be warriors. The individual as individual will lose all value, for all thought and energy will be channelled into the one purpose of preserving the State. The first person singular will become a linguistic atavism; every sentence will begin with "we" and end with "us." To be sure, the doctrine of "natural rights" will be abandoned in fact, as it has already been abandoned in theory, and the constitutional immunities of life, property and conscience will no longer be claimed. Within six months after hostilities begin, it is predicted, all the machinery of a military dictatorship will have been put into operation, including, above all, the means of suppressing dissident opinion.

Granted this eventuality, does it portend a continuing organization of life? Will it not be "for the duration" only? To which observation the prophets of gloom retort, how long will the "duration" endure? Even if military operations are terminated within a reasonably short time, even if one side is able quickly to impose its will on the other, the destruction of the world's economy, to say nothing of the explosive hatreds aroused, will necessitate a long period of world management by the victorious side; at least, the dictatorship will deem such management necessary. Or, as seems probable, if sheer exhaustion induces a stalemate and a truce, it is a certainty that both sides will start preparing themselves for another test of arms, which means a continuation of the dictatorships. In either event, the duration will be long enough—two or three generations at the least—for people to have acquired a new set of values and to have forgotten about the past. The habit of individualistic thought will have given way to a thorough adjustment to herd-living. Thus, the seed of a collectivized civilization implanted in our *mores* in the early part of the twentieth century will have been fertilized by the conditions of war—and that will be the successor to what we have known as western civilization.

The prophets adduce an historical argument to support their thesis. They point to the fact that the State never abdicates; it is constitutionally unable to do so. Its character demands that it accumulate power, always at the expense of society, and there is nothing else it can do. It is a beast of prey, without any means of sustenance other than what it can grab. When its confiscatory power reaches the point where it can and does absorb all the individual produces, above a bare living, the individual ceases to have any interest in production and then the State has little to live on; in that enervated condition the State is pushed out of the way by revolution and for a while the people enjoy freedom. But, that is a long-term process. In the meantime, the power acquired by the State during war—when fear of a foreign enemy reduces resistance to its encroachments—is never relinquished; each war strengthens the State and weakens Society. Following this historic pattern, the prospect is that World War III will completely obliterate the individualistic premise of western civilization and will introduce a long period of Statism.

The heart of a civilization consists of a body of values; its collapse means the loss of these values. Other casualties, like its accumulated knowledge and its physical appurtenances, can be counted by historians and archaeologists; but, buried in these observable ruins are the values of which they are but the expression, and the humanist of another generation, immersed in his own set of values, has difficulty in capturing them. What, for instance, did the Greeks of 500 B.C. really think and feel? What were their aspirations, their ideals? What pattern of thought motivated their manner of life? These are the difficult questions that a lost civilization presents to its successor.

To repeat, the key value of western civilization is the primacy of the individual; all the rest is but a manifestation of it. If World War III does in fact destroy this civilization, it will do nothing more than depersonalize the individual and reduce him to an automaton. The social organization will, as near as possible with human beings, follow the pattern of the ant society. The concept of inalienable rights, stemming from God, will be superceded by the doctrine of permissive rights, authored by the Great Leviathan. Since the first responsibility of the human being will be to the collectivity, operating through the State, the Judeo-Christian idea of a direct relationship between the individual soul and the Supreme Being will be untenable. The soul idea, in the new western civilization, will be a lost value.

Now, whether or not this is an exact picture of things to come, or is only the idle speculation of lugubrious poets, the outlines of it are all too visible to permit offhand dismissal. And the history of past civilizations keeps dinning its lessons into our ears. The thing can happen. The only question is, is this consequence of World War III inevitable, something ordained in God's plan, or is it, like the war itself, an evidence of human frailties? There are arguments for both theses.

For those of us who, while observing the panorama of our times, are concerned about the fate of the *one* value on which our civilization rests, perhaps because of a natural attachment to our offspring, the argument of inevitability has no weight. If the collapse of western civilization is determined by the ineluctable historical cycle, the living man cannot resign himself to it, but must work out his career in the light of his reason, his hopes and his ideals. The stars in the heavens tend to their eternal business, and we mortals must travel within our own specific orbits. After all, it was not an historical imperative that directed the pens of those who signed the Declaration of Independence; it was a force within each of them. And for those of us who still hold high the value of human dignity, our job, whether we like it or not, whether out of a sense of duty or an irrepressible inner compunction, is to keep polishing up this value so as to prevent its utter tarnishment. We must be the monks of western civilization.

The supreme task of the present is spiritual. We are not concerned with saving buildings or gadgets from the impending holocaust, nor even its precious literature. All the physical accomplishments of western civilization must take their chances along with human life. Some things and some people will escape. But, what will happen to the Judco-Christian tenet of the primacy of the person? Will anybody remember that "only the individual exists"? In the darkness and the stillness of universal Statism, will it be whispered that once there was a world built on the faith of the human being in himself and his God? All we can do now is to mobilize our forces in a struggle against the total obliteration of that value—and hope.

*1952*

# JOHN COURTNEY MURRAY

John Courtney Murray (1904–1967) was a Jesuit priest and theologian committed to reconciling Roman Catholicism with American-style religious pluralism.

———————

# E Pluribus Unum:
# The American Consensus

A S IT arose in America, the problem of pluralism was unique in the modern world, chiefly because pluralism was the native condition of American society. It was not, as in Europe and in England, the result of a disruption or decay of a previously existent religious unity. This fact created the possibility of a new solution; indeed, it created a demand for a new solution. The possibility was exploited and the demand was met by the American Constitution.

The question here concerns the position of the Catholic conscience in the face of the new American solution to a problem that for centuries has troubled, and still continues to trouble, various nations and societies. A new problem has been put to the universal Church by the fact of America—by the uniqueness of our social situation, by the genius of our newly conceived constitutional system, by the lessons of our singular national history, which has molded in a special way the consciousness and temper of the American people, within whose midst the Catholic stands, sharing with his fellow citizens the same national heritage. The Catholic community faces the task of making itself intellectually aware of the conditions of its own coexistence within the American pluralistic scene. We have behind us a lengthy historical tradition of acceptance of the special situation of the Church in America, in all its differences from the situations in which the Church elsewhere finds herself. But it is a question here of pursuing the subject, not in the horizontal dimension of history but in the vertical dimension of theory.

The argument readily falls into two parts. The first part is an analysis of the American Proposition with regard to political unity. The effort is to make a statement, later to be somewhat enlarged, of the essential contents of the American consensus, whereby we are made "e pluribus unum," one society subsisting amid multiple pluralisms. Simply to make this statement is to show why American Catholics participate with ready conviction in the American consensus. The second part of the argument, to be pursued in the next chapter, is an analysis of the American Proposition with regard to religious pluralism, especially as this proposition is embodied in our fundamental law. Again, simply to make this analysis is to lay bare the reasons why American Catholics accept on principle the unique American solution to the age-old problem.

## THE NATION UNDER GOD

The first truth to which the American Proposition makes appeal is stated in that landmark of Western political theory, the Declaration of Independence. It is a truth that lies beyond politics; it imparts to politics a fundamental human meaning. I mean the sovereignty of God over nations as well as over individual men. This is the principle that radically distinguishes the conservative Christian tradition of America from the Jacobin laicist tradition of Continental Europe. The Jacobin tradition proclaimed the autonomous reason of man to be the first and the sole principle of political organization. In contrast, the first article of the American political faith is that the political community, as a form of free and ordered human life, looks to the sovereignty of God as to the first principle of its organization. In the Jacobin tradition religion is at best a purely private concern, a matter of personal devotion, quite irrelevant to public affairs. Society as such, and the state which gives it legal form, and the government which is its organ of action are by definition agnostic or atheist. The statesman as such cannot be a believer, and his actions as a statesman are immune from any imperative or judgment higher than the will of the people, in whom resides ultimate and total sovereignty (one must remember that in the Jacobin tradition "the people" means "the party"). This whole manner of thought is altogether alien to the authentic American tradition.

From the point of view of the problem of pluralism this radical distinction between the American and the Jacobin traditions is of cardinal importance. The United States has had, and still has, its share of agnostics and unbelievers. But it has never known organized militant atheism on the Jacobin, doctrinaire Socialist, or Communist model; it has rejected parties and theories which erect atheism into a political principle. In 1799, the year of the Napoleonic *coup d'état* which overthrew the Directory and established a dictatorship in France, President John Adams stated the first of all American first principles in his remarkable proclamation of March 6:

> ... it is also most reasonable in itself that men who are capable of social arts and relations, who owe their improvements to the social state, and who derive their enjoyments from it, should, as a society, make acknowledgements of dependence and obligation to Him who hath endowed them with these capacities and elevated them in the scale of existence by these distinctions. . . .

President Lincoln on May 30, 1863, echoed the tradition in another proclamation:

> Whereas the Senate of the United States, devoutly recognizing the supreme authority and just government of Almighty God in all the affairs of men and nations, has by a resolution requested the President to designate and set apart a day for national prayer and humiliation; And whereas it is the duty of nations as well as of men to own their dependence upon the overruling power of God, to confess their sins and trespasses in humble sorrow, yet with the assured hope that genuine repentance will lead to mercy and pardon. . . .

The authentic voice of America speaks in these words. And it is a testimony to the enduring vitality of this first principle—the sovereignty of God over society as well as over individual men—that President Eisenhower in June, 1952, quoted these words of Lincoln in a proclamation of similar intent. There is, of course, dissent from this principle, uttered by American secularism (which, at that, is a force far different in content and purpose from Continental laicism). But the secularist dissent is clearly a dissent; it illustrates the existence of the American affirmation. And it is continually challenged. For instance, as late as 1952 an opinion of the United States Supreme Court challenged it by asserting: "We are a religious people whose institutions presuppose a Supreme Being." Three times before in its history—in 1815, 1892, and 1931—the Court had formally espoused this same principle.

## THE TRADITION OF NATURAL LAW

The affirmation in Lincoln's famous phrase, "this nation under God," sets the American proposition in fundamental continuity with the central political tradition of the West. But this continuity is more broadly and importantly visible in another, and related, respect. In 1884 the Third Plenary Council of Baltimore made this statement: "We consider the establishment of our country's independence, the shaping of its liberties and laws, as a work of special Providence, its framers 'building better than they knew,' the Almighty's hand guiding them." The providential aspect of the matter, and the reason for the better building, can be found in the fact that the American political community was organized in an era when the tradition of natural law and natural rights was still vigorous. Claiming no sanction other than its appeal to free minds, it still commanded universal acceptance. And it furnished the basic materials for the American consensus.

The evidence for this fact has been convincingly presented by Clinton Rossiter in his book, *Seedtime of the Republic,** a scholarly account of the "noble aggregate of 'self-evident truths' that vindicated the campaign of resistance (1765–1775), the resolution for independence (1776), and the establishment of the new state governments (1776–1780)." These truths, he adds, "had been no less self-evident to the preachers, merchants, planters, and lawyers who were the mind of colonial America." It might be further added that these truths firmly presided over the great time of study, discussion, and decision which produced the Federal Constitution. "The great political philosophy of

---

* New York: Harcourt, Brace and Co., 1953.

the Western world," Rossiter says, "enjoyed one of its proudest seasons in this time of resistance and revolution." By reason of this fact the American Revolution, quite unlike its French counterpart, was less a revolution than a conservation. It conserved, by giving newly vital form to, the liberal tradition of politics, whose ruin in Continental Europe was about to be consummated by the first great modern essay in totalitarianism.

The force for unity inherent in this tradition was of decisive importance in what concerns the problem of pluralism. Because it was conceived in the tradition of natural law the American Republic was rescued from the fate, still not overcome, that fell upon the European nations in which Continental Liberalism, a deformation of the liberal tradition, lodged itself, not least by the aid of the Lodges. There have never been "two Americas," in the sense in which there have been, and still are, "two Frances," "two Italys," "two Spains." Politically speaking, America has always been one. The reason is that a consensus was once established, and it still substantially endures, even in the quarters where its origins have been forgotten.

Formally and in the first instance this consensus was political, that is, it embraced a whole constellation of principles bearing upon the origin and nature of society, the function of the state as the legal order of society, and the scope and limitations of government. "Free government"—perhaps this typically American shorthand phrase sums up the consensus. "A free people under a limited government" puts the matter more exactly. It is a phrase that would have satisfied the first Whig, St. Thomas Aquinas.

To the early Americans government was not a phenomenon of force, as the later legal positivists would have it. Nor was it a "historical category," as Marx and his followers were to assert. Government did not mean simply the power to coerce, though this power was taken as integral to government. Government, properly speaking, was the right to command. It was authority. And its authority derived from law. By the same token its authority was limited by law. In his own way Tom Paine put the matter when he said, "In America Law is the King." But the matter had been better put by Henry of Bracton (d. 1268) when he said, "The king ought not to be under a man, but under God and under the law, because the law makes the king." This was the message of Magna Charta; this became the first structural rib of American constitutionalism.

Constitutionalism, the rule of law, the notion of sovereignty as purely political and therefore limited by law, the concept of government as an empire of laws and not of men—these were ancient ideas, deeply implanted in the British tradition at its origin in medieval times. The major American contribution to the tradition—a contribution that imposed itself on all subsequent political history in the Western world—was the written constitution. However, the American document was not the *constitution octroyée* of the nineteenth-century Restorations—a constitution graciously granted by the King or Prince-President. Through the American techniques of the constitutional convention and of popular ratification, the American Constitution is explicitly the act of the people. It embodies their consensus as to the purposes of government, its structure, the extent of its powers and the limitations on them, etc. By the Constitution the people define the areas where authority is legitimate and the areas where liberty is lawful. The Constitution is therefore at once a charter of freedom and a plan for political order.

## THE PRINCIPLE OF CONSENT

Here is the second aspect of the continuity between the American consensus and the ancient liberal tradition; I mean the affirmation of the principle of the consent of the governed. Sir John Fortescue (d. 1476), Chief Justice of the Court of King's Bench under Henry VI, had thus stated the tradition, in distinguishing between the absolute and the constitutional monarch: "The secounde king [the constitutional monarch] may not rule his people by other laws than such as thai assenten to. And therefore he may set uppon thaim non imposicions without their consent." The principle of consent was inherent in the medieval idea of kingship; the king was bound to seek the consent of his people to his legislation. The American consensus reaffirmed this principle, at the same time that it carried the principle to newly logical lengths. Americans agreed that they would consent to none other than their own legislation, as framed by their representatives, who would be responsible to them. In other words, the principle of consent was wed to the equally ancient principle of popular participation in rule. But, since this latter principle was given an amplitude of meaning never before known in history, the result was a new synthesis, whose formula is the phrase of Lincoln, "government by the people."

Americans agreed to make government constitutional and therefore limited in a new sense, because it is representative, republican, responsible government. It is limited not only by law but by the will of the people it represents. Not only do the people adopt the Constitution; through the techniques of representation, free elections, and frequent rotation of administrations they also have a share in the enactment of all subsequent statutory legislation. The people are really governed; American political theorists did not pursue the Rousseauist will-o'-the-wisp: how shall the individual in society come to obey only himself? Nevertheless, the people are governed because they consent to be governed; and they consent to be governed because in a true sense they govern themselves.

The American consensus therefore includes a great act of faith in the capacity of the people to govern themselves. The faith was not unrealistic. It was not supposed that everybody could master the technical aspects of government, even in a day when these aspects were far less complex than they now are. The supposition was that the people could understand the general objectives of governmental policy, the broad issues put to the decision of government, especially as these issues raised moral problems. The American consensus accepted the premise of medieval society, that there is a sense of justice inherent in the people, in virtue of which they are empowered, as the medieval phrase had it, to "judge, direct, and correct" the processes of government.

It was this political faith that compelled early American agreement to the institutions of a free speech and a free press. In the American concept of them, these institutions do not rest on the thin theory proper to eighteenth-century individualistic rationalism, that a man has a right to say what he thinks merely because he thinks it. The American agreement was to reject political censorship of opinion as unrightful, because unwise, imprudent, not to say impossible. However, the proper premise of these freedoms lay in the fact that they were social necessities. "Colonial thinking about each of these rights had a strong social rather than individualistic bias," Rossiter says. They were regarded as conditions essential to the conduct of free, representative, and responsible government. People who are called upon to obey have the right first to be heard. People who are to bear burdens and make sacrifices have the right first to pronounce on the purposes which their sacrifices serve. People who are summoned to contribute to the common good have the right first to pass their own judgment on the question, whether the good proposed be truly a good, the people's good, the common good. Through the technique of majority opinion this popular judgment becomes binding on government.

A second principle underlay these free institutions—the principle that the state is distinct from society and limited in its offices toward society. This principle too was inherent in the Great Tradition. Before it was cancelled out by the rise of the modern omnicompetent society-state, it had found expression in the distinction between the order of politics and the order of culture, or, in the language of the time, the distinction between *studium* and *imperium*. The whole order of ideas in general was autonomous in the face of government; it was immune from political discipline, which could only fall upon actions, not ideas. Even the medieval Inquisition respected this distinction of orders; it never recognized a crime of opinion, *crimen opinionis*; its competence extended only to the repression of organized conspiracy against public order and the common good. It was, if you will, a Committee on un-Christian Activities; it regarded activities, not ideas, as justiciable.

The American Proposition, in reviving the distinction between society and state, which had perished under the advance of absolutism, likewise renewed the principle of the incompetence of government in the field of opinion. Government submits itself to judgment by the truth of society; it is not itself a judge of the truth in society. Freedom of the means of communication whereby ideas are circulated and criticized, and the freedom of the academy (understanding by the term the range of institutions organized for the pursuit of truth and the perpetuation of the intellectual heritage of society) are immune from legal inhibition or government control. This immunity is a civil right of the first order, essential to the American concept of a free people under a limited government.

## A VIRTUOUS PEOPLE

"A free people": this term too has a special sense in the American Proposition. America has passionately pursued the ideal of freedom, expressed in a whole system of political and civil rights, to new lengths; but it has not pursued this ideal so madly as to rush over the edge of the abyss, into sheer libertarianism, into the chaos created by the nineteenth-century theory of the "outlaw conscience," *conscientia exlex*, the conscience that knows no law higher than its own subjective imperatives. Part of the inner architecture of the American ideal of freedom has been the profound conviction that only a virtuous people can be free. It is not an American belief that free government is inevitable, only that it is possible, and that its possibility can be realized only when the people as a whole are inwardly governed by the recognized imperatives of the universal moral law.

The American experiment reposes on Acton's postulate, that freedom is the highest phase of civil society. But it also reposes on Acton's further postulate, that the elevation of a people to this highest phase of social life supposes, as its condition, that they understand the ethical nature of political freedom. They must understand, in Acton's phrase, that freedom is "not the power of doing what we like, but the right of being able to do what we ought." The people claim this right, in all its articulated forms, in the face of government; in the name of this right, multiple limitations are put upon the power of government. But the claim can be made with the full resonance of moral authority only to the extent that it issues from an inner sense of responsibility to a higher law. In any phase civil society demands order. In its highest phase of freedom it demands that order should not be imposed from the top down, as it were, but should spontaneously flower outward from the free obedience to the restraints and imperatives that stem from inwardly possessed moral principle. In this sense democracy is more than a political experiment; it is a spiritual and moral enterprise. And its success depends upon the virtue of the people who undertake it. Men who would be politically free must discipline themselves. Likewise institutions which would pretend to be free with a human freedom must in their workings be governed from within and made to serve the ends of virtue. Political freedom is endangered in its foundations as soon as the universal moral values, upon whose shared possession the self-discipline of a free society depends, are no longer vigorous enough to restrain the passions and shatter the selfish inertia of men. The American ideal of freedom as ordered freedom, and therefore an ethical ideal, has traditionally reckoned with these truths, these truisms.

## HUMAN AND HISTORICAL RIGHTS

This brings us to the threshold of religion, and therefore to the other aspect of the problem of pluralism, the plurality of religions in America. However, before crossing this threshold one more characteristic of the American Proposition, as implying a consensus, needs mention, namely, the Bill of Rights. The philosophy of the Bill of Rights was also tributary to the tradition of natural law, to the idea that man has certain original responsibilities precisely as man, antecedent to his status as citizen. These responsibilities are creative of rights which inhere in man antecedent to any act of government; therefore they are not granted by government and they cannot be surrendered to government. They are as inalienable as they are inherent. Their proximate source is in nature, and in history insofar as history bears witness to the nature of man; their ultimate source, as the Declaration of Independence states, is in God, the Creator of nature and the Master of history. The power of this doctrine, as it inspired both the Revolution and the form of the Republic, lay in the fact that it drew an effective line of demarcation around the exercise of political or social authority. When government ventures over this line, it collides with the duty and right of resistance. Its authority becomes arbitrary and therefore nil; its act incurs the ultimate anathema, "unconstitutional."

One characteristic of the American Bill of Rights is important for the subject here, namely, the differences that separate it from the Declaration of the Rights of Man in the France of '89. In considerable part the latter was a parchment-child of the Enlightenment, a top-of-the-brain concoction of a set of men who did not understand that a political community, like man himself, has roots in history and in nature. They believed that a state could be simply a work of art, a sort of absolute beginning, an artifact of which abstract human reason could be the sole artisan. Moreover, their exaggerated individualism had shut them off from a view of the organic nature of the human community; their social atomism would permit no institutions or associations intermediate between the individual and the state.

In contrast, the men who framed the American Bill of Rights understood history and tradition, and they understood nature in the light of both. They too were individualists, but not to the point of ignoring the social nature of man. They did their thinking within the tradition of freedom that was their heritage from England. Its roots were not in the top of anyone's brain but in history. Importantly, its roots were in the medieval notion of the *homo liber et legalis*, the man whose freedom rests on law, whose law was the age-old custom in which the nature of man expressed itself, and whose lawful freedoms were possessed in association with his fellows. The rights for which the colonists contended against the English Crown were basically the rights of Englishmen. And these were substantially the rights written into the Bill of Rights.

Of freedom of religion there will be question later. For the rest, freedom of speech, assembly, association, and petition for the redress of grievances, security of person, home, and property—these were great historical as well as civil and natural rights. So too was the right to trial by jury, and all the procedural rights implied in the Fifth- and later in the Fourteenth-Amendment provision for "due process of law." The guarantee of these and other rights was new in that it was written, in that it envisioned these rights with an amplitude, and gave them a priority, that had not been known before in history. But the Bill of Rights was an effective instrument for the delimitation of government authority and social power, not because it was written on paper in 1789 or 1791, but because the rights it proclaims had already been engraved by history on the conscience of a people. The American Bill of Rights is not a piece of eighteenth-century rationalist theory; it is far more the product of Christian history. Behind it one can see, not the philosophy of the Enlightenment but the older philosophy that had been the matrix of the common law. The "man" whose rights are guaranteed in the face of law and government is, whether he knows it or not, the Christian man, who had learned to know his own personal dignity in the school of Christian faith.

## THE AMERICAN CONSENSUS TODAY

Americans have been traditionally proud of the earlier phases of their history—colonial and Revolutionary, constitutional and Federalist. This pride persists today. The question is, whether the American consensus still endures—the consensus whose essential contents have been sketched in the foregoing. A twofold answer may be given. The first answer is given by Professor Rossiter:

> Perhaps Americans could achieve a larger measure of liberty and prosperity and build a more successful government if they were to abandon the language and assumptions of men who lived almost two centuries ago. Yet the feeling cannot be downed that rude rejection of the past, rather than levelheaded respect for it, would be the huge mistake. Americans may eventually take the advice of their advanced philosophers and adopt a political theory that pays more attention to groups, classes, public opinion, power-élites, positive law, public administration, and other realities of twentieth-century America. Yet it seems safe to predict that the people, who occasionally prove themselves wiser than their philosophers, will go on thinking about the political community in terms of unalienable rights, popular sovereignty, consent, constitutionalism, separation of powers, morality, and limited government. The political theory of the American Revolution—a theory of ethical, ordered liberty—remains the political tradition of the American people.

This is a cheerful answer. I am not at all sure that it is correct, if it be taken to imply that the tradition of natural law, as the foundation of law and politics, has the same hold upon the mind of America today that it had upon the "preachers, merchants, planters, and lawyers who were the mind of colonial America." There is indeed talk today about a certain revival of this great tradition, notably among more thoughtful men in the legal profession. But the talk itself is significant. One would not talk of reviving the tradition, if it were in fact vigorously alive. Perhaps the American people have not taken the advice of their advanced philosophers. Perhaps they are wiser than their philosophers. Perhaps they still refuse to think of politics and law as their philosophers think—in purely positivist and pragmatist terms. The fact remains that this is the way the philosophers think. Not that they have made a "rude rejection of the past." They are never rude. And they can hardly be said to have rejected what they never knew or understood, because it was never taught to them and they never learned it. The tradition of natural law is not taught or learned in the American university. It has not been rejected, much less refuted. We do not refute our adversaries, said Santayana; we quietly bid them goodbye. I think, as I shall later say, that the American university long since bade a quiet goodbye to the whole notion of an American consensus, as implying that there are truths that we hold in common, and a natural law that makes known to all of us the structure of the moral universe in such wise that all of us are bound by it in a common obedience.

There is, however, a second answer to the question, whether the original American consensus still endures. It is certainly valid of a not inconsiderable portion of the American people, the Catholic community. The men of learning in it acknowledge certain real contributions made by positive sociological analysis of the political community. But both they and their less learned fellows still adhere, with all the conviction of intelligence, to the tradition of natural law as the basis of free and ordered political life. Historically, this tradition has found, and still finds, its intellectual home within the Catholic Church. It is indeed one of the ironies of history that the tradition should have so largely languished in the so-called Catholic nations of Europe at the same time that its enduring vigor was launching a new Republic across the broad ocean. There is also some paradox in the fact that a nation which has (rightly or wrongly) thought of its own genius in Protestant terms should have owed its origins and the stability of its political structure to a tradition whose genius is alien to current intellectualized versions of the Protestant religion, and even to certain individualistic exigencies of Protestant religiosity. These are special questions, not to be pursued here. The point here is that Catholic participation in the American consensus has been full and free, unreserved and unembarrassed, because the contents of this consensus—the ethical and political principles drawn from the tradition of natural law—approve themselves to the Catholic intelligence and conscience. Where this kind of language is talked, the Catholic joins the conversation with complete ease. It is his language. The ideas expressed are native to his own universe of discourse. Even the accent, being American, suits his tongue.

Another idiom now prevails. The possibility was inherent from the beginning. To the early American theorists and politicians the tradition of natural law was an inheritance. This was its strength; this was at the same time its weakness, especially since a subtle alteration of the tradition had already commenced. For a variety of reasons the intellectualist idea of law as reason had begun to cede to the voluntarist idea of law as will. One can note the change in Blackstone, for instance, even though he still stood within the tradition, and indeed drew whole generations of early American lawyers into it with him. (Part of American folklore is Sandburg's portrait of Abraham Lincoln, sitting barefoot on his woodpile, reading Blackstone.) Protestant Christianity, especially in its left wing (and its left wing has always been dominant in America), inevitably evolved away from the old English and American tradition. Grotius and the philosophers of the Enlightenment had cast up their secularized versions of the tradition. Their disciples were to better their instruction, as the impact of the methods of empirical science made itself felt even in those areas of human thought in which knowledge is noncumulative and to that extent recalcitrant to the methods of science. Seeds of dissolution were already present in the ancient heritage as it reached the shores of America.

Perhaps the dissolution, long since begun, may one day be consummated. Perhaps one day the noble many-storeyed mansion of democracy will be dismantled, levelled to the dimensions of a flat majoritarianism, which is no mansion but a barn, perhaps even a tool shed in which the weapons of tyranny may be forged. Perhaps there will one day be wide dissent even from the political principles which emerge from natural law, as well as dissent from the constellation of ideas that have historically undergirded these principles—the idea that government has a moral basis; that the universal moral law is the foundation of society; that the legal order of society—that is, the state—is subject to judgment by a law that is not statistical but inherent in the nature of man; that the eternal reason of God is the ultimate origin of all law; that this nation in all its aspects—as a society, a state, an ordered and free relationship between governors and governed—is under God. The possibility that widespread dissent from these principles should develop is not foreclosed. If that evil day should come, the results would introduce one more paradox into history. The Catholic community would still be speaking in the ethical and political idiom familiar to them as it was familiar to their fathers, both the Fathers of

the Church and the Fathers of the American Republic. The guardian-
ship of the original American consensus, based on the Western heritage, would have passed to the Catholic community, within which
the heritage was elaborated long before America was. And it would be
for others, not Catholics, to ask themselves whether they still shared
the consensus which first fashioned the American people into a body
politic and determined the structure of its fundamental law.

What has been said may suffice to show the grounds on which
Catholics participate in the American consensus. These grounds are
drawn from the materials of the consensus itself. It has been a greatly
providential blessing that the American Republic never put to the
Catholic conscience the questions raised, for instance, by the Third
Republic. There has never been a schism within the American Catholic
community, as there was among French Catholics, over the right attitude to adopt toward the established polity. There has never been the
necessity for nice distinctions between the regime and the legislation;
nor has there ever been the need to proclaim a policy of *ralliement*.
In America the *ralliement* has been original, spontaneous, universal.
It has been a matter of conscience and conviction, because its motive
was not expediency in the narrow sense—the need to accept what one
is powerless to change. Its motive was the evident coincidence of the
principles which inspired the American Republic with the principles
that are structural to the Western Christian political tradition.

*1960*

# WILLMOORE KENDALL

A brilliant man who never fulfilled his promise, Willmoore Kendall (1909–1967) was a peripatetic and prickly political theorist who made enemies more easily than friends. Kendall earned tenure at Yale, which then offered him several years' salary just to go away. He then spent time as a quarrelsome senior editor for William F. Buckley's *National Review*. Kendall ended his career at the University of Dallas, on the periphery of the nation's intellectual life.

---

## FROM *The Conservative Affirmation*

M Y PURPOSE in this chapter is neither to bury Joseph R. McCarthy, nor to praise him. As for burying him, that was done many years ago by more competent, and far more eager, hands than mine. As for praising him, that, like damning him, seems to me to have entered upon a phase in which everybody merely spins his wheels. The basic claims put forward on both sides—we should bless McCarthy's memory, we should rue the day he was born—no longer change; the claimants do not listen to, or even hear, one another, would not understand one another even if they did listen. They are likely, from now on, to persuade only themselves, and those who already agree with them. My purpose, I say, is neither to bury McCarthy nor to praise him but rather, starting out with one simple, non-controversial statement about the McCarthy episode (perhaps the only non-controversial statement that can be made about it), to raise and try to answer one simple question, which statement and which question I propose to put as follows: There were "McCarthyites," and there were "anti-McCarthyites," and they got mad at each other, very mad, and stayed mad at one another—if anything, got madder and madder at one another—through a period of several years.[1] And the question arises: What exactly was everybody so mad about? What was the issue?

Or, to expand the statement a little, there was a fight, if not a war at least a long, sustained battle; heavy artillery was brought into play on both sides; men fought in that battle with the kind of bitterness and acrimony that human beings appear to reserve for those occasions on which brother fights brother,[2] cousin fights cousin, Damon—yes, it was often so, as I can testify from personal experience—fights Pythias. For a long while smoke hung thick over the field of battle, so that visibility was poor and there was great confusion on the part of the observing public, not merely as to how, at any given moment, the battle was going, but even as to what precisely the fighting was about—as to what exactly was getting decided, as to what actually the victor, once he emerged triumphant, would have won. Moreover, so thick was the smoke that the combatants themselves often became hazy in their minds, even differed among themselves, as to who was whose enemy and as to the sense in which this or that "enemy," if he was an enemy, was an enemy. At the time, therefore (and even for a long while afterwards), the question I raise here—What was everybody so mad about?—probably could not have been answered in a satisfactory manner. There had to be time first for the smoke to clear, and then for McCarthy to be buried, and, finally, for McCarthy to be praised and damned to such a point that no single laudatory or vituperative word that could be said about him remained still to be said.

---

[1] Note the implication, which I believe to be correct, that at some point the two camps stopped being mad at each other, or at least *that* mad—a point to which I return *in extenso* below. I am not unaware, of course, that McCarthyism remains, especially in "intellectual" circles, a "touchy" subject, so that the hostess in those circles who likes everything to go nicely all evening keeps an ear cocked for McCarthy's name, remains constantly poised to intervene (even at the far end of the table) with if not the weather then something more adroit like, "Steve, did you read Arthur Krock's column yesterday?", and heaves a silent sigh of relief if the ploy works. But things have cooled down very considerably.

[2] See William F. Buckley, Jr., and L. Brent Bozell, *McCarthy and His Enemies* (Chicago: Henry Regnery, 1954 and 1962), *passim*. This remains the only serious book we have about the battle—as, to this day, it continues to await an intellectually responsible reply from those who disagree with its conclusions. Richard Rovere's *McCarthy* (New York: Harcourt, Brace & Co., 1959), is, by comparison, contemptible, especially as no one can plead in its defense that its author, one of the two most gifted Left-wing publicists of our day, is capable of nothing better.

By now, however—so at least I like to think—it should be otherwise; not only has the smoke lifted, but we have a whole generation amongst us who know of the battle only by hearsay; if we cannot answer the question now, we never shall be able to answer it. And it would, I submit, be sickening to have to conclude, as conclude we must if we cannot answer my question, that the fight was over nothing you can put your finger on; that the energies and heartaches that went into it were wasted energies and wasted heartaches; that, most horrible of all to contemplate, nobody won, nothing got decided, and it was all sound and fury, signifying nothing. My question, though simple, is also a grave question: either the McCarthyites and anti-McCarthyites got that mad at each other for some good and intelligible reason, or we all (for all of us of a certain age were, I suppose, one or the other, McCarthyites or anti-McCarthyites) made colossal fools of ourselves; and if we did we had best now face up to it, lest tomorrow we go make fools of ourselves again.[3]

Now let us, for the moment, postpone my question and, fixing attention on the statement itself, pause to say several things about it that need to be said in order to place it in its proper context:

First, that this sort of "getting-mad" is not usual in American politics. Our politics, as Professor Clinton Rossiter has observed at length in a recent book,[4] tend to be "low-key" politics, politics that precisely do not divide men on issues that are mad-making. And I have myself argued, in a book I wrote several years ago with a collaborator,[5] that the *genius* of our political system lies in the sloughing-off of genuinely controversial issues—sloughing them off in order for them either to be handled outside the system itself (or better still, to be handled not at all, that is, suppressed or[6] as sometimes happens, repressed—into

---

[3] Note, in anticipation of my subsequent argument, that the question "Were they mad at each other for some good and intelligible reason?" and the question, "Did anything get decided, did anybody win?" are different questions—so that the answer to the first could be "Yes" and that to the second "No," or if not "No" then "What got decided was to postpone a decision on the big issue."

[4] See Clinton Rossiter, *Parties and Politics in America* (Ithaca: Cornell University Press, 1960), *passim*.

[5] See Austin Ranney and Willmoore Kendall, *Democracy and the American Party System* (New York: Harcourt, Brace & Co., 1955).

[6] The classic case, perhaps, arose from an article by J. B. Matthews on the penetration of the Protestant churches by Communism. When, many months after its

the deep recesses of our collective unconscious, where, providentially, we can forget all about them). The McCarthy phase, or episode, or set-to—call it what you like—was then something presumptively special in our political history, something that we must not expect to explain to ourselves with everyday concepts and everyday tools of analysis. It was no mere quarrel, for example, over allocation of the contents of the porkbarrel or whether a businessman from Kansas City is to be confirmed as Ambassador to Ghana.

Secondly (that is, the second thing that needs to be said about how mad everybody got), we must not take for granted that the real issue ever, at the time, actually got put into words, ever actually thrust itself into the consciousness of the actors in the drama. To assume that the real issue was what got talked about—so we are assured by, variously, marriage counselors and trade-dispute arbitrators, all of whom are in debt here to the greatest of female political scientists in America, Mary Follett—to assume such a thing, they say, is to show ignorance of the way quarrels among human beings generate and develop. John and Mary may *think* they are quarreling about whether to send Jo-Ann to Mount Holyoke or Chicago, and end up getting very mad at each other about it, and staying mad weeks on end. But not so, says the marriage counselor; the issue must be one that goes to the very depths of the marriage relation between John and Mary. What is really being fought about is Mary's feeling that John somehow does not treat her as an equal, or if not that then some far-reaching sexual maladjustment that neither John nor Mary would dream of articulating and may not even be aware of, or John and Mary's shared but inarticulate feeling that John has turned out to be a second-rater in his profession. The quarrel, according to Miss Follett and her followers, must go on and on about this basically irrelevant issue or that one, go on and on and get worse and worse, either until it is repressed or until the real issue is somehow brought out into the open and, with or without the help of an outsider, dealt with on its merits.

Thirdly—a similar but not quite the same point—the chances are that the real issue, once out in the open, will prove to be far more

---

publication, the article became the topic of angry controversy, Dwight Eisenhower restored peace by proclaiming that the Protestant churches are among our basic institutions, and therefore could not be penetrated by Communism. The issue—I do not exaggerate—promptly disappeared.

"important" and difficult than the issue over which the quarrelers think they have been quarreling; that, concretely, it will prove to involve the meaning and quality and above all the destiny of the relatedness of the quarrelers. He who delves into the depths of a quarrel, an honest-to-goodness, bitter, and sustained quarrel, must not expect to come up with peanuts, or any known equivalent of peanuts.

Two other small points of that kind and we shall have done with preliminaries:

A. The McCarthyites were mad at the anti-McCarthyites, and the anti-McCarthyites were mad at the McCarthyites, which, I am saying, is unusual in our low-key politics. But to that I must now add (not, as I am tempted to do, that the anti-McCarthyites were madder than the McCarthyites—angrier, more bitter, more ready to paste someone in the nose—because that would perhaps slosh over into the controversial) that what is most unusual, and a different matter altogether, is that the anti-McCarthyites got mad at all. For the anti-McCarthyites were the Liberals; and the Liberals, as I understand them, have some built-in reasons for not getting mad that the McCarthyites, the anti-Liberals, do not have—built-in reasons connected, as I understand the matter, with the whole metaphysical and epistemological stance of contemporary American Liberalism. That is to say, the Liberals are usually the Tentative Ones of contemporary politics: they believe that everyone is entitled to his point of view, that in general one man's opinion is as good as another's, that, as I like to put it, all questions are open questions. Officially, therefore, they don't get mad—have, in point of fact, got really "fightin'" mad only twice within the memory of living man—once, of course, at Adolf Hitler, then a few years later and on their own principles equally unaccountably, at Joe McCarthy. Let us be quite clear about this. When A gets mad at B and sets out to defeat him cost what it may, A, whatever his metaphysics and whatever his epistemology, ends up saying, and saying in the most eloquent manner possible, which is by his actions: B is *wrong* about the issue over which we have fallen out, and *I* am *right*. Now A's metaphysical and epistemological commitments may or may not admit of his making any such assertion; if A is a Liberal, they certainly do not admit of it, because the Master, John Stuart Mill, taught above all that one does not assert one's "infallibility." In asserting it, A postpones until later (perhaps, as in the two cases mentioned, until the Greek kalends) a day of reckoning that, properly speaking, he has no right to sidestep (and along with it, the day on which he will get back to normal, which is to say: not be mad at Stalin, not be mad at World Communism, not be mad at Khrushchev—because who can say, after all, who is right and who is wrong in politics?). Yet, I am saying, A the Liberal did get mad at Joe McCarthy, did set out to defeat him *coûte que coûte*, did proclaim to the four winds that McCarthy was wrong and he was right. And this, I suggest, forces upon us a slightly revised but still more fascinating version of my original statement, namely that everybody got mad, including the professional Tentative Ones, the professional Don't-get-madders. At the same time, it lends color to our suspicion that the issue actually at stake went very deep, and never got itself stated in satisfactory terms. (As for the McCarthyites, they, unlike the Liberals, have built-in reasons for getting mad; they are the Non-tentative Ones of our politics, the Absolutists, the people who couldn't care less if they get caught assuming their own "infallibility." We have, therefore, less reason to be surprised at their getting mad. They are on the point of getting mad, and for good reason, all the time.)[7]

B. We might profitably, though without making too big a thing of it, remind ourselves of the other issues about which Americans, despite their low-key politics, have had big quarrels in the past. Mercifully, there have been very few of them; and conspicuously absent from among them, mercifully again, have been the Constitution, the Bill of Rights, and, surprisingly perhaps, the Amendments to the Constitution posterior to the Bill of Rights. Let us, by way of background, tick them off: During the years 1776–1779 there was the issue of *Loyalism*, which resulted in our driving the Loyalists into Canada. In the early years of the Republic there arose the issue of the Alien and Sedition Acts—which resulted in the silencing, nay, the persecution, of the alleged seditionists. During the years just before and during the Civil War, there was the issue of slavery. All three, I say, are cases where Americans got very mad at one another. They stayed mad for a long time, and were determined not to compromise, or let the matter drop, but to *win*—either to repudiate or perpetuate the authority of the King in Parliament, either to enforce or get rid of the Alien and Sedition

---

[7] See below, pp. 181–87.

Acts, either to abolish slavery or to save it as the South's "peculiar institution." And all three, as we can see in retrospect, involved an issue that bore, in the deepest and most direct manner possible to imagine, on the very destiny of the American people. All three involved, that is to say, a question that the American people must answer in order to know themselves as the kind of people they are, in order to achieve clarity as to their identity as a people, their mission in history, their responsibility under God—so, at least in those days, they would have put it—for the kind of political and social *order* they were to create and maintain in history. All three, let us note finally, are cases in which people kept on being mad until somebody won, and was understood by both sides to have won, and so made good its point about the destiny of America.

So much for preliminaries. I turn now to my question, and I propose to work my way toward an answer to it by taking up, then rejecting, in good Socratic manner, some "easy" answers that for one reason or another (as I hope to show) simply will not do. They are, as the reader will guess from my reference to Socratic method, the answers you will get if you go button-holing people down in the market place, putting the question to them, and listening attentively to what they come up with. I got mine by bringing the question up one evening in the Spring of 1962, at a "stag" dinner party made up of professors of political science at a well-known East Coast university. I shall, for convenience' sake, assign numbers to them, and devote a section of the present chapter to each.

## ANSWER NUMBER ONE

The issue was Joe McCarthy himself. McCarthy was rude, ruthless, fanatical. He lacked, as the good Mr. Welch[8] put it, all "sense of decency." He was a master of demagogy, of, to quote the Federalist Papers, those "vicious arts, by which elections are too often carried." He reflected a mood of "hysteria" amongst the electorate, was himself

---

[8] Counsel for the Government in the "famous" televised hearings.

hysterical, generated hysteria in others. He did not play politics according to the rules of the game as we understand them here in America. His conduct, as a Senate majority finally got around to putting it, was unbecoming a Senator and a gentleman. He browbeat witnesses. He took advantage of his senatorial immunity in order to blacken the reputations and assassinate the character of innocent persons; like Fr. Coughlin, like Gerald L. K. Smith, like Fritz Kuhn himself, he was a hater, a know-nothing, a man who knew and spoke no language other than that of hatred. He represented, in any case, a tendency that had to be nipped in the bud—lest it develop into an American version of that which it most resembled, namely, Nazism. He was, finally, a fraud; he never uncovered a single Communist. All you had to do was *see* him, on television, in order to realize that here was a man who must be struck down. What more natural, then, than that he should divide the country into two fanatically warring groups, namely, (a) those who like and go in for that kind of thing—of whom there are always only too many, all only too ready to respond with fury to any who resist them—and (b) the rest of us, who cling to at least minimum standards of civility?

That, I think, is a fair summary of the "case" against McCarthy as, say, a *Washington Post* editorial might have put it in 1952, or as a deeply convinced anti-McCarthyite (with, of course, a longer memory than most anti-McCarthyites have) would put it today.

Now, the McCarthyites among my readers would, no doubt, like me to linger over the charges, one by one, and refute them—as, for the most part anyhow, they have been refuted in The Book No Liberal Reads, Buckley and Bozell (see Note 2, above). I propose, however, to do nothing of the kind, since one of the advantages of my simple question—as compared to the questions on which discussion in this area has turned in recent years—is this: It frees us from the necessity of conducting the argument on that plane and enables us to take what we may, I think, fairly call higher ground. It enables us even to enter a demurrer—not, of course, to plead McCarthy guilty as charged, but to plead that the facts, even if they were as alleged, do not support the claim with which we are concerned, namely, that we have before us an answer to my simple question. The facts, as alleged, can at best illuminate only a small part of our problem, and for the following easy-to-document reason: The McCarthyites and anti-McCarthyites were mad at each other, "fightin'" mad at each other, before ever McCarthy appeared on the scene, and long, long before he became Chairman of the Committee on Government Operations. Which is to say, those who offer the answer before us are, quite simply, talking bad history and exaggerating out of all proportion the importance of McCarthy in the development of what I, at least, have no objection to calling McCarthyism. They are answering at most only a tiny part of our question, when what we want, what we must demand, is an answer to the whole question. McCarthy, like Achilles after the death of Patroclus, stepped into a battle that was already raging, one in which the lines were already drawn, one whose outcome he could and did still affect, but *not* one in which he could possibly become the issue being fought over. Never mind that the battle-waging armies ended up with new names—McCarthyites, anti-McCarthyites—because of his entry into the fray. Never mind, either, that the anti-McCarthyites do seem, as a matter of history, to have promptly got a lot madder at the McCarthyites than they had been before. Never mind, finally, that both armies increased considerably in size between the famous speech at Wheeling and the famous censure motion in the United States Senate. We are not asking why people got madder off at the end, or even why at some point the anger suddenly spread in ever-widening circles (as it did), but rather, What were people mad about to begin with? *What, for example, what were they mad about at the (earlier) time of the Hiss case?* What was the *real* issue? And the real issue was not, could not have been, McCarthy himself.

## ANSWER NUMBER TWO

The issue was an issue between two conflicting views of World Communism and the World Communist movement, between—I shall try here, as I did with Answer Number One, to put the thing from the side of the anti-McCarthyites, lest I be accused of stacking the cards in favor of the position with which, for good or ill, my own name is associated—those who are running scared in the presence of the so-called Communist threat, and those who are keeping their heads. Between those who would seek a false security by attempting to use against Communism the Communists' own weapons, and those who are prepared to settle for that degree of security that is possible, who believe that security can be achieved with an arsenal limited to democracy's normal weapons, which are those of negotiation and persuasion. Between those who think that by striking out at the Communist danger in all directions at once we can somehow eliminate it, somehow conjure it out of existence, and those who have got it through their heads that Communism, the Communist Empire on the world scene, the Communist minority at home, is something you have to learn to live with and ought to learn to live with because it is, after all, something that *we*, by our shortcomings, have brought upon ourselves. Between those who believe that the correct answer to Communism is military force internationally and coercive thought-control domestically, and those who know that these are not answers at all, that the struggle against Communism is a struggle over men's minds and hearts and souls, is in any case a battle that you win, if you win at all, by eliminating the poverty, the discrimination, the injustice, the inequality, that make Communism attractive and give the Communists their strategic opportunities. Between those who see the Communist danger as imposing upon us a choice between liberty and security, and would unhesitatingly sacrifice the former to the latter, and those of us who know for one thing that Communism is not that kind of danger, and know for another thing that the battle against Communism is not worth winning if, in winning it, we must lose our freedom. Between those who attribute to the Communists supernatural, nay, miraculous powers of seduction, of deceit, of winning against even the most unfavorable odds, and those who know that the Communists are mere men like ourselves, no more able to infiltrate our councils, our institutions, our high places, than we are to infiltrate theirs. Between those who have somehow convinced themselves that the Communists never sleep, and those of us who know that Communists, like other people, need their eight hours in the sack. Between those who think the Communists actually believe in their so-called ideology: Marxism, the inevitability of Communist victory, etc., and those of us sufficiently knowledgeable to take that sort of thing with a grain of salt, to realize that what we are up against is not something new and different properly called the Communist Empire, but something old and familiar properly called Russian nationalism. Between those who think that a Communist dictatorship can keep on being Communist and keep on being a dictatorship for ever and ever, and those of us who know that dictatorships, including Communist dictatorships, mellow and go soft as they get old, and that revolutionaries, even the wildest of revolutionaries, grow conservative and cautious as they become habituated to power. Between those who think the Communists will stop at nothing, not even totally destructive universal war, in their bid for world empire, and those of us who know that the Communists, the Russian government and the Russian people alike, want, above all, peace. Between those so addled in their wits by Communism that they think that even their next door neighbor may well be a Communist, and so see a Communist stripling behind every sapling, and those of us who remember, in the teeth of the Communist threat, that America is built upon trust among neighbors, that Americans do not sow the seeds of suspicion in each other's back yards. Between those who think the Communists really have found a way to repress, and hold in check, the forces that make for freedom in any society, and those of us who know that man's desire for freedom must in the end triumph over all obstacles. Between those who think the Communists mean it when they say they will "bury" us, and those of us who know that all that is just Communist "talk" and blustering. Between those who cling stubbornly to the notion that there are deep and irreconcilable differences between our so-called free society and the so-called slave society of the Soviet Union, and so take no cognizance of the political and economic and social change that goes forward within the Communist Empire, and those, better-informed, unencumbered by dogmatic preconceptions, who realize that with each passing day American society and Soviet society become "more alike"—become, each of them, a closer approximation to the universal society of the future, which will of course combine in beneficent union the better features of them both.

Answer Two is, clearly, a better answer than Answer One. It is, for one thing, better history. Through the period that we ought to have in mind when we speak of these matters, there have indeed been current among us two views of the nature and meaning of World Communism, two views of which, as I like to think anyhow, the little rundown I have just given provides a not inaccurate summary; two views and, in general, two groups of "those who's," respectively committed to the one or the other; two groups, moreover, whose stand on a whole series of issues in public policy that arose through the period tended to reflect the one or the other of the two views. No harm is done, furthermore, by calling the one of the two views the McCarthyite view and the other the anti-McCarthyite view—*provided*, however, that we remember, here as before, that both views had crystalized, and attracted numerous adherents, long before McCarthy appeared upon the scene; that the McCarthyite view was not invented by McCarthy; that it had, indeed, through the years in question, both more knowledgeable and more vigorous exponents than McCarthy; that, in a word, *it had best be thought of as having itself produced McCarthy rather than McCarthy it.* Insofar as it is correct, then, Answer Two has the further advantage of being correct for the whole period and not, like Number One, only for the years immediately following the Wheeling speech.

One easily sees, moreover, why those who entertained the McCarthyite view tended to get mad at those who entertained the anti-McCarthyite view. At least one of the two views, possibly perhaps both of them but at least one of them, must be wrong, intellectually incorrect, which is to say they cannot both be correct. Each of the two views, pretty clearly moreover, is pregnant with implications about policy, both foreign policy and internal security policy, that flatly contradict the implications of the other, so that any time a policy decision has to be made in either of those two areas the two groups are likely, other things being equal, to array themselves on opposite sides. Nor is that all. Since each view, from the standpoint of the other, would commit the nation to policies certain to turn out to be suicidal, we readily understand how and why the two groups did get mad at each other early in the period, and got madder and madder at each other as the period progressed. For each, in the eyes of the other, was guilty of an error of judgment so great as to seem unforgivable.

Indeed, Answer Two makes so much sense that we are tempted to adopt it out of hand as the correct answer to our question, and let it go at that. Our question is answered, and we can all settle back in our chairs and forget about it.

I suggest, nevertheless, that we take (but hold until we are sure we can do better) a rain-check on Answer Two as well as on Number One—not because Answer Two isn't correct as far as it goes (which I have conceded it is), but because, to me at least, it seems inadequate psychologically, and because its assumptions about the articulateness of American political struggles are somewhat more flattering than we deserve. Concretely, I find that Answer Two explains to me why some people got mad, but not why so many people got mad, or why anybody—to go back to my original form of words—got all *that* mad. The issue that Answer Two insists upon is (a) for the most part an issue about foreign policy, and I do not believe that Americans in general were at any time during that period that interested in foreign policy, and (b) an intellectual issue, where the ultimate crime the alleged criminals are being accused of is merely stupidity, and I do not believe we had yet reached the day when intellectual issues, issues ultimately capable of being talked out or, failing that, capable of being resolved by sound scholarship, arouse in us the kind of passions that were displayed in the clash between McCarthyism and anti-McCarthyism.[9] Millions of the persons who rallied around McCarthy, I should guess, and hundreds of thousands (for I do not believe there were millions) of the persons who rallied against him, entertained no view whatever on the nature of Communism, and, in any case, were not about to be moving in the direction of civil war against those who entertained a view different from their own. In other words, our correct and inclusive answer, if and when we find it, will tap a dimension that Answer Two conspicuously avoids, namely—for they were not a slip on my part, those words "civil war"—the civil war dimension, the dimension, if you like, of mutual accusations of heresy. And having said that, I can venture the following thesis: the ultimate crime of which McCarthyites and anti-McCarthyites were accusing one another was, make no mistake about it, that of heresy; the passions generated were, make again no mistake about it, passions appropriate not to an intellectual debate but to a heresy-hunt, and we shall not understand them, ever, unless we bear that in mind.

To which let me add, before passing on to Answer Number Three: if Answer Two were correct, people would evidently be madder today than they were in 1953, which in point of fact, as I have intimated above, they certainly are not. For the differences among us as to the

---

[9] Not that intellectual issues never arouse passions. They do, but exactly in the quarters where we are taught least to expect them, namely, those of the so-called "exact" physical scientists. On the latter point, see Michael Polanyi, *Personal Knowledge: Towards a Post-Critical Philosophy* (Chicago: University of Chicago, 1958), *passim.*

nature and meaning of Communism are no less deep, no less unresolved, than in 1952; nor, I feel safe in saying further, have the stakes,
which I repeat involve the very survival of the United States, got
any lower. The correct answer to our question, then, must be able to
explain why the clash between McCarthyites and anti-McCarthyites
seems not only not to have become sharper, but to be less sharp today
than it did nine years ago; and Answer Two cannot explain that for us.
The correct explanation, in short, must explain not only the storm,
but also the apparent ensuing calm.


## ANSWER NUMBER THREE

The clash between McCarthy and his enemies was merely another
chapter in the history of the separation and balancing of power within
the American political system. What was at issue was neither differing views of Communism as such (the clash might equally well have
occurred over some other topic), nor, to go back to Answer One,
McCarthy himself as such (although, say the proponents of this view,
McCarthy had personal qualities that made the dispute angrier than it
would otherwise have been, perhaps even innate tendencies of character that disposed him to play the role of hysteria-monger), since
the forces operating through McCarthy might equally have expressed
themselves through some other leader. The issue was, rather, that
of legislative encroachment on the constitutional powers of the
Executive. For one thing McCarthy pressed the prerogatives of congressional investigating committees to hitherto-unheard-of-lengths—
as witness, for example, his apparent belief that those prerogatives
extended even within the sacred precincts of the nation's universities. For another, even if we were to grant that Congress was acting
within its constitutional powers when it put the Internal Security
program on the statute books (even if we were, *per impossible*, to grant
that the program did not violate the freedom of speech clause of the
First Amendment), still enforcement of the relevant laws was the
proper business of the President and his subordinates in the executive
branch of government—with, of course, appeals where appeals might
be required to the courts of law. McCarthy's attempts to intervene in

the dispatch of individual cases, his explicit claim that the Committee on Government Operations was entitled to watch over and criticize the detail of internal security administration, therefore represented congressional self-aggrandizement in its most blatant and dangerous form. Nor is that all. McCarthy undermined discipline in the Executive Branch by openly inviting civil servants with tales to bear to break the chain of command and come directly to him; he would right all wrongs, punish all iniquities. Nor is even that all. The day came when foreign service officers were obliged to falsify their reports lest McCarthy haul them before his committee and, with his usual techniques of insinuation and innuendo, his usual willingness to assume a man guilty until proven innocent, crucify them for their alleged pro-Communist bias. Nay, still more. The day came when the foreign service could no longer attract able recruits because no young man in his senses would expose himself to the risks McCarthy had injected into the career of the foreign service officer; considerations alike of decency and of self-interest sent men of talent into other careers. Even McCarthy's "working capital," for that matter, the scraps of so-called "information" that he "held in his hand" and that enabled him to move in on his victims, came to him through violations of security regulations; his very possession of them was legislative encroachment. McCarthy, in short McCarthy every time he opened his mouth, upset the separation of powers equilibrium that is central and sacred in the American political tradition. He upset it, moreover (if we abstract from his having been a Senator not a member of the House of Representatives), in precisely the manner contemplated by the Founders of the Republic, namely, through the workings of a demagogically-led popular movement, adverse to natural rights and to the public interest, which sweeps through the country, establishes itself in Congress, finds itself unable to accomplish its objectives because of the defensive weapons the Constitution entrusts to the two other co-equal and coordinate branches of government—and must, willy-nilly, seek to concentrate all power in its own hands. The McCarthy movement did just that, and, naturally enough, all in America who love constitutional government, that is, limited government, saw in him a threat to all that they most value in the American political tradition, responded to him with righteous anger, struck back at him as best they could.

Nor, on the anti-McCarthy side at least, is any other answer needed to the question, "Why did people get so mad?"

Here, moreover, as with Answer Two though not with Answer One, the supposed issue is neat and symmetrical, that is, joined in almost identical terms from the other side: The Internal Security Program, or Loyalty Program as it was called in its early days, went onto the statute books by virtue of the exercise by Congress of powers clearly vested in it by the Constitution. The Executive Branch of government, the Department of State in particular, refused from the first moment to recognize the necessity for such legislation. It called its constitutionality into question, showed a complete lack of sympathy both with its underlying principles and its objectives, openly defied it, did everything it could to frustrate the committees—the Internal Security Committee in the Senate, the Committee on Un-American Activities in the House—Congress charged with responsibility for studying and reporting upon the Communist threat. The Executive withheld information from them (on the mostly spurious grounds of so-called "classification"), lied to them *ad libitum*, refused, even in the clearest cases, to act upon information provided by them—or, for that matter, upon information provided by their great ally within the Executive Branch itself, the F.B.I. The Executive kept in positions of high authority and honor men who obviously could not meet the loyalty-security standards set by the Congress. It moved—through the Truman Loyalty Order of 1947, which arbitrarily shifted the administrative standard in loyalty cases so as to give to the individual not the government the benefit of doubt—to emasculate the Program, starved the security offices in the great government departments, and mobilized against the Program not only the formidable opinion-making resources of its bureaucracy but also those of the newspapers and the radio and television networks. Subsequently, after McCarthy's appearance on the scene as a subcommittee chairman, it denied Congress' crystal-clear right to inquire whether its statutes were being faithfully executed. If there was encroachment, then it was clearly a matter of the Executive's encroaching upon Congress. Congress, off at the end, had no alternative but to raise up a McCarthy, and insist upon its right to exercise the investigative powers needed in order to prevent the Executive from becoming, quite simply, a law unto itself. Nor could any man capable of grasping the clear language of the Constitution hesitate as to where, in the interests of constitutional government and of the American political system as traditionally understood, to throw his support. If McCarthy had not existed it would have been necessary, for the sake of constitutional equilibrium, to invent him; and, naturally enough, the people, jealous always of the powers of that branch of government which, because closest to them in point both of time and of distance, they regard as peculiarly theirs, rallied around him. As for abuse of investigative powers, the Supreme Court is always there to set metes and bounds for congressional committees, and the records contain *no* Supreme Court decision that rules adversely to the McCarthy Subcommittee.

The issue, I repeat, is neat and symmetrical, but as regards an answer to our question we are back, I think, to where we were with Answer Two. Some people no doubt got mad about legislative encroachment in the area of internal security, and some no doubt about executive defiance of the will of Congress. Both groups, no doubt, got madder still because of the continuing dispute over the nature and meaning of the World Communist movement; but also no-one ever heard of anybody with a soft view of Communism getting worried, in those days, about *executive* encroachment, or of anybody with a tough view of Communism getting worried about *legislative* encroachment. Once again, therefore, the suspicion arises that we are flattering ourselves; that is, vastly exaggerating, this time, our capacity as a people to work ourselves up into a fury over an issue so legalistic and intellectual as separation of powers. The admittedly hard-to-read slogan emblazoned upon the banners of the McCarthyites, whatever it proclaimed, could not have proclaimed the principle: "All legislative powers herein granted shall be vested in a Congress of the United States. . . ." Answer Three is better than Answer Two in that it edges us over toward the kind of issue that could breed charges of heresy not stupidity. But we do not, I think, yet have hold of the right heresies.

## TESTS FOR A CORRECT ANSWER

I have now taken up one at a time, and examined, the three answers to our simple question that, as I put it to begin with, one is likely to encounter in the market place of contemporary American political discussion. I have in each case found the answer either unconvincing or, insofar as convincing, inadequate; that is, incapable of explaining the *whole* of the phenomenon that has engaged our curiosity. I should, however, be very sorry for the reader to conclude that we have wasted our time; that is, made no progress whatever with our task. For we have, I like to think, insofar as we have reasoned together correctly, begun to apprehend certain tests that a correct answer to our question must be able to meet, namely:

First, it must point to an issue deep enough to possess what, for lack of a better term, we may call *genuine civil war potential*, an issue capable, therefore, of being mentioned in the same breath with the slavery issue, the Loyalism issue during the American Revolution, and the issue (about which, let me say, we know all too little) posed, very early in our history as a nation, by the Alien and Sedition Acts.

Second, it must be an issue that large numbers of people are capable of grasping with hooks that are not precisely those of the intellect—an issue capable, I am tempted to say, of being grasped intuitively, of being felt as well as thought. "As well as," mind you, not "rather than," for I do not wish to imply that it must be an issue not susceptible of being put into words, or an issue that wholly eludes rational discussion.

Third, it must be an issue that, somewhere along the line, calls for an act, though not I should think necessarily a conscious act, of *moral choice* on the part of the man who "takes sides" on it. That is why I have stressed that one of its characteristics is that of not lending itself to resolution merely by sound scholarship, or to being just plain "talked out"—to a point where all may agree because all objections, on one side or the other, have been met and answered. That notion we may now refine a little by adding that it must be an issue that we would expect to be "talkable–outable," if I may put it so, only amongst men who move in their talk from common or at least reconcilable moral premises.

Fourth, the issue must meet certain historical tests or requirements. We must be able to see why, as a matter of history, it might well have begun to make itself felt (again, I stress "felt," for it will not necessarily have been clearly articulated), why people began to get mad about it at such and such a period rather than earlier.

Fifth, it must be an issue about which we can explain, not too unsatisfactorily, why it has seemed less sharp through the years since McCarthy's death than it did through the years preceding McCarthy's death.

Now I believe, as the reader will have guessed, that I know what the issue is, and I am going to try, in the next and concluding section of the present chapter, to get it into words and "justify" it over against the tests I have just enumerated.

## THE CORRECT ANSWER

Let us go right to the heart of the matter. By the late 1930's, that is, by the end of the second decade after the Communist Revolution, every free nation in the world, whether it realized it or not, faced the following question: Are we or are we not going to permit the emergence, within our midst, of totalitarian movements? Every free nation, in other words, was by that time already confronted with evidence that efforts would in due course be made to call such movements into being, that such efforts would be strongly supported from the home bases of the existing totalitarian movements, and that those efforts could, to some extent at least, be encouraged or discouraged by the action of its own government. Most free nations, to be sure, chose to ignore that evidence, and did not pose to themselves the question I have named, not even in some more cautious form such as "Are we at least going to try to prevent the emergence here of the totalitarian movements we see flourishing in other countries?" Not so, however, the United States. By the mid-1940's it had on its statute books an impressive array of legislation—the great names here, of course, are the Hatch Act, the Smith Act, and the so-called McCarran rider—which (a) reflected a very considerable awareness that the problem of encouraging or discouraging totalitarian movements existed, and called for some kind of answer, and (b) announced in effect: We—whatever other free nations may do or not do—are going to put certain major obstacles in the way of such movements; we at least are not going to facilitate their emergence; we at least are going to take some perfectly obvious immediate steps that should make clear alike to the self-appointed leaders of such minorities, to the world in general, and to ourselves, where we stand on the matter; and we at least regard the emergence and growth of such minorities as on the face of it undesirable. Let us proceed at once, then, to exclude representatives of such minorities from the service of our governments, national, state, and local; and let us proceed also to clip the wings of such minorities by forbidding them, on pain of imprisonment, to advocate the overthrow of the government of the United States. Opinions might differ, let us be fair and concede it at once, as to the moment the question narrowed in legislators' minds from one concerning totalitarian movements in general to one concerning a Communist minority in particular. Opinions might differ, too, as to the moment at which the Communist movement burgeoned, in legislators' minds, from the status of a logical possibility to that of a clear and present danger. Opinions might differ, finally, as to the moment at which the American Liberals decided that the question as to the future of totalitarian movements in the United States came under the general constitutional rubric of so-called freedom-of-speech questions, and therefore under the rubric of actions permitted or prohibited to the Congress of the United States by the First Amendment to the Constitution. But all three of these developments did, in due course, take place; and we must, in order to approach the correct answer to my question, get them clearly in mind—first of all as background for the following (in my opinion) crucial points:

First, the motive that underlay the original internal security legislation was certainly *not* that of impairing or limiting the Communists' freedom of speech. The Communist being struck at was for the most part the Communist who precisely did not exercise his constitutional right (if any) to freedom of speech in order to advocate Communism, but rather the man who, having transferred his allegiance from the United States to World Communism, set out to systematically conceal the fact from his fellow-citizens. The "freedom" at stake in the early legislation, then, assuming there was one worthy the name, was not freedom of speech, which the First Amendment does forbid the Congress to impair, but rather, if a "freedom" we must have, freedom of thought—the freedom to entertain such and such opinions in the United States without being subjected to such and such disabilities and such and such disagreeable consequences. Freedom of *thought*, I say, about which the Constitution of the United States says nothing at all. (Never mind that the Liberals say that when the Constitution says freedom of speech it means, must mean, freedom of thought. We have only their word for it.)

Second, the authors and supporters of the original legislation do not appear to have had, in passing the legislation, any freedom of speech "inhibitions," or for that matter any notion that the legislation they were putting on the statute books involved anything especially novel in the way of principle.

Third, it was, nevertheless, not long before one began to hear, from Liberal quarters of course, rumblings about freedom of speech, about the patent unconstitutionality of all such legislation, about, finally, the incompatibility of all such legislation with traditional American concepts of—of all things!—freedom.[10] The United States could not take preventive action against the emergence of a Communist movement because, precisely, of its commitment to liberty!

Fourth, after a certain moment in this train of events, everything, as I see it, conspired to conceal the issue actually, really and truly being fought over; everything but, as I have already intimated, two things: (a) Communism did at some moment acquire, in the eyes of Americans generally, the status of a "clear and present danger." And (b) the Liberals, at some moment, did pull in their horns, did change their public stance on anti-Communist legislation. Up to that moment (or those moments) what debate there was turned on the question, "Is the United States entitled to impose disabilities upon an emergent 'political' movement deemed undesirable even if it is not a clear and present danger?" or, variously, "Is there anything in the Constitution or in the American political tradition that prevents American government *or* American society from announcing: We intend to proscribe such and such 'political' opinions; to that end we intend to *persecute* those opinions, that is, to place the price of holding them—not expressing them, but holding them—so high that people will be forced to avoid them or, if they have already adopted them, to abandon them?" Up to that moment (or those moments) what debate there was was a matter of the legislators answering that question in the affirmative and the Liberals answering it in the negative. While after that moment (or

---

[10] The *locus classicus* remains the two-article series by Professor Thomas Emerson and David M. Helfeld, "Loyalty Amongst Government Employees," *Yale Law Journal*, Vol. 58, I and II (1948–1949).

those moments) the debate shifted to the very different question: "Is the United States entitled to strike at a body of opinion which constitutes a clear and present danger?", which question, because of the aforementioned shift on the part of the Liberals, almost everyone, the legislative majority and the Liberals alike, was suddenly answering in the affirmative. The original issue, in other words, simply disappeared, and, we may safely add, has hardly been heard of since.

Let me, so as to guard against any possible misunderstanding, say that over again in a slightly different way. First we get what amounts to the proscription of the Communist movement in America on the grounds merely that such a movement is undesirable in the United States, and that the proscription of an undesirable movement is clearly within the power of Congress—clearly, and without any complications about impairment of "freedom of speech" or "clear and present danger." The Liberals oppose the proscription, on the grounds that Congress has no power to proscribe—unless, just possibly, in the presence of a clear and present danger. A debate gets under way that, had the terms not changed, would have had to be decided one way or the other, yet could not have been decided one way or the other without (as I shall argue more concretely in a moment) what each party to the debate regarded as the very gravest implications as to the nature of our constitutional system. But the terms did change, because of two developments which, though more or less simultaneous, we must keep rigorously separated in our minds. First, Communism became, in the eyes of people generally, the kind of clear and present danger in the presence of which even the Liberals might concede Congress' power to act. Second, the Liberals, pretty certainly on straight strategic grounds, suddenly decided that they not only might but would give their blessing to the proscription of the Communist movement as, or insofar as it was, a clear and present danger. The original issue, therefore, promptly disappears, since all that remains to be talked about is whether, or the extent to which, Communism *is* a clear and present danger. The first development, in the absence of the second, would presumably have resulted only in redoubled effort on behalf of a course of action already decided upon before it occurred (just as more fire-fighting equipment is called in when what has seemed a routine fire suddenly threatens to become a conflagration). The second development, in the absence of the first (in the absence, that is, of a decision that the fire was not a routine fire), would merely have signalized overwhelming Liberal defeat on the original issue—which would, accordingly, have been decided in favor of the legislators. But the second development in the context of the first could only have the effect of spiriting the original issue away. Which is what it did.

Now my thesis is that the issue that really divided the McCarthyites and the anti-McCarthyites was, precisely, that original issue; that once we see that to be true, everything falls into place; and that, to anticipate a little, the disappearance of that original issue was, any way you look at it, a major national misfortune. And it remains for me only (a) to note that that original issue is merely an alternative statement of the issue that political philosophers debate under the heading "the open society," (b) to show that things do, once we recognize that as the issue at stake between the McCarthyites and the anti-McCarthyites, fall neatly into place, and (c) to make clear why I regard its eclipse as a "major national misfortune."

Let me put it this way: All political societies, all peoples, but especially I like to think our political society, this *"people of the United States,"* is founded upon what political philosophers call a *consensus;* that is, a hard core of shared beliefs. Those beliefs that the people share are what defines its character as a political society, what embodies its meaning as a political society, what, above all perhaps, expresses its understanding of itself as a political society, of its role and responsibility in history, of its very destiny. I say that is true especially of our political society because in our case the coming into existence as a people, a certain kind of people with a certain conception of its meaning and responsibility, takes place right out in the open for all to see, takes place unshrouded by the mists of remote history or the hazes of possibly inaccurate legend. "We," cries the people of the United States at the very moment of its birth (and we should be grateful to John Courtney Murray for having recently reminded us of the fact[11]), "We," cries the American people at that moment, "hold these *truths.*" That is, "we" believe there is such a thing as Truth, believe that the particular truths of which Truth is made up are discoverable by man's reason and thus by our reason, recognize *these* truths as those to which

---

[11] See especially the opening pages of his *We Hold These Truths* (New York: Sheed and Ward, 1961).

our reason and that of our forebears have led us, and agree with one another to *hold* these truths—that is, to cherish them as ours, to hand them down in their integrity to our descendants, to defend them against being crushed out of existence by enemies from without or corrupted out of all recognition by the acids of skepticism and disbelief working from within.

Now, such a consensus, conceived of as a body of truths actually held by the people whose consensus it is, is incomprehensible *save as we understand it* (in Murray's phrase) *to exclude ideas and opinions contrary to itself.* Discussion there is and must be, freedom of thought and freedom of expression there are and must be, but within limits set by the basic consensus; freedom of thought and freedom of expression there are and must be, but not anarchy of thought or anarchy of expression. In such a society by no means are *all* questions open questions; some questions involve matters so basic to the consensus that the society would, in declaring them open, abolish itself, commit suicide, terminate its existence as the kind of society it has hitherto understood itself to be. And it follows from that, as August follows July, that in such a society the doctrine according to which all questions are open questions, including, for example, the question as to the merits of Communism, is itself one of the excluded beliefs—one of the beliefs that are excluded because they involve, on the face of them, denial of the consensus that defines the society and sets its tone and character. And, having said that, we can get down to cases. What the McCarthyites distrusted and disliked and got mad about in the anti-McCarthyites was the at first explicit then tacit contention: We in America can't do anything about the Communists because America is a society in which all questions are open questions, a society dedicated to the proposition that *no* truth in particular is true, a society, in Justice Jackson's phrase, in which no one can speak properly of an orthodoxy—over against which any belief, however immoral, however extravagant, can be declared heretical and thus proscribed. And what the anti-McCarthyites distrusted and disliked and got mad about in the McCarthyites was the at first explicit and then tacit contention: America is not the kind of society you describe; the First Amendment does not have that meaning; America is a society whose essence is still to be found in the phrase "We hold these truths"; it *can* therefore proscribe certain doctrines and beliefs, and in the presence of the doctrines and beliefs of the Communists it cannot hesitate: it must proscribe them, and preferably long before they have had an opportunity to become a clear and present danger. Moreover, the McCarthyites knew, instinctively if not on the level of conscious articulation, that the anti-McCarthyites had good reason (long after they had dropped their principled opposition to the Internal Security Program) for continuing their opposition to it in the courts of law, for continuing to provide the most expensive of expensive legal talent for its so-called victims, and this quite regardless of whether or not they were so situated as to constitute a clear and present danger—had good reason because in their hearts they believed that no measures ought to be taken against the Communists at all. And the anti-McCarthyites knew that the McCarthyites, for all their willing talk of clear and present danger, had good reason for carrying the persecution of the Communists further, at every opportunity, than the clear and present danger doctrine called for; they believed in persecuting the Communists not because they were dangerous but because, from the standpoint of the consensus, their doctrines were wrong and immoral. Each group understood the other perfectly, and each was quite right in venting upon the other the fury reserved for heretics because each was, in the eyes of the other, *heretical*.

It is I repeat unfortunate for us all that the issue, once joined, did not stay joined, and that the question became so confused that each of the two groups emerged from the McCarthy period under the impression that it had won—the McCarthyites because they got the persecution of the Communists that their understanding of the American consensus demanded, the anti-McCarthyites because the persecution went forward with the incantations appropriate to the clear and present danger doctrine. Why unfortunate? Because until that issue is decided we no more understand ourselves as a nation than a schizophrenic understands himself as a person—so that, again in Murray's words, the American giant is likely to go lumbering about the world in ignorance even of who and what he is. And because—dare I say it?—next time around, people are going to get a whole lot madder.

*1963*

# HARRY V. JAFFA

Harry V. Jaffa (1918–2015) was a political philosopher and historian who spent the preponderance of his career teaching at Claremont McKenna College. Central to Jaffa's concerns were the moral foundations of the American political order, the meaning of original intent, and the relationship between the Declaration of Independence and the Constitution. Even among his fellow conservatives, his views generated considerable controversy, his critics deeming him excessively doctrinaire. In the debates that ensued, the combative Jaffa gave as good as he got.

## On the Nature of Civil and Religious Liberty: Reflections on the Centennial of the Gettysburg Address[1]

THERE is general agreement among Americans that the central political issue of our time is the world-wide conflict between Communist totalitarianism and political freedom, that freedom whose principles are affirmed in such documents as the Declaration of Independence and the Gettysburg Address. All decent Americans repudiate Communism and recognize their obligation to do what lies in their power to prevent its ascendancy or triumph. Yet in the field of civil liberties there is profound confusion as to what, in crucial cases, decent, freedom-loving citizens may do. With respect to freedom of speech and the closely related freedoms of assembly, association, and

---

[1] I would like to dedicate this essay to the memory of my Father, who died on November 19, 1958.—HVJ

188

the right of petition, the question continually arises: can we deny these freedoms or rights to Communists, or their agents or coadjutors, without ourselves ceasing, by that denial and to the extent of the denial, to constitute a free society? And, conversely, is it not true that if we do allow Communists the full advantage of these civil liberties we may allow them so to weaken and confuse our resistance that Communism may thereby be enabled to succeed? In short, may it not be true that the indispensable means for denying success to Communism are at the same time the necessary instruments for the self-immolation of freedom? That we may be confronted with such a dilemma has certainly puzzled the will of many conscientious lovers of freedom amongst us. Perhaps even more serious is the sharp conflict which has developed from time to time between those who have grasped one or another horn of the supposed dilemma.

This difficulty is not a new one in the experience of this republic under its present constitution. We should remember that if Thomas Jefferson opposed the Alien and Sedition Acts, George Washington favored them. The Civil War, however, presented the problem in its most acute form. It would perhaps not be inapt to sum up the experience of the years 1861 to 1865 by saying that no American statesman ever violated the ordinary maxims of civil liberties more than did Abraham Lincoln, and few seem to have been more careful of them than Jefferson Davis. Yet the cause for the sake of which the one slighted these maxims was human freedom, while the other, claiming to defend the forms of constitutional government, found in those forms a ground for defending and preserving human slavery. In his message to Congress on July 4, 1861, President Lincoln propounded the universal problem within the particular crisis in these words:

And this issue embraces more than the fate of these United States . . . It forces us to ask: "Is there, in all republics, this inherent and fatal weakness? Must a Government, of necessity, be too *strong* for the liberties of its own people, or too *weak* to maintain its own existence?"

That the liberties Lincoln had in mind were the civil liberties referred to above is shown by his defense, in a major section of that address, of his suspensions of the writ of habeas corpus. All civil liberties depend absolutely upon the privilege of this writ, since no one can exercise his freedom of speech or of association, for example, if he can be detained or imprisoned at the pleasure of any official. It is well then to consider that since the Constitution (Article I, Section 9) provides that the privilege of the writ of habeas corpus may be suspended "when in cases of rebellion or invasion the public safety may require it," the Constitution must contemplate the lawful abridgment under certain circumstances of the freedoms of the First Amendment. It must do so unless the First Amendment is supposed to have cancelled that part of the original Constitution which allows the suspension. No one seriously maintains this, however, because every good thing the people of the United States seek to accomplish in and through their government depends upon the ability of that government to preserve itself. And certainly nothing that led to the adoption of the First Amendment in any way affected the reasons for believing that "in cases of rebellion and invasion" the government might not be able to survive without suspending the writ.

When Lincoln defended his suspensions of the writ of habeas corpus in his Fourth of July message, he was mainly concerned to justify its suspension by the *Executive*. The provision of the Constitution in question is in the article that sets forth the powers (and the limitations upon the powers) of *Congress*. Lincoln's explanation of why the power to suspend cannot be confined to Congress is a masterly example of constitutional construction:

> Now, it is insisted that Congress, and not the Executive, is vested with this power. But the Constitution itself is silent as to which or who is to exercise the power; and as the provision was plainly made for a dangerous emergency, it cannot be believed the framers of the instrument intended that in every case the danger should run its course until Congress could be called together; the very assembling of which might be prevented, as was intended in this case, by the rebellion.

Earlier in the same message, however, Lincoln had taken much broader ground. Provisions of the Constitution, taken literally, can be in conflict, sometimes in direct contradiction, with each other. As we have seen, the command of the First Amendment that "Congress shall make no law . . . abridging the freedom of speech," is in a certain sense incompatible with the proposition that Congress may, in time of rebellion or invasion, suspend the writ of habeas corpus. And so

Lincoln, while denying that he had violated the Constitution, maintained nonetheless that if he had done so he would have been justified. For the Constitution also commanded him to "take care that the laws be faithfully executed," and he had sworn an oath so to execute them. All the laws were being resisted, and failing of execution, in nearly one-third of the states, and the whole government faced dissolution if its authority could not be restored. But, he asked, if the Constitution denied him the power to suspend the writ of habeas corpus, should he prefer the total destruction of all the laws, and the government, to the very limited violation of this one law? Lincoln summed the matter up in his usual succinct way:

> Are all the laws *but one* to go unexecuted, and the Government itself go to pieces, lest that one be violated?

It is the thesis of this paper that civil liberties are, as their name implies, liberties of men in civil society. As such, they are to be correlated with the duties of men in civil society, and they are therefore subject to that interpretation which is consistent with the duty of men to preserve the polity which incorporates their rights. But the preservation of a civil society does not and cannot mean merely its physical preservation or territorial integrity; nor can it mean merely its freedom from foreign domination or, for that matter, from domestic usurpation. For Lincoln, the preservation of the Union meant all of these things, but it meant above all the preservation of a body whose soul remained *dedicated* to the principles of the Declaration of Independence. The classic example of a dilemma in interpreting the Constitution, and one whose resolution may well serve as a guide for resolving the difficulty with which this paper began, is that afforded by the Fifth Amendment in the decades immediately preceding the Civil War. Among other things, the amendment charges Congress that "No person shall be ... deprived of life, liberty, or property, without due process of law." The pro-slavery Southerners maintained—and Chief Justice Taney in the Dred Scott decision upheld the assertion—that a congressional prohibition of slavery in any United States territory (as in the Missouri Compromise legislation of 1820) had the effect of freeing slaves that a man had lawfully brought with him into a territory. This, it was held, constituted an arbitrary deprivation of property. The anti-slavery Northerners, on the other hand, pointed to the fact that Negroes were recognized many times by the Constitution as persons (e.g., Article I, Section 2, par. 3.; ibid., Section 9, par. 1; and Article IV, Section 2, par. 3). They further insisted that by the terms of the same amendment, no Negro, being a person, might be held in slavery in a territory. The specific and immediate cause of the Civil War was precisely this difference over whether the Fifth Amendment made it the duty of Congress to prohibit or to protect slavery in the territories. Every candid student of this question must come to see, I believe, that the language of the Constitution admits with nearly perfect impartiality of either interpretation. In the so-called fugitive-slave clause of the Constitution—the word slave or slavery never occurs before the Thirteenth Amendment—a sanction undoubtedly is given to state laws which, in turn, treat certain "persons" as if they were not persons, that is, as if they were chattels. In short, the word "person" is treated in the Constitution in such ways that some persons may be either subjects of rights of their own, or mere objects of the rights of others. How to resolve this confusion in the text of the Constitution could not be decided by reference to the Constitution alone. As in many great matters, the meaning of the Constitution had and has to be sought outside the Constitution itself. The great debates that preceded the Civil War, above all the Lincoln-Douglas debates, turned on the question of the authority and meaning of the principles propounded in the Declaration of Independence, as the guide for interpreting the Constitution. For there could be no doubt that if the Declaration was authoritative, and if Negroes were included in the proposition that "all men are created equal," then the free-soil interpretation of the Fifth Amendment had to prevail, Chief Justice Taney to the contrary notwithstanding.[2] It is too little realized that the final word in the greatest of all American controversies is pronounced in the magisterial opening of the Gettysburg Address. Stephen A. Douglas had said, and the pro-slavery Southerners agreed, that we existed as a nation only in virtue of the Constitution, and the Constitution not only tolerated but gave legal guarantees to the institution of human slavery. When

---

[2] On this whole subject, see my *Crisis of the House Divided: An Interpretation of the Issues in the Lincoln-Douglas Debates*. New York: Doubleday, 1959, esp. Ch. XIV, The Universal Meaning of the Declaration of Independence.

Lincoln pronounced "Fourscore and seven years," he forever fixed the year 1776 as the year of the nation's nativity. In so doing he did not downgrade the Constitution, he merely affirmed in the most solemn manner what he held to be the essential cause of the dignity of the Constitution: that it was an instrument for better securing those human rights affirmed in the Declaration, that the Union which was to become "more perfect" took as its standard of perfection, its ends or principles, the "laws of Nature and of Nature's God" invoked in the earlier document.

The Union was created by its dedication to the equality of man. Slavery, Lincoln held, might be tolerated as a necessity, but only so long as it was understood to be a necessary evil. Douglas sought a middle position, a national "don't care" policy which would allow the settlers in the territories to decide as they wished in the matter of slavery. This, Lincoln said with scorn, attempted to treat as a matter of indifference something to which no human being could be indifferent. It was, he said, as vain as the search for a man who should be neither a living man nor a dead one. Lincoln preferred the candid pro-slavery argument, where the issue could be squarely joined. And he argued with unbreakable logic that if the slaveowners' interpretation of the Fifth Amendment were correct, and if the Negroes' humanity were either denied or treated as of no account, then the moral basis of the authority of the whole Constitution had to be called into question, and the American Revolution itself could be regarded as an expression of mere force without right.

Free government rests upon the consent or opinion of the governed. Law is an expression of opinion, and the opinion upon which the law rests is more fundamental than the law itself. "In this and like communities," Lincoln said in the first of his joint debates with Douglas, "public sentiment is everything. With public sentiment, nothing can fail; without it, nothing can succeed. Consequently, he who molds public sentiment, goes deeper than he who enacts statutes or pronounces decisions. He makes statutes and decisions possible or impossible to be executed." The Constitution was the creation of a people committed in the Declaration to the idea of human dignity. Although the people is sovereign, its sovereignty may not be exercised in a manner inconsistent with the moral ground of its own authority.

"All men are created equal," is called a self-evident truth. What does this mean? Not that all men are equal in intelligence, virtue, strength, or beauty. They are equal in certain "rights," and the meaning of these rights can perhaps be most easily expressed today in this negative way: there is no difference between man and man, such as there is between man and animals of other species, which makes any man, that is, any normal adult human being, the natural ruler of any man. Man is by nature the master of dog, horse, cow, or monkey. He is equally the master of the dangerous wild animals he cannot domesticate, because he can kill or capture them as a result of his natural superiority, and not because of mere accident. The rights which men evidently have over other animals, they do not, it is equally evident, have over each other. Men are not angels—who, it may be supposed, would require no government—nor are there angels to govern men. Government, which does not arise directly from *nature*, is then grounded upon *consent*. To repeat, government does not arise *directly* from nature, but it does arise *indirectly*, to the extent that consent, to be the ground of legitimate authority, must itself be based upon a recognition of the essential difference between man and the brutes. If the consent of the governed were given to a regime which treated the rulers as if they were gods or angels, differing essentially in their nature from the ruled, the regime would also be illegitimate. Deception and force are equally incapable of giving rise to legitimate authority. Legitimacy cannot then be claimed for any regime in which the rulers treat the ruled as if they are animals of another species, as if the governed can be used as mere instruments for the advantage of the rulers. Such a regime is illegitimate, we repeat, even if the ruled, for whatever reason, believe that their own highest good consists in gratifying the rulers. The governed, in a civilized regime must, by the principles of our Declaration, be treated as beings with ends of intrinsic worth, which ends the government serves. Cattle may be killed, their flesh eaten, and their skins used to clothe human bodies, because of the indefeasible, objective natural difference between the soul of a man and the soul of a brute.

The Declaration, as we have seen, speaks of the specific nature of man and, inferentially, of its difference from other species, as self-evident. By this it is meant that we cannot demonstrate the essential likeness of men to each other and their difference from other animals. This is because all understanding of the world, all demonstration about the world, proceeds *from* the experience by which we grasp the terms of such propositions as: "This is a man, this is a dog, this is a tree, etc." A self-evident truth is not one which everyone necessarily admits to be true; it is one the evidence for which is contained in the terms of the proposition, and which is admitted to be true by everyone *who already grasps the meaning of the terms*. Very young children, lunatics, and savages, are for various reasons deficient in those operations of the mind which issue in the abstractions, man, dog, horse, tree, etc. Hence, until their deficiencies are somehow overcome, they cannot be responsible members of civil society.

The men who founded our system of government were not moral or political relativists, as those terms are understood today. In affirming that all men are created equal, they expressed their conviction that human freedom depends upon the recognition of an order that man himself does not create. Man is not free to disregard the hierarchy of souls in nature. The equality of man flows from and corresponds to the inequality of the human and the subhuman, as it corresponds also to the inequality of the human and the superhuman. For man is part of the order of nature, and his dignity derives from the whole of which he is a part. This whole, being the cause of the dignity of the part which is man, is possessed of a dignity greater than man, for every cause is greater than the effects of which it is the cause. But the whole is not known to us as we and brute creation—the parts—are known. It is a mystery, but a mystery to which man alone in the universe is open. This fact is the ground of freedom of thought, which in turn is the ground of all other freedoms, including civil liberties. Freedom of thought is not freedom to deny that two and two is four. Someone who denies this may be more pitied than censured, but we do not see in his denial a consummation of his freedom. To repeat, all our liberties rest upon the objective fact of the specific difference of the human soul from subhuman souls, and the highest virtue of this difference is the human capacity to confront the mystery of the universe. This is what we mean when we say that the Declaration of Independence affirms the principle of the dignity of man. To call this principle an ideology—which means a mere rationalization of vulgar self-interest—is to demean and debase it. To call it a mere "ideal" is perhaps even worse. An ideal is distinguished from what is real, and the Declaration speaks not of something unreal, but of something real in the highest degree, namely, *truth*. Moreover, there are many ideals, but there is but one truth. To be guided by the laws of Nature and of Nature's God means to be guided not by multiple fantasies but by the unitary ground of actual existence. Present-day skepticism as to the laws of nature mentioned in the Declaration, does not supply us with an alternative ground for justifying civil liberty. Absolute skepticism is a self-devouring monster. Theoretically, it means doubting the ability to doubt. Practically, it teaches that if there is nothing that need be believed as true, neither is there anything that need be disbelieved. Unlimited skepticism quickly transforms itself into unlimited dogmatism. Political freedom exists only upon that wise and tolerant middle ground where men do not treat other men as brutes because they know that they themselves are not gods. But this restraint, this proud humility, is the attribute of those, and only those, who see in the order of nature the ground of the moral and political order.

Let us now turn to the problem with which we began. Does a free society prove false to itself if it denies civil liberties to Communists, Nazis, or anyone else who would use these liberties, if he could, as a means of destroying the free society? The answer, I believe, is now plain that it does not. In saying this I do not counsel, or even justify, any particular measure for dealing with persons of such description. What is right in any case depends upon the facts of that case, and I am here dealing only with principles, not their application. However, those who think that every denial of civil liberties is equally derogatory of the character of a free society, without reference to the character of the persons being denied, make this fundamental error: they confuse means with ends. Free speech is a priceless and indispensable attribute of a free society because it is a necessary means for deliberating upon public policy. But this deliberation does not extend to everything: above all, it does not extend to the question of whether the community shall exchange its freedom for slavery. Certain ends are fixed, and their fixity is the condition of mutability in other respects. The government may deliberate *how* to secure the rights to life and to liberty of all; it may never deliberate *whether* they shall be secured. Certain proposals can never be entertained by a civilized community. The essence of all such proposals would be to kill or enslave someone or some group in the community and distribute their property among the rest. Obviously, in any community in which such a proposal were seriously entertained, even for a moment, those who are proposed for proscription might rightfully consider themselves in a state of war with the rest, and feel justified in using every means to preserve themselves. But the right *not to be proscribed* is inherent in every part of the community, severally, and in the whole community, collectively. Hence *no one* ever has the right to introduce or advocate such a thing. Thus speech calling for the proscription of individuals or classes is inherently wrong, and there is an inherent right in every community to treat it as criminal, wholly apart from any consequences which can be foreseen at the moment.

Just as majority rule is a device for deciding matters of common interest where unanimity is impossible, but can never be rightfully used to destroy the minority, so free speech is a device for deliberating upon the common interest, but can never be rightfully employed to propose the destruction of either a majority or minority. Yet this is precisely what both Nazis and Communists do. Both are creeds calling for the proscription of individuals and groups innocent of any crime. The Nazis believe that one so-called race, the Aryan master race, is so superior to all others that it has the right to treat other men as if they were animals of another species. They do not hesitate to exterminate masses of human beings as if they were plague-bearing rats, or to use their skin as parchment, as if they were cattle. And Communists differ morally from Nazis only in proposing a so-called class, the proletariat, instead of a race, as the sole subject of moral right. For Nazis, morality is an intraracial, for Communists an intraclass phenomenon. Neither believe that faith is to be kept or, indeed, that there are any binding moral rules which extend beyond the barriers of race or class. The Nazis would, and have, proscribed every racial strain beyond the pale of their elite; and the Communists do the same with every class which they do not associate with the dictatorship of the proletariat. An American Communist is one who, if he knows the meaning, and accepts the discipline, of the Party, would use power arbitrarily to deprive his fellow citizens of their property and liberty and, if they resisted, their lives.

Communists and Nazis, I maintain, have no right to the use of free speech in a free society. However, whether it is wise or expedient to deny them its use is another matter. I believe that the United States is a sufficiently civilized and a sufficiently stable community to bear the advocacy of almost anything, whether it be National Socialism, Communism, or Cannibalism. I would take my stand with Jefferson, who in his first inaugural address said, "If there be any among us who would wish to dissolve this Union or to change its republican form, let them stand undisturbed as monuments of the safety with which error of opinion may be tolerated where reason is left free to combat it." But Jefferson only tolerated error; he did not in any way concede a right of the enemies of republican government to change it into a contrary form. As the context of this celebrated passage will show, it was only the impotence of the enemies of republican government which, in Jefferson's view, made it expedient, and right only because expedient, to tolerate them. And thus it was not inconsistent, as some critics have charged, for Jefferson to have instituted prosecutions by state officials for sedition, as he did, if experience revealed that the enemies of republican government were not as impotent as he had supposed. I would accordingly contend that, while it is seldom either expedient or wise to suppress the peaceful advocacy even of inhuman doctrines, in a community like ours, it is not for that reason unjust. But in communities very unlike ours—for example, in a new African nation, constantly threatened by relapse into primitive barbarism on the one hand, and by the barbarism of Communism on the other—the advocacy of many inhuman and indecent things would constantly have to be prohibited.

John Stuart Mill is the most famous of those who have or seem to have demanded absolute freedom of thought and expression. Yet, in the first chapter of his essay *On Liberty*, in the very next paragraph after he proposes his great libertarian principle, he adds a qualification which his present-day followers often overlook or disregard. "It is, perhaps hardly necessary to say," says Mill, quite mistaken as to the necessity, "that this doctrine is meant to apply only to human beings in the maturity of their faculties." The principle of liberty does not apply either to children or to those of less than legal age. Mill is very clear that he presupposes moral characters already formed, and not only able to distinguish right from wrong but disposed toward the right by a decent upbringing. Still further, Mill excludes from the application of his principle "those backward states of society in which the race itself may be considered in its nonage." Barbarians, like children, must be guided for their own good. "Despotism," he says, in a classic passage, "is a legitimate mode of government in dealing with barbarians, provided the end be their improvement, and the means justified by actually effecting that end. Liberty, as a principle, has no application to any state of things anterior to the time when mankind have become capable of being improved by free and equal discussion." I would ask those who today consider themselves followers of John Stuart Mill, what principle would exclude from the enjoyment of civil liberties the subjects of Akbar or Charlemagne, but admit the followers of Hitler or Stalin? Mill's great error was not that of believing moral qualifications were not necessary as a basis for the exercise of liberty. His error lay in his failure to discern that barbarism lurked as a potentiality of modern society no less than that of the Dark Ages. He perceived accurately the depth to which the spirit of modern science had penetrated the Western world, and he was right in believing that scientific progress in that world, and even beyond that world, was essentially irreversible. But he was utterly mistaken, in common with nearly all the thinkers of his time, in believing that the effect of the scientific spirit was to make men more temperate and just. The ability to be guided to improvement by conviction and persuasion, he said, had been "long since reached in all nations with whom we need here concern ourselves." He did not think it possible that a highly civilized modern nation could be persuaded to abandon the principle of persuasion. But we, who have seen Weimar Germany, the freest market place of ideas the world has ever known, give itself up to the Nazis, know differently. And we have also seen modern science flourish both in Hitler's Germany and Stalin's Russia. We know today that there is no necessary correlation between modern physics, chemistry, biology, and mathematics, not to mention the many branches of engineering, and a gentle and tolerant temper. Whatever the intention of the founders of modern science, there is nothing in its method which precludes its appropriation by men who are, in every other respect, barbarians.

There is no passage in the literature dealing with civil liberties more celebrated than the dissenting opinion of Mr. Justice Holmes in the Abrams case of 1919. The super-libertarians of our time quote it endlessly, and recite it as a litany, so much so that one wonders if many of them have not utterly forgotten the Declaration of Independence, with which it is, in many respects, in flagrant contradiction. We will present extensive selections.

> Persecution for the expression of opinions seems to me perfectly logical. If you have no doubt of your premises or your power and want a certain result with all your heart you naturally express your wishes in law and sweep away all opposition. To allow opposition by speech seems to indicate that you think the speech is impotent . . . or that you do not care wholeheartedly for the result, or that you doubt either your power or your premises. But when men have realized that time has upset many fighting faiths, they may come to believe even more than they believe the very foundations of their own conduct that the ultimate good desired is better reached by free trade in ideas—that the best test of truth is the power of the thought to get itself accepted in the competition of the market, and that truth is the only ground upon which their wishes safely can be carried out. That, at any rate, is the theory of our Constitution . . .
>
> . . . I think that we should be eternally vigilant against attempts to check the expression of opinions that we loathe and believe to be fraught with death, unless they so imminently threaten immediate interference with the lawful and pressing purposes of the law that an immediate check is required to save the country.
>
> I wholly disagree with the argument of the Government that the First Amendment left the common law as to seditious libel in force. History seems to me against the notion.

I should like first to notice Holmes' last point. No one today doubts that the First Amendment did leave the common law of seditious libel in force in the states in 1791. Since the publication of Leonard W. Levy's *Legacy of Suppression: Freedom of Speech and Press in Early American History* (Harvard University Press, 1960) all controversy on that subject seems to be at an end. Some doubt remains as to whether the First Amendment, which explicitly laid a prohibition only on *Congress*, allowed the *federal* courts to enforce the common law of seditious libel. But that the *states* remained free to enforce it, and did enforce it, is not in dispute. In his draft of the Kentucky Resolutions of 1798, in the third section, Jefferson cited the language of the Tenth Amendment, and then observed that

> no power over freedom of religion, freedom of speech, or freedom of the press being delegated to the United States by the Constitution, *nor prohibited by it to the States*, all lawful powers respecting the same did of right remain, and were reserved to the States or the people: that thus

was manifested their determination to retain to themselves the right
of judging how far licentiousness of speech and of the press may be
abridged without lessening their useful freedom . . . [italics added]

Nothing can be clearer than that, according to Jefferson, the First
Amendment laid a prohibition *only* on the federal government. So
far was Jefferson from any theoretical views that would prevent the
people or their governments from abridging freedom of speech and
press, that he insisted that the right of judging when and to what
degree they ought to be abridged was a right reserved to them by the
Tenth Amendment.

In the same section Jefferson went on to speak of religious freedom
in a way that distinguished it profoundly from other civil liberties. In
the Constitution, he said, the people "guarded against all abridgment
by the United States of the freedom of religious opinions and exercises,
and retain to themselves *the right of protecting* the same [italics added]
. . ." According to Jefferson the Constitution left to the states and the
people the right to judge how far freedom of speech and press might
be *abridged*, but left to the same authority the right only of *protecting*
freedom of religious opinions. For Jefferson this distinction between
religious opinion and other opinions was fundamental. In the *Notes
on Virginia*, Query XVII, he says that the legitimate powers of government extend only to those natural rights which we have submitted
to government and "The rights of conscience we never submitted, we
could not submit." It is in this context that he pronounces the famous
dictum, that "Reason and free inquiry are the only effectual agents
against error," adding immediately, "Give a loose to them, they will
support the true religion by bringing every false one to their tribunal."
In the Virginia Statute for Religious Freedom, again referring to religious truth and error, he wrote "that truth is great and will prevail if
left to herself . . . errors ceasing to be dangerous when it is permitted
freely to contradict them." Dumas Malone, in the latest volume of his
Jefferson biography (*Jefferson and the Ordeal of Liberty*. Boston: Little,
Brown and Company, 1962), searches the writings of his hero in vain
for even a single statement in which Jefferson defends unconditionally
any freedom of opinion other than religious opinion. He finally concludes (p. 393), quoting the "reason and free inquiry" passage, that for
Jefferson "freedom of thought was an absolute, and *it may be assumed*

that he applied [such maxims] not merely to religious opinion but to all opinion [italics added]." But Malone is wrong. It is no accident that he is forced to make such an assumption. The evidence does not exist because Jefferson did not say what he did not believe.

Freedom of thought was indeed an absolute for Jefferson. "The error seems not sufficiently eradicated, that the operations of the mind, as well as the acts of the body, are subject to the coercion of the laws," he also wrote in Query XVII. "The legitimate powers of government extend to such acts only as are injurious to others. But it does me no injury for my neighbor to say there are twenty gods, or no God. It neither picks my pocket nor breaks my leg." With the purely theoretical question of whether there is no God or twenty, Jefferson says government has no rightful business. But on the practical aspect of the question of whether the mind has a right to entertain such questions, and whether men must be left free by government to entertain them, there was no place in Jefferson's thinking for any neutrality. The error that the mind is not inherently free to speculate, is an error which, Jefferson says, seems not to be "sufficiently eradicated." To deny the power and right of the soul to confront the universe is a denial of human nature. Marxism, for example, by teaching that all opinions on the relation of man to God and to nature are nothing but ideology, that is, devices whereby the mind justifies and thereby cooperates in particular ways of relieving the demands of the body, treats the distinction between body and mind as essentially insignificant. It is no accident that every government professing Marxism therefore attempts to coerce the operations of the mind as well as those of the body. One cannot be equally tolerant then, and certainly Jefferson was not, of opinions destructive, and of opinions not destructive, of the regime of liberty itself. The sphere comprehended by what Jefferson called religious opinions, was essentially the sphere of theory. In his pungent phrase, it was the sphere in which a man's opinion, one way or another, neither picked Jefferson's pocket nor broke his leg. But political opinions, as they bore on the security of the government which preserved men's absolute liberty of theoretical opinion, were not matters of similar indifference. These Jefferson did not entrust to the mere hazard of any "market" of ideas. In his second inaugural address he wrote:

No inference is here intended, that the laws, provided by the State against false and defamatory publications, should not be enforced; he who has time, renders a service to public morals and public tranquillity, in reforming these abuses by the salutary coercions of the law . . .

Mr. Justice Holmes has written that persecution is perfectly logical if you do not doubt your premises or your power. But there are different kinds of "persecution." Jefferson was sick of the long, melancholy record of human government by superstition and terror. To be blunt, he had no doubt of the premises from which he deduced their illegitimacy, and he recorded his confidence when he proclaimed these premises to be self-evident truths. It was to end persecution that he and his partisans drew the sword of what was indeed a fighting faith. To persecute persecutors or to be intolerant of intolerance is then not the contradiction that dilettantes of political philosophy sometimes affect.

As the crisis of the Civil War approached, many frenzied efforts were made to placate Southern opinion. In 1860, in the wake of John Brown's raid, Senator Douglas of Illinois proposed a sedition law to punish abolitionist propaganda as an incitement to crime. In the Cooper Union speech, Lincoln argued against any such legislation. But he never even suggested that it would be wrong to pass such a law because it violated freedom of speech or of the press. "If slavery is right," said Lincoln, "all words, acts, laws, and constitutions against it, are themselves wrong, and should be silenced, and swept away . . . All they ask, we could readily grant, if we thought slavery right; all we ask, they could as readily grant, if they thought it wrong. Their thinking it right, and our thinking it wrong, is the precise fact upon which depends the whole controversy." Freedom of speech was logically subordinate to personal freedom, because a man who was a slave could not demand the right to speak. Lincoln argued over and over, with a logic which no one can now deny, that there was no principle by which the enslavement of Negroes could be justified, which could not also justify the enslavement of white men. The sheet-anchor of our liberties was not the Constitution but the principle of the Declaration of Independence, which alone gave life and meaning to the Constitution. To say that the Constitution protects the right to deny that all men are created equal, is as much as to say that it protects the right to deny any obligations to obey its law.

Lincoln and Jefferson both believed that a free government is the slowest and most reluctant to restrict the liberties even of its most dangerous and fanatical enemies. It is the one which least needs to protect itself by such distasteful means, because it is the one which commands the loyalty of the mass of the citizens by the benefits they feel in their daily lives. Still, it is necessary that our loyalty be enlightened, and to that end we must ever possess ourselves of the true standard by which to measure our blessings. If we fail to see the sanity and nobility of the charter of our own freedom, we will fail to recognize the barbarism of totalitarian doctrines. And it is much better if we repudiate the foul and perverted reasonings that would justify the bestiality of a Hitler or a Stalin, and all their regimes have spawned, by the force of opinion among us. For the more we accomplish by opinion, the less we will have to do by law.

*1964*

# JOAN DIDION

A novelist, screenwriter, essayist, and New Journalist, Joan Didion (b. 1934) earned wide acclaim for her acerbic and stylish assessments of the contemporary American scene. Here she fastens her gimlet eye on second-wave feminism. By her own admission, hers is an "unorthodox conservatism" that frequently places her at odds with defenders of orthodoxy.

## The Women's Movement

T O MAKE an omelette you need not only those broken eggs but someone "oppressed" to break them: every revolutionist is presumed to understand that, and also every woman, which either does or does not make fifty-one per cent of the population of the United States a potentially revolutionary class. The creation of this revolutionary "class" was from the virtual beginning the "idea" of the women's movement, and the tendency for popular discussion of the movement to center for so long around day-care centers is yet another instance of that studied resistance to political ideas which characterizes our national life.

"The new feminism is not just the revival of a serious political movement for social equality," the feminist theorist Shulamith Firestone announced flatly in 1970. "It is the second wave of the most important revolution in history." This was scarcely a statement of purpose anyone could find cryptic, and it was scarcely the only statement of its kind in the literature of the movement. Nonetheless, in 1972, in a "special issue" on women, *Time* was still musing genially that the movement might well succeed in bringing about "fewer diapers and more Dante."

That was a very pretty image, the idle ladies sitting in the gazebo and murmuring *lasciate ogni speranza*, but it depended entirely upon the popular view of the movement as some kind of collective inchoate yearning for "fulfillment," or "self-expression," a yearning absolutely devoid of ideas and capable of engendering only the most *pro forma* benevolent interest. In fact there was an idea, and the idea was Marxist, and it was precisely to the extent that there was this Marxist idea that the curious historical anomaly known as the women's movement would have seemed to have any interest at all. Marxism in this country had ever been an eccentric and quixotic passion. One oppressed class after another had seemed finally to miss the point. The have-nots, it turned out, aspired mainly to having. The minorities seemed to promise more, but finally disappointed: it developed that they actually cared about the issues, that they tended to see the integration of the luncheonette and the seat in the front of the bus as real goals, and only rarely as ploys, counters in a larger game. They resisted that essential inductive leap from the immediate reform to the social ideal, and, just as disappointingly, they failed to perceive their common cause with other minorities, continued to exhibit a self-interest disconcerting in the extreme to organizers steeped in the rhetoric of "brotherhood."

And then, at that exact dispirited moment when there seemed no one at all willing to play the proletariat, along came the women's movement, and the invention of women as a "class." One could not help admiring the radical simplicity of this instant transfiguration. The notion that, in the absence of a cooperative proletariat, a revolutionary class might simply be invented, made up, "named" and so brought into existence, seemed at once so pragmatic and so visionary, so precisely Emersonian, that it took the breath away, exactly confirmed one's idea of where nineteenth-century transcendental instincts, crossed with a late reading of Engels and Marx, might lead. To read the theorists of the women's movement was to think not of Mary Wollstonecraft but of Margaret Fuller at her most high-minded, of rushing position papers off to mimeo and drinking tea from paper cups in lieu of eating lunch; of thin raincoats on bitter nights. If the family was the last fortress of capitalism, then let us abolish the family. If the necessity for conventional reproduction of the species seemed unfair to women, then let us transcend, via technology, "the very organization of nature," the oppression, as Shulamith Firestone saw it, "that goes back through recorded history to the animal kingdom itself." *I accept the universe*, Margaret Fuller had finally allowed: Shulamith Firestone did not.

It seemed very New England, this febrile and cerebral passion. The solemn *a priori* idealism in the guise of radical materialism somehow bespoke old-fashioned self-reliance and prudent sacrifice. The clumsy torrent of words became a principle, a renunciation of style as unserious. The rhetorical willingness to break eggs became, in practice, only a thrifty capacity for finding the sermon in every stone. Burn the literature, Ti-Grace Atkinson said in effect when it was suggested that, even come the revolution, there would still remain the whole body of "sexist" Western literature. But of course no books would be burned: the women of this movement were perfectly capable of crafting didactic revisions of whatever apparently intractable material came to hand. "As a parent you should become an interpreter of myths," advised Letty Cottin Pogrebin in the preview issue of *Ms.* "Portions of any fairy tale or children's story can be salvaged during a critique session with your child." Other literary analysts devised ways to salvage other books: Isabel Archer in *The Portrait of a Lady* need no longer be the victim of her own idealism. She could be, instead, the victim of a sexist society, a woman who had "internalized the conventional definition of wife." The narrator of Mary McCarthy's *The Company She Keeps* could be seen as "enslaved because she persists in looking for her identity in a man." Similarly, Miss McCarthy's *The Group* could serve to illustrate "what happens to women who have been educated at first-rate women's colleges—taught philosophy and history—and then are consigned to breast-feeding and gourmet cooking."

The idea that fiction has certain irreducible ambiguities seemed never to occur to these women, nor should it have, for fiction is in most ways hostile to ideology. They had invented a class; now they had only to make that class conscious. They seized as a political technique a kind of shared testimony at first called a "rap session," then called "consciousness-raising," and in any case a therapeutically oriented American reinterpretation, according to the British feminist Juliet Mitchell, of a Chinese revolutionary practice known as "speaking bitterness." They purged and regrouped and purged again, worried out one another's errors and deviations, the "elitism" here, the "careerism" there. It would have been merely sententious to call some of their thinking Stalinist: of course it was. It would have been pointless even to speak of whether one considered these women "right" or "wrong," meaningless to dwell upon the obvious, upon the coarsening of moral imagination to which such social idealism so often leads. To believe in "the greater good" is to operate, necessarily, in a certain ethical suspension. Ask anyone committed to Marxist analysis how many angels on the head of a pin, and you will be asked in return to never mind the angels, tell me who controls the production of pins.

To those of us who remain committed mainly to the exploration of moral distinctions and ambiguities, the feminist analysis may have seemed a particularly narrow and cracked determinism. Nonetheless it was serious, and for these high-strung idealists to find themselves out of the mimeo room and onto the Cavett show must have been in certain ways more unsettling to them than it ever was to the viewers. They were being heard, and yet not really. Attention was finally being paid, and yet that attention was mired in the trivial. Even the brightest movement women found themselves engaged in sullen public colloquies about the inequities of dishwashing and the intolerable humiliations of being observed by construction workers on Sixth Avenue. (This grievance was not atypic in that discussion of it seemed always to take on unexplored Ms. Scarlett overtones, suggestions of fragile cultivated flowers being "spoken to," and therefore violated, by uppity proles.) They totted up the pans scoured, the towels picked off the bathroom floor, the loads of laundry done in a lifetime. Cooking a meal could only be "dogwork," and to claim any pleasure from it was evidence of craven acquiescence in one's own forced labor. Small children could only be odious mechanisms for the spilling and digesting of food, for robbing women of their "freedom." It was a long way from Simone de Beauvoir's grave and awesome recognition of woman's role as "the Other" to the notion that the first step in changing that role was Alix Kates Shulman's marriage contract ("wife strips beds, husband remakes them"), a document reproduced in *Ms.*, but it was toward just such trivialization that the women's movement seemed to be heading.

Of course this litany of trivia was crucial to the movement in the beginning, a key technique in the politicizing of women who had perhaps been conditioned to obscure their resentments even from themselves. Mrs. Shulman's discovery that she had less time than her husband seemed to have was precisely the kind of chord the movement had hoped to strike in all women (the "click! of recognition," as Jane O'Reilly described it), but such discoveries could be of no use at all if one refused to perceive the larger point, failed to make that inductive leap from the personal to the political. Splitting up the week into hours during which the children were directed to address their "personal questions" to either one parent or another might or might not have improved the quality of Mr. and Mrs. Shulman's marriage, but the improvement of marriages would not a revolution make. It could be very useful to call housework, as Lenin did, "the most unproductive, the most barbarous and the most arduous work a woman can do," but it could be useful only as the first step in a political process, only in the "awakening" of a class to its position, useful only as a metaphor: to believe, during the late Sixties and early Seventies in the United States of America, that the words had literal meaning was not only to stall the movement in the personal but to seriously delude oneself.

More and more, as the literature of the movement began to reflect the thinking of women who did not really understand the movement's ideological base, one had the sense of this stall, this delusion, the sense that the drilling of the theorists had struck only some psychic hardpan dense with superstitions and little sophistries, wish fulfillment, self-loathing and bitter fancies. To read even desultorily in this literature was to recognize instantly a certain dolorous phantasm, an imagined Everywoman with whom the authors seemed to identify all too entirely. This ubiquitous construct was everyone's victim but her own. She was persecuted even by her gynecologist, who made her beg in vain for contraceptives. She particularly needed contraceptives because she was raped on every date, raped by her husband, and raped finally on the abortionist's table. During the fashion for shoes with pointed toes, she, like "many women," had her toes amputated. She was so intimidated by cosmetics advertising that she would sleep "huge portions" of her day in order to forestall wrinkling, and when awake she was enslaved by detergent commercials on television. She sent her child to a nursery school where the little girls huddled in a "doll corner," and were forcibly restrained from playing with building blocks. Should she work she was paid "three to ten times less" than an (always) unqualified man holding the same job, was prevented from attending business lunches because she would be "embarrassed" to appear in public with a man not her husband, and, when she traveled alone, faced a choice between humiliation in a restaurant and "eating a doughnut" in her hotel room.

The half-truths, repeated, authenticated themselves. The bitter fancies assumed their own logic. To ask the obvious—why she did not get herself another gynecologist, another job, why she did not get out of bed and turn off the television set, or why, the most eccentric detail, she stayed in hotels where only doughnuts could be obtained from room service—was to join this argument at its own spooky level, a level which had only the most tenuous and unfortunate relationship to the actual condition of being a woman. That many women are victims of condescension and exploitation and sex-role stereotyping was scarcely news, but neither was it news that other women are not: nobody forces women to buy the package.

But of course something other than an objection to being "discriminated against" was at work here, something other than an aversion to being "stereotyped" in one's sex role. Increasingly it seemed that the aversion was to adult sexual life itself: how much cleaner to stay forever children. One is constantly struck, in the accounts of lesbian relationships which appear from time to time in movement literature, by the emphasis on the superior "tenderness" of the relationship, the "gentleness" of the sexual connection, as if the participants were wounded birds. The derogation of assertiveness as "machismo" has achieved such currency that one imagines several million women too delicate to deal at any level with an overtly heterosexual man. Just as one had gotten the unintended but inescapable suggestion, when told about the "terror and revulsion" experienced by women in the vicinity of construction sites, of creatures too "tender" for the abrasiveness of daily life, too fragile for the streets, so now one was getting, in the later literature of the movement, the impression of women too "sensitive" for the difficulties of adult life, women unequipped for reality and grasping at the movement as a rationale for denying that reality. The transient stab of dread and loss which accompanies menstruation simply never happens: we only thought it happened, because a male-chauvinist psychiatrist told us so. No woman need have bad dreams after an abortion: she has only been told she should. The power of sex is just an oppressive myth, no longer to be feared, because what the sexual connection really amounts to, we learn in one woman's account of a postmarital affair presented as liberated and liberating, is "wisecracking and laughing" and "lying together and then leaping up to play and sing the entire *Sesame Street Songbook.*" All one's actual apprehension of what it is like to be a woman, the irreconcilable difference of it—that sense of living one's deepest life underwater, that dark involvement with blood and birth and death—could now be declared invalid, unnecessary, *one never felt it at all.*

One was only told it, and now one is to be reprogrammed, fixed up, rendered again as inviolate and unstained as the "modern" little girls in the Tampax advertisements. More and more we have been hearing the wishful voices of just such perpetual adolescents, the voices of women scarred not by their class position as women but by the failure of their childhood expectations and misapprehensions. "Nobody ever so much as mentioned" to Susan Edmiston "that when you say 'I do,' what you are doing is not, as you thought, vowing your eternal love, but rather subscribing to a whole system of rights, obligations and responsibilities that may well be anathema to your most cherished beliefs." To Ellen Peck "the birth of children too often means the dissolution of romance, the loss of freedom, the abandonment of ideals to economics." A young woman described on the cover of *New York* as "The Suburban Housewife Who Bought the Promises of Women's Lib and Came to the City to Live Them" tells us what promises she bought: "The chance to respond to the bright lights and civilization of the Big Apple, yes. The chance to compete, yes. But most of all, the chance to have some fun. Fun is what's been missing."

Eternal love, romance, fun. The Big Apple. These are relatively rare expectations in the arrangements of consenting adults, although not in those of children, and it wrenches the heart to read about these women in their brave new lives. An ex-wife and mother of three speaks of her plan to "play out my college girl's dream. I am going to New York to become this famous writer. Or this working writer. Failing that, I will get a job in publishing." She mentions a friend, another young woman who "had never had any other life than as a daughter or wife or mother" but who is "just discovering herself to be a gifted potter." The childlike resourcefulness—to get a job in publishing, to become a gifted potter!—bewilders the imagination. The astral discontent with actual lives, actual men, the denial of the real generative possibilities of adult sexual life, somehow touches beyond words. "It is the right of the oppressed to organize around their oppression *as they see and define it*," the movement theorists insist doggedly in an effort to solve the question of these women, to convince themselves that what is going on is still a political process, but the handwriting is already on the wall. These are converts who want not a revolution but "romance," who believe not in the oppression of women but in their own chances for a new life in exactly the mold of their old life. In certain ways they tell us sadder things about what the culture has done to them than the theorists ever did, and they also tell us, I suspect, that the movement is no longer a cause but a symptom.

*1972*

# ALLAN BLOOM

Prior to the publication of *The Closing of the American Mind* in 1987, Allan Bloom (1930–1992) had quietly labored as a respected academic at the University of Chicago. His book, excerpted here, became a surprise blockbuster, celebrated by conservatives as an indictment of American culture and of the American university, which liberals had ostensibly brought to ruin. For his part, Bloom denied being a conservative.

———————

## Our Ignorance

IN REFLECTING on the language about which I have just written, the thought behind it and the way it has been received in America, I am reminded of one of my teachers, who wrote a Ten Commandments for Americans that began, "I am the Lord thy God who brought thee out of the house of the European tyrants into my own land, America: Relax!" As we have seen, these words we have half digested are the distillations of great questions that must be faced if one is to live a serious life: reason-revelation, freedom-necessity, democracy-aristocracy, good-evil, body-soul, self-other, city-man, eternity-time, being-nothing. Our condition of doubt makes us aware of alternatives but has not until recently given us the means to resolve our doubt about the primacy of any of the alternatives. A serious life means being fully aware of the alternatives, thinking about them with all the intensity one brings to bear on life-and-death questions, in full recognition that every choice is a great risk with necessary consequences that are hard to bear. That is what tragic literature is about. It articulates all the noble things men want and perhaps need and shows how unbearable it is when it appears that they cannot coexist harmoniously. One need

213

only remember what the choice between believing in God or rejecting Him used to entail for those who faced it. Or, to use a lesser but
equally relevant example, think of Tocqueville, one of the rarest flowers of the old French aristocracy, choosing equality over the splendor
of aristocracy because he believed it to be juster, even though it would
never be salubrious for a Pascal, a man who consumed himself in the
contemplation of God's existence, and even though the absence of
such intransigent confrontation with the grounds of all things would
impoverish the life of man and diminish his seriousness. These are real
choices, possible only for one who faces real questions.

We, on the other hand, have taken these words, which point toward
a rich lode of serious questions, and treated them as though they were
answers, in order to avoid confronting them ourselves. They are not
Sphinxlike riddles to which we must play the daring Oedipus, but
facts behind which we need not go and which structure the world of
concern to us. What has existentialism done to being-nothing for us?
Or value to good-evil; history to eternity-time; creativity to freedom-
necessity; the sacred to reason-revelation? The old tragic conflicts reappear newly labeled as assurances: "I'm OK, you're OK." *Choice* is all the
rage these days, but it does not mean what it used to mean. In a free
society where people are free—responsible—who can consistently not
be "pro-choice"? However, when the word still had some shape and
consistency, a difficult choice meant to accept difficult consequences
in the form of suffering, disapproval of others, ostracism, punishment
and guilt. Without this, choice was believed to have no significance.
Accepting the consequences for affirming what really counts is what
gives Antigone her nobility; unwillingness to do so is what makes
her sister Ismene less admirable. Now, when we speak of the right to
choice, we mean that there are no necessary consequences, that disapproval is only prejudice and guilt only a neurosis. Political activism
and psychiatry can handle it. In this optic Hester Prynne and Anna
Karenina are not ennobling exemplars of the intractability of human
problems and the significance of choice, but victims whose sufferings are no longer necessary in our enlightened age of heightened
consciousness. America has no-fault automobile accidents, no-fault
divorces, and it is moving with the aid of modern philosophy toward
no-fault choices.

Conflict is the evil we most want to avoid, among nations, among individuals and within ourselves. Nietzsche sought with his value philosophy to restore the harsh conflicts for which men were willing to die, to restore the tragic sense of life, at a moment when nature had been domesticated and men become tame. That value philosophy was used in America for exactly the opposite purpose—to promote conflict-resolution, bargaining, harmony. If it is only a difference of values, then conciliation is possible. We must respect values, but they must not get in the way of peace.[1] Thus Nietzsche contributed to what he was trying to cure. Conflict, the condition of creativity for Nietzsche, is for us a cry for therapy. I keep thinking of my Atlanta taxi driver and his Gestalt therapy. Kant argued that men are equal in dignity because of their capacity for moral choice. It is the business of society to provide the conditions for such choice and esteem for those who achieve it. With the intermediary of value relativism, we have been able to simplify the formula to: Men are equal in dignity. Our business is to distribute esteem equally. Rawls's *A Theory of Justice* is the instruction manual for such distribution. Kant's theory of justice makes it possible to understand *Anna Karenina* as a significant expression of our situation; Rawls's does the same for *Fear of Flying*.

Our desire for conflict reduction accounts for the great popularity of the word "dialectic"—in our sense, the Marxist sense—for, beginning in opposites it ends in synthesis, all charms and temptations united in harmony. In philosophy and morals the hardest and most essential rule is "You can't eat your cake and have it too," but dialectic overcomes this rule. Socratic dialectic takes place in speech and, although drawn forward by the search for synthesis, always culminates in doubt. Socrates' last word was that he knew that he knew nothing. Marx's dialectic takes place in deed and culminates in the classless society, which also puts an end to theoretical conflicts, now known as ideologies. Historical dialectic provides an absolute ground and happy resolution for our relative life-styles. Marx's formula that "Mankind never sets problems for itself which it cannot solve" suits one side of

---

[1] Nietzsche said that distrusting one's neighbor would be regarded as madness by last men, and they would go voluntarily to the madhouse if they suffered from it. Think of the use of the word "paranoid" today!

our national temper. Roosevelt said much the same thing when he announced, "We have nothing to fear but fear itself." This optimism is a national strength and is connected with our original project of mastering of nature. But that project itself is not unproblematic and makes sense only when kept within limits. One of these is the sanctity of human nature. It must not be mastered. Roosevelt's dictum is nonsense when blown up into cosmic proportions. Human nature must not be altered in order to have a problem-free world. Man is not just a problem-solving being, as behaviorists would wish us to believe, but a problem-recognizing and -accepting being.

Marx's appeal does, nonetheless, touch us close to home as the fulfillment of what we set out to do—solve problems that God and nature had previously seemed to make insoluble, and earlier men had made a virtue of living with. Man has always had to come to terms with God, love and death. They made it impossible to be perfectly at home on earth. But America is coming to terms with them in new ways. God was slowly executed here; it took two hundred years, but local theologians tell us He is now dead. His place has been taken by the sacred. Love was put to death by psychologists. Its place has been taken by sex and meaningful relationships. That has taken only about seventy-five years. It should not be surprising that a new science, thanatology, or death with dignity, is on the way to putting death to death. Coming to terms with the terror of death, Socrates' long and arduous education, learning how to die, will no longer be necessary. For death isn't what it used to be. What will take its place is not yet clear. Engels had a divination of what is needed when he said that the classless society would last, if not forever, a very long time. This reminds us of Dottore Dulcamare in *The Elixir of Love*, who says that he is known throughout the whole universe—and elsewhere. All one has to do is forget about eternity or blur the distinction between it and temporality; then the most intractable of man's problems will have been resolved. On Sunday mornings educated men used to be harangued about death and eternity, made to give them a bit of attention. This is not a danger to be run in doing battle with the Sunday *New York Times*. Forgetting, in a variety of subtle forms, is one of our primary modes of problem-solving. We are learning to "feel comfortable" with God, love, and even death.

The way we digest the European things is well illustrated by the influence of Thomas Mann's *Death in Venice* on American consciousness. The story was enormously popular with generations of university students, for it seemed to express the mysteries and sufferings of sophisticated Europeans. It fit in with our preoccupation of Freud and with the artist; its homosexual theme attracted curiosity, and much more than curiosity in some, at a time when imagination had little to feed on so far as forbidden themes were concerned. It was a little like a compendium of the best that was being said around the turn of the century. In *Death in Venice*, with what I believe to be a rather heavy Freudian hand, Mann analyzes the favorite subject and hero of poets and novelists since the invention of culture—the artist, that is, himself. The setting and the action of the story suggest the decline of the West; and the decay and demise of its hero, Aschenbach, teach the failure of sublimation, the shakiness and hollowness of his cultural superstructure. Underlying it all are hidden drives, primal, untamed, which are the real motives of his higher endeavor. Awareness of this undermines his life work without providing any acceptable alternatives. Much of this is a gloss on Mann's famous statement in *Tonio Kröger* that "the artist is a bourgeois with a guilty conscience," which I take to mean that he was experiencing all the post-romantic doubts about the artist's ground or his access to the sublime, that he thought the reality is the bourgeois, but that the artist's troubled conscience leads him somewhere out above, from the point of view of morals, and somewhere down below, from the point of view of motives. Aschenbach is a writer, an heir to the German tradition, but clearly not the spiritual aristocrat Goethe was. His self-possession is based on lack of self-knowledge. In Venice he touches the roots, finds out what he really wants; but there is nothing noble or even tolerable he can do with his awareness. He withers away horribly, finally dying of the plague afflicting that beautiful but decadent city. The Freudian view of sublimation, as opposed to the Nietzschean, is that there is a fixed goal of sexuality, a natural reality toward which it is pointed. Accordingly, civilized behavior rests on that foundation, is a secondary satisfaction and, hence, really not choiceworthy if the primary satisfaction were available. Freud's account of sexuality cannot help making the careful observer regret civilization and long for direct sexual satisfaction.

Nietzsche, on the other hand, thought that writing a poem could be as primary an erotic act as sexual intercourse. There is no fixed nature, just different levels of spirituality. From this point of view, Aschenbach represents both romanticism in its longing for lost nature and scientism in its bleak characterization of nature, with the addition of post-Nietzschean pathos. But *Death in Venice* does deal with the theme common to Freud and Nietzsche—the relation of sexual sublimation to culture. The coming to awareness of the infrastructure of culture is deadly to culture, and Mann is depicting the crisis of a civilization. Sublimation has lost its creative or molding power, and now there is desiccated culture and besmirched nature.

But I do not think this was how it was received by Americans. They were titillated and really took it as an early manifesto of the sexual-liberation movement. Even the most distinguished talents, or especially the most distinguished talents, suffer from these obscure longings repressed by society. There is nothing so bad about them; and people should not be intimidated by public opinion, should learn to accept themselves. They have nothing to fear but fear itself. In short, Aschenbach is a man aching to "come out of the closet." There may have been a bit of this in Mann, the need to be open about repressed desires, which, because of the climate of his time, had to come out in tragic garb, lacerating themselves, weeping and wailing. Surely Gide's Nietzscheanism was motivated largely by this. In order to be sexually liberated, so Gide seems to think, we must be supermen, beyond good and evil. He latches on to Nietzsche's immoralism for the sake of leveling bourgeois sexual morals, using a cannon to kill a gnat. Nietzsche would have had nothing but contempt for this. The man who said all greatness requires "semen in the blood" would not have sympathized with men obsessed by sexual repression, who could not make something sublime out of their eroticism, who longed for "natural" satisfaction and public approval to boot. To Nietzsche, Gide would have appeared to be a bourgeois in nihilistic drag. To the extent that such self-expression might have been Mann's intention, it would have been the sign of his own decadence, his creative impotence and desire to escape responsibility in aimless creature, as opposed to creator, pleasures.

The sexual interpretations of art and religion so powerfully made by Nietzsche, and less powerfully but more popularly made by Freud, had a corrupting effect on Americans. They noticed the sublime less than the sex in sexual sublimation. What in Nietzsche was intended to lead to the heights was used here to debunk the heights in favor of present desire. Any explanation of the higher in terms of the lower has that tendency, especially in a democracy, where there is envy of what makes special claims, and the good is supposed to be accessible to all. And this is one of the deep reasons why Freud found such an immediate audience in America. For all of the Continental *sturm und drang*, he believed in nature, and nature as Locke taught it, animal nature. He just added sex to work to compose his formula for healthy living—"love and work"—for he really could not explain love. This is what we were raised to believe. It accords with science rather than relying, as does Nietzsche, on poetic vapors. There is a solid ground, one that appeals to our native empiricism, in his interpretation of what eros really wants. Moreover, science rather than poetry is our preferred means of talking about the obscene. All this, plus the promise of some kind of satisfaction of our desires and relief from our miseries, made Freud a winner from the outset, the most accessible of all the great Continentals. He provided the license for the centrality of sex in public life, which is so characteristic of our day. He ultimately seemed too moralistic, not open enough. But all one had to do was imagine new social structures that demanded less repression for their functioning. This was where Marx was useful. Or one could simply forget about the problems concerning the relation between eros and culture, or else posit a natural harmony between the two. Freud, riding the crest of a wave of German philosophy, enabled Americans to think the satisfaction of their sexual desires was the most important element of happiness. He provided rationalization for instinct, although this was surely not his intention.

Sex immigrated to the United States with the special status given those who make scientific and literary contributions to our culture. But when it got here, it behaved just like everything else American. Gone was the plaintive tone, the poetry, the justification based on civilization's dependence on sublimation. Just as we had cut away the camouflage disguising economic needs—such as the Parthenon and Chartres—in order to concentrate efficiently on those needs themselves, so we demystified sexual desires, seeing them for what they really are, in order to satisfy them more efficiently. This brought into the Lockean world the second focus of human nature, the one concentrated on by Rousseau and those he influenced. The basic rights are "life, liberty, and the pursuit of property and sex." "Give us your poor, your sexually starved. . . ." Freud made it possible to consider sexual repression a medical complaint, and therefore endowed it with the prestige automatically enjoyed by anything having to do with health in a nation devoted to self-preservation. There is a tendency to neglect Rousseau's reminder that one does not die from not satisfying this hunger, and that even great seducers' lusts can be calmed by the certainty of the death penalty. Thus we demystify economy and sexuality, satisfying their primary demands, taking away what our philosophy tells us is their creative impulse, and then we complain we have no culture. We can always go to the opera between office and bed. In the Soviet Union they are dependent on operas from the bad old days, because tyranny prevents artistic expression; we are dependent on the same operas, because the thirsts that produced artistic need have been slaked. I cannot forget the Amherst freshman who asked in naive and good-natured bewilderment, "Should we go back to sublimation?" To the sugar-free diet substitute, as it were. This is what happened in America to the sublime, in all of the subtle meanings given to it from Rousseau and Kant to Nietzsche and Freud. I was charmed by the lad's candor but could not regard him as a serious candidate for culture. Because we have come to take the unnecessary to be necessary, we have lost all sense of necessity, either natural or cultural.

The crucial step was taken, however, when sex as life-style came on the scene. Up until then there was a certain rough-and-ready natural set of guidelines for sex. In the old America it was taken for granted that sex had a teleology—reproduction—and was treated as a means to this end. Everything not conducive to this is useless and even dangerous, to be forgotten or controlled by law, disapproval, conscience and, yes, reason. Freud had the effect of shaking sex loose from this definite connection. It is a force without an end, capable of serving many functions; and its wild, diffuse energies must be given some form if a person is to be happy. But Freud's real naturalism, underlying the explosive indeterminateness that he borrowed from Nietzsche, and the imperatives of health and the integrated personality provided limitations and a structure for legitimate sexual expression. There is no place in Freud for the satisfaction of the kinds of desire to which Mann gives voice in *Death in Venice*. They are explained and cured by Freud but not accepted on their own terms. In Mann they are somehow premonitory and like cries of the damned plunging into nothingness. Such desires search for significance—perhaps this is the case with everything erotic—but nothing in the world can give it to them. These desires are certainly not satisfied with the transfer of their cases from the tribunal of the judge and the priest to that of the doctor, or with being explained away. People can readily accept reductionism in everything except what most concerns them. Neither bourgeois society nor natural science has a place for the nonreproductive aspect of sex. With the slackening of bourgeois austerity and the concomitant emancipation of the harmless pleasures, a certain tolerance of harmless sex came into fashion. But this was not enough, because nobody really wants his dearest desires to be put in the same category as itching and scratching.

In America, especially, there is always a need for moral justification. Life-style—an expression that came out of the same school of thought as sublimation and was actually understood to be the product of sublimation, but had never been associated with it in America because of the division of labor that had Freud specializing in sublimation and Weber in life-style—turned out to be a godsend. "Life-style" justifies any way of life, as does "value" any opinion. It does away with the natural structure of the world, which is only raw material for the stylist's artistic hand. The very expression makes all moralisms and naturalisms stop short at the limit of the sacred ground, aware of their limits and respectful of creativity. Moreover, with our curious mixture of traditions, life-styles are accorded rights, so defense of them is a moral cause, justifying the sweet passions of indignation at the violators of human rights, against whom these tastes, before they became life-styles, were so politically and psychologically defenseless. Now they can call upon all the lovers of human rights throughout the world to join in their defense, for the threat to any group's rights is a threat to them all. Sadomasochists and Solidarity are bound together in the common cause of human rights, their fates depending on the success of the crusade in their favor. Sex is no longer an activity but a cause. In the past there was a respectable place for marginality, bohemia. But it had to justify its unorthodox practices by its intellectual and artistic achievement. Life-style is so much freer, easier, more authentic and democratic. No attention has to be paid to content.

Life-style was first popularized here to describe and make acceptable the lives of people who do attractive things that are frowned upon by society. It was identical to counterculture. Two great expressions in the American usage, draped in the authority lent by their philosophic genealogy, provided moral warrant for people to live exactly as they please. Counterculture, of course, enjoyed the dignity attaching to culture, and was intended as a reproach to the bourgeois excuse for a culture we see around us. What actually goes on in a counterculture or a life-style—whether it is ennobling or debasing—makes no difference. No one is forced to think through his practices. It is impossible to do so. Whatever you are, whoever you are, is the good. All this is testimony to the amazing power, about which Tocqueville speaks, of abstractions in a democratic society. The mere words change everything. It is also a commentary on our moralism. What begins in a search if not precisely for selfish pleasure—historians of the future will not look back on us as a race of hedonists who knew how to "enjoy," in spite of all of our talk about it—then at least for avoidance of and release from suffering or distress, transmogrified into a life-style and a *right*, becomes the ground of moral superiority. The comfortable, unconstrained life is morality.

One can see this in so many domains across the whole political spectrum. Self-serving is expressed as, and really believed to be, disinterested principle. When one looks at the earnest, middle-class proponents of birth control, abortion and easy divorce—with their social concern, their humorless self-confidence and masses of statistics—one cannot help thinking that all this serves them very well. This is not to deny the reality of the problems presented by too many children for the poor, the terrible consequences of rapes and battered wives. However, none of those problems really belongs to the middle classes, who are not reproducing themselves, are rarely raped or battered, but who are the best-rewarded beneficiaries of what they themselves propose. If one of their proposals entailed a sacrifice of freedom or pleasure for them or their class, they would be more morally plausible. As it is, all their proposals contribute to their own capacity to choose, in the contemporary sense of choice. Motives that could easily be so flawed should not be, but are, the basis for moral smugness. In this case, as in so many others, making sexual relations easy becomes identical to morality. I fear that the most self-righteous of Americans nowadays are precisely those who have most to gain from what they preach. This is made all the more distasteful when their weapons are constructed out of philosophic teachings the intentions of which are the opposite of theirs.

But what strikes me most about Mann's story, and makes me reflect on what has happened in America since such literature first attracted our attention, is his use of Plato. As Aschenbach becomes more and more obsessed by the boy on the beach, quotations from the *Phaedrus*, one of Plato's dialogues on love, keep coming into his head, expressing what he gradually and with horror recognizes is the character of his attraction. Plato had been incorporated into the German tradition, and the *Phaedrus* was probably one of the things Aschenbach was supposed to have read as a schoolboy while learning Greek. But its content, discourses on the love of a man for a boy, was not supposed to affect him. The dialogue, like so much that was in the German education, was another scrap of "culture," of historical information, which had not become a part of a vital, coherent whole. This is symptomatic of the deadness of Aschenbach's own cultural activity. Suddenly this scrap erupts into meaning, pointing the way down into the abyss of repressed desire. It is as a dream; and if you are a Freudian, you have keys for unlocking the meanings of dreams. Raw, physically unacceptable facts, inhabitants of the unconscious, express themselves in hidden ways, gaining covert satisfaction that way. They fasten themselves on consciously acceptable material, which then no longer really means what it seems to mean. It now does and does not express the true meaning. Plato's respectable dialogue is the intermediary between Aschenbach's good conscience and his carnality. Plato found a way of expressing and beautifying, of sublimating, perverse sexuality. So the story presents it. There is no indication that Mann thought one could learn much directly from Plato about eros. One could learn something by applying Freud's insights to Plato and seeing how desire finds rationalizations for itself. Plato was a vile body for scientific dissection. Mann was too caught up by the novelty of the Freudian teaching to

doubt whether sublimation can really account for the psychic phenomena it claims to explain. He was doctrinaire, or he was sure we
know better than did older thinkers. They are mythologists.

Freud and Plato agree about the pervasiveness of eroticism in everything human. But there the similarity ends. Anyone who wished to lay
aside his assurance about the superiority of modern psychology might
find in Plato a richer explanation of the diversity of erotic expression,
which so baffles us and has driven us to our present nonsense. He
would see there a rewarding articulation of the possibilities and impos-
sibilities of the fulfillment of erotic desires. Plato both enchants and
disenchants eros, and we need both. At least in Mann the tradition in
which we could refresh ourselves is present, if not exactly alive. With
what he gives us we might embark on our own journey and find more
interesting prey than is an Aschenbach. But in America that slender
thread, which was already almost stretched to its limit in Mann, has
broken. We have no more contact with the tradition. Eros is an obsession, but there is no thought about it, and no possibility of thought
about it, because we now take what were only interpretations of our
souls to be facts about them. Eros gradually becomes meaningless and
low; and there is nothing good for man which is not informed by
thought and affirmed by real choice, which means choice instructed
by deliberation. Saul Bellow has described his own intention as "the
rediscovery of the magic of the world under the debris of modern
ideas." That gray net of abstraction, used to cover the world in order
to simplify and explain it in a way that is pleasing to us, has become
the world in our eyes. The only way to see the phenomena, rather
than sterile distillations of them, to experience them in their ambiguity again, would be to have available alternate visions, a diversity of
profound opinions. But our ideas have made it difficult to have such
experiences in practice, and impossible in theory. How does a young-
ster who sees sublimation where Plato saw divination learn from Plato,
let alone think Plato can speak to him? Souls artificially constituted by
a new kind of education live in a world transformed by man's artifice
and believe that all values are relative and determined by the private
economic or sexual drives of those who hold them. How are they to
recover the primary natural experience?

I suspect that if we were to make a law forbidding the use of any
of the words on the imposing list in this section, a large part of the

population would be silenced. Technical discourse would continue; but all that concerns right and wrong, happiness, the way we ought to live, would become quite difficult to express. These words are there where thoughts should be, and their disappearance would reveal the void. The exercise would be an excellent one, for it might start people thinking about what they really believe, about what lies behind the formulas. Would "living exactly as I please" be speakable as a substitute for "life-style"? Would "my opinion" do for "values"? "My prejudices" for my "ideology"? Could "rabble-rousing" or "simply divine" stand in for "charisma"? Each of the standard words seems substantial and respectable. They appear to justify one's tastes and deeds, and human beings need to have such justification, no matter what they may say. We have to have reasons for what we do. It is the sign of our humanity and our possibility of community. I have never met a person who says, "I believe what I believe; these are just my values." There are always arguments. Nazis had them; Communists have them. Thieves and pimps have them. There may be some people who don't feel they have to make a case for themselves, but they must be either tramps or philosophers.

However, these words are not reasons, nor were they intended to be reasons. All to the contrary, they were meant to show that our deep human need to know what we are doing and to be good cannot be satisfied. By some miracle these very terms became our justification: nihilism as moralism. It is not the immorality of relativism that I find appalling. What is astounding and degrading is the dogmatism with which we accept such relativism, and our easygoing lack of concern about what that means for our lives. The one writer who does not appeal at all to Americans—who offers nothing for our Marxist, Freudian, feminist, deconstructionist, or structuralist critics to mangle, who provides no poses, sentimentalities or bromides that appeal to our young—is Louis-Ferdinand Céline, who best expresses how life looks to a man facing up to what we believe or don't believe. He is a far more talented artist and penetrating observer than the much more popular Mann or Camus. Robinson, the hero he admires in *Journey to the End of the Night*, is an utterly selfish liar, cheat, murderer for pay. Why does Ferdinand admire him? Partly for his honesty, but mostly because he allows himself to be shot and killed by his girlfriend rather than tell her he loves her. He believes in something, which Ferdinand is unable to do. American students are repelled, horrified by this novel, and turn away from it in disgust. If it could be force-fed to them, it might motivate them to reconsider, to regard it as urgent to think through their premises, to make their implicit nihilism explicit and examine it seriously. As an image of our current intellectual condition, I keep being reminded of the newsreel pictures of Frenchmen splashing happily in the water at the seashore, enjoying the paid annual vacations legislated by Léon Blum's Popular Front government. It was 1936, the same year Hitler was permitted to occupy the Rhineland. All our big causes amount to that kind of vacation.

What is so paradoxical is that our language is the product of the extraordinary thought and philosophical greatness at which this cursory and superficial survey has done nothing more than hint. There is a lifetime and more of study here, which would turn our impoverishing certitudes into humanizing doubts. To return to the reasons behind our language and weigh them against the reasons for other language would in itself liberate us. I have tried to provide the outline of an archeology of our souls as they are. We are like ignorant shepherds living on a site where great civilizations once flourished. The shepherds play with the fragments that pop up to the surface, having no notion of the beautiful structures of which they were once a part. All that is necessary is a careful excavation to provide them with life-enhancing models. We need history, not to tell us what happened, or to explain the past, but to make the past alive so that it can explain us and make a future possible. This is our educational crisis and opportunity. Western rationalism has culminated in a rejection of reason. Is this result necessary?

Many will say that my reports of the decisive influence of Continental, particularly German, philosophy on us are false or exaggerated and that, even if it were true that all this language comes from the source to which I attribute it, language does not have such effects. But the language is all around us. Its sources are also undeniable, as is the thought that produced the language. We know how the language was popularized. I need only think of my Amherst student or my Atlanta taxi driver to be persuaded that the categories of the mind determine the perceptions. If we can believe that Calvinist "worldviews" made capitalism, we can also credit the possibility that the overpowering visions of German philosophers are preparing the tyranny of the future.

I must reiterate that Rousseau, Kant, Hegel and Nietzsche are thinkers of the very highest order. This is, in fact, precisely my point. We must relearn what this means and also that there are others who belong in the same rank.

*1987*

# ANDREW SULLIVAN

Andrew Sullivan (b. 1963) is America's best-known openly gay self-described conservative who is also a practicing Catholic. Among intellectuals, one measure of influence is the capacity to transform a controversial point of view into the conventional wisdom, which thereafter becomes the law of the land. By that standard, Sullivan is arguably the most influential conservative public intellectual of his generation.

———————

# Here Comes the Groom:
# A (Conservative) Case For Gay Marriage

L AST MONTH in New York, a court ruled that a gay lover had the right to stay in his deceased partner's rent-control apartment because the lover qualified as a member of the deceased's family. The ruling deftly annoyed almost everybody. Conservatives saw judicial activism in favor of gay rent control: three reasons to be appalled. Chastened liberals (such as the *New York Times* editorial page), while endorsing the recognition of gay relationships, also worried about the abuse of already stretched entitlements that the ruling threatened. What neither side quite contemplated is that they both might be right, and that the way to tackle the issue of unconventional relationships in conventional society is to try something both more radical and more conservative than putting courts in the business of deciding what is and is not a family. That alternative is the legalization of civil gay marriage.

The New York rent-control case did not go anywhere near that far, which is the problem. The rent-control regulations merely stipulated that a "family" member had the right to remain in the apartment.

The judge ruled that to all intents and purposes a gay lover is part of his lover's family, inasmuch as a "family" merely means an inter-woven social life, emotional commitment, and some level of financial interdependence.

It's a principle now well established around the country. Several cities have "domestic partnership" laws, which allow relationships that do not fit into the category of heterosexual marriage to be regis-tered with the city and qualify for benefits that up till now have been reserved for straight married couples. San Francisco, Berkeley, Madison, and Los Angeles all have legislation, as does the politically correct Washington, D.C., suburb, Takoma Park. In these cities, a variety of interpersonal arrangements qualify for health insurance, bereavement leave, insurance, annuity and pension rights, housing rights (such as rent-control apartments), adoption and inheritance rights. Eventually, according to gay lobby groups, the aim is to include federal income tax and veterans' benefits as well. A recent case even involved the right to use a family member's accumulated frequent-flier points. Gays are not the only beneficiaries; heterosexual "live-togethers" also qualify.

There's an argument, of course, that the current legal advantages extended to married people unfairly discriminate against people who've shaped their lives in less conventional arrangements. But it doesn't take a genius to see that enshrining in the law a vague prin-ciple like "domestic partnership" is an invitation to qualify at little personal cost for a vast array of entitlements otherwise kept crudely under control.

To be sure, potential DPs have to prove financial interdependence, shared living arrangements, and a commitment to mutual caring. But they don't need to have a sexual relationship or even closely mirror old-style marriage. In principle, an elderly woman and her live-in nurse could qualify. A couple of uneuphemistically confirmed bachelors could be DPs. So could two close college students, a pair of seminarians, or a couple of frat buddies. Left as it is, the concept of domestic partnership could open a Pandora's box of litigation and subjective judicial decision-making about who qualifies. You either are or are not married; it's not a complex question. Whether you are in a "domestic partnership" is not so clear.

More important, the concept of domestic partnership chips away at the prestige of traditional relationships and undermines the priority we give them. This priority is not necessarily a product of heterosexism. Consider heterosexual couples. Society has good reason to extend legal advantages to heterosexuals who choose the formal sanction of marriage over simply living together. They make a deeper commitment to one another and to society; in exchange, society extends certain benefits to them. Marriage provides an anchor, if an arbitrary and weak one, in the chaos of sex and relationships to which we are all prone. It provides a mechanism for emotional stability, economic security, and the healthy rearing of the next generation. We rig the law in its favor not because we disparage all forms of relationship other than the nuclear family, but because we recognize that not to promote marriage would be to ask too much of human virtue. In the context of the weakened family's effect upon the poor, it might also invite social disintegration. One of the worst products of the New Right's "family values" campaign is that its extremism and hatred of diversity has disguised this more measured and more convincing case for the importance of the marital bond.

The concept of domestic partnership ignores these concerns, indeed directly attacks them; this is a pity, since one of its most important objectives—providing some civil recognition for gay relationships—is a noble cause and one completely compatible with the defense of the family. But the way to go about it is not to undermine straight marriage; it is to legalize old-style marriage for gays.

The gay movement has ducked this issue primarily out of fear of division. Much of the gay leadership clings to notions of gay life as essentially outsider, anti-bourgeois, radical. Marriage, for them, is co-optation into straight society. For the Stonewall generation, it is hard to see how this vision of conflict will ever fundamentally change. But for many other gays—my guess, a majority—while they don't deny the importance of rebellion 20 years ago and are grateful for what was done, there's now the sense of a new opportunity. A need to rebel has quietly ceded to a desire to belong. To be gay and to be bourgeois no longer seems such an absurd proposition. Certainly since AIDS, to be gay and to be responsible has become a necessity.

Gay marriage squares several circles at the heart of the domestic partnership debate. Unlike domestic partnership, it allows for recognition of gay relationships, while casting no aspersions on traditional marriage. It merely asks that gays be allowed to join in. Unlike domestic partnership, it doesn't open up avenues for heterosexuals to get benefits without the responsibilities of marriage, or a nightmare of definitional litigation. And unlike domestic partnership, it harnesses to an already established social convention the yearnings for stability and acceptance among a fast-maturing gay community.

Gay marriage also places more responsibilities upon gays: It says for the first time that gay relationships are not better or worse than straight relationships, and that the same is expected of them. And it's clear and dignified. There's a legal benefit to a clear, common symbol of commitment. There's also a personal benefit. One of the ironies of domestic partnership is that it's not only more complicated than marriage, it's more demanding, requiring an elaborate statement of intent to qualify. It amounts to a substantial invasion of privacy. Why, after all, should gays be required to prove commitment before they get married in a way we would never dream of asking of straights?

Legalizing gay marriage would offer homosexuals the same deal society now offers heterosexuals: general social approval and specific legal advantages in exchange for a deeper and harder-to-extract-yourself-from commitment to another human being. Like straight marriage, it would foster social cohesion, emotional security, and economic prudence. Since there's no reason gays should not be allowed to adopt or be foster parents, it could also help nurture children. And its introduction would not be some sort of radical break with social custom. As it has become more acceptable for gay people to acknowledge their loves publicly, more and more have committed themselves to one another for life in full view of their families and their friends. A law institutionalizing gay marriage would merely reinforce a healthy social trend. It would also, in the wake of AIDS, qualify as a genuine public health measure. Those conservatives who deplore promiscuity among some homosexuals should be among the first to support it. Burke could have written a powerful case for it.

The argument that gay marriage would subtly undermine the unique legitimacy of straight marriage is based upon a fallacy. For heterosexuals, straight marriage would remain the most significant—and only legal—social bond. Gay marriage could only delegitimize straight marriage if it were a real alternative to it, and this is clearly not true. To put it bluntly, there's precious little evidence that straights could be persuaded by any law to have sex with—let alone marry—someone of their own sex. The only possible effect of this sort would be to persuade gay men and women who force themselves into heterosexual marriage (often at appalling cost to themselves and their families) to find a focus for their family instincts in a more personally positive environment. But this is clearly a plus, not a minus: Gay marriage could both avoid a lot of tortured families and create the possibility for many happier ones. It is not, in short, a denial of family values. It's an extension of them.

Of course, some would claim that any legal recognition of homosexuality is a de facto attack upon heterosexuality. But even the most hardened conservatives recognize that gays are a permanent minority and aren't likely to go away. Since persecution is not an option in a civilized society, why not coax gays into traditional values rather than rail incoherently against them?

There's a less elaborate argument for gay marriage: It's good for gays. It provides role models for young gay people who, after the exhilaration of coming out, can easily lapse into short-term relationships and insecurity with no tangible goal in sight. My own guess is that most gays would embrace such a goal with as much (if not more) commitment as straights. Even in our society as it is, many lesbian relationships are virtual textbook cases of monogamous commitment. Legal gay marriage could also help bridge the gulf often found between gays and their parents. It could bring the essence of gay life—a gay couple—into the heart of the traditional straight family in a way the family can most understand and the gay offspring can most easily acknowledge. It could do as much to heal the gay-straight rift as any amount of gay rights legislation.

If these arguments sound socially conservative, that's no accident. It's one of the richest ironies of our society's blind spot toward gays that essentially conservative social goals should have the appearance of being so radical. But gay marriage is not a radical step. It avoids the mess of domestic partnership; it is humane; it is conservative in the best sense of the word. It's also practical. Given the fact that we already allow legal gay relationships, what possible social goal is advanced by framing the law to encourage these relationships to be unfaithful, undeveloped, and insecure?

*1989*

# SHELBY STEELE

Shelby Steele (b. 1946) is a senior fellow at the Hoover Institution, where his work focuses on race, multiculturalism, and affirmative action. A prolific writer and award-winning documentarian, he is a recipient of both the National Humanities Medal (2004) and the Bradley Prize (2006).

# Affirmative Action:
# The Price of Preference

I N A few short years, when my two children will be applying to college, the affirmative action policies by which most universities offer black students some form of preferential treatment will present me with a dilemma. I am a middle-class black, a college professor, far from wealthy, but also well-removed from the kind of deprivation that would qualify my children for the label "disadvantaged." Both of them have endured racial insensitivity from whites. They have been called names, have suffered slights, and have experienced firsthand the peculiar malevolence that racism brings out in people. Yet, they have never experienced racial discrimination, have never been stopped by their race on any path they have chosen to follow. Still, their society now tells them that if they will only designate themselves as black on their college applications, they will likely do better in the college lottery than if they conceal this fact. I think there is something of a Faustian bargain in this.

Of course, many blacks and a considerable number of whites would say that I was sanctimoniously making affirmative action into a test of character. They would say that this small preference is the meagerest recompense for centuries of unrelieved oppression. And to these arguments other very obvious facts must be added. In America, many marginally competent or flatly incompetent whites are hired everyday—some because their white skin suits the conscious or unconscious racial preference of their employer. The white children of alumni are often grandfathered into elite universities in what can only be seen as a residual benefit of historic white privilege. Worse, white incompetence is always an individual matter, while for blacks it is often confirmation of ugly stereotypes. The Peter Principle was not conceived with only blacks in mind. Given that unfairness cuts both ways, doesn't it only balance the scales of history that my children now receive a slight preference over whites? Doesn't this repay, in a small way, the systematic denial under which their grandfather lived out his days?

So, in theory, affirmative action certainly has all the moral symmetry that fairness requires—the injustice of historical and even contemporary white advantage is offset with black advantage; preference replaces prejudice, inclusion answers exclusion. It is reformist and corrective, even repentent and redemptive. And I would never sneer at these good intentions. Born in the late forties in Chicago, I started my education (a charitable term in this case) in a segregated school and suffered all the indignities that come to blacks in a segregated society. My father, born in the South, only made it to the third grade before the white man's fields took permanent priority over his formal education. And though he educated himself into an advanced reader with an almost professorial authority, he could only drive a truck for a living and never earned more than ninety dollars a week in his entire life. So yes, it is crucial to my sense of citizenship, to my ability to identify with the spirit and the interests of America, to know that this country, however imperfectly, recognizes its past sins and wishes to correct them.

Yet good intentions, because of the opportunity for innocence they offer us, are very seductive and can blind us to the effects they generate when implemented. In our society, affirmative action is, among other things, a testament to white goodwill and to black power, and in the midst of these heavy investments, its effects can be hard to see. But after twenty years of implementation, I think affirmative action has shown itself to be more bad than good and that blacks—whom I will focus on in this essay—now stand to lose more from it than they gain.

In talking with affirmative action administrators and with blacks and whites in general, it is clear that supporters of affirmative action focus on its good intentions while detractors emphasize its negative effects. Proponents talk about "diversity" and "pluralism"; opponents speak of "reverse discrimination," the unfairness of quotas and set-asides. It was virtually impossible to find people outside either camp. The closest I came was a white male manager at a large computer company who said, "I think it amounts to reverse discrimination, but I'll put up with a little of that for a little more diversity." I'll live with a little of the effect to gain a little of the intention, he seemed to be saying. But this only makes him a halfhearted supporter of affirmative action. I think many people who don't really like affirmative action support it to one degree or another anyway.

I believe they do this because of what happened to white and black Americans in the crucible of the sixties when whites were confronted with their racial guilt and blacks tasted their first real power. In this stormy time white absolution and black power coalesced into virtual mandates for society. Affirmative action became a meeting ground for these mandates in the law, and in the late sixties and early seventies it underwent a remarkable escalation of its mission from simple anti-discrimination enforcement to social engineering by means of quotas, goals, timetables, set-asides and other forms of preferential treatment.

Legally, this was achieved through a series of executive orders and EEOC guidelines that allowed racial imbalances in the workplace to stand as proof of racial discrimination. Once it could be assumed that discrimination explained racial imbalances, it became easy to justify group remedies to presumed discrimination, rather than the normal case-by-case redress for proven discrimination. Preferential treatment through quotas, goals, and so on is designed to correct imbalances based on the assumption that they always indicate discrimination. This expansion of what constitutes discrimination allowed affirmative action to escalate into the business of social engineering in the name of anti-discrimination, to push society toward statistically proportionate racial representation, without any obligation of proving actual discrimination.

What accounted for this shift, I believe, was the white mandate to achieve a new racial innocence and the black mandate to gain power.

Even though blacks had made great advances during the sixties without quotas, these mandates, which came to a head in the very late sixties, could no longer be satisfied by anything less than racial preferences. I don't think these mandates in themselves were wrong, since whites clearly needed to do better by blacks and blacks needed more real power in society. But, as they came together in affirmative action, their effect was to distort our understanding of racial discrimination in a way that allowed us to offer the remediation of preference on the basis of mere color rather than actual injury. By making black the color of preference, these mandates have reburdened society with the very marriage of color and preference (in reverse) that we set out to eradicate. The old sin is reaffirmed in a new guise.

But the essential problem with this form of affirmative action is the way it leaps over the hard business of developing a formerly oppressed people to the point where they can achieve proportionate representation on their own (given equal opportunity) and goes straight for the proportionate representation. This may satisfy some whites of their innocence and some blacks of their power, but it does very little to truly uplift blacks.

A white female affirmative action officer at an Ivy League university told me what many supporters of affirmative action now say: "We're after diversity. We ideally want a student body where racial and ethnic groups are represented according to their proportion in society." When affirmative action escalated into social engineering, diversity became a golden word. It grants whites an egalitarian fairness (innocence) and blacks an entitlement to proportionate representation (power). *Diversity* is a term that applies democratic principles to races and cultures rather than to citizens, despite the fact that there is nothing to indicate that real diversity is the same thing as proportionate representation. Too often the result of this on campuses (for example) has been a democracy of colors rather than of people, an artificial diversity that gives the appearance of an educational parity between black and white students that has not yet been achieved in reality. Here again, racial preferences allow society to leapfrog over the difficult problem of developing blacks to parity with whites and into a cosmetic diversity that covers the blemish of disparity—a full six years after admission, only about 26 percent of black students graduate from college.

Racial representation is not the same thing as racial development, yet affirmative action fosters a confusion of these very different needs. Representation can be manufactured; development is always hard-earned. However, it is the music of innocence and power that we hear in affirmative action that causes us to cling to it and to its distracting emphasis on representation. The fact is that after twenty years of racial preferences, the gap between white and black median income is greater than it was in the seventies. None of this is to say that blacks don't need policies that ensure our right to equal opportunity, but what we need more is the development that will let us take advantage of society's efforts to include us.

I think that one of the most troubling effects of racial preferences for blacks is a kind of demoralization, or put another way, an enlargement of self-doubt. Under affirmative action the quality that earns us preferential treatment is an implied inferiority. However this inferiority is explained—and it is easily enough explained by the myriad deprivations that grew out of our oppression—it is still inferiority. There are explanations, and then there is the fact. And the fact must be borne by the individual as a condition apart from the explanation, apart even from the fact that others like himself also bear this condition. In integrated situations where blacks must compete with whites who may be better prepared, these explanations may quickly wear thin and expose the individual to racial as well as personal self-doubt.

All of this is compounded by the cultural myth of black inferiority that blacks have always lived with. What this means in practical terms is that when blacks deliver themselves into integrated situations, they encounter a nasty little reflex in whites, a mindless, atavistic reflex that responds to the color black with alarm. Attributions may follow this alarm if the white cares to indulge them, and if they do, they will most likely be negative—one such attribution is intellectual ineptness. I think this reflex and the attributions that may follow it embarrass most whites today, therefore, it is usually quickly repressed. Nevertheless, on an equally atavistic level, the black will be aware of the reflex his color triggers and will feel a stab of horror at seeing himself reflected in this way. He, too, will do a quick repression, but a lifetime of such stabbings is what constitutes his inner realm of racial doubt.

The effects of this may be a subject for another essay. The point here is that the implication of inferiority that racial preferences engender in both the white and black mind expands rather than contracts this doubt. Even when the black sees no implication of inferiority in racial preferences, he knows that whites do, so that—consciously or unconsciously—the result is virtually the same. The effect of preferential treatment—the lowering of normal standards to increase black representation—puts blacks at war with an expanded realm of debilitating doubt, so that the doubt itself becomes an unrecognized preoccupation that undermines their ability to perform, especially in integrated situations. On largely white campuses, blacks are five times more likely to drop out than whites. Preferential treatment, no matter how it is justified in the light of day, subjects blacks to a midnight of self-doubt, and so often transforms their advantage into a revolving door.

Another liability of affirmative action comes from the fact that it indirectly encourages blacks to exploit their own past victimization as a source of power and privilege. Victimization, like implied inferiority, is what justifies preference, so that to receive the benefits of preferential treatment one must, to some extent, become invested in the view of one's self as a victim. In this way, affirmative action nurtures a victim-focused identity in blacks. The obvious irony here is that we become inadvertently invested in the very condition we are trying to overcome. Racial preferences send us the message that there is more power in our past suffering than our present achievements—none of which could bring us a *preference* over others.

When power itself grows out of suffering, then blacks are encouraged to expand the boundaries of what qualifies as racial oppression, a situation that can lead us to paint our victimization in vivid colors, even as we receive the benefits of preference. The same corporations and institutions that give us preference are also seen as our oppressors. At Stanford University minority students—some of whom enjoy as much as $15,000 a year in financial aid—recently took over the president's office demanding, among other things, more financial aid. The power to be found in victimization, like any power, is intoxicating and can lend itself to the creation of a new class of super-victims who can feel the pea of victimization under twenty mattresses. Preferential treatment rewards us for being underdogs rather than for moving beyond that status—a misplacement of incentives that, along with its deepening of our doubt, is more a yoke than a spur.

But, I think, one of the worst prices that blacks pay for preference has to do with an illusion. I saw this illusion at work recently in the mother of a middle-class black student who was going off to his first semester of college. "They owe us this, so don't think for a minute that you don't belong there." This is the logic by which many blacks, and some whites, justify affirmative action—it is something "owed," a form of reparation. But this logic overlooks a much harder and less digestible reality, that it is impossible to repay blacks living today for the historic suffering of the race. If all blacks were given a million dollars tomorrow morning it would not amount to a dime on the dollar of three centuries of oppression, nor would it obviate the residues of that oppression that we still carry today. The concept of historic reparation grows out of man's need to impose a degree of justice on the world that simply does not exist. Suffering can be endured and overcome, it cannot be repaid. Blacks cannot be repaid for the injustice done to the race, but we can be corrupted by society's guilty gestures of repayment.

Affirmative action is such a gesture. It tells us that racial preferences can do for us what we cannot do for ourselves. The corruption here is in the hidden incentive *not* to do what we believe preferences will do. This is an incentive to be reliant on others just as we are struggling for self-reliance. And it keeps alive the illusion that we can find some deliverance in repayment. The hardest thing for any sufferer to accept is that his suffering excuses him from very little and never has enough currency to restore him. To think otherwise is to prolong the suffering.

Several blacks I spoke with said they were still in favor of affirmative action because of the "subtle" discrimination blacks were subject to once on the job. One photojournalist said, "They have ways of ignoring you." A black female television producer said, "You can't file a lawsuit when your boss doesn't invite you to the insider meetings without ruining your career. So we still need affirmative action." Others mentioned the infamous "glass ceiling" through which blacks can see the top positions of authority but never reach them. But I don't think racial preferences are a protection against this subtle discrimination; I think they contribute to it.

In any workplace, racial preferences will always create two-tiered populations composed of preferreds and unpreferreds. This division makes automatic a perception of enhanced competence for the unpreferreds and of questionable competence for the preferreds—the former earned his way, even though others were given preference, while the latter made it by color as much as by competence. Racial preferences implicitly mark whites with an exaggerated superiority just as they mark blacks with an exaggerated inferiority. They not only reinforce America's oldest racial myth but, for blacks, they have the effect of stigmatizing the already stigmatized.

I think that much of the "subtle" discrimination that blacks talk about is often (not always) discrimination against the stigma of questionable competence that affirmative action delivers to blacks. In this sense, preferences scapegoat the very people they seek to help. And it may be that at a certain level employers impose a glass ceiling, but this may not be against the race so much as against the race's reputation for having advanced by color as much as by competence. Affirmative action makes a glass ceiling virtually necessary as a protection against the corruptions of preferential treatment. This ceiling is the point at which corporations shift the emphasis from color to competency and stop playing the affirmative action game. Here preference backfires for blacks and becomes a taint that holds them back. Of course, one could argue that this taint, which is, after all, in the minds of whites, becomes nothing more than an excuse to discriminate against blacks. And certainly the result is the same in either case—blacks don't get past the glass ceiling. But this argument does not get around the fact that racial preferences now taint this color with a new theme of suspicion that makes it even more vulnerable to the impulse in others to discriminate. In this crucial yet gray area of perceived competence, preferences make whites look better than they are and blacks worse, while doing nothing whatever to stop the very real discrimination that blacks may encounter. I don't wish to justify the glass ceiling here, but only to suggest the very subtle ways that affirmative action revives rather than extinguishes the old rationalizations for racial discrimination.

In education, a revolving door; in employment, a glass ceiling.

I believe affirmative action is problematic in our society because it tries to function like a social program. Rather than ask it to ensure equal opportunity we have demanded that it create parity between the races. But preferential treatment does not teach skills, or educate, or instill motivation. It only passes out entitlement by color, a situation that in my profession has created an unrealistically high demand for black professors. The social engineer's assumption is that this high demand will inspire more blacks to earn Ph.D.'s and join the profession. In fact, the number of blacks earning Ph.D.'s has declined in recent years. A Ph.D. must be developed from preschool on. He requires family and community support. He must acquire an entire system of values that enables him to work hard while delaying gratification. There are social programs, I believe, that can (and should) help blacks *develop* in all these areas, but entitlement by color is not a social program; it is a dubious reward for being black.

It now seems clear that the Supreme Court, in a series of recent decisions, is moving away from racial preferences. It has disallowed preferences except in instances of "identified discrimination," eroded the precedent that statistical racial imbalances are *prima facie* evidence of discrimination, and in effect granted white males the right to challenge consent degrees that use preference to achieve racial balances in the workplace. One civil rights leader said, "Night has fallen on civil rights." But I am not so sure. The effect of these decisions is to protect the constitutional rights of everyone rather than take rights away from blacks. What they do take away from blacks is the special entitlement to more rights than others that preferences always grant. Night has fallen on racial preferences, not on the fundamental rights of black Americans. The reason for this shift, I believe, is that the white mandate for absolution from past racial sins has weakened considerably during the eighties. Whites are now less willing to endure unfairness to themselves in order to grant special entitlements to blacks, even when these entitlements are justified in the name of past suffering. Yet the black mandate for more power in society has remained unchanged. And I think part of the anxiety that many blacks feel over these decisions has to do with the loss of black power they may signal. We had won a certain specialness and now we are losing it.

But the power we've lost by these decisions is really only the power that grows out of our victimization—the power to claim special entitlements under the law because of past oppression. This is not a very substantial or reliable power, and it is important that we know this so we can focus more exclusively on the kind of development that will bring enduring power. There is talk now that Congress will pass new legislation to compensate for these new limits on affirmative action.

If this happens, I hope that their focus will be on development and anti-discrimination rather than entitlement, on achieving racial parity rather than jerry-building racial diversity.

I would also like to see affirmative action go back to its original purpose of enforcing equal opportunity—a purpose that in itself disallows racial preferences. We cannot be sure that the discriminatory impulse in America has yet been shamed into extinction, and I believe affirmative action can make its greatest contribution by providing a rigorous vigilance in this area. It can guard constitutional rather than racial rights, and help institutions evolve standards of merit and selection that are appropriate to the institution's needs yet as free of racial bias as possible (again, with the understanding that racial imbalances are not always an indication of racial bias). One of the most important things affirmative action can do is to define exactly what racial discrimination is and how it might manifest itself within a specific institution. The impulse to discriminate *is* subtle and cannot be ferreted out unless its many guises are made clear to people. Along with this there should be monitoring of institutions and heavy sanctions brought to bear when actual discrimination is found. This is the sort of affirmative action that America owes to blacks and to itself. It goes after the evil of discrimination itself, while preferences only sidestep the evil and grant entitlement to its *presumed* victims.

But if not preferences, then what? I think we need social policies that are committed to two goals: the educational and economic development of disadvantaged people, regardless of race, and the eradication from our society—through close monitoring and severe sanctions—of racial, ethnic, or gender discrimination. Preferences will not deliver us to either of these goals, since they tend to benefit those who are not disadvantaged—middle-class white women and middle-class blacks—and attack one form of discrimination with another. Preferences are inexpensive and carry the glamour of good intentions—change the numbers and the good deed is done. To be against them is to be unkind. But I think the unkindest cut is to bestow on children like my own an undeserved advantage while neglecting the development of those disadvantaged children on the East Side of my city who will likely never be in a position to benefit from a preference. Give my children fairness; give disadvantaged children a better shot at development—better elementary and secondary schools, job training, safer neighborhoods, better financial assistance for college, and so on. Fewer blacks go to college today than ten years ago; more black males of college age are in prison or under the control of the criminal justice system than in college. This despite racial preferences.

The mandates of black power and white absolution out of which preferences emerged were not wrong in themselves. What was wrong was that both races focused more on the goals of these mandates than on the means to the goals. Blacks can have no real power without taking responsibility for their own educational and economic development. Whites can have no racial innocence without earning it by eradicating discrimination and helping the disadvantaged to develop. Because we ignored the means, the goals have not been reached, and the real work remains to be done.

*1991*

# RICHARD JOHN NEUHAUS

A Lutheran minister who became an ordained Catholic priest and an antiwar liberal who became a militant archconservative, Richard John Neuhaus (1936–2009) was the founding editor of the journal *First Things* and the author of many books.

———————

## Can Atheists Be Good Citizens?

THE QUESTION is asked whether atheists can be good citizens. I do not want to keep you in suspense. I would very much like to answer the question in the affirmative. It seems the decent and tolerant thing to do. But before we can answer the question posed, we should first determine what is meant by atheism. And, second, we must inquire more closely into what is required of a good citizen.

Consider our late friend Sidney Hook. Can anyone deny that he was a very good citizen indeed? During the long contest with totalitarianism he was a much better citizen than many believers, including numerous church leaders, who urged that the moral imperative was to split the difference between the evil empire and human fitness for freedom.

On the other hand, Sidney Hook was not really an atheist. He is more accurately described as a philosophical agnostic, one who says that the evidence is not sufficient to compel us either to deny or affirm the reality of God. Sidney was often asked what he would say when he died and God asked him why he did not believe. His standard answer was that he would say, "Lord, you didn't supply enough evidence." Some of us are rather confident that Sidney now has all the evidence that he wanted, and we dare to hope that the learning experience is not too painful for him. Unlike many atheists of our time, Sidney Hook believed in reason and evidence that yield what he did not hesitate to call truth. They may have been false gods, but he was not without his gods.

There is atheism and then there is atheism. The Greek *a-theos* meant one who is "without God." It had less to do with whether one believed in God than with whether one believed in the gods of the city or the empire. For his perceived disbelief in the gods, Socrates was charged with atheism. The early Christians were charged with atheism for their insistence that there is no god other than the God whom Jesus called Father. In the eyes of the ancients, to be a-theos was to be outside the civilizational circle of the *civitas*. To be an atheist was to be subversive. The atheist was a security risk, if not a traitor. Christians were thought to be atheists precisely because they professed the God who judges and debunks the false gods of the community. In the classical world, then, the answer to our question was decisively in the negative: No, an atheist could not be a good citizen. But those whom they called atheists then we do not call atheists today.

Those whom we call atheists in the modern period believe that they are denying what earlier "atheists," such as the Christians, affirmed. That is to say, they deny the reality of what they understand believing Jews and Christians to mean by God. This form of atheism is a post-Enlightenment and largely nineteenth-century phenomenon. It developed a vocabulary—first of course among intellectuals but then becoming culturally pervasive—that was strongly prejudiced against believers. Note the very use of the term "believer" to describe a person who is persuaded of the reality of God. The alternative to being a believer, of course, is to be a knower. Similarly, a curious usage developed with respect to the categories of faith and reason, the subjective and the objective, and, in the realm of morals, a sharp distinction between fact and value. Belief, faith, subjectivity, values—these were the soft and dubious words relevant to affirming God. Knowledge, reason, objectivity, fact—these were the hard and certain words relevant to denying God. This tendentious vocabulary of modern unbelief is still very much with us today.

Necessarily following from such distortive distinctions are common assumptions about the public and the private. One recalls A. N. Whitehead's axiom that religion is what a man does with his solitude.

Even one so religiously musical as William James could write, "Religion
. . . shall mean for us the feelings, acts, and experiences of individual
men in their solitude." (*The Varieties of Religious Experience*, Lecture 2)
In this construal of matters, we witness a radical departure from the
public nature of religion, whether that religion has to do with the
ancient gods of the city or with the biblical Lord who rules over the
nations. The gods of the city and the God of the Bible are emphatically
public. The confinement of the question of God or the gods to the
private sphere constitutes what might be described as political atheism. Many today who are believers in private have been persuaded, or
intimidated, into accepting political atheism.

Political atheism is a subspecies of practical or methodological
atheism. Practical or methodological atheism is, quite simply, the
assumption that we can get along with the business at hand without
addressing the question of God one way or another. Here the classic anecdote is the response of the Marquis de Laplace to Napoleon
Bonaparte. You will recall that when Napoleon observed that Laplace
had written a huge book on the system of the universe without men-
tioning the Author of the universe, Laplace replied, "Sire, I have no
need of that hypothesis." When God has become a hypothesis we have
traveled a very long way from both the gods of the ancient city and
the God of the Bible. Yet that distance was necessary to the emergence
of what the modern world has called atheism.

In his remarkable work, *At the Origins of Modern Atheism*, Michael
Buckley persuasively argues that the god denied by many moderns
is a strange god created by the attempts of misguided religionists to
demonstrate that god could be proven or known on philosophical
grounds alone.

> The extraordinary note about this emergence of the denial of the
> Christian god which Nietzsche celebrated is that Christianity as such,
> more specifically the person and teaching of Jesus or the experience
> and history of the Christian Church, did not enter the discussion. The
> absence of any consideration of Christology is so pervasive throughout
> serious discussion that it becomes taken for granted, yet it is so stunningly
> curious that it raises a fundamental issue of the modes of thought: How
> did the issue of Christianity vs. atheism become purely philosophical?

> To paraphrase Tertullian: How was it that the only arms to defend the temple were to be found in the Stoa?

As Nietzsche's god had nothing to do with Christology, so, needless to say, the god that he declared dead had nothing to do with Sinai, election, covenant, or messianic promise.

In his notebook, after his death, was found Pascal's famous assertion of trust in "the God of Abraham, the God of Isaac, the God of Jacob, not of philosophers and scholars." Modern atheism is the product not so much of anti-religion as of religion's replacement of the God of Abraham with the god of the philosophers, and of the philosophers' consequent rejection of that *ersatz* god. Descartes determined that he would accept as true nothing that could be reasonably doubted, and Christians set about to prove that the existence of God could not be reasonably doubted. Thus did the defenders of religion set faith against the doubt that is integral to the life of faith.

The very phrase, "the existence of God," gave away the game, as though God were one existent among other existents, one entity among other entities, one actor among other actors, whose actions must conform to standards that we have determined in advance are appropriate to being God. The transcendent, the ineffable, the totally other, the God who acts in history was tamed and domesticated in order to meet the philosophers' job description for the post of God. Not surprisingly, the philosophers determined that the candidates recommended by the friends of religion did not qualify for the post.

The American part of this story is well told by historian James Turner (*Without God, Without Creed: The Origins of Unbelief in America*). "The natural parents of modern unbelief," Turner writes, "turn out to have been the guardians of belief." Many thinking people came at last "to realize that it was religion, not science or social change, that gave birth to unbelief. Having made God more and more like man—intellectually, morally, emotionally—the shapers of religion made it feasible to abandon God, to believe simply in man." Turner's judgment is relentless: "In trying to adapt their religious beliefs to socioeconomic change, to new moral challenges, to novel problems of knowledge, to the tightening standards of science, the defenders of God slowly strangled Him. If anyone is to be arraigned for deicide, it is not Charles

Darwin but his adversary Bishop Samuel Wilberforce, not the godless Robert Ingersoll but the godly Beecher family."

H. L. Mencken observed that the great achievement of liberal Protestantism was to make God boring. That is unfair, of course, as Mencken was almost always unfair, but it is not untouched by truth. The god that was trimmed, accommodated, and retooled in order to be deemed respectable by the "modern mind" was increasingly uninteresting, because unnecessary. Dietrich Bonhoeffer described that god as a "god of the gaps," invoked to fill in those pieces of reality that human knowledge and control had not yet mastered. H. Richard Niebuhr's well-known and withering depiction of the gospel of liberal Christianity is very much to the point: "A God without wrath brought men without sin into a kingdom without judgment through the ministrations of a Christ without a Cross." Absent our sin and divine wrath, judgment, and redemption, it is not surprising that people came to dismiss the idea of God not because it is implausible but because it is superfluous, and, yes, boring.

It would no doubt be satisfying for Christian believers—and for Jews who identify themselves not by the accidents of Jewishness but by the truth of Judaism—to conclude that the God of Abraham, Isaac, Jacob, and Jesus has not been touched by the critiques of atheism. However, while it is true that the god denied by many atheists is not the God of the Bible affirmed by Christians and Jews, there are forms of atheism that do intend to preclude such affirmation, and certainly to preclude such affirmation in public. There is, for example, the more determined materialist who asserts that there simply is nothing and can be nothing outside a closed system of matter. This was the position of the late and unlamented "dialectical materialism" of Communism. It is the position of some scientists today, especially those in the biological sciences who are wedded to evolution as a belief system. (Physicists, as it turns out, are increasingly open to the metaphysical.)

Perhaps more commonly, one encounters varieties of logical positivism that hold that since assertions about God are not empirically verifiable—or, for that matter, falsifiable—they are simply meaningless. In a similar vein, analytical philosophers would instruct us that "God talk" is, quite precisely, non-sense. This is not atheism in the sense to which we have become accustomed, since it claims that denying God is as much nonsense as affirming God. It is atheism, however, in the original sense of a-theos, of being without God. Then there is the much more radical position that denies not only the possibility of truth claims about God but the possibility of claims to truth at all—at least as "truth" has usually been understood in our history. Perhaps today's most prominent proponent of this argument in America is Richard Rorty. This is not the atheism that pits reason against our knowledge of God; this is the atheism of unreason.

Rorty is sometimes portrayed, and portrays himself, as something of an eccentric gadfly. In fact, along with Derrida, Foucault, and other Heideggerian epigones of Nietzsche, Rorty is the guru of an academic establishment of increasing influence in our intellectual culture. Here we encounter the apostles of a relativism that denies it is relativism because it denies that there is any alternative to relativism, and therefore the term relativism is "meaningless." They are radically anti-foundationalist. That is to say, they contend that there are no conclusive arguments underlying our assertions, except the conclusive argument that there are no conclusive arguments. They reject any "correspondence theory" of truth. There is no coherent connection between what we think and say and the reality "out there." Truth is what the relevant community of discourse agrees to say is true.

The goal, in this way of thinking, is self-actualization, indeed self-creation. The successful life is the life lived as a *novum*, an autobiography that has escaped the "used vocabularies" of the past. This argument has its academic strongholds in literary criticism and sectors of philosophy, but it undergirds assumptions that are increasingly widespread in our intellectual culture. If personal and group self-actualization is the end, arguments claiming to deal with truth are but disguised stratagems for the exercise of will and the quest for power. Whether the issue is gender, sexual orientation, or race, we are told that the purpose is to change the ideational "power structure" presently controlled by oppressors who disingenuously try to protect the status quo by appeals to objective truth and intersubjective reason.

The only truth that matters is the truth that is instrumental to self-actualization. Thus truth is in service to "identity." If, for instance, one has the temerity to object that there is no evidence that Africans discovered the Americas before Columbus, he is promptly informed that he is the tool of hegemonic Eurocentrism. In such a view, the "social construction of reality" (to use the language of Peter Berger and Thomas Luckmann) takes on ominous new dimensions as it is asserted that all of reality, without remainder, is constructed to serve the will to power and self-actualization. Brevity requires that I describe this approach with broad strokes, but, alas, the description is no caricature.

But are people who embrace this view atheists? They brush aside the question as "not serious," for the theism upon which atheism depends is, in this view, not serious. As with relativism and irrationality, so also with atheism—the words only make sense in relation to the opposites from which they are derived. Of course privately, or for purposes of a particular community, any words might be deemed useful in creating the self. One might even find it meaningful to speak about "Nature and Nature's God." People can be permitted to talk that way, so long as they understand that such talk has no public purchase. Rorty's "liberal ironist" can employ any vocabulary, no matter how fantastical, so long as he does not insist that it is true in a way that makes a claim upon others, and so long as he does not act on that vocabulary in a manner that limits the freedom of others to construct their own realities.

There is indeed irony in the fact that some who think of themselves as theists eagerly embrace deconstructionism's operative atheism. Today's cultural scene is awash in what are called "new spiritualities." A recent anthology of "America's new spiritual voices" includes contributions promoting witchcraft, ecological mysticism, devotion to sundry gods and goddesses, and something that presents itself as Zen physio-psychoanalysis. All are deemed to be usable vocabularies for the creation of the self. The book is recommended by a Roman Catholic theologian who writes that it "turns us away from the 'truths' outside ourselves that lead to debate and division, and turns us toward the Inner Truth that is beyond debate." But theism—whether in relation to the gods of the *civitas* theism—whether in relation to the gods of the *civitas* or the God of Abraham—is devotion to that which is external to ourselves. In that light, it is evident that many of the burgeoning "spiritualities" in contemporary culture are richly religionized forms of atheism.

There is additional irony. Beyond pop-spiritualities and Rortian nihilism, a serious argument is being made today against a version of rationality upon which Enlightenment atheism was premised. Here one thinks preeminently of Alasdair MacIntyre, and especially of his most recent work, *Three Rival Versions of Moral Enquiry*. MacIntyre effectively polemicizes against a construal of rationality that understands itself to be universal, disinterested, autonomous, and transcending tradition. Our situation, he contends, is one of traditions of rationality in conflict. MacIntyre's favored tradition is Thomism's synthesis of Aristotle and Augustine. If I read him correctly, MacIntyre is prepared to join forces with the Rortians in debunking the hegemonic pretensions of the autonomous and foundational reason that has so long dominated our elite intellectual culture. After the great debunking, all the cognitive cards will have to be put on the table and we can then have at it. Presumably, the tradition that can provide the best account of reality will win out.

If that is MacIntyre's proposal, it strikes me as a very dangerous game. True, in exposing the fallacious value-neutrality of autonomous and traditionless reason, the academy is opened to the arguments of eminently reasonable theism. But, in the resulting free-for-all, it is opened to much else as well. It is made vulnerable to the Nietzschean will to power that sets the rules, and those rules are designed to preclude the return of the gods or God in a manner that claims public allegiance. For one tradition of reason (e.g., Thomism) to form a coalition, even a temporary coalition, with unreason in order to undo another tradition of reason (e.g., the autonomous "way of the mind") is a perilous tactic.

And yet something like this may be the future of our intellectual culture. In our universities, Christians, Jews, and, increasingly, Muslims will be free to contend for their truths. Just as lesbians, Marxists, Nietzscheans, and devotees of The Great Earth Goddess are free to contend for theirs. It is a matter of equal opportunity propaganda. But—and again there is delicious irony—the old methodological atheism and value-neutrality, against which the revolution was launched, may nonetheless prevail.

In other words, every party will be permitted to contend for their truths so long as they acknowledge that they are *their* truths, and not *the* truth. Each will be permitted to propagandize, each will *have* to propagandize if it is to hold its own, because it is acknowledged that there is no common ground for the alternative to propaganda, which is reasonable persuasion. Of course history, including the history of ideas, is full of surprises. But there is, I believe, reason to fear that theism, when it plays by the rules of the atheism of unreason, will be corrupted and eviscerated. The method becomes the message. Contemporary Christian theology already provides all too many instances of the peddling of truths that are in service to truths other than the truth of God.

## II

We have touched briefly, then, on the many faces of atheism—of living and thinking a-theos, without God or the gods. There is the atheism of the early Christians, who posited God against the gods. There is the atheism of Enlightenment rationalists who, committed to undoubtable certainty, rejected the god whom religionists designed to fit that criterion. There is the practical atheism of Laplace, who had no need of "that hypothesis" in order to get on with what he had to do. There is the weary atheism of those who grew bored with liberalism's god created in the image and likeness of good liberals. There is the more thorough atheism of Nietzschean relativism that dare not speak its name, that cannot speak its name, lest in doing so it implicitly acknowledge that there is an alternative to relativism. And, finally, there is the atheism of putative theists who peddle religious truths that are true for you, if you find it useful to believe them true.

Can these atheists be good citizens? It depends, I suppose, on what is meant by good citizenship. We may safely assume that the great majority of these people abide by the laws, pay their taxes, and may even be congenial and helpful neighbors. But can a person who does not acknowledge that he is accountable to a truth higher than the self, external to the self, really be trusted? Locke and Rousseau, among many other worthies, thought not. However confused their theology, they were sure that the social contract was based upon nature, upon the way the world really is. Rousseau's "civil religion" was apparently itself a social construct, but Locke was convinced that the fear of a higher judgment, even an eternal judgment, was essential to citizenship.

It follows that an atheist could not be trusted to be a good citizen, and therefore could not be a citizen at all. Locke is rightly celebrated as a champion of religious toleration, but not of irreligion. "Those are not at all to be tolerated who deny the being of a God," he writes in

*A Letter Concerning Toleration.* "Promises, covenants, and oaths, which are the bonds of human society, can have no hold upon an atheist. The taking away of God, though but even in thought, dissolves all." The taking away of God dissolves all. Every text becomes pretext, every interpretation misinterpretation, and every oath a deceit.

James Madison in his famed *Memorial and Remonstrance* of 1785 wrote to similar effect. It is always being forgotten that for Madison and the other founders religious freedom is an unalienable right that is premised upon unalienable duty. "It is the duty of every man to render to the Creator such homage and such only as he believes to be acceptable to him. This duty is precedent, both in order of time and in degree of obligation, to the claims of Civil Society." Then follows a passage that could hardly be more pertinent to the question that prompts our present reflection: "Before any man can be considered as a member of Civil Society, he must be considered as a subject of the Governour of the Universe: And if a member of Civil Society, who enters into any subordinate Association, must always do it with a reservation of his duty to the General Authority; much more must every man who becomes a member of any particular Civil Society, do it with a saving of his allegiance to the Universal Sovereign."

State constitutions could and did exclude atheists from public office. The federal Constitution, in Article VI, would simply impose no religious test. In reaction to the extreme secularist bias of much historical scholarship, some writers in recent years have attempted to portray the founders as Bible-believing, orthodox, even born-again evangelical Christians. That is much too much. It is well worth recalling, however, how much they had in common with respect to religious and philosophical beliefs. While a few were sympathetic to milder versions of Deism and some were rigorous Calvinists in the Puritan tradition, almost all assumed a clearly Christian, and clearly Protestant, construal of reality. In the language of contemporary discourse, the founders were "moral realists." This is amply demonstrated from many sources, not least the Declaration and the Constitution, and especially the preamble of the latter. The "good" was for the founders a reality not of their own fabrication, nor was it merely the "conventionalism" of received moral tradition.

The founders' notion of the social contract was not a truncated and mechanistic contrivance of calculated self-interest. Their understanding was more in the nature of a compact, premised upon a sense of covenantal purpose guiding this *novus ordo seclorum*. That understanding of a covenant encompassing the contract was, in a time of supreme testing, brought to full and magisterial articulation by Abraham Lincoln. The Constitution represented not a deal struck but a nation "so conceived and so dedicated."

In such a nation, an atheist can be a citizen, but he cannot be a good citizen. A good citizen does more than abide by the laws. A good citizen is able to give an account, a morally compelling account, of the regime of which he is part. He is able to justify its defense against its enemies, and to convincingly recommend its virtues to citizens of the next generation so that they, in turn, can transmit the regime to citizens yet unborn. This regime of liberal democracy, of republican self-governance, is not self-evidently good and just. An account must be given. Reasons must be given. They must be reasons that draw authority from that which is higher than the self, from that which is external to the self, from that to which the self is ultimately obliged.

An older form of atheism pitted reason against the knowledge of God. The newer atheism is the atheism of unreason. It is much the more dangerous because the more insidious. Fortunately, the overwhelming majority of Americans—and, I believe, the majority of our intellectual elites, if put to the test—are not atheists of any of the varieties we have discussed. They believe that there are good reasons for this ordering of the *civitas*, reasons that have public purchase, reasons that go beyond contingent convenience, reasons that entail what is just, the laws of nature, and maybe even the will of God.

The final irony, of course, is that those who believe in the God of Abraham, Isaac, Jacob, and Jesus turn out to be the best citizens. Those who were once called atheists are now the most reliable defenders not of the gods but of the good reasons for this regime of ordered liberty. Such people are the best citizens not despite but *because* their loyalty to the *civitas* is qualified by a higher loyalty. Among the best of the good reasons they give in justifying this regime is that it is a regime that makes a sharply limited claim upon the loyalty of its citizens. The ultimate allegiance of the faithful is not to the regime or to its constituting texts, but to the City of God and the sacred texts that guide our path toward that end for which we were created. They are dual citizens, so to speak, in a regime that, as Madison and others well understood, was designed for such duality. When the regime forgets itself and reestablishes the gods of the *civitas*, even if it be in the name of liberal democracy, the followers of the God of Abraham have no choice but to invite the opprobrium of once again being "atheists."

I am well aware that there are those who will agree with the gravamen of this argument but for quite different reasons. They do not themselves believe, but they recognize the importance of religion as a "useful lie" essential to securing this kind of public order. It is true, and it is sad. It is sad because they do not believe, and it is sadder because they are prepared to use, and thereby abuse, the name of the God whom they do not honor.

But of course they are right about religion and this public order. It is an order that was not conceived and dedicated by atheists, and cannot today be conceived and dedicated anew by atheists. In times of testing—and every time is a time of testing for this American experiment in ordered liberty—a morally convincing account must be given. You may well ask, Convincing to whom? One obvious answer in a democracy, although not the only answer, is this: convincing to a majority of their fellow citizens. Giving such an account is required of good citizens. And that is why, I reluctantly conclude, atheists cannot be good citizens.

*1991*

# MICHAEL NOVAK

For Michael Novak (1933–2017), democratic capitalism offers not only the best guarantee of political but also of religious freedom. Long a scholar-in-residence at the American Enterprise Institute in Washington, D.C., Novak was the author of many books, of which *The Catholic Ethic and the Spirit of Capitalism* (1993) is the best known. In 1994, he received the Templeton Prize for Progress in Religion.

---

## FROM *The Catholic Ethic and the Spirit of Capitalism*

### AMERICAN FOUNDING PRINCIPLES, CURRENT PRACTICE

L IKE our own elites, most of the world still neglects the American Revolution. The failed French Revolution of 1789 is seized upon as the great symbolic center of the modern era of liberty. Even Cardinal Ratzinger ignored the American (and cited only the French) Revolution in his second "Instruction on Christian Freedom and Liberation."[1] "The sad truth of the matter," Hannah Arendt has written, "is that the French Revolution, which ended in disaster, has made world history, while the American Revolution, so triumphantly successful, has remained an event of little more than local importance."[2] How sad this really is becomes clear from Professor Arendt's earlier line: "The colonization of North America and the republican government of the United States constitute perhaps the greatest, certainly the boldest, enterprise of European mankind."

Intellectually isolated from Europe, and separated from it by hundreds of tacit understandings, customs, habits, laws, and institutions, the United States is still the world's most original and most profound counterculture. Its underlying presuppositions are unknown to, or left inarticulate by, even the larger part of its own intellectual elite—that "adversary culture" which Lionel Trilling was the first to analyze.[3] "It is odd indeed," Arendt writes, "to see that twentieth-century *American* even more than European learned opinion often inclined to interpret the American Revolution in the light of the French Revolution, or to criticize it because it so obviously did not conform to the lessons learned from the latter."[4]

The U.S. system was in its beginnings unlike the European, and the Framers were quite aware of their originality.[5] Do not deny to us, James Madison in effect wrote in *Federalist* 14, the originality of our *novus ordo seclorum*, through which the American people "accomplished a revolution which has no parallel in the annals of human society. They reared the fabrics of governments which have no model on the face of the globe."[6] One of the original features of the new system erected by the people of the United States was the primacy it afforded to the institutions of conscience, information, and ideas—precisely to its moral culture—over the realms of politics (limited government) and economics (the least statist in history).

Another (and at first more striking) novelty, Prof. Arendt writes, is that the American experiment drew Europe's long-slumbering attention to "the social question." "America," she wrote, "had become the symbol of a society without poverty. . . . And only after this had happened and had become known to European mankind could *the social question* and the rebellion of the poor come to play a truly revolutionary role."[7] The American example awakened the conscience of Europe. Poverty no longer being inevitable or irreparable, its continued existence became for the first time in history a problem for human conscience.

Indeed, long after one Frenchman, Crèvecoeur, had reported back to Europe the amazing prosperity of those Americans who had not long since departed from Europe bitterly poor,[8] and about the same time as another, Alexis de Tocqueville, was describing the systemic prosperity and ordered liberty that "the hand of Providence"[9] had

launched in the world through the American experiment, Victor Hugo
was still able to describe the dejection and virtual hopelessness of *Les
Misérables* in the France of 1832. The poverty of the poor in France
already had shocked Jefferson some 40 years earlier, and the French
Revolution had done little to mitigate that poverty. Only gradually
did the example of the United States, in moving so many millions of
the poor out of poverty, awaken Europe to the social condition of its
own poor.

In 1886 the Liberal party of France (the party of Tocqueville), seeking to awaken the world again to the difference that the United States
had made to the history of liberty, commissioned and executed a
magnificent gift to the United States: the Statue of Liberty. Imagine
the work of its planning committee. "How shall we symbolize the specifically American idea of liberty?" they must have asked themselves.
Being French, they decided the symbol would be in the shape of a
woman, not a warrior. In this, they followed a tradition as old as the
image of Lady Philosophy in Boethius's *The Consolation of Philosophy*:
Woman as wisdom, bearing aloft in one hand the torch of understanding against the swirling mists of passion and the darkness of ignorance.
In her other hand, they placed a book of the law, inscribed "1776" to
signify the truths Americans hold dear. Her face would be resolute,
serious, purposive. This Lady symbolized not the French *Liberté* (the
prostitute on the altar of the Black Mass), but rather that "ordered
liberty" to which Pope John Paul II was to call attention in Miami
exactly 101 years later.[10] Thus the primacy of morals in the American
idea was fully and rightly grasped by the Liberal party of France, heirs
of Tocqueville.

*Virtue* is the pivotal and deepest American idea. Indeed, "Virtue"
was the inscription (later supplanted by *Novus Ordo Seclorum*) at first
inserted as the motto on the Great Seal of the United States. To imagine an experiment in republican government without virtue, Madison
had told the Virginia Assembly, is "chimerical."[11] For how could a
people, unable severally to govern their own passions, combine to govern their own body politic? Tied together in the then-novel conception of "political economy," neither a free polity nor a free economy
can long survive an incapacity among the people for the virtues that
make liberty possible.

According to the American idea (learned from Jerusalem, Athens, Rome, Paris, and London),[12] liberty springs from the human capacities for *reflection* and *choice*. These human capacities reflect the *Light* and *Love* that are the very names of God in Whose image humans are made, and by Whom they are endowed with "unalienable rights." Habits such as temperance, fortitude, justice, and prudence provide the calm that makes human acts of *reflection* and *choice* possible. The first paragraph of *The Federalist*[13] was addressed exactly to these capacities as the American people were making the precedent-shattering decision whether to constitute the new American republic or no.

The Framers appealed again and again to the primacy of morals, and indeed to God and to Providence (that is, the wise and knowing—"provident"—Creator) in whose image they believed the human capacities of reflection and choice were stamped. "The God who made us, made us free," Jefferson said. Hannah Arendt quotes John Adams (and could as well have quoted George Washington, Benjamin Franklin, James Madison, Alexis de Tocqueville, Abraham Lincoln, and others): "I always consider the settlement of America as the opening of a grand scheme and design in Providence for the illumination of the ignorant and the emancipation of the slavish part of mankind all over the earth."[14]

It is important to underline such a powerful stream of thought as this, and its embodiment in a thousand institutional and ritual ways, for it helps to understand how, to Americans, it is somehow fundamental to stand under the judgment of God. Like the ancient Israelites (to whom, John Adams said,[15] Americans owe more than to any other people), they know that no achievement of material prosperity or of military might would spare them a yet more demanding judgment. And this judgment would be rendered by a transcendent, almighty, and unswervingly *just* God, whose judgment was to be dreaded as "a terrible swift sword." The primacy of morals is written into America's very soul.

For this reason, Americans gave a privileged place to institutions of morals and culture: to churches preaching to the faithful, to universities (in whose support, more than any other people before or since, they have invested so many of their private and public energies), to learning, and to the press. Had he to choose between having a free government or a free press (and God forbid the choice, Jefferson said), he would prefer a free press.[16] If these moral and cultural institutions go sour, if that salt loses its savor, all the rest of ordered liberty is lost: The polity is doomed to division and self-destruction, the economy to hedonism and raw self-interest.

It is absolutely critical to the American experiment, therefore, that the institutions of conscience, information, culture, and moral reflection retain this primacy. Should there ever be a "treason of the clergy," all is lost.

We began with predictions of doom for American culture by Joseph Schumpeter and Daniel Bell. However accurate and penetrating their comments may be, their pessimism need not be paralyzing. For if the primary flaw in our political economy lies not so much in our political system (democracy being a flawed and poor type of governance, until compared to the alternatives), and not so much in our economic system (capitalism being a flawed and poor organization of economy, except compared to the alternatives), *but in our moral–cultural system*, then their prognosis may in the end be more hopeful than it first appears. For if the fatal flaw lies most of all in our ideas and morals, then its source lies not in our stars but in ourselves. And there, by the grace of God, we have a chance to mend our ways. Good ideas can (and often do) drive out bad ideas. If the flaw lies in ourselves—especially in our moral, intellectual, and cultural behavior—then we ourselves have a magnificent opportunity to do something about it. That is all that free women and men can ask. A chance. No guarantee, but a chance.

## THE POPE'S CHALLENGE TO THE U.S.

If I am not mistaken, this is more or less the diagnosis that Joseph Cardinal Ratzinger and Pope John Paul II have for several years now been applying to the United States. They appeal to our elites, most of all, on the plane of ideas and on the terrain of morals and of faith. They call us to step back from ourselves and to look at ourselves as others abroad see us. They ask us to look at the moral decadence visible to outsiders in American films, videotapes, music, television shows, magazines, newspapers, novels, and books, all of which our culture sends as emissaries across the world. Are we not embarrassed by *Dallas*, spoof though it may be, a series (at last count) being shown in 77 different nations of the earth? Just recently a young Korean-American attorney in Washington, DC, wrote that the young people of his nation of origin, just two decades ago wildly pro-American, have come to hold our nation in contempt for its inconstancy and change-ability, and for its public immorality. He begged the proper authorities to take American Armed Forces television off the airwaves, where it is shocking to South Koreans; but if we mean to keep it, at least to keep it on restricted cable lines which only Americans can watch, in quarantined self-corruption.[17]

In many ways, of course, U.S. culture is a much-admired model and pace-setter. Our films, our music, and even many of our books are both appreciated and imitated in every corner of the world. Nonetheless, it is also widely recognized that public exposure to various of the products of American pop culture do tend to generate a loosening of morals.

I do not think that our mass media are quite as decadent as some in our midst often say. Any well-told story requires the dramatization of the essential components of human moral action. Drama and narrative, even in the most attenuated forms, necessarily pay testimony to the basic capacities of the human soul for reflection and choice, and for the courage necessary to sustain both. Nonetheless, it can hardly be said that ours is an age of moral toughness, or that our public media of communication typically (or even often) present fully Christian or Jewish visions of the moral life. Such visions would have a great deal to say about our falls into temptation, about human sinfulness, and about the human weakness to which all of us are prey. It is not the portrayal of weakness and sinfulness that constitutes decadence; it is, rather, giving in to weakness and calling it virtue. It is not weakness that makes for decadence, but moral dishonesty. A fully Christian—or Jewish—vision cerainly would be much less likely than much of what we see today to call sin virtue, and virtue sin.

On a more profound level, the level of "serious" culture, Lionel Trilling—America's preeminent critic of culture—noted the detached (even hostile) point of view deeply embedded in today's cultural elites. It is not unusual for art to assume that at least some persons may "extricate themselves from the culture into which they were born."

It is not odd in literature to take virtually for granted "the adversary intention, the actually subversive intention, that characterizes modern writing." There is not even anything surprising in its clear purpose of "detaching the reader from the habits of thought and feeling that the larger culture imposes, of giving him a ground and a vantage point from which to judge and condemn, and perhaps revise, the culture that produced him."[18]

This adversary intention in modern art is more than a century old, Trilling continues, but

> the circumstances in which it has its existence have changed materially ... The difference can be expressed quite simply in numerical terms— there are a great many more people who adopt the adversary program than there formerly were. Between the end of the first quarter of the century into the present time there has grown up a populous group whose members take for granted the idea of the adversary culture. This group is to be described not only by its increasing size but by its increasing coherence. It is possible to think of it as a class. As such, it of course has its internal conflicts and contradictions but also its common interests and presuppositions and a considerable efficiency of organization, even of an institutional kind.[19]

Trilling notes that "Three or four decades ago, the university figured as the citadel of conservatism, even of reason." The phrase "ivory tower" suggested its safe removal from the acids of modernism. Taste, however, "has increasingly come under the control of criticism, which has made art out of what is not art and the other way around," and now this "making and unmaking of art is in the hands of university art departments and the agencies which derive from them, museums and professional publications."[20]

Trilling's is the classic text identifying a specific "adversary culture" within U.S. culture, a culture that now governs the mainstream in the universities, the magazines, movies, and television. Coincident with its rise is the gradual collapse of the prestige of scientific and technical elites, and even of the idea of progress. This adversary culture celebrates the antibourgeois virtues. By its own innermost intention, it defines itself *against* the common culture. It has increasingly lost its connection with ordinary people, whom it is inclined to scorn. *They* are religious, but the adversary culture is not. More than 100 million Americans attend church or synagogue every weekend, but the so-called popular culture of Hollywood and television is ignorant of this powerful vein of popular life.

The literature concerning the existence of this "new adversary class" is already vast.[21] Critics have long since linked Eastern European discussions of the new class in socialist societies, such as are found in the work of Milovan Djilas, with the adversary culture in Western societies.

Indeed, the hardest part of the moral task we now face is the immense power of that adversary culture. To oppose that power is to risk excommunication from the mainstream. Nonetheless, as Trilling (who loved modernist works) was compelled by intellectual honesty to state, the intention of the modernist project is to subvert the classic Jewish, Christian, and natural (as well as "bourgeois") virtues. It is to perform a massive transvaluation of values, to turn the moral world upside down. It is to insinuate that what Jews and Christians have for centuries called sin is actually a high form of liberation, and that what for centuries Jews and Christians have thought to be virtuous is actually vicious. It is to hate what Jews and Christians love, and to love what Jews and Christians hate.

Ironically, the very virtue of progressivism that is its most endearing quality—namely, its openmindedness—stands here defenseless. In trying to be broad-minded about the modernist subversion, even many Christians give it the best possible interpretation, and ascribe to the traditional Jewish and Christian agenda the most negative and hostile associations. Thus it happens that, in the name of launching a counterculture, some progressives baptize the worst features of the contemporary modernist project. In the name of openness, they try to shock the bourgeois middle class by collaborating in this deliberate transvaluation of values.

The truth is, there is all too little resistance to both the modernist project and the adversary culture. To oppose these would cause one to seem to be unsophisticated, backward, and unwashed. Thus does the treason of the intellectuals proceed as silently and effectively—and for the most part as undetectably—as a cloud of invisible but deadly gas.

To the extent that the Catholic Church is and must be countercultural, will it wish to link its criticism of U.S. culture with the criticism of that culture made by the new adversary class? This is certainly a temptation. It has tempted many socialists—particularly those in Latin cultures such as Southern Europe and Latin America who have become enamored of the project launched by the Italian communist Antonio Gramsci (1891–1937).[22] According to Gramsci, it is a mistake to understand socialism as an economic doctrine, and thus to tie socialism to the outmoded economic theories of the Marxists of the nineteenth century. On the contrary, democratic and capitalist societies have proven that they can raise up the proletariat into the middle class rather quickly. Therefore, Gramsci argued, the true socialist project lies not in the realm of economics, but in the realm of culture. The true socialist is an adversary of Western culture, both in its Christian and in its bourgeois aspects. A "long march through the institutions" (to borrow a later phrase) must be undertaken to subvert Western culture and its fundamental values.

In reviewing Michael Barone's book *Our Country: The Shaping of America from Roosevelt to Reagan,*[23] James Q. Wilson asked: Why did the American elite, which seemed so confident of its own policies and of the basic goodness of our system of governance at the beginning of the 1960s, turn so violently against it in the years centering on 1967 and 1968? I know that *I* did, in "The Secular Saint" (1967) and *A Theology for Radical Politics* (1969),[24] too much moved by the war in Vietnam, the rise of "black power," the moral arrogance of liberal technocrats on the campuses, the assassinations of John F. Kennedy, Robert F. Kennedy, and Martin Luther King, Jr. In any case, from pride in government service and optimism about "new frontiers," Jeff Bell points out, "Around 1967, the balance of powerful political and journalistic elites began to tip toward the views of society's harshest critics."[25]

Michael Barone, reviewing those events, writes: "The liberal elites, so smug and confident at the beginning of the decade, turned their face away from events that were in most cases the consequences of their own acts and found fault with the larger society instead."[26] Thus, the "adversary culture" of the 1950s became the "counterculture," a "movement" suddenly swollen by journalists, movie producers, TV stars, and radicalized professors whose favorite passion became rage— contempt for our own system.

As Jeff Bell shows, a great gap opened up between the elite and the people; a larger gap than ever. (This split is what worried me, and made me draw back, even in the last chapter of *A Theology for Radical Politics*.) It was particularly marked in the Democratic Party, whose strength had theretofore come from close cooperation between the intellectual elites and the people of the neighborhoods, unions, and city "machines." The party split asunder, and the "Reagan Democrats" began to emerge. The key differences were moral. Moral relativism and equality of result held primacy in the counterculture; the great bulk of the population retained traditional values. This was the theme of *The Rise of the Unmeltable Ethnics.*

Is the adversary culture the counterculture that the Catholic Church ought to join? The Gramsci project is aimed specifically at intellectual elites not only in the universities but also in the organs of mass culture and in the governmental bureaucracies that have administrative powers over the works of culture, wherever radio, television, and the arts are supported by the state. In this respect, the term "intellectuals" is to be understood in a very broad sense; it signifies the whole range of intellectual workers in the realm of symbol-making and the propagation of values. Both politically and intellectually, therefore, the central debate of our time has switched increasingly from politics and economics to culture. Christian and Jewish intellectuals will need to be very careful in choosing where and how to direct their efforts in this more general debate. As the Church arrives on the field, the battles have already been joined. The question now appears to be: Having at last reached this crucial battleground, what should we do?

## PROTECTING THE MORAL ECOLOGY

In the Jewish community, Irving Kristol has pointed out,[27] there has long been a division of labor. Receiving most notice down the ages have been the Jewish prophets of the Old Testament. But the prophets, Kristol notes, were relatively few in number and of considerably less than immediate relevance to the daily lives of most ordinary people. To meet these ordinary needs, the rabbinic tradition has nurtured the custom of practical commentary, carried through in the Talmud and in associated practical writings. The rabbis greatly outnumbered the prophets, not only in raw numbers but also in the magnitude of their daily influence.

In the Catholic tradition, by analogy, there have also been two major lines of development—one incarnational, the other eschatological.

More than typical Protestant communities, the Catholic community has tried to emphasize the presence of Christ in daily physical life, the incarnation of Christ in culture. It has blessed harvests, tools, and objects of daily living. It has tried to awaken the baptized to the reality that the kingdom of God has already begun in them and among them. Catholic faith welcomes ordinary life, even blesses it; this is, so to speak, its priestly or rabbinic work.

On the other hand, not only through its tradition of celibacy and the "setting aside" of a special way of life for nuns, priests, and brothers, the Catholic tradition has also tried to maintain an eschatological witness, a sense of rupture with this world and its ordinary demands, an anticipation of the kingdom to come. This witness is akin to that of the prophets of old. It is not a gnostic witness. Consistently, the Catholic Church has set its face against the "spiritualizers" and the "enthusiasts"[28]—that is, against those who would interpret Christianity as a project for fleeing from the world, for rejecting the world, or for merely condemning the world. Since "God so loved the world that he gave his only Son" (John 3:16), it affirms the goodness of each being and every event within the providential order. In every aspect of being, it has seen mystery, fruitfulness, and the presence of God.

In one moment, then, the Catholic tendency is to affirm every culture in which it finds itself. In another moment, it has always called every culture beyond itself and toward the kingdom yet to come and, thus, has set itself up as a counterculture. For the Catholic community to be truly Catholic, both moments are indispensable. Every Christian should represent in his or her own project in life both of these emphases. Each should be at home in the world, and work within it with affirmation and love; simultaneously, each should be in the world as a stranger.

But not so much as a stranger that one falls into uncritical lockstep with a treacherous ally. By now, the new adversary class has more than fulfilled its adversary intention. Hardly any aspect of the U.S. system—political, economic, and moral–cultural—escapes withering criticsm, often unfair and inaccurate criticism. Much of this criticism serves the self-interest of those who want to expand the powers and expenditures of the state. (There is profit in this prophet motive.) That such criticism is self-interested would matter little if it were accurate and fair. Most often, the appetite for prosecution outweighs the appetite for fair rebuttal. The sense of possessing a superior moral standing often overpowers a willingness to see the other side.

No democratic capitalist regime should pretend to be the kingdom of God. The U.S. regime, in particular, has been deliberately contrived to operate within a world of sin and fallibility, supplying to every ambition a counterambition. Such a political economy is self-consciously imperfect, flawed, and resolved to make the best out of the weak materials of human nature. "If men were angels, no government would be necessary," Madison wrote in *Federalist* 51. But men are not angels. Thus, criticism and prophecy do not of themselves injure a democratic capitalist regime. Even false prophecy and misplaced criticism may be put to creative use. Still, criticism and prophetic claims need to be assessed according to how accurately and creatively they are launched. Critics—and in particular the adversary culture—must in turn carry the burden of being *self*-critical. They must, if they are to be taken seriously, make sure that the interests they serve are truly just.

During the last 60 years or so, in interpreting the social doctrine of the Church, a great deal has been written about politics and (more recently) economics. No doubt this work has been necessary and valuable. It is surprising, however, to note the lack of sustained criticism regarding the culture of liberty. Neither a sound economy nor sound politics can be maintained for long in an atmosphere of decadence.

Pope John Paul II particularly has called upon U.S. Catholics to question our nation's widely diffused public morality as it is witnessed in the international media of communication that have so dramatic an effect upon the rest of the world. In raising this challenge, the Pope goes to the heart of our system's most glaring weakness (just when, ironically, many "progressive" Catholic theologians have been complaining that Rome does not understand U.S. culture). The Pope even raises the complementary question: Do American Catholic theologians *themselves* understand American culture? He has opened a debate about the true moral standing of U.S. culture: Is it really something that the rest of the world—including Rome—should emulate?

A distinction may be useful. There are certain virtues inherent in the successful practice of democratic polities and capitalist economies. These may be thought of as those parts of public morality that are embodied in *institutional* practices, and are accordingly thought of as the specifically "democratic" and "capitalist" virtues. But there are other virtues—equally necessary for the successful practice of democracy and capitalism—proper to the moral–cultural sphere itself.

When "progressive" Catholic theologians speak admiringly of the high moral standards of the U.S. experience, often they have in mind the panoply of virtues associated with democratic *institutions*: open inquiry, due process, judgment by a jury of one's peers, and the like. This, too, is a form of public morality. Both the political institutions and the economic institutions of the free society implicitly contain hidden references to the specific new virtues required to make these institutions function according to their own inner rules. Too seldom do we make these underlying virtues explicit in our thinking, despite the fact that they are quite different from the virtues of traditional societies. They include such modern virtues as the responsibilities of free, sovereign citizens, self-reliance, cooperativeness, openness, and personal economic enterprise. They are acquired during that long process of learning the habits of democratic living to which Tocqueville often refers.[29]

By comparison, the virtues proper to the moral–cultural system are distinct (but not separate) from the virtues proper to the political system. The founders of the U.S. order, such as Thomas Jefferson and James Madison, understood quite clearly the connection between the virtues of the moral order and those of the political order.

Thus, when Pope John Paul II suggests that the U.S. media of communication may be undercutting the practice of the moral virtues, he is implying, as well, a threat to the survival of democratic institutions. If true, this is a devastating criticism. It suggests that the very qualities of U.S. institutions that the "progressive" Catholic theologians profess to admire are being undermined by the widely broadcast public morality of our country's major media of communication. This would represent a form of pollution in the moral order even more destructive than the pollution of the physical environment. There is, so to speak, an ecology in morals as well as in the biosphere.[30]

The analysis offered by the Pope seems to be well aimed. Many important moral virtues *are* required to make a free and democratic society function according to its own inner logic; there is a set of moral virtues without which democratic institutions *cannot* be made to work. The fundamental premise of republican life is the concept of *ordered* liberty.[31]

The phrase "ordered liberty" follows the classical definition of practical wisdom, *recta ratio agendi* (the ordered reason in action). To hit the mark exactly, Aristotle observed, practical reason must be governed by (*recta*, corrected by) a good will. To do the truth, we must first love the truth—and love it well and accurately. In a similar way, to be truly free, our passions and appetites must be governed by a well-ordered love of the inner law of our humanity. In this sense, the exercise of freedom is a form of obedience to the truth—the truth about our own human nature.[32] For Christians, this truth is revealed only in Christ, the Logos "in whom, by whom, and with whom" were made all the things that were made. For those who are not Christian believers, the outlines of an analogous truth are also revealed in "the things that were made"—the habitual weakness of humans, combined with possibilities of love and renewal.[33]

## THE INSTITUTIONAL TASK

All around the world people who have suffered under socialist and traditionalist institutions are longing for a freer life. They dream of living under institutions that would liberate their human capacities for reflection and for choice. There is a longing in the human heart to live under a system of natural liberty—that is, under those sorts of institutions that allow the human soul to express itself naturally in all three major fields of life: political, economic, and moral–cultural. The vast majority of peoples on this planet, in the past and still today, have not lived under such institutions. But the broad outlines of these institutions are now fairly well known to most of the peoples of the world. They have glimpsed these outlines through their own harsh experiences under meaner alternatives.

Thus, with Pope John Paul II, most people seem to understand today that their best protection from torture, tyranny, and other forms of political oppression derives from living under institutions that are (a) subject to the consent of the governed, (b) protective of minority rights, and (c) designed around internal sets of checks and balances. We have in fact been hearing a great deal more about "democracy," even in cultures in which the very word has long been spoken of (as in "bourgeois democracy") with much disdain.

Similarly, since neither communist nor traditionalist societies seem to be capable of producing the goods which the poor of the world need and desire, the reputation of the hitherto much-scorned system, capitalism, is growing. In an ever-increasing number of countries one hears the demand for freer markets, for private property, and for incentives that reward greater labor and superior skills. Human beings can scarcely help desiring to express in their institutions and daily practices their God-given capacities for personal economic intitiative and creativity.

Finally, in such places as the former Soviet Union and the Peoples Republic of China, in South Africa and throughout Black Africa, in Latin America and elsewhere, the cry of most people is for "openness"—for institutions that permit the free exercise of liberty of conscience, inquiry, and expression.

In sum, most citizens of the world seek the three basic institutional liberations of human life: a free polity, a free economy, and a free moral–cultural system. This is seldom today a matter of ideology; it has arisen from harsh lessons of trial and error. One cannot speak of these three liberations without also speaking of *institutions*. And one can hardly speak of institutions without speaking of the *moral virtues* that sustain them.

For human rights are not protected by words on parchment. They are protected by habits, free associations, and independent judicial institutions. Moreover, the institutions that protect human rights do not *coerce* conscience, or *force* citizens to develop their individual moral and spiritual capacities. Those institutions create space for those achievements—but do not automatically produce them. Thus, the mere achievement of the basic institutions of political and economic liberty will not itself fulfill human moral and spiritual longing. Politics and economics are not enough. That is why the next frontier for those who think counterculturally concerns the moral and spiritual dimension of culture.

We come around then to the theme that Pope John Paul II set forth in the beginning as the *leitmotif* of his pontificate: the primacy of morals. Here is where the next and most important battles lie.

Solving serious national and international problems is not just a matter of economic production or of juridical or social organization, but calls for ethical and religious values. There is hope that the many people who profess no religion will also contribute to providing the necessary ethical foundation. But the Christian churches and the world religions will have a preeminent role in . . . building a society worthy of man.[34]

Building up civilizations that respect the true and nature-fulfilling "moral ecology" in which the virtues of ordered liberty flourish is a demanding task which will occupy the human race throughout the coming ages.

In this task, the institutions of the mass media—the much-vaunted "entertainment industry"—incur very high responsibilities, which they have barely begun to face. They, too, must be held to account. Because their influence upon the moral air we breathe and on the moral ecology we inhabit is vast, the prospects of the free society, and the virtues proper to ordered liberty, depend on their performance. The moral nobility of their task is far greater than they seem yet to recognize.

## NOTES

1. Congregation for the Doctrine of the Faith, "Instruction on Christian Freedom and Liberation" (Vatican City: Vatican Polyglot Press, 1986), 7.
2. Hannah Arendt, *On Revolution* (New York: The Viking Press, 1965), 49.
3. Lionel Trilling, *Beyond Culture: Essays on Literature and Learning* (New York: The Viking Press, 1968).
4. Arendt, 49 (italics added).
5. At a critical point in the Constitutional Convention on June 28, 1787, Franklin suggested the depths of the Framers' struggle to concur on a new order:

   We indeed seem to feel our own want of political wisdom, since we have been running about in search of it. We have gone back to ancient history for models of Government, and examined the different forms of those Republics which having been formed with the seeds of their own dissolution now no longer exist. And we have viewed Modern States all round Europe, but find none of their Constitutions suitable to our circumstances (Speech of Benjamin Franklin to the Federal Convention, June 28, 1787, cited in James Madison, *Notes of Debates in the Federal Convention of 1787* [New York: W. W. Norton & Co., 1987], 209).

6.  *The Federalist Papers*, No. 14.

7.  Arendt, 15.

8.  Crèvecoeur describes the new prosperity:

> The American ought therefore to love this country much better
> than that wherein either he or his forefathers were born. Here the
> rewards of his industry follow with equal steps the progress of his
> labour; his labour is founded on the basis of nature, *self-interest*; can
> it want a stronger allurement? Wives and children, who before in
> vain demanded of him a morsel of bread, now, fat and frolicsome,
> gladly help their father to clear those fields whence exuberant crops
> are to arise to feed and to clothe them all; without any part being
> claimed, either by a despotic prince, a rich abbot, or a mighty lord
> (Hector St. John Crèvecoeur, *Letter from an American Farmer* [1782;
> reprint ed., New York: Fox, Duffield & Co., 1904], 55).

9.  In Tocqueville's words:

> If patient observation and sincere meditation have led men of the
> present day to recognize that both the past and the future of their
> history consist in the gradual and measured advance of equality,
> that discovery in itself gives this progress the sacred character of
> the will of the Sovereign Master. In that case effort to halt democ-
> racy appears as a fight against God Himself, and nations have no
> alternative but to acquiesce in the social state imposed by Provi-
> dence (Alexis de Tocqueville, *Democracy in America*, trans. George
> Lawrence, ed. J. P. Mayer [Garden City: Anchor Books, 1969], 12).

10. "The Miami Meeting with President Reagan," *Origins* 17 (September 24,
    1987): 238.

11. "Is there no virtue among us?" asked Madison defiantly. "If there be not,
    we are in a wretched situation. No theoretical checks, no form of govern-
    ment, can render us secure. To suppose any form of government will
    secure liberty or happiness without any virtue in the people, is a chimeri-
    cal idea." Jonathan Elliot, ed., *Debates in the Several State Conventions on
    the Adoption of the Federal Constitution* (Philadelphia: Lippincott, 1907),
    Virginia, June 20, 1788.

12. Russell Kirk, *The Roots of American Order* (Washington, DC: Regnery Gate-
    way, 1992).

13. Hamilton wrote as follows (except for the italicizations) to the people of
    the United States, in *Federalist* 1:

> You are called upon to deliberate on a new Constitution for the
> United States of America. . . . It has frequently been remarked that it

seems to have been reserved to the people of this country, by their conduct and example, to decide the important question, whether societies of men are really capable or not of establishing good government from *reflection* and *choice*, or whether they are forever destined to depend for their political constitutions on accident and force.

14. Arendt, 15.

15. John Adams wrote in 1809:

> I will insist that the Hebrews have done more to civilize men than any other nation. If I were an atheist, and believed in blind eternal fate, I should still believe that fate had ordained the Jews to be the most essential instrument for civilizing the nations. If I were an athiest of the other sect, who believe or pretend to believe that all is ordered by chance, I should believe that chance had ordered the Jews to preserve and propagate to all mankind the doctrine of a supreme, intelligent, wise, almighty sovereign of the universe, which I believe to be the great essential principle of all morality, and consequently of all civilization (John Adams to F. A. Vanderkemp, February 16, 1809, in C. F. Adams, ed., *The Works of John Adams* [Boston: Little, Brown, 1854], 9: 609–10).

16. "The basis of our governments being the opinion of the people, the very first object should be to keep that right [a free press]; and were it left to me to decide whether we should have a government without newspapers, or newspapers without a government, I should not hesitate a moment to prefer the latter." Letter to Edward Carrington, January 16, 1787, in *Thomas Jefferson* (New York: Literary Classics of the United States, Inc., 1984), 880.

17. Sung-Chull Junn, "Why Koreans Think We're Jerks," *Washington Post*, "Outlook," April 9, 1989.

18. Trilling, xii. Irving Kristol adds an important clarification, which is that the new class is adversarial not just to the practices of the nation but to its ideals:

> We are so used to this fact of our lives, we take it so for granted, that we fail to realize how extraordinary it is. Has there ever been in all of recorded history, a civilization whose culture was at odds with the values and ideals of that civilization itself? It is not uncommon that a culture will be critical of the civilization that sustains it—and always critical of the failure of this civilization to realize perfectly the ideals that it claims as inspiration. Such criticism is implicit or

explicit in Aristophanes and Euripides, Dante and Shakespeare. But to take an adversary posture toward the ideals themselves? That is unprecedented. . . . The more "cultivated" a person is in our society, the more disaffected and malcontent he is likely to be—a disaffection, moreover, directed not only at the actuality of our society but at the ideality as well. Indeed, the ideality may be more strenuously opposed than the actuality (Irving Kristol, *Reflections of a Neoconservative: Looking Back, Looking Ahead* [New York: Basic Books, 1983], 27–28).

19. Trilling, xii.

20. Ibid., xiv–xv.

21. A useful introduction to the "new class" may be found in B. Bruce-Briggs, *The New Class?* (New Brunswick: Transaction Books, 1979). In *Beyond Culture*, Lionel Trilling showed the influence of the new class in literature; for the influence of the new class on politics and economics see, respectively, Jeane J. Kirkpatrick, "Politics and the 'New Class'," *Dictatorships and Double Standards: Rationalism and Reason in Politics* (New York: American Enterprise Institute and Simon and Schuster, 1982), 186–203; and Irving Kristol, *Two Cheers for Capitalism* (New York: Basic Books, 1978), chap. 2, "Business and the 'New Class'," 25–31.

   In Marxist countries the danger of a new class was discerned as early as 1939 by Bruno Rizzi; see his *The Bureaucratization of the World*, trans. with intro. by Adam Westoby (New York: The Free Press, 1986). Almost simultaneously, James Burnham discerned an equivalent to the new class in *The Managerial Revolution* (New York: John Day Co., 1941). The concept became prominent on the left with the publication of Milovan Djilas's *The New Class* (New York: Praeger, 1957). In the United States writers on the left, such as John Kenneth Galbraith, David T. Bazelon, and Michael Harrington began to point to the "new class" as a potential ally of—if not a replacement for—the proletariat. See Galbraith, *The Affluent Society* (Boston: Houghton Mifflin, 1967), and Harrington, *Toward a Democratic Left* (New York: Macmillan, 1968), 265–97.

22. See *Antonio Gramsci: Selections from Political Writings, 1910–1920*, trans. John Mathews (Ann Arbor: Books on Demand, UMI, 1976). See also Jaime Antunez, "Socialism Chic," *Crisis* 7 (April 1989): 38–40.

23. Jeffrey Bell, *Populism and Elitism: Politics in the Age of Equality* (Washington, DC: Regnery, 1992), xvi.

24. Michael Novak, "The Secular Saint," *Illinois State University Journal* 30 (September 1967): 3–35; id., *A Theology for Radical Politics* (New York: Herder & Herder, 1969).

25. Bell, xvi.
26. Ibid., xvii.
27. Kristol distinguishes two poles in the tradition:

    The terms "prophetic" and "rabbinic" which come, of course, from the Jewish tradition, indicate the two poles within which the Jewish tradition operates. They are not two equal poles: The rabbinic is the stronger pole, always. In an Orthodox Hebrew school, the prophets are read only by those who are far advanced. The rest of the students read the first five books of the Bible, and no more. They learn the Law. The prophets are only for people who are advanced in their learning and not likely to be misled by prophetic fever (Kristol, *Reflections of a Neoconservative*, 316–17).

28. See Ronald A. Knox, *Enthusiasm* (Westminster, MD: Christian Classics, 1983).
29. "It cannot be repeated too often: nothing is more fertile in marvels than the art of being free, but nothing is harder than freedom's apprenticeship. . . . But liberty is generally born in stormy weather, growing with difficulty amid civil discords, and only when it is already old does one see the blessings it has brought." Tocqueville, 240.

    Living on the boundary between the traditional society and the democratic society, Tocqueville himself saw more clearly than most the differences in the virtues required in the democratic, as opposed to aristocratic, societies. (He saw these as differences more clearly with respect to political institutions than he did with respect to economic institutions.)

30. "Yet more serious is the destruction of the *human environment*. People are rightly worried about the extinction of animal species, but too little effort is made to *safeguard the moral conditions for an authentic 'human ecology.'*" *Centesimus Annus*, #38.
31. "There is," writes Cotton Mather, "a *liberty* of corrupt nature, which is affected by *men* and *beasts* to do what they list; and this *liberty* is inconsistent with *authority*, impatient of all restraint; by this *liberty*, *Sumus Omnes Deteriores*, 'tis the grand enemy of *truth* and *peace*, and all the *ordinances* of God are bent against it. But there is a civil, a moral, a federal *liberty* . . . for that only which is *just* and *good*; for this *liberty* you are to stand with the hazard of your very *lives*." Cited in Tocqueville, 46.
32. This is clearly recognized in the recent encyclical:

    A person who is concerned solely or primarily with possessing and enjoying, who is no longer able to control his instincts and passions, or to subordinate them by obedience to the truth, cannot be free: *obedience to the truth* about God and man is the first condition of freedom, making it possible for a person to order his needs and desires and to choose the means of satisfying them according to a correct scale of values, so that the ownership of things may become an occasion of growth for him (*Centesimus Annus*, #41).

For the inseparability of obedience and freedom as understood by the Pope, see Karol Cardinal Wojtyla, "The Eucharist and Man's Hunger for Freedom," Homily given at the Forty-first International Eucharistic Congress in Philadelphia, August 3, 1976 (Daughters of St. Paul Pamphlets, 1978):

> Freedom has been given to him by his Creator not in order to commit what is evil (cf. Gal. 5:13), but to do good. God also bestowed upon man understanding and conscience to show him what is good and what ought to be done, what is wrong and what ought to be avoided. God's commandments help our understanding and our conscience on their way. The greatest commandment—that of love—leads the way to the fullest use of liberty (cf. 1 Cor. 9:19–22; 13:1–13). Freedom has been given to man in order to love, to love true good: to love God above all, to love man as his neighbor and brother (cf. Dt. 6:5; Lv. 19:18; Mk. 12:30–33). Those who obey this truth, this Gospel, the real disciples of eternal Wisdom, achieve thus, as the Council puts it, a state of "royal freedom," for they follow "that King whom to serve is to reign."
>
> Freedom is therefore offered to man and given to him as a task. He must not only possess it, but also conquer it. He must recognize the work of his life in a good use, in an increasingly good use of his liberty. This is the truly essential, the fundamental work on which the value and the sense of his whole life depend (7–8).

On this same occasion in Philadelphia, the Pope noted the common aspirations of the colonial Americans and his own Polish compatriots:

> This year is the bicentennial of the day when the hunger for freedom ripened in the American society and revealed itself in liberation and the Declaration of Independence of the United States. Tadeusz Kosciuszko and Kazimierz Pulaski, my compatriots, participated in this fight for independence. The heroes of the Polish nation became heroes of American independence. And all this took place at the time when the Polish Kingdom, a big state consisting of three nations, the Poles, the Lithuanians and the Ruthenians, was beginning to lose its independence, and by degrees became the prey of its rapacious neighbors, Russia, Germany and Austria. At the same time while the United States of America was gaining independence,

we were losing it for a period of more than a hundred years. And many heroic efforts and sacrifices, similar to those of Kosciuszko and Pulaski, had been necessary to ripen anew the freedom of the nation, to test it before all the world and to express it in time by the independence of our country (10–11).

33. See Michael Novak, "Christ: The Great Divide," *Crisis* (July–August 1992): 2–3.

34. *Centesimus Annus*, #60.

*1993*

# CHRISTOPHER LASCH

Historian, moralist, and social critic, Christopher Lasch (1932–1994) was himself not an avowed conservative. Yet in the last third of the twentieth century, no writer advanced a more trenchant critique of liberalism. For Lasch, it was of paramount importance to insulate the family from the fragmentation caused by relentless exposure to the forces of consumer capitalism and what he called, in the title of his most famous book, "the culture of narcissism."

———

## The Soul of Man under Secularism

M Y TITLE comes from a little book by Oscar Wilde, *The Soul of Man under Socialism*, which was published a little more than a hundred years ago, in February 1891. Wilde's intention, as always, was to dazzle and scandalize his readers, and *his* title served as a typically Wildean affront to respectable opinion. It linked a concept derived from religion, the soul, with an aggressively secular ideology that drew much of its inspiration from Marx's famous condemnation of religion as the opiate of the people.

This was perhaps the only Marxist dictum that Wilde could endorse without reservation. He was hardly an orthodox Socialist. "We are all of us more or less Socialists now-a-days," he told an interviewer in 1894, but his own version of the socialist creed celebrated the artist, not the horny-handed son of toil, and conceived of socialism, moreover, as the best hope for a new kind of individualism—a "new Hellenism," as he referred to it in the closing pages of his non-Communist manifesto. Orthodox Marxists ridiculed his aesthetic brand of socialism, but Wilde had the last laugh. His religion of art has survived the collapse of the Marxist utopia. Of all the secular religions that emerged in the nineteenth century, this one turned out to be the most durable—in its own way the most seductive and insidious as well.

Socialism, as Wilde understood it, was simply another name—in 1891, in the social circles in which Wilde was at home, a deliberately provocative name—for the elimination of drudgery by machines. Wilde had no patience with those who proclaimed the dignity of labor. "There is nothing necessarily dignified about manual labor at all, and most of it is absolutely degrading." In the future it would be done by sophisticated machinery. The progress of science and technology would gradually eliminate poverty, suffering, and injustice. The collectivization of production would liberate the poor from want, but it would also liberate the rich from the burden of managing and defending their property. If manual labor was degrading, property was a "bore," in Wilde's opinion. "Its duties make it unbearable. In the interest of the rich we must get rid of it." No less than manual labor, the administration of property distracted people from the real business of life: the cultivation and enjoyment of "personality." Once the state took over the production of useful objects, individuals could devote themselves to the production of "what is beautiful." The "true personality of man" would come into its own. "It will grow naturally and simply, flowerlike, or as a tree grows. . . . It will never argue or dispute. It will not be always meddling with others, or asking them to be like itself. It will love them because they will be different. . . . The personality of man will be very wonderful. It will be as wonderful as the personality of a child."

Socialism, in Wilde's conception, would not come about through the action of the masses. The masses were too stupefied by drudgery to be capable of emancipating themselves. They were "extraordinarily stupid" in their deference to authority. Indeed, they were "not really conscious" of their own suffering. "They have to be told of it by other people"—by "agitators," an "absolutely necessary" class without whom "there would be no advance towards civilization." Agitators were the political equivalent of artists: disturbers of the peace, enemies of conformity, rebels against custom. They shared with artists a hatred of authority, a contempt for tradition, and a refusal to court popular favor. Agitators and artists were the supreme embodiment of individualism, wishing only to please themselves. They took "no notice whatever of the public." Nor did they pay the slightest attention to the "sickly cant about doing what other people want because they want it; or any hideous cant about self-sacrifice." Artists were accountable only to themselves, and their selfishness, as it might be regarded from the point of view of conventional morality, was the precondition of any genuine achievement of the imagination. All the great leaders in history, according to Wilde, had the artistic temperament. Jesus Christ himself was an artist with an artist's message to the world. "He said to man, 'You have a wonderful personality. Develop it. Be yourself.'"

In his *De Profundis*, the long letter to Lord Alfred Douglas written six years later from the depths of his imprisonment in Reading Gaol, Wilde amplified this interpretation of "Christ as the precursor of the romantic movement in life," the "most supreme of individualists." Having "created himself" out of "his own imagination," Jesus of Nazareth preached the power of imagination as the "basis of all spiritual and material life," according to Wilde. He preached imaginative sympathy, not altruism, but his own powers of sympathetic identification made him the "mouthpiece" of the "entire world of the inarticulate, the voiceless world of pain." His life, as recorded in the Gospels, was "just like a work of art." He belonged "with the poets," and "his chief war was against the Philistines"—the "war that every child of light has to wage." Even in the depths of his own public degradation and despair, Wilde saw no reason to modify what he had written in *The Soul of Man under Socialism*: "that he who would lead a Christ-like life must be entirely and absolutely himself." As he put it in the earlier text, "The message of Christ to man was simply 'Be thyself.' That is the message of Christ."

This kind of message, whether or not it came from Christ and whether or not it was cast in a purely secular idiom or in the pseudo-spiritual idiom of *De Profundis*, appealed to intellectuals in search of a substitute for religious faiths by then widely regarded as offensive to the modern mind. In place of self-denial and self-control, it offered the seductive vision of selfhood unconstrained by civic, familial, or religious obligations. It confirmed artists and intellectuals in their sense of superiority to the common herd. It sanctioned their revolt against convention, against bourgeois solemnity, against stupidity and ugliness. By equating social justice with artistic freedom, the religion of art made socialism palatable to intellectuals who might otherwise have been repelled by its materialism. In the heyday of the socialist movement its attraction for intellectuals cannot be adequately explained without considering the way it overlapped with the bohemian critique of the bourgeoisie. Socialists and aesthetes shared a common enemy, the bourgeois philistine, and the unremitting onslaught against bourgeois culture was far more lasting in its effects, in the West at least and now probably in the East as well, than the attack on capitalism.

In the 1960s revolutionary students adopted slogans much closer in spirit to Wilde than to Marx: "All power to the imagination"; "It is forbidden to forbid." The continuing appeal of such ideas, thirty years later, should be obvious to anyone who casts an eye over the academic scene and the media. The postmodern mood, so called, is defined on the one hand by a disillusionment with grand historical theories or "metanarratives," including Marxism, and by an ideal of personal freedom, on the other hand, that derives in large part from the aesthetic revolt against middle-class culture. The postmodern sensibility rejects much of modernism as well, but it is rooted in the modernist ideal of individuals emancipated from convention, constructing identities for themselves as they choose, leading their own lives (as Oscar Wilde would have said) as if life itself were a work of art.

The tradition of romantic subjectivity had another advantage over Marxism and other ideologies more firmly rooted in the secularizing soil of the Enlightenment. As the child of the Counter-Enlightenment in Germany and England, the romantic tradition was more keenly aware of the limits of enlightened rationality. Without denying the achievements of the Enlightenment, it recognized the danger that the "disenchantment of the world," in Friedrich von Schiller's phrase, would lead to emotional and spiritual impoverishment. Max Weber seized on this phrase as the key to the historical process of rationalization, the central theme of his own work. Reason enhanced human control over nature, but it deprived humanity of the illusion that its activity had any significance beyond itself. Karl Mannheim, Weber's student and successor, referred to this as the "problem of ecstasy." In his essay "The Democratization of Culture," published in 1932, Mannheim reminded his readers that "a man for whom nothing exists beyond his immediate situation is not fully human." The disenchantment of the world made it "flat, uninspiring, and unhappy." It deprived men and women of the experience of ecstasy—literally the trancelike state of being beside oneself, more broadly a state of overmastering feeling, as of rapture. "There is no Beyond; the existing world is not a symbol for the eternal; immediate reality points to nothing beyond itself."

Mannheim believed that the reduction of "vertical distance," which he associated with democracy, at least created the possibility of authentic, "purely existential human relationships" unmediated by religion or by religiously derived ideologies like romantic love. Weber himself was less sanguine. The famous peroration of his *Protestant Ethic and the Spirit of Capitalism*—"specialists without spirit, sensualists without heart"—offered a chilling view of the human prospect. Like Freud, with whom he had much in common, Weber spurned the consolation of religion and its secular substitutes, insisting on the intellectual's duty to "bear the fate of the times like a man." Freud's tone, likewise, was wistful but firm: Let us put away childish things. Likening religion to a "childhood neurosis," Freud insisted that "men cannot remain children forever." He added that "it is something, at any rate, to know that one is thrown upon one's own resources," and there is a certain heroism in the determination of Freud and Weber to face unflinchingly facts that could not be altered, in their view, and to live without illusions.

Those who were looking for something to believe in could hardly find much comfort in this uncompromising commitment to "intellectual integrity," as Weber called it. They were more likely to be attracted to the aestheticism of Oscar Wilde or to Carl Jung's spiritualized version of psychoanalysis. Freud's version, according to Jung, could not "give modern man what he is looking for." It satisfied only "people who believe they have no spiritual needs or aspirations." Contrary to the Freudians, Jung claimed, spiritual needs were too urgent to be ignored. Treating those needs as if they were analogous to hunger or sexual desire, Jung insisted that they would always find expression in one "outlet" or another. Psychoanalysts accordingly discovered in the course of their practice that they could not escape "problems which, strictly speaking, belong to the theologian."

The beauty of Jung's system, for those threatened with "meaninglessness," as he liked to call it, was that it offered "meaning" without turning its back on modernity. Jung assured his followers, in effect, that they could remain thoroughly modern without sacrificing the emotional solace formerly provided by orthodox religion. His description of the modern condition began with the usual reference to the lost childhood of the race. The medieval world, in which "men were all children of God . . . and knew exactly what they should do and how they should conduct themselves," now lay "as far behind as childhood." Its innocence could not be recaptured; the world could only go forward to a "state of wider and higher consciousness." The fully modern man—"by no means the average man"—had to live without "metaphysical certainties"; he was "thrown back upon himself." But self-dependence contained unprecedented opportunities for self-discovery. Freedom was unnerving but exhilarating. Jung's portrait of modern man was more exuberant than Freud's. According to Freud, the disenchantment of the world had deprived people of the childlike security of dependence but at least given them science, which in his modest assessment had taught them "much since the days of the Deluge" and would gradually "increase their powers still further." In Jung's more enthusiastic formulation of this familiar story of enlightenment, modern man "stands upon a peak, or at the very edge of the world, the abyss of the future before him, above him the heavens, and below him the whole of mankind with a history that disappears in primeval mists." The view from the heights was vertiginous but commanding.

The unexamined premise that history can be compared with the individual's growth from childhood to maturity—the point of reference that Jung shared with Freud and Weber, indeed with most of those who speculate about such issues—made it possible to condemn any form of cultural conservatism, any respect for tradition, as an expression of the natural tendency to resist emotional and intellectual growth, to cling instead to the security of childhood. "Only the man who has outgrown the stages of consciousness belonging to the past . . . can achieve a full consciousness of the present."

It was the gifted individual, the one who accepted the burden of maturity, that Jung addressed in the essays collected in 1933 under the inevitable title *Modern Man in Search of a Soul*. By outgrowing tradition, the fully modern individual gained a wider perspective but unavoidably cut himself off from his more conservative fellows. A "fuller consciousness of the present removes him . . . from submersion in a common consciousness," from the "mass of men who live entirely within the bounds of tradition." This is why the solution of the "modern spiritual problem," as Jung called it, could not possibly lie in a return to "obsolete forms of religion," any more than it could lie in a purely secular world view. Neither the Freudian analyst nor the rabbi or pastor gave modern man "what he is looking for." (As the son of a Protestant minister and the spiritual son of Freud, Jung presumably knew what he was talking about. He spoke from direct experience of the rival traditions that competed for his allegiance, secular humanism and orthodox religion.) Freud ignored man's unappeasable hunger for some kind of transcendent "meaning," while conventional religion, on the other hand, ignored the creative individual's need "to break with tradition so that he can experiment with his life and determine what value and meanings things have in themselves, apart from traditional presuppositions." If the Freudian analyst backed away from questions of meaning and value, the pastor passed judgment all too quickly. Modern man, having "heard enough about guilt and sin," was rightly suspicious of "fixed ideas as to what is right," suspicious of spiritual counselors who "pretend to know what is right and what is not." Moral judgment, in any case, took "something away from the richness of experience." The old injunction to follow in the footsteps of the Lord had to be translated into a modern idiom. Sounding very much like Oscar Wilde, Jung took the position that imitation of Christ meant not that "we should copy his life" but that "we are to live with our own proper lives as truly as he lived his in all its implications."

Psychoanalysis served the same purpose in Jung's scheme of things that artistic imagination served in Wilde's. Reformulated so as to overcome Freud's unfortunate preoccupation with sex, it became the means by which to liberate the religious imagination from its enslavement to dying creeds. By providing access not only to the unconscious mental life of individuals but to the "collective unconscious" of the human race, Jungian psychoanalysis excavated the permanent structure of religious mythology, the raw material out of which the modern world might construct new forms of religious life appropriate to its needs. Jung invited his patients and readers to range through the whole array of mythologies and spiritual techniques—all of them equally available for inspection, thanks to the expansion of historical consciousness in the modern world—and to experiment with a variety of combinations until they found the one best suited to their individual requirements.

But I am less interested in Jung's remedy for the spiritual malaise of modernity than in his formulation of the problem and especially in the common assumptions Jung shared even with those who rejected his particular solution. The most important of these assumptions was that the inevitable unfolding of consciousness made it impossible, at least for the educated classes, to return to the childlike security of the past. The educated classes, unable to escape the burden of sophistica- tion, might envy the naïve faiths of the past; they might even envy the classes that continued unthinkingly to observe traditional faiths in the twentieth century, not yet having been exposed to the wintry blasts of modern critical thinking. They could not trade places with the unenlightened masses, however, any more than they could return to the past. Once the critical habit of mind had been fully assimilated, no one who understood its implications could find any refuge or resting place in premodern systems of thought and belief. It was this experi- ence of disillusionment, more than anything else, that was held to distinguish the artist and the intellectual from unreflective creatures of convention, who distrusted artists and intellectuals precisely because they could not bear to hear the bad news.

Unenlightened ages past might be forgiven for believing things no educated person could believe in the twentieth century or for taking literally mythologies better understood in a figurative or metaphori- cal sense; one might even forgive the modern proletarian, excluded from an education by virtue of his unremitting toil, but the bourgeois philistine lived in an enlightened age, with easy access to enlightened culture, yet deliberately chose not to see the light, lest it destroy the illusions essential to his peace of mind. The intellectual alone, in any case, looked straight into the light without blinking.

Disillusioned but undaunted: such is the self-image of modernity, so proud of its intellectual emancipation that it makes no effort to conceal the spiritual price that has to be paid. Again and again com- mentary on the spiritual condition of modernity—on the soul of man in the modern age, on the "modern temper," as Joseph Wood Krutch referred to it—again and again this commentary returns to its favorite biological analogy as the framing device that defines the problem. Krutch uses it too: *The Modern Temper*, published in 1929 and pre- dictably condemned by the philistines he was eager to offend as an overly pessimistic account of the contemporary plight, begins (no less predictably) with the contrast between childish innocence and experience. Krutch starts right off with Freud: "It is one of Freud's quaint conceits that the child in his mother's womb is the happiest of living creatures." Krutch does not reject this "quaint conceit," as his language might lead one to expect; instead he proceeds, as did Freud himself, to argue that "races as well as individuals have their infancy, their adolescence, and their maturity." As the race matures, "the universe becomes more and more what experience has revealed, less and less what imagination has created." Man reluctantly learns that he must depend on himself alone, not on supernatural powers created in his own image. "Like the child growing into manhood, he passes from a world which is fitted to him into a world for which he must fit himself." At the social level the process was still incomplete since the modern world had not completely outlived its past. Its "predicament" could be compared with that of the "adolescent who has not yet learned to orient himself without reference to the mythology amid which his childhood was passed."

There is a vast body of commentary on the modern spiritual plight, all of which assumes that the experience of doubt, moral relativism, and so on is distinctively modern. I have cited a few representative samples, but a more comprehensive and systematic survey of this literature would only confirm the central importance of imagery that links the history of culture to the life cycle of individuals. Following Krutch, we might call it a quaint conceit, this mental habit of playing off our disillusionment against the innocence of our ancestors, except that it originates in an impulse that is anything but quaint and leads to very serious consequences, not least of which is to prevent an understanding of vitally important matters. It betrays a predisposition to read history either as a tragedy of lost illusions or as the progress of critical reason. I say "either/or," but of course, these two versions of the modernist historical myth are closely related; indeed, they are symbiotically dependent on each other. It is the progress of critical reason that allegedly leads to lost illusions. Disillusionment represents the price of progress. Nostalgia and the idea of progress, as I have argued in *The True and Only Heaven*, go hand in hand. The assumption that our own civilization has achieved a level of unparalleled complexity gives rise to a nostalgic yearning for bygone simplicity. From this point of view, the relation of past to present is defined, above all, by the contrast between simplicity and sophistication.

The barrier that divides the past from the present—an impassable barrier, in the imagination of modernity—is the experience of disillusionment, which makes it impossible to recapture the innocence of earlier days. Disillusionment, we might say, is the characteristic form of modern pride, and this pride is no less evident in the nostalgic myth of the past than in the more aggressively triumphal version of cultural progress that dismisses the past without regrets. Nostalgia is superficially loving in its re-creation of the past, but it evokes the past only to bury it alive. It shares with the belief in progress, to which it is only superficially opposed, an eagerness to proclaim the death of the past and to deny history's hold on the present. Those who mourn the death of the past and those who acclaim it both take for granted that our age has outgrown its childhood. Both find it difficult to believe that history still haunts our enlightened, disillusioned adolescence or maturity or senility (whatever stage of the life cycle we have allegedly reached). Both are governed, in their attitude toward the past, by the prevailing disbelief in ghosts.

Perhaps the most important casualty of this habit of mind is a proper understanding of religion. In the commentary on the modern spiritual predicament, religion is consistently treated as a source of intellectual and emotional security, not as a challenge to complacency and pride. Its ethical teachings are misconstrued as a body of simple commandments leaving no room for ambiguity or doubt. Recall Jung's description of medieval Christians as "children of God [who] knew exactly what they should do and how they should conduct themselves." Krutch says much the same thing. Medieval theology, he thinks, made the conduct of life an "exact science." It offered a "plan of life" that was "delightfully simple." Medieval Christians "accepted the laws of God in a fashion exactly parallel to that in which the contemporary scientist accepts the Laws of Nature," and this unquestioning obedience to an authoritative science of morals, according to Krutch, is the only alternative to "moral nihilism." "As soon as one begins to doubt either the validity of the laws of God considered as the fundamental principles of a science which happens to be called theology, or as soon as one begins to raise a question as to the purpose of life," one begins to slide down the slippery slope to relativism, moral anarchy, and cultural despair.

What has to be questioned here is the assumption that religion ever provided a set of comprehensive and unambiguous answers to ethical questions, answers completely resistant to skepticism, or that it forestalled speculation about the meaning and purpose of life, or that religious people in the past were unacquainted with existential despair. The famous collection of songs written by medieval students preparing for the priesthood *Carmina Burana* would be enough in itself to dispel this notion; these disturbing compositions give voice to an age-old suspicion that the universe is ruled by Fortune, not by Providence, that life has no higher purpose at all, and that the better part of moral wisdom is to enjoy it while you can.

Or consider the varieties of religious experience analyzed by William James in his book of that name, one of the few books about the spiritual crisis of modernity (if that, in fact, is its subject) that has stood the test of time, in part—strange to say—because of its complete indifference to issues of historical chronology. To readers formed by the self-consciously modern tradition I have been referring to, this indifference to chronology might appear to be a weakness of James's book, but that is precisely his point: that the deepest variety of religious faith (the "twice-born type," as he calls it) always, in every age, arises out of a background of despair. Religious faith asserts the goodness of being in the face of suffering and evil. Black despair and alienation—which have their origin not in perceptions exclusively modern but in the bitterness always felt toward a God who allows evil and suffering to flourish—often become the prelude to conversion. An awareness of "radical evil" underlies the spiritual intoxication that finally comes with "yielding" and "self-surrender." The experience of the twice-born, according to James, is more painful but emotionally deeper than that of the "healthy-minded" because it is informed by the "iron of melancholy." Having no awareness of evil, the once-born type of religious experience cannot stand up to adversity. It offers sustenance only so long as it does not encounter "poisonous humiliations." "A little cooling down of animal excitability and instinct, a little loss of animal toughness, will bring the worm at the core of all our usual springs of delight into full view, and turn us into melancholy metaphysicians." When that happens, we need a more rugged form of faith, one that recognizes that "life and its negation are beaten up inextricably together" and that "all natural happiness thus seems infected with a contradiction." If nothing else, the shadow of death hangs over our pleasures and triumphs, calling them into question. "Back of everything is the great spectre of universal death, the all-encompassing blackness."

It needs to be emphasized, once again, that James is contrasting two types of temperament, not two ages of man. The modern world has no monopoly on the fear of death or the alienation from God. Alienation is the normal condition of human existence. Rebellion against God is the natural reaction to the discovery that the world was not made for our personal convenience. The further discovery that suffering is visited on the just and unjust alike is hard to square with a belief in a benign and omnipotent creator, as we know from the Book of Job. But it is the comfortable belief that the purposes of the Almighty coincide with our purely human purposes that religious faith requires us to renounce.

Krutch argues that religion gives man the agreeable illusion that he is the center of the universe, the object of God's loving-kindness and rapt attention. But it is just this illusion that the most radical form of religious faith relentlessly attacks. Thus Jonathan Edwards distinguishes between a "grateful good will"—the root of religious feeling, as he understands it—and the kind of gratitude that depends on being loved and appreciated—the kind of gratitude, in other words, that people might feel toward a creator presumed to have their interests at heart. "True virtue," Edwards wrote, "primarily consists, not in love of any particular Beings . . . nor in gratitude, because they love us, but in a propensity and union of heart to Being simply considered, exciting absolute benevolence . . . to Being in general." Man has no claim to God's favor, and a "grateful good will" has to be conceived, accordingly, not as an appropriate acknowledgment of the answer to our prayers, so to speak, but as the acknowledgment of God's life-giving power to order things as he pleases, without "giving any account of his matters," as Edwards puts it.

Edwards's view of God bears no resemblance to the benign father figure conjured up by childlike human beings, according to Freud, out of their unconscious need for dependence. Edwards's God is "absolutely perfect, and infinitely wise, and the fountain of all wisdom," and it is therefore "meet . . . that he should make himself his end, and that he should make nothing but his own wisdom his rule in pursuing that end, without asking leave or counsel of any." Freud, like Krutch, assumes that religion answers to the need for dependence, whereas Edwards speaks directly to those who proudly deny any such need— indeed, who find it galling to be reminded of their dependence on a power beyond their own control or at least beyond the control of humanity in general. Such people find it difficult to acknowledge the justice and goodness of this higher power when the world is so obviously full of evil. They find it difficult to reconcile their expectations of worldly success and happiness, so often undone by events, with the idea of a just, loving, and all-powerful creator. Unable to conceive of a God who does not regard human happiness as the be-all and end-all of creation, they cannot accept the central paradox of religious faith: that the secret of happiness lies in renouncing the right to be happy.

What makes the modern temper modern, then, is not that we have lost our childish sense of dependence but that the normal rebellion *against* dependence is more pervasive than it used to be. This rebellion is not new, as Flannery O'Connor reminds us when she observes that "there are long periods in the lives of all of us . . . when the truth as revealed by faith is hideous, emotionally disturbing, downright repulsive. Witness the dark night of the soul in individual saints." If the whole world now seems to be going through a dark night of the soul, it is because the normal rebellion against dependence appears to be sanctioned by our scientific control over nature, the same progress of science that has allegedly destroyed religious superstition.

Those wonderful machines that science has enabled us to construct have not eliminated drudgery, as Oscar Wilde and other false prophets so confidently predicted, but they have made it possible to imagine ourselves as masters of our fate. In an age that fancies itself as disillusioned, this is the one illusion—the illusion of mastery—that remains as tenacious as ever. But now that we are beginning to grasp the limits of our control over the natural world, it is an illusion—to invoke Freud once again—the future of which is very much in doubt, an illusion more problematical, certainly, than the future of religion.

*1995*

# GLENN LOURY

Glenn Loury (b. 1948) is the Merton P. Stoltz Professor of the Social Sciences and Professor of Economics at Brown University. A public intellectual and host of the podcast *The Glenn Show*, he also is, by his own account, a "chess player, lover of jazz, world traveler, and inveterate contrarian with the courage of my convictions." Race is a recurring subject of his contrarian views.

———

## Leadership Failure and the Loyalty Trap

S INCE THE late 1960s black American intellectuals and politicians have fallen prey to what amounts to a conspiracy of silence about the social and moral condition of the black lower classes. We return with trepidation to the places where we were born and raised, now communities unlike any we had known; we look despairingly at the tenements that once housed poor families in dignity but no longer do; we remain bewildered by the profound changes that have occurred in less than a generation. Yet we are unwilling to voice that bewilderment forthrightly, or to ask of today's residents, "How can you live like this?" We are participating in a conspiracy.

We have tolerated incompetence in the social and political institutions serving this population, because its source has been black. We have made excuses for and sometimes even glorified the supposedly rebellious actions of thugs, although those thugs have made poor black people their victims. We have strained our imaginations, and our fellow citizens' credulity, to find apologies for the able-bodied, healthy, and intelligent young men who father children and then walk away from the responsibility to support them. We have listened in silence, or sometimes with enthusiastic encouragement, to middle-class young black men and women at the best colleges and universities explain, in the terms of an ideology of "racist exploitation" that was not even valid in the 1960s and is much less so today, their failure to make full use of the opportunities presented to them. In the name of racial loyalty, and in an effort to keep alive the sense of oppression that fueled the revolts of our youth, we have engaged in an almost criminal abdication of responsibility.

Moreover, we have encouraged and enforced the exclusion from good standing in our ranks of those few (often called "bourgeois elit-ists," though their origins are usually lower working class) who have had the insight and courage to object to this transparently inadequate series of rationalizations. But it has been the black poor, not ourselves, who have paid the price for this folly.

We have embraced a false, enervating conception of racial loyalty. While it avoids giving aid and comfort to the enemy (that is, to the "white man"), it requires that we ignore the dictates of our forebears' traditions and deepest values. Seduced by the moral relativism that emerged triumphant in the 1960s, we blacks in the best position to do so now find ourselves without the will or self-confidence to pro-vide direction and set standards for our people. We have lapsed into the absurd posture of identifying true commitment to the cause with being uncritical of a person's deeds, however despicable, if that person is black. We act as if the historical fact of slavery and the associated culpability of America have endowed blacks with a fully paid insur-ance policy excusing whatever behavior ensues. Every personal failing of a black, even the illegal behavior of corrupt politicians, becomes evidence of the racism of whites. And every black individual who suc-ceeds by dint of hard work and self-sacrifice is an exception to the rule that pervasive white racism precludes the possibility of black progress.

Remarkably, we think that the mere announcement of the small number of blacks who attain a certain achievement constitutes an indictment of society, and not of ourselves. We practice an *exhibi-tionism of nonachievement*, hurrying to advertise every instance of our underrepresentation, not recognizing that in doing so we are only announcing our own failure. For it is an axiom of this credo of racial loyalty that when blacks do not succeed, it is whites who have failed. We display the false security of those who, having been violated historically, think they can do no wrong—that right must inexorably be on their side. Demagogues can run among us spewing hatred and venom, and we express the barest annoyance, reasoning that these haters are but the natural result of that ever-present, ultimately cleansing, oh-so-convenient hate we call white racism.

Lest the reader think the foregoing too extreme, consider some of the enormities that have driven me to this despairing conclusion. Between the summers of 1979 and 1981 there occurred a series of approximately two dozen child killings in Atlanta, plunging the city into a state of fear. All of the victims of these crimes were black. The black mayor, black police chief, and substantially black police force threw themselves into the hunt for the killer, calling on the FBI for assistance. In due course a suspect, Wayne Williams, was arrested, tried (before a black judge) for two of the murders—though evidence suggested his involvement in others—and convicted of the crimes. One might think this would be cause for rejoicing among Atlanta's blacks, but one would be wrong.

The fact that the convicted killer turned out to be a black man greatly disappointed many blacks in Atlanta and across the country. For months some had been insisting that the Ku Klux Klan was behind the child disappearances, and they continued to assert this despite the overwhelming evidence to the contrary presented at the trial. Others agreed with popular black activist Dick Gregory that the Centers for Disease Control in Atlanta were kidnapping and murdering young black boys for an exotic cancer-fighting drug to be found in the tips of their sex organs. The (largely black) jury's verdict is rejected by many blacks to this day.

It could hardly be otherwise, given the extent to which prominent blacks had used the killings to exemplify the fact that blacks continue to suffer the ravages of racism. Indeed, in 1981, before the Williams trial, Jesse Jackson had said of the killings: "It is open season on black people. . . . These murders can only be understood in the context of affirmative action and Ronald Reagan's conservative politics."

One victim's mother, derisively referring to Atlanta mayor Maynard Jackson as "that fat boy," led a campaign against the middle-class black Atlanta establishment, accusing it (in collaboration with the white "powers that be") of having found in Williams a convenient scapegoat. Rather than celebrate the cessation of a murder spree, the victims of which were black children, many chose instead to absolve the apparent perpetrator and use the case as a platform for expressing their discontent with American society. (This approach was taken to an extreme by James Baldwin in his 1985 meditation on the Atlanta child killings, *The Evidence of Things Not Seen*.) Evidently, no act of a black man, however willful and depraved, is unfit for exploitation in this manner. For the "sophisticated" observer, one seeing beneath the surface to the "true" nature of racial oppression, the formula injustice (a black man on trial for murder in white America is by definition a victim) proved more politically salient than the reality of mass killing being finally brought to a halt. This is a kind of collective madness. Are we so obsessed with our victimization by whites that we have lost the capacity to make moral judgments about other blacks, even the pathologically violent who prey on our children?

Consider how Charles Rangel, a black Democratic congressman from New York City, responded to the efforts of prominent New Yorkers to get him to condemn the speaking appearance of Louis Farrakhan at Madison Square Garden in October 1985. The Muslim minister's speech on that occasion, greeted by wild cheers, was described in one eyewitness account as follows:

> "The scriptures charge your people [the Jews] with killing the prophets of God." Farrakhan contended that God had not made the Jewish people pay for such deeds. However, if something happens to him, then God will make the Jews pay for all the prophets killed from biblical times to the present. "You cannot say 'never again' to God, because when God puts you in the oven, 'never again' don't mean a thing. If you fool with me, you court death itself. I will not run from you; I will run to you!" Farrakhan reserved a little of his hatred for black political leaders, telling the audience that "when a leader sells out the people, he should pay a price for that. Should a leader sell out the people and live?"

Not only did Representative Rangel refuse to issue a statement condemning this event, he went so far as to suggest that the pressure for him to do so constituted yet another example of white racism. In a public statement published in the *Washington Post* days after the speech, Rangel decried the "most objectionable assumption that I and other elected leaders who happen to be black have a special obligation to issue denunciations of Farrakhan on demand." He likened efforts to get him to make a statement to a requirement that he carry a "South African–like pass book stamped with issued denunciations" of the Muslim leader.

Rangel further suggested that "to renounce Farrakhan prior to his scheduled appearance at Madison Square Garden" would somehow have interfered with the minister's constitutional rights. He urged that we "differentiate between . . . the anti-Semitic garbage and the advocacy of discipline, self-help, and black pride" in Farrakhan's message, explaining that the real problem here is "the despair in the black community, the frustration and rage over America's failure to come to terms with its racism."

It is a measure of the great pressure this member of the U.S. House of Representatives was under that he would resort to such a transparently faulty attempt to evade his responsibilities as the principal national political spokesman for the blacks of Harlem. How would the public expression of his opinion regarding Farrakhan have limited the latter's right to speak? Why should it matter that "black pride" is also touted by one who preaches that no "leader [should] sell out the people and live?" While there were many thousands of Rangels constituents in that auditorium cheering on Mr. Farrakhan, many thousands more reject that hate-filled message. To whom else ought concerned observers have gone to ascertain whether the sentiments that were expressed there represented the views of the majority of black New Yorkers? Were Rangel the black representative of a farm district in Iowa, one might take more seriously his cry of "South African–like" racism when asked to respond. As it is, his talk of politicians who just "happen to be black" seems disingenuous at best. He would, after all, be among the first to insist that blackness is a primary qualification for one who would occupy the seat once held by Adam Clayton Powell.

There is a stunning moral insensitivity here, born of being too long in the habitual status of victim. Rangel ends up absolving Farrakhan's supporters of their anti-Semitic bigotry with his reference to "America's failure"; yet no white politician could similarly dismiss the expression of antiblack sentiments among his constituents, however impoverished.

In December 1984, Bernhard Goetz, the so-called subway vigilante, shot four black youths who, he claimed, were about to accost him on a New York subway. He instantly became a folk hero among many urban dwellers, black and white, who live in fear of victimization. In the ensuing public discussion of the problem of urban crime, Kenneth Clark, perhaps the most eminent living black social scientist, offered the theory that in today's big cities it is not poor young men but "society" that is the "real mugger." Writing in the *New York Times*, Clark condemned the unseemly vigilante sentiments evoked by the Goetz case, and he ascribed to "society" responsibility for the criminal acts of urban muggers. Those committing most street crimes, he asserted, have been mugged themselves: they are the victims of "pervasive community, economic, and educational muggings" perpetrated by a "hypocritical society," at the hands of which "their humanity is being systematically destroyed." The theft and violence that many city dwellers fear are, for Clark, but "the inevitable criminality that comes out of the degradation of human beings."

This is a remarkable argument, not only for its questionable sociology—some impoverished urban minority populations (the Chinese in San Francisco, for example) have very low crime rates—but more significantly for what it reveals about Dr. Clark's view of the values and capacities of the inner-city poor. Quite simply, he is willing to avoid judgments about the behavioral differences among blacks in the interest of portraying the problems of the community as due to racism. Yet it is factually inaccurate and morally disturbing to say of poor black persons generally that their economic deprivation has destroyed their humanity. Even in the harshest slums the vast majority of residents do not brutalize their neighbors; they can hardly be taken as aberrant exceptions to some sociological law requiring the unemployed to become, in Clark's words, "mindlessly anti-social."

Moreover, even the black poor who are violent must be held responsible for their conduct. Are they not made poorer still when they are not accorded the respect inherent in the equal application of the obligations and expectations of citizenship? What is most dangerous about Clark's social-muggings analogy is that it invites both blacks and whites to see the black poor as morally different, socially distorted human beings. What such a construction (which is but a restatement of the old blaming-the-victim argument) may "achieve" by way of fostering guilt and pity among the population at large would seem to be more than offset by the extent to which it directly undermines the dignity of these persons.

I will offer one final example. In January 1986 CBS aired a documentary, moderated by Bill Moyers, called "The Vanishing Black Family." It sensitively described the lives of three young families in Newark, New Jersey—the unwed mothers and their children struggling to survive on the meager public provisions available to them, and the unemployed fathers and their desultory lives in the ghetto subculture. One of the most striking figures was a young man named Timothy, the attractive, articulate father of the three children in one of the families. Timothy, having fathered a total of six children by four different women, expressed no regret about the fact that he supported none of them. He proudly bragged about his sexual prowess. When asked about his obligation to the women who bore his children, he said, "That's on them. . . . I ain't gonna let no woman stand in the way of my pleasures." He explained that he would like to marry the mother of three of his children, but only when he could afford "a big wedding . . . with all the trimmings." He seemed not even to be trying to provide financial help to his children, explaining, "What I don't do, the government does." Evidently a bright and artistically talented young man, Timothy spent his time "on the streets," with no visible means of support. He took great pride in his children, though, noting that if they were to accomplish great things in their lives, he would experience a vicarious feeling of achievement.

For many viewers, black and white, Timothy symbolized a great problem in the black ghettos—male irresponsibility toward their progeny. His attitude, and not simply the fact of his unemployment, seemed to be part of the problem. Indeed, the mother of Timothy's children openly complained to Moyers about his lack of support. Nevertheless, a number of influential blacks came to his defense and denounced Moyers for projecting false and damaging images of black family life.

Nationally syndicated columnist Carl Rowan was typical of these. Referring to the Moyers program as "just more slander of the black family," he declared himself "tired of seeing the black family analyzed" and worried that such analyses would only be used as an excuse for mean-spirited social policies. Rowan unabashedly defended Timothy as a victim, saying that he was "just this side of slavery," comparing his circumstance to that of a handicapped child and suggesting that he deserved our compassionate understanding rather than our condemnation. Rowan, caught up in the ostentatious exhibition of his finely honed moral outrage concerning American racism, found himself without the capacity to *judge* Timothy's behavior. Being a "loyal" black, he could thus only apologize for it. He seemed not even to notice how his line of apologia implicitly devalued the efforts and sacrifices of those many black young men and women who have faced the same hardship as Timothy, but who have married, worked when they could, and struggled against the odds to give their children a better life. By taking Timothy's behavior as beyond his control, as the necessary consequence of being born in the Newark ghetto, Rowan was dishonoring the accomplishments of millions of working-class black Americans and contributing to the intellectual malaise in which we blacks now find ourselves.

These examples serve to illustrate the contemporary crisis in black intellectual and political leadership. I have had quite enough of the timidity, wrongheadedness and moral relativism that characterizes so much of the commentary of contemporary black elites on the racial issues of our day. The time has come to break ranks with them. These elites are caught in a "loyalty trap." They are fearful of engaging in a candid, critical appraisal of the condition of our people because they do not want to appear to be disloyal to the race. But this rhetorical reticence has serious negative consequences for the ability of blacks as a group to grapple with the real problems that confront us. Moreover, it represents a failure of nerve in the face of adversity that may be more accurately characterized as intellectual treason than racial fealty. After all, what more important obligation can the privileged class of black elites have than to tell the truth to their own people?

For most people, loyalty is a highly prized trait. We expect it of our friends, demand it of our kin, and look down on those of our fellow citizens who evidence disloyalty to their nation. Yet it is not always so easy to say what really constitutes loyalty in any particular case. Was Elliot Richardson being disloyal when he refused to obey Richard Nixon's order to fire special prosecutor Archibald Cox? Or was he remaining true to a higher authority? Similarly, were those who protested the Vietnam War being disloyal Americans? Or were they showing us just what genuine loyalty is all about?

These questions are of particular importance to black Americans who may choose to depart from group consensus in order to stand up for what they believe. To criticize the civil rights leadership openly for their ineffective response to the social dissolution of much of black America is to invite being called a traitor, an Uncle Tom, or even a racist. To fail to jump for joy at the prospect that Jesse Jackson might become president of the United States is to be labeled, by the many self-appointed guardians of racial virtue who roam the landscape, as being either brain-dead or morally corrupt. The examples of intolerance for critical discourse by black American intellectuals at variance with the racial party line are legion.

Consider that Martin Luther King's much-honored widow, Coretta Scott King, and his former lieutenant, Andrew Young, were actually booed by the black supporters of Rev. Jesse Jackson at the Democratic National Convention in 1984 because they supported the Mondale campaign during the primaries. Political scientist Adolph Reed has observed that such intolerance has roots deep in the history of protest movements among blacks. In his book *The Jesse Jackson Phenomenon* he wrote: "The long-standing anti-participatory style of organic spokesmen has been reproduced among elective leadership, and as a result the entrenched elites have been able with impunity to identify collective racial interest with an exceedingly narrow class agenda. The main focus for practical political activity within the black community in this context must be breaking down the illusion of a single racial opinion."

When, in the 1970s, law professor Derrick Bell began to question the efficacy of busing as the primary remedy sought by civil rights advocates in school desegregation cases, he became *persona non grata* among those advocates. When economist Thomas Sowell began his sustained intellectual assault on the assumptions underlying the development of civil rights advocacy in the 1970s, pointing out that discrimination alone could not account for observed economic differences between racial groups, he was denounced in terms so vitriolic that one would have thought "Uncle" had become his first name. When sociologist William Julius Wilson published *The Declining Significance of Race*, a book with the principal argument that poor blacks suffered more because of their class status than their race, he was denounced as a tool of conservatives, in league with those who would reenslave America's black population.

Recent history demonstrates that we are entitled to question the conception of loyalty implicit in these denunciations, and to decry the limited debate to which it has led. The issue here is not whether the individuals subject to such attack have been treated unfairly, though it is arguable that they have. "The real issue," as Sowell has pointed out, "is whether the new McCarthyism creates an atmosphere in which only a handful of people dare to question publicly the prevailing vision. If it succeeds in discrediting ideas and facts it cannot answer, in intimidating others into silence, then the whole attempt to resolve urgent social issues will have to be abandoned to those with fashionable clichés and political cant."

Blacks confront economic, social, and political problems of staggering magnitude. Yet we have a leadership and intellectual class mired in a vision of racial advocacy more suited to the 1950s and 1960s than to the 1990s and beyond. Our professional racial advocacy organizations seem unable or unwilling to address these profound problems in an effectual way. While these conditions are clearly beyond the direct control of anyone in the black community, it is entirely appropriate to assess the quality of leadership by its response to this circumstance. Judged by this standard, the traditional civil rights leadership leaves much to be desired. In the face of a pervasive social pathology in the inner-city ghettos of this country, these spokesmen have found little else to do but repeat the litany of charges about slavery, racism, discrimination, and the callous policies of Republican administrations.

While they busy themselves with making excuses for failure, poor and working-class blacks live with its consequences. Murder is now the leading cause of death among black males under twenty-five, and more than 90 percent of the victims are killed by other blacks. Inner-city black women are more than twice as likely as urban white women to be rape victims, mostly at the hands of black men. Rampant drug use destroys the chances for many to find a way out. Irresponsible sexuality, with children produced without any provision being made for their support, makes it almost impossible for individuals to take advantage of the opportunities now widely available to black Americans.

It is now clear that protest marches, civil rights lawsuits, or affirmative action for millionaire black businessmen cannot be expected to bring about change for those living in the ghettos. It is obvious that racism—though continuing to exist—cannot be blamed for all that ails the black community. Yet the civil rights leadership continues to talk as if it were 1965. They have not noticed that most white Americans have long since stopped listening. In light of the failure of the policies and programs that these leaders have chosen to emphasize, it is vital that there occur a discourse among blacks regarding how things might be improved. Effective leadership for blacks requires creating an environment where critical intellectual exchange can occur without it undermining the basis for cooperative association among members of the group. Those who demand of all blacks blind loyalty to the agenda of the NAACP make this more difficult to achieve. Their natural distrust of the "heretics" must be suspended long enough for there to occur a serious reflection on whether the traditional positions of the racial advocacy groups continues to serve blacks' best interests.

We blacks who express deviant opinions risk ostracism and denunciation. This is no surprise; it is the price one pays for intellectual integrity. It is to be expected that most people will defend tradition, even when tradition is wrong. There should be a high threshold of resistance to change in long-standing, deeply held beliefs.

Throughout history, though, it has often been the case that profound change has come from those who are considered outsiders. There is also a noble tradition of courageous dissent from racial orthodoxy by black Americans. At the turn of the twentieth century W. E. B. Du Bois spoke out against the then dominant views of Booker T. Washington, who was urging that blacks moderate civil rights claims and seek accommodation with whites, despite the spread of lynchings and the enactment of Jim Crow laws. Du Bois objected, urging blacks to fight for all of their rights and going on to help found the NAACP. Though Du Bois paid a heavy price for this apostasy at the time, history has shown that his position had merit, and black people have been the beneficiaries of his courage and integrity.

Martin Luther King, Jr., also emphasized the crucial importance of open, critical discourse among blacks about our most serious problems.

In the last book he published during his lifetime, *Where Do We Go from Here: Chaos or Community*, he wrote the following:

> *It is not a sign of weakness, but a sign of high maturity, to rise to the level of self-criticism.* Through group unity we must convey to one another that our women must be respected, and that life is too precious to be destroyed in a Saturday night brawl, or a gang execution. Through community agencies and religious institutions we must develop a positive program through which Negro youth can become adjusted to urban living and improve their general level of behavior.

Were King at the helm of the civil rights movement today, I believe it is in this direction that he would be taking us.

*1995*

# ANTONIN SCALIA

In 1986, President Ronald Reagan nominated Antonin Scalia (1936–2016) to the Supreme Court. Confirmed by unanimous Senate vote, he remained on the court until his death, earning a reputation as one of its most colorful and outspoken members. Scalia was an "originalist," committed to discerning the intentions of the Constitution's framers and interpreting it accordingly.

## Dissent in *Obergefell v. Hodges*

I JOIN THE CHIEF JUSTICE's opinion in full. I write separately to call attention to this Court's threat to American democracy.

The substance of today's decree is not of immense personal importance to me. The law can recognize as marriage whatever sexual attachments and living arrangements it wishes, and can accord them favorable civil consequences, from tax treatment to rights of inheritance. Those civil consequences—and the public approval that conferring the name of marriage evidences—can perhaps have adverse social effects, but no more adverse than the effects of many other controversial laws. So it is not of special importance to me what the law says about marriage. It is of overwhelming importance, however, who it is that rules me. Today's decree says that my Ruler, and the Ruler of 320 million Americans coast-to-coast, is a majority of the nine lawyers on the Supreme Court. The opinion in these cases is the furthest extension in fact—and the furthest extension one can even imagine—of the Court's claimed power to create "liberties" that the Constitution and its Amendments neglect to mention. This practice of constitutional revision by an unelected committee of nine, always accompanied (as it is today) by extravagant praise of liberty, robs the People of the most important liberty they asserted in the Declaration of Independence and won in the Revolution of 1776: the freedom to govern themselves.

I

Until the courts put a stop to it, public debate over same-sex marriage displayed American democracy at its best. Individuals on both sides of the issue passionately, but respectfully, attempted to persuade their fellow citizens to accept their views. Americans considered the arguments and put the question to a vote. The electorates of 11 States, either directly or through their representatives, chose to expand the traditional definition of marriage. Many more decided not to.[1] Win or lose, advocates for both sides continued pressing their cases, secure in the knowledge that an electoral loss can be negated by a later electoral win. That is exactly how our system of government is supposed to work.[2]

The Constitution places some constraints on self-rule—constraints adopted *by the People themselves* when they ratified the Constitution and its Amendments. Forbidden are laws "impairing the Obligation of Contracts,"[3] denying "Full Faith and Credit" to the "public Acts" of other States,[4] prohibiting the free exercise of religion,[5] abridging the freedom of speech,[6] infringing the right to keep and bear arms,[7] authorizing unreasonable searches and seizures,[8] and so forth. Aside from these limitations, those powers "reserved to the States respectively, or to the people"[9] can be exercised as the States or the People desire. These cases ask us to decide whether the Fourteenth Amendment

---

[1] Brief for Respondents in No. 14–571, p. 14.
[2] Accord, *Schuette v. BAMN*, 572 U. S. ___, ___–___ (2014) (plurality opinion) (slip op., at 15–17).
[3] U. S. Const., Art. I, §10.
[4] Art. IV, §1.
[5] Amdt. 1.
[6] *Ibid.*
[7] Amdt. 2.
[8] Amdt. 4.
[9] Amdt. 10.

contains a limitation that requires the States to license and recognize marriages between two people of the same sex. Does it remove *that* issue from the political process?

Of course not. It would be surprising to find a prescription regarding marriage in the Federal Constitution since, as the author of today's opinion reminded us only two years ago (in an opinion joined by the same Justices who join him today):

> "[R]egulation of domestic relations is an area that has long been regarded as a virtually exclusive province of the States."[10]

> "[T]he Federal Government, through our history, has deferred to state-law policy decisions with respect to domestic relations."[11]

But we need not speculate. When the Fourteenth Amendment was ratified in 1868, every State limited marriage to one man and one woman, and no one doubted the constitutionality of doing so. That resolves these cases. When it comes to determining the meaning of a vague constitutional provision—such as "due process of law" or "equal protection of the laws"—it is unquestionable that the People who ratified that provision did not understand it to prohibit a practice that remained both universal and uncontroversial in the years after ratification.[12] We have no basis for striking down a practice that is not expressly prohibited by the Fourteenth Amendment's text, and that bears the endorsement of a long tradition of open, widespread, and unchallenged use dating back to the Amendment's ratification. Since there is no doubt whatever that the People never decided to prohibit the limitation of marriage to opposite-sex couples, the public debate over same-sex marriage must be allowed to continue.

But the Court ends this debate, in an opinion lacking even a thin veneer of law. Buried beneath the mummeries and straining-to-be-memorable passages of the opinion is a candid and startling assertion: No matter *what* it was the People ratified, the Fourteenth Amendment

---

[10] *United States v. Windsor*, 570 U. S. ___, ___ (2013) (slip op., at 16) (internal quotation marks and citation omitted).

[11] *Id.*, at ___ (slip op., at 17).

[12] See *Town of Greece v. Galloway*, 572 U. S. ___, ___–___ (2014) (slip op., at 7–8).

protects those rights that the Judiciary, in its "reasoned judgment," thinks the Fourteenth Amendment ought to protect.[13] That is so because "[t]he generations that wrote and ratified the Bill of Rights and the Fourteenth Amendment did not presume to know the extent of freedom in all of its dimensions. . . ."[14] One would think that sentence would continue: ". . . and therefore they provided for a means by which the People could amend the Constitution," or perhaps ". . . and therefore they left the creation of additional liberties, such as the freedom to marry someone of the same sex, to the People, through the never-ending process of legislation." But no. What logically follows, in the majority's judge-empowering estimation, is: "and so they entrusted to future generations a charter protecting the right of all persons to enjoy liberty as we learn its meaning."[15] The "we," needless to say, is the nine of us. "History and tradition guide and discipline [our] inquiry but do not set its outer boundaries."[16] Thus, rather than focusing on *the People's* understanding of "liberty"—at the time of ratification or even today—the majority focuses on four "principles and traditions" that, *in the majority's view*, prohibit States from defining marriage as an institution consisting of one man and one woman.[17]

This is a naked judicial claim to legislative—indeed, *super*-legislative—power; a claim fundamentally at odds with our system of government. Except as limited by a constitutional prohibition agreed to by the People, the States are free to adopt whatever laws they like, even those that offend the esteemed Justices' "reasoned judgment." A system of government that makes the People subordinate to a committee of nine unelected lawyers does not deserve to be called a democracy.

Judges are selected precisely for their skill as lawyers; whether they reflect the policy views of a particular constituency is not (or should not be) relevant. Not surprisingly then, the Federal Judiciary is hardly a cross-section of America. Take, for example, this Court, which consists of only nine men and women, all of them successful

---

[13] *Ante*, at 10.

[14] *Ante*, at 11.

[15] *Ibid*.

[16] *Ante*, at 10–11.

[17] *Ante*, at 12–18.

lawyers[18] who studied at Harvard or Yale Law School. Four of the nine are natives of New York City. Eight of them grew up in east- and west-coast States. Only one hails from the vast expanse in-between. Not a single Southwesterner or even, to tell the truth, a genuine Westerner (California does not count). Not a single evangelical Christian (a group that comprises about one quarter of Americans[19]), or even a Protestant of any denomination. The strikingly unrepresentative character of the body voting on today's social upheaval would be irrelevant if they were functioning as *judges*, answering the legal question whether the American people had ever ratified a constitutional provision that was understood to proscribe the traditional definition of marriage. But of course the Justices in today's majority are not voting on that basis; *they say they are not*. And to allow the policy question of same-sex marriage to be considered and resolved by a select, patrician, highly unrepresentative panel of nine is to violate a principle even more fundamental than no taxation without representation: no social transformation without representation.

## II

But what really astounds is the hubris reflected in today's judicial Putsch. The five Justices who compose today's majority are entirely comfortable concluding that every State violated the Constitution for all of the 135 years between the Fourteenth Amendment's ratification and Massachusetts' permitting of same-sex marriages in 2003.[20] They have discovered in the Fourteenth Amendment a "fundamental right" overlooked by every person alive at the time of ratification, and almost everyone else in the time since. They see what lesser legal minds—minds like Thomas Cooley, John Marshall Harlan, Oliver

---

[18] The predominant attitude of tall-building lawyers with respect to the questions presented in these cases is suggested by the fact that the American Bar Association deemed it in accord with the wishes of its members to file a brief in support of the petitioners. See Brief for American Bar Association as *Amicus Curiae* in Nos. 14–571 and 14–574, pp. 1–5.

[19] See Pew Research Center, America's Changing Religious Landscape 4 (May 12, 2015).

[20] *Goodridge v. Department of Public Health*, 440 Mass. 309, 798 N. E. 2d 941 (2003).

Wendell Holmes, Jr., Learned Hand, Louis Brandeis, William Howard Taft, Benjamin Cardozo, Hugo Black, Felix Frankfurter, Robert Jackson, and Henry Friendly—could not. They are certain that the People ratified the Fourteenth Amendment to bestow on them the power to remove questions from the democratic process when that is called for by their "reasoned judgment." These Justices *know* that limiting marriage to one man and one woman is contrary to reason; they *know* that an institution as old as government itself, and accepted by every nation in history until 15 years ago,[21] cannot possibly be supported by anything other than ignorance or bigotry. And they are willing to say that any citizen who does not agree with that, who adheres to what was, until 15 years ago, the unanimous judgment of all generations and all societies, stands against the Constitution.

The opinion is couched in a style that is as pretentious as its content is egotistic. It is one thing for separate concurring or dissenting opinions to contain extravagances, even silly extravagances, of thought and expression; it is something else for the official opinion of the Court to do so.[22] Of course the opinion's showy profundities are often profoundly incoherent. "The nature of marriage is that, through its enduring bond, two persons together can find other freedoms, such as expression, intimacy, and spirituality."[23] (Really? Who ever thought that intimacy and spirituality [whatever that means] were freedoms? And if intimacy is, one would think Freedom of Intimacy is abridged rather than expanded by marriage. Ask the nearest hippie. Expression, sure enough, *is* a freedom, but anyone in a long-lasting marriage will attest that that happy state constricts, rather than expands, what one can prudently say.) Rights, we are told, can "rise . . . from a better informed understanding of how constitutional imperatives define a liberty that remains urgent in our own era."[24] (Huh? How can a better informed understanding of how constitutional imperatives [whatever

---

[21] *Windsor*, 570 U. S., at ___ (Alito, J., dissenting) (slip op., at 7).

[22] If, even as the price to be paid for a fifth vote, I ever joined an opinion for the Court that began: "The Constitution promises liberty to all within its reach, a liberty that includes certain specific rights that allow persons, within a lawful realm, to define and express their identity," I would hide my head in a bag. The Supreme Court of the United States has descended from the disciplined legal reasoning of John Marshall and Joseph Story to the mystical aphorisms of the fortune cookie.

[23] *Ante*, at 13.

[24] *Ante*, at 19.

that means] define [whatever that means] an urgent liberty [never mind], give birth to a right?) And we are told that, "[i]n any particular case," either the Equal Protection or Due Process Clause "may be thought to capture the essence of [a] right in a more accurate and comprehensive way," than the other, "even as the two Clauses may converge in the identification and definition of the right."[25] (What say? What possible "essence" does substantive due process "capture" in an "accurate and comprehensive way"? It stands for nothing whatever, except those freedoms and entitlements that this Court *really* likes. And the Equal Protection Clause, as employed today, identifies nothing except a difference in treatment that this Court *really* dislikes. Hardly a distillation of essence. If the opinion is correct that the two clauses "converge in the identification and definition of [a] right," that is only because the majority's likes and dislikes are predictably compatible.) I could go on. The world does not expect logic and precision in poetry or inspirational pop-philosophy; it demands them in the law. The stuff contained in today's opinion has to diminish this Court's reputation for clear thinking and sober analysis.

\* \* \*

Hubris is sometimes defined as o'erweening pride; and pride, we know, goeth before a fall. The Judiciary is the "least dangerous" of the federal branches because it has "neither Force nor Will, but merely judgment; and must ultimately depend upon the aid of the executive arm" and the States, "even for the efficacy of its judgments."[26] With each decision of ours that takes from the People a question properly left to them—with each decision that is unabashedly based not on law, but on the "reasoned judgment" of a bare majority of this Court—we move one step closer to being reminded of our impotence.

*2015*

---

[25] *Ibid.*
[26] The Federalist No. 78, pp. 522, 523 (J. Cooke ed. 1961) (A. Hamilton).

# LIBERTY AND POWER

*The State and the Free Market*

# RANDOLPH BOURNE

As a very young man, Randolph Bourne (1886–1918) enjoyed spectacular success as a journalist of progressive inclinations. Yet Bourne parted company with his fellow progressives on the question of U.S. entry into World War I, which he adamantly opposed. That conviction all but destroyed his career, and he perished in the influenza pandemic of 1918. Posthumously, Bourne enjoys the enduring respect of libertarians and anti-militarists alike.

———◆———

## FROM *The State*

To MOST of the Americans of the classes which consider themselves significant the war brought a sense of the sanctity of the State, which, if they had had time to think about it, would have seemed a sudden and surprising alteration in their habits of thought. In times of peace, we usually ignore the State in favor of partisan political controversies, or personal struggles for office, or the pursuit of party policies. It is the Government rather than the State with which the politically minded are concerned. The State is reduced to a shadowy emblem which comes to consciousness only on occasions of patriotic holiday.

Government is obviously composed of common and unsanctified men, and is thus a legitimate object of criticism and even contempt. If your own party is in power, things may be assumed to be moving safely enough; but if the opposition is in, then clearly all safety and honor have fled the State. Yet you do not put it to yourself in quite that way. What you think is only that there are rascals to be turned out of a very practical machinery of offices and functions which you take for granted. When we say that Americans are lawless, we usually mean that they are less conscious than other peoples of the august majesty of the institution of the State as it stands behind the objective government of men and laws which we see. In a republic the men who hold office are indistinguishable from the mass. Very few of them possess the slightest personal dignity with which they could endow their political rôle; even if they ever thought of such a thing. And they have no class distinction to give them glamor. In a Republic the Government is obeyed grumblingly, because it has no bedazzlements or sanctities to gild it. If you are a good old-fashioned democrat, you rejoice at this fact, you glory in the plainness of a system where every citizen has become a king. If you are more sophisticated you bemoan the passing of dignity and honor from affairs of State. But in practice, the democrat does not in the least treat his elected citizen with the respect due to a king, nor does the sophisticated citizen pay tribute to the dignity even when he finds it. The republican state has almost no trappings to appeal to the common man's emotions. What it has are of military origin, and in an unmilitary era such as we have passed through since the Civil War, even military trappings have been scarcely seen. In such an era the sense of the State almost fades out of the consciousness of men.

With the shock of war, however, the State comes into its own again. The Government, with no mandate from the people, without consultation of the people, conducts all the negotiations, the backing and filling, the menaces and explanations, which slowly bring it into collision with some other Government, and gently and irresistibly slides the country into war. For the benefit of proud and haughty citizens, it is fortified with a list of the intolerable insults which have been hurled towards us by the other nations; for the benefit of the liberal and beneficent, it has a convincing set of moral purposes which our going to war will achieve; for the ambitious and aggressive classes, it can gently whisper of a bigger rôle in the destiny of the world. The result is that, even in those countries where the business of declaring war is theoretically in the hands of representatives of the people, no legislature has ever been known to decline the request of an Executive, which has conducted all foreign affairs in utter privacy and irresponsibility, that it order the nation into battle. Good democrats are wont to feel the crucial difference between a State in which the popular Parliament or Congress declares war, and the State in which an absolute monarch or ruling class declares war. But, put to the stern pragmatic test, the difference is not striking. In the freest of republics as well as in the most tyrannical of Empires, all foreign policy, the diplomatic negotiations which produce or forestall war, are equally the private property of the Executive part of the Government, and are equally exposed to no check whatever from popular bodies, or the people voting as a mass themselves.

The moment war is declared, however, the mass of the people, through some spiritual alchemy, become convinced that they have willed and executed the deed themselves. They then with the exception of a few malcontents, proceed to allow themselves to be regimented, coerced, deranged in all the environments of their lives, and turned into a solid manufactory of destruction toward whatever other people may have, in the appointed scheme of things, come within the range of the Government's disapprobation. The citizen throws off his contempt and indifference to Government, identifies himself with its purposes, revives all his military memories and symbols, and the State once more walks, an august presence, through the imaginations of men. Patriotism becomes the dominant feeling, and produces immediately that intense and hopeless confusion between the relations which the individual bears and should bear towards the society of which he is a part.

The patriot loses all sense of the distinction between State, nation and government. In our quieter moments, the Nation or Country forms the basic idea of society. We think vaguely of a loose population spreading over a certain geographical portion of the earth's surface, speaking a common language, and living in a homogeneous civilization. Our idea of Country concerns itself with the non-political aspects of a people, its ways of living, its personal traits, its literature and art, its characteristic attitudes towards life. We are Americans because we live in a certain bounded territory, because our ancestors have carried on a great enterprise of pioneering and colonization, because we live in certain kinds of communities which have a certain look and express their aspirations in certain ways. We can see that our civilization is different from contiguous civilizations like the Indian and Mexican. The institutions of our country form a certain network which affects us vitally and intrigues our thoughts in a way that these other civilizations do not. We are a part of country, for better or for worse. We have arrived in it through the operation of physiological laws, and not in any way through our own choice. By the time we have reached what are called years of discretion, its influences have molded our habits, our values, our ways of thinking, so that however aware we may become, we never really lose the stamp of our civilization, or could be mistaken for the child of any other country. Our feeling for our fellow-countrymen is one of similarity or of mere acquaintance. We may be intensely proud of and congenial to our particular network of civilization, or we may detest most of its qualities and rage at its defects. This does not alter the fact that we are inextricably bound up in it. The Country, as an inescapable group into which we are born, and which makes us its particular kind of a citizen of the world, seems to be a fundamental fact of our consciousness, an irreducible minimum of social feeling.

Now this feeling for country is essentially noncompetitive; we think of our own people merely as living on the earth's surface along with other groups, pleasant or objectionable as they may be, but fundamentally as sharing the earth with them. In our simple conception of country there is no more feeling of rivalry with other peoples than there is in our feeling for our family. Our interest turns within rather than without, is intensive and not belligerent. We grow up and our imaginations gradually stake out the world we live in, they need no greater conscious satisfaction for their gregarious impulses than this sense of a great mass of people to whom we are more or less attuned, and in whose institutions we are functioning. The feeling for country would be an uninflatable maximum were it not for the ideas of State and Government which are associated with it. Country is a concept of peace, of tolerance, of living and letting live. But State is essentially a concept of power, of competition; it signifies a group in its aggressive aspects. And we have the misfortune of being born not only into a country but into a State, and as we grow up we learn to mingle the two feelings into a hopeless confusion.

The State is the country acting as a political unit, it is the group acting as a repository of force, determiner of law, arbiter of justice. International politics is a "power politics" because it is a relation of States and that is what States infallibly and calamitously are, huge aggregations of human and industrial force that may be hurled against each other in war. When a country acts as a whole in relation to another country, or in imposing laws on its own inhabitants, or in coercing or punishing individuals or minorities, it is acting as a State. The history of America as a country is quite different from that of America as a State. In one case it is the drama of the pioneering conquest of the land, of the growth of wealth and the ways in which it was used, of the enterprise of education, and the carrying out of spiritual ideals, of the struggle of economic classes. But as a State, its history is that of playing a part in the world, making war, obstructing international trade, preventing itself from being split to pieces, punishing those citizens whom society agrees are offensive, and collecting money to pay for all.

Government, on the other hand, is synonymous with neither State nor Nation. It is the machinery by which the nation, organized as a State, carries out its State functions. Government is a framework of the administration of laws, and the carrying out of the public force. Government is the idea of the State put into practical operation in the hands of definite, concrete, fallible men. It is the visible sign of the invisible grace. It is the word made flesh. And it has necessarily the limitations inherent in all practicality. Government is the only form in which we can envisage the State, but it is by no means identical with it. That the State is a mystical conception is something that must never be forgotten. Its glamor and its significance linger behind the framework of Government and direct its activities.

Wartime brings the ideal of the State out into very clear relief, and reveals attitudes and tendencies that were hidden. In times of peace the sense of the State flags in a republic that is not militarized. For war is essentially the health of the State. The ideal of the State is that within its territory its power and influence should be universal. As the Church is the medium for the spiritual salvation of men, so the State is thought of as the medium for his political salvation. Its idealism is a rich blood flowing to all the members of the body politic. And it is precisely in war that the urgency for union seems greatest, and the necessity for universality seems most unquestioned. The State is the organization of the herd to act offensively or defensively against another herd similarly organized. The more terrifying the occasion for defense, the closer will become the organization and the more coercive the influence upon each member of the herd. War sends the current of purpose and activity flowing down to the lowest level of the herd, and to its most remote branches. All the activities of society are linked together as fast as possible to this central purpose of making a military offensive or a military defense, and the State becomes what in peacetimes it has vainly struggled to become—the inexorable arbiter and determinant of men's businesses and attitudes and opinions. The slack is taken up, the cross-currents fade out, and the nation moves lumberingly and slowly, but with ever accelerated speed and integration, towards the great end, towards that "peacefulness of being at war," of which L. P. Jacks has so unforgettably spoken.

The classes which are able to play an active and not merely a passive rôle in the organization for war get a tremendous liberation of activity and energy. Individuals are jolted out of their old routine, many of them are given new positions of responsibility, new techniques must be learnt. Wearing home ties are broken and women who would have remained attached with infantile bonds are liberated for service overseas. A vast sense of rejuvenescence pervades the significant classes, a sense of new importance in the world. Old national ideals are taken out, re-adapted to the purpose and used as universal touchstones, or molds into which all thought is poured. Every individual citizen who in peacetimes had no function to perform by which he could imagine himself an expression or living fragment of the State becomes an active amateur agent of the Government in reporting spies and disloyalists, in raising Government funds, or in propagating such measures as are considered necessary by officialdom. Minority opinion, which in times of peace, was only irritating and could not be dealt with by law unless it was conjoined with actual crime, becomes, with the outbreak of war, a case for outlawry. Criticism of the State, objections to war, lukewarm opinions concerning the necessity or the beauty of conscription, are made subject to ferocious penalties, far exceeding in severity those affixed to actual pragmatic crimes. Public opinion, as expressed in the newspapers, and the pulpits and the schools, becomes one solid block. "Loyalty," or rather war orthodoxy, becomes the sole test for all professions, techniques, occupations. Particularly is this true in the sphere of the intellectual life. There the smallest taint is held to spread over the whole soul, so that a professor of physics is *ipso facto* disqualified to teach physics or to hold honorable place in a university—the republic of learning—if he is at all unsound on the war. Even mere association with persons thus tainted is considered to disqualify a teacher. Anything pertaining to the enemy becomes taboo. His books are suppressed wherever possible, his language is forbidden. His artistic products are considered to convey in the subtlest spiritual way taints of vast poison to the soul that permits itself to enjoy them. So enemy music is suppressed, and energetic measures of opprobrium taken against those whose artistic consciences are not ready to perform such an act of self-sacrifice. The rage for loyal conformity works impartially, and often in diametric opposition to other orthodoxies and traditional conformities, or even ideals. The triumphant orthodoxy of the State is shown at its apex perhaps when Christian preachers lose their pulpits for taking more or less in literal terms the Sermon on the Mount, and Christian zealots are sent to prison for twenty years for distributing tracts which argue that war is unscriptural.

War is the health of the State. It automatically sets in motion throughout society those irresistible forces for uniformity, for passionate cooperation with the Government in coercing into obedience the minority groups and individuals which lack the larger herd sense. The machinery of government sets and enforces the drastic penalties, the minorities are either intimidated into silence, or brought slowly around by a subtle process of persuasion which may seem to them really to be converting them. Of course the ideal of perfect loyalty, perfect uniformity is never really attained. The classes upon whom the amateur work of coercion falls are unwearied in their zeal, but often their agitation, instead of converting, merely serves to stiffen their resistance. Minorities are rendered sullen, and some intellectual opinion bitter and satirical. But in general, the nation in war-time attains a uniformity of feeling, a hierarchy of values culminating at the undisputed apex of the State ideal, which could not possibly be produced through any other agency than war. Other values such as artistic creation, knowledge, reason, beauty, the enhancement of life, are instantly and almost unanimously sacrificed, and the significant classes who have constituted themselves the amateur agents of the State are engaged not only in sacrificing these values for themselves but in coercing all other persons into sacrificing them.

War—or at least modern war waged by a democratic republic against a powerful enemy—seems to achieve for a nation almost all that the most inflamed political idealist could desire. Citizens are no longer indifferent to their Government, but each cell of the body politic is brimming with life and activity. We are at last on the way to full realization of that collective community in which each individual somehow contains the virtue of the whole. In a nation at war, every citizen identifies himself with the whole, and feels immensely strengthened in that identification. The purpose and desire of the collective community live in each person who throws himself wholeheartedly into the cause of war. The impeding distinction between society and the individual is almost blotted out. At war, the individual becomes almost identical with his society. He achieves a superb self-assurance, an intuition of the rightness of all his ideas and emotions, so that in the suppression of opponents or heretics he is invincibly strong; he feels behind him all the power of the collective community. The individual as social being in war seems to have achieved almost his apotheosis. Not for any religious impulse could the American nation have been expected to show such devotion *en masse*, such sacrifice and labor. Certainly not for any secular good, such as universal education or the subjugation of nature, would it have poured forth its treasure and its life, or would it have permitted such stern coercive measures to be taken against it, such as conscripting its money and its men. But for the sake of a war of offensive self-defense, undertaken to support a difficult cause to the slogan of "democracy," it would reach the highest level ever known of collective effort.

For these secular goods, connected with the enhancement of life, the education of man and the use of the intelligence to realize reason and beauty in the nation's communal living, are alien to our traditional ideal of the State. The State is intimately connected with war, for it is the organization of the collective community when it acts in a political manner, and to act in a political manner towards a rival group has meant, throughout all history—war.

There is nothing invidious in the use of the term, "herd," in connection with the State. It is merely an attempt to reduce closer to first principles the nature of this institution in the shadow of which we all live, move and have our being. Ethnologists are generally agreed that human society made its first appearance as the human pack and not as a collection of individuals or of couples. The herd is in fact the original unit, and only as it was differentiated did personal individuality develop. All the most primitive surviving tribes of men are shown to live in a very complex but very rigid social organization where opportunity for individuation is scarcely given. These tribes remain strictly organized herds, and the difference between them and the modern State is one of degree of sophistication and variety of organization, and not of kind.

Psychologists recognize the gregarious impulse as one of the strongest primitive pulls which keeps together the herds of the different species of higher animals. Mankind is no exception. Our pugnacious evolutionary history has prevented the impulse from ever dying out. This gregarious impulse is the tendency to imitate, to conform, to coalesce together, and is most powerful when the herd believes itself threatened with attack. Animals crowd together for protection, and men become most conscious of their collectivity at the threat of war. Consciousness of collectivity brings confidence and a feeling of massed strength, which in turn arouses pugnacity and the battle is on. In civilized man, the gregarious impulse acts not only to produce concerted action for defense, but also to produce identity of opinion. Since thought is a form of behavior, the gregarious impulse floods up into its realms and demands that sense of uniform thought which wartime produces so successfully. And it is in this flooding of the conscious life of society that gregariousness works its havoc.

For just as in modern societies the sex-instinct is enormously oversupplied for the requirements of human propagation, so the gregarious impulse is enormously over-supplied for the work of protection which it is called upon to perform. It would be quite enough if we were gregarious enough to enjoy the companionship of others, to be able to coöperate with them, and to feel a slight malaise at solitude. Unfortunately, however, this impulse is not content with these reasonable and healthful demands, but insists that like-mindedness shall prevail everywhere, in all departments of life. So that all human progress, all novelty, and non-conformity, must be carried against the resistance of this tyrannical herd-instinct which drives the individual into obedience and conformity with the majority. Even in the most modern and enlightened societies this impulse shows little sign of abating. As it is driven by inexorable economic demand out of the sphere of utility, it seems to fasten itself ever more fiercely in the realm of feeling and opinion, so that conformity comes to be a thing aggressively desired and demanded.

The gregarious impulse keeps its hold all the more virulently because when the group is in motion or is taking any positive action, this feeling of being with and supported by the collective herd very greatly feeds that will to power, the nourishment of which the individual organism so constantly demands. You feel powerful by conforming, and you feel forlorn and helpless if you are out of the crowd. While even if you do not get any access of power by thinking and feeling just as everybody else in your group does, you get at least the warm feeling of obedience, the soothing irresponsibility of protection.

Joining as it does to these very vigorous tendencies of the individual—the pleasure in power and the pleasure in obedience—this gregarious impulse becomes irresistible in society. War stimulates it to the highest possible degree, sending the influences of its mysterious herd-current with its inflations of power and obedience to the farthest reaches of the society, to every individual and little group that can possibly be affected. And it is these impulses which the State—the organization of the entire herd, the entire collectivity—is founded on and makes use of.

There is, of course, in the feeling towards the State a large element of pure filial mysticism. The sense of insecurity, the desire for protection, sends one's desire back to the father and mother, with whom is associated the earliest feeling of protection. It is not for nothing that one's State is still thought of as Father or Motherland, that one's relation towards it is conceived in terms of family affection. The war has shown that nowhere under the shock of danger have these primitive childlike attitudes failed to assert themselves again, as much in this country as anywhere. If we have not the intense Father-sense of the German who worships his Vaterland, at least in Uncle Sam we have a symbol of protecting, kindly authority, and in the many Mother-posters of the Red Cross, we see how easily in the more tender functions of war service, the ruling organization is conceived in family terms. A people at war have become in the most literal sense obedient, respectful, trustful children again, full of that naïve faith in the all-wisdom and all-power of the adult who takes care of them, imposes his mild but necessary rule upon them and in whom they lose their responsibility and anxieties. In this recrudescence of the child, there is great comfort, and a certain influx of power. On most people the strain of being an independent adult weighs heavily, and upon none more than those members of the significant classes who have had bequeathed to them or have assumed the responsibilities of governing. The State provides the convenientest of symbols under which these classes can retain all the actual pragmatic satisfaction of governing, but can rid themselves of the psychic burden of adulthood. They continue to direct industry and government and all the institutions of society pretty much as before, but in their own conscious eyes and in the eyes of the general public, they are turned from their selfish and predatory ways, and have become loyal servants of society, or something greater than they—the State. The man who moves from the direction of a large business in New York to a post in the war management industrial service in Washington does not apparently alter very much his power or his administrative technique. But psychically, what a transfiguration has occurred! His is now not only the power but the glory! And his sense of satisfaction is directly proportional not to the genuine amount of personal sacrifice that may be involved in the change but to the extent to which he retains his industrial prerogatives and sense of command.

From members of this class a certain insuperable indignation arises if the change from private enterprise to State service involves any real loss of power and personal privilege. If there is to be pragmatic sacrifice, let it be, they feel, on the field of honor, in the traditionally acclaimed deaths by battle, in that detour to suicide, as Nietzsche calls war. The State in wartime supplies satisfaction for this very real craving, but its chief value is the opportunity it gives for this regression to infantile attitudes. In your reaction to an imagined attack on your country or an insult to its government, you draw closer to the herd for protection, you conform in word and deed, and you insist vehemently that everybody else shall think, speak and act together. And you fix your adoring gaze upon the State, with a truly filial look, as upon the Father of the flock, the quasi-personal symbol of the strength of the herd, and the leader and determinant of your definite action and ideas.

The members of the working-classes, that portion at least which does not identify itself with the significant classes and seek to imitate it and rise to it, are notoriously less affected by the symbolism of the

State, or, in other words, are less patriotic than the significant classes. For theirs is neither the power nor the glory. The State in wartime does not offer them the opportunity to regress, for, never having acquired social adulthood, they cannot lose it. If they have been drilled and regimented, as by the industrial régime of the last century, they go out docilely enough to do battle for their State, but they are almost entirely without that filial sense and even without that herd-intellect sense which operates so powerfully among their "betters." They live habitually in an industrial serfdom, by which though nominally free, they are in practice as a class bound to a system of machine-production the implements of which they do not own, and in the distribution of whose product they have not the slightest voice, except what they can occasionally exert by a veiled intimidation which draws slightly more of the product in their direction. From such serfdom, military conscription is not so great a change. But into the military enterprise they go, not with those hurrahs of the significant classes whose instincts war so powerfully feeds, but with the same apathy with which they enter and continue in the industrial enterprise.

From this point of view, war can be called almost an upper-class sport. The novel interests and excitements it provides, the inflations of power, the satisfaction it gives to those very tenacious human impulses—gregariousness and parent-regression—endow it with all the qualities of a luxurious collective game which is felt intensely just in proportion to the sense of significant rule the person has in the class-division of his society. A country at war—particularly our own country at war—does not act as a purely homogeneous herd. The significant classes have all the herd-feeling in all its primitive intensity, but there are barriers, or at least differentials of intensity, so that this feeling does not flow freely without impediment throughout the entire nation. A modern country represents a long historical and social process of disaggregation of the herd. The nation at peace is not a group, it is a network of myriads of groups representing the coöperation and similar feeling of men on all sorts of planes and in all sorts of human interests and enterprises. In every modern industrial country, there are parallel planes of economic classes with divergent attitudes and institutions and interests—bourgeois and proletariat, with their many subdivisions according to power and function, and even their interweaving, such as those more highly skilled workers who habitually identify themselves with the owning and the significant classes and strive to raise themselves to the bourgeois level, imitating their cultural standards and manners. Then there are religious groups with a certain definite, though weakening sense of kinship, and there are the powerful ethnic groups which behave almost as cultural colonies in the New World, clinging tenaciously to language and historical tradition, though their herdishness is usually founded on cultural rather than State symbols. There are even certain vague sectional groupings. All these small sects, political parties, classes, levels, interests, may act as foci for herd-feelings. They intersect and interweave, and the same person may be a member of several different groups lying at different planes. Different occasions will set off his herd-feeling in one direction or another. In a religious crisis he will be intensely conscious of the necessity that his sect (or sub-herd) may prevail; in a political campaign, that his party shall triumph.

To the spread of herd-feeling, therefore, all these smaller herds offer resistance. To the spread of that herd-feeling which arises from the threat of war, and which would normally involve the entire nation, the only groups which make serious resistance are those, of course, which continue to identify themselves with the other nation from which they or their parents have come. In times of peace they are for all practical purposes citizens of their new country. They keep alive their ethnic traditions more as a luxury than anything. Indeed these traditions tend rapidly to die out except where they connect with some still unresolved nationalistic cause abroad, with some struggle for freedom, or some irredentism. If they are consciously opposed by a too invidious policy of Americanism, they tend to be strengthened. And in time of war, these ethnic elements which have any traditional connection with the enemy, even though most of the individuals may have little real sympathy with the enemy's cause, are naturally lukewarm to the herd-feeling of the nation which goes back to State traditions in which they have no share. But to the natives imbued with State-feeling, any such resistance or apathy is intolerable. This herd-feeling, this newly awakened consciousness of the State, demands universality. The leaders of the significant classes, who feel most intensely this State-compulsion, demand a one hundred per cent. Americanism, among one hundred per cent. of the population. The State is a jealous God and will brook no rivals. Its sovereignty must pervade every one, and all feeling must be run into the stereotyped forms of romantic patriotic militarism which is the traditional expression of the State herd-feeling.

Thus arises conflict within the State. War becomes almost a sport between the hunters and the hunted. The pursuit of enemies within outweighs in psychic attractiveness the assault on the enemy without. The whole terrific force of the State is brought to bear against the heretics. The nation boils with a slow insistent fever. A white terrorism is carried on by the Government against pacifists, Socialists, enemy aliens, and a milder unofficial persecution against all persons or movements that can be imagined as connected with the enemy. War, which should be the health of the State, unifies all the bourgeois elements and the common people, and outlaws the rest. The revolutionary proletariat shows more resistance to this unification, is, as we have seen, psychically out of the current. Its vanguard, as the I. W. W., is remorselessly pursued, in spite of the proof that it is a symptom, not a cause, and its prosecution increases the disaffection of labor and intensifies the friction instead of lessening it.

But the emotions that play around the defense of the State do not take into consideration the pragmatic results. A nation at war, led by its significant classes, is engaged in liberating certain of its impulses which have had all too little exercise in the past. It is getting certain satisfactions, and the actual conduct of the war or the condition of the country are really incidental to the enjoyment of new forms of virtue and power and aggressiveness. If it could be shown conclusively that the persecution of slightly disaffected elements actually increased enormously the difficulties of production and the organization of the war technique, it would be found that public policy would scarcely change. The significant classes must have their pleasure in hunting down and chastizing everything that they feel instinctively to be not imbued with the current State-enthusiasm, though the State itself be actually impeded in its efforts to carry out those objects for which they are passionately contending. The best proof of this is that with a pursuit of plotters that has continued with ceaseless vigilance ever since the beginning of the war in Europe, the concrete crimes unearthed and punished have been fewer than those prosecutions for the mere crime of opinion or the expression of sentiments critical of the State or the national policy. The punishment for opinion has been far more ferocious and unintermittent than the punishment of pragmatic crime. Unimpeachable Anglo-Saxon Americans who were freer of pacifist or socialist utterance than the State-obsessed ruling public opinion, received heavier penalties and even greater opprobrium, in many instances, than the definitely hostile German plotter. A public opinion which, almost without protest, accepts as just, adequate, beautiful, deserved and in fitting harmony with ideals of liberty and freedom of speech, a sentence of twenty years in prison for mere utterances, no matter what they may be, shows itself to be suffering from a kind of social derangement of values, a sort of social neurosis, that deserves analysis and comprehension.

On our entrance into the war, there were many persons who predicted exactly this derangement of values, who feared lest democracy suffer more at home from an America at war than could be gained for democracy abroad. That fear has been amply justified. The question whether the American nation would act like an enlightened democracy going to war for the sake of high ideals, or like a State-obsessed herd, has been decisively answered. The record is written and cannot be erased. History will decide whether the terrorization of opinion, and the regimentation of life was justified under the most idealistic of democratic administrations. It will see that when the American nation had ostensibly a chance to conduct a gallant war, with scrupulous regard to the safety of democratic values at home, it chose rather to adopt all the most obnoxious and coercive techniques of the enemy and of the other countries at war, and to rival in intimidation and ferocity of punishment the worst governmental systems of the age. For its former unconsciousness and disrespect of the State ideal, the nation apparently paid the penalty in a violent swing to the other extreme. It acted so exactly like a herd in its irrational coercion of minorities that there is no artificiality in interpreting the progress of the war in terms of the herd psychology. It unwittingly brought out into the strongest relief the true characteristics of the State and its intimate alliance with war. It provided for the enemies of war and the critics of the State the most telling arguments possible. The new passion for the State ideal unwittingly set in motion and encouraged forces that threaten very materially to reform the State. It has shown those who are really determined to end war that the problem is not the mere simple one of finishing a war that will end war.

For war is a complicated way in which a nation acts, and it acts so out of a spiritual compulsion which pushes it on, perhaps against all its interests, all its real desires, and all its real sense of values. It is States that make wars and not nations, and the very thought and almost necessity of war is bound up with the ideal of the State. Not for centuries have nations made war; in fact the only historical example of nations making war is the great barbarian invasions into southern Europe, the invasions of Russia from the East, and perhaps the sweep of Islam through Northern Africa into Europe after Mohammed's death. And the motivations for such wars were either the restless expansion of migratory tribes or the flame of religious fanaticism. Perhaps these great movements could scarcely be called wars at all, for war implies an organized people drilled and led; in fact, it necessitates the State. Ever since Europe has had any such organization, such huge conflicts between nations—nations, that is, as cultural groups—have been unthinkable. It is preposterous to assume that for centuries in Europe there would have been any possibility of a people *en masse* (with their own leaders, and not with the leaders of their duly constituted State), rising up and overflowing their borders in a war raid upon a neighboring people. The wars of the Revolutionary armies of France were clearly in defense of an imperiled freedom, and, moreover, they were clearly directed not against other peoples, but against the autocratic governments that were combining to crush the Revolution. There is no instance in history of a genuinely national war. There are instances of national defenses, among primitive civilizations such as the Balkan peoples, against intolerable invasion by neighboring despots or oppression. But war, as such, cannot occur except in a system of competing States, which have relations with each other through the channels of diplomacy.

War is a function of this system of States, and could not occur except in such a system. Nations organized for internal administration, nations organized as a federation of free communities, nations organized in any way except that of a political centralization of a dynasty, or the reformed descendant of a dynasty, could not possibly make war upon each other. They would not only have no motive for conflict, but they would be unable to muster the concentrated force to make war effective. There might be all sorts of amateur marauding, there might be guerilla expeditions of group against group, but there could not be that terrible war *en masse* of the national State, that exploitation of the nation in the interests of the State, that abuse of the national life and resource in the frenzied mutual suicide, which is modern war.

It cannot be too firmly realized that war is a function of States and not of nations, indeed that it is the chief function of States. War is a very artificial thing. It is not the naïve spontaneous outburst of herd pugnacity; it is no more primary than is formal religion. War cannot exist without a military establishment, and a military establishment cannot exist without a State organization. War has an immemorial tradition and heredity only because the State has a long tradition and heredity. But they are inseparably and functionally joined. We cannot crusade against war without crusading implicitly against the State. And we cannot expect, or take measures to ensure, that this war is a war to end war, unless at the same time we take measures to end the State in its traditional form. The State is not the nation, and the State can be modified and even abolished in its present form, without harming the nation. On the contrary, with the passing of the dominance of the State, the genuine life-enhancing forces of the nation will be liberated. If the State's chief function is war, then the State must suck out of the nation a large part of its energy for its purely sterile purposes of defense and aggression. It devotes to waste or to actual destruction as much as it can of the vitality of the nation. No one will deny that war is a vast complex of life-destroying and life-crippling forces. If the State's chief function is war, then it is chiefly concerned with coördinating and developing the powers and techniques which make for destruction. And this means not only the actual and potential destruction of the enemy, but of the nation at home as well. For the very existence of a State in a system of States means that the nation lies always under a risk of war and invasion, and the calling away of energy into military pursuits means a crippling of the productive and life-enhancing processes of the national life.

All this organizing of death-dealing energy and technique is not a natural but a very sophisticated process. Particularly in modern nations, but also all through the course of modern European history, it could never exist without the State. For it meets the demands of no other institution, it follows the desires of no religious, industrial, political group. If the demand for military organization and a military establishment seems to come not from the officers of the State but from the public, it is only that it comes from the State-obsessed portion of the public, those groups which feel most keenly the State ideal. And in this country we have had evidence all too indubitable how powerless the pacifically minded officers of State may be in the face of a State-obsession of the significant classes. If a powerful section of the significant classes feels more intensely the attitudes of the State, then they will most infallibly mold the Government in time to their wishes, bring it back to act as the embodiment of the State which it pretends to be. In every country we have seen groups that were more loyal than the king—more patriotic than the Government—the Ulsterites in Great Britain, the Junkers in Prussia, l'Action Française in France, our patrioteers in America. These groups exist to keep the steering wheel of the State straight, and they prevent the nation from ever veering very far from the State ideal.

Militarism expresses the desires and satisfies the major impulse only of this class. The other classes, left to themselves, have too many necessities and interests and ambitions, to concern themselves with so expensive and destructive a game. But the State-obsessed group is either able to get control of the machinery of the State or to intimidate those in control, so that it is able through use of the collective force to regiment the other grudging and reluctant classes into a military programme. State idealism percolates down through the strata of society; capturing groups and individuals just in proportion to the prestige of this dominant class. So that we have the herd actually strung along between two extremes, the militaristic patriots at one end, who are scarcely distinguishable in attitude and animus from the most reactionary Bourbons of an Empire, and unskilled labor groups, which entirely lack the State sense. But the State acts as a whole, and the class that controls governmental machinery can swing the effective action of the herd as a whole. The herd is not actually a whole, emotionally. But by an ingenious mixture of cajolery, agitation, intimidation, the herd is licked into shape, into an effective mechanical unity, if not into a spiritual whole. Men are told simultaneously that they will enter the military establishment of their own volition, as their splendid sacrifice for their country's welfare, and that if they do not enter they will be hunted down and punished with the most horrid penalties; and under a most indescribable confusion of democratic pride and personal fear they submit to the destruction of their livelihood if not their lives, in a way that would formerly have seemed to them so obnoxious as to be incredible.

In this great herd-machinery, dissent is like sand in the bearings. The State ideal is primarily a sort of blind animal push towards military unity. Any interference with that unity turns the whole vast impulse towards crushing it. Dissent is speedily outlawed, and the Government, backed by the significant classes and those who in every locality, however small, identify themselves with them, proceeds against the outlaws, regardless of their value to the other institutions of the nation, or to the effect their persecution may have on public opinion. The herd becomes divided into the hunters and the hunted, and war-enterprise becomes not only a technical game but a sport as well.

It must never be forgotten that nations do not declare war on each other, nor in the strictest sense is it nations that fight each other. Much has been said to the effect that modern wars are wars of whole peoples and not of dynasties. Because the entire nation is regimented and the whole resources of the country are levied on for war, this does not mean that it is the country *qua* country which is fighting. It is the country organized as a State that is fighting, and only as a State would it possibly fight. So, literally, it is States which make war on each other and not peoples. Governments are the agents of States, and it is Governments which declare war on each other, acting truest to form in the interests of the great State ideal they represent. There is no case known in modern times of the people being consulted in the initiation of a war. The present demand for democratic control of foreign policy indicates how completely, even in the most democratic of modern nations, foreign policy has been the secret private possession of the executive branch of the Government.

However representative of the people Parliaments and Congresses may be in all that concerns the internal administration of a country's political affairs, in international relations it has never been possible to maintain that the popular body acted except as a wholly mechanical ratifier of the Executive's will. The formality by which Parliaments and Congresses declare war is the merest technicality. Before such a declaration can take place, the country will have been brought to the very brink of war by the foreign policy of the Executive. A long series of steps on the downward path, each one more fatally committing the unsuspecting country to a warlike course of action will have been taken without either the people or its representatives being consulted or expressing its feeling. When the declaration of war is finally demanded by the Executive, the Parliament or Congress could not refuse it without reversing the course of history, without repudiating what has been representing itself in the eyes of the other States as the symbol and interpreter of the nation's will and animus. To repudiate an Executive at that time would be to publish to the entire world the evidence that the country had been grossly deceived by its own Government, that the country with an almost criminal carelessness had allowed its Government to commit it to gigantic national enterprises in which it had no heart. In such a crisis, even a Parliament which in the most democratic States represents the common man and not the significant classes who most strongly cherish the State ideal, will cheerfully sustain the foreign policy which it understands even less than it would care for if it understood, and will vote almost unanimously for an incalculable war, in which the nation may be brought well nigh to ruin. That is why the referendum which was advocated by some people as a test of American sentiment in entering the war was considered even by thoughtful democrats to be something subtly improper. The die had been cast. Popular whim could only derange and bungle monstrously the majestic march of State policy in its new crusade for the peace of the world. The irresistible State ideal got hold of the bowels of men. Whereas up to this time, it had been irreproachable to be neutral in word and deed, for the foreign policy of the State had so decided it, henceforth it became the most arrant crime to remain neutral. The Middle West, which had been soddenly pacifistic in our days of neutrality, became in a few months just as soddenly bellicose, and in its zeal for witch-burnings and its scent for enemies within gave precedence to no section of the country. The herd-mind followed faithfully the State-mind and, the agitation for a referendum being soon forgotten, the country fell into the universal conclusion that, since its Congress had formally declared the war, the nation itself had in the most solemn and universal way devised and brought on the entire affair. Oppression of minorities became justified on the plea that the latter were perversely resisting the rationally constructed and solemnly declared will of a majority of the nation. The herd-coalescence of opinion which became inevitable the moment the State had set flowing the war-attitudes became interpreted as a pre-war popular decision, and disinclination to bow to the herd was treated as a monstrously anti-social act. So that the State, which had vigorously resisted the idea of a referendum and clung tenaciously and, of course, with entire success to its autocratic and absolute control of foreign policy, had the pleasure of seeing the country, within a few months, given over to the retrospective impression that a genuine referendum had taken place. When once a country has lapped up these State attitudes, its memory fades; it conceives itself not as merely accepting, but of having itself willed the whole policy and technique of war. The significant classes with their trailing satellites, identify themselves with the State, so that what the State, through the agency of the Government, has willed, this majority conceives itself to have willed.

All of which goes to show that the State represents all the autocratic, arbitrary, coercive, belligerent forces within a social group, it is a sort of complexus of everything most distasteful to the modern free creative spirit, the feeling for life, liberty and the pursuit of happiness. War is the health of the State. Only when the State is at war does the modern society function with that unity of sentiment, simple uncritical patriotic devotion, coöperation of services, which have always been the ideal of the State lover. With the ravages of democratic ideas, however, the modern republic cannot go to war under the old conceptions of autocracy and death-dealing belligerency. If a successful animus for war requires a renaissance of State ideals, they can only come back under democratic forms, under this retrospective conviction of democratic control of foreign policy, democratic desire for war, and particularly of this identification of the democracy with the State. How unregenerate the ancient State may be, however, is indicated by the laws against sedition, and by the Government's unreformed attitude on foreign policy. One of the first demands of the more far-seeing democrats in the democracies of the Alliance was that secret diplomacy must go. The war was seen to have been made possible by a web of secret agreements between States, alliances that were made by Governments without the shadow of popular support or even popular knowledge, and vague, half-understood commitments that scarcely reached the stage of a treaty or agreement, but which proved binding in the event. Certainly, said these democratic thinkers, war can scarcely be avoided unless this poisonous underground system of secret diplomacy is destroyed, this system by which a nation's power, wealth and manhood may be signed away like a blank check to an allied nation to be cashed in at some future crisis. Agreements which are to affect the lives of whole peoples must be made between peoples and not by Governments, or at least by their representatives in the full glare of publicity and criticism.

Such a demand for "democratic control of foreign policy" seemed axiomatic. Even if the country had been swung into war by steps taken secretly and announced to the public only after they had been consummated, it was felt that that attitude of the American State towards foreign policy was only a relic of the bad old days and must be superseded in the new order. The American President himself, the liberal hope of the world, had demanded, in the eyes of the world, open diplomacy, agreements freely and openly arrived at. Did this mean a genuine transference of power in this most crucial of State functions from Government to people? Not at all. When the question recently came to a challenge in Congress, and the implications of open discussion were somewhat specifically discussed, and the desirabilities frankly commended, the President let his disapproval be known in no uncertain way. No one ever accused Mr. Wilson of not being a State idealist, and whenever democratic aspirations swung ideals too far out of the State orbit, he could be counted on to react vigorously. Here was a clear case of conflict between democratic idealism and the very crux of the concept of the State. However unthinkingly he might have been led on to encourage open diplomacy in his liberalizing programme, when its implication was made vivid to him, he betrayed how mere a tool the idea had been in his mind to accentuate America's redeeming rôle. Not in any sense as a serious pragmatic technique had he thought of a genuinely open diplomacy. And how could he? For the last stronghold of State power is foreign policy. It is in foreign policy that the State acts most concentratedly as the organized herd, acts with fullest sense of aggressive power, acts with freest arbitrariness. In foreign policy, the State is most itself. States, with reference to each other, may be said to be in a continual state of latent war. The "armed truce," a phrase so familiar before 1914, was an accurate description of the normal relation of States when they are not at war. Indeed, it is not too much to say that the normal relation of States is war. Diplomacy is a disguised war, in which States seek to gain by barter and intrigue, by the cleverness of wits, the objectives which they would have to gain more clumsily by means of war. Diplomacy is used while the States are recuperating from conflicts in which they have exhausted themselves. It is the wheedling and the bargaining of the worn-out bullies as they rise from the ground and slowly restore their strength to begin fighting again. If diplomacy had been a moral equivalent for war, a higher stage in human progress, an inestimable means of making words prevail instead of blows, militarism would have broken down and given place to it. But since it is a mere temporary substitute, a mere appearance of war's energy under another form, a surrogate effect is almost exactly proportioned to the armed force behind it. When it fails, the recourse is immediate to the military technique whose thinly veiled arm it has been. A diplomacy that was the agency of popular democratic forces in their non-State manifestations would be no diplomacy at all. It would be no better than the Railway or Education Commissions that are sent from one country to another with rational constructive purpose. The State, acting as a diplomatic-military ideal, is eternally at war. Just as it must act arbitrarily and autocratically in time of war, it must act in time of peace in this particular rôle where it acts as a unit. Unified control is necessarily autocratic control. Democratic control of foreign policy is therefore a contradiction in terms. Open discussion destroys swiftness and certainty of action. The giant State is paralyzed. Mr. Wilson retains his full ideal of the State at the same time that he desires to eliminate war. He wishes to make the world safe for democracy as well as safe for diplomacy. When the two are in conflict, his clear political insight, his idealism of the State, tells him that it is the naïver democratic values that must be sacrificed. The world must primarily be made safe for diplomacy. The State must not be diminished.

What is the State essentially? The more closely we examine it, the more mystical and personal it becomes. On the Nation we can put our hand as a definite social group, with attitudes and qualities exact enough to mean something. On the Government we can put our hand as a certain organization of ruling functions, the machinery of law-making and law-enforcing. The Administration is a recognizable group of political functionaries, temporarily in charge of the government. But the State stands as an idea behind them all, eternal, sanctified, and from it Government and Administration conceive themselves to have the breath of life. Even the nation, especially in times of war—or at least, its significant classes—considers that it derives its authority, and its purpose from the idea of the State. Nation and State are scarcely differentiated, and the concrete, practical, apparent facts are sunk in the symbol. We reverence not our country but the flag. We may criticize ever so severely our country, but we are disrespectful to the flag at our peril. It is the flag and the uniform that make men's hearts beat high and fill them with noble emotions, not the thought of and pious hopes for America as a free and enlightened nation.

It cannot be said that the object of emotion is the same, because the flag is the symbol of the nation, so that in reverencing the American flag we are reverencing the nation. For the flag is not a symbol of the country as a cultural group, following certain ideals of life, but solely a symbol of the political State, inseparable from its prestige and expansion. The flag is most intimately connected with military achievement, military memory. It represents the country not in its intensive life, but in its far-flung challenge to the world. The flag is primarily the banner of war; it is allied with patriotic anthem and holiday. It recalls old martial memories. A nation's patriotic history is solely the history of its wars, that is, of the State in its health and glorious functioning. So in responding to the appeal of the flag, we are responding to the appeal of the State, to the symbol of the herd organized as an offensive and defensive body, conscious of its prowess and its mystical herd-strength.

*1918*

# ALBERT JAY NOCK

In intellectual circles, libertarians tend to be more passionate than numerous. In his day, Albert Jay Nock (1870–1945) was America's foremost libertarian—although he preferred the term "philosophical anarchist"—and was as critical of twentieth-century American liberalism as he was of totalitarianism in its various forms.

FROM *Our Enemy, The State*

## THREE INDEXES OF STATE POWER

IN THE United States at the present time, the principal indexes of the increase of State power are three in number. First, the point to which the centralization of State authority has been carried. Practically all the sovereign rights and powers of the smaller political units—all of them that are significant enough to be worth absorbing—have been absorbed by the federal unit; nor is this all. State power has not only been thus concentrated at Washington, but it has been so far concentrated into the hands of the Executive that the existing regime is a regime of personal government. It is nominally republican, but actually monocratic; a curious anomaly, but highly characteristic of a people little gifted with intellectual integrity. Personal government is not exercised here in the same ways as in Italy, Russia or Germany, for there is as yet no State interest to be served by so doing, but rather the contrary; while in those countries there is. But personal government is always personal government; the mode of its exercise is a matter of immediate political expediency, and is determined entirely by circumstances.

This regime was established by a *coup d'Etat* of a new and unusual kind practicable only in a rich country. It was effected, not by violence, like Louis-Napoleon's, or by terrorism, like Mussolini's, but by purchase. It therefore presents what might be called an American variant of the *coup d'Etat*.[1] Our national legislature was not suppressed by force of arms, like the French Assembly in 1851, but was bought out of its functions with public money; and as appeared most conspicuously in the elections of November, 1934, the consolidation of the *coup d'Etat* was effected by the same means; the corresponding functions in the smaller units were reduced under the personal control of the Executive.[2] This is a most remarkable phenomenon; possibly nothing quite like it ever took place; and its character and implications deserve the most careful attention.

A second index is supplied by the prodigious extension of the bureaucratic principle that is now observable. This is attested *prima facie* by the number of new boards, bureaux and commissions set up at Washington in the last two years. They are reported as representing something like 90,000 new employees appointed outside the civil service, and the total of the federal payroll in Washington is reported as something over three million dollars per month.[3] This, however, is relatively a small matter. The pressure of centralization has tended powerfully to convert every official and every political aspirant in the smaller units into a venal and complaisant agent of the federal bureaucracy. This presents an interesting parallel with the state of things prevailing in the Roman Empire in the last days of the Flavian dynasty, and afterwards. The rights and practices of local self-government, which were formerly very considerable in the provinces and much more so in the municipalities, were lost by surrender

---

[1] There is a sort of precedent for it in Roman history, if the story be true in all its details that the army sold the emperorship to Didius Julianus for something like five million dollars. Money has often been used to grease the wheels of a *coup d'Etat*, but straight over-the-counter purchase is unknown, I think, except in these two instances.

[2] On the day I write this, the newspapers say that the President is about to order a stoppage on the flow of federal relief-funds into Louisiana, for the purpose of bringing Senator Long to terms. I have seen no comment, however, on the propriety of this kind of procedure.

[3] A friend in the theatrical business tells me that from the box-office point of view, Washington is now the best theatre-town, concert-town and general-amusement town in the United States, far better than New York.

rather than by suppression. The imperial bureaucracy, which up to the second century was comparatively a modest affair, grew rapidly to great size, and local politicians were quick to see the advantage of being on terms with it. They came to Rome with their hats in their hands, as governors, Congressional aspirants and such-like now go to Washington. Their eyes and thoughts were constantly fixed on Rome, because recognition and preferment lay that way; and in their incorrigible sycophancy they became, as Plutarch says, like hypochondriacs who dare not eat or take a bath without consulting their physician.

A third index is seen in the erection of poverty and mendicancy into a permanent political asset. Two years ago, many of our people were in hard straits; to some extent, no doubt, through no fault of their own, though it is now clear that in the popular view of their case, as well as in the political view, the line between the deserving poor and the undeserving poor was not distinctly drawn. Popular feeling ran high at the time, and the prevailing wretchedness was regarded with undiscriminating emotion, as evidence of some general wrong done upon its victims by society at large, rather than as the natural penalty of greed, folly or actual misdoings; which in large part it was. The State, always instinctively "turning every contingency into a resource" for accelerating the conversion of social power into State power, was quick to take advantage of this state of mind. All that was needed to organize these unfortunates into an invaluable political property was to declare the doctrine that the State owes all its citizens a living, and this was accordingly done. It immediately precipitated an enormous mass of subsidized voting-power, an enormous resource for strengthening the State at the expense of society.[4]

## STATE POWER DOES NOT DIMINISH

There is an impression that the enhancement of State power which has taken place since 1932 is provisional and temporary, that the corresponding depletion of social power is by way of a kind of

---

[4] The feature of the approaching campaign of 1936 which will most interest the student of civilization will be the use of the four-billion-dollar relief-fund that has been placed at the President's disposal—the extent, that is, to which it will be distributed on a patronage-basis.

emergency-loan, and therefore is not to be scrutinized too closely. There is every probability that this belief is devoid of foundation. No doubt our present regime will be modified in one way and another; indeed, it must be, for the process of consolidation itself requires it. But any essential change would be quite unhistorical, quite without precedent, and is therefore most unlikely; and by any essential change, I mean one that will tend to redistribute actual power between the State and society.[5] In the nature of things, there is no reason why such a change should take place, and every reason why it should not. We shall see various apparent recessions, apparent compromises, but the one thing we may be quite sure of is that none of these will tend to diminish actual State power.

For example, we shall no doubt shortly see the great pressure-group of politically-organized poverty and mendicancy subsidized indirectly instead of directly, because State interest can not long keep pace with the hand-over-head disposition of the masses to loot their own Treasury. The method of direct subsidy, or sheer cash-purchase, will therefore in all probability soon give way to the indirect method of what is called "social legislation;" that is, a multiplex system of State-managed pensions, insurances and indemnities of various kinds. This is an apparent recession, and when it occurs it will no doubt be proclaimed as an actual recession, no doubt accepted as such; but is it? Does it actually tend to diminish State power and increase social power? Obviously not, but quite the opposite. It tends to consolidate firmly this particular fraction of State power, and opens the way to getting an indefinite increment upon it by the mere continuous invention of new courses and developments of State-administered social legislation, which is an extremely simple business. One may add the observation for whatever its evidential value may be worth, that if the effect of progressive social legislation upon the sum-total of State power were unfavourable or even nil, we should hardly have found

---

[5] It must always be kept in mind that there is a tidal-motion as well as a wave-motion in these matters, and that the wave-motion is of little importance, relatively. For instance, the Supreme Court's invalidation of the National Recovery Act counts for nothing in determining the actual status of personal government. The real question is not how much less the sum of personal government is now than it was before that decision, but how much greater it is normally now than it was in 1932, and in years preceding.

Prince de Bismarck and the British Liberal politicians of forty years ago going in for anything remotely resembling it.

When, therefore, the inquiring student of civilization has occasion to observe this or any other apparent recession upon any point of our present regime,[6] he may content himself with asking the one question, *What effect has this upon the sum-total of State power?* The answer he gives himself will show conclusively whether the recession is actual or apparent, and this is all he is concerned to know.

There is also an impression that if actual recessions do not come about of themselves, they may be brought about by the expedient of voting one political party out and another one in. This idea rests upon certain assumptions that experience has shown to be unsound; the first one being that the power of the ballot is what republican political theory makes it out to be, and that therefore the electorate has an effective choice in the matter. It is a matter of open and notorious fact that nothing like this is true. Our nominally republican system is actually built on an imperial model, with our professional politicians standing in the place of the praetorian guards; they meet from time to time, decide what can be "got away with," and how, and who is to do it; and the electorate votes according to their prescriptions. Under these conditions it is easy to provide the appearance of any desired concession of State power, without the reality; our history shows innumerable instances of very easy dealing with problems in practical politics much more difficult than that. One may remark in this connexion also the notoriously baseless assumption that party-designations connote principles, and that party-pledges imply performance. Moreover, underlying these assumptions and all others that faith in "political action" contemplates, is the assumption that the interests of the State and the interests of society are, at least theoretically, identical; whereas in theory they are directly opposed, and this opposition invariably declares itself in practice to the precise extent that circumstances permit.

However, without pursuing these matters further at the moment, it is probably enough to observe here that in the nature of things the exercise of personal government, the control of a huge and growing bureaucracy, and the management of an enormous mass of subsidized

---

[6] As, for example, the spectacular voiding of the National Recovery Act.

voting-power, are as agreeable to one stripe of politician as they are to another. Presumably they interest a Republican or a Progressive as much as they do a Democrat, Communist, Farmer-Labourite, Socialist, or whatever a politician may, for electioneering purposes, see fit to call himself. This was demonstrated in the local campaigns of 1934 by the practical attitude of politicians who represented nominal opposition parties. It is now being further demonstrated by the derisible haste that the leaders of the official opposition are making towards what they call "reorganization" of their party. One may well be inattentive to their words; their actions, however, mean simply that the recent accretions of State power are here to stay, and that they are aware of it; and that, such being the case, they are preparing to dispose themselves most advantageously in a contest for their control and management. This is all that "reorganization" of the Republican Party means, and all it is meant to mean; and this is in itself quite enough to show that any expectation of an essential change of regime through a change of party-administration is illusory. On the contrary, it is clear that whatever party-competition we shall see hereafter will be on the same terms as heretofore. It will be a competition for control and management, and it would naturally issue in still closer centralization, still further extension of the bureaucratic principle, and still larger concessions to subsidized voting-power. This course would be strictly historical, and is furthermore to be expected as lying in the nature of things, as it so obviously does.

Indeed, it is by this means that the aim of the collectivists seems likeliest to be attained in this country; this aim being the complete extinction of social power through absorption by the State. Their fundamental doctrine was formulated and invested with a quasi-religious sanction by the idealist philosophers of the last century; and among peoples who have accepted it in terms as well as in fact, it is expressed in formulas almost identical with theirs. Thus, for example, when Hitler says that "the State dominates the nation because it alone represents it," he is only putting into loose popular language the formula of Hegel, that "the State is the general substance, whereof individuals are but accidents." Or, again, when Mussolini says, "Everything for the State; nothing outside the State; nothing against the State," he is merely vulgarizing the doctrine of Fichte, that "the State is the superior power, ultimate and beyond appeal, absolutely independent."

It may be in place to remark here the essential identity of the various extant forms of collectivism. The superficial distinctions of Fascism, Bolshevism, Hitlerism, are the concern of journalists and publicists; the serious student[7] sees in them only the one root-idea of a complete conversion of social power into State power. When Hitler and Mussolini invoke a kind of debased and hoodwinking mysticism to aid their acceleration of this process, the student at once recognizes his old friend, the formula of Hegel, that "the State incarnates the Divine Idea upon earth," and he is not hoodwinked. The journalist and the impressionable traveller may make what they will of "the new religion of Bolshevism;" the student contents himself with remarking clearly the exact nature of the process which this inculcation is designed to sanction.

## THE NOISELESS REVOLUTION

This process—the conversion of social power into State power—has not been carried as far here as it has elsewhere; as it has in Russia, Italy or Germany, for example. Two things, however, are to be observed. First, that it has gone a long way, at a rate of progress which has of late been greatly accelerated. What has chiefly differentiated its progress here from its progress in other countries is its unspectacular character. Mr. Jefferson wrote in 1823 that there was no danger he dreaded so much as "the consolidation [i.e., centralization] of our government by the noiseless and therefore unalarming instrumentality of the Supreme Court." These words characterize every advance that we have made in State aggrandizement. Each one has been noiseless and therefore unalarming, especially to a people notoriously preoccupied, inattentive and incurious. Even the *coup d'Etat* of 1932 was noiseless and unalarming. In Russia, Italy, Germany, the *coup d'Etat* was violent and spectacular; it had to be; but here it was neither. Under cover of a nation-wide, State-managed mobilization of inane buffoonery and aimless commotion, it took place in so unspectacular a way that its

---

[7] This book is a sort of syllabus or precis of some lectures to students of American history and politics—mostly graduate students—and it therefore presupposes some little acquaintance with those subjects. The few references I have given, however, will put any reader in the way of documenting and amplifying it satisfactorily.

true nature escaped notice, and even now is not generally understood. The method of consolidating the ensuing regime, moreover, was also noiseless and un-alarming; it was merely the prosaic and unspectacular "higgling of the market," to which a long and uniform political experience had accustomed us. A visitor from a poorer and thriftier country might have regarded Mr. Farley's activities in the local campaigns of 1934 as striking or even spectacular, but they made no such impression on us. They seemed so familiar, so much the regular thing, that one heard little comment on them. Moreover, political habit led us to attribute whatever unfavourable comment we did hear, to interest; either partisan or monetary interest, or both. We put it down as the jaundiced judgment of persons with axes to grind; and naturally the regime did all it could to encourage this view.

The second thing to be observed is that certain formulas, certain arrangements of words, stand as an obstacle in the way of our perceiving how far the conversion of social power into State power has actually gone. The force of phrase and name distorts the identification of our own actual acceptances and acquiescences. We are accustomed to the rehearsal of certain poetic litanies, and provided their cadence be kept entire, we are indifferent to their correspondence with truth and fact. When Hegel's doctrine of the State, for example, is restated in terms by Hitler and Mussolini, it is distinctly offensive to us, and we congratulate ourselves on our freedom from the "yoke of a dictator's tyranny." No American politician would dream of breaking in on our routine of litanies with anything of the kind. We may imagine, for example, the shock to popular sentiment that would ensue upon Mr. Roosevelt's declaring publicly that "the State embrace, everything, and nothing has value outside the State. The State creates right." Yet an American politician, as long as he does not formulate that doctrine in set terms, may go further with it in a practical way than Mussolini has gone, and without trouble or question. Suppose Mr. Roosevelt should defend his regime by publicly reasserting Hegel's dictum that "the State alone possesses rights, because it is the strongest." One can hardly imagine that our public would get that down without a great deal of retching. Yet how far, really, is that doctrine alien to our public's actual acquiescences? Surely not far.

The point is that in respect of the relation between the theory and the actual practice of public affairs, the American is the most unphilosophical of beings. The rationalization of conduct in general is most repugnant to him; he prefers to emotionalize it. He is indifferent to the theory of things, so long as he may rehearse his formulas; and so long as he can listen to the patter of his litanies, no practical inconsistency disturbs him—indeed, he gives no evidence of even recognizing it as an inconsistency.

The ablest and most acute observer among the many who came from Europe to look us over in the early part of the last century was the one who is for some reason the most neglected, notwithstanding that in our present circumstances, especially, he is worth more to us than all the de Tocquevilles, Bryces, Trollopes and Chateaubriands put together. This was the noted St.-Simonien and political economist, Michel Chevalier. Professor Chinard, in his admirable biographical study of John Adams, has called attention to Chevalier's observation that the American people have "the morale of any army on the march." The more one thinks of this, the more clearly one sees how little there is in what our publicists are fond of calling the "American psychology" that it does not exactly account for; and it exactly accounts for the trait that we are considering.

An army on the march has no philosophy; it views itself as a creature of the moment. It does not rationalize conduct except in terms of an immediate end. As Tennyson observed, there is a pretty strict official understanding against its doing so; "theirs not to reason why." Emotionalizing conduct is another matter, and the more of it the better; it is encouraged by a whole elaborate paraphernalia of showy etiquette, flags, music, uniforms, decorations, and the careful cultivation of a very special sort of camaraderie. In every relation to "the reason of the thing," however—in the ability and eagerness, as Plato puts it, "to see things as they are"—the mentality of any army on the march is merely so much delayed adolescence; it remains persistently, incorrigibly and notoriously infantile.

Past generations of Americans, as Martin Chuzzlewit left record, erected this infantilism into a distinguishing virtue, and they took great pride in it as the mark of a chosen people, destined to live forever amidst the glory of their own unparalleled achievements *wie Gott in Frankreich*. Mr. Jefferson Brick, General Choke and the Honourable Elijah Pogram made a first-class job of indoctrinating their countrymen with the idea that a philosophy is wholly unnecessary, and that a concern with the theory of things is effeminate and unbecoming. An envious and presumably dissolute Frenchman may say what he likes about the morale of any army on the march, but the fact remains that it has brought us where we are, and has got us what we have. Look at a continent subdued, see the spread of our industry and commerce, our railways, newspapers, finance-companies, schools, colleges, what you will! Well, if all this has been done without a philosophy, if we have grown to this unrivalled greatness without any attention to the theory of things, does it not show that philosophy and the theory of things are all moonshine, and not worth a practical people's consideration? The morale of any army on the march is good enough for us, and we are proud of it.

The present generation does not speak in quite this tone of robust certitude. It seems, if anything, rather less openly contemptuous of philosophy; one even sees some signs of a suspicion that in our present circumstances the theory of things might be worth looking into, and it is especially towards the theory of sovereignty and rulership that this new attitude of hospitality appears to be developing. The condition of public affairs in all countries, notably in our own, has done more than bring under review the mere current practice of politics, the character and quality of representative politicians, and the relative merits of this-or-that form or mode of government. It has served to suggest attention to the one institution whereof all these forms or modes are but the several, and, from the theoretical point of view, indifferent, manifestations. It suggests that finality does not lie with consideration of species, but of genus; it does not lie with consideration of the characteristic marks that differentiate the republican State, monocratic State, constitutional, collectivist, totalitarian, Hitlerian, Bolshevist, what you will. It lies with consideration of the State itself.

*1935*

# RICHARD WEAVER

Born and raised in North Carolina, Richard Weaver (1910–1963) spent the preponderance of his professional career at the University of Chicago. Yet in a fundamental sense he never left the South, which he saw as a model of a society resistant to the rampant materialism that was destructive of civility and social cohesion. Weaver became the intellectual godfather of paleoconservatism, which stresses tradition and defense of the existing social order.

## The Great Stereopticon

> Sick are they always; they vomit their bile
> and call it a newspaper.
> —Nietzsche.

THE DISAPPEARANCE of the primordial synthesis has profound consequences which are felt even by those below the level of philosophy; and it is they, ironically, who make the first effort to repair the damage. It scarcely needs adding that their lack of penetration renders the effort abortive, for what they do, when fragmentation has reached the point of danger, is to attempt a restoration by physical means.

The problem which disintegration places in the lap of practical men, those in charge of states, of institutions, of businesses, is how to persuade to communal activity people who no longer have the same ideas about the most fundamental things. In an age of shared belief, this problem does not exist, for there is a wide area of basic agreement, and dissent is viewed not as a claim to egotistic distinction but as a sort of excommunication. The entire group is conscious of the tendency,

347

which furnishes standards for value judgments. When the goal of life becomes self-realization, however, this vanishes. It vanishes right at that point where the ego asserts its independence; thereafter what reconciliation can there be between authority and individual will? The politicians and businessmen are not interested in saving souls, but they are interested in preserving a minimum of organization, for upon that depend their posts and their incomes.

These leaders adopted the liberal's solution to their problem. That was to let religion go but to replace it with education, which supposedly would exercise the same efficacy. The separation of education from religion, one of the proudest achievements of modernism, is but an extension of the separation of knowledge from metaphysics. And the education thus separated can provide their kind of indoctrination. We include here, of course, the education of the classroom, for all such institutionalized instruction proceeds on the assumptions of the state. But the education which best accomplishes their purpose is the systematic indoctrination from day to day of the whole citizenry through channels of information and entertainment.

The vested interests of our age, which, from all kinds of motives, desire to maintain traditional values or to get new values set up in their place, have constructed a wonderful machine, which we shall call the Great Stereopticon. It is the function of this machine to project selected pictures of life in the hope that what is seen will be imitated. All of us of the West who are within the long reach of technology are sitting in the audience. We are told the time to laugh and the time to cry, and signs are not wanting that the audience grows ever more responsive to its cues.

A great point is sometimes made of the fact that modern man no longer sees above his head a revolving dome with fixed stars and glimpses of the *primum mobile*. True enough, but he sees something similar when he looks at his daily newspaper. He sees the events of the day refracted through a medium which colors them as effectively as the cosmology of the medieval scientist determined his view of the starry heavens. The newspaper is a man-made cosmos of the world of events around us at the time. For the average reader it is a construct with a set of significances which he no more thinks of examining than did his pious forebear of the thirteenth century—whom he pities for sitting in medieval darkness—think of questioning the cosmology.

This modern man, too, lives under a dome, whose theoretical aspect has been made to harmonize with a materialistic conception of the world. And he employs its conjunctions and oppositions to explain the occurrences of his time with all the confidence of the now supplanted disciple of astrology.

The Great Stereopticon, like most gadgets, has been progressively improved and added to until today it is a machine of three parts: the press, the motion picture, and the radio. Together they present a version of life quite as controlled as that taught by medieval religionists, though feeble in moral inspiration, as we shall see. It is now our object to look at the effects of each in turn.

No one is prepared to understand the influence of journalism on the public mind until he appreciates the fact that the newspaper is a spawn of the machine. A mechanism itself, it has ever been closely linked with the kind of exploitation, financial and political, which accompanies industrialism. The press is the great scribe, possessed of that preponderance of means which technology always provides. The ease with which it multiplies stereotypes makes it the ideal servant of progress. It thrives on an endlessness of dissemination. Its progeny, like the frogs of Egypt, come up into our very kneading troughs. But, just because the mechanical victory of the press is so complete, we are likely to ignore the conditions on which its work proceeds.

I serve notice, therefore, that we here approach a question of blasphemous nature, a question whose mere asking disturbs the deepest complacency of the age. And that is: Has the art of writing proved an unmixed blessing? The thought challenges so many assumptions that to consider it requires almost a fresh orientation in philosophy; but we must recall that it occurred to Plato, who answered the question in the negative. With him it concerned the issue of whether philosophy should be written down, and his conclusion was that philosophy exists best in discourse between persons, the truth leaping up between them "like a flame."

In explanation of this important point he makes Socrates relate a myth about the Egyptian god Theuth, a mighty inventor, who carried his inventions before King Thamus, desiring that they be made available to the people. Some of the inventions the King praised; but he stood firmly against that of writing, declaring that it could be only a means of propagating false knowledge and an encouragement to forgetfulness. Socrates adds the view that anyone who leaves writing behind on the supposition that it will be "intelligible or certain" or who believes that writing is better than knowledge present to the mind is badly mistaken.

Now Plato was disturbed by written discourse because it has "no reticences or proprieties toward different classes of persons" and because, if an individual goes to it with a question in his mind, it "always gives one unvarying answer." And we find him making in the seventh *Epistle* the extraordinary statement that "no intelligent man will ever be so bold as to put into language those things which his reason has contemplated, especially not into a form that is unalterable,—which must be the case with what is expressed in written symbols." Obviously, here is a paradox, and the present writer is aware of risking another in a book which calls attention to the sin of writing. The answer to the problem seems to be that written discourse *is* under a limitation and that whether we wish to accept that limitation to secure other advantages must be decided after due reference to purposes and circumstances. In the Good Society it is quite possible that man will not be so dependent on the written word.

In any case, for Plato, truth was a living thing, never wholly captured by men even in animated discourse and in its purest form, certainly, never brought to paper. In our day it would seem that a contrary presumption has grown up. The more firmly an utterance is stereotyped, the more likely it is to win credit. It is assumed that engines as expensive and as powerful as the modern printing press will naturally be placed in the hands of men of knowledge. Faith in the printed word has raised journalists to the rank of oracles; yet could there be a better description of them than these lines from the *Phaedrus*: "They will appear to be omniscient and will generally know nothing; they will be tiresome, having the reputation of knowledge without the reality"?

If the realization of truth is the product of a meeting of minds, we may be skeptical of the physical ability of the mechanism to propagate it as long as that propagation is limited to the printing and distribution of stories which give "one unvarying answer." And this circumstance brings up at once the question of the intention of the rulers of the press. There is much to indicate that modern publication wishes to minimize discussion. Despite many artful pretensions to the contrary, it does not want an exchange of views, save perhaps on academic matters. Instead, it encourages men to read in the hope that they will absorb. For one thing, there is the technique of display, with its implied evaluations. This does more of the average man's thinking for him than he suspects. For another, there is the stereotyping of whole phrases. These are carefully chosen not to stimulate reflection but to evoke stock responses of approbation or disapprobation. Headlines and advertising teem with them, and we seem to approach a point at which failure to make the stock response is regarded as faintly treasonable, like refusal to salute the flag. Especially do the journals of mass circulation exploit the automatic response. So journalism becomes a monstrous discourse of Protagoras, which charms by hypnotizing and thwarts that participation without which one is not a thinking man. If our newspaper reader were trained to look for assumptions, if he were conscious of the rhetoric in lively reporting, we might not fear this product of the printer's art; but that would be to grant that he is educated. As the modern world is organized, the ordinary reader seems to lose means of private judgment, and the decay of conversation has about destroyed the practice of dialectic. Consequently the habit of credulity grows.

There is yet another circumstance which raises grave doubts about the contribution of journalism to the public weal. Newspapers are under strong pressure to distort in the interest of holding attention. I think we might well afford to overlook the pressure of advertisers upon news and editorial policy. This source of distortion has been fully described and is perhaps sufficiently discounted; but there is at work a far more insidious urge to exaggerate and to color beyond necessity. It is an inescapable fact that newspapers thrive on friction and conflict. One has only to survey the headlines of some popular journal, often presented symbolically in red, to note the *kind* of thing which is considered news. Behind the big story there nearly always lies a battle of some sort. Conflict, after all, is the essence of drama, and it is a truism that newspapers deliberately start and prolong quarrels; by allegation, by artful quotation, by the accentuation of unimportant differences, they create antagonism where none was felt to exist before. And this is profitable practically, for the opportunity to dramatize a fight is an opportunity for news. Journalism, on the whole, is glad to see a quarrel start and sorry to see it end. In the more sensational publications this spirit of passion and violence, manifested in a certain recklessness of diction, with vivid verbs and fortissimo adjectives, creeps into the very language. By the attention it gives their misdeeds it makes criminals heroic and politicians larger than life. I have felt that the way in which newspapers raked over every aspect of Adolf Hitler's life and personality since the end of the war shows that they really have missed him; they now have no one to play anti-Christ against the bourgeois righteousness they represent.

In reviewing the persistent tendency of the newspaper to corrupt, I shall cite a passage from James Fenimore Cooper. Though Cooper lived before the advent of yellow journalism, he seems to have stated the essential situation with a truth and eloquence impossible to improve on when he said in *The American Democrat*: "As the press of this country now exists, it would seem to be expressly devised by the great agent of mischief, to depress and destroy all that is good, and to elevate and advance all that is evil in the nation. The little truth that is urged, is usually urged coarsely, weakened and rendered vicious, by personalities; while those who live by falsehoods, fallacies, enmities, partialities and the schemes of the designing, find the press the very instrument that the devils would invent to effect their designs." A hundred years later Huey Long made a statement of impolitic truth when he called his tax on newspapers a "lie tax."

How, in the light of these facts, can one hesitate to conclude that we would live in greater peace and enjoy sounder moral health if the institution of the newspaper were abolished entirely? Jefferson observed at one time that it would be better to have newspapers and lack a government than to have a government and be without newspapers. Yet we find him in his seventieth year writing to John Adams: "I have given up newspapers in exchange for Tacitus and Thucydides, for Newton and Euclid, and I find myself much the happier."

The Russians, with their customary logical realism, which ought to come as a solemn admonition to the Western mind, have concluded that freedom to initiate conflicts is not one of the legitimate freedoms. They have therefore established state control of journalism. If newspapers can do nothing but lie, they will at least lie in the interest of the state, which, according to the philosophy of statism, is not lying at all. Certainly it remains to be seen whether the Western democracies with their strong divisive forces can continue to allow a real freedom of the press. In limited areas, indeed, there are now signs that the day of that freedom is over.

We see this silently arising in the appearance of the press agent and the public-relations officer. More institutions of every kind are coming to feel that they cannot permit an unrestricted access to news about themselves. What they do is simply set up an office of publicity in which writers skilled in propaganda prepare the kinds of stories those institutions wish to see circulated. Inevitably this organization serves at the same time as an office of censorship, de-emphasizing, or withholding entirely, news which would be damaging to prestige. It is easy, of course, to disguise such an office as a facility created to keep the public better informed, but this does not alter the fact that where interpretation counts, control of source is decisive. During the Second World War the United States government set up a vast office of war information, the object of which was to interpret the struggle from the point of view of an administration which had been all along pro-war. In this day of skilled competition for public favor, even separate departments of government have their public information services. I shall illustrate by citing in some detail from a recent press dispatch from Washington: "The United States Navy, which in pre-war days hid its light under a bushel, has decided to embark on a high-powered publicity program." Its plan, the account goes on to say, is to gather a staff of five hundred men the duties of which will be to provide "photographs, radio programs, and other public information about the navy." The development resulted, it is explained, from a realization that during the war "the publicity machines of the army and the army air forces were able to capture public support to the detriment of the navy's reputation." In the course of the war, this candid correspondent declares, the Navy made some effort to get in step with the times when it "introduced modern advertising agency methods and discarded the traditional name of 'office of public relations' for the more euphemistic 'office of public information.'" Such is the policy of seeing that there is enough news and that it originates in the proper hands. The practice is becoming universal; not only departments of governments and private businesses but even universities have concluded that freedom of access to news turns out to be expensive and embarrassing.

So much for forces which keep this part of the Stereopticon from giving us the living truth; now let us turn to the second part.

Every student of the motion picture has been impressed with the great resourcefulness of this medium. The movie producer is a maker almost to the extent of the poet, for he is working with a means capable of transforming subject matter. His production carries the evaluative power implicit in all dramatic representation, and it is, in the usual course of affairs, employed for purposes of entertainment. These two points bear consideration.

We need not speak of the enormous influence of this synoptic depiction of life upon children and adolescents. That is a point concerning reticences and proprieties toward different classes of persons; our interest is rather in the deleterious effects of movie-going upon even adult mentalities that find satisfaction in it. That the public as a whole misses the issue of the motion picture's influence can be seen from its attitude toward censorship. For what the public is reconciled to seeing censored are just the little breaches of decorum which fret bourgeois respectability and sense of security. The truth is that these are so far removed from the heart of the problem that they could well be ignored. The thing that needs to be censored is not the length of the kisses but the egotistic, selfish, and self-flaunting hero; not the relative proportion of undraped breast but the flippant, vacuous-minded, and also egotistic heroine. Let us not worry about the jokes of dubious propriety; let us rather object to the whole story, with its complacent assertion of the virtues of materialist society. We are speaking here, of course, from the fundamental point of view. A censorship of the movies, to be worthy of the name, would mean a complete reinterpretation of most of their themes, for the beliefs which underlie virtually every movie story are precisely the ones which are hurrying us on to perdition. The entire globe is becoming imbued with the notion that there is something normative about the insane sort of life lived in New York and Hollywood—even after that life has been exaggerated to suit the morbid appetite of the thrill-seeker.

The spurious nature of the "interest" of the ordinary movie shows an indifference to the real issues of life. The producer, in order to make his offerings attractions, that is, in order to make them beguiling, must present them as slick and false as advertising. It has been said that tragedy is for aristocrats, comedy is for bourgeoisie, and farce is for peasants. What percentage of the output of motion-picture factories can qualify as tragedy?[1] With the animated cartoon, a growing percentage qualifies as farce. But romance and comedy—these measure the depth of the world which movie audiences wish to see.

The third part of the Great Stereopticon is the radio and television. Because they bring the human voice, unique opportunities are open to them.

The primary effect of the radio is to disorder further our picture of the world by diminishing the opportunity for genuine selection (in its system of programs it has achieved a "rationalization" which results in the wildly irrational). One skims through a newspaper, practicing a certain art of rejection; the movie he may stay away from, but the radio is insistently present; indeed the victims of this publicity are virtually hunted down. In few public places do we escape it, and our neighbor's loud-speaker may penetrate the very sanctum of our privacy. In our listening, voluntary or not, we are made to grow accustomed to the weirdest of juxtapositions: the serious and the trivial, the comic and the tragic, follow one another in mechanical sequence without real transition. During the recent war what person of feeling was not struck by the insanity of hearing advertisements for laxatives between announcements of the destruction of famous cities by aerial bombardment? Is it not a travesty of all sense to hear reports fraught with disaster followed by the comedy-variety with its cheap wit and arranged applause (this applause, of course, tells the listeners when to react and how and so further submerges them in massness).[2]

Here, it would seem, is the apotheosis; here is the final collapsing of values, a fantasia of effects, suggesting in its wild disorder the debris left by a storm. Here is the daily mechanical wrecking of hierarchy.

Not to be overlooked in any gauging of influence is the voice of announcer and commentator. The metaphysical dream of progress

---

[1] A different but more serious question is what percentage of genuine tragedies could be identified as tragedies by a modern audience? For the inability of the contemporary mind to recognize tragedy when it is presented see Robert B. Heilman's "Melpomene as Wallflower," *Sewanee Review*, winter, 1947.

[2] It is a fact in keeping with others which we have cited that rural and urban tastes in radio differ. An official survey made by the Bureau of Agricultural Economics found that whereas with city people "comedy-variety shows are the overwhelming favorites, rural people generally seemed to prefer the more serious type of programs, such as news and market reports, religious music and sermons."

dictates the tone, which is one of cheery confidence, assuring us in the face of all contrary evidence that the best is yet to be. Recalling the war years once more, who has not heard the news of some terrible tragedy, which might stagger the imagination and cause the conscientious artist to hesitate at the thought of its depiction, given to the world in the same tone that commends a brand of soap or predicts fair weather for the morrow? There were commentators, it is true, who got the spirit of gravity into their speech, but behind them stood always the announcer, denying by his formula of regular inflection the poignancy of their message. The radio, more than press or screen, is the cheerful liar.

Thus the broadcast of chaos comes in a curious monotone. This is the voice of the Hollow Men, who can see the toppling walls of Jerusalem, Athens, and Rome without enough soul to sense tragedy. It is the tone of those dead to sentiment. But this is as we predicted; the closer man stands to ruin, the duller grows his realization; the annihilation of spiritual being precedes the destruction of temple walls.

The radio is, last of all, a prime instrument for discouraging the thought of participation. It is the natural monopoly of communication. For turning whole populations into mute recipients of authoritative edicts, what better means could there be? A national radio hookup is like the loud-speaker system of a battleship or a factory, from which the post of command can transmit orders to every part. If we grant the assumptions of the materialists that society must conform to the developments of science, we may as well prepare ourselves for the monolithic state.

Thus far we have been speaking of specific temptations to suppress and distort; it is now time to look at the fundamental source of the harm done by the Great Stereopticon. If we are pleading for unity of mind and if we admit the necessity for some degree of subjective determination, it might appear that this machine, with its power to make the entire environment rhetorical, is a heaven-sent answer to our needs. We do not in the final reckoning desire uninterpreted data; it is precisely the interpretation which holds our interest. But the great fault is that data, as it passes through the machine, takes its significance from a sickly metaphysical dream. The ultimate source of evaluation ceases to be the dream of beauty and truth and becomes that of psychopathia, of fragmentation, of disharmony and nonbeing. The operators of the Stereopticon by their very selection of matter make horrifying assumptions about reality. For its audience that overarching dome becomes a sort of miasmic cloud, a breeder of strife and degradation and of the subhuman. What person taking the affirmative view of life can deny that the world served up daily by press, movie, and radio is a world of evil and negation? There is iron in our nature sufficient to withstand any fact that is present in a context of affirmation, but we cannot remain unaffected by the continued assertion of cynicism and brutality. Yet these are what the materialists in control of publicity give us.

The sickly metaphysical dream is not the creation solely of those who have cast restraint to the winds to seek profit in sensationalism. It is the work, too, of many who profess higher ideals but who cannot see where their assumptions lead. Fundamental to the dream, of course, is the dogma of progress, with its postulate of the endlessness of becoming. The habit of judging all things by their departure from the things of yesterday is reflected in most journalistic interpretation. Hence the restlessness and the criteria of magnitude and popularity. The fact that capitalism seems to flourish only by expansion is no doubt connected with this; but, whatever the cause may be, there is no law of perfection where there are no standards of measure. The touchstone of progress simply schools the millions in shallow evaluation.

Somewhere, moreover, the metaphysicians of publicity have absorbed the idea that the goal of life is happiness through comfort. It is a state of complacency supposed to ensue when the physical appetites have been well satisfied. Advertising fosters the concept, social democracy approves it, and the acceptance is so wide that it is virtually impossible today, except from the religious rostrum, to teach that life means discipline and sacrifice. It means, in the world picture of press agency, a job, domesticity, interest in some harmless diversion such as baseball and fishing, and a strong antipathy toward abstract ideas. This is the Philistine version of man in pursuit of happiness. Even Carlyle's doctrine of blessedness through work has overtones of strenuousness which are repugnant to the man of today. Because the journalist-philosophers evaluate the multifarious objects and events of the world by their appeal to the greatest possible number of this type, it is not to be expected that they will recommend the arduous road of spiritualization.

As for the latter, it cannot be said too emphatically that the operators of the Great Stereopticon have an interest in keeping people from breaking through to deeper significances. Not only is the philosopher a notoriously poor consumer; he is also an unsettling influence on societies careless of justice. That there are abysses of meaning beneath his daily routine, the common man occasionally suspects; to have him realize them in some apocalyptic revelation might well threaten the foundations of materialist civilization. It is no wonder that experienced employers advertise for workers who are married and sober, for the other type sometimes begins to wonder which is the *real* reality, and they cannot afford help which might behave as Santayana, when he reportedly deserted the Harvard lecture room at the voice of spring, or Sherwood Anderson, when he left without adieu the Ohio paint factory.

The speculations of journalism seldom go beyond the confines of business and propriety, and its oracles have been quick to assail those who come with disturbing notions—quick and unscrupulous, too, if they sense that the notions contain some necessary truth. In this they bear out the observation of Socrates that society does not mind an individual's being wise; only when he begins to make others wise does it become apprehensive. This is to say that they fear the spread of what has truth and reason on its side. Has any brilliant social critic of the last century received something better than a sneer from the pundits of journalism until his appreciation by the thoughtful forced a grudging recognition? A Nietzsche, a Kierkegaard, a Péguy, a Spengler—it is impossible for journalism to take these people seriously. The existence of the one threatens the existence of the other. The proprietors of the Stereopticon have a pretty clear idea of the level at which thinking is safe for the established order. They are protecting a materialist civilization growing more insecure and panicky as awareness filters through that it is over an abyss.

Thus, by insisting upon the dogma of progress, by picturing physical sufficiency as the goal of living, by insulating the mind against thoughts of an immanent reality, the Great Stereopticon keeps the ordinary citizen from perceiving "the vanity of his bookkeeping and the emptiness of his domestic felicities." It is the great projection machine of the bourgeois mentality, which we have already seen to be psychopathic in its alienation from reality.

It is curious to see how this mentality impresses those brought up under differing conditions. I recall with especial vividness a passage from Walter Hines Page's *The Autobiography of Nicholas Worth*. Page, who grew up in the Reconstruction South and later went North to school, had received his earliest impressions in a society where catastrophe and privation had laid bare some of the primal realities, including the existence of evil—a society, too, in which the "primitive infection" of the African race, to use a term employed by Jung, had developed in the white man some psychological cunning. It seemed to Page that his northern acquaintances had "minds of logical simplicity."[3] Such, I think, must be the feeling of anyone who comes out of a natural environment into one in which education, however lengthy and laborious, is based on bourgeois assumptions about the real character of the world. It is a mind which learns to play with counters and arrives at answers which work—in a bourgeois environment. If we reverse this process and send the "mind of logical simplicity" into regions where mystery and contingency are recognized, we re-enact the plot of Conrad's *Lord Jim*. There is a world of terrifying reality to which the tidy moralities of an Anglican parsonage do not seem applicable.[4]

Seen from another point of view, the Great Stereopticon is a translation into actuality of Plato's celebrated figure of the cave. The defect of the prisoners, let us recall, is that they cannot perceive the truth. The wall before them, on which the shadows play, is the screen on which press, motion picture, and radio project their account of life. The chains which keep the prisoners from turning their heads are the physical monopoly which the engines of publicity naturally possess. And is it not pathetically true that these victims, with their limited

---

[3] In his novel *The Bostonians*, which deserves to be better known, Henry James sends the "southern" type of mind into a northern environment, with consequences that corroborate Page's thesis.

[4] An anthropologist related to me that certain Negro tribes of West Africa have a symbol for the white man consisting of a figure seated on the deck of a steamer in a position of stiffest rigidity. The straight, uncompromising lines are the betrayal; the primitive artist has caught the white man's unnatural rigor, which contrasts, ominously for him, with the native's sinuous adaptation.

A mind nurtured on press, motion picture, and radio cannot be otherwise in relation to the complexity of the world. Its instructors do not teach it to use the "proper reticences and proprieties" toward different things, and so its ideas may be comical simplifications.

vision, are "in the habit of conferring honors among themselves to those who are quickest to observe the passing shadows and to remark which of them went before and which followed after, and which were together"?

The result is that insulation by technology has made the task of disseminating wisdom more difficult since Plato's day. In Athenian sophistry and demagoguery Plato faced evils of the same kind, but they could not work behind such strategic entrenchment, and it was hardly as difficult for the wise man to make himself heard in centers of influence. Nothing is more natural than that, in an age dominated by materialism, authority should attach to those who possess. What chance today, to make the situation concrete, has a street-corner preacher, without means and without institutional sponsorship, in competition with the glib assertions of a radio oracle? The denizens of the cave have never been so firmly enchained as in this age, which uses liberty as a veritable incantation.

There are, it is true, certain hopeful signs of restiveness growing out of our condition. Most of us have observed among ordinary people a deep suspicion of propaganda since the First World War. The lesson of that disillusionment has lasted surprisingly. So intense has been this distrust that during the recent conflict the most authentic stories of outrages, documented and proved in every possible way, either were met with outright disbelief or were accepted gingerly and with reservations. The common man realizes that he has been misled and that there are those who would mislead him again; but, lacking analytical power, he tends to group every instance of organized expression with propaganda. In times of peace, too, he has exhibited a certain hard-headed resistance to attempts to drive or cajole him. We have seen in this country politicians elected in the face of almost unanimous press opposition; we note oftentimes a cagey dismissal of the obvious falsification in advertising, and I have heard simple men remark that newspapers should not print items of a private and distressing nature such as we have classified as obscene.

In serious writing, too, there are some hopeful portents of change. It has been noted how modern poets have reacted against the debased coinage of cliché language; and indications appear in other types of literature that the middle-class world picture is being abandoned. Perhaps Arthur Koestler is right: as the bourgeois novel flickers out, an

entirely new type of writer is destined to appear: "airmen, revolutionaries, adventurers, men who lead the dangerous life." Such, indeed,
seem Silone, Saint-Exupéry, Hemingway. They will carry the gift for
reflection into experiences of intense physical distress, and they will
emerge with a more genuine contempt for materialist explanations
than has been seen for centuries. When Saint-Exupéry, for example,
declares that "the physical drama itself cannot touch us until someone
points out its spiritual sense," he makes an affirmation of tragedy and
significance. In a way, these men have the same recourse as medieval
mystics, who, in suffering, caught the vision. And, since their faith
has been tested by fire, they cannot be intimidated by those things
which reduce the armchair philosopher to meekness. They have broken through the falsity and have returned to tell that the world is not
at all what it has been made to seem—not after one has cut loose from
security and comfort and achieved a kind of freedom far different from
that promised by political liberals, who are themselves pushing slides
into the Stereopticon. In reflecting on what is taught by extremities,
one is reminded of Yeats's saying that saints and drunkards are never
Whigs.

It will certainly have to be asked whether European fascism was not
just this impulse vulgarized and perverted. The rebellion of youth, the
repudiation of bourgeois complacency, the attempt to renew the sense
of "holiness and heroism," appear the beginning of a revolt at least as
deep-seated as that which made the French Revolution. The revolt was
led by ignorant spirits who were impelled from behind by resentment
and who, through their determination to invert the Christian ethic,
made an unexampled fiasco. There is no reason to believe, however,
that the deep dissatisfaction with the superficiality of Western life has
been removed or even mitigated. And this is why we wonder how long
the Stereopticon can preserve the inane world which the bourgeois
finds congenial. It is, after all, only a mechanical means of unifying
empirical communities.

In summary, the plea that the press, motion picture, and radio justify themselves by keeping people well informed turns out to be misleading. If one thinks merely of facts and of vivid sensations, the claim
has some foundation, but if he thinks of encouragement to meditation, the contrary rather is true. For by keeping the time element con-
tinuously present—and one may recall Henry James's description of

journalism as criticism of the moment at the moment—they discourage composition and so promote the fragmentation already reviewed. We have seen in other connections how specialization is hostile to all kinds of organization, whether that organization is expressed as image, as whole, or as generalization. In the last analysis this reveals itself as an attempt to prevent the simultaneous perception of successive events, which is the achievement of the philosopher. Materialism and success require the "decomposed eternity" of time for their operation, and this is why we have these hidden but persistent attacks on memory, which holds successive events in a single picture. The successive perception of successive events is empiricism; the simultaneous perception is idealism. Need we go further to account for the current dislike of long memories and for the hatred of the past?

Recurring to Plato's observation that a philosopher must have a good memory, let us inquire whether the continuous dissemination of news by the media under discussion does not produce the provincial in time. The constant stream of sensation, eulogized as lively propagation of what the public wants to hear, discourages the pulling-together of events from past time into a whole for contemplation. Thus, absence of reflection keeps the individual from being aware of his former selves, and it is highly questionable whether anyone can be a member of a metaphysical community who does not preserve such memory. Upon the presence of the past in the present depends all conduct directed by knowledge.

There can be little doubt that this condition of mind is a large factor in the low political morality of our age. Oswald Garrison Villard, a political journalist of the old school, who spent half a century crusading for standards of probity in public administration, once declared that he had never ceased to marvel at the shortness of the public's memory, at the rapidity with which it forgets episodes of scandal and incompetence. It sometimes appeared to him of little use to attack a party for its unethical conduct, for the voters would have no recollection of it. The glee with which the epithet "ancient history" is applied to what is out of sight is of course a part of this barbarous attitude. The man of culture finds the whole past relevant; the bourgeois and the barbarian find relevant only what has some pressing connection with their appetites. Those who remember alone have a sense of relatedness, but whoever has a sense of relatedness is in at least the first grade of philosophy. Henry Ford's statement that history is bunk is a perfectly proper observation for a bourgeois industrialist, and it was followed with equal propriety by another: "Creeds must go." Technology emancipates not only from memory but also from faith.

What humane spirit, after reading a newspaper or attending a popular motion picture or listening to the farrago of nonsense on a radio program, has not found relief in fixing his gaze upon some characteristic bit of nature? It is escape from the sickly metaphysical dream. Out of the surfeit of falsity born of technology and commercialism we rejoice in returning to primary data and to assurance that the world is a world of enduring forms which in themselves are neither brutal nor sentimental.

*1948*

# JOHN T. FLYNN

John Thomas Flynn (1882–1964) was a leading figure of the Old Right, opposing the New Deal, the U.S. entry into World War II (and, retrospectively, World War I), and the militarized interventionist tendencies of U.S. foreign policy during the Cold War. Here Flynn sounds the alarm not only about communism but also about the expansion of the welfare state in the Western democracies, especially in Great Britain after the end of World War II.

## FROM *The Road Ahead*

M Y PURPOSE in writing this book is to attempt to describe the road along which this country is traveling to its destruction.

Human societies come under the influence of great tides of thought and appetite that run unseen deeply below the surface of society. After a while these powerful streams of opinion and desire move the whole social mass along with them without the individuals in the mass being aware of the direction in which they are going. Up to a certain point it is possible to resist these controlling tides and to reverse them, but a time comes when they are so strong that society loses its power of decision over the direction in which it is going.

I believe we are now moving along under the dominion of such tides and that all the things we do to deal with our accumulating perils are futile because we do not understand the tides nor the direction in which they are carrying us. I believe that we still have in our hands the means of checking this onrush to disaster. We still may consciously control our destiny. But I feel sure that we are moving toward a crisis which will be for us the moment of decision. It will be at that point we will either use or lose our final opportunity to determine the direction along which this nation will travel.

For a while, as the war came to an end, our people were nervous about what was supposed to be the reconversion problem and the inevitable deflation. At the end of a year there was no sign of the crisis. Despite solemn predictions in the second year, the crisis did not come, nor in the third nor fourth year after peace was concluded. Even business men began to wonder about this. Can it be that this new thing works? Maybe, they thought, there will be no crisis. This feeling had settled fairly snugly into the plans and hopes of almost every class. Our economic system had been altered—and our political system as well. Of course the explanation of this continuing war boom was quite obvious. The hot war had ended and the cold war had been launched. Having lost Japan and Germany as enemies, we managed to acquire a new one—Russia. And so, instead of ending our vast war expenditures wholly, we continued to spend billions a year on our military establishments, plus more billions to reconstruct Europe and save her from being engulfed by the Communist terror.

Obviously we cannot go on the way we are now traveling. We do have a very large number of people employed, though unemployment has risen to 4,000,000 workers and the number continues to increase with each month. This employment, under the present system, is made possible by what is called the cold war. We are spending 15 billion dollars on our defenses because of the threat of war with Russia. We are spending about five billion more to rehabilitate Europe—spending the money in our factories and on our farms to send supplies abroad. We now propose to spend another 1.5 billion to rearm Europe. But suppose the cold war were to come to an end? We cannot seriously contemplate keeping it up forever. Suppose we had to cut our military outlays to a peacetime basis and make an end of attempting to support and arm western Europe. This would immediately result in throwing at least four million people out of work in the first place and at least four or five million more when the first four million quit buying at the stores. In short, our economic system is now a "war" economy—a "cold war" economy. If the cold war should end without becoming a hot war, what then would we do?

Of course it is now beginning to seep into the minds of our people that we could have an economic crisis here even before this cold war ends. In any case, the cold war has had one significant effect. It has forced us to look at Russia for what she is and not as she was pictured to us when she was "our noble ally." And this has forced us to turn our attention to our American Communist movement. We have, as a consequence, been making war on the Communists. This has had one very serious by-product. It has dramatized the American Communist Party and its dupes as the chief internal enemy of our economic system and our form of government. And it is widely feared that a crisis here would present our native Communists with their great opportunity.

This I hold to be a mistake of the first magnitude. I insist that if every Communist in America were rounded up and liquidated, the great menace to our form of social organization would be still among us. I do not mean to underestimate the danger from the Communists. They are interested at the moment in serving the purposes of the great enemy of the whole western world—Russia. They are a traitorous bloc in our midst and they have frightening potentialities for harm in our foreign relations. But they are not as dangerous to us in the struggle now under way to change our internal institutions as another wholly indigenous movement. The leaders of this movement now actually seek to outdo us in berating the Communists with whom they were marching together but two or three years ago. They are more dangerous because they are more numerous and more respectable and they are not tainted with the odium of treachery. They are more dangerous because, as a matter of fact, they are now occupying positions of great power, have in their hands immense sections of our political machinery and are actually hailed as our brothers in the battle against the Reds. Every day that passes reduces the power of the Communists to mislead us or to promote their program among us. But every day that passes enlarges the opportunities of our real internal enemies to confuse us, to arouse us and to entice us to travel the dark road that has led every country in Europe to its doom. Acting under false colors and a name designed to conceal their real purpose and using words chosen to deceive, they are now well advanced in a sneak attack upon our whole way of life.

Our people, despite our international wars, have been so far removed from the European scene that they have not observed very closely the play of forces which in the last 30 years has been eating away the foundations of European civilization. It is very difficult for us to credit the influence which certain human appetites and frustrations and hatreds can exercise upon the mass mind of a whole nation. Our history had been, up to 20 years ago, one of almost continuous advance. We have encountered difficulties but we have managed somehow to struggle or blunder our way out of them. We have no talent as a people for pessimism. In prosperity we convinced ourselves it would last forever. When the Depression came we were always sure recovery was just ahead. No one could convince us we would ever go into another European war. When the war came we were quite sure it would end swiftly and when the enemy surrendered we fondly imagined peace would attend us as a matter of course. And now, after four years of the mess which we call the "cold war" we persist in our confidence that somehow some friendly deity will save us from drifting into that kind of social disorder which has engulfed all of Europe.

Yet while we cherish this fatuous dream the same forces that ruined Germany and Italy and France and Britain are mobilizing to repeat their work of destruction upon us. The germs of that fatal sickness—the sickness of the twentieth century which has circled the western world—are already fastened in the very vitals of our economic and political organisms. And we can no longer refuse to recognize them.

Most of the countries in Europe have moved into the Socialist camp. The two which concern us most are Russia and Great Britain. Each has moved into socialism by a different route. Each has organized its Socialist society upon a different model. But both are Socialist. Russia was conquered overnight by a sudden, violent revolutionary convulsion. Great Britain managed its revolution upon a peaceful and gradualist pattern. It moved into socialism a little at a time. The journey took almost 40 years.

We are following, not in the footsteps of Russia, but in the footsteps of England. We are being drawn into socialism on the British gradualist model. We are well on the road—much further along than our people suspect. And if we do not clearly recognize that fact and abandon that fatal route, we will inevitably, perhaps in less than a decade, arrive at that state of socialization now before us in England. Not until we recognize this fact and all its implications will we be able to recognize "where we are and whither we are tending." Not until then will we be able to judge "what to do, and how to do it."

In England we have a perfect case history of the infection and progress of the Socialist disease—for despite the glowing terms in which its apostles promote it, socialism is a disease which fastens itself upon the body of a weakened society. This book is about America, but I must ask the reader to pause for a moment and go with me through a brief inspection of the rise of socialism in England and its swift conquest of that great nation. England was a free society more nearly resembling our own than any other European country and, until recently, the richest and most powerful nation in the world. What has happened there is far more informative for us than the story of the onset of socialism in any other country.

The Socialist government in Britain did not come into power by accident. It arrived in power in England as the result of a plan—a carefully concerted plan, laid down with great intelligence many years ago. In the next chapter I propose to describe for you step by step the unfolding of the British plan by which that once great country—the home of modern capitalism and modern free government—was led stealthily, with the aid of two "victorious" wars, to her present state.

*We must see this English experiment clearly because the plan by which England was sneaked into socialism is now being promoted in this country by a coalition of politicians and revolutionary crusaders who are the counterpart of the British Fabian Socialists. It is being carried out with startling fidelity and promptness with the aid of the ignorance of the American business man and politician. And it is a grave question whether or not the program has been already so far advanced that reversal may be impossible. But this much is certain—it must be reversed and that at once or we will find ourselves trapped in a Socialist system in a far shorter time than was required to conquer England.*

*1949*

# MILTON FRIEDMAN

Milton Friedman (1912–2006) founded what has become known as the Chicago School of economics, which sought to minimize if not abolish altogether government interference with the workings of the free market. He was, in that sense, a classical liberal. Yet it was postwar conservatives who proved most attracted to his theories. In 1976, he was awarded the Nobel Prize.

## Capitalism and Freedom

I N DISCUSSING the principles of a free society it is desirable to have a convenient label and this has become extremely difficult. In the late 18th and early 19th centuries, an intellectual movement developed that went under the name of liberalism. This development, which was a reaction against the authoritarian elements in the prior society, emphasized freedom as the ultimate goal and the individual as the ultimate entity in the society. It supported *laissez faire* at home as a means of reducing the role of the state in economic affairs and thereby avoiding interfering with the individual; it supported free trade abroad as a means of linking the nations of the world together peacefully and democratically. In political matters, it supported the development of representative government and of parliamentary institutions, reduction in the arbitrary power of the state, and protection of the civil freedoms of individuals.

Beginning in the late 19th century, the intellectual ideas associated with the term *liberalism* came to have a very different emphasis, particularly in the economic area. Whereas 19th-century liberalism emphasized freedom, 20th-century liberalism tended to emphasize welfare. I would say welfare instead of freedom though the 20th-century liberal would no doubt say welfare in addition to freedom. The 20th-century liberal puts his reliance primarily upon the state rather than on private voluntary arrangements.

The difference between the two doctrines is most striking in the economic sphere, less extreme in the political sphere. The 20th-century liberal, like the 19th-century liberal, puts emphasis on parliamentary institutions, representative government, civil rights, and so on. And yet even here there is an important difference. Faced with the choice between having the state intervene or not, the 20th-century liberal is likely to resolve any doubt in favor of intervention; the 19th-century liberal, in the other direction. When the question arises at what level of government something should be done, the 20th-century liberal is likely to resolve any doubt in favor of the more centralized level—the state instead of the city, the federal government instead of the state, a world organization instead of a federal government. The 19th-century liberal is likely to resolve any doubt in the other direction and to emphasize a decentralization of power.

This use of the term *liberalism* in these two quite different senses renders it difficult to have a convenient label for the principles I shall be talking about. I shall resolve these difficulties by using the word liberalism in its original sense. Liberalism of what I have called the 20th-century variety has by now become orthodox and indeed reactionary. Consequently, the views I shall present might equally be entitled, under current conditions, the "new liberalism," a more attractive designation than "nineteenth-century liberalism."

It is widely believed that economic arrangements are one thing and political arrangements another, that any kind of economic arrangement can be associated with any kind of political arrangement. This is the idea that underlies such a term as "democratic socialism." The essential thesis, I believe, of a new liberal is that this idea is invalid, that "democratic socialism" is a contradiction in terms, that there is an intimate connection between economic arrangements and political arrangements, and that only certain combinations are possible.

It is important to emphasize that economic arrangements play a dual role in the promotion of a free society. On the one hand, "freedom" in economic arrangements is itself a component of freedom broadly understood, so "economic freedom" is an end in itself to a believer in freedom. In the second place, economic freedom is also an indispensable means toward the achievement of political freedom.

The first of these roles of economic freedom needs special emphasis. The citizen of Great Britain who after World War II was not permitted, by law, to spend his vacation in the United States because of exchange control was being deprived of an essential freedom no less than the citizen of the United States who was denied the opportunity to spend his vacation in Russia on the grounds of his political views. The one was ostensibly an economic limitation on freedom and the other a political limitation, yet there is no essential difference between the two.

The citizen of the United States who is compelled by law to devote something like 10% of his income to the purchase of a particular kind of retirement contract, administered by the government, is being deprived of a corresponding part of his own personal freedom. How strongly this particular deprivation may be felt, and its closeness to the deprivation of religious freedom, which all would regard as "civil" or "political" rather than "economic," was dramatized by the recent episode involving a group of Ohio or Pennsylvania farmers of a particular religious sect. On grounds of principle, this group regarded compulsory federal old age programs as an infringement on their own personal individual freedom and refused to pay taxes or accept benefits. As a result, some of their livestock were sold at auction in order to satisfy claims for social security levies. A citizen of the United States who under the laws of various states is not free to follow the occupation of his own choosing unless he can get a license for it is likewise being deprived of an essential part of his freedom. So economic freedom, in and of itself, is an extremely important part of total freedom.

The reason it is important to emphasize this point is because intellectuals in particular have a strong bias against regarding this aspect of freedom as important. They tend to express contempt for what they regard as material aspects of life and to regard their own pursuit of allegedly higher values as on a different plane of significance and as deserving special attention. But for the ordinary citizen of the country, for the great masses of the people, the direct importance of economic freedom is in many cases of at least comparable importance to the indirect importance of economic freedom as a means of political freedom.

Viewed as a means to the end of political freedom, economic arrangements are essential because of the effect which they have on the concentration or the deconcentration of power. A major thesis of the new
liberal is that the kind of economic organization that provides economic freedom directly, namely, organization of economic activities
through a largely free market and private enterprise, in short through
competitive capitalism, is also a necessary though not a sufficient
condition for political freedom. The central reason why this is true
is because such a form of economic organization separates economic
power from political power and in this way enables the one to be an
offset to the other. Historical evidence speaks with a single voice on
the relation between political and economic freedom. I cannot think
of a single example at any time or any place where there was a large
measure of political freedom without there also being something comparable to a private enterprise market form of economic organization
for the bulk of economic activity.

Because we live in a largely free society, we tend to forget how limited is the span of time and the part of the globe for which there has
ever been anything like political freedom. The 19th century and the
early 20th century in the Western world stand out as striking exceptions from the general trend of historical development. It is clear that
freedom in this instance came along with the free market and the
development of capitalist institutions.

History suggests only that economic freedom is a necessary condition for political freedom. Clearly it is not a sufficient condition. Fascist
Italy or Fascist Spain, Germany at various times in the last 70 years,
Japan before World Wars I and II, Czarist Russia in the decades before
World War I are all societies that cannot conceivably be described as
politically free yet in which private enterprise was the dominant form
of economic organization. So it is possible to have economic arrangements that are fundamentally capitalist and yet political arrangements
that are not free.

Yet, even in those cases, the citizenry had a good deal more freedom than citizens of a modern totalitarian state like Russia or Nazi
Germany in which economic totalitarianism is combined with political totalitarianism. Even in Russia under the czars it was possible for
some citizens under some circumstances to change their jobs without
getting permission from political authority because the existence of

private property and of capitalism provided some kind of offset to the centralized power of the state.

The relation between political and economic freedom is complex and by no means unilateral. In the early 19th century, Bentham and the Philosophical Radicals were inclined to regard political freedom as a means to economic freedom. Their view was that the masses were being hampered by the restrictions that were being imposed upon them, that if political reform gave the bulk of the people the vote, they would do what was good for them, which was to vote for *laissez faire*. In retrospect, it is hard to say that they were wrong. There was a large measure of political reform that was accompanied by economic reform in the direction of a great deal of *laissez faire*. And an enormous increase in the well-being of the masses followed this change in economic arrangements.

Later in the 19th century, when there began to be a movement away from freer economic arrangements and *laissez faire* toward a greater measure of collectivism and centralization, the view developed, as expressed for example by Lord Acton and in the 20th century by Henry Simons and Friedrich Hayek, that the relation was more nearly the opposite—that economic freedom was the means to political freedom.

In the period since World War II, I think we have seen still a different interconnection between political and economic freedom. In the post-war period, the fears that economic intervention would destroy political freedom seemed to be on the way to being realized. Various countries, and again Britain is perhaps the outstanding example because it has been so much a leader in the realm of ideas and social arrangements, did extend very greatly the area of state intervention into economic affairs and this did threaten political freedom. But the result was rather surprising. Instead of political freedom giving way, what happened in many cases was that economic intervention was discarded. The striking example in British post-war development was the Control-of-Engagements Order issued by the Labour Government. In trying to carry out their economic plans, the Labour Government found it necessary to do something which several years before it had said it would never do, namely, to exercise control over the jobs which people could take. Thanks to widespread popular objection, the legislation was never enforced at all extensively. After being on the books for one year, it was repealed. It seems clear that it was repealed precisely because it quite directly threatened a cherished political freedom. And from that day to this, there has been a trend toward a reduction in the extent of political intervention in economic affairs.

The dismantling of controls dates from the repeal of the Control-of-Engagements Order; it would have occurred even if the Labour Government had stayed in power. This may, of course, turn out to be a purely temporary interlude, a minor halt in the march of affairs toward a greater degree of intervention into economic affairs. Perhaps only innate optimism leads me to believe that it is more than that. Whether this be so or not, it illustrates again in striking fashion the close connection between economic arrangements and political arrangements. Not only in Britain but in other countries of the world as well, the post-war period has seen the same tendency for economic arrangements to interfere with political freedom and for the economic intervention frequently to give way.

Historical evidence that the development of freedom and of capitalist and market institutions have coincided in time can never by itself be persuasive. Why should there be a connection? What are the logical links between economic and political freedom? In discussing these questions, I shall first consider the market as a direct component of freedom and then the indirect relation between market arrangements and political freedom. In the process, I shall in effect outline the ideal economic arrangements of the new liberal.

The new liberal takes freedom of the individual as his ultimate goal in judging social arrangements. Freedom as a value in this sense has to do with the interrelations among people; it has no meaning whatsoever to a Robinson Crusoe on an isolated island (without his man Friday). Robinson Crusoe on his island is subject to "constraint," he has limited "power," he has only a limited number of alternatives, but there is no problem of freedom in the sense that is relevant to the present discussion. Similarly, in a society, freedom has nothing to say about what an individual does with his freedom; it isn't an all-embracing ethic by any manner of means. Indeed, a major aim of the believer in freedom is to leave the ethical problem for the individual to wrestle with. The "really" important ethical problems are those that face an individual in a free society—what an individual should do with his freedom. There are thus two sets of values that a liberal will emphasize—the values relevant to relations among people which is the context in which he assigns first priority to freedom; and the values that are relevant to the individual in the exercise of his freedom, which is the realm of individual ethics and philosophy.

Fundamentally there are only two ways in which the activities of a large number of people can be co-ordinated: by central direction, which is the technique of the army and of the totalitarian state and involves some people telling other people what to do; or by voluntary co-operation, which is the technique of the marketplace and of arrangements involving voluntary exchange. The possibility of voluntary co-operation in its turn rests fundamentally on the proposition that both parties to an exchange can benefit from it. If it is voluntary and reasonably well informed, the exchange will not take place unless both parties do benefit from it.

The simplest way to see the principle at work is to go back to the economist's favorite abstraction of Robinson Crusoe, only to have a number of Robinson Crusoe households on different islands, each of which is initially self-sufficient. Let the households come into contact with one another. The possibility of trade now emerges. What is it that gives them an incentive to trade? The answer clearly is that if each household concentrates on a small range of activities, producing things for itself indirectly, by trade, rather than doing everything for itself, everybody can be better off. This possibility arises for two reasons: one is that an individual can achieve a higher degree of competence in an activity if he specializes in it rather than engaging in many activities; the other, closely associated but not identical, is that people are different and each can specialize in those activities for which he has special capacities. Even if everyone were identical in all his capacities and abilities, there would still be a gain from division of labor which would make a larger total return possible because each individual could concentrate on a particular activity. But in addition, diversity among people becomes a source of strength because each individual can concentrate on doing those things that he can do best. So the incentive for the households to engage in trade and to specialize is the possibility of a greater total output.

The protection to Household A is that it need not enter into an exchange with Household B unless both parties benefit. If exchange is voluntary, it will take place if, and only if, both parties do benefit.

Each individual always has the alternative of going back to producing for himself what he did before so he can never be worse off; he can only be better off.

Of course, specialization of function and division of labor would not go far if the ultimate productive unit were the household. In a modern society, we have gone much farther. We have introduced enterprises which are intermediaries between individuals in their capacities as suppliers of services and as purchasers of goods. And similarly, specialization of function and division of labor could not go very far if we had to continue to rely on the barter of product for product. In consequence, money has been introduced as a means of facilitating exchange and of enabling the act of purchase and of sale to be separated into two parts.

The introduction of enterprises and the introduction of money raise most of the really difficult problems for economics as a science. But from the point of view of the principles of social organization, they do not fundamentally alter the essential character of economic arrangements. In a modern complex society using enterprises and money it is no less true than in the simple idealized world that co-ordination through the markets is a system of voluntary co-operation in which all parties to the bargain gain.

So long as effective freedom of exchange is maintained, the essential feature of the market is that it enables people to co-operate voluntarily in complex tasks without any individual being in a position to interfere with any other. Many of the difficult technical problems that arise in applying our principles to actual economic arrangements are concerned with assuring effective freedom to enter or not to enter into exchanges. But so long as people are effectively free to enter into an exchange and are reasonably well informed the essential feature of the market remains that of our ideal example. It provides for co-operation without coercion; it prevents one person from interfering with another. The employer is protected from being interfered with or coerced by his employees by the existence of other employees whom he can hire. The employee is protected from being coerced by his employer by the existence of other employers for whom he can work; the customer by the existence of other sellers, and so on.

Of course, it is partly this feature of the market that leads many people to be opposed to it. What most people really object to when they object to a free market is that it is so hard for them to shape it to their own will. The market gives people what the people want instead of what other people think they ought to want. At the bottom of many criticisms of the market economy is really lack of belief in freedom itself.

The essence of political freedom is the absence of coercion of one man by his fellow men. The fundamental danger to political freedom is the concentration of power. The existence of a large measure of power in the hands of a relatively few individuals enables them to use it to coerce their fellow man. Preservation of freedom requires either the elimination of power where that is possible, or its dispersal where it cannot be eliminated. It essentially requires a system of checks and balances, like that explicitly incorporated in our Constitution. One way to think of a market system is as part of a broader system of checks and balances, as a system under which economic power can be a check to political power instead of an addition to it.

If I may speculate in an area in which I have little competence, there seems to be a really essential difference between political power and economic power that is at the heart of the use of a market mechanism to preserve freedom. With respect to political power, there is something like a law of conservation of energy or power. The notion that what one man gains another man loses has more applicability in the realm of politics than in the realm of economic arrangements. One can have many different small governments, but it is hard to think of having many different small centers of political power in any single government. It is hard for there to be more than one really outstanding leader, one person on whom the energies and enthusiasms and so on of his countrymen are centered. If the central government gains power, it is likely to do so at the expense of local governments. While I do not know how to formulate the statement precisely, there seems to be something like a fixed total of political power to be distributed.

There is no such fixed total, no law of conservation of power, with respect to economic power. You cannot very well have two presidents in a country, although you may have two separate countries, but it is perfectly possible to have a large number of additional million-aires. You can have an additional millionaire without there being any fewer millionaires anywhere else. If somebody discovers a way to make resources more productive than they were before, he will simply add to the grand total of economic wealth. Economic power can thus be more readily dispersed than political power. There can be a larger number of independent foci of power. Further, if economic power is kept in separate hands from political power, it can serve as a check and an offset to political power.

This is a very abstract argument and I think I can illustrate its force for our purpose best by turning to some examples. I would like to discuss first a hypothetical example that helps to bring out the principles involved and then an actual example from recent experience that also illustrates the way in which the market works to preserve political freedom.

I think that most of us will agree that an essential element of political freedom is the freedom to advocate and to try to promote radical changes in the organization of society. It is a manifestation of political freedom in our capitalist society that people are free to advocate, and to try to persuade others to favor socialism or communism. I want to contemplate for a moment the reverse problem. It would be a sign of political freedom in a socialist society that people in that society should be free to advocate, and try to persuade others to favor capitalism. I want to ask the hypothetical question: how could a socialist society preserve the freedom to advocate capitalism? I shall assume that the leading people and the public at large seriously wish to do so and ask how they could set up the institutional arrangements that would make this possible.

The first problem is that the advocates of capitalism must be able to earn a living. Since in a socialist society all persons get their incomes from the state as employees or dependents of employees of the state, this already creates quite a problem. It is one thing to permit private individuals to advocate radical change. It is another thing to permit governmental employees to do so. Our whole post-war experience with un-American activities' committees and the McCarthy investigations and so on shows how difficult a problem it is to carry over this notion to governmental employees. The first thing that would be necessary would therefore be essentially a self-denying ordinance on the part of the government that would not discharge from public employment individuals who advocate subversive doctrines—since of course, in a socialist state the doctrine that capitalism should be restored would be a subversive doctrine. Let us suppose this hurdle, which is the least of the hurdles, is surmounted.

Next, in order to be able to advocate anything effectively it is necessary to be able to raise some money to finance meetings, propaganda, publications, writings and so on. In a socialist society, there might still be men of great wealth. There is no reason why a socialist society shouldn't have a wide and unequal distribution of income and of wealth. It is clear, however, that most, if not all of the people, of great wealth or income would be the leading figures in the government, directly or indirectly—high-level civil servants or favored authors, actors, and the like. Perhaps it doesn't strain the bounds of credulity greatly to suppose that the government would countenance and tolerate the advocacy of capitalism by minor civil servants. It's almost incredible that it could tolerate the financing of subversive activity by leading civil servants. It is, therefore, hard to believe that these wealthy or high-income individuals could be a source of finance. The only other recourse would be to try to get small sums from a large number of people. But this evades the issue. In order to get a lot of people to contribute you first have to persuade them. How do you get started persuading?

Note that in a capitalistic society radical movements have never been financed by small amounts from many people. They have been financed by a small number of wealthy people being willing to foot the bill. To take an example that is quite old but very striking, who financed Karl Marx? It was Engels, and where did Engels get his money? He was an independent businessman of wealth. (In the modern day it's the Anita McCormick Blaines and Frederick Vanderbilt Fields, the Corliss Lamonts and so on who have been the source of finance of the radical movement.) This is the important source of the strength of freedom in a capitalist society. It means that anybody who has a "crazy" idea that he wants to propagate and promote has only to persuade a small number out of a very large number of potential backers in order to be able to get an opportunity to try out his crazy notions in the marketplace of ideas.

Moreover, the situation is even more extreme. Suppose somebody has an idea that he thinks will appeal to a large number of people. He doesn't even have to persuade somebody that he is right. He just has to persuade some capitalist in the society—in this particular case say a publisher or a magazine editor—that there's a chance that a lot of people will be willing to pay to read about his idea. A publisher, for example, will have an incentive to publish a book with whose ideas he doesn't agree in the slightest, if there is a substantial chance that the book will sell enough copies to make money.

By contrast, let's go back to the hypothetical socialist society. How does the proponent of capitalism in such a society raise money to propagate his ideas? He can't get it from the wealthy individuals in the society. It is hard to believe that it is feasible for him to raise the necessary amount by getting small sums from a large number of people. Perhaps one can conceive of the socialist society being sufficiently aware of this problem and sufficiently anxious to preserve freedom to set up a governmental fund for the financing of subversive activities. It is a little difficult to conceive of this being done, but even if it were done it would not meet the problem. How would it be decided who should be supported from the fund? If subversive activity is made a profitable enterprise, it is clear that there will be an ample supply of people willing to take money for this purpose. If money is to be got for the asking, there will be plenty of asking. There must be some way of rationing. How could it be rationed?

Even if this problem were solved, the socialist society would still have difficulties in preserving freedom. The advocate of capitalism must not only have money, he must also be able to buy paper, print his material, distribute it, hold meetings, and the like. And, in the socialist society, in each instance this would involve dealing with an instrumentality of the government. The seller of paper in a capitalist society doesn't care or indeed know whether the paper he's selling is going to be used to print the *Wall Street Journal* or the *Worker*.

In the circumstances envisaged in the socialist society, the man who wants to print the paper to promote capitalism has to persuade a government mill to sell him the paper, a government printing press to print it, a government post office to distribute it among the people, a government agency to rent him a hall in which to talk and so on. Maybe there is some way in which one could make arrangements under a socialist society to preserve freedom and to make this possible. I certainly cannot say that it is utterly impossible. What is clear is that there are very real difficulties in preserving dissent and that, so far as I know, none of the people who have been in favor of socialism and also in favor of freedom have really faced up to this issue or made even a respectable start at developing the institutional arrangements that would permit freedom under socialism. By contrast, it is clear how a free market capitalist society fosters freedom.

A striking example, which may be found in the January 26, 1959, issue of *Time*, has to do with the "Blacklist Fadeout." Says the *Time* story, "The Oscar-awarding ritual is Hollywood's biggest pitch for dignity, but two years ago dignity suffered. When one Robert Rich was announced as top original writer for *The Brave One*, he never stepped forward. Robert Rich was a pseudonym, masking one of about 150 actors [. . .] blacklisted by the industry since 1947 as suspected Communists or fellow travelers. The case was particularly embarrassing to the Motion Picture Academy because it had barred any Communist or Fifth Amendment pleader from Oscar competition. Last week both the Communist rule and the mystery of Rich's identity were suddenly rescripted.

"Rich turned out to be Dalton (*Johnny Got His Gun*) Trumbo, one of the original 'Hollywood Ten' writers who refused to testify at the 1947 hearing on Communism in the movie industry. Said producer Frank King, who had stoutly insisted that Robert Rich was 'a young guy in Spain with a beard': 'We have an obligation to our stockholders to buy the best scripts we can. Trumbo brought us *The Brave One* and we bought it . . .' [. . .] In effect it was the formal end of the Hollywood blacklist. For barred writers, the informal end came long ago. At least 15% of current Hollywood films are reportedly written by blacklist members. Says producer King: 'There are more ghosts in Hollywood than in Forest Lawn. Every company in town has used the work of blacklisted people. We're just the first to confirm what everybody knows.'"

One may believe, as I do, that Communism would destroy all of our freedoms, and one may be opposed to it as firmly and as strongly as possible and yet at the same time also believe that in a free society it is intolerable for a man to be prevented from earning his living because he believes in or is trying to promote Communism. His freedom includes his freedom to promote Communism. The Hollywood black-list is a thoroughly unfree act that destroys freedom. It didn't work, however, precisely because the market made it costly for people to pre-serve the blacklist. The commercial emphasis, the fact that people who are running enterprises have an incentive to make as much money as they can, protected the freedom of the individuals who were black-listed by providing them with an alternative form of employment, and by giving people an incentive to employ them.

If Hollywood and the movie industry had been government enter-prises or if in England it had been a question of employment by the BBC it is difficult to believe that the Hollywood Ten or their equivalent would have found employment.

The essential feature of the market which is brought out by these examples, and one could multiply them many fold, is essentially that it separates the economic activities of the individual from his politi-cal ideas or activities and in this way provides individuals with an effective support for personal freedom. The person who buys bread doesn't know whether the wheat from which it was made was grown by a pleader of the 5th Amendment or a McCarthyite, by a person whose skin is black or whose skin is white. The market is an imper-sonal mechanism that separates economic activities of individuals from their personal characteristics. It enables people to co-operate in the economic realm regardless of any differences of opinion or views or attitudes they may have in other areas. You and I may buy Mennen drug products even though we may think "Soapy" Williams was a ter-rible governor of the state of Michigan. This is the fundamental way in which a free-market capitalist organization of economic activity promotes personal freedom and political freedom.

*1962*

# IRVING KRISTOL

Irving Kristol (1920–2009) was a journalist and editor, who was frequently referred to as the "godfather of neoconservatism." While publishing widely in a variety of important publications, Kristol made his most enduring contribution to American intellectual life by helping to launch and sustain two important quarterlies that took direct aim at liberal orthodoxy. These were *The Public Interest*, founded in 1965 and focused on domestic affairs, and *The National Interest*, founded in 1985 and focused on foreign policy.

## "When Virtue Loses All Her Loveliness": Some Reflections on Capitalism and "the Free Society"

W HEN WE lack the will to see things as they really are, there is nothing so mystifying as the obvious. This is the case, I think, with the new upsurge of radicalism that is now shaking much of Western society to its foundations. We have constructed the most ingenious sociological and psychological theories—as well as a few disingenuously naive ones—to explain this phenomenon. But there is in truth no mystery here. Our youthful rebels are anything but inarticulate; and though they utter a great deal of nonsense, the import of what they are saying is clear enough. What they are saying is that they dislike—to put it mildly—the liberal, individualist, capitalist civilization that stands ready to receive them as citizens. They are rejecting this offer of citizenship and are declaring their desire to see some other kind of civilization replace it.

That most of them do not always put the matter as explicitly or as candidly as this is beside the point. Some of them do, of course; we try to dismiss them as "the lunatic fringe." But the mass of dissident young are not, after all, sufficiently educated to understand the implications of everything they say. Besides, it is so much easier for the less bold among them to insist that what they find outrageous are the defects and shortcomings of the present system. Such shortcomings undeniably exist and are easy polemical marks. And, at the other end, it is so much easier for the adult generations to accept such polemics as representing the sum and substance of their dissatisfaction. It is consoling to think that the turmoil among them is provoked by the extent to which our society falls short of realizing its ideals. But the plain truth is that it is these ideals themselves that are being rejected. Our young radicals are far less dismayed at America's failure to become what it ought to be than they are contemptuous of what it thinks it ought to be. For them, as for Oscar Wilde, it is not the average American who is disgusting; it is the ideal American.

This is why one can make so little impression on them with arguments about how much progress has been made in the past decades, or is being made today, toward racial equality, or abolishing poverty, or fighting pollution, or whatever it is that we conventionally take as a sign of "progress." The obstinacy with which they remain deaf to such "liberal" arguments is not all perverse or irrational, as some would like to think. It arises, rather, out of a perfectly sincere, if often inchoate, animus against the American system itself. This animus stands for a commitment—*to* what, remains to be seen, but *against* what is already only too evident.

## CAPITALISM'S THREE PROMISES

Dissatisfaction with the liberal-capitalist ideal, as distinct from indignation at failures to realize this ideal, are coterminous with the history of capitalism itself. Indeed, the cultural history of the capitalist epoch is not much more than a record of the varying ways such dissatisfaction could be expressed—in poetry, in the novel, in the drama, in painting, and today even in the movies. Nor, again, is there any great mystery why, from the first stirrings of the romantic movement, poets and philosophers have never had much regard for the capitalist civilization in which they lived and worked. But to understand this fully, one must be able to step outside the "progressive" ideology which makes us assume that liberal capitalism is the "natural" state of man toward which humanity has always aspired. There is nothing more natural about capitalist civilization than about many others that have had, or will have, their day. Capitalism represents a sum of human choices about the good life and the good society. These choices inevitably have their associated costs, and after two hundred years the conviction seems to be spreading that the costs have got out of line.

What did capitalism promise? First of all, it promised continued improvement in the material conditions of all its citizens, a promise without precedent in human history. Secondly, it promised an equally unprecedented measure of individual freedom for all of these same citizens. And lastly, it held out the promise that, amidst this prosperity and liberty, the individual could satisfy his instinct for self-perfection—for leading a virtuous life that satisfied the demands of his spirit (or, as one used to say, his soul)—and that the free exercise of such individual virtue would aggregate into a just society.

Now, it is important to realize that, though these aims were in one sense more ambitious than any previously set forth by a political ideology, in another sense they were far more modest. Whereas, as Joseph Cropsey has pointed out, Adam Smith defined "prudence" democratically as "the care of the health, of the fortune, of the rank of the individual," Aristotle had defined that term aristocratically, to mean "the quality of mind concerned with things just and noble and good for man." By this standard, all pre-capitalist systems had been, to one degree or another, Aristotelian: they were interested in creating a high and memorable civilization even if this were shared only by a tiny minority. In contrast, capitalism lowered its sights, but offered its shares in bourgeois civilization to the entire citizenry. Tocqueville, as usual, astutely caught this difference between the aristocratic civilizations of the past and the new liberal capitalism he saw emerging in the United States:

In aristocratic societies the class that gives the tone to opinion and has the guidance of affairs, being permanently and hereditarily placed above the multitude, naturally conceives a lofty idea of itself and man. It loves to invent for him noble pleasures, to carve out splendid objects for his ambition. Aristocracies often commit very tyrannical and inhuman actions, but they rarely entertain groveling thoughts. . . .

[In democracies, in contrast] there is little energy of character but customs are mild and laws humane. If there are few instances of exalted heroism or of virtues of the highest, brightest, and purest temper, men's habits are regular, violence is rare, and cruelty almost unknown. . . . Genius becomes rare, information more diffused. . . . There is less perfection, but more abundance, in all the productions of the arts.

It is because "high culture" inevitably has an aristocratic bias—it would not be "high" if it did not—that, from the beginnings of the capitalist era, it has always felt contempt for the bourgeois mode of existence. That mode of existence purposively depreciated the very issues that were its *raison d'être*. It did so by making them, as no society had ever dared or desired to do, matters of personal taste, according to the prescription of Adam Smith in his *Theory of Moral Sentiments*:

Though you despise that picture, or that poem, or even that system of philosophy, which I admire, there is little danger of our quarreling upon that account. Neither of us can reasonably be much interested about them. They ought all of them to be matters of great indifference to us both; so that, though our opinions may be opposite, our affections shall be very nearly the same.

In short, an amiable philistinism was inherent in bourgeois society, and this was bound to place its artists and intellectuals in an antagonistic posture toward it. This antagonism was irrepressible—the bourgeois world could not suppress it without violating its own liberal creed; the artists could not refrain from expressing their hostility without denying their most authentic selves. But the conflict could, and was, contained so long as capitalist civilization delivered on its three basic promises. It was only when the third promise, of a virtuous life and a just society, was subverted by the dynamics of capitalism itself, as it strove to fulfill the other two—affluence and liberty—that the bourgeois order came, in the minds of the young especially, to possess a questionable legitimacy.

## FROM BOURGEOIS SOCIETY TO A "FREE SOCIETY"

I can think of no better way of indicating the distance that capitalism has travelled from its original ideological origins than by contrasting the most intelligent defender of capitalism today with his predecessors. I refer to Friedrich von Hayek, who has as fine and as powerful a mind as is to be found anywhere, and whose *Constitution of Liberty* is one of the most thoughtful works of the last decades. In that book, he offers the following argument against viewing capitalism as a system that incarnates any idea of justice:

> Most people will object not to the bare fact of inequality but to the fact that the differences in reward do not correspond to any recognizable differences in the merit of those who receive them. The answer commonly given to this is that a free society on the whole achieves this kind of justice. This, however, is an indefensible contention if by justice is meant proportionality of reward to moral merit. Any attempt to found the case for freedom on this argument is very damaging to it, since it concedes that material rewards ought to be made to correspond to recognizable merit and then opposes the conclusion that most people will draw from this by an assertion which is untrue. The proper answer is that in a free society it is neither desirable nor practicable that material rewards should be made generally to correspond to what men recognize as merit and that it is an essential characteristic of a free society that an individual's position should not necessarily depend on the views that his fellows hold about the merit he has acquired. . . . A society in which the position of the individual was made to correspond to human ideas of moral merit would therefore be the exact opposite of a free society. It would be a society in which people were rewarded for duty performed instead of for success. . . . But if nobody's knowledge is sufficient to guide all human action, there is also no human being who is competent to reward all efforts according to merit.

This argument is admirable both for its utter candor and for its firm opposition to all those modern authoritarian ideologies, whether rationalist or irrationalist, which give a self-selected elite the right to shape men's lives and fix their destinies according to its preconceived notions of good and evil, merit and demerit. But it is interesting to note what Hayek is doing: he is opposing a *free* society to a *just* society—because, he says, while we know what freedom is, we have no generally accepted knowledge of what justice is. Elsewhere he writes:

> Since they [i.e., differentials in wealth and income] are not the effect of
> anyone's design or intentions, it is meaningless to describe the manner
> in which the market distributed the good things of this world among
> particular people as just or unjust. . . . No test or criteria have been
> found or can be found by which such rules of "social justice" can be
> assessed. . . . They would have to be determined by the arbitrary will of
> the holders of power.

Now, it may be that this is the best possible defense that can be
made of a free society. But if this is the case, one can fairly say that
"capitalism" is (or was) one thing, and a "free society" another. For
capitalism, during the first hundred years or so of its existence, did lay
claim to being a just social order, in the meaning later given to that
concept by Paul Elmer More: ". . . Such a distribution of power and
privilege, and of property as the symbol and instrument of these, as
at once will satisfy the distinctions of reason among the superior, and
will not outrage the feelings of the inferior." As a matter of fact, capitalism at its apogee saw itself as the most just social order the world
has ever witnessed, because it replaced all arbitrary (e.g., inherited)
distributions of power, privilege, and property with a distribution that
was directly and intimately linked to personal merit—this latter term
being inclusive of both personal abilities and personal virtues.

Writing shortly before the Civil War, George Fitzhugh, the most
gifted of Southern apologists for slavery, attacked the capitalist North
in these terms:

> In a free society none but the selfish virtues are in repute, because none
> other help a man in the race of competition. In such a society virtue
> loses all her loveliness, because of her selfish aims. Good men and bad
> men have the same end in view—self-promotion and self-elevation. . . .

At the time, this accusation was a half-truth. The North was not
yet "a free society," in Hayek's sense or Fitzhugh's. It was still in good
measure a bourgeois society in which the capitalist mode of existence involved moral self-discipline and had a visible aura of spiritual
grace. It was a society in which "success" was indeed seen as having
what Hayek has said it ought never to have: a firm connection with
"duty performed." It was a society in which Theodore Parker could
write of a leading merchant: "He had no uncommon culture of the

understanding or the imagination, and of the higher reason still less. But in respect of the *greater faculties*—in respect of conscience, affection, the religious element—he was well born, well bred." In short, it was a society still permeated by the Puritan ethic, the Protestant ethic, the capitalist ethic—call it what you will. It was a society in which it was agreed that there was a strong correlation between certain personal virtues—frugality, industry, sobriety, reliability, piety—and the way in which power, privilege, and property were distributed. And this correlation was taken to be the sign of a just society, not merely of a free one. Samuel Smiles or Horatio Alger would have regarded Professor Hayek's writings as slanderous of his fellow Christians, blasphemous of God, and ultimately subversive of the social order. I am not sure about the first two of these accusations, but I am fairly certain of the validity of the last.

This is not the place to recount the history and eventual degradation of the capitalist ethic in America.[1] Suffice it to say that, with every passing decade, Fitzhugh's charge, that "virtue loses all her loveliness, because of her selfish aims," became more valid. From having been a *capitalist, republican community*, with shared values and a quite unambiguous claim to the title of a just order, the United States became a *free, democratic society* where the will to success and privilege was severed from its moral moorings.

## THREE CURRENT APOLOGIA

But can men live in a free society if they have no reason to believe it is also a just society? I do not think so. My reading of history is that, in the same way as men cannot for long tolerate a sense of spiritual meaninglessness in their individual lives, so they cannot for long accept a society in which power, privilege, and property are not distributed according to some morally meaningful criteria. Nor is equality itself any more acceptable than inequality—neither is more "natural" than the other—if equality is merely a brute fact rather than a

---

[1] See Daniel Bell's essay, "The Cultural Contradictions of Capitalism," for a more detailed analysis of what happened and why.

consequence of an ideology or social philosophy. This explains what otherwise seems paradoxical: that small inequalities in capitalist countries can become the source of intense controversy while relatively larger inequalities in socialist or communist countries are blandly overlooked. Thus, those same young radicals who are infuriated by trivial inequalities in the American economic system are quite blind to grosser inequalities in the Cuban system. This is usually taken as evidence of hyprocrisy or self-deception. I would say it shows, rather, that people's notions of equality or inequality have extraordinarily little to do with arithmetic and almost everything to do with political philosophy.

I believe that what holds for equality also holds for liberty. People feel free when they subscribe to a prevailing social philosophy; they feel unfree when the prevailing social philosophy is unpersuasive; and the existence of constitutions or laws or judiciaries have precious little to do with these basic feelings. The average working man in nineteenth-century America had far fewer "rights" than his counterpart today; but he was far more likely to boast about his being a free man.

So I conclude, despite Professor Hayek's ingenious analysis, that men cannot accept the historical accidents of the marketplace—seen merely as accidents—as the basis for an enduring and legitimate entitlement to power, privilege, and property. And, in actual fact, Professor Hayek's rationale for modern capitalism is never used outside a small academic enclave; I even suspect it cannot be believed except by those whose minds have been shaped by overlong exposure to scholasticism. Instead, the arguments offered to justify the social structure of capitalism now fall into three main categories:

1) *The Protestant Ethic*—This, however, is now reserved for the lower socioeconomic levels. It is still believed, and it is still reasonable to believe, that worldly success among the working class, lower-middle class, and even middle class has a definite connection with personal virtues such as diligence, rectitude, sobriety, honest ambition, etc., etc. And, so far as I can see, the connection is not only credible but demonstrable. It does seem that the traditional bourgeois virtues are efficacious among these classes—at least, it is rare to find successful men emerging from these classes who do not to a significant degree exemplify them. But no one seriously claims that these traditional

virtues will open the corridors of corporate power to anyone, or that the men who now occupy the executive suites are—or even aspire to be—models of bourgeois virtue.

2) *The Darwinian Ethic*—This is to be found mainly among small businessmen who are fond of thinking that their "making it" is to be explained as "the survival of the fittest." They are frequently quite right, of course, in believing the metaphor appropriate to their condition and to the ways in which they achieved it. But it is preposterous to think that the mass of men will ever accept as legitimate a social order formed in accordance with the laws of the jungle. Men may be animals, but they are political animals—and, what comes to not such a different thing, moral animals too. The fact that for several decades after the Civil War, the Darwinian ethic, as popularized by Herbert Spencer, could be taken seriously by so many social theorists represents one of the most bizarre and sordid episodes in American intellectual history. It could not last; and did not.

3) *The Technocratic Ethic*—This is the most prevalent justification of corporate capitalism today, and finds expression in an insistence on "performance." Those who occupy the seats of corporate power, and enjoy the prerogatives and privileges thereof, are said to acquire legitimacy by their superior ability to achieve superior "performance"—in economic growth, managerial efficiency, technological innovation. In a sense, what is claimed is that these men are accomplishing social tasks, and fulfilling social responsibilities, in an especially efficacious way.

There are, however, two fatal flaws in this argument. First, if one defines "performance" in a strictly limited and measurable sense, then one is applying a test that any ruling class is bound, on fairly frequent occasions, to fail. Life has its ups and downs; so do history and economics; and men who can only claim legitimacy *via* performance are going to have to spend an awful lot of time and energy explaining why things are not going as well as they ought to. Such repeated, defensive apologias, in the end, will be hollow and unconvincing. Indeed, the very concept of "legitimacy," in its historical usages, is supposed to take account of and make allowances for all those rough passages a society will have to navigate. If the landed gentry of Britain during those centuries of its dominance, or the business class in the United

States during the first century and a half of our national history, had insisted that it be judged by performance alone, it would have flunked out of history. So would every other ruling class that ever existed.

Secondly, if one tries to avoid this dilemma by giving the term "performance" a broader and larger meaning, then one inevitably finds oneself passing beyond the boundaries of bourgeois propriety. It is one thing to say with Samuel Johnson that men honestly engaged in business are doing the least mischief that men are capable of; it is quite another thing to assert that they are doing the greatest good—this is only too patently untrue. For the achievement of the greatest good, more than successful performance in business is necessary. Witness how vulnerable our corporate managers are to accusations that they are befouling our environment. What these accusations really add up to is the statement that the business system in the United States does not create a beautiful, refined, gracious, and tranquil civilization. To which our corporate leaders are replying: "Oh, we can perform that mission too—just give us time." But there is no good reason to think they can accomplish this noncapitalist mission; nor is there any reason to believe that they have any proper entitlement even to try.

## "PARTICIPATION" OR LEADERSHIP?

It is, I think, because of the decline of the bourgeois ethic, and the consequent drainage of legitimacy out of the business system, that the issue of "participation" has emerged with such urgency during these past years. It is a common error to take this word at its face value—to assume that, in our organized and bureaucratized society, the average person is more isolated, alienated, or powerless than ever before, and that the proper remedy is to open new avenues of "participation." We are then perplexed when, the avenues having been open, we find so little traffic passing through. We give college students the right to representation on all sorts of committees—and then discover they never bother to come to meetings. We create new popularly-elected "community" organizations in the ghettos—and then discover that ghetto residents won't come out to vote. We decentralize New York City's school system—only to discover that the populace is singularly uninterested in local school board elections.

I doubt very much that the average American is actually more iso-lated or powerless today than in the past. The few serious studies that have been made on this subject indicate that we have highly roman-ticized notions of the past—of the degree to which ordinary people were ever involved in community activities—and highly apocalyptic notions of the present. If one takes membership in civic-minded orga-nizations as a criterion, people are unquestionably more "involved" today than ever before in our history. Maybe that's not such a good criterion; but it is a revealing aspect of this whole problem that those who make large statements on this matter rarely give us any workable or testable criteria at all.

But I would not deny that more people, even if more specifically "involved" than ever before, also feel more "alienated" in a general way. And this, I would suggest, is because the institutions of our soci-ety have lost their vital connection with the values which are sup-posed to govern the private lives of our citizenry. They no longer exemplify these values; they no longer magnify them; they no longer reassuringly sustain them. When it is said that the institutions of our society have become appallingly "impersonal," I take this to mean that they have lost any shape that is congruent with the private moral codes which presumably govern individual life. (That presumption, of course, may be factually weak; but it is nonetheless efficacious so long as people hold it.) The "outside" of our social life has ceased being harmonious with the "inside"—the mode of distribution of power, privilege, and property, and hence the very principle of authority, no longer "makes sense" to the bewildered citizen. And when institutions cease to "make sense" in this way, all the familiar criteria of success or failure become utterly irrelevant.

As I see it, then, the demand for "participation" is best appreciated as a demand for authority—for leadership that holds the promise of reconciling the inner and outer worlds of the citizen. So far from its being a hopeful reawakening of the democratic spirit, it signifies a hunger for authority that leads toward some kind of plebiscitary democracy at best, and is in any case not easy to reconcile with lib-eral democracy as we traditionally have known it. I find it instructive that such old-fashioned populists as Hubert Humphrey and Edmund Muskie, whose notions of "participation" are both liberal and tra-ditional, fail to catch the imagination of our dissidents in the way that Robert Kennedy did. The late Senator Kennedy was very much a leader—one can imagine Humphrey or Muskie participating in an old-fashioned town meeting, one can only envision Kennedy dominating a town rally. One can also envision those who "participated" in such a rally feeling that they had achieved a kind of "representation" previously denied them.

## A CASE OF REGRESSION

For a system of liberal, representative government to work, free elections are not enough. The results of the political process and of the exercise of individual freedom—the distribution of power, privilege, and property—must also be seen as in some profound sense expressive of the values that govern the lives of individuals. An idea of self-government, if it is to be viable, must encompass both the private and the public sectors. If it does not—if the principles that organize public life seem to have little relation to those that shape private lives—you have "alienation," and *anomie*, and a melting away of established principles of authority.

Milton Friedman, arguing in favor of Hayek's extreme libertarian position, has written that the free man "recognizes no national purpose except as it is the consensus of the purposes for which the citizens severally strive." If he is using the term "consensus" seriously, then he must be assuming that there is a strong homogeneity of values among the citizenry, and that these values give a certain corresponding shape to the various institutions of society, political and economic. Were that the case, then it is indeed true that a "national purpose" arises automatically and organically out of the social order itself. Something like this did happen when liberal capitalism was in its prime, vigorous and self-confident. But is that our condition today? I think not—just as I think Mr. Friedman doesn't really mean "consensus" but rather the mere aggregation of selfish aims. In such a blind and accidental arithmetic, the sum floats free from the addenda, and its legitimacy is infinitely questionable.

The inner spiritual chaos of the times, so powerfully created by the dynamics of capitalism itself, is such as to make nihilism an easy temptation. A "free society" in Hayek's sense gives birth in massive numbers to "free spirits"—emptied of moral substance but still driven by primordial moral aspirations. Such people are capable of the most irrational actions. Indeed, it is my impression that, under the strain of modern life, whole classes of our population—and the educated classes most of all—are entering what can only be called, in the strictly clinical sense, a phase of infantile regression. With every passing year, public discourse becomes sillier and more petulant, while human emotions become, apparently, more ungovernable. Some of our most intelligent university professors are now loudly saying things that, had they been uttered by one of their students twenty years ago, would have called forth gentle and urbane reproof.

## THE REFORMING SPIRIT AND THE
## CONSERVATIVE IDEAL

And yet, if the situation of liberal capitalism today seems so precarious, it is likely nevertheless to survive for a long while, if only because the modern era has failed to come up with any plausible alternatives. Socialism, communism, and fascism have all turned out to be either utopian illusions or sordid frauds. So we shall have time—though not an endless amount of it, for we have already wasted a great deal. We are today in a situation not very different from that described by Herbert Croly in *The Promise of American Life* (1912):

> The substance of our national Promise has consisted ... of an improving popular economic condition, guaranteed by democratic political institutions, and resulting in moral and social amelioration. These manifold benefits were to be obtained merely by liberating the enlightened self-enterprise of the American people. . . . The fulfillment of the American Promise was considered inevitable because it was based upon a combination of self-interest and the natural goodness of human nature. On the other hand, if the fulfillment of our national Promise can no longer be considered inevitable, if it must be considered as equivalent to a conscious national purpose instead of an inexorable national destiny, the implication necessarily is that the trust reposed in individual self-interest has been in some measure betrayed. No pre-established harmony can then exist between the free and abundant satisfaction of private needs and the accomplishment of a morally and socially desirable result.

Croly is not much read these days. He was a liberal reformer with essentially conservative goals. So was Matthew Arnold, fifty years earlier—and he isn't much read these days, either. Neither of them can pass into the conventional anthologies of liberal or conservative thought. I think this is a sad commentary on the ideological barrenness of the liberal and conservative creeds. I also think it is a great pity. For if our private and public worlds are ever again, in our lifetimes, to have a congenial relationship—if virtue is to regain her lost loveliness—then some such combination of the reforming spirit with the conservative ideal seems to me to be what is most desperately wanted.

I use the word "conservative" advisedly. Though the discontents of our civilization express themselves in the rhetoric of "liberation" and "equality," one can detect beneath the surface an acute yearning for order and stability—but a legitimate order, of course, and a legitimized stability. In this connection, I find the increasing skepticism as to the benefits of economic growth and technological innovation most suggestive. Such skepticism has been characteristic of conservative critics of liberal capitalism since the beginning of the nineteenth century. One finds it in Coleridge, Carlyle, and Newman—in all those who found it impossible to acquiesce in a "progressive" notion of human history or social evolution. Our dissidents today may think they are exceedingly progressive; but no one who puts greater emphasis on "the quality of life" than on "mere" material enrichment can properly be placed in that category. For the idea of progress in the modern era has always signified that the quality of life would inevitably be improved by material enrichment. To doubt this is to doubt the political metaphysics of modernity and to start the long trek back to pre-modern political philosophy—Plato, Aristotle, Thomas Aquinas, Hooker, Calvin, etc. It seems to me that this trip is quite necessary. Perhaps there we shall discover some of those elements that are most desperately needed by the spiritually impoverished civilization that we have constructed on what once seemed to be sturdy bourgeois foundations.

*1970*

# MURRAY ROTHBARD

A principled if idiosyncratic libertarian, Murray Rothbard (1926–1995) explained his views in over twenty books and played a key role in the creation of such libertarian outposts as the Center for Libertarian Studies (1976) and the Ludwig von Mises Institute (1983).

—————

## FROM *For a New Liberty*

### THE STATE AND THE INTELLECTUALS

SINCE THE early origins of the State, its rulers have always turned, as a necessary bolster to their rule, to an alliance with society's class of intellectuals. The masses do not create their own abstract ideas, or indeed think through these ideas independently; they follow passively the ideas adopted and promulgated by the body of intellectuals, who become the effective "opinion moulders" in society. And since it is precisely a moulding of opinion on behalf of the rulers that the State almost desperately needs, this forms a firm basis for the age-old alliance of the intellectuals and the ruling classes of the State. The alliance is based on a *quid pro quo*: on the one hand, the intellectuals spread among the masses the idea that the State and its rulers are wise, good, sometimes divine, and at the very least inevitable and better than any conceivable alternatives. In return for this panoply of ideology, the State incorporates the intellectuals as part of the ruling elite, granting them power, status, prestige, and material security. Furthermore, intellectuals are needed to staff the bureaucracy and to "plan" the economy and society.

Before the modern era, particularly potent among the intellectual handmaidens of the State was the priestly caste, cementing the powerful and terrible alliance of warrior chief and medicine man, of Throne and Altar. The State "established" the Church and conferred upon it power, prestige, and wealth extracted from its subjects. In return, the Church anointed the State with divine sanction and inculcated this sanction into the populace. In the modern era, when theocratic arguments have lost much of their lustre among the public, the intellectuals have posed as the scientific cadre of "experts" and have been busy informing the hapless public that political affairs, foreign and domestic, are much too complex for the average person to bother his head about. Only the State and its corps of intellectual experts, planners, scientists, economists, and "national security managers" can possibly hope to deal with these problems. The role of the masses, even in "democracies," is to ratify and assent to the decisions of their knowledgeable rulers.

Historically, the union of Church and State, of Throne and Altar, has been the most effective device for inducing obedience and support among the subjects. Burnham attests to the power of myth and mystery in inducing support when he writes that "In ancient times, before the illusions of science had corrupted traditional wisdom, the founders of Cities were known to be gods or demi-gods."[1] To the established priestcraft, the ruler was either anointed by God or, in the case of the absolute rule of many Oriental despotisms, was even himself God; hence, any questioning or resistance to his rule would be blasphemy.

Many and subtle are the ideological weapons the State and its intellectuals have used over the centuries to induce their subjects to accept their rule. One excellent weapon has been the power of *tradition*. The longer lasting the rule of any given State, the more powerful this weapon; for then the X-Dynasty or the Y-State has the seeming weight of centuries of tradition behind it. Worship of one's ancestors then becomes a none-too-subtle means of cultivating worship of

[1] James Burnham, *Congress and the American Tradition* (Chicago: Henry Regnery, 1959), p. 3.

one's ancestral rulers. The force of tradition is, of course, bolstered by ancient *habit*, which confirms the subjects in the seeming propriety and legitimacy of the rule under which they live. Thus, the political theorist Bertrand De Jouvenel has written:

> The essential reason for obedience is that it has become a habit of the species. . . . Power is for us a fact of nature. From the earliest days of recorded history it has always presided over human destinies . . . the authorities which ruled . . . in former times did not disappear without bequeathing to their successors their privilege nor without leaving in men's minds imprints which are cumulative in their effect. The succession of governments which, in the course of centuries, rule the same society may be looked on as one underlying government which takes on continuous accretions.[2]

Another potent ideological force is for the State to deprecate the *individual* and exalt either the past or the present collectivity of society. Any isolated voice, any raiser of new doubts, can then be attacked as a profane violator of the wisdom of his ancestors. Moreover, any new idea, much less any new *critical* idea, must necessarily *begin* as a small minority opinion. Therefore, in order to ward off any potentially dangerous idea from threatening majority acceptance of its rule, the State will try to nip the new idea in the bud by ridiculing any view that sets itself against mass opinion. The ways in which the State rulers in ancient Chinese despotisms used religion as a method of binding the individual to the State-run society were summarized by Norman Jacobs:

> Chinese religion is a social religion, seeking to solve the problems of social interests, not individual interests. . . . Religion is essentially a force of impersonal social adjustment and control—rather than a medium for the personal solutions of the individual—and social adjustment and control are effected through education and reverence for superiors. . . . Reverence for superiors—superior in age and hence in education and experience—is the ethical foundation of social adjustment and control. . . . In China, the inter-relationship of political authority with orthodox religion equated heterodoxy with political error. The orthodox

---

[2] Bertrand De Jouvenel, *On Power* (New York: Viking Press, 1949), p. 22.

religion was particularly active in persecuting and destroying heterodox sects; in this it was backed by the secular power.[3]

The general tendency of government to seek out and thwart any heterodox views was outlined, in typically witty and delightful style, by the libertarian writer H. L. Mencken:

> All [that government] can see in an original idea is potential change, and hence an invasion of its prerogatives. The most dangerous man, to any government, is the man who is able to think things out for himself, without regard to the prevailing superstitions and taboos. Almost inevitably he comes to the conclusion that the government he lives under is dishonest, insane and intolerable, and so, if he is romantic, he tries to change it. And even if he is not romantic personally he is very apt to spread discontent among those who are.[4]

It is also particularly important for the State to make its rule seem *inevitable*: even if its reign is disliked, as it often is, it will then be met with the passive resignation expressed in the familiar coupling of "death and taxes." One method is to bring to its side historical determinism: if X-State rules us, then this has been inevitably decreed for us by the Inexorable Laws of History (or the Divine Will, or the Absolute, or the Material Productive Forces), and nothing that any puny individuals may do can change the inevitable. It is also important for the State to inculcate in its subjects an aversion to any outcropping of what is now called "a conspiracy theory of history." For a search for "conspiracies," as misguided as the results often are, means a search for motives, and an attribution of individual responsibility for the historical misdeeds of ruling elites. If, however, any tyranny or venality or aggressive war imposed by the State was brought about *not* by particular State rulers but by mysterious and arcane "social forces," or by the imperfect state of the world—or if, in some way, *everyone* was guilty ("We are *all* murderers," proclaims a common slogan), then there is no point in anyone's becoming indignant or rising up against

---

[3] Norman Jacobs, *The Origin of Modern Capitalism and Eastern Asia* (Hong Kong: Hong Kong University Press, 1958), pp. 161–63, 185. The great work on all aspects of Oriental despotism is Karl A. Wittfogel, *Oriental Despotism: A Comparative Study of Total Power* (New Haven: Yale University Press, 1957).

[4] H. L. Mencken, *A Mencken Crestomathy* (New York: Alfred A. Knopf, 1949), p. 145.

such misdeeds. Furthermore, a discrediting of "conspiracy theories"—
or indeed, of anything smacking of "economic determinism"—will
make the subjects more likely to believe the "general welfare" reasons
that are invariably put forth by the modern State for engaging in any
aggressive actions.

The rule of the State is thus made to seem inevitable. Furthermore,
any alternative to the existing State is encased in an aura of fear.
Neglecting its own monopoly of theft and predation, the State raises
the spectre among its subjects of the chaos that would supposedly
ensue if the State should disappear. The people on their own, it is
maintained, could not possibly supply their own protection against
sporadic criminals and marauders. Furthermore, each State has been
particularly successful over the centuries in instilling fear among its
subjects of *other* State rulers. With the land area of the globe now
parcelled out among particular States, one of the basic doctrines and
tactics of the rulers of each State has been to identify *itself* with the
territory it governs. Since most men tend to love their homeland, the
identification of that land and its population with the State is a means
of making natural patriotism work to the State's advantage. If, then,
"Ruritania" is attacked by "Walldavia," the first task of the Ruritanian
State and its intellectuals is to convince the people of Ruritania that
the attack is really upon *them*, and not simply upon their ruling class.
In this way, a war between *rulers* is converted into a war between
*peoples*, with each people rushing to the defense of their rulers in the
mistaken belief that the rulers are busily defending *them*. This device
of nationalism has been particularly successful in recent centuries;
it was not very long ago, at least in Western Europe, when the mass
of subjects regarded wars as irrelevant battles between various sets of
nobles and their retinues.

Another tried and true method for bending subjects to one's will is
the infusion of guilt. Any increase in private well-being can be attacked
as "unconscionable greed," "materialism," or "excessive affluence";
and mutually beneficial exchanges in the market can be denounced as
"selfish." Somehow the conclusion always drawn is that more resources
should be expropriated from the private sector and siphoned into the
parasitic "public," or State, sector. Often the call upon the public to
yield more resources is couched in a stern call by the ruling elite for
more "sacrifices" for the national or the common weal. Somehow,

however, while the public is supposed to sacrifice and curtail its "materialistic greed," the sacrifices are always one way. The *State* does not sacrifice; the State eagerly grabs more and more of the public's material resources. Indeed, it is a useful rule of thumb: when your ruler calls aloud for "sacrifices," look to your own life and pocketbook!

This sort of argumentation reflects a general double standard of morality that is always applied to State rulers but not to anyone else. No one, for example, is surprised or horrified to learn that businessmen are seeking higher profits. No one is horrified if workers leave lower-paying for higher-paying jobs. All this is considered proper and normal behavior. But if anyone should dare assert that politicians and bureaucrats are motivated by the desire to maximize *their* incomes, the hue and cry of "conspiracy theorist" or "economic determinist" spreads throughout the land. The general opinion—carefully cultivated, of course, by the State itself—is that men enter politics or government purely out of devoted concern for the common good and the public weal. What gives the gentlemen of the State apparatus their superior moral patina? Perhaps it is the dim and instinctive knowledge of the populace that the State *is* engaged in systematic theft and predation, and they may feel that only a dedication to altruism on the part of the State makes these actions tolerable. To consider politicians and bureaucrats subject to the same monetary aims as everyone else would strip the Robin Hood veil from State predation. For it would then be clear that, in the Oppenheimer phrasing, ordinary citizens were pursuing the peaceful, productive "economic means" to wealth, while the State apparatus was devoting itself to the coercive and exploitative organized "political means." The emperor's clothes of supposed altruistic concern for the common weal would then be stripped from him.

The intellectual arguments used by the State throughout history to "engineer consent" by the public can be classified into two parts: (1) that rule by the existing government is inevitable, absolutely necessary, and far better than the indescribable evils that would ensue upon its downfall; and (2) that the State rulers are especially great, wise, and altruistic men—far greater, wiser, and better than their simple subjects. In former times, the latter argument took the form of rule by "divine right" or by the "divine ruler" himself, or by an "aristocracy" of men. In modern times, as we indicated earlier, this argument stresses not so much divine approval as rule by a wise guild of "scientific experts" especially endowed in knowledge of statesmanship and the arcane facts of the world. The increasing use of scientific jargon, especially in the social sciences, has permitted intellectuals to weave apologia for State rule which rival the ancient priestcraft in obscurantism. For example, a thief who presumed to justify his theft by saying that he was really helping his victims by his spending, thus giving retail trade a needed boost, would be hooted down without delay. But when this same theory is clothed in Keynesian mathematical equations and impressive references to the "multiplier effect," it carries far more conviction with a bamboozled public.

In recent years, we have seen the development in the United States of a profession of "national security managers," of bureaucrats who never face electoral procedures, but who continue, through admin- istration after administration, secretly using their supposed special expertise to plan wars, interventions, and military adventures. Only their egregious blunders in the Vietnam war have called their activi- ties into any sort of public question; before that, they were able to ride high, wide, and handsome over the public they saw mostly as cannon fodder for their own purposes.

A public debate between "isolationist" Senator Robert A. Taft and one of the leading national security intellectuals, McGeorge Bundy, was instructive in demarking both the issues at stake and the attitude of the intellectual ruling elite. Bundy attacked Taft in early 1951 for opening a public debate on the waging of the Korean war. Bundy insisted that only the executive policy leaders were equipped to manipulate diplomatic and military force in a lengthy decades-long period of limited war against the communist nations. It was important, Bundy maintained, that public opinion and public debate be excluded from promulgating any policy role in this area. For, he warned, the public was unfortunately not committed to the rigid national pur- poses discerned by the policy managers; it merely responded to the *ad hoc* realities of given situations. Bundy also maintained that there should be no recriminations or even examinations of the decisions of the policy managers, because it was important that the public accept their decisions without question. Taft, in contrast, denounced the secret decision-making by military advisers and specialists in the exec- utive branch, decisions effectively sealed off from public scrutiny. Furthermore, he complained, "If anyone dared to suggest criticism or even a thorough debate, he was at once branded as an isolationist and a saboteur of unity and the bipartisan foreign policy."[5]

Similarly, at a time when President Eisenhower and Secretary of State Dulles were privately contemplating going to war in Indochina, another prominent national security manager, George F. Kennan, was advising the public that "There are times when, having elected a government, we will be best advised to let it govern and let it speak for us as it will in the councils of the nations."[6]

We see clearly why the State needs the intellectuals; but why do the intellectuals need the State? Put simply, the intellectual's livelihood in the free market is generally none too secure; for the intellectual, like everyone else on the market, must depend on the values and choices of the masses of his fellow men, and it is characteristic of these masses that they are generally uninterested in intellectual concerns. The State, on the other hand, is willing to offer the intellectuals a warm, secure, and permanent berth in its apparatus, a secure income, and the panoply of prestige.

The eager alliance between the State and the intellectuals was symbolized by the avid desire of the professors at the University of Berlin, in the nineteenth century, to form themselves into what they themselves proclaimed as the "intellectual bodyguard of the House of Hohenzollern." From a superficially different ideological perspective, it can be seen in the revealingly outraged reaction of the eminent Marxist scholar of ancient China, Joseph Needham, to Karl Wittfogel's acidulous critique of ancient Chinese despotism. Wittfogel had shown the importance for bolstering the system of the Confucian glorification of the gentleman-scholar officials who manned the ruling bureaucracy of despotic China. Needham charged indignantly that the "civilization which Professor Wittfogel is so bitterly attacking was one which could make poets and scholars into officials."[7] What matter

---

[5] See Leonard P. Liggio, *Why the Futile Crusade?* (New York: Center for Libertarian Studies, April 1978), pp. 41–43.

[6] George F. Kennan, *Realities of American Foreign Policy* (Princeton: Princeton University Press, 1954), pp. 95–96.

[7] Joseph Needham, "Review of Karl A. Wittfogel, *Oriental Despotism*," *Science and Society* (1958), p. 65. For an attitude in contrast to Needham's, see John Lukacs, "Intellectual Class or Intellectual Profession?," in George B. deHuszar, ed., *The Intellectuals* (Glencoe, Ill.: The Free Press, 1960), p. 522.

the totalitarianism so long as the ruling class is abundantly staffed by certified intellectuals!

The worshipful and fawning attitude of intellectuals toward their rulers has been illustrated many times throughout history. A contemporary American counterpart to the "intellectual bodyguard of the House of Hohenzollern" is the attitude of so many liberal intellectuals toward the office and person of the President. Thus, to political scientist Professor Richard Neustadt, the President is the "sole crownlike symbol of the Union." And policy manager Townsend Hoopes, in the winter of 1960, wrote that "under our system the people can look only to the President to define the nature of our foreign policy problem and the national programs and sacrifices required to meet it with effectiveness."[8] After generations of such rhetoric, it is no wonder that Richard Nixon, on the eve of his election as President, should thus describe his role: "He [the President] must articulate the nation's values, define its goals and marshall its will." Nixon's conception of his role is hauntingly similar to Ernst Huber's articulation, in the Germany of the 1930s, of the *Constitutional Law of the Greater German Reich*. Huber wrote that the head of State "sets up the great ends which are to be attained and draws up the plans for the utilization of all national powers in the achievement of the common goals . . . he gives the national life its true purpose and value."[9]

The attitude and motivation of the contemporary national security intellectual bodyguard of the State has been caustically described by Marcus Raskin, who was a staff member of the National Security Council during the Kennedy administration. Calling them "megadeath intellectuals," Raskin writes that:

> . . . their most important function is to justify and extend the existence of their employers. . . . In order to justify the continued large-scale production of these [thermonuclear] bombs and missiles, military and industrial leaders needed some kind of theory to rationalize their use. . . . This became particularly urgent during the late 1950's, when

---

[8] Richard Neustadt, "Presidency at Mid-Century," *Law and Contemporary Problems* (Autumn, 1956), pp. 609–45; Townsend Hoopes, "The Persistence of Illusion: The Soviet Economic Drive and American National Interest," *Yale Review* (March 1960), p. 336.

[9] Quoted in Thomas Reeves and Karl Hess, *The End of the Draft* (New York: Vintage Books, 1970), pp. 64–65.

economy-minded members of the Eisenhower Administration began to wonder why so much money, thought, and resources were being spent on weapons if their use could not be justified. And so began a series of rationalizations by the "defense intellectuals" in and out of the universities. . . . Military procurement will continue to flourish, and they will continue to demonstrate why it must. In this respect they are no different from the great majority of modern specialists who accept the assumptions of the organizations which employ them because of the rewards in money and power and prestige. . . . They know enough not to question their employers' right to exist.[10]

This is not to say that all intellectuals everywhere have been "court intellectuals," servitors and junior partners of power. But this has been the ruling condition in the history of civilizations—generally in the form of a priestcraft—just as the ruling condition in those civilizations has been one or another form of despotism. There have been glorious exceptions, however, particularly in the history of Western civilization, where intellectuals have often been trenchant critics and opponents of State power, and have used their intellectual gifts to fashion theoretical systems which could be used in the struggle for liberation from that power. But invariably, these intellectuals have only been able to arise as a significant force when they have been able to operate from an independent power base—an independent property base—separate from the apparatus of the State. For wherever the State controls all property, wealth, and employment, everyone is economically dependent on it, and it becomes difficult, if not impossible, for such independent criticism to arise. It has been in the West, with its decentralized foci of power, its independent sources of property and employment, and therefore of bases from which to criticize the State, where a body of intellectual critics has been able to flourish. In the Middle Ages, the Roman Catholic Church, which was at least separate if not independent from the State, and the new free towns were able to serve as centers of intellectual and also of substantive opposition. In later centuries, teachers, ministers, and pamphleteers in a relatively free society were able to use their independence from

---

[10] Marcus Raskin, "The Megadeath Intellectuals," *The New York Review of Books* (November 14, 1963), pp. 6–7. Also see Martin Nicolaus, "The Professor, the Policeman, and the Peasant," *Viet-Report* (June–July 1966), pp. 15–19.

the State to agitate for further expansion of freedom. In contrast, one of the first libertarian philosophers, Lao-tse, living in the midst of ancient Chinese despotism, saw no hope for achieving liberty in that totalitarian society except by counseling quietism, to the point of the individual's dropping out of social life altogether.

With decentralized power, with a Church separate from the State, with flourishing towns and cities able to develop outside the feudal power structure, and with freedom in society, the economy was able to develop in Western Europe in a way that transcended all previous civilizations. Furthermore, the Germanic—and particularly the Celtic—tribal structure which succeeded the disintegrating Roman Empire had strong libertarian elements. Instead of a mighty State apparatus exerting a monopoly of violence, disputes were solved by contending tribesmen consulting the elders of the tribe on the nature and application of the tribe's customary and common law. The "chief" was generally merely a war leader who was only called into his warrior role whenever war with other tribes was under way. There was no permanent war or military bureaucracy in the tribes. In Western Europe, as in many other civilizations, the typical model of the origin of the State was not via a voluntary "social contract" but by the conquest of one tribe by another. The original liberty of the tribe or the peasantry thus falls victim to the conquerors. At first, the conquering tribe killed and looted the victims and rode on. But at some time the conquerors decided that it would be more profitable to settle down among the conquered peasantry and rule and loot them on a permanent and systematic basis. The periodic tribute exacted from the conquered subjects eventually came to be called "taxation." And, with equal generality, the conquering chieftains parcelled out the land of the peasantry to the various warlords, who were then able to settle down and collect feudal "rent" from the peasantry. The peasants were often enslaved, or rather enserfed, to the land itself to provide a continuing source of exploited labor for the feudal lords.[11]

---

[11] On the typical genesis of the State, see Oppenheimer, *op. cit.*, Chapter II. While scholars such as Lowie and Wittfogel (*op. cit.*, pp. 324–25) dispute the Gumplowicz-Oppenheimer-Rüstow thesis that the State *always* originated in conquest, they concede that conquest often entered into the alleged internal development of States. Furthermore, there is evidence that in the first great civilization, Sumer,

We may note a few prominent instances of the birth of a modern
State through conquest. One was the military conquest of the Indian
peasantry in Latin America by the Spaniards. The conquering Spanish
not only established a new State over the Indians, but the land of the
peasantry was parcelled out among the conquering warlords, who were
ever after to collect rent from the tillers of the land. Another instance
was the new political form imposed upon the Saxons of England after
their conquest by the Normans in 1066. The land of England was
parcelled out among the Norman warrior lords, who thereby formed a
State and feudal-land apparatus of rule over the subject population. For
the libertarian, the most interesting and certainly the most poignant
example of the creation of a State through conquest was the destruction of the libertarian society of ancient Ireland by England in the
seventeenth century, a conquest which established an imperial State
and ejected numerous Irish from their cherished land. The libertarian
society of Ireland, which lasted for a thousand years was able to resist
English conquest for hundreds of years because of the absence of a
State which could be conquered easily and then used by the conquerors to rule over the native population.

But while throughout Western history, intellectuals have formulated theories designed to check and limit State power, each State has
been able to use its own intellectuals to turn those ideas around into
further legitimations of its own advance of power. Thus, originally,
in Western Europe the concept of the "divine right of kings" was a
doctrine promoted by the Church to *limit* State power. The idea was
that the king could not just impose his arbitrary will. His edicts were
limited to conforming with the divine law. As absolute monarchy
advanced, however, the kings were able to turn the concept around
to the idea that God put his stamp of approval on any of the king's
actions; that he ruled by "divine right."

Similarly, the concept of parliamentary democracy began as a popular check on the absolute rule of the monarch. The king was limited by
the power of parliament to grant him tax revenues. Gradually, however, as parliament displaced the king as head of State, the parliament

---

a prosperous, free and Stateless society existed until military *defense* against conquest induced the development of a permanent military and State bureaucracy. Cf.
Samual Noah Kramer, *The Sumerians* (Chicago: University of Chicago Press, 1963),
pp. 73ff.

itself became the unchecked State sovereign. In the early nineteenth century, English utilitarians, who advocated additional individual liberty in the name of social utility and the general welfare, were to see these concepts turned into sanctions for expanding the power of the State.

As De Jouvenel writes:

> Many writers on theories of sovereignty have worked out one or the other of these restrictive devices. But in the end every single such theory has, sooner or later, lost its original purpose, and come to act merely as a springboard to Power, by providing it with the powerful aid of an invisible sovereign with whom it could in time successfully identify itself.[12]

Certainly, the most ambitious attempt in history to impose limits on the State was the Bill of Rights and other restrictive parts of the United States Constitution. Here, written limits on government became the fundamental law, to be interpreted by a judiciary supposedly independent of the other branches of government. All Americans are familiar with the process by which John C. Calhoun's prophetic analysis has been vindicated; the State's own monopoly judiciary has inexorably broadened the construction of State power over the last century and a half. But few have been as keen as liberal Professor Charles Black—who hails the process—in seeing that the State has been able to transform judicial review itself from a limiting device into a powerful instrument for gaining legitimacy for its actions in the minds of the public. If a judicial decree of "unconstitutional" is a mighty check on governmental power, so too a verdict of "constitutional" is an equally mighty weapon for fostering public acceptance of ever greater governmental power.

Professor Black begins his analysis by pointing out the crucial necessity for "legitimacy" of any government in order to endure; that is, basic majority acceptance of the government and its actions. Acceptance of legitimacy, however, becomes a real problem in a country like the United States, where "substantive limitations are built into the theory on which the government rests." What is needed, adds Black, is a method by which the government can assure the public

---

[12] De Jouvenel, *op. cit.*, p. 27.

that its expanding powers are indeed "constitutional." And this, he concludes, has been the major historic function of judicial review. Let Black illustrate the problem:

> The supreme risk [to the government] is that of disaffection and a feeling of outrage widely disseminated throughout the population, and loss of moral authority by the government as such, however long it may be propped up by force or inertia or the lack of an appealing and immediately available alternative. Almost everybody living under a government of limited powers, must sooner or later be subjected to some governmental action which as a matter of private opinion he regards as outside the power of government or positively forbidden to government. A man is drafted, though he finds nothing in the Constitution about being drafted. . . . A farmer is told how much wheat he can raise; he believes, and he discovers that some respectable lawyers believe with him, that the government has no more right to tell him how much wheat he can grow than it has to tell his daughter whom she can marry. A man goes to the federal penitentiary for saying what he wants to, and he paces his cell reciting . . . "Congress shall make no laws abridging the freedom of speech." . . . A businessman is told what he can ask, and must ask, for buttermilk.
>
> The danger is real enough that each of these people (and who is not of their number?) will confront the concept of governmental limitation with the reality (as he sees it) of the flagrant overstepping of actual limits, and draw the obvious conclusion as to the status of his government with respect to legitimacy.[13]

This danger is averted, Black adds, by the State's propounding the doctrine that *some one* agency must have the ultimate decision on constitutionality, and that this agency must be part of the federal government itself. For while the seeming independence of the federal judiciary has played a vital role in making its actions virtual Holy Writ for the bulk of the population, it is also true that the judiciary is part and parcel of the government apparatus and is appointed by the executive and legislative branches. Professor Black concedes that the government has thereby set itself up as a judge in its own case, and has thus violated a basic juridical principle for arriving at any kind of just decision. But Black is remarkably lighthearted about this fundamental

---

[13] Charles L. Black, Jr., *The People and the Court* (New York: Macmillan, 1960), pp. 42–43.

breach: "The final power of the State . . . must stop where the law stops it. And who shall set the limit, and who shall enforce the stopping, against the mightiest power? Why, the State itself, of course, through its judges and its laws. Who controls the temperate? Who teaches the wise? . . ."[14] And so Black admits that when we have a State, we hand over all our weapons and means of coercion to the State apparatus, we turn over all of our powers of ultimate decision-making to this deified group, and *then* we must jolly well sit back quietly and await the unending stream of justice that will pour forth from these institutions—even though they are basically judging their own case. Black sees no conceivable alternative to this coercive monopoly of judicial decisions enforced by the State, but here is precisely where our new movement challenges this conventional view and asserts that there *is* a viable alternative: libertarianism.

Seeing no such alternative, Professor Black falls back on mysticism in his defense of the State, for in the final analysis he finds the achievement of justice and legitimacy from the State's perpetual judging of its own cause to be "something of a miracle." In this way, the liberal Black joins the conservative Burnham in falling back on the miraculous and thereby admitting that there is no satisfactory rational argument in support of the State.[15]

Applying his realistic view of the Supreme Court to the famous conflict between the Court and the New Deal in the 1930s, Professor Black chides his liberal colleagues for their shortsightedness in denouncing judicial obstructionism:

> . . . the standard version of the story of the New Deal and the Court, though accurate in its way, displaces the emphasis. . . . It concentrates on the difficulties; it almost forgets how the whole thing turned out. The upshot of the matter was (and this is what I like to emphasize) that after some twenty-four months of balking . . . the Supreme Court, without a single change in the law of its composition, or, indeed, in its actual

---

[14] *Ibid.*, pp. 32–33.

[15] In contrast to the complacency of Black was the trenchant critique of the Constitution and the powers of the Supreme Court by the political scientist J. Allen Smith. Smith wrote that "Clearly, common sense required that no organ of the government should be able to determine its own powers." J. Allen Smith, *The Growth and Decadence of Constitutional Government* (New York: Henry Holt and Co., 1930), p. 87. Clearly, common sense and "miracles" dictate very different views of government.

manning, *placed the affirmative stamp of legitimacy on the New Deal, and on the whole new conception of government in America. [Italics the author's.]*[16]

In this way, the Supreme Court was able to put the quietus to the large body of Americans who had strong constitutional objections to the expanded powers of the New Deal:

> Of course, not everyone was satisfied. The Bonnie Prince Charlie of constitutionally commanded laissez-faire still stirs the hearts of a few zealots in the Highlands of choleric unreality. But there is no longer any significant or dangerous public doubt as to the constitutional power of Congress to deal as it does with the national economy. . . . We had no means, other than the Supreme Court, for imparting legitimacy to the New Deal.[17]

Thus, even in the United States, unique among governments in having a constitution, parts of which at least were meant to impose strict and solemn limits upon its actions, even here the Constitution has proved to be an instrument for ratifying the expansion of State power rather than the opposite. As Calhoun saw, any written limits that leave it to government to interpret its own powers are bound to be interpreted as sanctions for expanding and not binding those powers. In a profound sense, the idea of binding down power with the chains of a written constitution has proved to be a noble experiment that failed. The idea of a strictly limited government has proved to be utopian; some other, more radical means must be found to prevent the growth of the aggressive State. The libertarian system would meet this problem by scrapping the entire notion of creating a government—an institution with a coercive monopoly of force over a given territory— and *then* hoping to find ways to keep that government from expanding. The libertarian alternative is to abstain from such a monopoly government to begin with.

We will explore the entire notion of a State-less society, a society without formal government, in later chapters. But one instructive exercise is to try to abandon the habitual ways of seeing things, and to consider the argument for the State *de novo*. Let us try to transcend

---

[16] *Ibid.*, p. 64.

[17] *Ibid.*, p. 65.

the fact that for as long as we can remember, the State has monopo-lized police and judicial services in society. Suppose that we were all starting completely from scratch, and that millions of us had been dropped down upon the earth, fully grown and developed, from some other planet. Debate begins as to how protection (police and judicial services) will be provided. Someone says: "Let's all give all of our weap-ons to Joe Jones over there, and to his relatives. And let Jones and his family decide all disputes among us. In that way, the Joneses will be able to protect all of us from any aggression or fraud that anyone else may commit. With all the power and all the ability to make ultimate decisions on disputes in the hands of Jones, we will all be protected from one another. And then let us allow the Joneses to obtain their income from this great service by using their weapons, and by exact-ing as much revenue by coercion as they shall desire." Surely in that sort of situation, no one would treat this proposal with anything but ridicule. For it would be starkly evident that there would be no way, in that case, for any of us to protect ourselves from the aggressions, or the depredations, of the Joneses themselves. No one would then have the total folly to respond to that long-standing and most perceptive query: "Who shall guard the guardians?" by answering with Professor Black's blithe: "Who controls the temperate?" It is only because we have become accustomed over thousands of years to the existence of the State that we now give precisely this kind of absurd answer to the problem of social protection and defense.

And, of course, the State never really did begin with this sort of "social contract." As Oppenheimer pointed out, the State generally began in violence and conquest; even if at times internal processes gave rise to the State, it was certainly never by general consensus or contract.

The libertarian creed can now be summed up as (1) the absolute right of every man to the ownership of his own body; (2) the equally absolute right to own and therefore to control the material resources he has found and transformed; and (3) therefore, the absolute right to exchange or give away the ownership to such titles to whoever is willing to exchange or receive them. As we have seen, each of these steps involves *property* rights, but even if we call step (1) "personal" rights, we shall see that problems about "personal liberty" inextricably involve the rights of material property or free exchange. Or, briefly, the rights of personal liberty and "freedom of enterprise" almost invariably intertwine and cannot really be separated.

We have seen that the exercise of personal "freedom of speech," for example, almost invariably involves the exercise of "economic freedom"—i.e., freedom to own and exchange material property. The holding of a meeting to exercise freedom of speech involves the hiring of a hall, traveling to the hall over roads, and using some form of transportation, etc. The closely related "freedom of the press" even more evidently involves the cost of printing and of using a press, the sale of leaflets to willing buyers—in short, all the ingredients of "economic freedom." Furthermore, our example of "shouting 'fire' in a crowded theater" provides us with the clear guideline for deciding *whose* rights must be defended in any given situation—the guidelines being provided by our criterion: the rights of property.

*1973*

# PATRICK DENEEN

Patrick Deneen (b. 1964) is a professor of political science at the University of Notre Dame and author of the book *Why Liberalism Failed* (2018). A democratic communitarian, he is deeply skeptical of the moral claims of unrestrained capitalism, sexual liberation, radical individualism, and of forms of recent technology that, as he and others have argued, undermine genuine social relationships.

————

# Unsustainable Liberalism

FOR MOST people of the West, the idea of a time and way of life after liberalism is as plausible as the idea of living on Mars. Yet liberalism is a bold political and social experiment that is far from certain to succeed. Its very apparent strengths rest upon a large number of pre-, non-, and even antiliberal institutions and resources that it has not replenished, and in recent years has actively sought to undermine. This "drawing down" on its preliberal inheritance is not contingent or accidental but in fact an inherent feature of liberalism.

Thus the liberal experiment contradicts itself, and a liberal society will inevitably become "postliberal." The postliberal condition can retain many aspects that are regarded as liberalism's triumphs—equal dignity of persons, in particular—while envisioning an alternative understanding of the human person, human community, politics, and the relationship of the cities of Man to the city of God. Envisioning a condition after liberalism calls us not to restore something that once was but to consider something that might yet be; it is a project not of nostalgia but of vision, imagination, and construction.

Many of what are considered liberalism's signal features—particularly political arrangements such as constitutionalism, the rule of law, rights and privileges of citizens, separation of powers, the free exchange of goods and services in markets, and federalism—are to be found in medieval thought. Inviolable human dignity, constitutional limits upon central power, and equality under law are part of a preliberal legacy.

The strictly political arrangements of modern constitutionalism do not per se constitute a liberal regime. Rather, liberalism is constituted by a pair of deeper anthropological assumptions that give liberal institutions a particular orientation and cast: 1) anthropological individualism and the voluntarist conception of choice, and 2) human separation from and opposition to nature. These two revolutions in the understanding of human nature and society constitute "liberalism" inasmuch as they introduce a radically new definition of "liberty."

Liberalism introduces a particular cast to its preliberal inheritance mainly by ceasing to account for the implications of choices made by individuals upon community, society, and future generations. Liberalism did not introduce the idea of choice. It dismissed the idea that there are wrong or bad choices, and thereby rejected the accompanying social structures and institutions that were ordered to restrain the temptation toward self-centered calculation.

The first revolution, and the most basic and distinctive aspect of liberalism, is to base politics upon the idea of voluntarism—the free, unfettered, and autonomous choice of individuals. This argument was first articulated in the proto-liberal defense of monarchy by Thomas Hobbes. According to Hobbes, human beings exist by nature in a state of radical independence and autonomy. Recognizing the fragility of a condition in which life is "nasty, brutish, and short," they employ their rational self-interest to sacrifice most of their natural rights in order to secure the protection and security of a sovereign. Legitimacy is conferred by consent.

The state is created to restrain the external actions of individuals and legally restricts the potentially destructive activity of radically separate human beings. Law is a set of practical restraints upon self-interested individuals; there is no assumption of the existence of self-restraint born of mutual concern. As Hobbes writes in *Leviathan*, law is comparable to hedges that are set "not to stop travelers, but to keep them in the way"; that is, law restrains people's natural tendency to act on "impetuous desires, rashness or indiscretion," and so are always "rules authorized" as external constraints upon what is otherwise our natural liberty. "Where the law is silent," people are free, obligated only insofar as the "authorized" rules of the state are explicit. All legitimate authority is vested in the state. It is the sole creator and enforcer of positive law and even determines legitimate and illegitimate expressions of religious belief. The state is charged with the maintenance of social stability and with preventing a return to natural anarchy; in discharging these duties, it "secures" our natural rights.

Human beings are by nature, therefore, "non-relational" creatures, separate and autonomous. Liberalism thus begins a project by which the legitimacy of all human relationships—beginning with, but not limited to, political bonds—becomes increasingly subject to the criterion of whether or not they have been *chosen*, and chosen upon the basis of their service to rational self-interest.

As Hobbes' philosophical successor John Locke understood, voluntarist logic ultimately affects all relationships, including the familial. Locke—the first philosopher of liberalism—on the one hand acknowledges in his *Second Treatise on Government* that the duties of parents to raise children and the corresponding duties of children to obey spring from the commandment to "honor thy father and thy mother," but further claims that every child must ultimately subject his inheritance to the logic of consent beginning in a version of the state of nature, in which we act as autonomous choosing individuals. "For every man's children being by nature as free as himself, or any of his ancestors ever were, may, whilst they are in that freedom, choose what society they will join themselves to, what commonwealths they will put themselves under. But if they will enjoy the inheritance of their ancestors, they must take it on the same terms their ancestors had it, and submit to all the conditions annex'd to such a possession." Even those who adopt the inheritance of their parents in every regard only do so through the logic of consent, even if theirs is only tacit consent.

Even marriage, Locke holds, is finally to be understood as a contract whose conditions are temporary and subject to revision, particularly once the duties of child-rearing are completed. If this encompassing logic of choice applies to the most elemental and basic relationships of the family, then it applies all the more to the looser ties that bind people to other institutions and associations, in which continued membership is subject to constant monitoring and assessment of whether it benefits or unduly burdens any person's individual rights.

This is not to suggest that a preliberal era dismissed the idea of the free choice of individuals. Among other significant ways that preliberal Christianity contributed to an expansion of human choice was to transform the idea of marriage from an institution based upon considerations of family and property to one based upon the choice and consent of individuals united in sacramental love. What it is to suggest is that the default basis for evaluating institutions, society, affiliations, memberships, and even personal relationships becomes dominated by considerations of individual choice based upon the calculation of individual self-interest, and without broader considerations of the impact one's choices have upon the community—present and future—and of one's obligations to the created order and ultimately to God.

Liberalism began with the explicit assertion, and has continued to claim, that it merely *describes* our political, social, and private decision-making. Yet implicitly it was constituted as a constructive or normative project: What it presented as a description of human voluntarism in fact had to displace a very different form of human self-understanding and long-standing experience. In effect, liberal theory sought to educate people to think differently about themselves and their relationships. Liberalism often claims neutrality about the choices people make in liberal society; it is the defender of "Right," not of any particular conception of the "Good."

Yet it is not neutral about the basis on which people make their decisions. In the same way that courses in economics claiming merely to describe human beings as utility-maximizing individual actors in fact influence students to act more selfishly, so liberalism teaches a people to hedge commitments and adopt flexible relationships and bonds. Not only are all political and economic relationships fungible and subject to constant redefinition, but so are *all* relationships—to place, to neighborhood, to nation, to family, and to religion. Liberalism tends to encourage loose connections.

The second revolution, and the second anthropological assumption that constitutes liberalism, is less visibly political. Premodern political thought—ancient and medieval, particularly that informed by an Aristotelian understanding of natural science—understood the human creature to be part of a comprehensive natural order. Man was understood to have a *telos*, a fixed end, given by nature and unalterable. Human nature was continuous with the order of the natural world, and so humanity was required to conform both to its own nature as well as, in a broader sense, to the natural order of which human beings were a part. Human beings could freely act against their own nature and the natural order, but such actions deformed them and harmed the good of human beings and the world. Aristotle's *Ethics* and Aquinas' *Summa Theologica* are alike efforts to delineate the limits that nature—thus, natural law—places upon human beings, and each seeks to educate man about how best to live within those limits, through the practice of virtues, in order to achieve a condition of human flourishing.

Liberal philosophy rejected this requirement of human self-limitation. It first displaced the idea of a natural order to which humanity is subject and thereafter the very notion of human nature itself. Liberalism inaugurated a transformation in the natural and human sciences, premised on the transformation of the view of human nature and on humanity's relationship to the natural world.

The first wave of this revolution—inaugurated by early-modern thinkers dating back to the Renaissance—insisted that man should seek the mastery of nature by employing natural science and a transformed economic system supportive of such an undertaking. The second wave—developed largely by various historicist schools of thought, especially in the nineteenth century—replaced belief in the idea of a fixed human nature with a belief in human "plasticity" and capacity for moral progress and transformation. While these two iterations of liberalism—often labeled "conservative" and "progressive"—contend today for ascendance, we would do better to understand their deep interconnection.

The "proto-liberal" thinker who ushered in the "first wave" of liberalism's transformation was Francis Bacon. Like Hobbes (who was Bacon's secretary), he attacked the ancient Aristotelian and Thomistic understanding of nature and natural law alike and argued for the human capacity to "master" or "control" nature—even at one point comparing nature to a prisoner withholding secrets from an inquisitor and requiring the inquirer (the scientist) to subject it to torture—all with an aim to providing "relief of the human estate."

Liberalism became closely bound up with the embrace of this new orientation of the natural sciences and also advanced an economic system—market-based free enterprise—that similarly promoted the expansion of human use, conquest, and mastery of the natural world. Early-modern liberalism held the view that *human* nature was unchangeable—human beings were, by nature, self-interested creatures whose base impulses could be harnessed but not fundamentally altered—but could, if usefully channeled, promote an economic and scientific system that increased human freedom through the active and expanding capacity of human beings to exert their mastery over natural phenomena.

The "second wave" of this revolution began as an explicit criticism of this view of humanity. Thinkers ranging from Rousseau to Marx, from Mill to Dewey, and from Richard Rorty to contemporary "transhumanists" reject the idea that human nature is in any way fixed. Adopting the insight of first-wave theorists, they extend to human nature itself the idea that nature is subject to human conquest.

And so first-wave liberals are today represented by "conservatives" who stress the need for the scientific and economic mastery of nature but stop short of extending this project fully to human nature. They support nearly any utilitarian use of the world for economic ends but oppose most forms of biotechnological "enhancement." Second-wave liberals increasingly approve nearly any technical means of liberating man from the biological imperatives of our own bodies. Today's political debates occur largely and almost exclusively between liberals, first-wave and second-wave, neither of whom confront the fundamentally alternative understanding of human nature and the human relationship to nature that the preliberal tradition defended.

Liberalism is thus not merely a narrowly political project of constitutional government and juridical defense of rights, as it is too often portrayed. Rather, it seeks the transformation of the entirety of human life and the world. Its two revolutions—its anthropological individualism and the voluntarist conception of choice, and its insistence on the human separation from and opposition to nature—created its distinctive and new understanding of liberty as the most extensive possible expansion of the human sphere of autonomous activity in the service of the fulfillment of the self. Liberalism rejects the ancient and preliberal conception of liberty as the learned capacity of human beings to govern their base and hedonistic desires. This kind of liberty is a condition of self-governance of both city and soul, drawing closely together the individual cultivation and practice of virtue and the shared activities of self-legislation. Societies that understand liberty this way pursue the comprehensive formation and education of individuals and citizens in the art and virtue of self-rule.

Liberalism instead understands liberty as the condition in which one can act freely within the sphere that is unconstrained by positive law. Liberalism effectively remakes the world in the image of its vision of the state of nature, shaping a world in which the theory of natural human individualism becomes ever more a reality, secured through the architecture of law, politics, economics, and society. Under liberalism, human beings increasingly live in a condition of autonomy such as that first imagined by theorists of the state of nature, except that the anarchy that threatens to develop from that purportedly natural condition is controlled and suppressed through the imposition of laws and the corresponding growth of the state. With man liberated from constitutive communities (leaving only loose connections) and nature harnessed and controlled, the constructed sphere of autonomous liberty expands seemingly without limit.

Ironically, the more complete the securing of a sphere of autonomy, the more encompassing and comprehensive the state must become. Liberty, so defined, requires in the first instance liberation from all forms of associations and relationships—from the family, church, and schools to the village and neighborhood and the community broadly defined—that exerted strong control over behavior largely through informal and habituated expectations and norms.

These forms of control were largely *cultural*, not political—law was generally less extensive, and existed largely as a continuation of cultural norms, the informal expectations of behavior that were largely learned through family, church, and community. With the liberation of individuals from these associations and membership based upon individual choice, the need for impositions of positive law to regulate behavior grows. At the same time, as the authority of social norms dissipates, they are increasingly felt to be residual, arbitrary, and oppressive, motivating calls for the state to actively work toward their eradication through the rationalization of law and regulation.

Liberalism thus culminates in two ontological points: the liberated individual and the controlling state. Hobbes's *Leviathan* perfectly portrayed those two realities: The state consists solely of autonomous (and non-grouped) individuals, and the individuals are "contained" by the state. No other grouping is granted ontological reality.

In this world, gratitude to the past and obligations to the future are replaced by a near-universal pursuit of immediate gratification: Culture, rather than imparting the wisdom and experience of the past toward the end of cultivating virtues of self-restraint and civility, instead becomes synonymous with hedonic titillation, visceral crudeness, and distraction, all oriented toward promoting a culture of consumption, appetite, and detachment. As a result, seemingly self-maximizing but socially destructive behaviors begin to predominate in society.

In schools, norms of modesty, comportment, and academic honesty are replaced by widespread activities of lawlessness and cheating (along with the rise of forms of surveillance of youth), while in the fraught realm of coming-of-age, courtship norms are replaced by hookups and utilitarian sexual encounters. The norm of stable, lifelong marriage fades, replaced by various arrangements that ensure the fundamental autonomy of the individuals, whether married or not. Children are increasingly viewed as a limitation upon individual freedom, even to the point of justifying widespread infanticide under the banner of "choice," while overall birthrates decline across the developed world. In the economic realm, get-rich-quick schemes replace investment and trusteeship. And, in our relationship to the natural world, short-term exploitation of the earth's bounty becomes our birthright, whether or not its result for our children might be shortages of life-sustaining resources such as topsoil and potable water. Restraint of any of these activities is understood to be the domain of the state's exercise of positive law and not the result of cultivated self-governance born of cultural norms and institutions.

Premised on the idea that the basic activity of life is the inescapable pursuit of what Hobbes called the "power after power that ceaseth only in death"—Alexis de Tocqueville would later describe it as "inquietude" or "restlessness"—the endless quest for fewer obstacles to self-fulfillment and greater power to actuate the ceaseless cravings of the human soul requires ever-accelerating forms of economic growth and pervasive consumption. Liberal society can barely survive the slowing of such growth and would collapse if it were to stop or reverse for an extended period of time. The sole object and justification of this indifference to human ends—of the emphasis on "Right" over the "Good"—is nevertheless premised on the embrace of the liberal human as a self-fashioning individual and self-expressive consumer. This default aspiration requires that no truly hard choices be made between lifestyle options.

Liberalism's founders tended to take for granted the persistence of social norms, even as they sought to liberate individuals from those constitutive associations and the accompanying education in self-limitation that sustained these norms. In its earliest moments, the health and continuity of good families, schools, and communities was assumed, though their bases were philosophically undermined. The philosophical undermining led to the undermining of these goods in reality, as the norm-shaping authoritative institutions become tenuous with liberalism's advance. In its advanced stage, the passive depletion has become active destruction: Remnants of associations historically charged with the cultivation of norms are increasingly seen as obstacles to autonomous liberty, and the apparatus of the state is directed toward the task of liberating individuals from any such bonds.

In a similar way—in the material and economic realm—liberalism has drawn down on age-old reservoirs of resources in its endeavor to conquer nature. An extended inability to provide for seemingly endless choice would result in a systemic crisis, requiring the state to face down a populace suddenly confronted with the one unacceptable "choice" of restricted choices. Liberalism can function only by the constant *increase* of available and consumable material goods and satisfactions, and thus by constantly expanding humanity's conquest and mastery of nature. No matter the political program of today's leaders, *more* is the incontestable program. No person can aspire to a position of political leadership through a call for limits and self-command.

Liberalism was a wager of titanic proportions, a wager that ancient norms of behavior could be abolished in the name of a new form of liberation and that the conquest of nature would supply the fuel that would permit near-infinite choices. The twin outcomes of this effort, the depletion of moral self-command and the depletion of material resources, make inevitable an inquiry into what comes after liberalism.

Liberalism's defenders fear that any compromise of liberal principles will result in the resurgence of religious warfare, the re-enslavement of various populations, the loss of the independence of women, and the abandonment of rights and equality under law. If I am right, however, a reconsideration of liberalism's two main commitments will not compromise but instead be the preconditions for securing equal human dignity and ordered liberty. The conception of inviolable human dignity, of constitutional limits upon central power, of equality under law, and of the free exchange of goods and services in markets is, again, part of a preliberal legacy.

The creation of a world after liberalism would not require, as some might fear, the dismantling of the Constitution and the Bill of Rights, nor the cessation of free markets. Instead, what would be required is a fundamental rethinking of how law and economics are understood and employed to undergird the liberal vision of society. Such a rethinking is by necessity taking place, in many ways. As government is able to provide fewer and fewer services to people facing challenging times (the claims of the political left notwithstanding), people will necessarily turn to the very constitutive relationships that liberalism regarded as limitations upon our autonomy: family, neighborhood, and community. Breakdowns in the market similarly call for strengthening such institutions. The economic crisis has, for example, resulted in greater understanding of the need to rely upon the help of families and communities, as shown in the growth of multigenerational homes, which were the norm for much of human history.

Contemporary "conservatism" does not offer an answer to liberalism, because it is itself a species of liberalism. While the elders on the political right continue to rail against "environmentalists," they fail to detect how deeply conservative (conservationist) is the impulse among the young who see clearly the limits of the consumptive economy and the ravages it bequeaths to their generation. What these elders have generally lacked is a recognition that one cannot revise one of liberalism's main commitments, today characterized as "progressivism," while ignoring the other, particularly economic liberalism. A different paradigm is needed, one that intimately connects the cultivation of self-limitation and self-governance among constitutive associations and communities with a general ethic of thrift, frugality, saving, hard work, stewardship, and care. So long as the dominant narrative of individual choice aimed at the satisfaction of appetite and consumption dominates in the personal or economic realms, the ethic of liberalism will continue to dominate our society.

Both the left and the right effectively enact a pincer movement in which local associations and groups are engulfed by an expanding state and by the market, each moving toward singularity in each realm: one state and one market. If the left insists on the liberal interpretation of our constitutional and political institutions in an uncompromising effort to defend the ever-expanding role of the state to secure the practical liberty of individuals, the right defends the free-market system and uncompromisingly rejects any restraint on the unfettered economic choices of individuals. The right embraces a market orthodoxy that places the choosing, autonomous individual at the center of its economic theory and accepts the larger liberal frame in which the only alternative to this free-market, individualist orthodoxy is statism and collectivism. It seeks to promote family values but denies that the market undermines many of the values that undergird family life. The left commends sexual liberation as the best avenue to achieve individual autonomy, while nonsensically condemning the immorality of a marketplace in which sex is the best sales pitch. The encompassing Leviathan daily attains more reality.

A different trajectory does not require a change of institutions; it requires a change in how we understand the human person in relationship to other persons, to nature, and the source of creation. While the Constitution consolidated a number of political activities in the center, it left considerable room for local entities. The return to a more robust form of federalism would allow for greater local autonomy in establishing and cultivating local forms of culture and self-governance.

This will provide space for the nuanced discussions between what sociologist Robert Nisbet called the "laissez-faire of social groups." Recommending federalism always meets the response that local self-rule and culture will reinstitute local prejudices. That argument is a strained effort not to defend the great and I think irreversible achievement of Christendom's embrace of the imago Dei, but instead to defend the state's intervention in every sphere of life, justified on the grounds that local norms and prohibitions express bigotry and lead directly to oppression.

A wide variety of local norms and beliefs should be permitted, within limits that would exclude egregious limits upon human liberty. These authoritative norm-shaping institutions and behaviors are the only credible mechanisms for advancing the substantial withering away of the state. These local norms and beliefs would afford a different experience of liberty, one about which liberalism has been silent, one that stresses self-governance and self-limitation achieved primarily through the cultivation of practices and virtues. Such a cultivation of ordered liberty would restrain the pursuit of libertine liberty, and restrain the tendency toward the expansion of state and market, which together increasingly undermine constitutive social institutions, thereby leaving the individual "free" to be shaped by popular culture and advertising mostly aimed to encourage the appetites fed by the enticements of a globalized market.

The recognition of the central and constitutive role and the necessity of the varied institutions that exist between the state and the individual has been a staple observation of thinkers from Tocqueville to contemporary thinkers on both the nominal right and nominal left, such as Bertrand de Jouvenel, Robert Nisbet, Russell Kirk, Christopher Lasch, Alasdair MacIntyre, Wilson Carey McWilliams, and Jean Bethke Elshtain. As they have argued, family, citizenship, church, neighborhood, community, schools, and markets need to be drawn closer together in a more integrated whole, in every aspect ranging from the built environment to the cultivation of genuine local cultures arising from the varying circumstances of diverse places. Drawing them together requires an ethic of self-command. So long as the right tries to defend them without offering a broader ecology of a deeply integrated and formative community—something broader, for example, than the long-standing defense of "family values" that denigrates the idea that there is a relationship between the family and the village—it can offer no real alternative to liberalism.

If I am right that the liberal project is ultimately self-contradictory, culminating in the twin depletions of moral and material reservoirs upon which it has relied even without replenishing them, then we face a choice. We can pursue more local forms of self-government by choice or suffer by default an oscillation between growing anarchy and likely martial imposition of order by an increasingly desperate state.

If my analysis is fundamentally accurate, liberalism's endgame is unsustainable in every respect: It cannot perpetually enforce order upon a collection of autonomous individuals increasingly shorn of constitutive social norms, nor can it continually provide endless material growth in a world of limits. We can either elect a future of self-limitation born of the practice and experience of self-governance in local communities, or we can back slowly but inexorably into a future in which extreme license invites extreme oppression.

The ancient claim that man is by nature a political animal and must in and through the exercise and practice of virtue learned in communities achieve a form of local and communal self-limitation—a condition properly understood as liberty—cannot be denied forever without cost. Currently we lament and attempt to treat the numerous social, economic, and political symptoms of liberalism's idea of liberty but not the deeper sources of those symptoms deriving from the underlying pathology of liberalism's philosophic commitments.

While most commentators today regard our current crises—whether understood morally or economically or, as they are rarely understood, as both moral and economic—as technical problems to be solved by better policy, our most thoughtful citizens must consider whether these crises are the foreshocks of a more systemic quake that awaits us. Unlike the ancient Romans, confident in their eternal city, who could not imagine a condition "after Rome," we should ponder the prospect that a better way awaits after liberalism.

*2012*

# THE TIES THAT BIND

*The Local and Familiar*

# JOHN CROWE RANSOM

In 1930, a group identifying themselves as "Twelve Southerners" published the agrarian manifesto *I'll Take My Stand*. Among them was the prize-winning poet John Crowe Ransom (1888–1974), who as a critic and essayist would later be associated with New Criticism, an influential approach to literary analysis. In his contribution to *I'll Take My Stand*, Ransom links the local culture of the South to nineteenth-century English values and what he regarded as "the core of unadulterated Europeanism, with its self-sufficient, backward-looking, intensely provincial communities."

## Reconstructed but Unregenerate

I

IT IS out of fashion in these days to look backward rather than forward. About the only American given to it is some unreconstructed Southerner, who persists in his regard for a certain terrain, a certain history, and a certain inherited way of living. He is punished as his crime deserves. He feels himself in the American scene as an anachronism, and knows he is felt by his neighbors as a reproach.

Of course he is a tolerably harmless reproach. He is like some quaint local character of eccentric but fixed principles who is thoroughly and almost pridefully accepted by the village as a rare exhibit in the antique kind. His position is secure from the interference of the police, but it is of a rather ambiguous dignity.

I wish now that he were not so entirely taken for granted, and that as a reproach he might bear a barb and inflict a sting. I wish that the whole force of my own generation in the South would get behind his principles and make them an ideal which the nation at large would have to reckon with. But first I will describe him in the light of the position he seems now to occupy actually before the public.

His fierce devotion is to a lost cause—though it grieves me that his contemporaries are so sure it is lost. They are so far from fearing him and his example that they even in the excess of confidence offer him a little honor, a little petting. As a Southerner I have observed this indulgence and I try to be grateful. Obviously it does not constitute a danger to the Republic; distinctly it is not treasonable. They are good enough to attribute a sort of glamour to the Southern life as it is defined for them in a popular tradition. They like to use the South as the nearest available locus for the scenes of their sentimental songs, and sometimes they send their daughters to the Southern seminaries. Not too much, of course, is to be made of this last gesture, for they do not expose to this hazard their sons, who in our still very masculine order will have to discharge the functions of citizenship, and who must accordingly be sternly educated in the principles of progress at progressive institutions of learning. But it does not seem to make so much difference what principles of a general character the young women acquire, since they are not likely to be impaired by principles in their peculiar functions, such as virtue and the domestic duties. And so, at suitable seasons, and on the main-line trains, one may see them in some numbers, flying south or flying north like migratory birds; and one may wonder to what extent their philosophy of life will be affected by two or three years in the South. One must remember that probably their parents have already made this calculation and are prepared to answer, Not much.

The Southerner must know, and in fact he does very well know, that his antique conservatism does not exert a great influence against the American progressivist doctrine. The Southern idea today is down, and the progressive or American idea is up. But the historian and the philosopher, who take views that are thought to be respectively longer and deeper than most, may very well reverse this order and find that the Southern idea rather than the American has in its favor the authority of example and the approval of theory. And some prophet may even find it possible to expect that it will yet rise again.

I will propose a thesis which seems to have about as much cogency as generalizations usually have: The South is unique on this continent for having founded and defended a culture which was according to the European principles of culture; and the European principles had better look to the South if they are to be perpetuated in this country.

II

The nearest of the European cultures which we could examine is that of England; and this is of course the right one in the case, quite aside from our convenience. England was actually the model employed by the South, in so far as Southern culture was not quite indigenous. And there is in the South even today an Anglophile sentiment quite anomalous in the American scene.

England differs from America doubtless in several respects, but most notably in the fact that England did her pioneering an indefinite number of centuries ago, did it well enough, and has been living pretty tranquilly on her establishment ever since, with infrequent upheavals and replacements. The customs and institutions of England seem to the American observer very fixed and ancient. There is no doubt that the English tradition expresses itself in many more or less intangible ways, but it expresses itself most importantly in a material establishment; and by this I mean the stable economic system by which Englishmen are content to take their livelihood from the physical environment. The chief concern of England's half-mythical pioneers, as with pioneers anywhere, was with finding the way to make a living. Evidently they found it. But fortunately the methods they worked out proved transmissible, proved, in fact, the main reliance of the succeeding generations. The pioneers explored the soil, determined what concessions it might reasonably be expected to make them, housed themselves, developed all their necessary trades, and arrived by painful experiment at a thousand satisfactory recipes by which they might secure their material necessities. Their descendants have had the good sense to consider that this establishment was good enough for them. They have elected to live their comparatively easy and routine lives in accordance with the tradition which they inherited, and they have consequently enjoyed a leisure, a security, and an intellectual freedom that were never the portion of pioneers.

The pioneering life is not the normal life, whatever some Americans may suppose. It is not, if we look for the meaning of European history. The lesson of each of the European cultures now extant is in this—that European opinion does not make too much of the intense practical enterprises, but is at pains to define rather narrowly the practical effort which is prerequisite to the reflective and aesthetic life. Boys are very well pleased to employ their muscles almost exclusively, but men prefer to exercise their minds. It is the European intention to live materially along the inherited line of least resistance, in order to put the surplus of energy into the free life of the mind. Thus is engendered that famous, or infamous, European conservatism, which will appear stupid, necessarily, to men still fascinated by materialistic projects, men in a state of arrested adolescence; for instance, to some very large if indefinite fraction of the population of these United States.

I have in mind here the core of unadulterated Europeanism, with its self-sufficient, backward-looking, intensely provincial communities. The human life of English provinces long ago came to terms with nature, fixed its roots somewhere in the spaces between the rocks and in the shade of the trees, founded its comfortable institutions, secured its modest prosperity—and then willed the whole in perpetuity to the generations which should come after, in the ingenuous confidence that it would afford them all the essential human satisfactions. For it is the character of a seasoned provincial life that it is realistic, or successfully adapted to its natural environment, and that as a consequence it is stable, or hereditable. But it is the character of our urbanized, anti-provincial, progressive, and mobile American life that it is in a condition of eternal flux. Affections, and long memories, attach to the ancient bowers of life in the provinces; but they will not attach to what is always changing. Americans, however, are peculiar in being somewhat averse to these affections for natural objects, and to these memories.

Memories of the past are attended with a certain pain called nostalgia. It is hardly a technical term in our sociology or our psychiatry, but it might well be. Nostalgia is a kind of growing-pain, psychically speaking. It occurs to our sorrow when we have decided that it is time for us, marching to some magnificent destiny, to abandon an old home, an old provincial setting, or an old way of living to which we had become habituated. It is the complaint of human nature in its vegetative aspect, when it is plucked up by the roots from the place of its origin and transplanted in foreign soil, or even left dangling in the air. And it must be nothing else but nostalgia, the instinctive objection to being transplanted, that chiefly prevents the deracination of human communities and their complete geographical dispersion as the casualties of an insatiable wanderlust.

Deracination in our Western life is the strange discipline which individuals turn upon themselves, enticed by the blandishments of such fine words as Progressive, Liberal, and Forward-looking. The progressivist says in effect: Do not allow yourself to feel homesick; form no such powerful attachments that you will feel a pain in cutting them loose; prepare your spirit to be always on the move. According to this gospel, there is no rest for the weary, not even in heaven. The poet Browning expresses an ungrateful intention, the moment he shall enter into his reward, to "fight onward, there as here." The progressivist H. G. Wells has outlined very neatly his scheme of progress, the only disheartening feature being that he has had to revise it a good many times, and that the state to which he wants us to progress never has any finality or definition. Browning and Wells would have made very good Americans, and I am sure they have got the most of their disciples on this side of the Atlantic; they have not been good Europeans. But all the true progressivists intend to have a program so elastic that they can always propose new worlds to conquer. If his Utopia were practicable really, and if the progressivist should secure it, he would then have to defend it from further progress, which would mean his transformation from a progressivist into a conservative. Which is unthinkable.

The gospel of Progress is a curious development, which does not reflect great credit on the supposed capacity of our species for formulating its own behavior. Evidently the formula may involve its practitioners in self-torture and suicide just as readily as in the enjoyment of life. In most societies man has adapted himself to environment with plenty of intelligence to secure easily his material necessities from the graceful bounty of nature. And then, ordinarily, he concludes a truce with nature, and he and nature seem to live on terms of mutual respect and amity, and his loving arts, religions, and philosophies come spontaneously into being: these are the blessings of peace. But the latter-day societies have been seized—none quite so violently as our American one—with the strange idea that the human destiny is not to secure an honorable peace with nature, but to wage an unrelenting war on nature. Men, therefore, determine to conquer nature to a degree which is quite beyond reason so far as specific human advantage is concerned, and which enslaves them to toil and turnover. Man is boastfully declared to be a natural scientist essentially, whose strength is capable of crushing and making over to his own desires the brute materiality which is nature; but in his infinite contention with this materiality he is really capitulating to it. His engines transform the face of nature—a little—but when they have been perfected, he must invent new engines that will perform even more heroically. And always the next engine of his invention, even though it be that engine which is to invade the material atom and exploit the most secret treasury of nature's wealth, will be a physical engine; and the man who uses it will be engaged in substantially the same struggle as was the primitive Man with the Hoe.

This is simply to say that Progress never defines its ultimate objective, but thrusts its victims at once into an infinite series. Our vast industrial machine, with its laboratory centers of experimentation, and its far-flung organs of mass production, is like a Prussianized state which is organized strictly for war and can never consent to peace. Or, returning to the original figure, our progressivists are the latest version of those pioneers who conquered the wilderness, except that they are pioneering on principle, or from force of habit, and without any recollection of what pioneering was for.

III

Along with the gospel of Progress goes the gospel of Service. They work beautifully as a team.

Americans are still dreaming the materialistic dreams of their youth. The stuff these dreams were made on was the illusion of preëminent personal success over a material opposition. Their tone was belligerence, and the euphemism under which it masqueraded was ambition. But men are not lovely, and men are not happy, for being too ambitious. Let us distinguish two forms under which ambition drives men on their materialistic projects; a masculine and a feminine.

Ambitious men fight, first of all, against nature; they propose to put nature under their heel; this is the dream of scientists burrowing in their cells, and then of the industrial men who beg of their secret knowledge and go out to trouble the earth. But after a certain point this struggle is vain, and we only use ourselves up if we prolong it. Nature wears out man before man can wear out nature; only a city man, a laboratory man, a man cloistered from the normal contacts with the soil, will deny that. It seems wiser to be moderate in our expectations of nature, and respectful; and out of so simple a thing as respect for the physical earth and its teeming life comes a primary joy, which is an inexhaustible source of arts and religions and philosophies.

Ambitious men are belligerent also in the way they look narrowly and enviously upon one another; and I do not refer to such obvious disasters as wars and the rumors of wars. Ambition of the first form was primary and masculine, but there is a secondary form which is typically feminine, though the distribution between the sexes may not be without the usual exceptions. If it is Adam's curse to will perpetually to work his mastery upon nature, it is Eve's curse to prompt Adam every morning to keep up with the best people in the neighborhood in taking the measure of his success. There can never be stability and establishment in a community whose every lady member is sworn to see that her mate is not eclipsed in the competition for material advantages; that community will fume and ferment, and every constituent part will be in perpetual physical motion. The good life depends on leisure, but leisure depends on an establishment, and the establishment depends on a prevailing magnanimity which scorns personal advancement at the expense of the free activity of the mind.

The masculine form is hallowed by Americans, as I have said, under the name of Progress. The concept of Progress is the concept of man's increasing command, and eventually perfect command, over the forces of nature; a concept which enhances too readily our conceit, and brutalizes our life. I believe there is possible no deep sense of beauty, no heroism of conduct, and no sublimity of religion, which is not informed by the humble sense of man's precarious position in the universe. The feminine form is likewise hallowed among us under the name of Service. The term has many meanings, but we come finally to the one which is critical for the moderns; service means the function of Eve, it means the seducing of laggard men into fresh struggles with nature. It has special application to the apparently stagnant sections of mankind, it busies itself with the heathen Chinee, with the Roman Catholic Mexican, with the "lower" classes in our own society. Its motive is missionary. Its watchwords are such as Protestantism, Individualism, Democracy, and the point of its appeal is a discontent, generally labeled "divine."

Progress and Service are not European slogans, they are Americanisms. We alone have devoted our lives to ideals which are admirable within their proper limits, but which expose us to slavery when pursued without critical intelligence. Some Europeans are taken in by these ideals, but hardly the American communities on the whole. Herr Spengler, with a gesture of defeat, glorifies the modern American captain of industry when he compares his positive achievements with the futilities of modern poets and artists. Whereupon we may well wish to save Europe from even so formidable a European as Spengler, hoping that he may not convert Europe to his view. And it is hardly likely; Europe is founded on a principle of conservatism, and is deeply scornful of the American and pioneer doctrine of the strenuous life. In 1918 there was danger that Europe might ask to be Americanized, and American missionaries were quite prepared to answer the call. But since then there has been a revulsion in European opinion, and this particular missionary enterprise confronts now an almost solid barrier of hostility. Europe is not going to be Americanized through falling suddenly in love with strenuousness. It only remains to be seen whether Europe may not be Americanized after all through envy, and through being reminded ceaselessly of our superior prosperity. That is an event to be determined by the force of European magnanimity; Europe's problem, not ours.


IV


The Southern states were settled, of course, by miscellaneous strains. But evidently the one which determined the peculiar tradition of the South was the one which came out of Europe most convinced of the virtues of establishment, contrasting with those strains which seem for the most part to have dominated the other sections, and which came out of Europe feeling rebellious toward all establishments. There are a good many faults to be found with the old South, but hardly the fault of being intemperately addicted to work and to gross material prosperity. The South never conceded that the whole duty of man was to increase material production, or that the index to the degree of his culture was the volume of his material production. His business seemed to be rather to envelop both his work and his play with a leisure which permitted the activity of intelligence. On this assumption the South pioneered her way to a sufficiently comfortable and rural sort of establishment, considered that an establishment was something stable, and proceeded to enjoy the fruits thereof. The arts of the section, such as they were, were not immensely passionate, creative, and romantic; they were the eighteenth-century social arts of dress, conversation, manners, the table, the hunt, politics, oratory, the pulpit. These were arts of living and not arts of escape; they were also community arts, in which every class of society could participate after its kind. The South took life easy, which is itself a tolerably comprehensive art.

But so did other communities in 1850, I believe. And doubtless some others do so yet; in parts of New England, for example. If there are such communities, this is their token, that they are settled. Their citizens are comparatively satisfied with the life they have inherited, and are careful to look backward quite as much as they look forward. Before the Civil War there must have been many such communities this side of the frontier. The difference between the North and the South was that the South was constituted by such communities and made solid. But solid is only a comparative term here. The South as a culture had more solidity than another section, but there were plenty of gaps in it. The most we can say is that the Southern establishment was completed in a good many of the Southern communities, and that this establishment was an active formative influence on the spaces between, and on the frontier spaces outlying, which had not yet perfected their organization of the economic life.

The old Southern life was of course not so fine as some of the traditionalists like to believe. It did not offer serious competition against the glory that was Greece or the grandeur that was Rome. It hardly began to match the finish of the English, or any other important European civilization. It is quite enough to say that it was a way of life which had been considered and authorized. The establishment had a sufficient economic base, it was meant to be stable rather than provisional, it had got beyond the pioneering stage, it provided leisure, and its benefits were already being enjoyed. It may as well be admitted that Southern society was not an institution of very showy elegance, for the so-called aristocrats were mostly home-made and countrified. Aristocracy is not the word which defines this social organization so well as squirearchy, which I borrow from a recent article by Mr. William Frierson in the *Sewanee Review*. And even the squires, and the other classes, too, did not define themselves very strictly. They were loosely graduated social orders, not fixed as in Europe. Their relations were personal and friendly. It was a kindly society, yet a realistic one; for it was a failure if it could not be said that people were for the most part in their right places. Slavery was a feature monstrous enough in theory, but, more often than not, humane in practice; and it is impossible to believe that its abolition alone could have effected any great revolution in society.

The fullness of life as it was lived in the ante-bellum South by the different social orders can be estimated today only by the application of some difficult sociological technique. It is my thesis that all were committed to a form of leisure, and that their labor itself was leisurely. The only Southerners who went abroad to Washington and elsewhere, and put themselves into the record, were those from the top of the pyramid. They held their own with their American contemporaries. They were not intellectually as seasoned as good Europeans, but then the Southern culture had had no very long time to grow, as time is reckoned in these matters: it would have borne a better fruit eventually. They had a certain amount of learning, which was not as formidable as it might have been: but at least it was classical and humanistic learning, not highly scientific, and not wildly scattered about over a variety of special studies.


V


Then the North and the South fought, and the consequences were disastrous to both. The Northern temper was one of jubilation and expansiveness, and now it was no longer shackled by the weight of the conservative Southern tradition. Industrialism, the latest form of pioneering and the worst, presently overtook the North, and in due time has now produced our present American civilization. Poverty and pride overtook the South; poverty to bring her institutions into disrepute and to sap continually at her courage; and a false pride to inspire a distaste for the thought of fresh pioneering projects, and to doom her to an increasing physical enfeeblement.

It is only too easy to define the malignant meaning of industrialism. It is the contemporary form of pioneering; yet since it never consents to define its goal, it is a pioneering on principle, and with an accelerating speed. Industrialism is a program under which men, using the latest scientific paraphernalia, sacrifice comfort, leisure, and the enjoyment of life to win Pyrrhic victories from nature at points of no strategic importance. Ruskin and Carlyle feared it nearly a hundred years ago, and now it may be said that their fears have been realized partly in England, and with almost fatal completeness in America. Industrialism is an insidious spirit, full of false promises and generally fatal to establishments since, when it once gets into them for a little renovation, it proposes never again to leave them in peace. Industrialism is rightfully a menial, of almost miraculous cunning but no intelligence; it needs to be strongly governed or it will destroy the economy of the household. Only a community of tough conservative habit can master it.

The South did not become industrialized; she did not repair the damage to her old establishment, either, and it was in part because she did not try hard enough. Hers is the case to cite when we would show how the good life depends on an adequate pioneering, and how the pioneering energy must be kept ready for call when the establishment needs overhauling. The Southern tradition came to look rather pitiable in its persistence when the twentieth century had arrived, for the establishment was quite depreciated. Unregenerate Southerners were trying to live the good life on a shabby equipment, and they were grotesque in their effort to make an art out of living when they were not decently making the living. In the country districts great numbers of these broken-down Southerners are still to be seen in patched blue-jeans, sitting on ancestral fences, shotguns across their laps and hound-dogs at their feet, surveying their unkempt acres while they comment shrewdly on the ways of God. It is their defect that they have driven a too-easy, an unmanly bargain with nature, and that their æstheticism is based on insufficient labor.

But there is something heroic, and there may prove to be yet something very valuable to the Union, in their extreme attachment to a certain theory of life. They have kept up a faith which was on the point of perishing from this continent.

Of course it was only after the Civil War that the North and the South came to stand in polar opposition to each other. Immediately after Appomattox it was impossible for the South to resume even that give-and-take of ideas which had marked her ante-bellum relations with the North. She was offered such terms that acquiescence would have been abject. She retired within her borders in rage and held the minimum of commerce with the enemy. Persecution intensified her tradition, and made the South more solid and more Southern in the year 1875, or thereabouts, than ever before. When the oppression was left off, naturally her guard relaxed. But though the period of persecution had not been long, nevertheless the Southern tradition found itself then the less capable of uniting gracefully with the life of the Union; for that life in the meantime had been moving on in an opposite direction. The American progressive principle was like a ball rolling down the hill with an increasing momentum, and by 1890 or 1900 it was clear to any intelligent Southerner that it was a principle of boundless aggression against nature which could hardly offer much to a society devoted to the arts of peace.

But to keep on living shabbily on an insufficient patrimony is to decline, both physically and spiritually. The South declined.


VI


And now the crisis in the South's decline has been reached.

Industrialism has arrived in the South. Already the local chambers of commerce exhibit the formidable data of Southern progress. A considerable party of Southern opinion, which might be called the New South party, is well pleased with the recent industrial accomplishments of the South and anxious for many more. Southerners of another school, who might be said to compose an Old South party, are apprehensive lest the section become completely and uncritically devoted to the industrial ideal precisely as the other sections of the Union are. But reconstruction is actually under way. Tied politically and economically to the Union, her borders wholly violable, the South now sees very well that she can restore her prosperity only within the competition of an industrial system.

After the war the Southern plantations were often broken up into small farms. These have yielded less and less of a living, and it said that they will never yield a good living until once more they are integrated into large units. But these units will be industrial units, controlled by a board of directors or an executive rather than a squire, worked with machinery, and manned not by farmers living at home, but by "labor." Even so they will not, according to Mr. Henry Ford, support the population that wants to live on them. In the off seasons the laborers will have to work in factories, which henceforth are to be counted on as among the charming features of Southern landscape. The Southern problem is complicated, but at its center is the farmer's problem, and this problem is simply the most acute version of that general agrarian problem which inspires the despair of many thoughtful Americans today.

The agrarian discontent in America is deeply grounded in the love of the tiller for the soil, which is probably, it must be confessed, not peculiar to the Southern specimen, but one of the more ineradicable human attachments, be the tiller as progressive as he may. In proposing to wean men from this foolish attachment, industrialism sets itself against the most ancient and the most humane of all the modes of human livelihood. Do Mr. Hoover and the distinguished thinkers at Washington see how essential is the mutual hatred between the industrialists and the farmers, and how mortal is their conflict? The gentlemen at Washington are mostly preaching and legislating to secure the fabulous "blessings" of industrial progress; they are on the industrial side. The industrialists have a doctrine which is monstrous, but they are not monsters personally; they are forward-lookers with nice manners, and no American progressivist is against them. The farmers are boorish and inarticulate by comparison. Progressivism is against them in their fight, though their traditional status is still so strong that soft words are still spoken to them. All the solutions recommended for their difficulties are really enticements held out to them to become a little more coöperative, more mechanical, more mobile—in short, a little more industrialized. But the farmer who is not a mere laborer, even the farmer of the comparatively new places like Iowa and Nebraska, is necessarily among the more stable and less progressive elements of society. He refuses to mobilize himself and become a unit in the industrial army, because he does not approve of army life.

I will use some terms which are hardly in his vernacular. He identifies himself with a spot of ground, and this ground carries a good deal of meaning; it defines itself for him as nature. He would till it not too hurriedly and not too mechanically to observe in it the contingency and the infinitude of nature; and so his life acquires its philosophical and even its cosmic consciousness. A man can contemplate and explore, respect and love, an object as substantial as a farm or a native province. But he cannot contemplate nor explore, respect nor love, a mere turnover, such as an assemblage of "natural resources," a pile of money, a volume of produce, a market, or a credit system. It is into precisely these intangibles that industrialism would translate the farmer's farm. It means the dehumanization of his life.

However that may be, the South at last, looking defensively about her in all directions upon an industrial world, fingers the weapons of industrialism. There is one powerful voice in the South which, tired of a long status of disrepute, would see the South made at once into a section second to none in wealth, as that is statistically reckoned, and in progressiveness, as that might be estimated by the rapidity of the industrial turnover. This desire offends those who would still like to regard the South as, in the old sense, a home; but its expression is loud and insistent. The urban South, with its heavy importation of regular American ways and regular American citizens, has nearly capitulated to these novelties. It is the village South and the rural South which supply the resistance, and it is lucky for them that they represent a vast quantity of inertia.

Will the Southern establishment, the most substantial exhibit on this continent of a society of the European and historic order, be completely crumbled by the powerful acid of the Great Progressive Principle? Will there be no more looking backward but only looking forward? Is our New World to be dedicated forever to the doctrine of newness?

It is in the interest of America as a whole, as well as in the interest of the South, that these questions press for an answer. I will enter here the most important items of the situation as well as I can; doubtless they will appear a little over-sharpened for the sake of exhibition.

(1) The intention of Americans at large appears now to be what it was always in danger of becoming: an intention of being infinitely progressive. But this intention cannot permit of an established order of human existence, and of that leisure which conditions the life of intelligence and the arts.

(2) The old South, if it must be defined in a word, practiced the contrary and European philosophy of establishment as the foundation of the life of the spirit. The ante-bellum Union possessed, to say the least, a wholesome variety of doctrine.

(3) But the South was defeated by the Union on the battlefield with remarkable decisiveness, and the two consequences have been dire: the Southern tradition was physically impaired, and has ever since been unable to offer an attractive example of its philosophy in action; and the American progressive principle has developed into a pure industrialism without any check from a Southern minority whose voice ceased to make itself heard.

(4) The further survival of the Southern tradition as a detached local remnant is now unlikely. It is agreed that the South must make contact again with the Union. And in adapting itself to the actual state of the Union, the Southern tradition will have to consent to a certain industrialization of its own.

(5) The question at issue is whether the South will permit herself to be so industrialized as to lose entirely her historic identity, and to remove the last substantial barrier that has stood in the way of American progressivism; or will accept industrialism, but with a very bad grace, and will manage to maintain a good deal of her traditional philosophy.

VII

The hope which is inherent in the situation is evident from the terms in which it is stated. The South must be industrialized—but to a certain extent only, in moderation. The program which now engages the Southern leaders is to see how the South may handle this fire without being burnt badly. The South at last is to be physically reconstructed;

but it will be fatal if the South should conceive it as her duty to be regenerated and get her spirit reborn with a totally different orientation toward life.

Fortunately, the Southern program does not have to be perfectly vague. There are at least two definite lines, along either of which an intelligent Southern policy may move in the right general direction; it may even move back and forth between them and still advance.

The first course would be for the Southern leaders to arouse the sectional feeling of the South to its highest pitch of excitement in defense of all the old ways that are threatened. It might seem ungrateful to the kind industrialists to accept their handsome services in such a churlish spirit. But if one thing is more certain than another, it is that these gentlemen will not pine away in their discouragement; they have an inextinguishable enthusiasm for their rôle. The attitude that needs artificial respiration is the attitude of resistance on the part of the natives to the salesmen of industrialism. It will be fiercest and most effective if industrialism is represented to the Southern people as—what it undoubtedly is for the most part—a foreign invasion of Southern soil, which is capable of doing more devastation than was wrought when Sherman marched to the sea. From this point of view it will be a great gain if the usually-peaceful invasion forgets itself now and then, is less peaceful, and commits indiscretions. The native and the invader will be sure to come to an occasional clash, and that will offer the chance to revive ancient and almost forgotten animosities. It will be in order to proclaim to Southerners that the carpet-baggers are again in their midst. And it will be well to seize upon and advertise certain Northern industrial communities as horrible examples of a way of life we detest—not failing to point out the human catastrophe which occurs when a Southern village or rural community becomes the cheap labor of a miserable factory system. It will be a little bit harder to impress the people with the fact that the new so-called industrial "slavery" fastens not only upon the poor, but upon the middle and better classes of society, too. To make this point it may be necessary to revive such an antiquity as the old Southern gentleman and his lady, and their scorn for the dollar-chasers.

Such a policy as this would show decidedly a sense of what the Germans call *Realpolitik*. It could be nasty and it could be effective.

Its net result might be to give to the South eventually a position in the Union analogous more or less to the position of Scotland under the British crown—a section with a very local and peculiar culture that would, nevertheless, be secure and respected. And Southern traditionalists may take courage from the fact that it was Scottish stubbornness which obtained this position for Scotland; it did not come gratuitously; it was the consequence of an intense sectionalism that fought for a good many years before its fight was won.

That is one policy. Though it is not the only one, it may be necessary to employ it, with discretion, and to bear in mind its Scottish analogue. But it is hardly handsome enough for the best Southerners. Its methods are too easily abused; it offers too much room for the professional demagogue; and one would only as a last resort like to have the South stake upon it her whole chance of survival. After all, the reconstruction may be undertaken with some imagination, and not necessarily under the formula of a literal restoration. It does not greatly matter to what extent the identical features of the old Southern establishment are restored; the important consideration is that there be an establishment for the sake of stability.

The other course may not be so easily practicable, but it is certainly more statesmanlike. That course is for the South to reënter the American political field with a determination and an address quite beyond anything she has exhibited during her half-hearted national life of the last half a century. And this means specifically that she may pool her own stakes with the stakes of other minority groups in the Union which are circumstanced similarly. There is in active American politics already, to start with, a very belligerent if somewhat uninformed Western agrarian party. Between this party and the South there is much community of interest; both desire to defend home, stability of life, the practice of leisure, and the natural enemy of both is the insidious industrial system. There are also, scattered here and there, numerous elements with the same general attitude which would have some power if united: the persons and even communities who are thoroughly tired of progressivism and its spurious benefits, and those who have recently acquired, or miraculously through the generations preserved, a European point of view—sociologists, educators, artists, religionists, and ancient New England townships. The combination of these elements with the Western farmers and the old-fashioned South would make a formidable bloc. The South is numerically much the most substantial of these three groups, but has done next to nothing to make the cause prevail by working inside the American political system.

The unifying effective bond between these geographically diverse elements of public opinion will be the clean-cut policy that the rural life of America must be defended, and the world made safe for the farmers. My friends are often quick to tell me that against the power of the industrial spirit no such hope can be entertained. But there are some protests in these days rising against the industrial ideal, even from the centers where its grip is the stoutest; and this would indicate that our human intelligence is beginning again to assert itself. Of course this is all the truer of the European countries, which have required less of the bitter schooling of experience. Thus Dean Inge declares himself in his Romanes Lecture on "The Idea of Progress":

> I believe that the dissatisfaction with things as they are is caused not only by the failure of nineteenth-century civilization, but partly also by its success. We no longer wish to progress on those lines if we could. Our apocalyptic dream is vanishing into thin air. It may be that the industrial revolution which began in the reign of George the Third has produced most of its fruits, and has had its day. We may have to look forward to such a change as is imagined by Anatole France at the end of his *Isle of the Penguins*, when, after an orgy of revolution and destruction, we shall slide back into the quiet rural life of the early modern period. If so, the authors of the revolution will have cut their own throats, for there can be no great manufacturing towns in such a society. Their disappearance will be no great loss. The race will have tried a great experiment, and will have rejected it as unsatisfying.

The South has an important part to play, if she will, in such a counter-revolution. But what pitiful service have the inept Southern politicians for many years been rendering to the cause! Their Southern loyalty at Washington has rarely had any more imaginative manifestation than to scramble vigorously for a Southern share in the federal pie. They will have to be miraculously enlightened.

I get quickly beyond my depth in sounding these political possibilities. I will utter one last fantastic thought.

No Southerner ever dreams of heaven, or pictures his Utopia on earth, without providing room for the Democratic Party. Is it really possible that the Democratic Party can be held to a principle, and that the principle can now be defined as agrarian, conservative, anti-industrial? It may not be impossible, after all. If it proves possible, then the South may yet be rewarded for a sentimental affection that has persisted in the face of many betrayals.

*1930*

# ROBERT NISBET

Robert A. Nisbet (1913–1996) was a sociologist whose writings centered on the growing loneliness and alienation in American life. These by-products of modernity were destroying the prospect that genuine forms of community could be sustained in the United States. The only antidote, he argued, was to rehabilitate and enhance nonstate institutions, above all the family.

———

## The Loss of Community

O NE MAY paraphrase the famous words of Karl Marx and say that a specter is haunting the modern mind, the specter of insecurity. Surely the outstanding characteristic of contemporary thought on man and society is the preoccupation with personal alienation and cultural disintegration. The fears of the nineteenth-century conservatives in Western Europe, expressed against a background of increasing individualism, secularism, and social dislocation, have become, to an extraordinary degree, the insights and hypotheses of present-day students of man in society. The widening concern with insecurity and disintegration is accompanied by a profound regard for the values of status, membership, and community.

In every age there are certain key words which by their repetitive use and re-definition mark the distinctive channels of faith and thought. Such words have symbolic values which exert greater influence upon the nature and direction of men's thinking than the techniques used in the study or laboratory or the immediate empirical problems chosen for research. In the nineteenth century, the age of individualism and rationalism, such words as *individual, change, progress, reason,* and *freedom* were notable not merely for their wide use as linguistic tools in books, essays, and lectures but for their symbolic value in the convictions of immense numbers of men. These words were both the outcome of thought and the elicitors of thought. Men were fascinated by their referents and properties.

All of these words reflected a temper of mind that found the essence of society to lie in the solid fact of the discrete individual—autonomous, self-sufficing, and stable—and the essence of history to lie in the progressive emancipation of the individual from the tyrannous and irrational statuses handed down from the past. Competition, individuation, dislocation of status and custom, impersonality, and moral anonymity were hailed by the rationalist because these were the forces that would be most instrumental in emancipating man from the dead hand of the past and because through them the naturally stable and rational individual would be given an environment in which he could develop illimitably his inherent potentialities. Man was the primary and solid fact; relationships were purely derivative. All that was necessary was a scene cleared of the debris of the past.

If there were some, like Taine, Ruskin, and William Morris, who called attention to the cultural and moral costs involved—the uprooting of family ties, the disintegration of villages, the displacement of craftsmen, and the atomization of ancient securities—the apostles of rationalism could reply that these were the inevitable costs of Progress. After all, it was argued—argued by liberals and radicals alike—in all great ages of achievement there is a degree of disorder, a snapping of the ties of tradition and security. How else can the creative individual find release for his pent-up powers of discovery and reason if the chains of tradition are not forcibly struck off?

This was the age of optimism, of faith in the abstract individual and in the harmonies of nature. In Mark Twain's *Huckleberry Finn*, what we are given, as Parrington points out in his great study of American thought, is the matchless picture of a child of nature revolting against the tyrannies of village, family, and conventional morality. It is a revolt characterized, not by apprehensiveness and insecurity, but by all the confidence of the frontier. In the felicities and equalities of nature Huck finds joyous release from the cloistering prejudices and conventions of old morality. Truth, justice, and happiness lie in man alone.

In many areas of thought and imagination we find like perspectives. The eradication of old restraints, together with the prospect of new and more natural relationships in society, relationships arising directly from the innate resources of individuals, prompted a glowing vision of society in which there would be forever abolished the parochialisms and animosities of a world founded upon kinship, village, and church. Reason, founded upon natural interest, would replace the wisdom Burke and his fellow-conservatives had claimed to find in historical processes of use and wont, of habit and prejudice.

"The psychological process which social relations were undergoing," Ostrogorski has written of the nineteenth century, "led to the same conclusions as rationalism and by the same logical path—abstraction and generalization." Henceforth, man's social relations "were bound to be guided not so much by sentiment, which expressed the perception of the particular, as by general principles, less intense in their nature perhaps, but sufficiently comprehensive to take in the shifting multitudes of which the abstract social groups were henceforth composed, groups continually subject to expansion by reason of their continual motion."[1]

Between philosophers as far removed as Spencer and Marx there was a common faith in the organizational powers of history and in the self-sufficiency of the individual. All that was needed was calm recognition of the historically inevitable. In man and his natural affinities lay the bases of order and freedom. These were the affirmations that so largely dominated the thought, lay as well as scholarly, of the nineteenth and early twentieth century. All of the enmity of the French Enlightenment toward the social relationships that were the heritage of the Middle Ages became translated, during the nineteenth century, into a theoretical indifference to problems of the relation of individual security and motivation to contexts of association and cultural norm. Both freedom and order were envisaged generally in terms of the psychology and politics of individual release from the old.

We see this in the social sciences of the age. What was scientific psychology but the study of forces and states of mind within the natural individual, assumed always to be autonomous and stable? Political science and economics were, in their dominant forms, concerned with legal and economic atoms—abstract human beings—and with impersonal relationships supplied by the market or by limited general legislation. All social and cultural differences were resolved by the rationalist into differences of quantity and intensity of individual passions and desires. The stability of the individual was a function of his unalterable instincts and his sovereign reason; the stability of society was guaranteed by the laws of historical change. The two goals of scientific universality and moral emancipation from the past became largely indistinguishable in the philosophy and the social science of the age. Bentham's boast that he could legislate wisely for all of India from the recesses of his own study was hardly a piece of personal eccentricity. It sprang from a confidence both in reason and in the ineradicable sameness and stability of individuals everywhere.

Above everything towered the rationalist's monumental conviction of the *organizational* character of history—needing occasionally to be facilitated, perhaps, but never directed—and of the self-sufficing *stability* of the discrete individual.

## TWO

Today a different set of words and symbols dominates the intellectual and moral scene. It is impossible to overlook, in modern lexicons, the importance of such words as *disorganization, disintegration, decline, insecurity, breakdown, instability,* and the like. What the nineteenth-century rationalist took for granted about society and the nature of man's existence, as the result of an encompassing faith in the creative and organizational powers of history, the contemporary student of society makes the object of increasing apprehension and uncertainty.

At the present time there is in numerous areas of thought a profound reaction to the rationalist point of view. No longer are we convinced that basic organizational problems in human relations are automatically solved by readjustments of political or economic structures. There is a decided weakening of faith in the inherent stability of the individual and in the psychological and moral benefits of social impersonality. Impersonality, moral neutrality, individualism, and mechanism have become, in recent decades, terms to describe pathological conditions of society. Nearly gone is the sanguine confidence in the power of history itself to engender out of the soil of disorganization seeds of new and more successful forms of social and moral security.

A concern with cultural disorganization underlies almost every major philosophy of history in our time. The monumental historical synthesis of a Toynbee represents anew the effort of the prophetic historian to find in the casual forces of history meanings that will illuminate the darkness of the present age. Like St. Augustine's *City of God*, written to sustain the faith of fifth-century Christians, Toynbee's volumes, with all their magnificent learning and religious insight, are directed to the feelings of men who live beneath the pall of insecurity that overhangs the present age. One cannot resist the suspicion that for most of Toynbee's readers the governing interest is in the sections of *A Study of History* that deal not with genesis and development but with decline and disintegration. And it is hard to put aside the suspicion that Toynbee himself has reserved his greatest interpretative skill for the melancholy phenomena of death and decay, a circumstance which, like Milton's characterization of Satan, may bespeak an irresistible, if morally reluctant, love for his subject. Toynbee's cataloguing of historic stigmata of social dissolution—schism in society and the soul, archaism, futurism, and above all, the process of "deracination," the genesis of the proletariat—reads like a list of dominant themes in contemporary thought.

Are not the works of the major prophets of the age, Niebuhr, Bernanos, Berdyaev, Sorokin, Spengler, and others, based foremost upon the conviction that ours is a sick culture, marked by the pathologies of defeat and failure of regenerative processes? Is it not extraordinary how many of the major novelists and poets and playwrights of the present age have given imaginative expression to themes of dissolution and decay—of class, family, community, and morality? Not only are these themes to be seen among the Titans—Proust, Mann, Joyce, Kafka, Eliot—but among a large and increasing number of secondary or popular writers. It is hard to miss the centrality of themes of dissolution in contemporary religious and literary expressions and the fascination that is exerted by the terminology of failure and defeat. Disaster is seen as the consequence of process rather than event, of "whimper" rather than "bang," to use the words of T. S. Eliot.

How extraordinary, when compared with the optimism of half a century ago, is the present ideology of lament. There is now a sense of disorganization that ranges all the way from the sociologist's concern with disintegration of the family and small community to the religious prophet's intuition that moral decay is enveloping the whole of Western society. Premonitions of disaster have been present in all ages, along with millennial hopes for the termination of the mundane world. But the present sense of dissolution is of a radically different sort. It looks to no clear salvation and it is held to be the consequence neither of Divine decree nor of fortuitous catastrophe. It is a sense of disorganization that takes root in the very conditions which to earlier generations of rationalists appeared as the necessary circumstances of progress. Where the nineteenth-century rationalist saw progressively higher forms of order and freedom emerging from the destruction of the old, the contemporary sociologist is not so sanguine. He is likely to see not creative emancipation but sterile insecurity, not the framework of the new but the shell of the old.

There is a large and growing area of psychology and social science that emphasizes this contemporary preoccupation with disintegration and disorganization. Innumerable studies of community disorganization, family disorganization, personality disintegration, not to mention the myriad investigations of industrial strife and the dissolution of ethnic subcultures and "folk" areas, all serve to point up the idea of disorganization in present-day social science. The contemporary student of man is no more able to resist the lure of the evidences of social disorganization than his nineteenth-century predecessor could resist the manifest evidences of creative emancipation and reorganization. However empirical his studies of social relationships, however bravely he rearranges the semantic elements of his terminology, to support belief in his own moral detachment, and however confidently he may sometimes look to the salvational possibilities of political legislation for moral relief, it is plain that the contemporary student of human relations is haunted by perceptions of disorganization and the possibility of endemic collapse.[2]

THREE

A further manifestation of the collapse of the rationalist view of man, and even more revealing, is the conception of man's moral estrangement and spiritual isolation that pervades our age. Despite the influence and power of the contemporary State there is a true sense in which the present age is more individualistic than any other in European history. To examine the whole literature of lament of our time—in the social sciences, moral philosophy, theology, the novel, the theater—and to observe the frantic efforts of millions of individuals to find some kind of security of mind is to open our eyes to the perplexities and frustrations that have emerged from the widening gulf between the individual and those social relationships within which goals and purposes take on meaning. The sense of cultural disintegration is but the obverse side of the sense of individual isolation.

The historic triumph of secularism and individualism has presented a set of problems that looms large in contemporary thought. The modern release of the individual from traditional ties of class, religion, and kinship has made him free; but, on the testimony of innumerable works in our age, this freedom is accompanied not by the sense of creative release but by the sense of disenchantment and alienation. The alienation of man from historic moral certitudes has been followed by the sense of man's alienation from fellow man.

Where the lone individual was once held to contain within himself all the propensities of order and progress, he is now quite generally regarded as the very symbol of society's anxiety and insecurity. He is the consequence, we are now prone to say, not of moral progress but of social disintegration.

*Frustration, anxiety, insecurity,* as descriptive words, have achieved a degree of importance in present-day thought and writing that is astonishing. Common to all of them and their many synonyms is the basic conception of man's alienation from society's relationships and moral values. If in Renaissance thought it was the myth of reasonable man which predominated; if in the eighteenth century it was natural man; and, in the nineteenth century, economic or political man, it is by no means unlikely that for our own age it is alienated or maladjusted man who will appear to later historians as the key figure of twentieth-century thought. Inadequate man, insufficient man, disenchanted man, as terms, reflect a multitude of themes in contemporary writing. Thus Berdyaev sees before him in the modern world the "disintegration of the human image"; Toynbee sees the proletarian, he who has lost all sense of identity and belonging; for Ortega y Gasset it is mass man, the anonymous creature of the market place and the mass ballot;

for John Dewey, it is the lost individual—bereft of the loyalties and values which once endowed life with meaning.

"The natural state of twentieth-century man," the protagonist of a recent novel declares, "is anxiety." At the very least, anxiety has become a major state of mind in contemporary imaginative writing. Underlying many works is the conception of man as lost, baffled, and obsessed. It is not strange that for so many intellectuals the novels and stories of Franz Kafka should be, or have been until recently, the basis of almost a cult. Whatever the complexity and many-sidedness of Kafka's themes, whatever the deepest roots of his inspiration, such novels as *The Trial* and *The Castle* are, as many critics have observed, allegories of alienation and receding certainty. The residual meaning of these novels may well be man's relation to God, a universal and timeless theme. But it is nearly impossible not to see them also as symbolizations of man's effort to achieve status, to uncover meaning in the society around him, and to discover guilts and innocences in a world where the boundaries between guilt and innocence become more and more obscured. The plight of Kafka's hero is the plight of many persons in the living world: isolation, estrangement, and the compulsive search for fortresses of certainty and the equities of judgment.

The theme of the individual uprooted, without status, struggling for revelations of meaning, seeking fellowship in some kind of moral community, is as recurrent in our age as was, in an earlier age, that of the individual's release from the pressure of certainty, of his triumph over tribal or communal laws of conformity. In a variety of ways this contemporary theme finds its way into popular writing, into the literature of adventure and the murder mystery. The notion of an impersonal, even hostile, society is common—a society in which all actions and motives seem to have equal values and to be perversely detached from human direction. Common too is the helplessness of the individual before alien forces—not the hero who does things but, as Wyndham Lewis has put it, the hero to whom things are done. The disenchanted, lonely figure, searching for ethical significance in the smallest of things, struggling for identification with race or class or group, incessantly striving to answer the question, "Who am I, What am I," has become, especially in Europe, almost the central literary type of the age.

Not even with Richard III's sense of bleak triumph does the modern protagonist cry out, "I am myself alone." Where in an earlier literature the release of the hero from society's folkways and moral injunctions and corporate protections was the basis of joyous, confident, assertive individualism, the same release in contemporary literature is more commonly the occasion for morbidity and obsession. Not the free individual but the lost individual; not independence but isolation; not self-discovery but self-obsession; not to conquer but to be conquered: these are major states of mind in contemporary imaginative literature.

They are not new ideas. A whole school of literary criticism has devoted itself in recent years to the reinterpretation of writers in other ages who, like Hawthorne, Melville, and Dostoevsky, portrayed the misery of estrangement, the horror of aloneness.[3] In Tolstoy's *Ivan Ilyich* and in almost all of Dostoevsky's novels we learn that the greatest of all vices is to claim spiritual and moral autonomy and to cast off the ties that bind man to his fellows. So too in the theological writings of Kierkegaard there is luminously revealed the dread reality of man, solitary and tormented, in a hostile universe. In the writings of the Philosophical Conservatives, at the very beginning of the nineteenth century, the vision was central of man's isolation and impotence once he had got loose from society's traditions and moral constraints. Far from being new ideas these are as old as moral prophecy itself.

What is now so distinctive about these ideas is their penetration into so many areas of thought which, until recently, stressed a totally different conception of the nature of man. For a long time in modern European thought the rationalist view of self-sufficing, self-stabilizing man was ascendant in moral philosophy, Protestant theology, and social science. Few were the works that did not take the integrity and self-sufficiency of man before God as almost axiomatic. But now in widening spheres of thought we find a different concept of man.

Thus the theologian Paul Tillich sees before him in the Western world today a culture compounded not of traditional faith and confidence, but one agitated by feelings of fear and anxiety, uncertainty, loneliness, and meaninglessness. So long as a strong cultural heritage existed, and with it a sense of membership, the modern ethic of individualism was tolerable. "But when the remnants of a common world broke down, the individual was thrown into complete loneliness and the despair connected with it."[4]

Historically, Protestantism has given its emphasis to the immediacy of the individual to God, and, in theory, has relied little on the corporate nature of ecclesiastical society or the principle of hierarchical intermediation. Popularly, religion was directed not to Kierkegaard's solitary, tormented individual, alone in a hostile universe, but to the confident, self-sufficing man who carried within himself the seeds not only of faith and righteousness but of spiritual stability as well.

But this faith in the spiritual integrity of the lone individual is perceptibly declining in much Protestant thought of the present time. Today there are many leaders of the Protestant churches who have come to realize the inadequacy and irrelevance of the historic emphasis upon the church invisible and the supposedly autonomous man of faith. "It is this autonomous individual who really ushers in modern civilization and who is completely annihilated in the final stages of that civilization," declares Reinhold Niebuhr.[5]

Behind the rising tide of alienation and spiritual insecurity in contemporary society, more and more theologians, Jewish, Catholic, and Protestant alike, find the long-celebrated Western tradition of secular individualism. The historic emphasis upon the individual has been at the expense of the associative and symbolic relationships that must in fact uphold the individual's own sense of integrity. Buber, Maritain, Brunner, Niebuhr, and Demant are but the major names in the group that has come to recognize the atomizing effects of the long tradition of Western individualism upon man's relation to both society and God. "When the relation between man and God is subjective, interior (as in Luther) or in timeless acts and logic (as in Calvin) man's utter dependence upon God is not mediated through the concrete facts of historical life," writes Canon Demant.[6] And when it is not so mediated, the relation with God becomes tenuous, amorphous, and insupportable.

For more and more theologians of today the solitary individual before God has his inevitable future in Jung's "modern man in search of a soul." Man's alienation from man must lead in time to man's alienation from God. The loss of the sense of visible community in Christ will be followed by the loss of the sense of the invisible. The decline of community in the modern world has as its inevitable religious consequence the creation of masses of helpless, bewildered individuals who are unable to find solace in Christianity regarded merely as creed. The stress upon the individual, at the expense of the churchly community, has led remorselessly to the isolation of the individual, to the shattering of the man-God relationship, and to the atomization of personality. This is the testimony of a large number of theologians in our day.

So too in the social sciences has the vision of the lost individual become central. It was the brilliant French sociologist Emile Durkheim who, at the beginning of the present century, called attention to the consequences of moral and economic individualism in modern life. Individualism has resulted in masses of normless, unattached, insecure individuals who lose even the capacity for independent, creative living. The highest rates of suicide and insanity, Durkheim discovered, are to be found in those areas of society in which moral and social individualism is greatest.

Suicide varies inversely with the degree of integration in society. Hence, as Durkheim pointed out in studies which have been confirmed by the researches of many others, there is a higher rate of suicide among Protestants, among urban dwellers, among industrial workers, among the unmarried, among, in short, all those whose lives are characterized by relative tenuousness of social ties.[7]

When the individual is thrown back upon his own inner resources, when he loses the sense of moral and social involvement with others, he becomes prey to sensations of anxiety and guilt. Self-destruction is frequently his only way out. Such sensations, Durkheim concluded from his studies of modern society, are on the increase in Western society. For, in the process of modern industrial and political development, established social contexts have become weak, and fewer individuals have the secure interpersonal relations which formerly gave meaning and stability to existence.

At the present time, in all the social sciences, the various synonyms of alienation have a foremost place in studies of human relations. Investigations of the "unattached," the "marginal," the "obsessive," the "normless," and the "isolated" individual all testify to the central place occupied by the hypothesis of alienation in contemporary social science.

In studies of the aged, the adolescent, and the infant; of marriage, the neighborhood, and the factory; of the worker, the unemployed, the intellectual, and the bureaucrat; of crime, insanity, alcoholism, and of mass movements in politics, the hypothesis of alienation has reached an extraordinary degree of importance. It has become nearly as prevalent as the doctrine of enlightened self-interest was two generations ago. It is more than a hypothesis; it is a perspective.

Thus Elton Mayo and his colleagues, in their pioneering studies of industrial organization in the Western Electric plant, found that increasingly modern industry tends to predispose workers to obsessive responses, and the number of unhappy individuals increases. "Forced back upon himself, with no immediate or real social duties, the individual becomes a prey to unhappy and obsessive personal preoccupations." There is something about the nature of modern industry that inevitably creates a sense of void and aloneness. The change from what Mayo calls an *established* to an *adaptive* society has resulted for the worker in a "profound loss of security and certainty in his actual living and in the background of his thinking . . . Where groups change ceaselessly, as jobs and mechanical processes change, the individual experiences a sense of void, of emptiness, where his fathers knew the joy of comradeship and security."[8]

Similarly in innumerable studies of the community, especially the urban community, the process of alienation is emphasized. "The urban mode of life," we read, "tends to create solitary souls, to uproot the individual from his customs, to confront him with a social void, and to weaken traditional restraints on personal conduct . . . Personal existence and social solidarity in the urban community appear to hang by a slender thread. The tenuous relations between men, based for the most part upon a pecuniary nexus, make urban existence seem very fragile and capable of being disturbed by a multitude of forces over which the individual has little or no control. This may lead some to evince the most fruitful ingenuity and heroic courage, while it overpowers others with a paralyzing sense of individual helplessness and despair."[9]

Perceptions of alienation are not confined to studies of Western urban culture. In recent years the attention of more and more anthropologists has been focused on the effects that Western culture has had upon the lives and thought of individuals in pre-literate or folk societies. The phenomenon of detribalization has of course been long noted. But where most early students of native cultures were generally reassured by the preconceptions of rationalism, seeing in this detribalization the manifold opportunities of psychological release and cultural progress, recent students have come more and more to emphasize the characteristics of alienation which are the consequence of the destruction of traditional groups and values.

It has become apparent to many anthropologists that the loss of allegiance to caste, clan, tribe, or community—a common consequence of what Margaret Mead has called the West's "psychic imperialism"—coupled with the native's inability to find secure membership in the new modes of authority and responsibility, leads to the same kind of behavior observed by sociologists and psychologists in many Western areas. "The new individual," writes one anthropologist, himself a South African native, "is in a spiritual and moral void. Partial civilization means . . . a shattering of ancient beliefs and superstitions. They are shattered but not replaced by any new beliefs. Customs and traditions are despised and rejected, but no new customs and traditions are acquired, or can be acquired."[10] So too have the more recent observations and writings of such anthropologists as Malinowski, Thurnwald, and many others emphasized the rising incidence of personal alienation, of feelings of insecurity and abandonment, among individuals in native cultures throughout the world.

In no sphere of contemporary thought has the image of the lost individual become more dominant and directive than in the fields of psychiatry and social psychology. A large number of pathological states of mind which, even a short generation ago, were presumed to be manifestations of complexes embedded in the innate neurological structure of the individual, or to be the consequence of some early traumatic experience in childhood, are now widely regarded as the outcome of a disturbed relation between the individual patient and the culture around him. The older rationalist conception of stable, self-sufficing man has been replaced, in large measure, by a conception of man as unstable, inadequate, and insecure when he is cut off from the channels of social membership and clear belief. Changes and dislocations in the cultural environment will be followed by dislocations in personality itself.

From the writings of such psychiatrists as Karen Horney, Erich Fromm, and the late Harry Stack Sullivan we learn that in our culture, with its cherished values of individual self-reliance and self-sufficiency, surrounded by relationships which become ever more impersonal and by authorities which become ever more remote, there is a rising tendency, even among the "normal" elements of the population, toward increased feelings of aloneness and insecurity. Because the basic moral values of our culture come to seem more and more inaccessible, because the line between right and wrong, good and bad, just and unjust, becomes ever less distinct, there is produced a kind of cultural "set" toward unease and chronic disquiet.

From such "normal" conditions arise the typical neuroses of contemporary middle-class society. The neurotic is, quite generally, the human being in whom these sensations of disquiet and rootlessness become chronic and unmanageable. He is the victim of intensified feelings of insecurity and anxiety and intolerable aloneness. From his conviction of aloneness he tends to derive convictions of the hostility of society toward him. Many a psychiatrist has observed with Karen Horney that among neurotics there is, in striking degree, "the incapacity to be alone, varying from slight uneasiness and restlessness to a definite terror of solitude . . . These persons have the feeling of drifting forlornly in the universe, and any human contact is a relief to them."[11]

What is of importance here is not so much the diagnoses of neurosis which are to be found in the writings of the new school of psychiatry but, rather, the implied diagnosis or evaluation of the society in which neurotics live. Two generations ago when the foundations of clinical psychiatry were being laid by Freud, there was, for all the keen interest in neurotic behavior, little doubt of the fundamental stability of society. Then, the tendency was to ascribe neurotic behavior to certain conflicts between the nature of man and the stern demands of a highly stable, even oppressive, society. This tendency has not, to be sure, disappeared. But it is now matched, and probably exceeded, by tendencies to ascribe the roots of neurosis to the structure of society itself. The human person has not been forgotten, but more and more psychiatrists are prone to follow Harry Stack Sullivan in regarding personality as but an aspect of interpersonal relations and personality disorders as but manifestations of social instability. And with these judgments there is the further, more drastic judgment, that contemporary society, especially middle-class society, tends by its very structure to produce the alienated, the disenchanted, the rootless, and the neurotic.

FOUR

Despite the matchless control of physical environment, the accumulations of material wealth, and the unprecedented diffusion of culture
in the lives of the masses, all of which lend glory to the present age,
there is much reason for supposing that we are already entering a new
Age of Pessimism. More than one prophet of our day has discovered
contemporary relevance in Sir Gilbert Murray's celebrated characterization of the ancient Athens that lay in the wake of the disastrous
Peloponnesian Wars as suffering from a "failure of nerve." Ours also
is an age, on the testimony of much writing, of amorphous, distracted
multitudes and of solitary, inward-turning individuals. Gone is the
widespread confidence in the automatic workings of history to provide
cultural redemption, and gone, even more strikingly, is the rationalist
faith in the individual. Whether in the novel, the morality play, or in
the sociological treatise, what we are given to contemplate is, typically,
an age of uncertainty, disintegration, and spiritual aloneness.

To be sure it is by no means certain how far the preoccupations of
intellectuals, whether novelists or sociologists, may be safely regarded
as an index to the conditions of a culture at large. It may be argued
that in such themes of estrangement we are dealing with rootless shadowy apprehensions of the intellectual rather than with the empirical
realities of the world around us. Extreme and habitual intellectualism
may, it is sometimes said, produce tendencies of a somewhat morbid
nature—inner tendencies that the intellectual is too frequently unable
to resist endowing with external reality.

Doubtless there is something in this diagnosis. The prophet,
whether he be theologian or social scientist, is necessarily detached in
some degree from the common currents of his age. From this detachment may come illuminative imagination and insight. But from this
same detachment may come also an unrepresentative sense of aloneness, of alienation. However brilliant the searchlight of imagination,
the direction of its brilliance is inevitably selective and always subjective to some extent.

Nevertheless, making all allowance for the possibly unrepresentative nature of much of the literature of decline and alienation, we are
still left with its astonishing diversity and almost massive clustering
in our age. Were themes of isolation and disintegration confined to

a coterie, to writers manifestly of the ivory tower, there would be more to support the view of the unrepresentative nature of the present literature of lament. But such themes extend beyond the area of imaginative literature and moral prophecy. They are incorporated in the works of those who are most closely and empirically concerned with the behavior of human beings.

Nor can we overlook the fact that between the mind of the intellectual and the interests and cravings of the public there is always a positive connection of some kind. We need not go as far as Toynbee, Mannheim, and T. S. Eliot in their conceptions of creative minorities, élites, and classes to recognize that in any society there is a close and continuing relation between the actual condition of a culture and the image of that culture which directs the minds of its intellectual leaders—its philosophers, artists, scientists, and theologians. In the nineteenth century and for a decade or two after, the intellectual's faith in the inevitability of progress and the self-sufficiency of man were matched by broad, popular convictions. And in the mid-twentieth century there is a good deal of evidence to suggest that philosophical intimations of alienation and dissolution are set in a context of analogous mass intimations.

There are of course prophets of optimism who find hope in the monumental technological achievements of the age and in the manifest capacity of our industrial machine to provide food and comfort for the many. Such minds see in present conditions of social and moral distress only an ephemeral lag between man's still incompletely evolved moral nature and his technological achievements. In the long run, it is argued, the material progress of society will not be denied, and with the diffusion of material goods and technical services there will be an ever constant lessening of present disquietudes.

But it has become obvious, surely, that technological progress and the relative satisfaction of material needs in a population offer no guarantee of the resolution of all deprivations and frustrations. Human needs seem to form a kind of hierarchy, ranging from those of a purely physical and self-preservative nature at the bottom to needs of a social and spiritual nature at the top. During a period when a population is concerned largely with achieving satisfaction of the lower order of needs—satisfaction in the form of production and distribution of material goods—the higher order of needs may scarcely be felt by the majority of persons. But with the satisfaction of the prime, material needs, those of a social and spiritual nature become ever more pressing and ever more decisive in the total scheme of things. Desires for cultural participation, social belonging, and personal status become irresistible and their frustrations galling. Material improvement that is unaccompanied by a sense of personal belonging may actually intensify social dislocation and personal frustration.

"The true hall-mark of the proletarian," Toynbee warns us, "is neither poverty nor humble birth, but a consciousness—and the resentment which this consciousness inspires—of being disinherited from his ancestral place in society and being unwanted in a community which is his rightful home; and this subjective proletarianism is not incompatible with the possession of material assets."[12]

Whether or not it is the presence of the machine and its iron discipline that creates, as so many argue in our day, the conditions of depersonalization and alienation in modern mass culture, the fact is plain that the contemporary sense of anxiety and insecurity is associated with not merely an unparalleled mechanical control of environment but, more importantly, with widespread *faith* in such control. Fears of famine, pestilence, destruction, and death have been present in all ages and have been allayed by appropriate mechanisms of relief. What is so striking about the present sense of anxiety is that it has little determinable relation to these timeless afflictions and is rooted in an age when their control has reached unprecedented heights of success.

It is impossible to escape the melancholy conclusion that man's belief in himself has become weakest in the very age when his control of environment is greatest. This is the irony of ironies. Not the most saturnine inhabitant of Thomas Love Peacock's *Nightmare Abbey*, not even the author of that nineteenth-century dirge, *The City of Dreadful Night*, foresaw the Devil in the guise he has taken.

## NOTES

1.  *Democracy and the Organization of Political Parties* (London, 1902), vol. 1, p. 50.
2.  "Can the anonymity, mobility, impersonality, specialization, and sophistication of the city become the attributes of a stable society, or will society

fall apart?" asks one of America's foremost sociologists, Kingsley Davis, in his *Human Society* (New York, 1949), p. 342. Questions of this sort form the moral perspective of a great deal of theoretical and empirical work in the contemporary sciences of human behavior.

3. See, for example, such recent studies as Philip Rahv, *Image and Idea* (New York, 1949), Newton Arvin, *Hawthorne's Short Stories* (New York, 1947), and the superb appraisal of Dostoevsky and his critics, "The Insufficient Man," *Times Literary Supplement*, 20 September 1947.

4. *The Protestant Era* (University of Chicago, 1948), pp. 245–6.

5. *The Nature and Destiny of Man* (London, 1941), vol. 1, p. 59.

6. *Christian Polity* (London, 1936), p. 87.

7. See Durkheim's *Suicide* (Paris, 1897), especially the final chapters. The writings of Durkheim's German contemporary, Georg Simmel, have had something of the same influence upon modern thought.

8. *The Social Problems of an Industrial Civilization* (Harvard University, 1945), pp. 7, 56.

9. National Resources Committee, *Our Cities* (Washington, D.C., 1937), p. 53.

10. S. M. Molema, *The Bantu, Past and Present* (Edinburgh, 1920), p. 308.

11. *The Neurotic Personality of Our Time* (New York, 1937), p. 117.

12. *A Study of History* (London, 1946), vol. 5, p. 63.

*1953*

# EUGENE GENOVESE

Eugene Genovese (1930–2012) was never one to shy away from controversy. During the 1960s, as a swaggeringly unapologetic Marxist historian, he notoriously declared that he hoped for a Communist victory in the Vietnam War. Yet Genovese was also remarkably heterodox in his intellectual outlook. *Roll Jordan, Roll* (1974) was a groundbreaking study of slave society in the South, one that recognized modes of slave resistance. In subsequent work, Genovese unearthed in the worldview of slaveholders and their intellectual defenders much to admire. In their critique of industrial capitalism, he glimpsed values that might provide the basis for a more humane alternative.

---

## FROM *The Southern Tradition*

S INCE THE 1930s southerners, conservative and other, have left little doubt about where they stand on fascism. In an essay titled "The South and the Revolution of Nihilism," Weaver accurately noted: "That the South was the first section of the United States to sense an enemy in fascism was indicated not only by the polls of opinion, but also by its ardor in preparing for the fight." Weaver launched into another of his attacks on unbridled capitalism, which he regarded as an invitation to fascist tyranny: "Centralism always points to an alliance between the mass as such and the single leader purporting to be their champion; and, conversely, decentralization leaves the way open for local authority and provides opportunity for individuals to express themselves as such ... It [the South] understands correctly that the promise of fascism to restore the ancient virtues is counteracted by this process, and that the denial of an ethical basis for the state means the loss of freedom and humanity."

Weaver, sorting out the threads of the southern legacy, expressed displeasure at George Fitzhugh's assault on free society, with "its remarkable foreshadowing of the modern corporate state . . . an outline of the totalitarian state, which substitutes for individual liberty and free competition a fixed hierarchy and state provision for all classes." Weaver misread Fitzhugh and would have done better to invoke Henry Hughes of Mississippi. No matter. His strictures lay bare his hostility to fascism and, more instructively, his hostility to the translation of natural inequality and hierarchy into an excuse for social immobility, the drawing of caste lines, and the state's assumption of power over the whole life of the individual.[1]

The southern conservatives' attitude toward war proves no less revealing. They have not glorified war, despite outbursts of the bloody-mindedness that disgrace people in all political camps whenever they have to justify a particular war. That charge might be leveled at the proslavery wing of Young America and those who have, ever since, shouted their allegiance to egalitarian democracy, although even they might resist the charge as unfair. At the most, southern conservatives have agreed with Freud and Einstein that human nature contains an aggressive instinct that makes perpetual peace unrealizable.[2] Fear and an acceptance of a perceived reality do not constitute glorification and are not incompatible with a commitment to do everything in one's power to settle international affairs amicably. More to the point, the views of southern conservatives must be evaluated in the context of their emphatic protest against total war—against the so-called people's wars that have become the norm during our blood-drenched century.

Thus, they have resisted, albeit not always firmly, holy wars aimed at the imposition of an ideology and way of life on others. Weaver was never more eloquent than in his condemnation of the people of South Carolina for accepting nuclear installations on their soil, the more so for their having done it for economic advantage: "There is no more melancholy spectacle on the American scene than the fact South Carolina, which in former times set the best example of the ideal of chivalry, is now the site of the hydrogen bomb project, which prepares for indiscriminate slaughter on a scale not hitherto contemplated."[3] In contrast, Gentile justified war as necessary to the health of the state, and, in good totalitarian fashion, he laid down a dictum that could only appall southern conservatives. A defeated enemy, he declared as if with an eye on America in 1865, must accept the will of its conqueror as its own.[4]

The attitude toward war also exposes the political gap between the southern conservatives and their preferred mass base, as may be seen in their awkward relation to the religious fundamentalists, with whom they are often confused. Southern conservatives share with other transatlantic traditionalists a theological orientation, however much it is secularized by individual theorists. Yet despite having orthodox Christian prejudices, few if any leading conservatives have believed in biblical inerrancy or have had much stomach for theological rigidity of any kind. The tension may be illustrated by a glance at foreign policy. During the Cold War both groups wanted a hard line against the Soviet Union, but for radically different reasons. For many religious fundamentalists, the Cold War was a holy crusade against a satanic empire and a sign of the coming apocalypse. But most conservatives have distrusted ideological crusades, especially those which remind them of Lincoln, Grant, and Sherman and profess to stand at Armageddon and battle for the Lord.

For these conservatives, the Cold War concerned a massive threat to American national-state interests, albeit a threat ideologically driven. They wanted to lift that threat, not to tell other people how to live. No one, therefore, ought to have been surprised when leading southern conservatives poured out their wrath on President Bush for his intervention in the Persian Gulf, denouncing American policy as imperialist, rapacious, and one more example of Yankee presumption, meddling, greed, and violence.[5]

Opposition to fascism and resistance to ideological holy wars flow from southern conservatives' hostility to the centralization of political and economic power and from their preference for community decisionmaking. But they know that real communities, in contradistinction to those projected by utopian imaginations, must be creatures of the historical evolution of shared experience and faith. Thus, they face a dilemma, for they know perfectly well that the hitherto solid communities of the South, like those of the North, are wilting under rapid demographic and technological change in a new era of intense international competition. For the most part they seek, as do others across the ideological spectrum, to find a way to recreate the essence of their preferred rural and small-town communities in the big cities. How they expect to accomplish this feat without government intervention remains unclear.

The difficulties that southern conservatives are having with economic issues help explain their increasing attempt to influence opinion in the North while they worry about the spread of liberalism in the South. John Shelton Reed, our most perceptive student of white southern folkways, explains:

> [Individualism] has always coexisted with some other "Southern" traits—in particular, those that the South has shared with other "folk cultures," traits that characterize all rural, village, and peasant societies—which is what the South has been in the American context, until very recently: . . . parochialism, fatalism, authoritarianism, ethnocentrism, and categorical resistance to innovation . . .
>
> Alongside the folkish, organic strain in our region's culture, however, there has always been a stubborn, individualist, "I'm as good as you" outlook, a collection of cultural themes that competed with and undermined the demands of prescription, hierarchy, and organic community. The openness of early Southern society, the possibilities for individual mobility, meant that would-be hierarchs of the South had to resort to slavery to keep their retainers in place . . .
>
> The erosion of the folkish South by twentieth-century economic and demographic changes has left the South's version of laissez-faire free to develop relatively unchecked by prescriptive obligations and restraints based on family position, rank, class, or even race. (Sex remains perhaps a different matter.)
>
> A respect for individualism and self-reliance is also increasingly evident in Southerners' economic views . . . Public opinion polls have shown a substantial increase of late in the proportion of Southerners who support "conservative" (that is, laissez-faire) economic policies, along with an increase in those who support "liberal" social policies.[6]

An alternate policy remains implicit in the southern-conservative resistance to Leviathan. Any policy aimed at the strengthening of communities must simultaneously strengthen the autonomy of private and even public institutions. First, historically grounded communities or even new but solid ones require considerable government action of the kind that Owsley advocated during and after the Great Depression.

And in fact Owsley's critics were not above attacking him for advocating policies described as "Kremlinesque."[7]

Second, any government, unless rigorously circumscribed, would likely end by imposing the very centralization it is designed to reduce. For typically, proposals to share power—say, between the national and state governments—wind up being formulas to allow the national government to decide all important questions of policy and to allow the states to administer policies handed to them by bureaucracies with agendas that do not necessarily accord with those of the people they are called upon to serve. We are told that he who pays the piper calls the tune. But this line implies that the national bureaucracy is paying the piper, when in fact it is distributing the people's money. Even if the people assume power over their own money, Calhoun's problem would remain with us. For if we define "the people" as the majority of the country at large, with power over everything, then institutional and community autonomy cannot survive. It can survive only if the people restrain themselves in their own collective interest and agree to constitutional sanction for expenditures on causes that lack the support of a national majority.

To illustrate from the condition of our universities:[8] It is argued that if professors or students experience negatively the policies and arrangements of a university, they ought to be able to move to one that is more congenial.[9] But if the oppression experienced by those professors or students stems from the imposition of a national rather than a local consensus, then the reigning attitudes may be expected to reappear in the substituted university and to produce a similar result. The only assurance against such institutional flattening would lie in the university's ability to project and defend autonomous goals and procedures and to assert dissident values. If all were compelled to adhere to standards established in society as a whole, whether established democratically or no, the freedom to move would become a sham. And an appeal to a plethora of communities and institutions within society only brings us back to the same problem.

Specifically, since the Catholic Church, appealing to the revealed word of God, regards homosexuality as a sin, it could not readily countenance homosexuality on its campuses without prostituting itself. More generally, a Catholic university must discriminate in the hiring of its faculty and infuse its curriculum, not merely its theology courses, with its own version of Christian ethics, or it must cease to be Catholic in any respect other than in its claims on government subsidies. To be sure, some Catholic universities do just that—which means only that a good deal of prostitution is taking place. A Catholic university must be allowed to discriminate and to stand on its prejudices. But to be allowed to do so, society must acknowledge the legitimacy of some claims of discrimination and prejudice. It does not follow that any institution should be allowed to discriminate at will. Collective historical experience has prior claims. The United States has paid a terrible price for racism, and nothing should prevent its placing racial discrimination beyond the pale. But it does follow that such strictures should be held to the barest minimum.

It also follows that a democracy imposed upon, say, a Catholic university would threaten institutional autonomy and distinctiveness, especially if the university were prevented from prejudicing the hiring of faculty to guarantee a critical mass of Catholics. At that, anyone who has received the sacrament of confirmation could claim to be a Catholic and yet be ready, as so many are these days, to treat the standards of the Church with contempt. How long would it take for such a faculty, acting democratically, to destroy the very Catholicity of the university? To put it another way, only a strong dose of institutional authority and hierarchy could preserve the distinctiveness essential to the preservation of freedom—and even of democracy, sensibly construed—in the larger society.

Beyond the universities lie the churches themselves. Are we prepared to impose egalitarian and antihierarchical notions upon the episcopal and other noncongregational churches? If so, what becomes of religious freedom? And never mind that liberals could reasonably crow that, even in the Catholic Church, the laity is doing the job for them. Sanity may yet return to the laity, or the laity may be put down by the Pope, who, whatever his faults, gives no sign of being a fool or a marshmallow.

Our institutions, voluntary and not-so-voluntary, are the closest thing we have to the historically evolved communities so dear to the hearts of traditionalists. They require governmental nurturing in a world increasingly dominated by corporate conglomerates that live easily with the cultural radicalism which threatens to bring all institutions and communities under the rule of a nationally numerical but economically powerless majority. The process of political centralization and democratization is strengthening—by no means weakening—an economic centralization that is indifferent to moral considerations.

According to the free marketeer's best-case scenario, a well ordered international economy should be able to deliver affluence to enough Americans to allow us to write off the rest—with or without an occasional crackdown on the lower-class losers in the competitive struggle. Even Francis Fukuyama, the leading exponent of the "end of history" thesis, describes multinational finance capitalism as inherently and indeed proudly amoral and notes that the emerging business and technocratic elite can live happily with a wide array of social policies, just so long as they do not seriously interfere with business. Social and moral questions are beside the point. We may very well be on the threshold of that brave new world of affluent depravity for many people and unspeakable misery for many others which Weaver described as a world of animal relationships. Fukuyama observes: "It should not be surprising that the strength of community life has declined in America. This decline has occurred not *despite* liberal principles, but because of them. This suggests that no fundamental strengthening of community life will be possible unless individuals give back certain of their rights to communities, and accept the return of certain historical forms of intolerance."[10]

The perspectives offered by southern conservatives, which I have hastily sketched, remain alive, if at bay: opposition to finance capitalism and, more broadly, to the attempt to substitute the market for society itself; opposition to the radical individualism that is today sweeping America; support for broad property ownership and a market economy subject to socially determined moral restraints; adherence to a Christian individualism that condemns personal license and demands submission to a moral consensus rooted in elementary piety; and an insistence that every people must develop its own genius, based upon its special history, and must reject siren calls to an internationalism—or rather, a cosmopolitanism—that would eradicate local and national cultures and standards of personal conduct by reducing morals and all else to commodities.

Consider these perspectives in the wake of the collapse of socialism and the astonishing worldwide economic integration that is taking place under the aegis of multinational corporate conglomerates. We are today staring at statistics that project the destruction of much of the young black male population of the United States. If the projection proves accurate, a substantial majority of black males by age twenty-five or so will be dead, in jail, on drugs, effectively uneducated, or unemployable. The faceless makers and shakers of the emerging world economic order neither desire that result nor are conspiring to bring it about. It is just not their problem, any more than the collapse of the family, the inundation of society by drugs, pornography, and sheer filth, or a host of other matters are their problems. Filth, like everything else, is a commodity, and if people choose to buy and sell it, very well. They will thereby create jobs in a burgeoning industry.

The basic problem with the ascendancy of the multinationals is not that they are hierarchical, cruel, or ill intentioned, however much they may be charged on all counts. Rather, it is that they are literally irresponsible. They operate under few if any moral constraints and can, with formal justification, claim not to be responsible for the creeping genocide in America or the savaging of the Third World, or the moral degeneracy of modern life.

Yet if a return to small private property is a will-o'-the-wisp, the substitution of state property for private has everywhere generated terrifying political regimes and, for good measure, economic incompetence. Thus, either we rethink the nature of property itself and devise forms that combine private ownership with a high level of social participation and control, or we decide to live in the world of Richard Weaver's "moral idiots"—a world comfortable for some or even many and brutal beyond description for the rest.

The southern conservatives' critique of capitalism has always existed in severe tension with their distrust of big government. Those who, notwithstanding a renewed fervor for protectionism in foreign trade, condemn the atomizing effects of finance capitalism continue to gag on the government intervention in the economy that, under present international conditions, may well be essential to combat it. In the ideal world of the southern conservatives, we would be our brothers' keepers, but only as individuals or through our families, churches, and local communities. Time has run out for a substantial realization of any such dream. The restoration—or, better, the recasting—of the traditional family would itself require considerable interaction among government, churches, and other private institutions.

Meanwhile, we continue to be inundated with nihilistic assaults on the very notion of legitimate authority and with appeals to a personal liberation that would unleash the worst in all of us. Consider the Critical Legal Studies movement, which embraces many of the best minds on the American Left and unselfishly defends the poor and vulnerable against palpable injustices. Its theorists rail endlessly against "illegitimate authority" but have yet to present their own notion of legitimate authority. We may, if we wish, sneer at southern-conservative calls for piety and respect for natural law—that is, for recognition that there are many things no regime has a right to do to people, no matter how wide and democratically constructed the consensus behind it. But it remains unclear that we have anything to put in their place.

The fashionable calls for ever more participatory democracy, combined with contempt for authority and social discipline, logically ought to lead to a demand for the very decentralization of power that the southern conservatives have always stood for. Unfortunately, decentralization of power often produces local policies other than those which radical democrats want. In consequence, not only do we end up with support for Jacobin centralization, but, since the people cannot be trusted on that level either, we end up with demands that the courts and the bureaucracy—the institutions farthest removed from popular control—legislate for us on such burning issues as abortion and homosexuality. One would think that democrats, especially radical democrats, would want such questions settled directly by the people or their elected representatives.

We face the contradictions and dangers inherent in all political and ideological camps. The reemergence of nationalisms and tribalisms demonstrates the desperate attempt of peoples to take their lives into their own hands in the wake of an unprecedented concentration of power by international economic and cultural elites. Simultaneously, it is unleashing a new wave of barbarism and massive bloodletting. Calhoun's questions are striking back at us. How do we strengthen the political power of states and communities while recognizing the indispensability of the federal government in the solution of vast international as well as national problems? How do we resist a transformation of the market from a necessary center of the economy into a substitute for society itself? How do we recover a sense of national purpose and moral consensus while reinvigorating family and community autonomy?

Southern conservatives as well as Marxists may here appeal to a rich historical experience to sustain their view that the ownership and effective management of property remain essential. If so, then in the revolutionary economic transformation of our time the whole people must acquire not merely a stake in ownership but the ultimate control of management. True, private ownership and the exercise of firm authority in management are essential for economic efficiency as well as the preservation of freedom. But then, the alternative to present arrangements may well reside in the extension of republican political principles to the economy—to a constitutional arrangement that protects private interests, including the right to inherit property, while it respects the ultimate power of the people, acting collectively, to establish proper limits on individual action. At issue here is the challenge to devise property relations that can sustain a "social bond individualism" strong enough to repress both personal license and totalitarian tendencies.

If we need to devise a creative system that combines social and private property ownership and renders it politically responsible; if we need to find ways to strengthen the political power of states and communities while recognizing the indispensability of a strong federal government in the solution of vast problems; if we are not to transform the market as a necessary center of the economy into a substitute for society itself; if we are to recover a sense of national purpose and moral consensus—then southern conservative thought, shorn of its errors and irrationalities, has at least as strong a claim to a respectful hearing as any competing body of doctrine.

A few grim thoughts are nonetheless in order. The southern-conservative intellectuals dare not drift too far from their political base. We saw the results of their being imprisoned by racism during the struggle for racial integration. Recently, in Louisiana they faced a formidable challenge from the latest of those anything-but-conservative politicians who steal their thunder and play to the worst instincts of white people. David Duke may look like a messiah to those dispossessed, alienated, and ignored souls for whom southern conservatives have always tried to speak. Primarily, however, we need fear him as a political John the Baptist who has prepared the way for a more plausible leader without a neo-Nazi past. Should the dark clouds on the international economic horizon thicken, the David Dukes may yet inherit the American earth—the northern earth even more readily than the southern. If so, the intellectual efforts of the southern conservatives are likely to reduce to little more than ill-digested fodder for demagogues who appeal to selected portions of the letter of their teachings while destroying the spirit.

The free marketeers wish no one ill, but their happy dream of a well ordered international economy of morally indifferent affluence for many and misery for those who cannot compete—a dream that constitutes my own private nightmare—is becoming a reality. We may indeed be on the threshold of a brave new world of affluent depravity for a good many people, perhaps even a majority of Americans. If so, I am glad to be too old to have to live with the worst of what is coming.

The current national drift into an ever deepening moral and political paralysis can be arrested. Here, too, the southern experience counsels against gloom and passivity. The people of the South have suffered defeat in war, have seen the collapse of their fondest expectations, and have accepted it all as God's will. However distasteful many of their reactions in time and place, they have struggled bravely against cynicism and despair and have been well served by their trust in God and in their own free will.[11] In their own way they have lived by Romain Rolland's great dictum, "Pessimism of the intellect! Optimism of the will!" As to the prospects for a constructive outcome to the time of troubles in which we live, the more generous and worldly side of the southern tradition offers its own special combination of hope and caution. Robert E. Lee expressed it well shortly before he died. General Lee, then a college president, jotted down these few lines, for what purpose we do not know:

> My experience of men has neither disposed me to think worse of them; nor indisposed me to serve them; nor in spite of failures, which I lament, of errors, which I now see and acknowledge, or of the present state of affairs, do I despair of the future. The march of Providence is so slow, and our desires so impatient, the work of progress is so immense, and our means of aiding it so feeble, the life of humanity is so long, and that of the individual so brief, that we often see only the ebb of the advancing wave, and are thus discouraged. It is history that teaches us to hope.[12]

## NOTES

1.  Richard M. Weaver, *The Southern Tradition at Bay* (Washington, D.C.: Regnery Gateway, 1989), p. 73. Finally, we have a much needed first-rate study of Henry Hughes. See Douglas Ambrose, "'The Man for Times Coming': The Life and Thought of Henry Hughes" (diss.: State University of New York at Binghamton, 1991), a revised version of which will soon be published.

    Parenthetically, southern conservatives have had a hard time sorting out their attitudes toward the Populists, fearing their social radicalism and the threat posed by the very existence of their movement to the unity of the community, but admiring their opposition to big business and their defense of the small farmer. And when the Watsons and Tillmans emerged as race-baiting demagogues, the more genteel of the conservatives drew back in disgust. The result in the complex politics of the South has been the failure of southern conservatism to confront the Populist experience and to formulate a critique of its strengths and weaknesses. Bradford, however, did take up this subject in "Word from the Forks of the Creek: The Revolution and the Populist Heritage," *A Better Guide than Reason: Studies in the American Revolution* (La Salle, Ill.: Sherwood Sugden, 1979), pp. 59–76. Also Havard and Sullivan, "Introduction," in *Band of Prophets*, p. 5.

2.  Albert Einstein invited Sigmund Freud to offer an analysis of the prospects for world peace. Freud, as might have been expected, was not optimistic. In a response that occasioned some surprise, Einstein, although cautiously optimistic, agreed with Freud's claim that there is an aggressive instinct in human beings. See Albert Einstein and Sigmund Freud, *Why War?* trans. Stuart Gilbert (Geneva: International Institute of Intellectual Co-Operation, League of Nations, 1933).

3.  Weaver, "The Tennessee Agrarians," in *Southern Essays*, p. 12; also, idem, "Southern Chivalry and Total War," p. 169. See also Bradford, *Reactionary Imperative*, pp. 94–95, 205–217. The language used by Pope John Paul II in his critique of scientism and its outcome in the threat of nuclear war strongly resembles that of the Agrarians, Weaver, and Bradford. See the encyclical *Centesimus Annus* (Washington: U.S. Catholic Conference, 1981), no. 18.

    Weaver's stance here recalls that of his German contemporary Carl Schmitt, who sought to reassert Vattel's effort to accept war with limits to its legitimate goals and practices—that is, to treat war as a limited quarrel between states rather than as an ideological crusade. Alas, Schmitt eventually joined the Nazi Party, apparently in the forlorn hope that he could help civilize the powers-that-be. Notwithstanding Schmitt's services to the Nazis, his political theory proved largely unassimilable to their ideology. See Paul A. Gottfried, *Carl Schmitt: Politics and Theory* (New York: Greenwood Press, 1990), pp. 9–10, 27, 80–81.

4.  Gentile, *Genesis and Structure of Society*, p. 164. Gentile, here and elsewhere, seems to have made concessions to those fascist intransigents who berated him as a closet liberal, but on this issue the intransigents, not Gentile, set the party line.

5.  See *Chronicles: A Magazine of American Culture*, the issues during the war in the Persian Gulf.

6.  Reed, "The Same Old Stand," in Fifteen Southerners, *Why the South Will Survive*, pp. 21–22.

7.  For a critical discussion of Owsley's views, see Reed, "For Dixieland: The Sectionalism of *I'll Take My Stand*," in Havard and Sullivan, eds., *Band of Prophets*, p. 50.

8.  A caveat: A left-wing friend who read a draft of this book remarked, "I'd like to agree with your discussion of universities, but alas, I don't. I think the real universities of the future will probably be found in basements, backrooms, and garages—and will probably be illegal." He may well be right. But here, I am discussing principles and possibilities, not prophesying. The current situation is appalling and will probably get worse. But as my friend would agree, that probability is no excuse for fatalism and apathy.

9.  For an elaboration, see Eugene D. Genovese, "Critical Legal Studies as Radical Politics and World View," *Yale Journal of Law and Humanities* 3 (Winter 1991): 131–156, from which I have lifted some passages.

10. Francis Fukuyama, *The End of History and the Last Man* (New York: Free Press, 1992), p. 328.

11. Yes, trust in their own free will. The widespread notion that the South was conquered by Calvinist predestinarianism is a figment of historians' imagination, as Elizabeth Fox-Genovese and I shall try to demonstrate in a forthcoming book on the life and mind of the slaveholders.

12. Quoted in Richard Weaver, "Lee the Philosopher," *Southern Essays*, pp. 179–180.

*1993*

# WENDELL BERRY

Poet, novelist, environmentalist, cultural critic, political activist, and Kentucky farmer, Wendell Berry (b. 1934) is the intellectual heir of the Agrarians of the 1930s.

―――――

# Local Knowledge in the
# Age of Information

I N 1983, reviewing a book of agricultural essays by Wes Jackson and one by me, Lewis Hyde suggested that our two books were part of an effort of the periphery to be heard by the center. This has stayed in my mind as perhaps the most useful thing that has been said about my agricultural writing and that of my allies. It is useful because the dichotomy between center and periphery does in fact exist, as does the tendency of the center to be ignorant of the periphery.

These terms appear to be plain enough, but as I am going to use them here they may need a little clarification. We can say, for example, that a land grant university is a center with a designated periphery which it is supposed to maintain and improve. Or an industrial city is a center with a periphery which it is bound to influence and which, according to its politics and its power, it may either conserve or damage. Or a national or a state government is a center solemnly entrusted with responsibility for peripheral places, but in general it extends its protections and favors to the commercial centers, which outvote or out-"contribute" the periphery. But above all, now, as a sort of center of centers, is the global "free market" economy of the great corporations, the periphery of which is everywhere, and for its periphery this center expresses no concern and acknowledges no responsibility.

The global economy is a development—it is intended apparently as the culmination—of the technological and commercial colonialist orthodoxy that has dominated the world increasingly since the Renaissance, the principle of the orthodoxy being that any commercial entity is entitled to wealth according to its power. A center, then, as I will use the term, is wherever the wealth, power, and knowledge of this overbearing economy have accumulated. Modern technology, as it has developed from oceanic navigation to the World Wide Web, has been increasingly a centralizing force, enabling ever larger accumulations of wealth, power, and knowledge in an ever smaller number of centers.

Since my concern here is with the need for communication—or, as I would prefer to say, conversation—between periphery and center, I must begin with the center's characteristic ignorance of the periphery. This, I suppose, must always have been so, even of the market towns of the world before the Renaissance. But in that older world, the cities and towns mostly (though with significant exceptions) could take for granted that their tributary landscapes were populated by established rural communities that knew both how to make the land produce and how to take care of it.

It is still true that the center is supported by the periphery. All human economy is still land-based. To the extent that we must eat and drink and be clothed, sheltered, and warmed, we live from the land. The idea that we have now progressed from a land-based economy to an economy based on information is a fantasy.

It is still true also that the people of the center believe that the people of the periphery will always supply their needs from the land and will always keep the land productive: there will always be an abundance of food, fiber, timber, and fuel. This too is a fantasy. It is not known, but is simply taken for granted.

As its power of attraction increases, the center becomes more ignorant of the periphery. And under the pervasive influence of the center, the economic landscapes of the periphery have fewer and fewer inhabitants who know them well and know how to care properly for them. Many rural areas are now populated mostly by urban people.

In the *New York Review of Books* of March 24, 2005, Clifford Geertz wrote that tsunamis and other large-scale disasters threaten "the conviction that perhaps most reconciles many of us . . . to our own mortality: that, though we ourselves may perish, the community into which we were born, and the sort of life it supports, will somehow live on." But except for a few of the better-established Amish communities, this conviction is an illusion; one cannot imagine how Mr. Geertz has held onto it. No matter even if "we" have stayed put geographically, if we are over thirty, or maybe even twenty, the community in which we live is by now radically unlike "the community in which we were born." In fact, there are now many people whose native communities have not only been radically changed but have been completely destroyed by some form of "development." Since the end of World War II, the economic, technological, and social forces of industrialism have pretty thoroughly disintegrated the rural communities of the United States and, I believe, of other parts of the world also, inducing in them a "mobility" that has boiled over in the cities, disintegrating them as well.

The loss of the old life of the rural communities has usually been written off as an improvement, and only sometimes lamented. Nowhere that I know has it been more knowingly and poignantly lamented than in Ernest J. Gaines's novel, *A Gathering of Old Men*, set on a sugarcane plantation in Louisiana. Here the man named Johnny Paul is speaking for the community of black field hands that he knew as a growing boy:

> Thirty, forty of us going out in the field with cane knives, hoes, plows—name it. Sunup to sundown, hard, miserable work, but we managed to get it done. We stuck together, shared what little we had, and loved and respected each other.
>
> But just look at things today. Where the people? Where the roses? Where the four-o'clocks? The palm-of-Christians? Where the people used to sing and pray in the church? I'll tell you. Under them trees back there, that's where. And where they used to stay, the weeds got it now, just waiting for the tractor to come plow it up.
>
> .   .   .   .   .   .   .   .   .   .   .   .   .   .   .   .   .   .   .   .   .
>
> You had to be here then to be able to don't see it . . . now. But I was here then, and I don't see it now . . . I was scared . . . one day that tractor was go'n come in there and plow up them graves, getting rid of all proof that we ever was. Like now they trying to get rid of all proof that black people ever farmed this land with plows and mules—like if

they had nothing from the starten but motor machines. . . . Mama and
Papa worked too hard in these fields. They mama and they papa worked
too hard in these same fields. They mama and they papa people worked
too hard, too hard to have that tractor just come in that graveyard and
destroy all proof that they ever was. I'm the last one left.

This too is part of an effort of the periphery to be heard by the center.

Johnny Paul's speech, of which I have quoted only a part, is obviously eloquent and as deeply moving as he is deeply moved, but still
we are left with the question: Was what he was lamenting actually
lamentable? To begin to answer that question, we have to answer
another: Was what those people knew about their place of any value
to their place and to people in other places? Or, to state the question
a little more thematically, is there a practical reason for the periphery
to be heard by the center?

Insofar as the center is utterly dependent upon the periphery, its ignorance of the periphery is not natural or necessary, but is merely dangerous. The danger is increased when this ignorance protects itself by
contempt for the people who know. If the most intimate knowledge of
the land from which you live belongs to people whom you consider to
be provincials or field niggers or hillbillies or hicks or rednecks, then
you are not likely ever to learn very much.

Furthermore, the danger increases as the periphery is enlarged; the
vulnerability of long supply lines is well understood. To give the most
obvious example, the United States has chosen (if that is the right
word) to become an import-dependent society rather than to live principally from its own land and the work of its own people, as if dependence on imported goods and labor can be consistent with political
independence and self-determination. This inconsistency is making
us, willy-nilly, an imperial power, which perhaps increases "business
opportunities" for our government's corporate sponsors, but certainly
increases our fragility and our peril. The economic independence of
families, communities, and even regions has now been almost completely destroyed.

Far from caring for our land and our rural people, as we would do
if we understood our dependence on them, we have not, as a nation,
given them so much as a serious thought for half a century. I read, I

believe, my full share of commentary on politics and economics by accredited experts, and I can assure you that you will rarely find in any of them even a passing reference to agriculture or forestry. Our great politicians seem only dimly aware that an actual *country* lies out there beyond the places of power, wealth, and knowledge. The ultimate official word on agriculture seems to have been spoken by Dwight Eisenhower's secretary of agriculture, Ezra Taft Benson, who told the farmers to "Get big or get out."

A predominantly urban population that is contemptuous of the working people of the farms and forests cannot know enough about the country to exercise a proper responsibility for its good use. And ignorance in the center promotes ignorance on the periphery. Knowledge that is not properly valued decreases in value, and so finally is lost. It is not possible to uproot virtually the whole agricultural population by economic adversity, replacing it with machines and chemicals, and still keep local knowledge of the land and land use at a high level of competence. We still know how to make the land produce, but only temporarily, for we are losing the knowledge of how to keep it productive. Wes Jackson has written and often said that when the ratio of eyes to acres in agricultural landscapes becomes too wide, when the number of caretakers declines below a level that varies from place to place but is reckonable for every place, then good husbandry of the land becomes impossible.

The general complacency about such matters seems to rest on the assumption that science can serve as a secure connection between land and people, designing beneficent means and methods of land use and assuring the quality and purity of our food. But we cannot escape or ignore the evidence that this assumption is false.

There is, to begin with, too great a gap between the science and the practice of agriculture. This gap is inherent in the present organization of intellectual and academic life, and it formalizes the differences between knowing and doing, the laboratory or classroom and the world. It is generally true that agricultural scientists are consumers rather than producers of agricultural products. They eat with the same freedom from farmwork, weather, and the farm economy as other consumers, and perhaps with the same naïve confidence that a demand will dependably call forth a supply.

Moreover, the official agriculture of science, government, and agribusiness has been concerned almost exclusively with the ability of the land to produce food and fiber, and ultimately salaries, grants, and profits. It has correspondingly neglected its ecological and social responsibilities, and also, in many ways, its agricultural ones. It has ignored agriculture's continuing obligations to be diverse, conservative of its means, and respectful of its natural supports.

The assumption that science can serve as an adequate connector between people and land, and thus can effectively replace the common knowledge and culture of local farm communities, by now has the status of an official program—though the aim of science, more often than not, is to connect capital with profit. The ascendancy of the expert involves a withdrawal or relinquishment of confidence in local intelligence—that is, in the knowledge, experience, and mental competence of ordinary people doing ordinary work. The result, naturally, is that the competence of local intelligence has declined. We are losing the use of local minds at work on local problems. The right way to deal with a problem, supposedly, is to summon an expert from government, industry, or a university, who will recommend the newest centrally-devised mechanical or chemical solution. Thus capital supposedly replaces intelligence as the basis of work, just as information supposedly replaces land as the basis of the economy.

This would be fine, of course, if the recommended solutions were in fact solving the problems. But too often they not only fail to solve the problems, but either make them worse or replace them with new problems. And so, as we continue our enterprise of "sound science" and technological progress, our agriculture becomes more and more toxic, specialized, and impoverished of genes, breeds, and varieties; we deplete the aquifers and the rivers; our rural communities die; our fields and our food become less healthful; our food supply becomes ever more dependent on long-distance transportation and immigrant labor; our water becomes less drinkable; the hypoxic zone grows in the Gulf of Mexico.

These calamities of industrial agriculture define our need to take seriously Wes Jackson's insistence that we need a farm population large, alert, and skilled enough, not just to make the land produce, but to take the best possible care of it as well. At present we are so far from this goal that a number of depopulated rural communities in the prairie states are offering free land and other economic incentives to new settlers.

But we need to consider the possibility that even our remnant farm population possesses knowledge and experience that is indispensable in a rapidly urbanizing world. The center may need to pay attention to the periphery and accept its influence simply in order to survive. I have at hand three testimonials to the value of peripheral knowledge, and remarkably they all come from scientists. The first is from Robert B. Weeden, a biologist and writer who has done much of his work in Alaska:

> If science took on a regional/local focus, one result would be that, for the first time in three centuries, the gap between scientist and citizen would start to close. . . . [W]hat we would see is that the conduct of critiqued experiment (science) and the close observation of unfolding life (common sense) would form a team. I watched this notion be born and begin its childhood in Alaska's north. Scientists, newcomers from the south, were hired by federal agencies and oil corporations to find out something about the environments in which petroleum exploration and production would occur. Time was scarcer than money. Some of the scientists had enough casual conversation with Inuit and Yupik people to realize that if you wanted guides to the seasonal behavior of sea ice and its inhabitants, local people were far better sources than the thin and inadequate records of earlier scientists. The informal conversation grew into formal conferences, funding, and ongoing committees. To be honest, government and corporate motives were mixed, because, in addition to knowing something, native people also controlled access to places the oil folk wanted to explore. Nevertheless, two systems of knowledge did come together.

My second witness is the geographer, Carl Sauer, who wrote:

> If I should move to the center of the mass I should feel that the germinal potential was out there on the periphery.

And, finally, I offer a rather emphatic statement from the biologist Roger Payne's book, *Among Whales*:

> [A]ny observant local knows more than any visiting scientist. Always. No exceptions.

That the center at present is ignorantly dependent on the periphery does not suggest that the center is somehow inherently worthless. It is not. The periphery needs a center, just as a center needs a periphery. One is unthinkable without the other. The center collects and stores things of value. It is a place of economic and cultural exchange. It is the right place for a stockyard or a university. The distinction I am working toward is that between an ignorant center and one that is properly knowledgeable, and also that between an ignorant periphery and one that is properly knowledgeable. The critical point is that to be properly knowledgeable each must be in conversation with the other. They must know the truth of their interdependence; they must know what they *owe* to each other.

To speak of a need for knowledge, I know, is to put oneself in danger of being run over by the information economy and the communications industry hastening to the rescue with computers, data banks, PA systems, photocopiers, leaflets, and PowerPoint presentations. Despite my reputation as a Luddite, I don't want to say that the information economy is useless, but I would like to say several things meant to burden it and slow it down, and (let us hope) improve it.

First, let us consider how we have degraded this word *information*. As you would expect, in-form-ation in its root meaning has to do with the idea of form: a pattern, structure, or ordering principle. To in-form is to form from within. *Information*, in this sense, refers to teaching and learning, to the formation of a person's mind or character. But we seem to be using the word now almost exclusively to refer to a random accumulation of facts, all having the one common characteristic of availability; they can, as we are too likely to say, be "accessed." Sometimes they are available at little cost—from a public library, say, or an Extension Service bulletin. Sometimes they are available only as "intellectual property," which is available at the seller's price. At whatever cost this information is made available to its potential users, it arrives unformed and unexperienced. There is nothing deader or of more questionable value than facts in isolation.

And this exposes the problem of an information economy. The problem is in determining the value of the commodity, information being much harder to evaluate than real goods such as food, clothing, and shelter. The value of information is in its usefulness in manipulating, for better or worse, the natural world. If the result is "for better," then the information can be accounted an asset; if "for worse," then it must be booked as a liability, of less than no value. But until the information is shaped into knowledge in some particular mind and applied with or without harm to an actual place, we will not know whether or not it is an asset or how valuable an asset it is.

This warehousing of accessible information is obviously an activity of the center. Information of this sort is one of the commodities that the center collects and dispenses to the periphery. The center, as we now say, "communicates" with the periphery, the market or the factory or the university communicates with the countryside, by means of this information. Sometimes the information is sent out encoded in various kinds of technology, sometimes in printed instructions or reports, sometimes in radio or television broadcasts. And this communication is a connection between the center and the periphery.

But let us consider, secondly, that this is only half a connection. It is a one-way communication between an active sender and a passive receiver. This is why I said earlier that I prefer conversation to communication. Communication, as we have learned from our experience with the media, goes one way, from the center outward to the periphery. But a conversation goes two ways; in a conversation the communication goes back and forth. A conversation, unlike a "communication," cannot be prepared ahead of time, and it is changed as it goes along by what is said. Nobody beginning a conversation can know how it will end. And there is always the possibility that a conversation, by bringing its participants under one another's influence, will change them, possibly for the better. (*Conversation*, as I understand the term, refers to talk between or among people for their mutual edification. This excludes talk shows or call-in programs, which are commodities for consumption by a nonparticipating audience.)

Once we have proposed a conversation between center and periphery, we see immediately that what the periphery has to say to the center is critically different from what the center has to say, or at least from what it presently is saying, to the periphery.

The information that is accumulated at the center—at the corporate or academic or governmental end of the information economy—and then dispersed to the periphery tends necessarily toward the abstract or universal, toward general applicability. The Holstein cow and the

Roundup-ready soybean are, in this sense, abstractions: the artifacts of a centrally divised agriculture, in use everywhere without respect to place or to any need for local adaptation. When the periphery accepts these things uncritically, adopting the ideas and the language of the center, then it has begun to belong to the center, and usually at a considerable long-term cost to itself. The immediate cost is the loss of knowledge and language specific to localities.

But the question we are trying to raise here is: How can the best work be done? Or: How can we give the best possible care to our highly variable economic landscapes, in which no two woodlands, no two farms, and no two fields are exactly alike? If we are ever to get the right answers to this question, then the people of the periphery will have to cultivate and cherish knowledge of their places and communities, which are always to some extent unique. This will be *placed* knowledge; out of place, it is little better than ignorance; and it is learnable only at home. To speak of it will require a *placed* language, made in reference to local names, conditions, and needs. Moreover, the people of the center need to know that this local knowledge is a necessary knowledge of *their* world. They need to hear the local languages with understanding and respect—no more talk about "hicks" and "provincials" and "rednecks." A refined, discriminating knowledge of localities by the local people is indispensable if we want the most sensitive application of intelligence to local problems, if we want the best work to be done, if we want the world to last. If we give up the old orientation of agriculture to the nature of individual farms and fields, and reorient it to industry, industrial technology, and the global economy, then the result is uniformity, oversimplification, overspecialization, and (inevitably) destruction.

To use the handiest practical example, I am talking about the need for a two-way communication, a conversation, between a land grant university and the region for and to which it is responsible. The idea of the extension service should be applied to the whole institution. Not just the agricultural extension agents, but also the graduate teachers, doctors, lawyers, and other community servants should be involved. They should be carrying news from the university out into its region, of course. But this would be extension in two directions: They would also be carrying back into the university news of what is happening that works well, what is succeeding according to the best standards, what works locally. And they should be carrying back criticism also: what is *not* working, what the university is not doing that it should do, what it is doing that it should do better.

Communication is not necessarily cooperative. "Get big or get out" is a communication, and hardly expectant of a reply. But conversation is necessarily cooperative, and it can carry us, far beyond the principle of competition, to an understanding of common interest. By conversation a university or a city and its region could define themselves as one community rather than an assortment of competing interests. Center and periphery, city and country, consumers and producers do not have to define themselves as economic adversaries. They can begin to be a community simply by asking: What can we do for each other? What do you need that we can supply you with or do for you? What do you need to know that we can tell you?

Once the conversation has started, it will quickly become obvious, I think, that there must be a common, agreed-upon standard of judgment; and I think this will have to be health: the health of ecosystems and of human communities.

There will have to be also a common idea, or hope, of economic justice. The operative principles here would be production controls, to prevent surpluses from being used as a weapon against producers; and fairness, granting to small producers and tradespeople the same marketing advantages as to large ones. And so good-bye to volume discounts.

My third point is that the means of human communication are limited, and that we dare not forget this. There is some knowledge that cannot be communicated by communication technology, the accumulation of tape-recorded "oral histories" notwithstanding. For what may be the most essential knowledge, how to work well in one's place, language simply is not an adequate vehicle. To return again to land use as an example, farming itself, like life itself, is different from information or knowledge or anything else that can be verbally communicated. It is not just the local application of science; it is also the local practice of a local art and the living of a local life.

As farmers never tire of repeating, you can't learn to farm by reading a book, and you can't *tell* somebody how to farm. Older farmers I knew used to be fond of saying, "I can't tell you how to do that, but

I can put you where you can learn." There is such a thing, then, as incommunicable knowledge, knowledge that comes only by experience and by association.

There is in addition for us humans, always, the unknown, things perhaps that we need to know that we do not know and are never going to know. There is mystery. Obvious as it is, we easily forget that beyond our sciences and our arts, beyond our technology and our language, is the irreducible reality of our precious world that somehow, so far, has withstood our demands and accommodated our life, and of which we will always be dangerously ignorant.

Our great modern powers of science, technology, and industry are always offering themselves to us with the suggestion that we know enough to use them well, that we are intelligent enough to act without limit in our own behalf. But the evidence is now rapidly mounting against us. By living as we do, in our ignorance and our pride, we are diminishing our world and the possibility of life.

This is a plea for humility.

*2005*

# THE EXCEPTIONAL NATION

*America and the World*

# THEODORE ROOSEVELT

The twenty-sixth U.S. president, Theodore Roosevelt (1858–1919), was a nationalist, a war hero, and an unapologetic imperialist. He was also an explorer, conservationist, prolific writer, and ardent promoter of what were known in his day as manly virtues. This speech, delivered early in his ascent to prominence, captures several facets of Roosevelt's worldview, notably his belief in the importance of moral character.

———

# The Strenuous Life

I N SPEAKING to you, men of the greatest city of the West, men of the State which gave to the country Lincoln and Grant, men who preëminently and distinctly embody all that is most American in the American character, I wish to preach, not the doctrine of ignoble ease, but the doctrine of the strenuous life, the life of toil and effort, of labor and strife; to preach that highest form of success which comes, not to the man who desires mere easy peace, but to the man who does not shrink from danger, from hardship, or from bitter toil, and who out of these wins the splendid ultimate triumph.

A life of slothful ease, a life of that peace which springs merely from lack either of desire or of power to strive after great things, is as little worthy of a nation as of an individual. I ask only that what every self-respecting American demands from himself and from his sons shall be demanded of the American nation as a whole. Who among you would teach your boys that ease, that peace, is to be the first consideration in their eyes—to be the ultimate goal after which they strive? You men of Chicago have made this city great, you men of Illinois have done your share, and more than your share, in making America great, because you neither preach nor practise such a doctrine. You work yourselves, and you bring up your sons to work. If you are rich and are worth your salt, you will teach your sons that though they may have leisure, it is not to be spent in idleness; for wisely used leisure merely means that those who possess it, being free from the necessity of working for their livelihood, are all the more bound to carry on some kind of non-remunerative work in science, in letters, in art, in exploration, in historical research—work of the type we most need in this country, the successful carrying out of which reflects most honor upon the nation. We do not admire the man of timid peace. We admire the man who embodies victorious effort; the man who never wrongs his neighbor, who is prompt to help a friend, but who has those virile qualities necessary to win in the stern strife of actual life. It is hard to fail, but it is worse never to have tried to succeed. In this life we get nothing save by effort. Freedom from effort in the present merely means that there has been stored up effort in the past. A man can be freed from the necessity of work only by the fact that he or his fathers before him have worked to good purpose. If the freedom thus purchased is used aright, and the man still does actual work, though of a different kind, whether as a writer or a general, whether in the field of politics or in the field of exploration and adventure, he shows he deserves his good fortune. But if he treats this period of freedom from the need of actual labor as a period, not of preparation, but of mere enjoyment, even though perhaps not of vicious enjoyment, he shows that he is simply a cumberer of the earth's surface, and he surely unfits himself to hold his own with his fellows if the need to do so should again arise. A mere life of ease is not in the end a very satisfactory life, and, above all, it is a life which ultimately unfits those who follow it for serious work in the world.

In the last analysis a healthy state can exist only when the men and women who make it up lead clean, vigorous, healthy lives; when the children are so trained that they shall endeavor, not to shirk difficulties, but to overcome them; not to seek ease, but to know how to wrest triumph from toil and risk. The man must be glad to do a man's work, to dare and endure and to labor; to keep himself, and to keep those dependent upon him. The woman must be the housewife, the helpmeet of the homemaker, the wise and fearless mother of many healthy children. In one of Daudet's powerful and melancholy books he speaks of "the fear of maternity, the haunting terror of the young wife of the present day." When such words can be truthfully written of a nation, that nation is rotten to the heart's core. When men fear work or fear righteous war, when women fear motherhood, they tremble on the brink of doom; and well it is that they should vanish from the earth, where they are fit subjects for the scorn of all men and women who are themselves strong and brave and high-minded.

As it is with the individual, so it is with the nation. It is a base untruth to say that happy is the nation that has no history. Thrice happy is the nation that has a glorious history. Far better it is to dare mighty things, to win glorious triumphs, even though checkered by failure, than to take rank with those poor spirits who neither enjoy much nor suffer much, because they live in the gray twilight that knows not victory nor defeat. If in 1861 the men who loved the Union had believed that peace was the end of all things, and war and strife the worst of all things, and had acted up to their belief, we would have saved hundreds of thousands of lives, we would have saved hundreds of millions of dollars. Moreover, besides saving all the blood and treasure we then lavished, we would have prevented the heartbreak of many women, the dissolution of many homes, and we would have spared the country those months of gloom and shame when it seemed as if our armies marched only to defeat. We could have avoided all this suffering simply by shrinking from strife. And if we had thus avoided it, we would have shown that we were weaklings, and that we were unfit to stand among the great nations of the earth. Thank God for the iron in the blood of our fathers, the men who upheld the wisdom of Lincoln, and bore sword or rifle in the armies of Grant! Let us, the children of the men who proved themselves equal to the mighty days, let us, the children of the men who carried the great Civil War to a triumphant conclusion, praise the God of our fathers that the ignoble counsels of peace were rejected; that the suffering and loss, the blackness of sorrow and despair, were unflinchingly faced, and the years of strife endured; for in the end the slave was freed, the Union restored, and the mighty American republic placed once more as a helmeted queen among nations.

We of this generation do not have to face a task such as that our fathers faced, but we have our tasks, and woe to us if we fail to perform them! We cannot, if we would, play the part of China, and be content to rot by inches in ignoble ease within our borders, taking no interest in what goes on beyond them, sunk in a scrambling commercialism; heedless of the higher life, the life of aspiration, of toil and risk, busying ourselves only with the wants of our bodies for the day, until suddenly we should find, beyond a shadow of question, what China has already found, that in this world the nation that has trained itself to a career of unwarlike and isolated ease is bound, in the end, to go down before other nations which have not lost the manly and adventurous qualities. If we are to be a really great people, we must strive in good faith to play a great part in the world. We cannot avoid meeting great issues. All that we can determine for ourselves is whether we shall meet them well or ill. In 1898 we could not help being brought face to face with the problem of war with Spain. All we could decide was whether we should shrink like cowards from the contest, or enter into it as beseemed a brave and high-spirited people; and, once in, whether failure or success should crown our banners. So it is now. We cannot avoid the responsibilities that confront us in Hawaii, Cuba, Porto Rico, and the Philippines. All we can decide is whether we shall meet them in a way that will redound to the national credit, or whether we shall make of our dealings with these new problems a dark and shameful page in our history. To refuse to deal with them at all merely amounts to dealing with them badly. We have a given problem to solve. If we undertake the solution, there is, of course, always danger that we may not solve it aright; but to refuse to undertake the solution simply renders it certain that we cannot possibly solve it aright. The timid man, the lazy man, the man who distrusts his country, the over-civilized man, who has lost the great fighting, masterful virtues, the ignorant man, and the man of dull mind, whose soul is incapable of feeling the mighty lift that thrills "stern men with empires in their brains"—all these, of course, shrink from seeing the nation undertake its new duties; shrink from seeing us build a navy and an army adequate to our needs; shrink from seeing us do our share of the world's work, by bringing order out of chaos in the great, fair tropic islands from which the valor of our soldiers and sailors has driven the Spanish flag. These are the men who fear the strenuous life, who fear the only national life which is really worth leading. They believe in that cloistered life which saps the hardy virtues in a nation, as it saps them in the individual; or else they are wedded to that base spirit of gain and greed which recognizes in commercialism the be-all and end-all of national life, instead of realizing that, though an indispensable element, it is, after all, but one of the many elements that go to make up true national greatness. No country can long endure if its foundations are not laid deep in the material prosperity which comes from thrift, from business energy and enterprise, from hard, unsparing effort in the fields of industrial activity; but neither was any nation ever yet truly great if it relied upon material prosperity alone. All honor must be paid to the architects of our material prosperity, to the great captains of industry who have built our factories and our railroads, to the strong men who toil for wealth with brain or hand; for great is the debt of the nation to these and their kind. But our debt is yet greater to the men whose highest type is to be found in a statesman like Lincoln, a soldier like Grant. They showed by their lives that they recognized the law of work, the law of strife; they toiled to win a competence for themselves and those dependent upon them; but they recognized that there were yet other and even loftier duties—duties to the nation and duties to the race.

We cannot sit huddled within our own borders and avow ourselves merely an assemblage of well-to-do hucksters who care nothing for what happens beyond. Such a policy would defeat even its own end; for as the nations grow to have ever wider and wider interests, and are brought into closer and closer contact, if we are to hold our own in the struggle for naval and commercial supremacy, we must build up our power without our own borders. We must build the isthmian canal, and we must grasp the points of vantage which will enable us to have our say in deciding the destiny of the oceans of the East and the West.

So much for the commercial side. From the standpoint of international honor the argument is even stronger. The guns that thundered off Manila and Santiago left us echoes of glory, but they also left us a legacy of duty. If we drove out a mediæval tyranny only to make room for savage anarchy, we had better not have begun the task at all. It is worse than idle to say that we have no duty to perform, and can leave to their fates the islands we have conquered. Such a course would be the course of infamy. It would be followed at once by utter chaos in the wretched islands themselves. Some stronger, manlier power would have to step in and do the work, and we would have shown ourselves weaklings, unable to carry to successful completion the labors that great and high-spirited nations are eager to undertake.

The work must be done; we cannot escape our responsibility; and if we are worth our salt, we shall be glad of the chance to do the work—glad of the chance to show ourselves equal to one of the great tasks set modern civilization. But let us not deceive ourselves as to the importance of the task. Let us not be misled by vainglory into underestimating the strain it will put on our powers. Above all, let us, as we value our own self-respect, face the responsibilities with proper seriousness, courage, and high resolve. We must demand the highest order of integrity and ability in our public men who are to grapple with these new problems. We must hold to a rigid accountability those public servants who show unfaithfulness to the interests of the nation or inability to rise to the high level of the new demands upon our strength and our resources.

Of course we must remember not to judge any public servant by any one act, and especially should we beware of attacking the men who are merely the occasions and not the causes of disaster. Let me illustrate what I mean by the army and the navy. If twenty years ago we had gone to war, we should have found the navy as absolutely unprepared as the army. At that time our ships could not have encountered with success the fleets of Spain any more than nowadays we can put untrained soldiers, no matter how brave, who are armed with archaic black-powder weapons, against well-drilled regulars armed with the highest type of modern repeating rifle. But in the early eighties the attention of the nation became directed to our naval needs. Congress most wisely made a series of appropriations to build up a new navy, and under a succession of able and patriotic secretaries, of both political parties, the navy was gradually built up, until its material became equal to its splendid personnel, with the result that in the summer of 1898 it leaped to its proper place as one of the most brilliant and formidable fighting navies in the entire world. We rightly pay all honor to the men controlling the navy at the time it won these great deeds, honor to Secretary Long and Admiral Dewey, to the captains who handled the ships in action, to the daring lieutenants who braved death in the smaller craft, and to the heads of bureaus at Washington who saw that the ships were so commanded, so armed, so equipped, so well engined, as to insure the best results. But let us also keep ever in mind that all of this would not have availed if it had not been for the wisdom of the men who during the preceding fifteen years had built up the navy. Keep in mind the secretaries of the navy during those years; keep in mind the senators and congressmen who by their votes gave the money necessary to build and to armor the ships, to construct the great guns, and to train the crews; remember also those who actually did build the ships, the armor, and the guns; and remember the admirals and captains who handled battle-ship, cruiser, and torpedo-boat on the high seas, alone and in squadrons, developing the seamanship, the gunnery, and the power of acting together, which their successors utilized so gloriously at Manila and off Santiago. And, gentlemen, remember the converse, too. Remember that justice has two sides. Be just to those who built up the navy, and, for the sake of the future of the country, keep in mind those who opposed its building up. Read the "Congressional Record." Find out the senators and congressmen who opposed the grants for building the new ships; who opposed the purchase of armor, without which the ships were worthless; who opposed any adequate maintenance for the Navy Department, and strove to cut down the number of men necessary to man our fleets. The men who did these things were one and all working to bring disaster on the country. They have no share in the glory of Manila, in the honor of Santiago. They have no cause to feel proud of the valor of our sea-captains, of the renown of our flag. Their motives may or may not have been good, but their acts were heavily fraught with evil. They did ill for the national honor, and we won in spite of their sinister opposition.

Now, apply all this to our public men of to-day. Our army has never been built up as it should be built up. I shall not discuss with an audience like this the puerile suggestion that a nation of seventy millions of freemen is in danger of losing its liberties from the existence of an army of one hundred thousand men, three fourths of whom will be employed in certain foreign islands, in certain coast fortresses, and on Indian reservations. No man of good sense and stout heart can take such a proposition seriously. If we are such weaklings as the proposition implies, then we are unworthy of freedom in any event. To no body of men in the United States is the country so much indebted as to the splendid officers and enlisted men of the regular army and navy. There is no body from which the country has less to fear, and none of which it should be prouder, none which it should be more anxious to upbuild.

Our army needs complete reorganization,—not merely enlarging,—and the reorganization can only come as the result of legislation. A proper general staff should be established, and the positions of ordnance, commissary, and quartermaster officers should be filled by detail from the line. Above all, the army must be given the chance to exercise in large bodies. Never again should we see, as we saw in the Spanish war, major-generals in command of divisions who had never before commanded three companies together in the field. Yet, incredible to relate, Congress has shown a queer inability to learn some of the lessons of the war. There were large bodies of men in both branches who opposed the declaration of war, who opposed the ratification of peace, who opposed the upbuilding of the army, and who even opposed the purchase of armor at a reasonable price for the battle-ships and cruisers, thereby putting an absolute stop to the building of any new fighting-ships for the navy. If, during the years to come, any disaster should befall our arms, afloat or ashore, and thereby any shame come to the United States, remember that the blame will lie upon the men whose names appear upon the roll-calls of Congress on the wrong side of these great questions. On them will lie the burden of any loss of our soldiers and sailors, of any dishonor to the flag; and upon you and the people of this country will lie the blame if you do not repudiate, in no unmistakable way, what these men have done. The blame will not rest upon the untrained commander of untried troops, upon the civil officers of a department the organization of which has been left utterly inadequate, or upon the admiral with an insufficient number of ships; but upon the public men who have so lamentably failed in forethought as to refuse to remedy these evils long in advance, and upon the nation that stands behind those public men.

So, at the present hour, no small share of the responsibility for the blood shed in the Philippines, the blood of our brothers, and the blood of their wild and ignorant foes, lies at the thresholds of those who so long delayed the adoption of the treaty of peace, and of those who by their worse than foolish words deliberately invited a savage people to plunge into a war fraught with sure disaster for them—a war, too, in which our own brave men who follow the flag must pay with their blood for the silly, mock humanitarianism of the prattlers who sit at home in peace.

The army and the navy are the sword and the shield which this nation must carry if she is to do her duty among the nations of the earth—if she is not to stand merely as the China of the western hemisphere. Our proper conduct toward the tropic islands we have wrested from Spain is merely the form which our duty has taken at the moment. Of course we are bound to handle the affairs of our own household well. We must see that there is civic honesty, civic cleanliness, civic good sense in our home administration of city, State, and nation. We must strive for honesty in office, for honesty toward the creditors of the nation and of the individual; for the widest freedom of individual initiative where possible, and for the wisest control of individual initiative where it is hostile to the welfare of the many. But because we set our own household in order we are not thereby excused from playing our part in the great affairs of the world. A man's first duty is to his own home, but he is not thereby excused from doing his duty to the State; for if he fails in this second duty it is under the penalty of ceasing to be a free-man. In the same way, while a nation's first duty is within its own borders, it is not thereby absolved from facing its duties in the world as a whole; and if it refuses to do so, it merely forfeits its right to struggle for a place among the peoples that shape the destiny of mankind.

In the West Indies and the Philippines alike we are confronted by most difficult problems. It is cowardly to shrink from solving them in the proper way; for solved they must be, if not by us, then by some stronger and more manful race. If we are too weak, too selfish, or too foolish to solve them, some bolder and abler people must undertake the solution. Personally, I am far too firm a believer in the greatness of my country and the power of my countrymen to admit for one moment that we shall ever be driven to the ignoble alternative.

The problems are different for the different islands. Porto Rico is not large enough to stand alone. We must govern it wisely and well, primarily in the interest of its own people. Cuba is, in my judgment, entitled ultimately to settle for itself whether it shall be an independent state or an integral portion of the mightiest of republics. But until order and stable liberty are secured, we must remain in the island to insure them, and infinite tact, judgment, moderation, and courage must be shown by our military and civil representatives in keeping the island pacified, in relentlessly stamping out brigandage, in protecting all alike, and yet in showing proper recognition to the men who have fought for Cuban liberty. The Philippines offer a yet graver problem. Their population includes half-caste and native Christians, warlike Moslems, and wild pagans. Many of their people are utterly unfit for self-government, and show no signs of becoming fit. Others may in time become fit but at present can only take part in self-government under a wise supervision, at once firm and beneficent. We have driven Spanish tyranny from the islands. If we now let it be replaced by savage anarchy, our work has been for harm and not for good. I have scant patience with those who fear to undertake the task of governing the Philippines, and who openly avow that they do fear to undertake it, or that they shrink from it because of the expense and trouble; but I have even scanter patience with those who make a pretense of humanitarianism to hide and cover their timidity, and who cant about "liberty" and the "consent of the governed," in order to excuse themselves for their unwillingness to play the part of men. Their doctrines, if carried out, would make it incumbent upon us to leave the Apaches of Arizona to work out their own salvation, and to decline to interfere in a single Indian reservation. Their doctrines condemn your forefathers and mine for ever having settled in these United States.

England's rule in India and Egypt has been of great benefit to England, for it has trained up generations of men accustomed to look at the larger and loftier side of public life. It has been of even greater benefit to India and Egypt. And finally, and most of all, it has advanced the cause of civilization. So, if we do our duty aright in the Philippines, we will add to that national renown which is the highest and finest part of national life, will greatly benefit the people of the Philippine Islands, and, above all, we will play our part well in the great work of uplifting mankind. But to do this work, keep ever in mind that we must show in a very high degree the qualities of courage, of honesty, and of good judgment. Resistance must be stamped out. The first and all-important work to be done is to establish the supremacy of our flag. We must put down armed resistance before we can accomplish anything else, and there should be no parleying, no faltering, in dealing with our foe. As for those in our own country who encourage the foe, we can afford contemptuously to disregard them; but it must be remembered that their utterances are not saved from being treasonable merely by the fact that they are despicable.

When once we have put down armed resistance, when once our rule is acknowledged, then an even more difficult task will begin, for then we must see to it that the islands are administered with absolute honesty and with good judgment. If we let the public service of the islands be turned into the prey of the spoils politician, we shall have begun to tread the path which Spain trod to her own destruction. We must send out there only good and able men, chosen for their fitness, and not because of their partizan service, and these men must not only administer impartial justice to the natives and serve their own government with honesty and fidelity, but must show the utmost tact and firmness, remembering that, with such people as those with whom we are to deal, weakness is the greatest of crimes, and that next to weakness comes lack of consideration for their principles and prejudices.

I preach to you, then, my countrymen, that our country calls not for the life of ease but for the life of strenuous endeavor. The twentieth century looms before us big with the fate of many nations. If we stand idly by, if we seek merely swollen, slothful ease and ignoble peace, if we shrink from the hard contests where men must win at hazard of their lives and at the risk of all they hold dear, then the bolder and stronger peoples will pass us by, and will win for themselves the domination of the world. Let us therefore boldly face the life of strife, resolute to do our duty well and manfully; resolute to uphold righteousness by deed and by word; resolute to be both honest and brave, to serve high ideals, yet to use practical methods. Above all, let us shrink from no strife, moral or physical, within or without the nation, provided we are certain that the strife is justified, for it is only through strife, through hard and dangerous endeavor, that we shall ultimately win the goal of true national greatness.

*1899*

# HENRY CABOT LODGE

Henry Cabot Lodge (1850–1924) served as U.S. senator from Massachusetts from 1893 until his death. In 1919, as chair of the Senate Foreign Relations Committee, he led the Republican opposition to U.S. membership in the proposed League of Nations. A dramatic confrontation with Democratic president Woodrow Wilson ensued. In this speech, delivered on the floor of the Senate, Lodge explains why he opposes the League.

## Speech in the U.S. Senate on the League of Nations

M R. PRESIDENT, in the Essays of Elia, one of the most delightful is that entitled "Popular Fallacies." There is one very popular fallacy, however, which Lamb did not include in his list, and that is the common saying that history repeats itself. Universal negatives are always dangerous, but if there is anything which is fairly certain, it is that history never exactly repeats itself. Popular fallacies, nevertheless, generally have some basis, and this saying springs from the undoubted truth that mankind from generation to generation is constantly repeating itself. We have an excellent illustration of this fact in the proposed experiment now before us, of making arrangements to secure the permanent peace of the world. To assure the peace of the world by a combination of the nations is no new idea. Leaving out the leagues of antiquity and of mediæval times and going back no further than the treaty of Utrecht, at the beginning of the eighteenth century, we find that at that period a project of a treaty to establish perpetual peace was brought forward in 1713 by the Abbé de Saint-Pierre. The treaty of Utrecht was to be the basis of an international system. A

European league or Christian republic was to be set up, under which the members were to renounce the right of making war against each other and submit their disputes for arbitration to a central tribunal of the allies, the decisions of which were to be enforced by a common armament. I need not point out the resemblance between this theory and that which underlies the present league of nations. It was widely discussed during the eighteenth century, receiving much support in public opinion; and Voltaire said that the nations of Europe, united by ties of religion, institutions, and culture, were really but a single family. The idea remained in an academic condition until 1791, when under the pressure of the French Revolution Count Kaunitz sent out a circular letter in the name of Leopold, of Austria, urging that it was the duty of all the powers to make common cause for the purpose of "preserving public peace, tranquillity of States, the inviolability of possession, and the faith of treaties," which has a very familiar sound. Napoleon had a scheme of his own for consolidating the Great European peoples and establishing a central assembly, but the Napoleonic idea differed from that of the eighteenth century, as one would expect. A single great personality dominated and hovered over all. In 1804 the Emperor Alexander took up the question and urged a general treaty for the formation of a European confederation. "Why could one not submit to it," the Emperor asked, "the positive rights of nations, assure the privilege of neutrality, insert the obligation of never beginning war until all the resources which the mediation of a third party could offer have been exhausted, until the grievances have by this means been brought to light, and an effort to remove them has been made? On principles such as these one could proceed to a general pacification, and give birth to a league of which the stipulations would form, so to speak, a new code of the law of nations, while those who should try to infringe it would risk bringing upon themselves the forces of the new union."

The Emperor, moved by more immediately alluring visions, put aside this scheme at the treaty of Tilsit and then decided that peace could best be restored to the world by having two all-powerful emperors, one of the east and one of the west. After the Moscow campaign, however, he returned to his early dream. Under the influence of the Baroness von Krudener he became a devotee of a certain mystic pietism which for some time guided his public acts, and I think it may be fairly said that his liberal and popular ideas of that period, however vague and uncertain, were sufficiently genuine. Based upon the treaties of alliance against France, those of Chaumont and of Vienna, was the final treaty of Paris, of November 20, 1815. In the preamble the signatories, who were Great Britain, Austria, Russia, and Prussia, stated that it is the purpose of the ensuing treaty and their desire "to employ all their means to prevent the general tranquillity—the object of the wishes of mankind and the constant end of their efforts—from being again disturbed; desirous, moreover, to draw closer the ties which unite them for the common interests of their people, have resolved to give to the principles solemnly laid down in the treaties of Chaumont of March 1, 1814, and of Vienna of March 25, 1815, the application the most analogous to the present state of affairs, and to fix beforehand by a solemn treaty the principles which they propose to follow, in order to guarantee Europe from dangers by which she may still be menaced."

Then follow five articles which are devoted to an agreement to hold France in control and checks, based largely on other more detailed agreements. But in article 6 it is said:

> To facilitate and to secure the execution of the present treaty, and to consolidate the connections which at the present moment so closely unite the four sovereigns for the happiness of the world, the high contracting parties have agreed to renew their meeting at fixed periods, either under the immediate auspices of the sovereigns themselves, or by their respective ministers, for the purpose of consulting upon their common interests, and for the consideration of the measures which at each of those periods shall be considered the most salutary for the repose and prosperity of nations and for the maintenance of the peace of Europe.

Certainly nothing could be more ingenuous or more praiseworthy than the purposes of the alliance then formed, and yet it was this very combination of powers which was destined to grow into what has been known, and we might add cursed, throughout history as the Holy Alliance.

As early as 1818 it had become apparent that upon this innocent statement might be built an alliance which was to be used to suppress the rights of nationalities and every attempt of any oppressed people to secure their freedom. Lord Castlereagh was a Tory of the Tories, but at that time, only three years after the treaty of Paris, when the representatives of the alliance met at Aix-la-Chapelle, he began to suspect that this new European system was wholly inconsistent with the liberties to which Englishmen of all types were devoted. At the succeeding meetings, at Troppau and Laibach, his suspicion was confirmed, and England began to draw away from her partners. He had indeed determined to break with the alliance before the Congress of Verona, but his death threw the question into the hands of George Canning, who stands forth as the man who separated Great Britain from the combination of the continental powers. The attitude of England, which was defined in a memorandum where it was said that nothing could be more injurious to the idea of government generally than the belief that their force was collectively to be prostituted to the support of an established power without any consideration of the extent to which it was to be abused, led to a compromise in 1818 in which it was declared that it was the intention of the five powers, France being invited to adhere, "to maintain the intimate union, strengthened by the ties of Christian brotherhood, contracted by the sovereigns; to pronounce the object of this union to be the preservation of peace on the basis of respect for treaties." Admirable and gentle words these, setting forth purposes which all men must approve.

In 1820 the British Government stated that they were prepared to fulfill all treaty obligations, but that if it was desired "to extend the alliance, so as to include all objects, present and future, foreseen and unforeseen, it would change its character to such an extent and carry us so far that we should see in it an additional motive for adhering to our course at the risk of seeing the alliance move away from us, without our having quitted it." The Czar Alexander abandoned his Liberal theories and threw himself into the arms of Metternich, as mean a tyrant as history can show, whose sinister designs probably caused as much misery and oppression in the years which followed as have ever been evolved by one man of second-rate abilities. The three powers, Russia, Austria, and Prussia, then put out a famous protocol in which it was said that the "States which have undergone a change of government due to revolution, the results of which threaten other States, *ipso facto* cease to be members of the European alliance and remain excluded from it until their situation gives guaranties for legal order and stability. If, owing to such alterations, immediate danger threatens other States, the powers bind themselves, by peaceful means, or, if need be, by arms, to bring back the guilty State into the bosom of the great alliance." To this point had the innocent and laudable declaration of the treaty of Paris already developed. In 1822 England broke away, and Canning made no secret of his pleasure at the breach. In a letter to the British minister at St. Petersburg he said:

> So things are getting back to a wholesome state again. Every nation for itself, and God for us all. The time for Areopagus, and the like of that, is gone by.

He also said, in the same year, 1823:

> What is the influence we have had in the counsels of the alliance, and which Prince Metternich exhorts us to be so careful not to throw away? We protested at Laibach; we remonstrated at Verona. Our protest was treated as waste paper; our remonstrances mingled with the air. Our influence, if it is to be maintained abroad, must be secured in the source of strength at home; and the sources of that strength are in sympathy between the people and the Government; in the union of the public sentiment with the public counsels; in the reciprocal confidence and cooperation of the House of Commons and the Crown.

These words of Canning are as applicable and as weighty now as when they were uttered and as worthy of consideration.

The Holy Alliance, thus developed by the three continental powers and accepted by France under the Bourbons, proceeded to restore the inquisition in Spain, to establish the Neapolitan Bourbons, who for 40 years were to subject the people of southern Italy to one of the most detestable tyrannies ever known, and proposed further to interfere against the colonies in South America which had revolted from Spain and to have their case submitted to a congress of the powers. It was then that Canning made his famous statement, "We have called a new world into existence to redress the balance of the old." It was at this point also that the United States intervened. The famous message of Monroe, sent to Congress on December 2, 1823, put an end to any danger of European influence in the American Continents. A distinguished English historian, Mr. William Alison Phillips, says:

The attitude of the United States effectually prevented the attempt to extend the dictatorship of the alliance beyond the bounds of Europe, in itself a great service to mankind.

In 1825 Great Britain recognized the South American Republics. So far as the New World was concerned the Holy Alliance had failed. It was deprived of the support of France by the revolution of 1830, but it continued to exist under the guidance of Metternich and its last exploit was in 1849, when the Emperor Nicholas sent a Russian army into Hungary to crush out the struggle of Kossuth for freedom and independence.

I have taken the trouble to trace in the merest outline the development of the Holy Alliance, so hostile and dangerous to human freedom, because I think it carries with it a lesson for us at the present moment, showing as it does what may come from general propositions and declarations of purposes in which all the world agrees. Turn to the preamble of the covenant of the league of nations now before us, which states the object of the league. It is formed "in order to promote international cooperation and to achieve international peace and security by the acceptance of obligations not to resort to war, by the prescription of open, just, and honorable relations between nations, by the firm establishment of the understandings of international laws as the actual rule of conduct among governments and by the maintenance of justice and a scrupulous respect for all treaty obligations in the dealings of organized peoples with one another."

No one would contest the loftiness or the benevolence of these purposes. Brave words, indeed! They do not differ essentially from the preamble of the treaty of Paris, from which sprang the Holy Alliance. But the covenant of this league contains a provision which I do not find in the treaty of Paris, and which is as follows:

The assembly may deal at its meetings with any matter within the sphere of action of the league or affecting the peace of the world.

There is no such sweeping or far-reaching provision as that in the treaty of Paris, and yet able men developed from that treaty the Holy Alliance, which England, and later France were forced to abandon and which, for 35 years, was an unmitigated curse to the world. England broke from the Holy Alliance and the breach began three years after it was formed, because English statesmen saw that it was intended to turn the alliance—and this league is an alliance—into a means of repressing internal revolutions or insurrections. There was nothing in the treaty of Paris which warranted such action, but in this covenant of the league of nations the authority is clearly given in the third paragraph of article 3, where it is said:

> The assembly may deal at its meetings with any matter within the sphere of action of the league or affecting the peace of the world.

No revolutionary movement, no internal conflict of any magnitude can fail to affect the peace of the world. The French Revolution, which was wholly internal at the beginning, affected the peace of the world to such an extent that it brought on a world war which lasted some 25 years. Can anyone say that our Civil War did not affect the peace of the world? At this very moment, who would deny that the condition of Russia, with internal conflicts raging in all parts of that great Empire, does not affect the peace of the world and therefore come properly within the jurisdiction of the league. "Any matter affecting the peace of the world" is a very broad statement which could be made to justify almost any interference on the part of the league with the internal affairs of other countries. That this fair and obvious interpretation is the one given to it abroad is made perfectly apparent in the direct and vigorous statement of M. Clemenceau in his letter to Mr. Paderewski, in which he takes the ground in behalf of the Jews and other nationalities in Poland that they should be protected, and where he says that the associated powers would feel themselves bound to secure guaranties in Poland "of certain essential rights which will afford to the inhabitants the necessary protection, whatever changes may take place in the internal constitution of the Polish Republic." He contemplates and defends interference with the internal affairs of Poland— among other things—in behalf of a complete religious freedom, a purpose with which we all deeply sympathize. These promises of the French prime minister are embodied in effective clauses in the treaties with Germany and with Poland and deal with the internal affairs of nations, and their execution is intrusted to the "principal allied and associated powers"; that is, to the United States, Great Britain,

France, Italy, and Japan. This is a practical demonstration of what can be done under article 3 and under article 11 of the league covenant, and the authority which permits interference in behalf of religious freedom, an admirable object, is easily extended to the repression of internal disturbances which may well prove a less admirable purpose. If Europe desires such an alliance or league with a power of this kind, so be it. I have no objection, provided they do not interfere with the American Continents or force us against our will but bound by a moral obligation into all the quarrels of Europe. If England, abandoning the policy of Canning, desires to be a member of a league which has such powers as this, I have not a word to say. But I object in the strongest possible way to having the United States agree, directly or indirectly, to be controlled by a league which may at any time, and perfectly lawfully and in accordance with the terms of the covenant, be drawn in to deal with internal conflicts in other countries, no matter what those conflicts may be. We should never permit the United States to be involved in any internal conflict in another country, except by the will of her people expressed through the Congress which represents them.

With regard to wars of external aggression on a member of the league the case is perfectly clear. There can be no genuine dispute whatever about the meaning of the first clause of article 10. In the first place, it differs from every other obligation in being individual and placed upon each nation without the intervention of the league. Each nation for itself promises to respect and preserve as against external aggression the boundaries and the political independence of every member of the league. Of the right of the United States to give such a guaranty I have never had the slightest doubt, and the elaborate arguments which have been made here and the learning which has been displayed about our treaty with Granada, now Colombia, and with Panama, were not necessary for me, because, I repeat, there can be no doubt of our right to give a guaranty to another nation that we will protect its boundaries and independence. The point I wish to make is that the pledge is an individual pledge. We have, for example, given guaranties to Panama and for obvious and sufficient reasons. The application of that guaranty would not be in the slightest degree affected by 10 or 20 other nations giving the same pledge if Panama, when in danger, appealed to us to fulfill our obligation. We should be bound to do so without the slightest reference to the other guarantors. In article 10 the United States is bound on the appeal of any member of the league not only to respect but to preserve its independence and its boundaries, and that pledge if we give it, must be fulfilled.

There is to me no distinction whatever in a treaty between what some persons are pleased to call legal and moral obligations. A treaty rests and must rest, except where it is imposed under duress and securities and hostages are taken for its fulfillment, upon moral obligations. No doubt a great power impossible of coercion can cast aside a moral obligation if it sees fit and escape from the performance of the duty which it promises. The pathway of dishonor is always open. I, for one, however, cannot conceive of voting for a clause of which I disapprove because I know it can be escaped in that way. Whatever the United States agrees to, by that agreement she must abide. Nothing could so surely destroy all prospects of the world's peace as to have any powerful nation refuse to carry out an obligation, direct or indirect, because it rests only on moral grounds. Whatever we promise we must carry out to the full, "without mental reservation or purpose of evasion." To me any other attitude is inconceivable. Without the most absolute and minute good faith in carrying out a treaty to which we have agreed, without ever resorting to doubtful interpretations or to the plea that it is only a moral obligation, treaties are worthless. The greatest foundation of peace is the scrupulous observance of every promise, express or implied, of every pledge, whether it can be described as legal or moral. No vote should be given to any clause in any treaty or to any treaty except in this spirit and with this understanding.

I return, then, to the first clause of article 10. It is, I repeat, an individual obligation. It requires no action on the part of the league, except that in the second sentence the authorities of the league are to have the power to advise as to the means to be employed in order to fulfill the purpose of the first sentence. But that is a detail of execution, and I consider that we are morally and in honor bound to accept and act upon that advice. The broad fact remains that if any member of the league suffering from external aggression should appeal directly to the United States for support the United States would be bound to give that support in its own capacity and without reference to the action of other powers because the United States itself is bound, and I hope the day will never come when the United States will not carry out its promises. If that day should come, and the United States or any other great country should refuse, no matter how specious the reasons, to fulfill both in letter and spirit every obligation in this covenant, the United States would be dishonored and the league would crumble into dust, leaving behind it a legacy of wars. If China should rise up and attack Japan in an effort to undo the great wrong of the cession of the control of Shantung to that power, we should be bound under the terms of article 10 to sustain Japan against China, and a guaranty of that sort is never involved except when the question has passed beyond the stage of negotiation and has become a question for the application of force. I do not like the prospect. It shall not come into existence by any vote of mine.

Article 11 carries this danger still further, for it says:

Any war or threat of war, whether immediately affecting any of the members of the league or not, is hereby declared a matter of concern to the whole league, and the league shall take any action that shall be deemed wise and effectual to safeguard the peace of nations.

"Any war or threat of war"—that means both external aggression and internal disturbance, as I have already pointed out in dealing with article 3. "Any action" covers military action, because it covers action of any sort or kind. Let me take an example, not an imaginary case, but one which may have been overlooked because most people have not the slightest idea where or what a King of the Hedjaz is. The following dispatch appeared recently in the newspapers:

HEDJAZ AGAINST BEDOUINS.

The forces of Emir Abdullah recently suffered a grave defeat, the Wahabis attacking and capturing Kurma, east of Mecca. Ibn Savond is believed to be working in harmony with the Wahabis. A squadron of the royal air force was ordered recently to go to the assistance of King Hussein.

Hussein I take to be the Sultan of Hedjaz. He is being attacked by the Bedouins, as they are known to us, although I fancy the general knowledge about the Wahabis and Ibn Savond and Emir Abdullah is slight and the names mean but little to the American people. Nevertheless, here is a case of a member of the league—for the King of Hedjaz is such a member in good and regular standing and signed the treaty by his representatives, Mr. Rustem Haidar and Mr. Abdul Havi Aouni.

Under article 10, if King Hussein appealed to us for aid and protection against external aggression affecting his independence and the boundaries of his Kingdom, we should be bound to give that aid and protection and to send American soldiers to Arabia. It is not relevant to say that this is unlikely to occur; that Great Britain is quite able to take care of King Hussein, who is her fair creation, reminding one a little of the Mosquito King, a monarch once developed by Great Britain on the Mosquito Coast of Central America. The fact that we should not be called upon does not alter the right which the King of Hedjaz possesses to demand the sending of American troops to Arabia in order to preserve his independence against the assaults of the Wahabis or Bedouins. I am unwilling to give that right to King Hussein, and this illustrates the point which is to me the most objectionable in the league as it stands; the right of other powers to call out American troops and American ships to go to any part of the world, an obligation we are bound to fulfill under the terms of this treaty. I know the answer well—that of course they could not be sent without action by Congress. Congress would have no choice if acting in good faith, and if under article 10 any member of the league summoned us, or if under article 11 the league itself summoned us, we should be bound in honor and morally to obey. There would be no escape except by a breach of faith, and legislation by Congress under those circumstances would be a mockery of independent action. Is it too much to ask that provision should be made that American troops and American ships should never be sent anywhere or ordered to take part in any conflict except after the deliberate action of the American people, expressed according to the Constitution through their chosen representatives in Congress?

Let me now briefly point out the insuperable difficulty which I find in article 15. It begins: "If there should arise between members of the league any dispute likely to lead to a rupture." "Any dispute" covers every possible dispute. It therefore covers a dispute over tariff duties and over immigration. Suppose we have a dispute with Japan or with some European country as to immigration. I put aside tariff duties as less important than immigration. This is not an imaginary case. Of late years there has probably been more international discussion and negotiation about questions growing out of immigration laws than any other one subject. It comes within the definition of "any dispute" at the beginning of article 15. In the eighth paragraph of that article it is said that "if the dispute between the parties is claimed by one of them, and is found by the council to arise out of a matter which, by international law, is solely within the domestic jurisdiction of that party, the council shall so report and shall make no recommendation as to its settlement." That is one of the statements, of which there are several in this treaty, where words are used which it is difficult to believe their authors could have written down in seriousness. They seem to have been put in for the same purpose as what is known in natural history as protective coloring. Protective coloring is intended so to merge the animal, the bird, or the insect in its background that it will be indistinguishable from its surroundings and difficult, if not impossible, to find the elusive and hidden bird, animal, or insect. Protective coloring here is used in the form of words to give an impression that we are perfectly safe upon immigration and tariffs, for example, because questions which international law holds to be solely within domestic jurisdiction are not to have any recommendation from the council, but the dangers are there just the same, like the cunningly colored insect on the tree or the young bird crouching motionless upon the sand. The words and the coloring are alike intended to deceive. I wish somebody would point out to me those provisions of international law which make a list of questions which are hard and fast within the domestic jurisdiction. No such distinction can be applied to tariff duties or immigration, nor indeed finally and conclusively to any subject. Have we not seen the school laws of California, most domestic of subjects, rise to the dignity of a grave international dispute? No doubt both import duties and immigration are primarily domestic questions, but they both constantly involve and will continue to involve international effects. Like the protective coloration, this paragraph is wholly worthless unless it is successful in screening from the observer the existence of the animal, insect, or bird which it is desired to conceal. It fails to do so and the real object is detected. But even if this bit of deception was omitted—and so far as the question of immigration or tariff questions are concerned it might as well be—the ninth paragraph brings the important point clearly to the front. Immigration, which is the example I took, cannot escape the action of the league by any claim of domestic jurisdiction; it has too many international aspects.

Article 9 says:

> The council may, in any case under this article, refer the dispute to the assembly.

We have our dispute as to immigration with Japan or with one of the Balkan States, let us say. The council has the power to refer the dispute to the assembly. Moreover the dispute shall be so referred at the request of either party to the dispute, provided that such request be made within 14 days after the submission of the dispute to the council. So that Japan or the Balkan States, for example, with which we may easily have the dispute, ask that it be referred to the assembly and the immigration question between the United States and Jugoslavia or Japan as the case may be, goes to the assembly. The United States and Japan or Jugoslavia are excluded from voting and the provision of article 12, relating to the action and powers of the council apply to the action and powers of the assembly provided, as set forth in article 15, that a report made by the assembly "if concurred in by the representatives of those members of the league represented on the council and of a majority of the other members of the league, exclusive in each case of the representatives of the parties to the dispute, shall have the same force as a report by the council concurred in by all the members thereof other than the representatives of one or more of the parties to the dispute." This course of procedure having been pursued, we find the question of immigration between the United States and Japan is before the assembly for decision. The representatives of the council, except the delegates of the United States and of Japan or Jugoslavia, must all vote unanimously upon it as I understand it, but a majority of the entire assembly, where the council will have only seven votes, will decide. Can anyone say beforehand what the decision of that assembly will be, in which the United States and Jugoslavia or Japan will have no vote? The question in one case may affect immigration from every country in Europe, although the dispute exists only for one, and in the other the whole matter of Asiatic immigration is involved. Is it too fanciful to think that it might be decided against us? For my purpose it matters not whether it is decided for or against us. An immigration dispute or a dispute over tariff duties, met by the procedure set forth in article 15, comes before the assembly of delegates for a decision by what is practically a majority vote of the entire assembly. That is something to which I do not find myself able to give my assent. So far as immigration is concerned, and also so far as tariff duties, although less important, are concerned, I deny the jurisdiction. There should be no possibility of other nations deciding who shall come into the United States, or under what conditions they shall enter. The right to say who shall come into a country is one of the very highest attributes of sovereignty. If a nation cannot say without appeal who shall come within its gates and become a part of its citizenship it has ceased to be a sovereign nation. It has become a tributary and a subject nation, and it makes no difference whether it is subject to a league or to a conqueror.

If other nations are willing to subject themselves to such a domination, the United States, to which many immigrants have come and many more will come, ought never to submit to it for a moment. They tell us that so far as Asiatic emigration is concerned there is not the slightest danger that that will ever be forced upon us by the league, because Australia and Canada and New Zealand are equally opposed to it. I think it highly improbable that it would be forced upon us under those conditions, but it is by no means impossible. It is true the United States has one vote and that England, if you count the King of the Hedjaz, has seven—in all eight—votes; yet it might not be impossible for Japan and China and Siam to rally enough other votes to defeat us; but whether we are protected in that way or not does not matter. The very offering of that explanation accepts the jurisdiction of the league, and personally, I cannot consent to putting the protection of my country and of her workingmen against undesirable immigration, out of our own hands. We and we alone must say who shall come into the United States and become citizens of this Republic, and no one else should have any power to utter one word in regard to it.

Article 21 says:

Nothing in this covenant shall be deemed to affect the validity of international engagements, such as treaties of arbitration or regional understandings like the Monroe doctrine for securing the maintenance of peace.

The provision did not appear in the first draft of the covenant, and when the President explained the second draft of the convention in the peace conference he said:

Article 21 is new.

And that was all he said. No one can question the truth of the remark, but I trust I shall not be considered disrespectful if I say that it was not an illuminating statement. The article was new, but the fact of its novelty, which the President declared, was known to everyone who had taken the trouble to read the two documents. We were not left, however, without a fitting explanation. The British delegation took it upon themselves to explain article 21 at some length, and this is what they said:

Article 21 makes it clear that the covenant is not intended to abrogate or weaken any other agreements, so long as they are consistent with its own terms, into which members of the league may have entered or may hereafter enter for the assurance of peace. Such agreements would include special treaties for compulsory arbitration and military conventions that are genuinely defensive.

The Monroe doctrine and similar understandings are put in the same category. They have shown themselves in history to be not instruments of national ambition, but guarantees of peace. The origin of the Monroe doctrine is well known. It was proclaimed in 1823 to prevent America from becoming a theater for intrigues of European absolutism. At first a principle of American foreign policy, it has become an international understanding, and it is not illegitimate for the people of the United States to say that the covenant should recognize that fact.

In its essence it is consistent with the spirit of the covenant, and, indeed, the principles of the league, as expressed in article 10, represent the extension to the whole world of the principles of the doctrine, while, should any dispute as to the meaning of the latter ever arise between the American and European powers, the league is there to settle it.

The explanation of Great Britain received the assent of France.

It seems to me monumentally paradoxical and a trifle infantile—

Says M. Lausanne, editor of the *Matin* and a chief spokesman for M. Clemenceau—

to pretend the contrary.

When the executive council of the league of nations fixes the "reasonable limits of the armament of Peru"; when it shall demand information concerning the naval program of Brazil (art. 7 of the covenant); when it shall tell Argentina what shall be the measure of the "contribution to the armed forces to protect the signature of the social covenant" (art. 16); when it shall demand the immediate registration of the treaty between the United States and Canada at the seat of the league, it will control, whether it wills or not, the destinies of America.

And when the American States shall be obliged to take a hand in every war or menace of war in Europe (art. 11) they will necessarily fall afoul of the fundamental principle laid down by Monroe.

* * * If the league takes in the world, then Europe must mix in the affairs of America; if only Europe is included, then America will violate of necessity her own doctrine by intermixing in the affairs of Europe.

It has seemed to me that the British delegation traveled a little out of the precincts of the peace conference when they undertook to explain the Monroe doctrine and tell the United States what it was and what it was not proposed to do with it under the new article. That, however, is merely a matter of taste and judgment. Their statement that the Monroe doctrine under this article, if any question arose in regard to it, would be passed upon and interpreted by the league of nations is absolutely correct. There is no doubt that this is what the article means. Great Britain so stated it, and no American authority, whether friendly or unfriendly to the league, has dared to question it. I have wondered a little why it was left to the British delegation to explain this article, which so nearly concerns the United States, but that was merely a fugitive thought upon which I will not dwell. The statement of M. Lausanne is equally explicit and truthful, but he makes one mistake. He says, in substance, that if we are to meddle in Europe, Europe cannot be excluded from the Americas. He overlooks the fact that the Monroe doctrine also says:

> Our policy in regard to Europe, which was adopted at an early stage of the wars which have so long agitated that quarter of the globe, nevertheless remains the same, which is not to interfere in the internal concerns of any of the powers.

The Monroe doctrine was the corollary of Washington's neutrality policy and of his injunction against permanent alliances. It reiterates and reaffirms the principle. We do not seek to meddle in the affairs of Europe and keep Europe out of the Americas. It is as important to keep the United States out of European affairs as to keep Europe out of the American Continents. Let us maintain the Monroe doctrine, then, in its entirety, and not only preserve our own safety, but in this way best promote the real peace of the world. Whenever the preservation of freedom and civilization and the overthrow of a menacing world conqueror summon us we shall respond fully and nobly, as we did in 1917. He who doubts that we could do so has little faith in America. But let it be our own act and not done reluctantly by the coercion of other nations, at the bidding or by the permission of other countries.

Let me now deal with the article itself. We have here some protective coloration again. The Monroe doctrine is described as a "regional understanding" whatever that may mean. The boundaries between the States of the Union, I suppose, are "regional understandings," if anyone chooses to apply to them that somewhat swollen phraseology. But the Monroe doctrine is no more a regional understanding than it is an "international engagement." The Monroe doctrine was a policy declared by President Monroe. Its immediate purpose was to shut out Europe from interfering with the South American Republics, which the Holy Alliance designed to do. It was stated broadly, however, as we all know, and went much further than that. It was, as I have just said, the corollary of Washington's declaration against our interfering in European questions. It was so regarded by Jefferson at the time and by John Quincy Adams, who formulated it, and by President Monroe, who declared it. It rested firmly on the great law of self-preservation, which is the basic principle of every independent State.

It is not necessary to trace its history or to point out the extensions which it has received or its universal acceptance by all American statesmen without regard to party. All Americans have always been for it. They may not have known its details or read all the many discussions in regard to it, but they knew that it was an American doctrine and that, broadly stated, it meant the exclusion of Europe from interference with American affairs and from any attempt to colonize or set up new States within the boundaries of the American Continent. I repeat it was purely an American doctrine, a purely American policy, designed and wisely designed for our defense. It has never been an "international engagement." No nation has ever formally recognized it. It has been the subject of reservation at international conventions by American delegates. It has never been a "regional understanding" or an understanding of any kind with anybody. It was the declaration of the United States of America, in their own behalf, supported by their own power. They brought it into being, and its life was predicated on the force which the United States could place behind it. Unless the United States could sustain it it would die. The United States has supported it. It has lived—strong, efficient, respected. It is now proposed to kill it by a provision in a treaty for a league of nations.

The instant that the United States, who declared, interpreted, and sustained the doctrine, ceases to be the sole judge of what it means, that instant the Monroe doctrine ceases and disappears from history and from the face of the earth. I think it is just as undesirable to have Europe interfere in American affairs now as Mr. Monroe thought it was in 1823, and equally undesirable that we should be compelled to involve ourselves in all the wars and brawls of Europe. The Monroe doctrine has made for peace. Without the Monroe doctrine we should have had many a struggle with European powers to save ourselves from possible assault and certainly from the necessity of becoming a great military power, always under arms and always ready to resist invasion from States in our near neighborhood. In the interests of the peace of the world it is now proposed to wipe away this American policy, which has been a bulwark and a barrier for peace. With one exception it has always been successful, and then success was only delayed. When we were torn by civil war France saw fit to enter Mexico and endeavored to establish an empire there. When our hands were once free the empire perished, and with it the unhappy tool of the third Napoleon. If the United States had not been rent by civil war no such attempt would have been made, and nothing better illustrates the value to the cause of peace of the Monroe doctrine. Why, in the name of peace, should we extinguish it? Why, in the name of peace, should we be called upon to leave the interpretation of the Monroe doctrine to other nations? It is an American policy. It is our own. It has guarded us well, and I, for one, can never find consent in my heart to destroy it by a clause in a treaty and hand over its body for dissection to the nations of Europe. If we need authority to demonstrate what the Monroe doctrine has meant to the United States we cannot do better than quote the words of Grover Cleveland, who directed Mr. Olney to notify the world that "to-day the United States is practically sovereign on this continent, and its fiat is law to which it confines its interposition." Theodore Roosevelt, in the last article written before his death, warned us, his countrymen, that we are "in honor bound to keep ourselves so prepared that the Monroe doctrine shall be accepted as immutable international law." Grover Cleveland was a Democrat and Theodore Roosevelt was a Republican, but they were both Americans, and it is the American spirit which has carried this country always to victory and which should govern us to-day, and not the international spirit which would in the name of peace hand the United States over bound hand and foot to obey the fiat of other powers.

Another point in this covenant where change must be made in order to protect the safety of the United States in the future is in article 1, where withdrawal is provided for. This provision was an attempt to meet the very general objection to the first draft of the league, that there was no means of getting out of it without denouncing the treaty; that is, there was no arrangement for the withdrawal of any nation. As it now stands it reads that—

> "Any member of the league may, after two years' notice of its intention to do so, withdraw from the league, provided that all its international obligations, and all its obligations under this covenant shall have been fulfilled at the time of its withdrawal."

The right of withdrawal is given by this clause, although the time for notice, two years, is altogether too long. Six months or a year would be found, I think, in most treaties to be the normal period fixed for notice of withdrawal. But whatever virtue there may be in the right thus conferred is completely nullified by the proviso. The right of withdrawal cannot be exercised until all the international obligations and all the obligations of the withdrawing nations have been fulfilled. The league alone can decide whether "all international obligations and all obligations under this covenant" have been fulfilled, and this would require, under the provisions of the league, a unanimous vote so that any nation desiring to withdraw could not do so, even on the two years' notice, if one nation voted that the obligations had not been fulfilled. Remember that this gives the league not only power to review all our obligations under the covenant but all our treaties with all nations for every one of those is an "international obligation."

Are we deliberately to put ourselves in fetters and be examined by the league of nations as to whether we have kept faith with Cuba or Panama before we can be permitted to leave the league? This seems to me humiliating to say the least. The right of withdrawal, if it is to be of any value whatever, must be absolute, because otherwise a nation desiring to withdraw could be held in the league by objections from other nations until the very act which induces the nation to withdraw had been completed; until the withdrawing nation had been forced to send troops to take part in a war with which it had no concern and upon which it did not desire to enter. It seems to me vital to the safety of the United States not only that this provision should be eliminated and the right to withdraw made absolute but that the period of withdrawal should be much reduced. As it stands it is practically no better in this respect than the first league draft which contained no provision for withdrawal at all, because the proviso here inserted so incumbers it that every nation to all intents and purposes must remain a member of the league indefinitely unless all the other members are willing that it should retire. Such a provision as this, ostensibly framed to meet the objection, has the defect which other similar gestures to give an impression of meeting objections have, that it apparently keeps the promise to the ear but most certainly breaks it to the hope.

I have dwelt only upon those points which seem to me most dangerous. There are, of course, many others, but these points, in the interest not only of the safety of the United States but of the maintenance of the treaty and the peace of the world, should be dealt with here before it is too late. Once in the league the chance of amendment is so slight that it is not worth considering. Any analysis of the provisions of this league covenant, however, brings out in startling relief one great fact. Whatever may be said, it is not a league of peace; it is an alliance, dominated at the present moment by five great powers, really by three, and it has all the marks of an alliance. The development of international law is neglected. The court which is to decide disputes brought before it fills but a small place. The conditions for which this league really provides with the utmost care are political conditions, not judicial questions, to be reached by the executive council and the assembly, purely political bodies without any trace of a judicial character about them. Such being its machinery, the control being in the hands of political appointees whose votes will be controlled by interest

and expedience, it exhibits that most marked characteristic of an alliance—that its decisions are to be carried out by force. Those articles
upon which the whole structure rests are articles which provide for the
use of force; that is, for war. This league to enforce peace does a great
deal for enforcement and very little for peace. It makes more essential
provisions looking to war than to peace, for the settlement of disputes.

Article 10 I have already discussed. There is no question that the
preservation of a State against external aggression can contemplate
nothing but war. In article 11, again, the league is authorized to take
any action which may be necessary to safeguard the peace of the
world. "Any action" includes war. We also have specific provisions
for a boycott, which is a form of economic warfare. The use of troops
might be avoided but the enforcement of a boycott would require
blockades in all probability, and certainly a boycott in its essence is
simply an effort to starve a people into submission, to ruin their trade,
and, in the case of nations which are not self-supporting, to cut off
their food supply. The misery and suffering caused by such a measure
as this may easily rival that caused by actual war. Article 16 embodies the boycott and also, in the last paragraph, provides explicitly for
war. We are told that the word "recommends" has no binding force;
it constitutes a moral obligation, that is all. But it means that if we,
for example, should refuse to accept the recommendation, we should
nullify the operation of article 16 and, to that extent, of the league.
It seems to me that to attempt to relieve us of clearly imposed duties
by saying that the word "recommend" is not binding is an escape of
which no nation regarding the sanctity of treaties and its own honor
would care to avail itself. The provisions of article 16 are extended to
States outside the league who refuse to obey its command to come in
and submit themselves to its jurisdiction; another provision for war.

Taken altogether, these provisions for war present what to my mind
is the gravest objection to this league in its present form. We are told
that of course nothing will be done in the way of warlike acts without
the assent of Congress. If that is true, let us say so in the covenant.
But as it stands there is no doubt whatever in my mind that American
troops and American ships may be ordered to any part of the world
by nations other than the United States, and that is a proposition to
which I for one can never assent. It must be made perfectly clear that
no American soldiers, not even a corporal's guard, that no American

sailors, not even the crew of a submarine, can ever be engaged in war or ordered anywhere except by the constitutional authorities of the United States. To Congress is granted by the Constitution the right to declare war, and nothing that would take the troops out of the country at the bidding or demand of other nations should ever be permitted except through congressional action. The lives of Americans must never be sacrificed except by the will of the American people expressed through their chosen Representatives in Congress. This is a point upon which no doubt can be permitted. American soldiers and American sailors have never failed the country when the country called upon them. They went in their hundreds of thousands into the war just closed. They went to die for the great cause of freedom and of civilization. They went at their country's bidding and because their country summoned them to service. We were late in entering the war. We made no preparation as we ought to have done, for the ordeal which was clearly coming upon us; but we went and we turned the wavering scale. It was done by the American soldier, the American sailor, and the spirit and energy of the American people. They overrode all obstacles and all shortcomings on the part of the administration or of Congress, and gave to their country a great place in the great victory. It was the first time we had been called upon to rescue the civilized world. Did we fail? On the contrary, we succeeded, we succeeded largely and nobly, and we did it without any command from any league of nations. When the emergency came we met it and we were able to meet it because we had built up on this continent the greatest and most powerful nation in the world, built it up under our own policies, in our own way, and one great element of our strength was the fact that we had held aloof and had not thrust ourselves into European quarrels; that we had no selfish interest to serve. We made great sacrifices. We have done splendid work. I believe that we do not require to be told by foreign nations when we shall do work which freedom and civilization require. I think we can move to victory much better under our own command than under the command of others. Let us unite with the world to promote the peaceable settlement of all international disputes. Let us try to develop international law. Let us associate ourselves with the other nations for these purposes. But let us retain in our own hands and in our own control the lives of the youth of the land. Let no American be sent into battle except by the constituted authorities of his own country and by the will of the people of the United States.

Those of us, Mr. President, who are either wholly opposed to the league or who are trying to preserve the independence and the safety of the United States by changing the terms of the league and who are endeavoring to make the league, if we are to be a member of it, less certain to promote war instead of peace, have been reproached with selfishness in our outlook and with a desire to keep our country in a state of isolation. So far as the question of isolation goes, it is impossible to isolate the United States. I well remember the time, 20 years ago, when eminent Senators and other distinguished gentlemen who were opposing the Philippines and shrieking about imperialism, sneered at the statement made by some of us, that the United States had become a world power. I think no one now would question that the Spanish War marked the entrance of the United States into world affairs to a degree which had never obtained before. It was both an inevitable and an irrevocable step, and our entrance into the war with Germany certainly showed once and for all that the United States was not unmindful of its world responsibilities. We may set aside all this empty talk about isolation. Nobody expects to isolate the United States or to make it a hermit Nation, which is a sheer absurdity. But there is a wide difference between taking a suitable part and bearing a due responsibility in world affairs and plunging the United States into every controversy and conflict on the face of the globe. By meddling in all the differences which may arise among any portion or fragment of humankind we simply fritter away our influence and injure ourselves to no good purpose. We shall be of far more value to the world and its peace by occupying, so far as possible, the situation which we have occupied for the last 20 years and by adhering to the policy of Washington and Hamilton, of Jefferson and Monroe, under which we have risen to our present greatness and prosperity. The fact that we have been separated by our geographical situation and by our consistent policy from the broils of Europe has made us more than any one thing capable of performing the great work which we performed in the war against Germany, and our disinterestedness is of far more value to the world than our eternal meddling in every possible dispute could ever be.

Now, as to our selfishness. I have no desire to boast that we are better than our neighbors, but the fact remains that this Nation in making peace with Germany had not a single selfish or individual interest to serve. All we asked was that Germany should be rendered incapable of again breaking forth, with all the horrors incident to German warfare, upon an unoffending world, and that demand was shared by every free nation and indeed by humanity itself. For ourselves we asked absolutely nothing. We have not asked any government or governments to guarantee our boundaries or our political independence. We have no fear in regard to either. We have sought no territory, no privileges, no advantages, for ourselves. That is the fact. It is apparent on the face of the treaty. I do not mean to reflect upon a single one of the powers with which we have been associated in the war against Germany, but there is not one of them which has not sought individual advantages for their own national benefit. I do not criticize their desires at all. The services and sacrifices of England and France and Belgium and Italy are beyond estimate and beyond praise. I am glad they should have what they desire for their own welfare and safety. But they all receive under the peace territorial and commercial benefits. We are asked to give, and we in no way seek to take. Surely it is not too much to insist that when we are offered nothing but the opportunity to give and to aid others we should have the right to say what sacrifices we shall make and what the magnitude of our gifts shall be. In the prosecution of the war we gave unstintedly American lives and American treasure. When the war closed we had 3,000,000 men under arms. We were turning the country into a vast workshop for war. We advanced ten billions to our allies. We refused no assistance that we could possibly render. All the great energy and power of the Republic were put at the service of the good cause. We have not been ungenerous. We have been devoted to the cause of freedom, humanity, and civilization everywhere. Now we are asked, in the making of peace, to sacrifice our sovereignty in important respects, to involve ourselves almost without limit in the affairs of other nations, and to yield up policies and rights which we have maintained throughout our history. We are asked to incur liabilities to an unlimited extent and furnish assets at the same time which no man can measure. I think it is not only our right but our duty to determine how far we shall go. Not only must we look carefully to see where we are being led into endless disputes and entanglements, but we must not forget that we have in this country millions of people of foreign birth and parentage.

Our one great object is to make all these people Americans so that we may call on them to place America first and serve America as they have done in the war just closed. We cannot Americanize them if we are continually thrusting them back into the quarrels and difficulties of the countries from which they came to us. We shall fill this land with political disputes about the troubles and quarrels of other countries. We shall have a large portion of our people voting not on American questions and not on what concerns the United States but dividing on issues which concern foreign countries alone. That is an unwholesome and perilous condition to force upon this country. We must avoid it. We ought to reduce to the lowest possible point the foreign questions in which we involve ourselves. Never forget that this league is primarily—I might say overwhelmingly—a political organization, and I object strongly to having the politics of the United States turn upon disputes where deep feeling is aroused but in which we have no direct interest. It will all tend to delay the Americanization of our great population, and it is more important not only to the United States but to the peace of the world to make all these people good Americans than it is to determine that some piece of territory should belong to one European country rather than to another. For this reason I wish to limit strictly our interference in the affairs of Europe and of Africa. We have interests of our own in Asia and in the Pacific which we must guard upon our own account, but the less we undertake to play the part of umpire and thrust ourselves into European conflicts the better for the United States and for the world.

It has been reiterated here on this floor, and reiterated to the point of weariness, that in every treaty there is some sacrifice of sovereignty. That is not a universal truth by any means, but it is true of some treaties and it is a platitude which does not require reiteration. The question and the only question before us here is how much of our sovereignty we are justified in sacrificing. In what I have already said about other nations putting us into war I have covered one point of sovereignty which ought never to be yielded, the power to send American soldiers and sailors everywhere, which ought never to be taken from the American people or impaired in the slightest degree. Let us beware how we palter with our independence. We have not reached the great position from which we were able to come down into the field of battle and help to save the world from tyranny by being guided by others. Our vast power has all been built up and gathered together by ourselves alone. We forced our way upward from the days of the Revolution, through a world often hostile and always indifferent. We owe no debt to anyone except to France in that Revolution, and those policies and those rights on which our power has been founded should never be lessened or weakened. It will be no service to the world to do so and it will be of intolerable injury to the United States. We will do our share. We are ready and anxious to help in all ways to preserve the world's peace. But we can do it best by not crippling ourselves.

I am as anxious as any human being can be to have the United States render every possible service to the civilization and the peace of mankind, but I am certain we can do it best by not putting ourselves in leading strings or subjecting our policies and our sovereignty to other nations. The independence of the United States is not only more precious to ourselves but to the world than any single possession. Look at the United States to-day. We have made mistakes in the past. We have had shortcomings. We shall make mistakes in the future and fall short of our own best hopes. But none the less is there any country to-day on the face of the earth which can compare with this in ordered liberty, in peace, and in the largest freedom? I feel that I can say this without being accused of undue boastfulness, for it is the simple fact, and in making this treaty and taking on these obligations all that we do is in a spirit of unselfishness and in a desire for the good of mankind. But it is well to remember that we are dealing with nations every one of which has a direct individual interest to serve and there is grave danger in an unshared idealism. Contrast the United States with any country on the face of the earth to-day and ask yourself whether the situation of the United States is not the best to be found. I will go as far as anyone in world service, but the first step to world service is the maintenance of the United States. You may call me selfish if you will, conservative or reactionary, or use any other harsh adjective you see fit to apply, but an American I was born, an American I have remained all my life. I can never be anything else but an American, and I must think of the United States first, and when I think of the United States first in an arrangement like this I am thinking of what is best for the world, for if the United States fails the best hopes of mankind fail with it. I have never had but one allegiance—I cannot divide it now. I have loved but one flag and I cannot share that devotion and give affection to the mongrel banner invented for a league. Internationalism, illustrated by the Bolshevik and by the men to whom all countries are alike provided they can make money out of them, is to me repulsive. National I must remain, and in that way I, like all other Americans, can render the amplest service to the world. The United States is the world's best hope, but if you fetter her in the interests and quarrels of other nations, if you tangle her in the intrigues of Europe, you will destroy her power for good and endanger her very existence. Leave her to march freely through the centuries to come as in the years that have gone. Strong, generous, and confident, she has nobly served mankind. Beware how you trifle with your marvelous inheritance, this great land of ordered liberty, for if we stumble and fall, freedom and civilization everywhere will go down in ruin.

We are told that we shall "break the heart of the world" if we do not take this league just as it stands. I fear that the hearts of the vast majority of mankind would beat on strongly and steadily and without any quickening if the league were to perish altogether. If it should be effectively and beneficently changed the people who would lie awake in sorrow for a single night could be easily gathered in one not very large room, but those who would draw a long breath of relief would reach to millions.

We hear much of visions and I trust we shall continue to have visions and dream dreams of a fairer future for the race. But visions are one thing and visionaries are another, and the mechanical appliances of the rhetorician designed to give a picture of a present which does not exist and of a future which no man can predict are as unreal and shortlived as the steam or canvas clouds, the angels suspended on wires, and the artificial lights of the stage. They pass with the moment of effect and are shabby and tawdry in the daylight. Let us at least be real. Washington's entire honesty of mind and his fearless look into the face of all facts are qualities which can never go out of fashion and which we should all do well to imitate.

Ideals have been thrust upon us as an argument for the league until the healthy mind, which rejects cant, revolts from them. Are ideals confined to this deformed experiment upon a noble purpose, tainted as it is with bargains, and tied to a peace treaty which might have been disposed of long ago to the great benefit of the world if it had not been compelled to carry this rider on its back? *"Post equitem sedet atra cura,"* Horace tells us, but no blacker care ever sat behind any rider than we shall find in this covenant of doubtful and disputed interpretation as it now perches upon the treaty of peace.

No doubt many excellent and patriotic people see a coming fulfill-ment of noble ideals in the words "league for peace." We all respect and share these aspirations and desires, but some of us see no hope, but rather defeat, for them in this murky covenant. For we, too, have our ideals, even if we differ from those who have tried to establish a monopoly of idealism. Our first ideal is our country, and we see her in the future, as in the past, giving service to all her people and to the world. Our ideal of the future is that she should continue to render that service of her own free will. She has great problems of her own to solve, very grim and perilous problems, and a right solution, if we can attain to it, would largely benefit mankind. We would have our country strong to resist a peril from the West, as she has flung back the German menace from the East. We would not have our politics distracted and embittered by the dissensions of other lands. We would not have our country's vigor exhausted or her moral force abated by everlasting meddling and muddling in every quarrel, great and small, which afflicts the world. Our ideal is to make her ever stronger and better and finer, because in that way alone, as we believe, can she be of the greatest service to the world's peace and to the welfare of mankind. [Prolonged applause in the galleries.]

*1919*

# CHARLES BEARD

During the first half of the twentieth century, historians figured prominently not only in interpreting America's past but in shaping the debate on
contemporary issues. None exercised more influence over a longer period
of time than Charles Beard (1874–1948). The prolific Beard eluded easy
categorization. To some he seemed a dangerous radical. Others classified
him as an out-of-step reactionary. In the years leading up to Pearl Harbor,
Beard argued vociferously that the U.S. should not enter the war against
Nazi Germany, a position that ultimately demolished his reputation. This
famous essay captures the essence of his anti-interventionist stance.

## Giddy Minds and Foreign Quarrels: An Estimate of American Foreign Policy

I N THE fourth act of "Henry IV" the King on his death-bed gives his
son and heir the ancient advice dear to the hearts of rulers in dire
straits at home:

> I . . . had a purpose now
> To lead out many to the Holy Land,
> Lest rest and lying still might make them look
> Too near unto my state. Therefore, my Harry,
> Be it thy course, to busy giddy minds
> With foreign quarrels; that action, hence borne out,
> May waste the memory of the former days.

Since the foundation of the American Republic there has been an
endless procession of foreign quarrels with which giddy minds could

have been busied. The following brief citations from the record hint at the thousands of possibilities scattered through the days and years from George Washington's Administration to the advent of Theodore Roosevelt:

1793–1815, Revolutionary and Napoleonic wars.
1815, Alliance of England, Russia, Prussia, and Austria to hold down republican and democratic agitations.
1817, Popular outburst at Wartburg.
1819, Carlsbad decrees establish despotism in German confederation.
1820, Revolutions in Spain and Italy.
1821, War for Greek independence opens.
1822, "Triumph" of Holy Alliance over democratic movements.
1827, English Russian, and French fleets crush the Sultan's fleet at Navarino.
1828–29, Russian war on Turkey.
1830, Revolutions in France and Belgium; uprising in Poland.
1831, Insurrections in central Italy.
1838–42, British war on Afghanistan.
1840, British opium war in China.
1845, British war in the Punjab.
1847, France finishes conquest of Algeria.
1848, Revolution in France; spreads to Hungary, Germany, and Austria.
1849, Violent reaction, Austrian war on Hungary.
1851, Louis Napoleon makes a coup d'état in France.
1852, Napoleon III establishes an eighteen-year dictatorship in France.
1853, T'ai-p'ing rebellion starts in China; millions killed; great cities destroyed.
1854–56, England, France, Sardinia, and Turkey wage war on Russia.
1856–60, France and England wage war on China.
1857, Sepoy mutiny in India; vigorous suppression.
1859–60, France and Sardinia wage war on Austria.
1861, England, France, and Spain act against Mexico.
1863, Insurrection in Poland.
1864, Prussia attacks Denmark and seizes Schleswig-Holstein.
1865, Insurrection in Spain.
1866, German-Italian axis treaty; Germany wages war on Austria.
1867, Insurrection in Spain; Fenian uprisings in Ireland.
1868, Overthrow of Spanish monarchy.

1870–71, Franco-Prussian war.

1873–75, Establishment and subsequent overthrow of the Spanish republic.

1875, Insurrection against Turkey in Herzegovina.

1876, Palace revolution in Turkey and Bulgarian atrocities.

1877, Russia wages war on Turkey.

1881, France finishes conquest of Tunis.

1882, Italy makes an axis with Austria and Germany; British seize Cairo.

1883, France finishes conquest of Annam.

1885, France takes Tonkin from China by war; Serbo-Bulgarian war.

1889, Boulangism flares up and bursts in France.

1891, Franco-Russian Alliance.

1894, Persecution of Dreyfus begins.

1895, Japan finishes war on China; Jameson raid in the Transvaal.

1896, Italian war on Abyssinia.

1897, Germany seizes Kiao-chau in China; missionary troubles.

1898, Bloody uprising in Milan; British reconquer the Sudan.

1899, Britain opens war on Boer republics.

1900, Boxer rebellion.

1901, Peaceful era of Queen Victoria closes.


Until near the end of that "wonderful" century of "peace, religion, and international good faith" the Government of the United States kept aloof from the aggressions, wars, and quarrels of Europe. It proposed no world conferences for correcting the wicked, settling conflicts, and curing unrest in the four corners of the earth. From time to time, it is true, groups of American people held meetings in favor of one country or party or another, but even they did not try to force their Government to play the role of universal preceptor and manufacturer of rules for settling everybody and everything under threats of armed intervention. Only in relatively recent times has wholesale interference with foreign quarrels and disturbances become a major concern of the intelligentsia, the press, and professional politicians in the United States.

But frenetic preoccupation with foreign quarrels has now reached the proportion of a heavy industry in this country. All our universities have funds and endowments for teaching what is called "international relations," and since about 1918 a large part of this instruction has been stripped of all scientific pretensions and has been little more than propaganda for the League of Nations, collective security, collaboration with Great Britain and France, or some kind of regularized intervention by the United States Government in foreign controversies everywhere, except perhaps at Amritsar or in Syria. Hundreds of professors, instructors, and assistants, sustained by endowments, lecture to students, forums, women's clubs, academies, and dinner parties on their favorite theme—the duty of the United States to set the world aright. Peace societies, associations for the "study" of foreign affairs, councils, leagues, and committees for this and that, with millions of dollars at their disposal, are engaged in the same kind of propaganda, openly or under the guise of contemporary "scholarship."

In fact, advocacy of American interventionism and adventurism abroad has become a huge vested interest. The daily press and the radio, thriving on hourly sensations, do their best to inflame readers, listeners, and lookers with a passion for putting down the wicked abroad. Foreign propagandists, often well paid by American audiences, play the same game. And brash young tom-tom beaters in journalism, who know no history beyond a few days ago, write books on the "inside" of this or that, all directed profitably to the same end. How did we get this way? This is the fundamental question for all of us who are trying to take bearings.

II

The era of universal American jitters over foreign affairs of no vital interest to the United States was opened in full blast about 1890 by four of the most powerful agitators that ever afflicted any nation: Alfred Thayer Mahan, Theodore Roosevelt, Henry Cabot Lodge, and Albert J. Beveridge. These were the chief manufacturers of the new doctrine correctly characterized as "imperialism for America," and all of them were primarily phrase-makers, not men of hard economic experience.

The ideology for this adventure was cooked up by the bookish Mahan and was promulgated by politicians. It was "sold" to the country amid the great fright induced by the specter of Bryanism, and amid the din of the wars on Spain and the Filipinos. As the British agent who framed a portion of the new gospel for John Hay, Secretary of State presumably for the United States, shrewdly observed, this was one way of smashing the populist uprising and getting the country in hand. It was not Woodrow Wilson, the schoolmaster, who first invented the policy of running out and telling the whole world just the right thing to do. It was the new men of imperialism.

The heady ideology put forth to sustain the imperialist policy may be summarized as follows: America has grown up, has acquired man's stature and put on long pants; the frontier has passed; the continent has been rounded out; America must put aside childish things, become a great big world power, follow the example of Great Britain, France, and Germany, build a monster navy, grab colonies, sea bases, and trading posts throughout the world, plunge into every big dispute among European powers, and carry "civilization" to "backward" races.

For this creed of lunging and plunging Alfred Thayer Mahan caught the clew from Mommsen's history of Rome and furnished the sea-power slogans. An army of literary artists supplied sentimental prose and poetry. Clergymen did their bit by citing the rich opportunity to "Christianize" the heathen. Steel makers and other naval merchants put sinews of war into the propaganda chest of the Navy League and pronounced it good for business—their business, at least. Shipyard constituencies whipped up political support. The middle classes, terrorized by populism, applauded.

Albert J. Beveridge provided the eloquence: "American factories are making more than the American people can use; American soil is producing more than they can consume. Fate has written our policy for us; the trade of the world must and shall be ours. And we shall get it as our mother [England] has told us how. We will establish trading posts throughout the world. . . . We will cover the ocean with our merchant marine. We will build a navy to the measure of our greatness. Great colonies governing themselves, flying our flag and trading with us will grow about our posts of trade. Our institutions will follow our flag on the wings of our commerce. And American law, American order, American civilization, and the American flag will plant themselves on shores hitherto bloody and benighted, but by those agencies of God henceforth to be made beautiful and bright." Cheers, cheers, cheers. And mighty men among the intelligentsia joined the

Mahan-Lodge-Roosevelt-Beveridge storm troops in full cry, shouting for the new gospel, while damning Bryan as a fool, Altgeld as an anarchist, and opponents of imperialism as "white-livered cowards" and "little Americans." What a Roman holiday!

Taking advantage of the national furor over the war against Spain and the unrest created by the populist upheaval at home, the imperialist agitators "put their creed over on the country" for a brief season. As an accident of politics, Theodore Roosevelt became President of the United States and started his big parade. The water-cure torture was administered to recalcitrant Filipinos. Endless notes were written to Kaiser Wilhelm II. The Navy was sent around the world. The big stick was brandished furiously. The United States participated in the conference of the great powers at Algeciras and helped to dish Germany in a quarrel that had no relation whatever to any vital interests of this country. But from the point of view of finding outlets for "our surpluses" and bolstering up national security, the show was a farce. In an economic sense it brought an enormous expense to the nation, not the promised profit. In respect of national defense, it gave us the Achilles heel of the Philippines.

For a time the monster demonstration entertained the intelligentsia and the mobs, like a Roman circus. But underneath it all there was a revolt. The sober second sense of the country gradually came to estimate it at its true worth, that is, as a frenzy. Despite the big carousel, "pusillanimous, cowardly, contemptible mollycoddles" at home continued to insist on devoting attention to the state of the American Union.

By one of the ironies of history it fell to the lot of Wilson, whom Theodore Roosevelt hated like poison, to mount the world stage and outdo Roosevelt in using the power of the United States to set the whole world aright. Roosevelt had lunged and plunged here and there—at Pekin, Algeciras, Morocco, and other troubled spots. Wilson's ambitions were without limit. He proposed to make the wide world safe for the American brand of democracy and transform backward places into mandated trusts for civilization.

The lines of the Wilsonian creed of world interventionism and adventurism are in substance: Imperialism is bad (well, partly); every nation must have a nice constitutional government, more or less like ours; if any government dislikes the settlement made at Versailles it must put up its guns and sit down with its well-armed neighbors for a "friendly" conference; trade barriers are to be lowered and that will make everybody round the globe prosperous (almost, if not entirely); backward peoples are to be kept in order but otherwise treated nicely, as wards; the old history, full of troubles, is to be closed; brethren, and presumably sisters, are to dwell together in unity; everything in the world is to be managed as decorously as a Baptist convention presided over by the Honorable Cordell Hull; if not, we propose to fight disturbers everywhere (well, nearly everywhere). The American people did not vote for exactly this in 1916. At the very first chance, the congressional election of 1918, they expressed decided distrust and in 1920 they seemed to express more than distrust. But the intelligentsia of world affairs continued unshaken in their faith, agitation, and propaganda.

Although the Republican Party was dubbed "isolationist" after 1920, its politicians in power were really nothing of the sort. On the contrary they tried to combine the two kinds of jitters over foreign affairs that had recently been sponsored by Theodore Roosevelt and Woodrow Wilson. They sought to make the most of both kinds. They played the old Roosevelt-Lodge-Beveridge game of imperialism wherever they could and whenever they had a chance, in the Far East and in the Near East. They turned the Government of the United States into a big drumming agency for pushing the sale of goods and the lending of money abroad, and they talked vociferously about the open doors everywhere except at home. On the other hand, they lectured Soviet Russia and discoursed sagely on peace for worried mankind in the best Wilsonian style. It was near the high noon of Normalcy, while the American marines were waging peace in the Caribbean, that the State Department proudly arranged for the Kellogg Pact and the powers of the earth solemnly renounced war forever as an instrument of national policy.

But this experiment in combining two kinds of jitters did not fare any better than the experiment in taking on each kind separately. The big drumming game blew up. Foreign bonds to the tune of billions went into default. The Kellogg Pact became a gibbering ghost. The industrial boom, fed by pump priming abroad at the expense of

American investors, burst with a terrific explosion which produced the ruins amid which we now sit in sackcloth and ashes.

## III

For a brief season the American people had enough jitters at home to keep their giddy minds away from foreign affairs, and in a quest for relief they swept into office Franklin D. Roosevelt, who promised to get them out of the slough of economic despond. At first President Roosevelt concentrated his energies on those domestic measures of reform and salvation known as the New Deal. He scouted the idea that world economic conferences, tariff tinkering, and diplomatic notes could contribute materially to relieving the frightful distress at home. Slowly, however, he veered in the direction of world lecturing and interventionism, and now he displays a firm resolve to interfere with the affairs of Europe and Asia as if he were arbiter of international relations and commissioned to set the world aright. The causes of this reversal are obscure, but the fact remains. Internal and external changes may partly account for it. The state of jitters in domestic economy has not been cured by the New Deal, despite the best of intentions. And Great Britain, after playing Germany off against France and treating Russia with studied contempt, has once more got what Henry Adams called "the grizzly German terror" on her doorstep, and needs American help again.

The veering tendencies of the Roosevelt Administration are to be observed in every phase of our foreign affairs. At the outset Latin-American countries were informed that the good old imperialism of earlier times was to be renounced. In 1934 the provision of the Platt Amendment which gave the United States the "legal" right to military intervention in Cuba was abrogated. American marines were withdrawn from various places in the Caribbean region. Latin-American governments were allowed to default on their bonds held in the United States and to seize property owned by American citizens, without evoking anything stronger than diplomatic notes from Washington. Instead of thundering and drawing the sword after the style of Theodore Roosevelt and Albert Fall, the Administration has resorted to negotiation. Instead of sending marines to collect on defaulted bonds, it is arranging to use public money to revive the trade which collapsed after private lending had ended in disaster for American investors. Thus Latin-American politicians have been given smaller excuses for straining their lungs over "Yankee imperialism" and seeking counter weights in Europe.

Yet through the Latin-American negotiations, especially since 1936, the Roosevelt Administration has evidently been seeking to line up Latin-American governments in defense of "democracy," shrewdly with an eye to developing a "united front" against Hitler and Mussolini. These two disturbers of the order in Europe are not making any demands on the United States, but their efforts to get trade and win supporters in countries to the south of the Rio Grande furnish points for the Roosevelt Administration's agitation against them in Europe and at home. Things have been brought to such a pass that American citizens given to alarms are imagining German planes from Bolivia dropping bombs on peaceful people in Keokuk or Kankakee.

Schemes for promoting "democracy" in Latin America have been less successful. The people of the United States have only vague ideas about the countries below the Rio Grande, but they know enough to know that most governments in that vast region are not and never have been democracies. At the close of the year 1938, according to J. Fred Rippy, at least twelve of the twenty Latin-American countries were governed by dictators of their own and if the term is interpreted broadly, "perhaps two or three more should be added to the list." These twelve dictators "were ruling seventy-five million people in Latin America—three-fifths of its population—and dominating a land area almost twice the size of the United States." It would seem, therefore, that the rhetoric of democratic solidarity in this hemisphere does not get very far below the surface of things.

In respect of Far Eastern affairs, the Roosevelt Administration, early in its career, made a brave gesture in the direction of anti-imperialism by accepting the act of Congress granting conditional independence to the Philippines. At the moment this maneuver was widely interpreted to mean that the United States intended to withdraw its armed forces from the Orient and fix its front upon the Hawaiian line. Organized agriculture was dead set against competitive imports from the Philippines. Organized labor was firm in its opposition to the immigration of "our little brown brothers" and to the importation of cheap goods made by them in their island home. Against these two forces organized business could make no headway. From an economic point of view the whole experiment in the Philippines had been a costly fiasco, as more than one copious balance sheet demonstrated. Imperialism certainly did not provide the outlets for American "surpluses" which Senator Beveridge had promised. Besides, even amateur strategists discovered, as Theodore Roosevelt had done after the first uprush of his berserk enthusiasm, that the Philippines were the Achilles heel of American defense.

Nevertheless, the question of naval bases in the Philippines has been left hanging in the air under the terms of the independence act, and the outburst in Washington last winter over the preliminaries to the fortification of Guam indicates that someone in the Capital is toying with the idea of transforming our obvious liability in the Western Pacific into what is euphoniously called "an asset of naval power"—for exerting pressure in Asiatic affairs. That the Philippines, with Singapore not far away, could be used as a lever in world politics is obvious.

While Philippine "independence" was being promised with a great flourish and the American people were busy with their jitters at home, the Roosevelt Administration put aside the old delusion that booming "the China trade" would help in getting the country out of a depression through the sale of "our surpluses." In fact, that balloon has completely burst. For years Western merchants and their intellectual retainers, including consular agents, filled the air with a great noise about how much money could be made in China as soon as four hundred million customers got round to buying automobiles, bath-tubs, typewriters, radios, refrigerators, and sewing machines. Probably a few of these myth makers were honest. But many among them must have realized that this swarm of customers had neither the money nor the goods with which to pay for Western gadgets. However that may be, and despite tons of diplomatic notes, despite gunboats, marines, soldiers, Open Doors, and all the rest, the trade of the United States with China has been and remains relatively insignificant; in an absolute sense it is of no vital importance to the United States.

Notwithstanding this well-known fact the Roosevelt Administration, from the very outset, in dealing with China has followed rather closely the old Hay-Knox-Hughes imperialist line, laid down in the Open Door fiction supplied to the United States by British negotiators—that curious form of direct interventionism that was sold to the country as "a fair deal." Even before he was inaugurated in 1933 Franklin D. Roosevelt apparently committed himself to that amazing fantasy known as the Hoover, or Stimson, doctrine. We were "never" going to recognize any conquest of territory made contrary to treaties, especially the Kellogg "Pact." So efforts were made to induce other co-signers of Open Door and peace treaties, especially Britain and France, to join in putting the screws on Japan. But those two democracies wriggled out of the net.

Later, when Japan again started to make war on China, the President managed to instigate another European "conference," composed of governments solemnly committed to the Open Door. Our peripatetic ambassador-extraordinary, Norman Davis, was sent over the sea, to take part in the feast of reason and flow of soul. When Mr. Davis returned home a reporter asked him point blank, "Was it a bust?" He could not quite admit that, but the reporter was right. It was a bust. Yet the Roosevelt Administration still labors hard at taking the Open Door delusion seriously, and still seems to regard it as a tangible asset, at least in the manipulations of world politics.

After the Japanese invasion of China flamed up in a major war the Roosevelt Administration blew hot and cold, but ended by using the affair to strengthen its general campaign for setting the world aright. At one time it declared that it did not intend to keep American forces in China for the purpose of protecting American citizens who refused to withdraw from the war zones. American merchants in Shanghai emitted a vigorous protest. Then Secretary Hull put the soft pedal on the notion that the Government of the United States was not duty bound to uphold American rights to do business even on Chinese battlefields, and the Administration tried to make a national sensation out of the *Panay* incident.

Yet, curiously enough, this same Administration refused to find a state of war existing in China and to apply the munitions embargo to the belligerents. Voices were heard saying that an embargo would hurt China more than Japan. Perhaps that was so. Perhaps not. Anyway, Americans made hay while the sun shone by selling Japan enormous quantities of munitions and raw materials of war. The Roosevelt

Administration had run into a violent economic slump and that trade was good for American business. Every little bit of profit helped in the gray days of 1937 and 1938. Even so, Japan was included among the enemies of the United States in the Chicago speech of October 5, 1937.

The sharp shift from focussing attention on the disturbing plight of domestic economy to the concentration of attention on foreign affairs is most clearly evident in respect of European relations. Shortly after the Roosevelt Administration opened in 1933 it took part in the London world economic conference, for which President Hoover and Congress had made preparations. True to his economic style, Secretary Hull, at this mondial assembly, derided "isolationism," ridiculed the efforts of nations "by bootstrap methods" to lift themselves out of the economic crisis, declared that each nation by domestic action could improve its condition only "to a moderate extent," and offered a plan of salvation in lower trade barriers. But President Roosevelt took the onus of putting a stop to the palaver in London. The affair was another failure from the outset. If the President had waited a few months the conference would doubtless have worn itself out and adjourned. He did not wait. By a sharp message to the august assembly he exploded the works. In so doing he declared that "the sound internal economic system of a nation is a greater factor in its well being than the price of its currency in changing terms of the currencies of other nations." After proclaiming this policy he turned to the business of trying to stimulate domestic agriculture and industry by domestic action.

For a considerable time after the explosion in London, President Roosevelt gave his special attention to domestic affairs. It is true that he signed the Reciprocal Trade bill, so dear to Secretary Hull's heart, and allowed the State Department to set out on its crusade to "lower trade barriers," but at the same time he tried to keep on good terms with George N. Peek, who believed that Secretary Hull was employing sentiment—not hard-headedness—in driving trade bargains. When the plan for taking the United States into the World Court was before the Senate, the President endorsed it, but lukewarmly, and put no heavy pressure on his party's Senators to force ratification. The defeat of the project gave him no sleepless nights. By recognizing Soviet Russia he yanked the State Department out of the high dudgeon stirred up in Wilson's Administration and kept going by Hughes, Kellogg, and Stimson, and simply restored the old policy, consecrated by usage, of maintaining diplomatic relations with saints and villains abroad. This looked like attending to our own business.

The real reversal of American policy and return to constant jitters over European affairs came after the election of 1936. In the campaign of that year President Roosevelt gave no hint that he intended to take a strong hand in European quarrels. The Democratic platform, made in his own office, declared positively: "We shall continue to observe a true neutrality in the disputes of others; to be prepared resolutely to resist aggression against ourselves; to work for peace and to take the profits out of war; to guard against being drawn, by political commitments, international banking, or private trading, into any war which may develop anywhere." This looked like a pledge to keep out of foreign conflicts and wars. The pledge President Roosevelt confirmed in his Chautauqua address of August 14, 1936: "We can keep out of war if those who watch and decide have a sufficiently detailed understanding of international affairs to make certain that the small decisions of each day do not lead toward war and if, at the same time, they possess the courage to say 'no' to those who selfishly or unwisely would let us go to war." If words meant anything in 1936, those words confirmed an evident desire to avoid meddling with the incessant quarrels of Europe and Asia.

Although his platform declared that "we shall continue to observe a true neutrality in the disputes of others," President Roosevelt, in December 1936, a little more than a month after his victory in the election, moved to violate neutrality in connection with the civil war in Spain. On his initiative a bill was drafted and jammed through Congress putting an embargo on munitions to the Loyalist government at Madrid. Whether he took this action at the suggestion of Great Britain, or to parallel British action in the Non-intervention Committee, so farcical in its operations, the upshot pointed in one direction—intervention in European affairs. The embargo was a violation of international law. It was a violation of a specific treaty with Spain. It was an insult to the government of Madrid, which the Government of the United States recognized as *de facto* and *de jure*. It smoothed the way for those non-interveners, Hitler and Mussolini, to destroy that government. Whatever may have been President Roosevelt's intentions, he violated neutrality and entered into collaboration with Great Britain and France in a fateful policy which was responsible for the triumph of despotism, Hitler, and Mussolini, in Spain—the very kind of despotism and two of the biggest despots that he now denounces to the world.

The pledge of the Democratic platform stood written in the record. The Chautauqua speech of 1936 stood there also. But on October 5, 1937, President Roosevelt went to Chicago and called, in effect, for collective action by all the "democracies" against Germany, Italy, and Japan. He declared that if a holocaust came the United States could not avoid it and appealed to "the peace loving nations" to put a quarantine on aggressors. The significance of this address was grasped immediately. Advocates of collective security and collaboration with Britain and France hailed it as a sharp change of front on the part of the President. But the counter blast of criticism from all parts of the country was startling and for a few weeks President Roosevelt lapsed into silence. Nevertheless he had evidently made up his mind that he was going to take a big hand in European and Asiatic affairs anyway and that the country would have to bend to his will or break.

Additional proof of his resolve soon came. On January 28, 1938, President Roosevelt sent a resounding message to Congress on the subject of armaments. He demanded an enormous increase in naval outlays, with special emphasis on battleships, and called for a mobilization bill which had no meaning unless he wanted a huge army that could be used in Europe. This increase in armaments, he said, was made necessary by the growth of land and sea forces in other countries which "involve a threat to world peace and security." One week before this bombshell message landed in Congress, the House of Representatives had passed the regular naval appropriation bill granting the Navy substantially all that it had called for in the largest peacetime naval appropriation in the history of the country. Why had the Navy Department suddenly discovered that it needed another billion or more? This question was put to Admiral Leahy by a member of the House Committee on naval affairs, and the honest old sailor blurted out: "I am not accurately informed in regard to that."

This was the cold truth. The sudden demand for an immense increase in the Navy had not come from the Navy Department. It had come from the White House. It was not related to defending the American zone of interest in the Western hemisphere. Admiral Leahy testified that the Navy was then ready to defend this zone. The new bill took on significance and utility only in relation to the President's resolve to act as a kind of arbiter in world affairs. It is true that the Democratic managers in Congress, while pushing the bill through the House and Senate, repudiated all "quarantine" doctrines and rested their case on grounds of continental security, but by citations from the testimony of naval experts the opposition demonstrated the hollowness of all such pretensions.

Victorious in securing his extraordinary naval authorization, President Roosevelt renewed his battle in 1939. His message to Congress in January vibrated with emotions connected with foreign tumults and asserted that the United States is directly menaced by "storms from abroad." These storms, the President said, challenge "three institutions indispensable to Americans. The first is religion. It is the source of the other two—democracy and international good faith." Evidently he was clearing a way to make the next war a real holy war. This clarion call President Roosevelt followed by another demand for an increase in armaments on a scale more vast.

As if undaunted by all that had happened in the previous autumn when he had, metaphorically and yet truly speaking, gone to Munich with Chamberlain and Daladier, President Roosevelt, on April 14, 1939, issued to the world a peace appeal to Hitler and offered in exchange another round-table on disarmament and another economic conference. All the while the Tory government in Great Britain and the reactionary government in France were playing with Hitler and Mussolini and aiding in the destruction of the Spanish Republic.

Apparently indifferent to the real nature of British and French tactics, President Roosevelt and Secretary Hull grew bolder in their determination to help Britain and France in whatever they were doing. In the summer of 1939 they opened a public campaign to break down the provision of the Neutrality Act which imposed an embargo on munitions in case of a foreign war "found" by the President. They had all along covertly fought this provision, without taking the risk of officially and openly denouncing it in the name of the Administration. The will of the country to stay out of foreign wars had been too strong. That will would have to be crushed. The President and the Secretary of State were well aware that Congress was not likely to give them the coveted power to name "aggressors" and throw the country into a conflict on the side of "peace lovers"; but they were none the less resolved if possible to erase every line of the Neutrality Act that stood in the way of their running the foreign affairs of the United States on the basis of constant participation in the quarrels of Europe and Asia, with war as their *ultima ratio*.

Now President Roosevelt's foreign policy is clear as daylight. He proposes to collaborate actively with Great Britain and France in their everlasting wrangle with Germany, Italy, and Japan. He wants to wring from Congress the power to throw the whole weight of the United States on the side of Great Britain and France in negotiations, and in war if they manage to bungle the game. That using measures short of war would, it is highly probable, lead the United States into full war must be evident to all who take thought about such tactics.


IV


From the point of view of the interest of the United States as a continental nation in this hemisphere, the Roosevelt policy is, in my opinion, quixotic and dangerous. It is quixotic for the reason that it is not based upon a realistic comprehension of the long-time history of Europe and Asia and of the limited power which the United States has over the underlying economies and interests of those two continents. It assumes that the United States can in fact bring those continents into a kind of stable equilibrium, assure them the materials of a peaceful economic life, and close their history in a grand conference of the powers—perhaps as successfully as Locarno. It assumes that somebody in the White House or State Department can calculate the consequences likely to come out of the explosive forces which are hidden in the civilizations of those immense areas.

Does anyone in this country really know what is going on in Europe, behind the headlines, underneath the diplomatic documents? Is it true, as French publicists contend, that the Pope, having blessed the triumph of Franco in Spain, is striving for a union of fascist and other powers, for the secret purpose of liquidating Soviet Russia? Has Russia just grounds for distrusting the governments of Chamberlain and Daladier? If Hitler and Mussolini are liquidated either by pressure or by war, will the outcome be a Victorian democracy, a communistic revolution, or a general disintegration? Are not the powers immediately and directly entangled in all this strife in a better position to adjust their disputes than President Roosevelt and his assistants in the State Department?

Even assuming that the United States ought to do its best to help the "democracies" in Europe and Asia, the Roosevelt policy is quixotic in that it does not look far beyond a temporary pacification—a pacification that might be affected by a mere show of force or by another war. It does not propose any fundamental adjustment in the economies of nations which would provide any guarantee of peace after the temporary pacification, either by pressure or by war. And if the United States really had the knowledge, good will, and intention necessary to construct a formula for such a permanent economic peace, it does not and cannot have the power to force it upon other nations. In my opinion it does not have the knowledge, the will, or the intention.

Hence, in my judgment, it is folly for the people of the United States to embark on a vast and risky program of world pacification. We can enjoy the luxury of hating certain nations. We can indulge in the satisfaction that comes from contemplating a war to destroy them. We can rush into a combination that might temporarily check them. But, it seems to me, it would be wiser to suggest that those countries of Europe which are immediately menaced by Germany and Italy put aside their jealousies, quarrels, and enmities, and join in a combination of their own to effect control over the aggressors. If countries whose very existence seems at stake will not unite for self-protection, how can the United States hope to effect a union among them? After temporary pacification what? After war what? After peace what? To these questions the Roosevelt foreign policy makes no answer. And they are the fundamental questions.

The Roosevelt foreign policy is also quixotic because it is based on the assumption that the economy and democracy of the United States are secure, that our industry, agriculture, farmers, workers, share croppers, tenants, and millions of unemployed are safe, that the state of our public finances is impregnable, and that the future of our democracy is scatheless; so that we have the power to force pacification, self-government, and economic prosperity upon recalcitrant nations beyond two oceans. Is the management of our own affairs so efficient and so evidently successful that we may take up the role of showing other countries just how to manage their internal economies? Have we the economic and military power required to set their systems in an order to suit our predilections, even assuming that we could get wholehearted collaboration from the Tory government of Great Britain, the reactionary government of France, and the communist government of Russia? If the very idea of world economic pacification in such circumstances is not a dream of Sancho Panza, then I am unacquainted with Cervantes.

V

On what then should the foreign policy of the United States be based? Here is one answer and it is not excogitated in any professor's study or supplied by political agitators. It is the doctrine formulated by George Washington, supplemented by James Monroe, and followed by the Government of the United States until near the end of the nineteenth century, when the frenzy for foreign adventurism burst upon the country. This doctrine is simple. Europe has a set of "primary interests" which have little or no relation to us, and is constantly vexed by "ambition, rivalship, interest, humor, or caprice." The United States is a continental power separated from Europe by a wide ocean which, despite all changes in warfare, is still a powerful asset of defense. In the ordinary or regular vicissitudes of European politics the United States should not become implicated by any permanent ties. We should promote commerce, but force "nothing." We should steer clear of hates and loves. We should maintain correct and formal relations with all established governments without respect to their forms or their religions, whether Christian, Mohammedan, or Shinto, or what have you. Efforts of any European powers to seize more colonies or to oppress independent states in this hemisphere, or to extend their systems of despotism to the New World will be regarded as a matter of concern to the United States as soon as they are immediately threatened and begin to assume tangible shape.

This policy was stated positively in the early days of our Republic. It was clear. It was definite. It gave the powers of the earth something they could understand and count upon in adjusting their policies and conflicts. It was not only stated. It was acted upon with a high degree of consistency until the great frenzy overtook us. It enabled the

American people to go ahead under the principles of 1776, conquering a continent and building here a civilization which, with all its faults, has precious merits for us and is, at all events, our own. Under the shelter of this doctrine, human beings were set free to see what they could do on this continent, when emancipated from the privilege-encrusted institutions of Europe and from entanglement in the endless revolutions and wars of that continent.

Grounded in strong common sense, based on deep and bitter experience, Washington's doctrine has remained a tenacious heritage, despite the hectic interludes of the past fifty years. Owing to the growth of our nation, the development of our own industries, the expulsion of Spain from this hemisphere, and the limitations now imposed upon British ambition by European pressures, the United States can pursue this policy more securely and more effectively today than at any time in our history. In an economic sense the United States is far more independent than it was in 1783, when the Republic was launched and, what is more, is better able to defend itself against all comers. Why, as Washington asked, quit our own to stand on foreign ground?

This is a policy founded upon our geographical position and our practical interests. It can be maintained by appropriate military and naval establishments. Beyond its continental zone and adjacent waters, in Latin America, the United States should have a care; but it is sheer folly to go into hysterics and double military and naval expenditures on the rumor that Hitler or Mussolini is about to seize Brazil, or that the Japanese are building gun emplacements in Costa Rica. Beyond this hemisphere, the United States should leave disputes over territory, over the ambitions of warriors, over the intrigues of hierarchies, over forms of government, over passing myths known as ideologies—all to the nations and peoples immediately and directly affected. They have more knowledge and power in the premises than have the people and Government of the United States.

This foreign policy for the United States is based upon a recognition of the fact that no kind of international drum beating, conferring, and trading can do anything material to set our industries in full motion, raise the country from the deeps of the depression. Foreign trade is important, no doubt, but the main support for our American life is production and distribution in the United States and the way out of the present economic morass lies in the acceleration of this production and distribution at home, by domestic measures. Nothing that the United States can do in foreign negotiations can raise domestic production to the hundred billions a year that we need to put our national life, our democracy, on a foundation of internal security which will relax the present tensions and hatreds.

It is a fact, stubborn and inescapable, that since the year 1900 the annual value of American goods exported has never risen above ten per cent of the total value of exportable or movable goods produced in the United States, except during the abnormal conditions of the war years. The exact percentage was 9.7 in 1914, 9.8 in 1929, and 7.3 in 1931. If experience is any guide we may expect the amount of exportable goods actually exported to be about ten per cent of the total, and the amount consumed at home to be about ninety per cent. High tariff or low tariff, little Navy or big, good neighbor policy or saber-rattling policy, hot air or cold air, this proportion seems to be in the nature of a fixed law, certainly more fixed than most of the so-called laws of political economy.

Since this is so, then why all the furor about attaining full prosperity by "increasing" our foreign trade? Why not apply stimulants to domestic production on which we can act directly? I can conceive of no reason for all this palaver except to divert the attention of the American people from things they can do at home to things they cannot do abroad.

In the rest of the world, outside this hemisphere, our interests are remote and our power to enforce our will is relatively slight. Nothing we can do for Europeans will substantially increase our trade or add to our, or their, well-being. Nothing we can do for Asiatics will materially increase our trade or add to our, or their, well-being. With all countries in Europe and Asia, our relations should be formal and correct. As individuals we may indulge in hate and love, but the Government of the United States embarks on stormy seas when it begins to love one power and hate another officially. Great Britain has never done it. She has paid Prussians to beat Frenchmen and helped Frenchmen to beat Prussians, without official love or hatred, save in wartime, and always in the interest of her security. The charge of perfidy hurled against

Britain has been the charge of hypocrites living in glass houses while throwing bricks.

Not until some formidable European power comes into the western Atlantic, breathing the fire of aggression and conquest, need the United States become alarmed about the ups and downs of European conflicts, intrigues, aggressions, and wars. And this peril is slight at worst. To take on worries is to add useless burdens, to breed distempers at home, and to discover, in the course of time, how foolish and vain it all has been. The destiny of Europe and Asia has not been committed, under God, to the keeping of the United States; and only conceit, dreams of grandeur, vain imaginings, lust for power, or a desire to escape from our domestic perils and obligations could possibly make us suppose that Providence has appointed us his chosen people for the pacification of the earth.

And what should those who hold to such a continental policy for the United States say to the powers of Europe? They ought not to say: "Let Europe stew in its own juice; European statesmen are mere cunning intriguers; and we will have nothing to do with Europe." A wiser and juster course would be to say: "We cannot and will not underwrite in advance any power or combination of powers; let them make as best they can the adjustments required by their immediate interests in Europe, Africa, and Asia, about which they know more and over which they have great force; no European power or combination of powers can count upon material aid from the United States while pursuing a course of power politics designed to bolster up its economic interests and its military dominance; in the nature of things American sympathy will be on the side of nations that practice self-government, liberty of opinion and person, and toleration and freedom of thought and inquiry—but the United States has had one war for democracy; the United States will not guarantee the present distribution of imperial domains in Africa and Asia; it will tolerate no attempt to conquer independent states in this hemisphere and make them imperial possessions; in all sincere undertakings to make economic adjustments, reduce armaments, and co-operate in specific cases of international utility and welfare that comport with our national interest, the United States will participate within the framework of its fundamental policy respecting this hemisphere; this much, nations of Europe, and may good fortune attend you."

VI

Some of our fellow-citizens of course do not believe that America can deny or refuse to accept the obligation of directing world destiny. Mr. Walter Lippmann is among them. "Our foreign policy," he has recently said in a tone of contempt, "is regulated finally by an attempt to neutralize the fact that America has preponderant power and decisive influence in the affairs of the world. . . . What Rome was to the ancient world, what Great Britain has been to the modern world, America is to be to the world of to-morrow. . . . We cling to the mentality of a little nation on the frontiers of the civilized world, though we have the opportunity, the power, and the responsibilities of a very great nation at the center of the civilized world." These are ornate, glistening, masculine words, but are they true words and what do they mean in terms of action?

America has "preponderant power." According to the most encyclopaedic dictionary of the English language, "preponderant" means "surpassing in weight, outweighing, heavier; surpassing in influence, power, or importance." It is a word of comparison. If Mr. Lippmann's statement has a meaning that corresponds to exact usage, it means that America outweighs the rest of the world, surpasses it in influence and power. This, I submit, is false. Mr. Lippmann's "fact" is not a "fact." It is an illusion. America has power in the world, but it is not preponderant anywhere outside of this hemisphere. A lust for unattainable preponderance and a lack of sense for the limitations of power have probably done more damage to nations and the world than any other psychological force in history.

The same may be said of Mr. Lippmann's "decisive influence." Decisive means having the quality that determines a contest. There are some conceivable contests in which America could presumably exercise a determining power. Given the status of things in 1917, America probably did determine the combat outcome of the World War. But in fact America did not determine the larger outcome of the World War, either the little phase at Versailles or the multitudinous results that flowed from it. America certainly has influence in the world. Within its competence it may exercise a decisive influence in particular contests. But America does not have a decisive influence on the larger course of European and Asiatic history.

Mr. Lippmann says that America is to be "what Rome was to the ancient world." That sounds big, but the test of facts bursts the bubble. Rome conquered, ruled, and robbed other peoples from the frontier in Scotland to the sands of Arabia, from the Rhine to the Sahara, and then crumbled to ruins. Does anybody in his right mind really believe that the United States can or ought to play that role in the future, or anything akin to it? America is to be "what Great Britain has been to the modern world." Well, what has Great Britain been to the modern world? Many fine and good things, no doubt. But in terms of foreign policy, Britain swept the Spanish, the Dutch, the French, and the Germans from the surface of the seven seas. During the past three hundred years Britain has waged numerous wars on the Continent to maintain, among other things, the balance of power. Britain has wrested colonies from the Spanish, the Dutch, the French, and the Germans, has conquered, ruled, and dictated to a large part of the globe. Does anyone really believe that the United States can or ought to do all these things, or anything akin to them?

Mr. Lippmann's new brew of Roman grandeur and British philanthropy is of the same vat now used by British propagandists in appealing to Americans who have a frontier "mentality." These propagandists have at last learned that, between the submarine and airplane on the one side and events in Russia, Germany, and Italy on the other, the jig is up for British imperial dictatorship in the old style. So they welcome the rise of the United States as a sea power to help maintain "security and order," that is, the British Empire. With this, for obvious reasons, French propagandists agree. But Americans who are bent on making a civilization in the United States and defending it here will beware of all such Greeks bearing gifts and set about their own work on this continent.

Is this retreat or cowardice? Walter Lippmann says that Americans are suffering from "a national neurosis," defeatism, and "wishing to escape from their opportunities and responsibilities." In my opinion the exact opposite is the truth. American people are resolutely taking stock of their past follies. Forty years ago bright young men of tongue and pen told them they had an opportunity and responsibility to go forth and, after the manner of Rome and Britain, conquer, rule, and civilize backward peoples. And the same bright boys told them that all of this would "pay," that it would find outlets for their "surpluses" of manufactures and farm produce. It did not. Twenty-two years ago American people were told that they were to make the world safe for democracy. They nobly responded. Before they got through they heard about the secret treaties by which the Allies divided the loot. They saw the Treaty of Versailles which distributed the spoils and made an impossible "peace." What did they get out of the adventure? Wounds and deaths. The contempt of former associates—until the Americans were needed again in another war for democracy. A repudiation of debts. A huge bill of expenses. A false boom. A terrific crisis.

Those Americans who refuse to plunge blindly into the maelstrom of European and Asiatic politics are not defeatist or neurotic. They are giving evidence of sanity, not cowardice; of adult thinking as distinguished from infantilism. Experience has educated them and made them all the more determined to concentrate their energies on the making of a civilization within the circle of their continental domain. They do not propose to withdraw from the world, but they propose to deal with the world as it is and not as romantic propagandists picture it. They propose to deal with it in American terms, that is, in terms of national interest and security on this continent. Like their ancestors who made a revolution, built the Republic, and made it stick, they intend to preserve and defend the Republic, and under its shelter carry forward the work of employing their talents and resources in enriching American life. They know that this task will call for all the enlightened statesmanship, the constructive energy, and imaginative intelligence that the nation can command. America is not to be Rome or Britain. It is to be America.

*1939*

# JAMES BURNHAM

As a young academic teaching at New York University, James Burnham (1905–1987) became an enthusiastic Trotskyist. While his infatuation with left-wing radicalism had passed by the beginning of World War II, during which Burnham served in the Office of Strategic Services (OSS), the tendency toward portentousness persisted. Soon enough, he became a stalwart Cold Warrior, using the pages of William F. Buckley's *National Review* to sound the alert at any signs of backsliding in the face of evil. In that sense, Burnham was a forerunner of the neoconservatism that came to prominence around the turn of the twenty-first century.

---

## FROM *The Struggle for the World*

### THE MAIN LINE OF WORLD POLITICS

THE GREAT captains of military history, varied as they have been in every other respect, have all been noted for their grasp of what military writers call "the key to the situation." At each level of military struggle, from a brief skirmish to the grand strategy of a war or series of wars, they have understood that there is one crucial element which is this key to the situation. The key may be almost anything: a ford across a river, or a hill like Cemetery Ridge at Gettysburg; a swift blow at the enemy reserve, or the smashing of the enemy fleet as at Trafalgar or Salamis; stiff discipline on the flanks as at Cannæ, or a slow strangling blockade for an entire war; a long defensive delay to train an army or win an ally, or a surprise attack on a capital; control of the seas, the destruction of supplies, or the capture of a hero.

The great captain concentrates on the key to the situation. He sim-
plifies, even over-simplifies, knowing that, though the key alone is
not enough, without it he will never open the door. He may, if that
is his temperament, concern himself also with a thousand details. He
never allows details to distract his attention, to divert him from the
key. Often he turns the details, which in quantitative bulk total much
larger than the key, over to his subordinates. That is why the genius of
the great captain is often not apparent to others. He may seem a mere
figurehead, indolent, lethargic, letting the real work be done by those
around him. They fail to comprehend that the secret of his genius is
to know the key, to have it always in mind, and to reserve his supreme
exertion for the key, for what decides the issue.

The principles of political struggle are identical with those of military struggle. Success in both political knowledge and political practice
depends finally, as in military affairs, upon the grasp of the key to the
situation. The exact moment for the insurrection, the one issue upon
which the election will in reality revolve, the most vulnerable figure in
the opposition's leadership, the deeply felt complaint that will rouse
the masses, the particular concession that will clinch a coalition, the
guarded silence that will permit an exposure to be forgotten, the exact
bribe that will open up a new Middle Eastern sphere of influence, the
precise hour for a great speech: at each stage and level of the political
process there is just one element, or at most a very small number of
elements, which determines, which decides.

The great political leader (who is often also a great captain)—
Pericles or the elder Cato or Mohammed or Cæsar or Henry of Navarre
or Bismarck or Hamilton or Lenin or Innocent III or the younger
Pitt—focuses on the key. He feels whether it is a time for expansion
or recovery, whether the opposition will be dismayed or stimulated
by a vigorous attack, whether internal problems or external affairs are
taking political precedence. He knows, in each political phase, what
is the central challenge.

During the late 12th and for most of the 13th centuries, the Papacy
struggled with the Hohenstaufen Empire, and concluded by destroying the Hohenstaufen. For all of Italy that struggle was in those times
the key to the general political situation, no matter how it appeared to
those whose political sense was distracted by temporary and episodic

details. For the first generation of the 5th century B.C., the political key in the Aegean was the attempt of Persia to conquer the Hellenic world. All of the contests among the Greek states, and all their internal city squabbles, were in reality subordinate to the relation with Persia. For a generation in America, until it was decided by the Civil War, the key was the struggle for a united nation. Everything else in politics, foreign or domestic, was secondary. For Western Civilization as a whole at the turn of the 19th century, the key was the contest between England and France. England won, perhaps, because her governing class concentrated on the key, whereas Napoleon, only vaguely glimpsing the key with its shaft of sea power, dissipated his energies.

For a given nation, the political key is located sometimes among internal, sometimes among foreign affairs. For the United States, the key during most of its independent history has been internal: union or slavery or the opening of the West or industrialization or monopoly. For England, quite naturally, it has been more ordinarily, though by no means always, an external relation. It may be the church or the army or the peasant problem, or, for a brief period, a spectacular scandal like the Dreyfus affair or the South Sea Bubble or Teapot Dome.

We have entered a period of history in which world politics take precedence over national and internal politics, and in which world politics literally involve the entire world. During this period, now and until this period ends with the settlement, one way or another, of the problems which determine the nature of the period, all of world politics, and all of what is most important in the internal politics of each nation, are oriented around the struggle for world power between Soviet-based communism and the United States. This is now the key to the political situation. Everything else is secondary, subordinate.

The key is, much of the time, hidden. The determining struggle is not apparent in the form of individual political issues, as they arise week by week. The deceptive surface is the cause of the political disorientation and futility of so many of the observers and actors, which so particularly infect the citizens and leaders of the United States. They base their ideas and actions on the temporary form of political events, not on the controlling reality.

Yugoslavia disputes with Italy over Trieste. Chiang Kai-shek fights with Chou En-lai over North China. Armenians begin to clamor for an independent Armenia. The new Philippine government confronts a revolt of the Hukbalahaps. Poland argues with Mexico in the Security Council. The French Cabinet calls for an immediate break with Franco. Harry Lundberg and the communists fight for control of the United States waterfront. The American Labor Party and the Liberal Party jockey for position in New York State. The British Communists apply for admission to the Labour Party. The World Federation of Trade Unions demands an official voice in the United Nations. The International Harvester Company objects to sending tractors to the Balkans. Japanese printers' unions refuse to set up editorials they don't like. Sweden signs a commercial agreement with Moscow. The United States asks for bases in Iceland or the Azores. Bulgaria, Yugoslavia and Albania arm and succor Macedonian partisans. Joseph Clark Baldwin, ousted by the New York Republicans, is endorsed by Vito Marcantonio. Australia objects to the veto power.

The eyes of the public become entangled in the many-colored surface. The exact ethnic complexion of Venezia Giulia is debated with ponderous statistics. Owen Lattimore proves at length that Chiang is not quite democratic and that many peasants support Yenan. Arthur Upham Pope explains that there are reactionary landlords in Iran. Henry Wallace describes the geography of Siberia. *The Nation* catalogues the villainies of Franco. *PM* sturdily denounces the crimes of Greek Royalists. *The New Republic* gives the history of agricultural oppression in the Philippines. The innocent bystanders send in their dollars, join committees, and sign open letters.

The statistics and records and swarms of historical facts are admirable enough to have at hand. But by themselves they are shadows, ashes. If we do not look through them to the living body, the focal fire, we know nothing. If we do not grasp that Trieste and Thrace, and Armenia and Iran and North China and Sweden and Greece are the border marches between the communist power and the American power, and that all the statistics and records are filigree work on the historical structure, then we know nothing. We know less than nothing, and we fall into the trap which those who do know deliberately bait with all the statistics and records. It is their purpose to deceive us with the shadows and to prevent us from seeing the body. If we do not know that the American Labor Party has nothing to do with America or with Labor or with any of the issues stated in its program and speeches, but is simply a disguised colony of the communist power planted within the enemy territory, then, politically, we know nothing. If we do not understand that the World Federation of Trade Unions is merely a device manipulated by the N.K.V.D. to further the communist objective of infiltrating and demoralizing the opponents in the Third World War, then we have not begun to realize what is at issue in the world. The central point is not whether Chiang is a democrat—though that too is an important point—but that he is, in his own fashion, a shield of the United States against the thrust of communist power out of the Heartland. The debates in the Security Council are not really over the absurd procedural ritual that appears on the surface of the minutes. The ritual is like a stylized formal dance reflecting in art the battle of the Titans.

Walter Lippmann, after a tour of Europe in the Spring of 1946, told us in a widely publicized series of articles that the main issue of world politics was the contest between England and the Soviet Union, which was coming to a head in the struggle over Germany. The United States he found to be in the comfortable position of an impartial umpire who could generously intervene to mediate and settle the dispute. Mr. Lippmann was right in insisting on the crucial present role of the fight for Germany. But one look at the political map of Europe, with a side-glance at the state of India and the British colonies, should be enough to demonstrate that England could not possibly stand up as principal in a challenge to the communist power. England in Germany, whatever her intentions, functions as a detachment of the greater power which is the only existing rival in the championship class. If it were really England, and if the pressure of the United States were withdrawn from the European arena, the decision over Germany would long since have been announced.

The determining facts are merely these: Western Civilization has reached the stage in its development that calls for the creation of its Universal Empire. The technological and institutional character of Western Civilization is such that a Universal Empire of Western Civilization would necessarily at the same time be a World Empire. In the world there are only two power centers adequate to make a serious attempt to meet this challenge. The simultaneous existence of these two centers, and only these two, introduces into world political relationships an intolerable disequilibrium. The whole problem is made incomparably sharper and more immediate by the discovery of atomic weapons, and by the race between the two power centers for atomic supremacy, which, independently of all other historical considerations, could likewise be secured only through World Empire.

One of the two power centers is itself a child, a border area, of Western Civilization. For this reason, the United States, crude, awkward, semi-barbarian, nevertheless enters this irreconcilable conflict as the representative of Western culture. The other center, though it has already subdued great areas and populations of the West, and though it has adapted for its own use many technological and organizational devices of the West, is alien to the West in origin and fundamental nature. Its victory would, therefore, signify the reduction of all Western society to the status of a subject colony. Once again, the settled peoples of the Plains would bow to the yoke of the erupting Nomads of the Steppes. This time the Nomads have taken care to equip themselves from the arsenal of the intended slaves. The horses and dogs have been transformed into tanks and bombs. And this time the Plains are the entire Earth.

Between the two great antagonists there is this other difference, that may decide. The communist power moves toward the climax self-consciously, deliberately. Its leaders understand what is at stake. They have made their choice. All their energies, their resources, their determination, are fixed on the goal. But the Western power gropes and lurches. Few of its leaders even want to understand. Like an adolescent plunged into his first great moral problem, it wishes, above all, to avoid the responsibility for choice. Genuine moral problems are, however, inescapable, and the refusal to make a choice is also a moral decision. If a child is drowning at our feet, to turn away is to decide, as fully as to save him or to push him under. It is not our individual minds or desires, but the condition of world society, that today poses for the Soviet Union, as representative of communism, and for the United States, as representative of Western Civilization, the issue of world leadership. No wish or thought of ours can charm this issue away.

This issue will be decided, and in our day. In the course of the decision, both of the present antagonists may, it is true, be destroyed. But one of them must be.

[. . .]

## WORLD EMPIRE AND THE BALANCE OF POWER

A world federation initiated and led by the United States would be, we have recognized, a World Empire. In this imperial federation, the United States, with a monopoly of atomic weapons, would hold a preponderance of decisive material power over all the rest of the world. In world politics, that is to say, there would not be a "balance of power."

To those commentators who feel that they are displaying a badge of political virtue when they denounce the "balance of power," the prospect of its elimination ought to seem a prime asset of the policy here under discussion. Those who are not impressed with the rhetorical surface of politics will be less pleased.

At whatever level of social life, from a small community to the world at large, a balance of power is the only sure protection of individual or group liberties. Since we cannot get rid of power, the real political choice is between a balance of diverse powers and a monopoly of power. Either one power outweighs all the rest, or separately located powers check and countercheck each other. If one power outweighs all the rest, there is no effective guarantee against the abuse of that power by the group which wields it. It will seem desirable and necessary to buttress still further the power dominance, to take measures against any future threat to the power relations, to cut off at the source any trickle of potential opposition. It will seem right that those with the over-weening power should also receive material privilege commensurate with their power ranking. Only power can be counted on to check power and to hinder its abuse. Liberty, always precarious, arises out of the unstable equilibrium that results from the conflict of competing powers.

As a solution for the present crisis, might it not therefore seem that there is little objective reason to prefer a world federation under United States leadership to a communist World Empire? Of course, we might, not altogether cynically, reflect that even if our choice is only between jailers to preside over our common prison, that is still not an occasion for indifference. But is anything more at stake? Would not the United States also, if it became world leader, turn out in the end to be world tyrant?

We must begin by replying, as we have so often: it might be so. There can be no certainty against it. We must say even more than this.

There is in American life a strain of callow brutality. This betrays itself no less in the lynching and gangsterism at home than in the arrogance and hooliganism of soldiers or tourists abroad. The provincialism of the American mind expresses itself in a lack of sensitivity toward other peoples and other cultures. There is in many Americans an ignorant contempt for ideas and tradition and history, a complacency with the trifles of merely material triumph. Who, listening a few hours to the American radio, could repress a shudder if he thought that the price of survival would be the Americanization of the world?

2

We have already observed that the idea of "empire" carries with it a confused set of associations that is only remotely related to historical experience. There have been many empires, of many kinds, differing in almost every imaginable way in their social and political content. The only constant, the factor that leads us to call the given political aggregate an "empire," is the predominance—perhaps only to a very small degree—of a part over the whole.

It is by no means true that all empires are tyrannies. The Athenian Empire of the 5th century B.C. was for most of its history little more than a strengthened federation. Within the imperial state, Athens itself, there flourished the most vigorous political democracy of the ancient world, and in some respects of all time. Though Athens controlled the foreign policy of the federated cities and islands, in many instances she used her influence to promote democratic changes of their internal regimes.

The hand of England has been heavy on India, Malaysia, Ceylon, but she can hardly be accused of destroying there a liberty which never existed. And in what independent states has there been found more liberty than in her loosely dependent Dominions?

The imperial rule of Rome, especially if compared to the preexisting regimes of the areas to which it was gradually extended, was far from an unmixed despotism. For hundreds of years it was centered in an imperial state which was itself a Republic. Many of the cities and states which were added by force or maneuver were, upon affiliation, cemented by the grant not of slavery but of Roman citizenship. It would be hard to prove that Roman power meant less liberty for the inhabitants of Egypt or Thrace or Parthia.

Even the Ottoman Empire, which, entering from outside, took over the rule of the enfeebled Byzantine states in Asia Minor, the Balkans, and parts of Africa, is hardly responsible for the end of liberties which had never grown on Byzantine soil. Under the Ottoman Turks, the Christians, permitted the free practice of their religion, and eligible through the peculiar device of the slave household of the capital to the highest military and administrative positions, were more free than had been heathens or heterodox Christian sects under the Byzantine power.

I am not, certainly, trying to suggest that building an empire is the best way to protect freedom. The empires of the Mongols, of the Egyptians, the Incaic and Aztec and Babylonian and Hittite empires will scarcely be included among the friends of liberty. It does, however, seem to be the case that there is no very close causal relation between empire and liberty. The lack of liberty among the Andean or Mexican Indians, the Egyptians or Mongolians or Hittites, cannot be blamed on the imperial structures into which their societies were, at various periods, politically articulated. Within their cultures, social and political liberties, as we understand them, did not exist at any time, whether or not they were organized as empires. The degree of liberty which exists within an empire seems to be relatively independent of the mere fact of the imperial political superstructure.

The extension of an empire does, by its very nature, mean at least some reduction in the independence, or sovereignty, of whatever nations or peoples become part of the empire. This is sometimes felt as a grievous loss by these nations or peoples, almost always so felt by the governing class which has previously been their unrestricted rulers—perhaps their tyrants. But this partial loss of independence need not at all mean a loss of concrete liberties for the population, may even mean their considerable development, and may bring also a great gain to civilization and world political order. Untrammeled national independence is a dubious blessing, consistent with complete despotism inside the given nation, and premise of an international anarchy that derives precisely from separatist independence.

I did not attempt to deduce the totalitarian tyranny of a communist World Empire from the mere fact that it would be an empire. This conclusion was based upon the analysis of the nature of communism, as revealed in ideology, organization, and historical practice. Though it must be granted that an imperial world federation led by the United States might also develop into a tyranny, the fact of empire does not, in this case either, make the conclusion necessary.

3

The development of an industrial economy world-wide in scope, the breakdown of the international political order, and the existence of atomic weapons are, we observed at the beginning of our discussion, the elements of the world crisis as well as the occasion for the attempt to construct a world imperial federation. This world federation is made possible by the material and social conditions, is demanded by the catastrophic acuteness of the crisis, and at the same time is a means for solving the crisis. The nature of the federation cannot be deduced from definition, but must be understood in relation to the historical circumstances out of which it may arise.

From the point of view of the United States, and of the non-communist world generally, the world federation is required in order to perform two inter-related tasks, which cannot be performed without the federation: to control atomic weapons, and to prevent mass, total, world war. With United States leadership, and only with its leadership, a federation able to perform these tasks could be built, and built in time. With the performance of these tasks, the federation would be accomplishing what might be called its "historical purpose"; it would be fulfilling the requirements which prompted its creation. The minimum content of the "American world empire" would thus be no more than that of a protective association of nations and peoples in which, for a restricted special purpose, a special power—the power of atomic weapons—would be guarded in the beginning by one member of the association.

At first there would be, perhaps, little more to the federation than this minimum content—which, after all, would not be such an unmitigated blow to the liberties of mankind. It is not, however, to be expected that the federation would remain long at this bare level. It would develop; the content would deepen. How it would develop is a question not decided in advance. If the direction might be toward a tyrannous despotism on the part of the initially favored nation, there is no reason to rule out a development in a quite opposite direction, toward the fuller freedoms and humanity of a genuine world state and world society.

The danger to liberties would be the power predominance of the United States in the beginning of the federation. Fortunately for liberty, there are objective factors of very great weight that would operate against any attempt by the United States to institute a totalitarian world tyranny.

Not unimportant among these factors is the historical tradition which is the past of the United States social present. I have mentioned the brutality, provincialism, and cultural insensitivity which are not infrequent in United States behavior. These are, however, characteristics to be expected in a young and "semi-barbarian superstate of the cultural periphery" (I use, again, Toynbee's phrase). There is nothing totalitarian about them. Their rather anarchic, somewhat lawless, disruptive manifestations are on the whole anti-totalitarian in effect. Americans do, most of them, have a contempt for ideas; but that very contempt gives them a certain immunity to mental capture by an integral ideology of the totalitarian kind. It is less easy for a nation to escape from its past than many optimists, and pessimists, imagine. The past can be a millstone around the neck, but it can also be an anchor bringing safety. The United States may become totalitarian. It seems to me unlikely, however, that this will come about through a natural internal evolution. Totalitarianism would have to be brought from without, as it would have been by a world-victorious Nazi Germany, as it will be by the communists, if they are allowed to continue.

A second factor on the side of liberty is the inadequate power of the United States. The United States has today very great power, greater than its own spokesmen realize, great enough to build a world federation, to defeat communism, and to ensure control of atomic weapons. It does not have enough power to impose a totalitarian rule on the rest of the world. Even if the United States could concentrate enough in the form of purely military power, it lacks sufficient manpower and sufficient political experience.

What this means is that the United States can lead only by accepting others as partners, only by combining the methods of conciliation and concession with the methods of power, only by guarding the rights of others as jealously as its own privileges. If the United States refuses this mode of leadership, if it should try instead to be world despot, it might still, for a short while, subdue the world beneath an atomic terror. But the end would be swift and certain. Mankind would be avenged, and the United States destroyed. The only question would be whether all civilization would be brought down in the process.

Looked at somewhat differently, this indicates that in the projected world federation the principle of the balance of power would not in reality be suspended. At the one, narrowly military level, a balance would be replaced by United States preponderance. But military force, especially in the technical sense which is alone at stake in the control of atomic weapons, is by no means the only form of social power. In terms of population, material resources, cultural skills and experience, the United States would not at all outweigh the other members of the federation. Within the framework of the federation, divided powers would continue to interact. Through their mutual checks and balancings, they would operate to prevent any totalitarian crystallization of all power.

A third, ironic protection of liberty is the unwillingness of the United States to rule the world. No people, pushed by forces they cannot control, ever entered on the paths of world power with less taste for the journey, with more nostalgic backward glances. This distaste, indeed, is so profound that it is primarily significant not so much as a protection against the abuse of United States power, but rather as a tragic handicap to the sufficient utilization of that power.

There is a fourth major factor which will challenge any despotic presumption on the part of the United States. In the world today there are many millions of men and women who know the meaning of totalitarian tyranny, often through the frightful lessons of direct experience, and who are resolved, if any chance is given them, to fight against it. They are within the United States itself, as within every other nation, not the least firm among them silent for the moment under the stranglehold of the communist power. The loss of liberty teaches best, perhaps, its meaning. Though they are now, after so many betrayals and vain hopes, close to despair, they are still ready to act again.

They are ready, since there is no other way, to accept and follow the leadership of the United States, but only if they are given reason to believe that United States leadership will bring both power and justice: power so that there will be a chance to win, and justice so that the victory will be worth winning. They will follow not as subjects of the United States, but, in their own minds, as citizens of the world. For them, all governments and all power are suspect. They will be— they are—stern judges of the United States; they are acquainted with the symptoms of tyranny; they will observe and resist every invasion of liberty. If experience should prove to them that their hope in the United States is also empty, then they will abandon the United States.

The United States cannot compete in tyranny with the communists. The communists have cornered that political market. The peoples of the world will reason that if it is to be totalitarianism anyway, then it had might as well be the tried and tested brand. The United States will not win the peoples to her side—and the struggle in the end is for them, is not merely military—unless her leadership is anti-totalitarian, unless she can make herself the instrument of the hope, not the fear, of mankind.

4

In Chapter 3 we reached the conclusion that a genuine world government was not a possible solution of the present world political crisis. At the same time we found no reason for abandoning the ideal of a genuine world government or even the far nobler ideal of a world society in which the coercion and violence which are always part of any government would be replaced by the free, cooperative union of all mankind.

Those men who are dedicated to these ideals, who have rid their hearts forever of the bitter nationalist shell that divides them from their brothers who are all men, cannot remain satisfied with any such perspective as we have been examining. With the best of chances, a world federation led, however generously and discreetly, by the United

States would still retain its gross flaw of imperial inequality. Must they, then, these dedicated men, reject and condemn this perspective?

I think they need not, if their ideal is more than self-indulgence, if they know that their ideal must be realized within and through the harsh, real world of history. For them, this is the means; there is no other way. They cannot want for its own sake a federation of unequals, led by the United States. But they must want it as the necessary step toward their own goal of a world society of equals, in which they will continue to believe, and toward which their influence will try to direct the future of the federation.

5

Let us assume that I am correct in maintaining that world organization under communist leadership and world organization under United States leadership are the only two real alternatives in the present world political situation.

Communism, consistent in itself, is not troubled by any seeming disparities between the various propaganda masks through which it faces the world. From one mouth, it will tell us that all is well within the Soviet Union and among communists everywhere, and that any story of communist villainy is a fascist slander and a counter-revolutionary lie. If we have learned too much to be in this way quite lulled, communism will change mouths, and say: of course communists are now and then guilty of excesses, and there has been some Soviet trouble, but is this not the way of the world? How can the United States, with its own eye so full of beams, object to those Soviet motes? If communists are rather bad, well, at any rate Americans are no better.

This adoit maneuver, playing as it does so skillfully on all the strings of our own guilt, has a paralyzing effect on the minds and wills of honest men. Is it not true that we oppress a subject race, that we grab military bases, that our soldiers rape and rob, that we have dismal slums, that our propaganda is often false and hypocritical, that much of our press serves rich and wicked men, that we have grafters and absentee landlords and exploiters? What right do we have, then, to criticize communism, to set up our own way against its way? What choice is there between us? And, above all, what right have we to ask the world to choose?

Because I have not tried to conceal either the present defects in our society or the threats of future danger, but rather to force these out into the open, I feel it necessary to comment on the subtle, pseudo-humility of this attitude.

The truth is this. Our way is not the communist way. There is a difference, and there is a choice, as profound as any that men have in history confronted. We do not ever have, in history, a choice between absolutes, between Good and Evil, God and Satan. Evil, along with good, pervades the fabric of the City of the World; Satan, if not enthroned, is always present at the world's assemblies. Our choice is always between gray mixtures of good and evil; our right choice can never gain more than the lesser evil. What is always relevant, therefore, is the exact composition of the mixture, the degree, the measure.

It is true that we discriminate against the Negro race; but the most oppressed Negro in the United States has ten times more freedom than nine-tenths of the persons subject to the communist power. It is true that there are some frauds in our elections; but the whole electoral system of the Soviet Union is nothing but a gigantic fraud and farce. It is true, and wrong, that our press sometimes distorts news for the sake of selfish owners; but the entire communist press is simply the voice of a total lie. Some of our workers and farmers live in poverty and slums; but all Soviet workers live, under communist rule, in poverty and slums; all are hounded by a secret police and tied to the state by labor passports, and fifteen or twenty million of them are herded into the slave-gangs of the N.K.V.D. Our soldiers, occupying a country, are, some of them, brutal; but the communists, occupying a country, suck it dry, destroy its independent life, ship hundreds of thousands of its inhabitants back to the slave-gangs, and torture and kill every even potential opponent. Our police occasionally knock a striker over the head, or beat up a harmless drunk; but the communist police torture and frame and exile and murder millions of innocent men and women, and by means of spies and provocateurs reach into every factory and farm and home. Our employers and authorities sometimes try to break a strike; under a communist regime the very mention of a strike is punishable by death. We sometimes punish a poor man who in desperation steals, say, a jewel from a rich waster; in the Soviet Union a starving peasant who takes, to feed his children, a bushel of wheat from the farm he works, can legally be sentenced to exile or death for what, in the pious cant, is called "the theft of socialist property." In communist law and practice, it is a crime not to be a stoolpigeon, and a duty to betray friends and wife and family. Among us, the poor and weak do not have an equal chance against the rich and powerful; under the communists the poor and weak must not only obey, but praise and fawn on their masters.

It is far from my purpose to list these comparisons in order to suggest any complacency on our part. Our evils are still evil, even if there are worse. It is no less our duty to reject and overcome them. Every one of them, every added one, it may be noted, is a weapon contributed to communism. But it is necessary to guard against a false and in reality cynical indifference which escapes the responsibility for choice by the plea that all roads are alike, and alike lead to ruin. It is well to recall that there is something, after all, to lose.

It will be useful to give a name to the supreme policy which I have formulated. It is neither "imperial" nor "American" in any sense that would be ordinarily communicated by these words. The partial leadership which it allots to the United States follows not from any nationalist bias but from the nature and possibilities of existing world power relationships. Because this policy is the only answer to the communist plan for a universal totalitarianism, because it is the only chance for preserving the measure of liberty that is possible for us in our Time of Troubles, and because it proposes the sole route now open toward a free world society, I shall henceforth refer to it as *the policy of democratic world order.*

*1947*

# ROBERT A. TAFT

Known to his admirers as "Mr. Republican," Robert A. Taft (1889–1953) served as a U.S. senator for Ohio from 1939 to his death. A proponent of small government, he was wary of misusing military power and urged restraint in foreign policy. With the onset of World War II, soon followed by the Cold War, his principled anti-interventionism fell out of fashion.

———————

## FROM *A Foreign Policy for Americans*

### 1.
### WHAT ARE THE PURPOSES OF A FOREIGN POLICY?

NO ONE can think intelligently on the many complicated problems of American foreign policy unless he decides first what he considers the real purpose and object of that policy. In the letters which I receive from all parts of the country I find a complete confusion in the minds of the people as to our purposes in the world—and therefore scores of reasons which often seem to me completely unsound or inadequate for supporting or opposing some act of the Government. Confusion has been produced because there has been no consistent purpose in our foreign policy for a good many years past. In many cases the reason stated for some action—and blazoned forth on the radio to secure popular approval—has not been the real reason which animated the Administration.

Fundamentally, I believe the ultimate purpose of our foreign policy must be to protect the liberty of the people of the United States. The American Revolution was fought to establish a nation "conceived in liberty." That liberty has been defended in many wars since that day.

That liberty has enabled our people to increase steadily their material welfare and their spiritual freedom. To achieve that liberty we have gone to war, and to protect it we would go to war again.

Only second to liberty is the maintenance of peace. The results of war may be almost as bad as the destruction of liberty and, in fact, may lead, even if the war is won, to something very close to the destruction of liberty at home. War not only produces pitiful human suffering and utter destruction of many things worth-while, but it is almost as disastrous for the victor as for the vanquished. From our experience in the last two world wars, it actually promotes dictatorship and totalitarian government throughout the world. Much of the glamour has gone from it, and war today is murder by machine. World War II killed millions of innocent civilians as well as those in uniform and in many countries wiped out the product of hundreds of years of civilization. Two hundred and fifty thousand American boys were killed in World War II and hundreds of thousands permanently maimed or disabled, their lives often completely wrecked. Millions of families mourn their losses. War, undertaken even for justifiable purposes, such as to punish aggression in Korea, has often had the principal results of wrecking the country intended to be saved and spreading death and destruction among an innocent civilian population. Even more than Sherman knew in 1864, "war is hell." War should never be undertaken or seriously risked except to protect American liberty.

Our traditional policy of neutrality and non-interference with other nations was based on the principle that this policy was the best way to avoid disputes with other nations and to maintain the liberty of this country without war. From the days of George Washington that has been the policy of the United States. It has never been isolationism; but it has always avoided alliances and interference in foreign quarrels as a preventive against possible war, and it has always opposed any commitment by the United States, in advance, to take any military action outside of our territory. It would leave us free to interfere or not interfere according to whether we consider the case of sufficiently vital interest to the liberty of this country. It was the policy of the free hand.

I have always felt, however, that we should depart from this principle if we could set up an effective international organization, because in the long run the success of such an organization should be the most effective assurance of world peace and therefore of American peace. I regretted that we did not join the League of Nations.

We have now taken the lead in establishing the United Nations. The purpose is to establish a rule of law throughout the world and protect the people of the United States by punishing aggression the moment it starts and deterring future aggression through joint action of the members of such an organization.

I think we must recognize that this involves the theory of a preventive war, a dangerous undertaking at any time. If, therefore, we are going to join in such an organization it is essential that it be effective. It must be a joint enterprise. Our Korean adventure shows the tremendous danger, if the new organization is badly organized or improperly supported by its members and by the public opinion of the people of the world.

The United Nations has failed to protect our peace, I believe, because it was organized on an unsound basis with a veto power in five nations and is based, in fact, on the joint power of such nations, effective only so long as they agree. I believe the concept can only be successful if based on a rule of law and justice between nations and willingness on the part of all nations to abide by the decisions of an impartial tribunal.

The fact that the present organization has largely failed in its purpose has forced us to use other means to meet the present emergency, but there is no reason to abandon the concept of collective security which, by discouraging and preventing the use of war as national policy, can ultimately protect the liberty of the people of the United States and enforce peace.

2

I do not believe it is a selfish goal for us to insist that the overriding purpose of all American foreign policy should be the maintenance of the liberty and the peace of the people of the United States, so that they may achieve that intellectual and material improvement which is their genius and in which they can set an example for all peoples. By that example we can do an even greater service to mankind than we can by billions of material assistance—and more than we can ever do by war.

Just as our nation can be destroyed by war it can also be destroyed by a political or economic policy at home which destroys liberty or breaks down the fiscal and economic structure of the United States. We cannot adopt a foreign policy which gives away all of our people's earnings or imposes such a tremendous burden on the individual American as, in effect, to destroy his incentive and his ability to increase production and productivity and his standard of living. We cannot assume a financial burden in our foreign policy so great that it threatens liberty at home.

It follows that except as such policies may ultimately protect our own security, we have no primary interest as a national policy to improve conditions or material welfare in other parts of the world or to change other forms of government. Certainly we should not engage in war to achieve such purposes. I don't mean to say that, as responsible citizens of the world, we should not gladly extend charity or assistance to those in need. I do not mean to say that we should not align ourselves with the advocates of freedom everywhere. We did this kind of thing for many years, and we were respected as the most disinterested and charitable nation in the world.

But the contribution of supplies to meet extraordinary droughts or famine or refugee problems or other emergencies is very different from a global plan for general free assistance to all mankind on an organized scale as part of our foreign policy. Such a plan, as carried out today, can only be justified on a temporary basis as part of the battle against communism, to prevent communism from taking over more of the world and becoming a still more dangerous threat to our security. It has been undertaken as an emergency measure. Our foreign policy in ordinary times should not be primarily inspired by the motive of raising the standard of living of millions throughout the world, because that is utterly beyond our capacity. I believe it is impossible with American money or other outside aid to raise in any substantial degree the standard of living of the millions throughout the world who have created their own problems of soil destruction or overpopulation. Fundamentally, I doubt if the standard of living of any people can be successfully raised to any appreciable degree except by their own efforts. We can advise; we can assist, if the initiative and the desire and the energy to improve themselves is present. But our assistance cannot be a principal motive for foreign policy or a justification for going to war.

We hear a great deal of argument that if we do not deliberately, as part of a world welfare program, contribute to the raising of standards of living of peoples with low income they will turn Communist and go to war against us. Apart from such emergency situations as justified the Marshall Plan, following World War II, I see no evidence that this is true. Recent wars have not been started by poverty-stricken peoples, as in China or India, but by prosperous peoples, as in a Germany led by dictators. The standard of living of China or India could be tripled and yet would still be so far below the United States that the Communists could play with equal force on the comparative hardships the people were suffering. Communism is stronger today in France and Italy than in India, though the standard of living and distribution is infinitely better in the first two countries.

However, I think as a general incident to our policy of protecting the peace and liberty of the people of the United States it is most important that we prevent the building up of any great resentment against the success and the wealth which we have achieved. In other words, I believe that our international trade relations should be scrupulously fair and generous and should make it clear to the other peoples of the world that we intend to be fair and generous.

For the same reason, and as a contribution to world economic progress, I believe that some program like the Point Four program is justified to a limited extent, even if the Russian threat were completely removed. I supported the general project of a loan to Brazil to enable that country to build up a steel industry to use the natural resources which are available there. I believe that the policy not only assisted the development of that country in some degree but that in the long run it contributed to the growth of trade between Brazil and the United States and therefore to our own success in that field. But such programs should be sound economic projects, for the most part undertaken by private enterprise. Any United States Government contribution is in the nature of charity to poor countries and should be limited in amount. We make no such contribution to similar projects in the United States. It seems to me that we should not undertake any such project in such a way as to make it a global plan for sending Americans all over the world in unlimited number to find projects upon which American money can be spent. We ought only to receive with sympathy any application from these other nations and give it fair consideration.

Nor do I believe we can justify war by our natural desire to bring freedom to others throughout the world, although it is perfectly proper to encourage and promote freedom. In 1941 President Roosevelt announced that we were going to establish a moral order throughout the world: freedom of speech and expression, "everywhere in the world"; freedom to worship God "everywhere in the world"; freedom from want, and freedom from fear "everywhere in the world." I pointed out then that the forcing of any special brand of freedom and democracy on a people, whether they want it or not, by the brute force of war will be a denial of those very democratic principles which we are striving to advance.

The impracticability of such a battle was certainly shown by the progress of World War II. We were forced into an alliance with Communist Russia. I said on June 25, 1941, "To spread the four freedoms throughout the world we will ship airplanes and tanks and guns to Communist Russia. If, through our aid, Stalin is continued in power, do you suppose he will spread the four freedoms through Finland and Estonia and Latvia and Lithuania? Do you suppose that anybody in Russia itself will ever hear of the four freedoms after the war?" Certainly if World War II was undertaken to spread freedom throughout the world it was a failure. As a matter of fact, Franklin Roosevelt never dared to go to war for that purpose, and we only went to war when our own security was attacked at Pearl Harbor.

3

There are a good many Americans who talk about an American century in which America will dominate the world. They rightly point out that the United States is so powerful today that we should assume a moral leadership in the world to solve all the troubles of mankind. I quite agree that we need that moral leadership not only abroad but also at home. We can take the moral leadership in trying to improve the international organization for peace. I think we can take leadership in the providing of example and advice for the improvement of material standards of living throughout the world. Above all, I think we can take the leadership in proclaiming the doctrines of liberty and justice and in impressing on the world that only through liberty and law and justice, and not through socialism or communism, can the world hope to obtain the standards which we have attained in the United States. Our leaders can at least stop apologizing for the American system, as they have been apologizing for the past fifteen years.

If we confine our activities to the field of moral leadership we shall be successful if our philosophy is sound and appeals to the people of the world. The trouble with those who advocate this policy is that they really do not confine themselves to moral leadership. They are inspired with the same kind of New Deal planned-control ideas abroad as recent Administrations have desired to enforce at home. In their hearts they want to force on these foreign peoples through the use of American money and even, perhaps, American arms the policies which moral leadership is able to advance only through the sound strength of its principles and the force of its persuasion. I do not think this moral leadership ideal justifies our engaging in any preventive war, or going to the defense of one country against another, or getting ourselves into a vulnerable fiscal and economic position at home which may invite war. I do not believe any policy which has behind it the threat of military force is justified as part of the basic foreign policy of the United States except to defend the liberty of our own people.


4


In order to justify a lend-lease policy or the Atlantic Pact program for mutual aid and for arming Europe in time of peace or the Marshall Plan or the Point Four program beyond a selective and limited extent, any such program must be related to the liberty of the United States. Our active partisanship in World War II was based on the theory that a Hitler victory would make Germany a serious threat to the liberty of the United States. I did not believe that Germany would be such a threat, particularly after Hitler brought Russia into the war, and that is the reason I opposed the war policy of the Administration from the elections of 1940 to the attack on the United States at Pearl Harbor in December 1941. The more recent measures for Marshall Plan aid on a global scale—and to the extent of billions of dollars of American taxpayers' money—and the Atlantic Pact arms program are and must be based on the theory that Russia today presents a real threat to the security of the United States.

While I may differ on the extent of some of these measures, I agree that there is such a threat. This is due principally to the facts that air power has made distances so short and the atomic bomb has made air power so potentially effective that Russia today could do what Hitler never could do—inflict serious and perhaps crippling injury on our cities and on our industrial plants and the other production resources which are so essential to our victory in war.

Furthermore, the Russians combine with great military and air power a fanatical devotion to communism not unlike that which inspired the Moslem invasion of Europe in the Middle Ages. The crusading spirit makes possible a fifth-column adjunct to military attack which adds tremendously to the power and danger of Russian aggression. The Russian threat has become so serious today that in defense of the liberty and peace of the people of the United States I think we are justified in extending economic aid and military aid to many countries, but only when it can be clearly shown in each case that such aid will be an effective means of combating Communist aggression. We have now felt it necessary in order to protect the liberty of the United States against an extraordinary special threat to adopt a policy which I do not believe should be considered as part of any permanent foreign policy. We have been forced into this not only because of the power of Soviet Russia but because the United Nations has shown that it is wholly ineffective under its present charter. The new temporary policy may be outlined as follows:

1. We have had to set up a much larger armed force than we have ever had to do before in time of peace, in order to meet the Communist threat. I believe this effort should be directed particularly toward a development of an all-powerful air force.

2. We have had to adopt as a temporary measure the policy of extending economic and military aid to all those countries which,

with the use of such aid, can perhaps prevent the extension of Russian military power or Russian or Communist influence. We have backed that up by announcing definitely to Russia that if it undertakes aggression against certain countries whose independence is important to us it will find itself at war with us. This is a kind of Monroe Doctrine for Europe.

3. We have had to adopt a policy of military alliances to deter, at least, the spread of Communist power. To control sea and air throughout the world, the British alliance is peculiarly important. Again, we hope that with the decline of Russian power and the re-establishment of an international organization for peace such alliances may be unnecessary.

I opposed that feature of the Atlantic Pact which looked toward a commitment of the United States to fight a land war on the continent of Europe and therefore opposed, except to a limited degree, the commitment of land troops to Europe. Except as we find it absolutely essential to our security, I do not believe we should depart from the principle of maintaining a free hand to fight a war which may be forced upon us, in such a manner and in such places as are best suited at the time to meet those conditions which are changing so rapidly in the modern world. Nothing is so dangerous as to commit the United States to a course which is beyond its capacity to perform with success.

In the course of later chapters I shall discuss the wisdom of this temporary policy and apply it to the particular situations which we face throughout the world. But it must always be considered, I believe, as a temporary expedient. It cannot avoid the possible danger of involving us in war with Soviet Russia, but it should not provoke a war which otherwise might not occur.

5

The main point of this preliminary statement, however, is to emphasize that our foreign policy must always keep in mind, as its ultimate goal, the peace and security of the people of the United States. Most of our Presidents have been imbued with a real determination to keep the country at peace. I feel that the last two Presidents have put all kinds of political and policy considerations ahead of their interest in liberty and peace. No foreign policy can be justified except a policy devoted without reservation or diversion to the protection of the liberty of the American people, with war only as the last resort and only to preserve that liberty.

*1951*

# REINHOLD NIEBUHR

Arguably the most influential public intellectual of mid-twentieth-century America, Reinhold Niebuhr (1892–1971) played many roles, making his mark as a theologian, teacher, polemicist, political activist, and the founding editor of *Christianity & Crisis*, the leading journal of liberal American Protestantism for half a century. His early pacifism and socialism yielded to a more nuanced approach marked by his concept of "Christian realism," a central theme of his book *The Irony of American History* (1952), excerpted here. Although a man of the political left, and a lifelong champion of progressive Democratic Party politicians and civil rights leaders (Martin Luther King and Barack Obama both cited him as a crucial intellectual inspiration), Niebuhr has also had an important influence on American conservative thought.

———————

FROM *The Irony of American History*

O UR FOREIGN policy reveals even more marked contradictions between our early illusions of innocency and the hard realities of the present day than do our domestic policies. We lived for a century not only in the illusion but in the reality of innocency in our foreign relations. We lacked the power in the first instance to become involved in the guilt of its use. As we gradually achieved power, through the economic consequences of our richly stored continent, the continental unity of our economy and the technical efficiency of our business and industrial enterprise, we sought for a time to preserve innocency by disavowing the responsibilities of power. We were, of course, never as innocent as we pretended to be, even as a child is not as innocent as is implied in the use of the child as the symbol of innocence. The surge of our infant strength over a continent, which claimed Oregon, California, Florida and Texas against any sovereignty which may have stood in our way, was not innocent. It was the expression of a will-to-power of a new community in which the land-hunger of hardy pioneers and settlers furnished the force of imperial expansion. The organs of government, whether political or military, played only a secondary role. From those early days to the present moment we have frequently been honestly deceived because our power availed itself of covert rather than overt instruments. One of the most prolific causes of delusion about power in a commercial society is that economic power is more covert than political or military power.

We believed, until the outbreak of the First World War, that there was a generic difference between us and the other nations of the world. This was proved by the difference between their power rivalries and our alleged contentment with our lot. The same President of the United States who ultimately interpreted the First World War as a crusade to "make the world safe for democracy" reacted to its first alarms with the reassuring judgment that the conflict represented trade rivalries with which we need not be concerned. We were drawn into the war by considerations of national interest, which we hardly dared to confess to ourselves. Our European critics may, however, overshoot the mark if they insist that the slogan of making "the world safe for democracy" was merely an expression of that moral cant which we seemed to have inherited from the British, only to express it with less subtlety than they. For the fact is that every nation is caught in the moral paradox of refusing to go to war unless it can be proved that the national interest is imperiled, and of continuing in the war only by proving that something much more than national interest is at stake. Our nation is not the only community of mankind which is tempted to hypocrisy. Every nation must come to terms with the fact that, though the force of collective self-interest is so great, that national policy must be based upon it; yet also the sensitive conscience recognizes that the moral obligation of the individual transcends his particular community. Loyalty to the community is therefore morally tolerable only if it includes values wider than those of the community.

More significant than our actions and interpretations in the First World War was our mood after its conclusion. Our "realists" feared that our sense of responsibility toward a nascent world community had exceeded the canons of a prudent self-interest. Our idealists, of the thirties, sought to preserve our innocence by neutrality. The main force of isolationism came from the "realists," as the slogan "America First" signifies. But the abortive effort to defy the forces of history which were both creating a potential world community and increasing the power of America beyond that of any other nation, was supported by pacifist idealists, Christian and secular, and by other visionaries who desired to preserve our innocency. They had a dim and dark understanding of the fact that power cannot be wielded without guilt, since it is never transcendent over interest, even when it tries to subject itself to universal standards and places itself under the control of a nascent world-wide community. They did not understand that the disavowal of the responsibilities of power can involve an individual or nation in even more grievous guilt.

There are two ways of denying our responsibilities to our fellow-men. The one is the way of imperialism, expressed in seeking to dominate them by our power. The other is the way of isolationism, expressed in seeking to withdraw from our responsibilities to them. Geographic circumstances and the myths of our youth rendered us more susceptible to the latter than the former temptation. This has given our national life a unique color, which is not without some moral advantages. No powerful nation in history has ever been more reluctant to acknowledge the position it has achieved in the world than we. The moral advantage lies in the fact that we do not have a strong lust of power, though we are quickly acquiring the pride of power which always accompanies its possession. Our lack of the lust of power makes the fulminations of our foes against us singularly inept. On the other hand, we have been so deluded by the concept of our innocency that we are ill prepared to deal with the temptations of power which now assail us.

The Second World War quickly dispelled the illusions of both our realists and idealists; and also proved the vanity of the hopes of the legalists who thought that rigorous neutrality laws could abort the historical tendencies which were pushing our nation into the center of the world community. We emerged from that war the most powerful nation on earth. To the surprise of our friends and critics we seemed also to have sloughed off the tendencies toward irresponsibility which had characterized us in the long armistice between the world wars. We were determined to exercise the responsibilities of our power.

The exercise of this power required us to hold back the threat of Europe's inundation by communism through the development of all kinds of instruments of mass destruction, including atomic weapons. Thus an "innocent" nation finally arrives at the ironic climax of its history. It finds itself the custodian of the ultimate weapon which perfectly embodies and symbolizes the moral ambiguity of physical warfare. We could not disavow the possible use of the weapon, partly because no imperiled nation is morally able to dispense with weapons which might insure its survival. All nations, unlike some individuals, lack the capacity to prefer a noble death to a morally ambiguous survival. But we also could not renounce the weapon because the freedom or survival of our allies depended upon the threat of its use. Of this at least Mr. Winston Churchill and other Europeans have assured us. Yet if we should use it, we shall cover ourselves with a terrible guilt. We might insure our survival in a world in which it might be better not to be alive. Thus the moral predicament in which all human striving is involved has been raised to a final pitch for a culture and for a nation which thought it an easy matter to distinguish between justice and injustice and believed itself to be peculiarly innocent. In this way the perennial moral predicaments of human history have caught up with a culture which knew nothing of sin or guilt, and with a nation which seemed to be the most perfect fruit of that culture.

In this as in every other ironic situation of American history there is a footnote which accentuates the incongruity. This footnote is added by the fact that the greatness of our power is derived on the one hand from the technical efficiency of our industrial establishment and on the other from the success of our natural scientists. Yet it was assumed that science and business enterprise would insure the triumph of reason over power and passion in human history.

Naturally, a culture so confident of the possibility of resolving all incongruities in life and history was bound to make strenuous efforts to escape the tragic dilemma in which we find ourselves. These efforts fall into two categories, idealistic and realistic. The idealists naturally believe that we could escape the dilemma if we made sufficiently strenuous rational and moral efforts; if for instance we tried to establish a world government. Unfortunately the obvious necessity of integrating the global community politically does not guarantee its possibility. And all the arguments of the idealists finally rest upon a logic which derives the possibility of an achievement from its necessity. Other idealists believe that a renunciation of the use of atomic weapons would free us from the dilemma. But this is merely the old pacifist escape from the dilemma of war itself.

The realists on the other hand are inclined to argue that a good cause will hallow any weapon. They are convinced that the evils of communism are so great that we are justified in using any weapon against them. Thereby they closely approach the communist ruthlessness. The inadequacy of both types of escape from our moral dilemma proves that there is no purely moral solution for the ultimate moral issues of life; but neither is there a viable solution which disregards the moral factors. Men and nations must use their power with the purpose of making it an instrument of justice and a servant of interests broader than their own. Yet they must be ready to use it though they become aware that the power of a particular nation or individual, even when under strong religious and social sanctions, is never so used that there is a perfect coincidence between the value which justifies it and the interest of the wielder of it.

One difficulty of a nation, such as ours, which manifests itself long before we reach the ultimate dilemma of warfare with weapons of mass destruction, is that we have reached our position in the world community through forms of power which are essentially covert rather than overt. Or rather the overt military power which we wield has been directly drawn from the economic power, derived from the wealth of our natural resources and our technical efficiency. We have had little experience in the claims and counter-claims of man's social existence, either domestically or internationally. We therefore do not know social existence as an encounter between life and life, or interest with interest in which moral and non-moral factors are curiously compounded. It is therefore a weakness of our foreign policy, particularly as our business community conceives it, that we move inconsistently from policies which would overcome animosities toward us by the offer of economic assistance to policies which would destroy resistance by the use of pure military might. We can understand the neat logic of either economic reciprocity or the show of pure power. But we are

mystified by the endless complexities of human motives and the varied compounds of ethnic loyalties, cultural traditions, social hopes,
envies and fears which enter into the policies of nations, and which
lie at the foundation of their political cohesion.

In our relations with Asia these inconsistencies are particularly baf-
fling. We expect Asians to be grateful to us for such assistance as we
have given them; and are hurt when we discover that Asians envy,
rather than admire, our prosperity and regard us as imperialistic when
we are "by definition" a non-imperialistic nation.

Nations are hardly capable of the spirit of forgiveness which is the
final oil of harmony in all human relations and which rests upon
the contrite recognition that our actions and attitudes are inevitably
interpreted in a different light by our friends as well as foes than we
interpret them. Yet it is necessary to acquire a measure of this spirit
in the collective relations of mankind. Nations, as individuals, who
are completely innocent in their own esteem, are insufferable in their
human contacts. The whole world suffers from the pretensions of the
communist oligarchs. Our pretensions are of a different order because
they are not as consistently held. In any event, we have preserved a
system of freedom in which they may be challenged. Yet our American
nation, involved in its vast responsibilities, must slough off many illusions which were derived both from the experiences and the ideologies
of its childhood. Otherwise either we will seek escape from responsibilities which involve unavoidable guilt, or we will be plunged into
avoidable guilt by too great confidence in our virtue.

*1952*

# RONALD REAGAN

After achieving considerable success as a Hollywood actor, Ronald Wilson Reagan (1911–2004) found a new calling in politics. As a young man, Reagan had been a liberal Democrat and a strong supporter of President Franklin Roosevelt. By the 1960s, however, he had moved to the right. Running as a conservative Republican, he won two terms as governor of California, serving from 1967 to 1975, followed by two terms as the fortieth U.S. president from 1981 to 1989.

———————◆———————

## Address to Members of Parliament
## London, June 8, 1982

My Lord Chancellor, Mr. Speaker:
The journey of which this visit forms a part is a long one. Already it has taken me to two great cities of the West, Rome and Paris, and to the economic summit at Versailles. And there, once again, our sister democracies have proved that even in a time of severe economic strain, free peoples can work together freely and voluntarily to address problems as serious as inflation, unemployment, trade, and economic development in a spirit of cooperation and solidarity.

Other milestones lie ahead. Later this week, in Germany, we and our NATO allies will discuss measures for our joint defense and America's latest initiatives for a more peaceful, secure world through arms reductions.

Each stop of this trip is important, but among them all, this moment occupies a special place in my heart and in the hearts of my countrymen—a moment of kinship and homecoming in these hallowed halls.

Speaking for all Americans, I want to say how very much at home we feel in your house. Every American would, because this is, as we have been so eloquently told, one of democracy's shrines. Here the rights of free people and the processes of representation have been debated and refined.

It has been said that an institution is the lengthening shadow of a man. This institution is the lengthening shadow of all the men and women who have sat here and all those who have voted to send representatives here.

This is my second visit to Great Britain as President of the United States. My first opportunity to stand on British soil occurred almost a year and a half ago when your Prime Minister graciously hosted a diplomatic dinner at the British Embassy in Washington. Mrs. Thatcher said then that she hoped I was not distressed to find staring down at me from the grand staircase a portrait of His Royal Majesty King George III. She suggested it was best to let bygones be bygones, and in view of our two countries' remarkable friendship in succeeding years, she added that most Englishmen today would agree with Thomas Jefferson that "a little rebellion now and then is a very good thing." [*Laughter*]

Well, from here I will go to Bonn and then Berlin, where there stands a grim symbol of power untamed. The Berlin Wall, that dreadful gray gash across the city, is in its third decade. It is the fitting signature of the regime that built it.

And a few hundred kilometers behind the Berlin Wall, there is another symbol. In the center of Warsaw, there is a sign that notes the distances to two capitals. In one direction it points toward Moscow. In the other it points toward Brussels, headquarters of Western Europe's tangible unity. The marker says that the distances from Warsaw to Moscow and Warsaw to Brussels are equal. The sign makes this point: Poland is not East or West. Poland is at the center of European civilization. It has contributed mightily to that civilization. It is doing so today by being magnificently unreconciled to oppression.

Poland's struggle to be Poland and to secure the basic rights we often take for granted demonstrates why we dare not take those rights for granted. Gladstone, defending the Reform Bill of 1866, declared, "You cannot fight against the future. Time is on our side." It was easier to believe in the march of democracy in Gladstone's day—in that high noon of Victorian optimism.

We're approaching the end of a bloody century plagued by a terrible political invention—totalitarianism. Optimism comes less easily today, not because democracy is less vigorous, but because democracy's enemies have refined their instruments of repression. Yet optimism is in order, because day by day democracy is proving itself to be a not-at-all-fragile flower. From Stettin on the Baltic to Varna on the Black Sea, the regimes planted by totalitarianism have had more than 30 years to establish their legitimacy. But none—not one regime—has yet been able to risk free elections. Regimes planted by bayonets do not take root.

The strength of the Solidarity movement in Poland demonstrates the truth told in an underground joke in the Soviet Union. It is that the Soviet Union would remain a one-party nation even if an opposition party were permitted, because everyone would join the opposition party. [*Laughter*]

America's time as a player on the stage of world history has been brief. I think understanding this fact has always made you patient with your younger cousins—well, not always patient. I do recall that on one occasion, Sir Winston Churchill said in exasperation about one of our most distinguished diplomats: "He is the only case I know of a bull who carries his china shop with him." [*Laughter*]

But witty as Sir Winston was, he also had that special attribute of great statesmen—the gift of vision, the willingness to see the future based on the experience of the past. It is this sense of history, this understanding of the past that I want to talk with you about today, for it is in remembering what we share of the past that our two nations can make common cause for the future.

We have not inherited an easy world. If developments like the Industrial Revolution, which began here in England, and the gifts of science and technology have made life much easier for us, they have also made it more dangerous. There are threats now to our freedom, indeed to our very existence, that other generations could never even have imagined.

There is first the threat of global war. No President, no Congress, no Prime Minister, no Parliament can spend a day entirely free of this threat. And I don't have to tell you that in today's world the existence of nuclear weapons could mean, if not the extinction of mankind, then surely the end of civilization as we know it. That's why negotiations on intermediate-range nuclear forces now underway in Europe and the START talks—Strategic Arms Reduction Talks—which will begin later this month, are not just critical to American or Western policy; they are critical to mankind. Our commitment to early success in these negotiations is firm and unshakable, and our purpose is clear: reducing the risk of war by reducing the means of waging war on both sides.

At the same time there is a threat posed to human freedom by the enormous power of the modern state. History teaches the dangers of government that overreaches—political control taking precedence over free economic growth, secret police, mindless bureaucracy, all combining to stifle individual excellence and personal freedom.

Now, I'm aware that among us here and throughout Europe there is legitimate disagreement over the extent to which the public sector should play a role in a nation's economy and life. But on one point all of us are united—our abhorrence of dictatorship in all its forms, but most particularly totalitarianism and the terrible inhumanities it has caused in our time—the great purge, Auschwitz and Dachau, the Gulag, and Cambodia.

Historians looking back at our time will note the consistent restraint and peaceful intentions of the West. They will note that it was the democracies who refused to use the threat of their nuclear monopoly in the forties and early fifties for territorial or imperial gain. Had that nuclear monopoly been in the hands of the Communist world, the map of Europe—indeed, the world—would look very different today. And certainly they will note it was not the democracies that invaded Afghanistan or suppressed Polish Solidarity or used chemical and toxin warfare in Afghanistan and Southeast Asia.

If history teaches anything it teaches self-delusion in the face of unpleasant facts is folly. We see around us today the marks of our terrible dilemma—predictions of doomsday, antinuclear demonstrations, an arms race in which the West must, for its own protection, be an unwilling participant. At the same time we see totalitarian forces in the world who seek subversion and conflict around the globe to further their barbarous assault on the human spirit. What, then, is our course? Must civilization perish in a hail of fiery atoms? Must freedom wither in a quiet, deadening accommodation with totalitarian evil?

Sir Winston Churchill refused to accept the inevitability of war or even that it was imminent. He said, "I do not believe that Soviet Russia desires war. What they desire is the fruits of war and the indefinite expansion of their power and doctrines. But what we have to consider here today while time remains is the permanent prevention of war and the establishment of conditions of freedom and democracy as rapidly as possible in all countries."

Well, this is precisely our mission today: to preserve freedom as well as peace. It may not be easy to see; but I believe we live now at a turning point.

In an ironic sense Karl Marx was right. We are witnessing today a great revolutionary crisis, a crisis where the demands of the economic order are conflicting directly with those of the political order. But the crisis is happening not in the free, non-Marxist West, but in the home of Marxist-Leninism, the Soviet Union. It is the Soviet Union that runs against the tide of history by denying human freedom and human dignity to its citizens. It also is in deep economic difficulty. The rate of growth in the national product has been steadily declining since the fifties and is less than half of what it was then.

The dimensions of this failure are astounding: a country which employs one-fifth of its population in agriculture is unable to feed its own people. Were it not for the private sector, the tiny private sector tolerated in Soviet agriculture, the country might be on the brink of famine. These private plots occupy a bare 3 percent of the arable land but account for nearly one-quarter of Soviet farm output and nearly one-third of meat products and vegetables. Overcentralized, with little or no incentives, year after year the Soviet system pours its best resource into the making of instruments of destruction. The constant shrinkage of economic growth combined with the growth of military production is putting a heavy strain on the Soviet people. What we see here is a political structure that no longer corresponds to its economic base, a society where productive forces are hampered by political ones.

The decay of the Soviet experiment should come as no surprise to us. Wherever the comparisons have been made between free and closed societies—West Germany and East Germany, Austria and

Czechoslovakia, Malaysia and Vietnam—it is the democratic countries that are prosperous and responsive to the needs of their people. And one of the simple but overwhelming facts of our time is this: Of all the millions of refugees we've seen in the modern world, their flight is always away from, not toward the Communist world. Today on the NATO line, our military forces face east to prevent a possible invasion. On the other side of the line, the Soviet forces also face east to prevent their people from leaving.

The hard evidence of totalitarian rule has caused in mankind an uprising of the intellect and will. Whether it is the growth of the new schools of economics in America or England or the appearance of the so-called new philosophers in France, there is one unifying thread running through the intellectual work of these groups—rejection of the arbitrary power of the state, the refusal to subordinate the rights of the individual to the superstate, the realization that collectivism stifles all the best human impulses.

Since the exodus from Egypt, historians have written of those who sacrificed and struggled for freedom—the stand at Thermopylae, the revolt of Spartacus, the storming of the Bastille, the Warsaw uprising in World War II. More recently we've seen evidence of this same human impulse in one of the developing nations in Central America. For months and months the world news media covered the fighting in El Salvador. Day after day we were treated to stories and film slanted toward the brave freedom-fighters battling oppressive government forces in behalf of the silent, suffering people of that tortured country.

And then one day those silent, suffering people were offered a chance to vote, to choose the kind of government they wanted. Suddenly the freedom-fighters in the hills were exposed for what they really are—Cuban-backed guerrillas who want power for themselves, and their backers, not democracy for the people. They threatened death to any who voted, and destroyed hundreds of buses and trucks to keep the people from getting to the polling places. But on election day, the people of El Salvador, an unprecedented 1.4 million of them, braved ambush and gunfire, and trudged for miles to vote for freedom.

They stood for hours in the hot sun waiting for their turn to vote. Members of our Congress who went there as observers told me of a woman who was wounded by rifle fire on the way to the polls, who refused to leave the line to have her wound treated until after she had voted. A grandmother, who had been told by the guerrillas she would be killed when she returned from the polls, and she told the guerrillas, "You can kill me, you can kill my family, kill my neighbors, but you can't kill us all." The real freedom-fighters of El Salvador turned out to be the people of that country—the young, the old, the in-between.

Strange, but in my own country there's been little if any news coverage of that war since the election. Now, perhaps they'll say it's—well, because there are newer struggles now.

On distant islands in the South Atlantic young men are fighting for Britain. And, yes, voices have been raised protesting their sacrifice for lumps of rock and earth so far away. But those young men aren't fighting for mere real estate. They fight for a cause—for the belief that armed aggression must not be allowed to succeed, and the people must participate in the decisions of government—[*applause*]—the decisions of government under the rule of law. If there had been firmer support for that principle some 45 years ago, perhaps our generation wouldn't have suffered the bloodletting of World War II.

In the Middle East now the guns sound once more, this time in Lebanon, a country that for too long has had to endure the tragedy of civil war, terrorism, and foreign intervention and occupation. The fighting in Lebanon on the part of all parties must stop, and Israel should bring its forces home. But this is not enough. We must all work to stamp out the scourge of terrorism that in the Middle East makes war an ever-present threat.

But beyond the troublespots lies a deeper, more positive pattern. Around the world today, the democratic revolution is gathering new strength. In India a critical test has been passed with the peaceful change of governing political parties. In Africa, Nigeria is moving into remarkable and unmistakable ways to build and strengthen its democratic institutions. In the Caribbean and Central America, 16 of 24 countries have freely elected governments. And in the United Nations, 8 of the 10 developing nations which have joined that body in the past 5 years are democracies.

In the Communist world as well, man's instinctive desire for freedom and self-determination surfaces again and again. To be sure, there are grim reminders of how brutally the police state attempts to snuff out this quest for self-rule—1953 in East Germany, 1956 in Hungary, 1968 in Czechoslovakia, 1981 in Poland. But the struggle continues in

Poland. And we know that there are even those who strive and suffer for freedom within the confines of the Soviet Union itself. How we conduct ourselves here in the Western democracies will determine whether this trend continues.

No, democracy is not a fragile flower. Still it needs cultivating. If the rest of this century is to witness the gradual growth of freedom and democratic ideals, we must take actions to assist the campaign for democracy.

Some argue that we should encourage democratic change in right-wing dictatorships, but not in Communist regimes. Well, to accept this preposterous notion—as some well-meaning people have—is to invite the argument that once countries achieve a nuclear capability, they should be allowed an undisturbed reign of terror over their own citizens. We reject this course.

As for the Soviet view, Chairman Brezhnev repeatedly has stressed that the competition of ideas and systems must continue and that this is entirely consistent with relaxation of tensions and peace.

Well, we ask only that these systems begin by living up to their own constitutions, abiding by their own laws, and complying with the international obligations they have undertaken. We ask only for a process, a direction, a basic code of decency, not for an instant transformation.

We cannot ignore the fact that even without our encouragement there has been and will continue to be repeated explosions against repression and dictatorships. The Soviet Union itself is not immune to this reality. Any system is inherently unstable that has no peaceful means to legitimize its leaders. In such cases, the very repressiveness of the state ultimately drives people to resist it, if necessary, by force.

While we must be cautious about forcing the pace of change, we must not hesitate to declare our ultimate objectives and to take concrete actions to move toward them. We must be staunch in our conviction that freedom is not the sole prerogative of a lucky few, but the inalienable and universal right of all human beings. So states the United Nations Universal Declaration of Human Rights, which, among other things, guarantees free elections.

The objective I propose is quite simple to state: to foster the infrastructure of democracy, the system of a free press, unions, political parties, universities, which allows a people to choose their own way to develop their own culture, to reconcile their own differences through peaceful means.

This is not cultural imperialism, it is providing the means for genuine self-determination and protection for diversity. Democracy already flourishes in countries with very different cultures and historical experiences. It would be cultural condescension, or worse, to say that any people prefer dictatorship to democracy. Who would voluntarily choose not to have the right to vote, decide to purchase government propaganda handouts instead of independent newspapers, prefer government to worker-controlled unions, opt for land to be owned by the state instead of those who till it, want government repression of religious liberty, a single political party instead of a free choice, a rigid cultural orthodoxy instead of democratic tolerance and diversity?

Since 1917 the Soviet Union has given covert political training and assistance to Marxist-Leninists in many countries. Of course, it also has promoted the use of violence and subversion by these same forces. Over the past several decades, West European and other Social Democrats, Christian Democrats, and leaders have offered open assistance to fraternal, political, and social institutions to bring about peaceful and democratic progress. Appropriately, for a vigorous new democracy, the Federal Republic of Germany's political foundations have become a major force in this effort.

We in America now intend to take additional steps, as many of our allies have already done, toward realizing this same goal. The chairmen and other leaders of the national Republican and Democratic Party organizations are initiating a study with the bipartisan American political foundation to determine how the United States can best contribute as a nation to the global campaign for democracy now gathering force. They will have the cooperation of congressional leaders of both parties, along with representatives of business, labor, and other major institutions in our society. I look forward to receiving their recommendations and to working with these institutions and the Congress in the common task of strengthening democracy throughout the world.

It is time that we committed ourselves as a nation—in both the public and private sectors—to assisting democratic development.

We plan to consult with leaders of other nations as well. There is a proposal before the Council of Europe to invite parliamentarians from democratic countries to a meeting next year in Strasbourg. That prestigious gathering could consider ways to help democratic political movements.

This November in Washington there will take place an international meeting on free elections. And next spring there will be a conference of world authorities on constitutionalism and self-government hosted by the Chief Justice of the United States. Authorities from a number of developing and developed countries—judges, philosophers, and politicians with practical experience—have agreed to explore how to turn principle into practice and further the rule of law.

At the same time, we invite the Soviet Union to consider with us how the competition of ideas and values—which it is committed to support—can be conducted on a peaceful and reciprocal basis. For example, I am prepared to offer President Brezhnev an opportunity to speak to the American people on our television if he will allow me the same opportunity with the Soviet people. We also suggest that panels of our newsmen periodically appear on each other's television to discuss major events.

Now, I don't wish to sound overly optimistic, yet the Soviet Union is not immune from the reality of what is going on in the world. It has happened in the past—a small ruling elite either mistakenly attempts to ease domestic unrest through greater repression and foreign adventure, or it chooses a wiser course. It begins to allow its people a voice in their own destiny. Even if this latter process is not realized soon, I believe the renewed strength of the democratic movement, complemented by a global campaign for freedom, will strengthen the prospects for arms control and a world at peace.

I have discussed on other occasions, including my address on May 9th, the elements of Western policies toward the Soviet Union to safeguard our interests and protect the peace. What I am describing now is a plan and a hope for the long term—the march of freedom and democracy which will leave Marxism-Leninism on the ash-heap of history as it has left other tyrannies which stifle the freedom and muzzle the self-expression of the people. And that's why we must continue our efforts to strengthen NATO even as we move forward with our Zero-Option initiative in the negotiations on intermediate-range forces and our proposal for a one-third reduction in strategic ballistic missile warheads.

Our military strength is a prerequisite to peace, but let it be clear we maintain this strength in the hope it will never be used, for the ultimate determinant in the struggle that's now going on in the world will not be bombs and rockets, but a test of wills and ideas, a trial of spiritual resolve, the values we hold, the beliefs we cherish, the ideals to which we are dedicated.

The British people know that, given strong leadership, time and a little bit of hope, the forces of good ultimately rally and triumph over evil. Here among you is the cradle of self-government, the Mother of Parliaments. Here is the enduring greatness of the British contribution to mankind, the great civilized ideas: individual liberty, representative government, and the rule of law under God.

I've often wondered about the shyness of some of us in the West about standing for these ideals that have done so much to ease the plight of man and the hardships of our imperfect world. This reluctance to use those vast resources at our command reminds me of the elderly lady whose home was bombed in the Blitz. As the rescuers moved about, they found a bottle of brandy she'd stored behind the staircase, which was all that was left standing. And since she was barely conscious, one of the workers pulled the cork to give her a taste of it. She came around immediately and said, "Here now—there now, put it back. That's for emergencies." [*Laughter*]

Well, the emergency is upon us. Let us be shy no longer. Let us go to our strength. Let us offer hope. Let us tell the world that a new age is not only possible but probable.

During the dark days of the Second World War, when this island was incandescent with courage, Winston Churchill exclaimed about Britain's adversaries, "What kind of a people do they think we are?" Well, Britain's adversaries found out what extraordinary people the British are. But all the democracies paid a terrible price for allowing the dictators to underestimate us. We dare not make that mistake again. So, let us ask ourselves, "What kind of people do we think we are?" And let us answer, "Free people, worthy of freedom and determined not only to remain so but to help others gain their freedom as well."

Sir Winston led his people to great victory in war and then lost an election just as the fruits of victory were about to be enjoyed. But he left office honorably, and, as it turned out, temporarily, knowing that the liberty of his people was more important than the fate of any single leader. History recalls his greatness in ways no dictator will ever know. And he left us a message of hope for the future, as timely now as when he first uttered it, as opposition leader in the Commons nearly 27 years ago, when he said, "When we look back on all the perils through which we have passed and at the mighty foes that we have laid low and all the dark and deadly designs that we have frustrated, why should we fear for our future? We have," he said, "come safely through the worst."

Well, the task I've set forth will long outlive our own generation. But together, we too have come through the worst. Let us now begin a major effort to secure the best—a crusade for freedom that will engage the faith and fortitude of the next generation. For the sake of peace and justice, let us move toward a world in which all people are at last free to determine their own destiny.

Thank you.

*1982*

# WILLIAM PFAFF

William Pfaff (1928–2015) was born in Iowa, raised in Georgia, and educated at Notre Dame, but for much of his life chose to reside in Paris,
writing a regular column for the *International Herald-Tribune*. He became
a respected critic of U.S. foreign policy, contributing to *The New York
Review of Books*, *The New Yorker*, *Harper's*, and other publications. Here, in
an excerpt from the last of his several books, he voices a long-standing
skepticism toward our nation's enthusiasm for foreign entanglements.

FROM *The Irony of Manifest Destiny*

T HERE HAS always been, and remains, a noninterventionist alternative to the foreign policy followed by the United States since the
beginning of the 1960s. This would discard ideological and historicist
generalizations, minimize interference in the affairs of other societies,
and accept the existence of an international system of plural, legitimate, and autonomous powers and interests.*

It would emphasize pragmatic and empirical judgment of the interests and needs of the American nation, and of others. It would accept
the realism of George Kennan's stark judgment that democracy along
West European and American lines cannot prevail internationally.

---

* Confusion is sometimes produced because the "realist" and noninterventionist
policy recommendations put forward in the 1950s and 1960s were at the time
pejoratively called "neo-isolationist," which they were not (whatever that term may
mean in contemporary practice). The possibility of a modern American isolationist
foreign policy was exhaustively considered by the Brown University political scientist Eric A. Nordlinger in his 1995 book (pre-globalism and pre-9/11), *Isolationism
Reconfigured: American Foreign Policy for a New Century*. It ends (unhelpfully) by
recommending "moderated idealistic activism."

"To have real self-government, a people must understand what this means, want it, and be willing to sacrifice for it." Many nondemocratic systems are inherently unstable. "But so what?" Kennan asked in 1993. "We are not their keepers. We never will be." He did not anticipate that before his death, at the age of 101 in 2005, his country would have committed itself to a huge effort to become the world's "keeper." He recommended asking only from foreign nations, "governed or misgoverned as habit or tradition will dictate," that "their governing cliques observe, in their bilateral relations with the United States, and with the remainder of the world community, the minimum standards of civilized diplomatic intercourse."[1]

A policy of nonintervention would rely heavily on diplomacy and analytical intelligence, with particular attention to history, since nearly all serious problems among nations are recurrent or have important recurring elements in them. Current crises concerning Iran, Afghanistan, Pakistan, Iraq, Lebanon, and Palestine-Israel all have origins in the European imperial systems and their dismantlement in the aftermath of the twentieth century's totalitarian wars. They are the legacy or in a sense the residue of the history of the last century, and their resolution must be sought in terms of that experience, a fact generally ignored in American political and press references to history—which, despite the frequent polemical citation of historical "lessons," is usually poorly known.

A noninterventionist American foreign policy requires a White House that will understand its primary responsibility to be the well-being and quality of American life. It would curtail nonessential external commitments and support multilateral methods and forums for dealing with international problems and crises, to the extent that this is useful. It would redefine its national security strategy narrowly so as to make its priorities the protection of the American polity and its constitutional government, and its security against military threat. It would reduce military expenditures to levels commensurate with the actual problems of the contemporary world and not the hypothetical threats of science fiction. It would regard nonstate threats of subversion and terrorism as primarily matters for the criminal police and other civilian agencies of security. It would honor the security guarantees given foreign nations and would make the well-being of states historically close to the United States, and to which it is allied by treaty, its concern, but would cease to make military sales and assistance routine instruments of American diplomacy. It is not in the American interest to supply backward governments with the weapons to fight one another, or to repress their own populations.

Such a noninterventionist policy would rely primarily on trade and the market, rather than on territorial control or military intimidation, to provide the resources and energy the United States needs. American security deployments abroad would be reexamined with attention to whether they might actually be impediments to solutions of the conflicts of clients, or might empower civil war or nationalist irredentism, as in Georgia and East Africa.

It would undertake the inevitably controversial reduction of America's global military command structure, recognizing that too often it has been a provocation to nationalist hostility towards the United States and an inspiration to radical forces and the extremist violence it is intended to prevent—in practice a program that automatically generates its own contradiction.

It would assume that nations are responsible for their own political affairs so long as these do not directly threaten the larger interests of the international community. It would act on the assumption that American intervention in others' affairs, even when benevolent, is more likely to turn small problems into big ones. This would seem a position attractive to an American public that traditionally has believed in individual responsibility and the autonomy of markets, considers itself hostile to political ideology (largely unaware of its own), and professes to be governed by pragmatism, compromise, and constitutional order. This was the case in the era of the republic's beginnings, but it no longer seems to be the national taste, or at least not that of its leadership.

Had a noninterventionist policy been followed in the 1960s, there would have been no American war in Indochina. The struggle there would have been recognized as nationalist in motivation, unsusceptible to solution by foreigners, and inherently limited in its international consequences, whatever they might be—as proved to be the case. The United States would never have been defeated, its army demoralized, or its students radicalized. There would have been no

American invasion of Cambodia and no Khmer Rouge genocide. Laos and its tribal peoples would have been spared their ordeal.

The United States would not have suffered its catastrophic implication in what was essentially a domestic crisis in Iran in 1979, which still poisons Near and Middle Eastern affairs, since there would never have been the Nixon administration's huge and provocative investment in the Shah's regime as America's "gendarme" in the region, compromising the Shah and contributing to that fundamentalist backlash against his secularizing modernization that provoked the Islamists' revolution.

Instead of a general assurance in his Cairo speech in June 2009, addressed to the Muslim world, that the United States intended to withdraw its troops from Iraq and Afghanistan and wished to have no bases there, to which there has been no sequel, President Barack Obama might have actually asked the governments of the region for their political assistance to the United States in accomplishing these desirable ends, as well as offering a withdrawal of American forces from South and Central Asia as a whole, and from the Middle East, whose well-being, manner of self-rule, and social and religious affairs might be considered of inherently limited importance to the United States and the affair of the peoples themselves rather than of Washington officials.

Without entering further into what could become a futile discussion of the "mights" or "might nots" of the last half-century, one can say that the United States would certainly not have found itself at war in 2010 in Afghanistan and Pakistan (and indirectly in Somalia, Yemen, and elsewhere in Africa), while still trying to extricate itself from the consequences of its invasion of Iraq seven years earlier.

Israel, with its conventional and unconventional arms, is capable of assuring its own defense against external aggression, even if newly aware of the limits of its ability to win victories against irregular local and foreign resistance to its occupation of the Palestinian territories which can only increase as its demographic disadvantage mounts. It cannot expect total security without political resolution of the Palestinian question, a problem only it can solve, presumably by withdrawing from the illegally occupied Palestinian territories. With the arrival of the Obama administration in Washington, Israel was once again urged to search for such a solution but was given no new incentive to do so. Forty years of past American involvement have mainly enabled, or indeed encouraged, the Israelis to avoid facing facts, facilitating its colonization of Palestine, accompanied by the emergence of quasi-fascist settler groups hostile to the Israeli government itself, all contributing to that radicalization of Islamic society that inspires a continuing search for revenge. The major shifts in Israeli public opinion and in government policy following the attack on Gaza in the winter of 2008–2009 produced the formation of a government encouraging further seizure of Palestinian territory, a policy inviting new resistance.[2] Elsewhere, a noninterventionist Washington might reasonably consider people who are victims of domestic despots, such as the Iraqis before 2003, to be responsible for their own solutions and usually capable of their own revolutions—if they really do want change or revolution. No foreign power occupied Iraq in 2003, imposing Saddam Hussein's dictatorship, and as 2010 began, the only foreign intervention in Afghanistan and Pakistan is America's (and NATO's).

This may be considered a hard-headed, or hard-hearted, doctrine concerning the responsibilities of people themselves, even shocking when international media audiences witness atrocities in Darfur and elsewhere. It does not necessarily imply passivity in the face of atrocity. The appalling nonintervention of the Western powers in Yugoslav ethnic cleansing during the initial UN intervention in that country in 1992 occurred because the Security Council (under U.S. pressure, motivated by Washington's unwillingness to get involved) pusillanimously limited the UN mission to "peace-keeping" even while a war of aggression was taking place. Only after the Bosnian Serbs attacked UN soldiers, taking prisoners, was military intervention decided by the European governments involved, which the United States then insisted be placed under NATO command. The Dayton agreement that followed separated the combatants, but the situation of Kosovo, its Serbian minority population, and the Albanians of the region is still without a reliable settlement.

A noninterventionist foreign policy is entirely compatible with multilateral international reaction to atrocious public crimes and the existence of international criminal courts (which the United States has generally opposed because of its present vulnerability to indictments and prosecution for a number of practices that have been or are national policy). However, it is extremely difficult to conduct international interventions in such matters with more positive than negative results, since many such emergencies have causes beyond decisive international remedy. The ultimate roots of the Darfur crisis are ethnic and climatic, since many arable regions of sub-Saharan Africa are experiencing gradual desertification, which causes conflict between the agricultural peoples of the border region and the nomadic or semi-nomadic people beyond, who are forced inland to feed their herds. Well-meant Western proposals to identify "villains" in such cases and impose military reprisals are usually futile. The Rwanda genocide was the result of the hypocrisies of colonialism and of decolonization and "democratization." It was both ethnic in nature and a "class" war between the historically oppressed Hutu and their historic rulers, the Tutsi. The ironic outcome is that the ultimate consequence of the genocidal attack by the democratically empowered Hutu majority upon the Tutsi minority has been to restore Tutsi power in Rwanda. Humanitarian intervention itself often creates problems, as nongovernmental groups now readily acknowledge. UN and NGO action to feed and support refugees and casualties can, for example, reward an aggressor by taking his victims off his hands.

At the time of the U.S. invasion of Iraq, when "humanitarian intervention" continued to be a subject of controversy and political manipulation, the Canadian intellectual and now Liberal Party leader Michael Ignatieff wrote that the United States was the "last hope for democracy and stability" in failed states. Since the Iraq invasion and what has followed, this is no longer a widely held view. Direct American intervention polarizes and politicizes, given not only the widespread present unpopularity of the United States in the non-Western world, but also the frequent incompetence and destructiveness of these interventions.

My argument from the beginning of this essay has been that the United States is reenacting in war and politics a classic progression in humanity's collective as well as individual destiny in which the successive stages have consisted in the acquisition of great power—the increasing abuses of power that characterized the Cold War, the

Vietnam War, and the eight years of the Bush administration, and thus far of its aftermath, with a subordination of ethical values to an ideology of national triumphalism. A conception of American Manifest Destiny as of universal relevance and validity has been held to justify the arbitrary use of power to impose the national will.

This sequence of events is not the result of any law of history, although humans experience its recurrence. It is recognized in literature, philosophy, and history as a characteristic pattern of human action. What is its culmination? How does it normally end? Aristotle, and the philosophers and artists of his time and before, found "pity and terror" in the artistic representation of such events and a moral catharsis in witnessing their tragic conclusion, considered ineluctable. Can tragedy and failure be avoided in the American case? George Kennan believed that it could if Americans looked within themselves. The nation might eventually discover that it is unable "to find in our relations with other countries or other parts of the world relief from the painful domestic confrontation with ourselves." He wrote in 1993, "We are, for the love of God, only human beings, the descendants of human beings, the bearers, like our ancestors, of all the usual human frailties. Divine hands may occasionally reach down to support us in our struggles, as individuals, with our divided nature; but no divine hand has ever reached down to make us, as a national community, anything more than what we are, or to elevate us in that capacity over the remainder of mankind."[3]

Those were the words of an old man of eighty-nine, whose belief in the American republic remained very much alive. They might find a different validation in the nation's simply becoming so distracted by simultaneous and continuing economic and domestic social crises and loss, and the loss of international economic and financial primacy, that it finds itself forced by uncontrollable forces to abandon military and political fantasy and retreat into a healing isolation.

A second relatively simple possibility is that the nation's attempt by military means to control the evolution of radical and puritanical political forces in Islamic society, as well as the concomitant ills that afflict the modern world elsewhere, might simply exhaust itself in repeated and extensive military frustration. This could take a long time, as the recognition of failure will be resisted, ignored, or distorted in the minds of American leaders and policy thinkers, convinced that power has given them the means to "make new realities" (as the George W. Bush government tried and failed to do), able to overcome the grinding inertia of existing reality. Such would be a further exhibition of pride, one of the components of Hubris, introduction to Nemesis.

Another result of such failures, if accompanied by national humiliation, could produce hatred against those Americans held responsible for the failure, as after America's defeat in Vietnam. One must note that the most intense post-Vietnam hatred was not for those responsible for the war, but for those who had opposed it—and ominously, for those who had fought it: its veterans to an extent found themselves pariahs, incomprehensibly to themselves. Anger may mount against enemies in the Muslim world, their allies, and their sympathizers, and also against the "so-called allies" who fail to support the United States.

It was not an isolated segment of opinion that expressed the domestic bitterness that followed the Vietnam War. It included leading figures in the Republican Party and inside the army and air force who held the war's opponents responsible for having blocked the measures of unlimited war they claimed could still have won in Vietnam (to what purpose, as we now have to ask). This certainly could happen again, and it may even be likely if the war in Asia lengthens, as the president warned the Veterans of Foreign Wars in August 2009 that it would.

The Vietnam War aroused an enduring and corrosive hatred between certain groups of Americans. This hatred has reappeared since the 2008 presidential election. The conflicts that have followed have all seemed too intense for their articulated causes. Some said this was a return of racism, suppressed during the presidential campaign. I think not. It was as if a huge, uncomprehending disappointment lay across the land, especially among the poor and middle classes who had most believed in the American Dream and felt most betrayed by what the United States had become by 2010. I would think this is why Barack Obama has so stubbornly sought reconciliation and cooperation in governing the nation. This was to be his greatness. He has yet to find it. In matters of international policy he has followed the road laid out by his immediate predecessors, and by the dominant policy elites and interests that already have failed the nation.

Imperial failure is more likely to begin in detail than in drama. The Swiss philosopher Denis de Rougemont has noted that

> one of the minor prophets of the modern era, Joseph de Maistre, wrote under Napoleon, "When a too preponderant power terrifies the universe, one is irritated to find no means to stop it; one abounds in bitter reproaches against the egoism and immorality of governments, which prevent them from uniting to confront the common danger. But at bottom these complaints are ill-founded. A coalition among sovereigns, formed on the principles of a pure and disinterested morality, would be a miracle. God, who owes no one any miracles, and who makes no useless ones, employs two simple means to reestablish the equilibrium: sometimes the giant cuts his own throat, sometimes a greatly inferior power throws in his path an imperceptible obstacle which, no one knows how, subsequently grows and becomes insurmountable; like a feeble reed, caught in the current of a river, which in the end produces an accumulation of silt which changes its course."[4]

The United States may simply find itself with no choice but to fall back on itself, no doubt embittered by disappointment. That might provide a soft ending to empire. The hard ending would be palpable defeat in crucial undertakings. These would have to be defeats that cut through the insulation of ignorance, misinformation, and complacency that has prevailed in the country during the first decade of the new century and such is perhaps impossible. The external crisis would have to be deeper, and be more personal in its effects, than the Vietnam defeat, and that too seems unlikely. The American army thwarted in Vietnam was the people's army: hence millions of men and their families were involved. It was the corrupted remnant of those American people's armies that fought the Revolutionary, Civil (on two sides), and world wars, in which, in this new Vietnam version, the privileged of society, and the cowards, stood aside, finding themselves with "other priorities"—as former vice president Richard Cheney told us—and were able to find the complacent doctor, academic dean, or draft board to make it happen. The new all-volunteer American army is working and lower-middle class, and it increasingly is composed of, and recruited from, poor foreigners, in need of a route to legal immigration.

I suppose there could also be a catastrophic end, in which a maddened American elite would show an ungrateful world why all those nuclear weapons had been saved. That is harder to imagine, almost impossible, but as I have suggested, the personalities and ideologies to constitute an elite of revenge-seekers clearly are latent in modern American political society, having already revealed themselves by their responsibility for American torture sites around the world, our hired assassins, and all the others who have pitilessly killed or been killed in empty causes since 2001. Even to speak of such a possibility is con-firmation that the post-Enlightenment crisis of Western civilization is not over.

Today the conviction is all but unanimous that the First World War was purposeless, entered into without objective cause and finished in general ruin. Everyone agrees that the totalitarian-instigated Second World War, and the delirious ambitions of those who caused that war, displayed man at his most bestial. What then should we say about today's worldwide struggle between Americans and "the rest" that does not have behind it even a convincing positive ideological cause—such as Marxism-Leninism, which was plausible and seemingly progres-sive to many in the circumstances of those times? The struggle is not powered by a claim to national vindication after defeat and seeming betrayal—as in Germany's case after 1918, put together by Hitler with a national project of racial conquest, national expansion, and world domination. America's only rationale is that as the sole superpower it seems inevitable that it impose its own values as universal.

Thucydides, writing of the war between Athens and Sparta, dis-misses, as if beyond comment, the evidence of human bestiality loosed on the weak, the arrogance of leaders, the greed of the profiteers, and the criminal complacence of the demagogue, in order to speak of something more important: political stupidity.

The stupidity is "the belief that military measures and massacres can resolve intricate political-territorial contrarieties of interest; the collective folly that seems to infect civic sensibility, making it tribal and infantile, in moments of victory; the incapacity of statecraft and sheer common sense to halt, to reexamine rationally the mechanism of waste and of mutual crippling, which wars set in motion."[5]

Americans today conduct a colossally militarized but morally nuga-tory global mission supported by apparent majorities of the political, intellectual, and academic elites of the nation. It has lacked from the very beginning an attainable goal. It cannot succeed. George W. Bush is quoted by Bob Woodward as having said that American strategy was "to create chaos, to create vacuum," in his enemies' countries. This was very unwise. The United States risks becoming such a strategy's ultimate victim.

## NOTES

1.  George F. Kennan, *Around the Cragged Hill: A Personal and Political Philosophy* (New York and London: W.W. Norton and Company, Inc., 1993), chapter 9, passim.
2.  Former Israeli prime minister Ehud Olmert said on September 29, 2008, what "everybody" had already known but no Israeli leader in power had had the courage to say: "That Israel must withdraw from nearly all of the West Bank and East Jerusalem to attain peace with the Palestinians and that any occupied land that it held on to would have to be exchanged for the same quantity of Israeli territory." Interview in the newspaper *Yediot Aharonot*, as reported in the *International Herald Tribune* on September 30, 2008. Unfortunately, Olmert on September 29, 2008, was caretaker prime minister and was incapable of acting on his words.
3.  Kennan, *Around the Cragged Hill*.
4.  *The Devil's Share: An Essay on the Diabolic in Modern Society* (Washington, D.C.: Bollingen Series of the Old Dominion Foundation, 1994), 199–200. Copyright assigned to Bollingen Foundation, Inc., New York, NY. Meridian edition first published March 1956.
5.  See George Steiner, review of Donald Kagan, *The Peloponnesian War*, in *The New Yorker*, March 11, 1991.

*2010*

# Sources and Acknowledgments

Russell Kirk, Conservatism Defined, *The Portable Conservative Reader*, ed. Russell Kirk (New York: Viking Penguin, 1982). The title given here has been provided by this volume's editor. Copyright © 1982 by Penguin Random House LLC. Used by permission of Viking Books, an imprint of Penguin Random House LLC. All rights reserved.

William F. Buckley, Notes Toward an Empirical Definition of Conservatism: William F. Buckley, *The Jeweler's Eye* (New York: G. P. Putnam and Sons, 1968). Copyright © 1958, 1962, 1963, 1964, 1965, 1966, 1967, 1968 by William F. Buckley, Jr. Reprinted by permission of The Wallace Literary Agency.

Frank S. Meyer, The Recrudescent American Conservatism: *Left, Right, Center*, ed. Robert Goldwin (Skokie, IL: Rand McNally, 1965), as "Conservatism."

Henry Adams, The Dynamo and the Virgin: *Henry Adams, Novels, Mont Saint Michel, The Education*, eds. Ernst Samuels and Jayne Samuels (New York: Library of America, 1983).

Walter Lippmann, from Journalism and the Higher Law: Walter Lippmann, *Liberty and the News* (New York: Harcourt, Brace & Howe, 1920).

George Santayana, Materialism and Idealism in American Life: George Santayana, *Character and Opinion in the United States* (New York: Charles Scribner's Sons, 1921).

Herbert Hoover, from *American Individualism*: Herbert Hoover, *American Individualism* (Garden City, NY: Doubleday, Page & Company, 1922).

Zora Neale Hurston, How It Feels to Be Colored Me: *Zora Neale Hurston, Folklore, Memoirs, & Other Writings*, ed. Cheryl Wall (New York: Library of America, 1995).

Irving Babbitt, What I Believe: Rousseau and Religion: *Forum* 83 (1930): 80–87.

William Henry Chamberlin, The Choice Before Civilization: William Henry Chamberlin, *Collectivism: A False Utopia* (New York: Macmillan, 1937). Copyright © 1937 by The Macmillan Company, renewed 1965 by William Henry Chamberlin. Reprinted with the permission of Scribner, a division of Simon & Schuster, Inc. All rights reserved.

Whittaker Chambers, Foreword in the Form of a Letter to My Children: Whittaker Chambers, *Witness* (New York: Random House, 1952). Copyright © 1952. Reprinted by permission of Regnery Publishing, Inc.

Frank Chodorov, The Most Precious Heirloom: Frank Chodorov, *One Is a Crowd: Reflections of an Individualist* (New York: Devin-Adair Company, 1952). Copyright © 1952. Reprinted by permission of Ludwig von Mises Institute.

John Courtney Murray, E Pluribus Unum: John Courtney Murray, *We Hold These Truths* (New York: Sheed and Ward, 1960). Copyright © 1960. Reprinted by permission of Rowman & Littlefield Publishing Group.

Wilmoore Kendall, from *The Conservative Affirmation*: Wilmoore Kendall, *The Conservative Affirmation* (Chicago: Henry Regnery, 1963). Copyright © 1963. Reprinted by permission of Regnery Publishing, Inc.

Harry A. Jaffa, On the Nature of Civil and Religious Liberty: *The Conservative Papers*, ed. Ralph de Toledano and Karl Hess (New York: Doubleday Anchor, 1964). Copyright © 1964 by Ralph de Toledano and Karl Hess. Used by permission of Doubleday, an imprint of the Knopf Doubleday Publishing Group, a division of Random House LLC. All rights reserved.

Joan Didion, The Women's Movement: Joan Didion, *The White Album* (New York: Simon & Schuster, 1979). Copyright © 1979 by Joan Didion. Reprinted by permission of Farrar, Straus & Giroux.

Allan Bloom, Our Ignorance: Alan Bloom, *The Closing of the American Mind* (New York: Simon & Schuster, 1987). Copyright © 1987 by Allan Bloom. Reprinted with the permission of Simon & Schuster, Inc. All rights reserved.

Andrew Sullivan, Here Comes the Groom: *The New Republic*, August 28, 1989. Copyright © 1989 by Andrew Sullivan, used by permission of The Wylie Agency LLC.

Shelby Steele, Affirmative Action: The Price of Preference: Shelby Steele, *The Content of Our Character* (New York: St. Martin's, 1990). Copyright © 1990 by Shelby Steele. Reprinted by permission of St. Martin's Press. All rights reserved.

Richard John Neuhaus, Can Atheists Be Good Citizens? *First Things*, August 1991. Copyright © 1991. Reprinted by permission of *First Things*.

Michael Novak, from *The Catholic Ethic and the Spirit of Capitalism*: Michael Novak, *The Catholic Ethic and the Spirit of Capitalism* (New York: Free Press, 1993). Copyright © 1993 by Michael Novak. Reprinted with the permission of The Free Press, a division of Simon & Schuster, Inc. All rights reserved.

Christopher Lasch, The Soul of Man under Secularism: Christopher Lasch, *The Revolt of the Elites and the Betrayal of Democracy* (New York: W. W. Norton, 1994). Copyright © 1994 by Christopher Lasch. Reprinted by permission of Nell Lasch.

Glenn Loury, Leadership Failure and the Loyalty Trap: Glenn Loury, *One by One from the Inside Out: Essays and Reviews on Race and Responsibility in America*

(New York: The Free Press, 1995). Copyright © 1995 by Glenn C. Loury. Reprinted with the permission of The Free Press, a division of Simon & Schuster, Inc. All rights reserved.

Antonin Scalia, Dissent in *Obergefell v. Hodges*: *Obergefell v. Hodges*, 135 S. Ct. 2584 (2015).

Randolph Bourne, from *The State*: Randolph Bourne, *The Radical Will: Selected Writings 1911–1917*, ed. Olaf Hansen. New York: Urizen Books, 1977.

Albert Jay Nock, from *Our Enemy, The State*: Albert Jay Nock, *Our Enemy, The State* (New York: William Morrow and Company, 1935). Copyright © 1935 by Albert Jay Nock. Reprinted by permission of HarperCollins Publishers.

Richard Weaver, The Great Stereopticon: Richard Weaver, *Ideas Have Consequences* (Chicago: The University of Chicago Press, 1948). Copyright © 1948 by Richard M. Weaver. Republished with permission of The University of Chicago Press; permission conveyed through Copyright Clearance Center, Inc.

John T. Flynn, from *The Road Ahead*: John Flynn, *The Road Ahead* (New York: Devin-Adair, 1949).

Milton Friedman, Capitalism and Freedom: *New Individualist Review* 1 (April 1961): 3–10. Copyright © 1961 by Milton Friedman. Reprinted with permission of the Center for the Study of Public Choice.

Irving Kristol, When Virtue Loses All Her Loveliness—Some Reflections on Capitalism and "the Free Society": *Two Cheers for Capitalism* (New York: Basic Books, 1978). Copyright © 1978 by Irving Kristol. Used by permission of the Estate of Irving Kristol c/o Writers Representatives LLC, New York, NY 10011. All rights reserved.

Murray Rothbard, from *For a New Liberty*: Murray Rothbard, *For a New Liberty* (New York: Collier Macmillan, 1973). Copyright © 1973, 1978 by Murray N. Rothbard, copyright © 2006 by Ludwig von Mises Institute. Reprinted by permission of Ludwig von Mises Institute.

Patrick Deneen, Unsustainable Liberalism: *First Things*, August 2012. Reprinted in Patrick Deneen, *Why Liberalism Failed* (New Haven, CT: Yale University Press, 2018), 21–42. Copyright © 2018 by Yale University Press. Reprinted by permission of Yale University Press.

John Crowe Ransom, Reconstructed but Unregenerate, *I'll Take My Stand* (New York: Harper & Brothers, 1930). Copyright 1930 by Harper & Brothers, copyright renewed 1958 by Donald Davidson. Reprinted 1977, 2006 by Louisiana State University Press. Reprinted with permission of Louisiana State University Press.

Robert Nisbet, The Loss of Community: *The Quest for Community* (Oxford: Oxford University Press, 1953), chapter 1. Copyright © 1953, 1981 by

Robert Nisbet, reprinted by the Intercollegiate Studies Institute in 2010. Reprinted by permission of the Intercollegiate Studies Institute, Inc.

Eugene Genovese, from *The Southern Tradition*: Eugene Genovese, *The Southern Tradition: The Achievement and Limitations of an American Conservatism* (Cambridge, MA: Harvard University Press, 1994). Copyright © 1994 by the President and Fellows of Harvard College. Reprinted with permission.

Wendell Berry, Local Knowledge in an Age of Information: Wendell Berry, *The Way of Ignorance and Other Essays* (Washington, DC: Shoemaker and Hoard, 2005). Copyright © 2005 by Wendell Berry. Reprinted with permission of Counterpoint Press.

Theodore Roosevelt, The Strenuous Life: *American Speeches: Political Oratory from Abraham Lincoln to Bill Clinton*, ed. Ted Widmer (New York: Library of America, 2006).

Henry Cabot Lodge, Speech in the U.S. Senate on the League of Nations: *American Speeches: Political Oratory from Abraham Lincoln to Bill Clinton*, ed. Ted Widmer (New York: Library of America, 2006).

Charles Beard, *Giddy Minds and Foreign Quarrels*: Charles Beard, *Giddy Minds and Foreign Quarrels* (New York: Macmillan, 1939).

James Burnham, from *The Struggle for the World*: James Burnham, *The Struggle for the World* (New York: John Day, 1947). Copyright © 1947 by James Burnham. Reprinted with permission of the Estate of James Burnham.

Robert A. Taft, from *A Foreign Policy for Americans*: Robert A. Taft, *A Foreign Policy for Americans: The Senator from Ohio Substitutes Sane Analysis for Expediency* (New York: Doubleday, 1951). Copyright © 1951 by Robert A. Taft, renewed 1979 by Robert A. Taft Jr. Used by permission of Doubleday, an imprint of the Knopf Doubleday Publishing Group, a division of Random House LLC. All rights reserved.

Reinhold Niebuhr, from *The Irony of American History*: Reinhold Niebuhr, *The Irony of American History* (New York: Scribner, 1952). Copyright © 1952 by Reinhold Niebuhr, renewed 1980 by Ursula Keppel-Compton Niebuhr. Reprinted by permission of The Estate of Elisabeth Sifton.

Ronald Reagan, Address to Members of Parliament (1982): *American Speeches: Political Oratory from Abraham Lincoln to Bill Clinton*, ed. Ted Widmer (New York: Library of America, 2006).

William Pfaff, from *The Irony of Manifest Destiny*: William Pfaff, *The Irony of Manifest Destiny* (New York: Walker and Company, 2010). Copyright © 2010 by William Pfaff. Reprinted with permission of Bloomsbury Publishing, Inc.

# Index

Abdullah, Emir, 515
Abolition, 169, 203, 440
Abortion, 476
Abraham, 247–48, 250, 254–55
Action Française, 330
Acton, Baron (John Dalberg-Acton), 89, 156, 373
Adam and Eve, 68–69, 437–38
Adams, Franklin P., 58
Adams, Henry, 541; "The Dynamo and the Virgin," 47–56
Adams, James Truslow: "The Mucker Pose," 93
Adams, John, 150, 259, 273, 345, 352
Adams, John Quincy, 522
Adversary culture, 262–64, 267
Advertising, 351, 357, 360
Affirmative action, 233–43, 301
Afghanistan, 593, 603, 605–6
African Americans, 64, 110, 192–93, 203, 264, 359, 475, 483–84, 573; and affirmative action, 233–43; conservative, 84–88; racial loyalty of, 291–302
Agnosticism, 25, 149
Agriculture: collectives, 105–6, 594; decline of rural communities, 481–92; in the South, 443, 449
AIDS, 230–31
Akbar the Great, 199
Akhnaten, 29
Alaska, 487
Albania, 561, 606
Alexander I, 507, 509
Algeciras Conference, 539
Alger, Horatio, 389

Alien and Sedition Acts, 168–69, 180, 189
Alienation, 288, 393, 450, 456–66
Alliances, 508–13, 521–22, 525, 529, 551, 582, 603, 609
Altgeld, John Peter, 539
Altruism, 80–81, 94, 280
American Bar Association, 307
American Conservative Union, 36–37
American Enterprise Institute, 256
American Indians, 315, 408, 487, 504, 566
Americanism, 325, 438
Americanization, 530, 565
Amiens Cathedral, 53–55
Amish, 483
Anarchism, xvi, 6, 8, 17–18, 20, 337, 539
Anderson, Martin, 43
Anderson, Sherwood, 358
Antigone, 214
Anti-Saloon League, 102
Aouni, Abdul Havi, 516
Apaches, 504
Appomattox, surrender at, 442
Aquinas, Thomas, 56, 89, 152, 251, 396; *Summa Theologica*, 419
Arabia, 515–16, 519
Archaism, 29, 454
Arendt, Hannah, 256–57, 259
Argentina, 521
Aristocracy, 108–9, 117, 385–86, 440
Aristophanes, 6, 274
Aristotle, 89, 102, 251, 269, 385, 396, 608; *Ethics*, 419
Arizona, 504

Armenia, 560–61
Army, U.S., 111, 500–502, 547, 610
Arnold, Matthew, 55, 396
Artists, 107–10, 220, 279–81, 284, 319, 360–61
Assembly, freedom of, 104, 158, 188
Association, freedom of, 158, 188
Atheism, 23–26, 149–50, 244–55, 273
Athens, ancient, 29, 259, 356, 464, 565, 611
Atkinson, Ti-Grace, 207
Atlanta, Ga., 293–94
Atlantic Pact, 580–82
Auerbach, Morton: *The Conservative Illusion*, 30
Augustine, 89, 96, 251; *City of God*, 454
Auschwitz concentration camp, 593
Australia, 8, 519, 561
Austria, 7, 76, 507–11, 594
Authoritarianism, 38–39, 356, 387, 426
Azores, 561
Aztecs, 566

Babbitt, Irving, xvii; "What I Believe: Rousseau and Religion," 89–103
Babylon, ancient, 566
Bacon, Francis, 47, 92–93, 98, 102, 419–20
Bagehot, Walter, 7, 11
Baldwin, James: "The Evidence of Things Not Seen," 293
Baldwin, Joseph Clark, 561
Balkans, 328, 518, 561, 566, 606
Baltimore, Md., 132, 151
Barbarism, 104–5, 198–99, 204, 328, 362, 476, 563, 568
Barnard College, 86
Barone, Michael: *Our Country*, 264
Bavarian Soviet Republic, 122
Beard, Charles A., xviii; "Giddy Minds and Foreign Quarrels:

An Estimate of American Foreign Policy," 534–57
Beauvoir, Simone de, 208
Bedouins, 515–16
Beecher, Henry Ward, 248
Beethoven, Ludwig van, 136
Behaviorism, 95, 216
Beijing, China, xv, 539
Belgium, 529
Bell, Daniel, 260; "The Cultural Contradictions of Capitalism," 389
Bell, Derrick, 299
Bell, Jeffrey, 264
Bellow, Saul, 224
Benson, Ezra Taft, 485
Bentham, Jeremy, 7, 9, 373, 453
Berdyaev, Nikolai, 454, 456
Berger, Peter, 250
Bergson, Henri, 99
Berkeley, Calif., 229
Berlin, Germany, 106, 131, 591
Berlin Wall, 591
Bernanos, Georges, 454; *Diary of a Country Priest*, 18
Berry, Wendell, xviii; "Local Knowledge in the Age of Information," 481–92
Beveridge, Albert J., 537–40, 543
Bible, 133, 246, 248, 253–54, 265–66, 275–76, 280, 289
Bierce, Ambrose: *The Devil's Dictionary*, 5
Bill of Rights, U.S., 157–58, 168, 176, 182, 186, 190–93, 200–201, 306, 381–82, 409, 424. *See also* Constitution, U.S.
Bismarck, Otto von, 341, 559
Black, Charles: *The People and the Court*, 409–13
Black, Hugo, 308
Blacklist, 381–82
Blackstone, William, 161
Blaine, Anita McCormick, 379
Bloom, Allan: *The Closing of the American Mind*, 213–27

Blum, Léon, 226
Boethius: *Consolation of Philosophy*, 258
Bolivia, 542
Bolsheviks, 81, 114, 343, 346, 532
Bonald, Louis de, 7
Bonhoeffer, Dietrich, 248
Bosnia, 606
Boston, Mass., 51, 54, 57, 62
Bourbon dynasty, 330, 510
Bourne, Randolph, xviii; *The State*, 313–36
Bozell, L. Brent: *McCarthy and His Enemies*, xv, 164, 170
Brandeis, Louis, 308
Branly, Édouard, 49, 52
*Brave One, The*, 381
Brazil, 521, 552, 578
Brezhnev, Leonid, 597, 599
Britain, 62, 82, 89, 96, 106, 161, 207, 382, 391, 516, 541, 560–62, 585; alliance with United States, 582; alliances after Napoleonic wars, 508–13; Conservative Party, 7–9, 548, 551; and culture of American South, 433–34, 439, 441, 447–48; and divine right of kings, 117; economic freedom in, 371; education in, 101; English Civil War, 6, 29, 111; foreign policy in late 1930s, 546, 548–49, 551–57; as home of modern capitalism, 368; imperialism of, 504, 544, 565; journalism in, 60; Labour Party, 373–74; and League of Nations, 513, 519–21, 537; Liberal Party, 341; loyalty in, 330; Magna Carta, 153; navy of, 538; Parliament, 168, 408–9, 510, 590–601; reform in, 591; religion in, 72, 148; rights in, 158; romanticism in, 281; socialism in, 31, 111, 367–68;

welfare state in, 364; in World War I, 529
British Broadcasting Corporation, 382
Browder, Earl, 112
Browning, Robert, 435
Brownson, Orestes, 7
Brown University, 291
Brunner, Emil, 459
Brussels, Belgium, 591
Bryan, William Jennings, 537, 539
Bryce, James, 345
Buber, Martin, 459
Buchanan, Patrick, xviii
Buckley, Michael: *At the Origins of Modern Atheism*, 245–46
Buckley, William F., Jr., 163, 558; *McCarthy and His Enemies*, xv, 164, 170; "Notes Toward an Empirical Definition of Conservatism," 12–27; "Our Mission Statement," xv
Buddhism, 97, 250
Buffalo, N.Y., 71–72
Bukharin, Nicolai, 114
Bulgaria, 561
Bundy, McGeorge, 403
Bureaucracy, 113, 177–78, 265, 338–39, 342, 378–79, 392, 398, 403, 407, 472, 476, 593
Bureau of Agricultural Economics, 355
Burke, Edmund, 5–7, 9–11, 25, 30, 92, 94, 231, 452; *Reflections on the Revolution in France*, 7
Burnham, James: *Congress and the American Tradition*, 398; *The Struggle for the World*, 558–73
Bush, George H. W., 470
Bush, George W., 608–9, 611–12
Business, xiv, 116, 391–92, 474–75, 481, 484
Byzantine Empire, 566

Caesar, Julius, 559
Cairo, Egypt, 605

Calhoun, John C., 7, 409, 412, 472, 476
California, 517, 585, 590
Calvin, John, 396, 459
Calvinism, 226, 253, 480
Cambodia, 593, 605
Camus, Albert, 225
Canada, 168, 519, 521, 607
Cannae, battle of, 558
Canning, George, 509–10, 513
Canton, China, 131
Capitalism, 76–77, 79, 81, 91, 278, 383, 394; created by Calvinism, 226; democratic, 256, 267–68; developed in Britain, 368; and family, 206; flaws of, 112–13, 260, 281; and freedom, 369–82; and free society, 388–89; industrial, 468; and justice, 387; justifications for, 390–91; liberal, 384–85, 394–96; multinational finance, 474–75; promises of, 384–86; state, 116; unrestrained, 415; and working class, 264
Capone, Al, 106
Cardozo, Benjamin, 308
Carlyle, Thomas, 97, 357, 396, 441
Carmina Burana, 288
Castlereagh, Viscount (Robert Stewart), 509
Catholics, 12, 94–95, 148–49, 151, 160–62, 228, 244, 250, 256, 263–68, 406, 438, 459, 472–73
Cato the Elder, 559
Cavett, Dick, 208
CBS-TV, 297
Céline, Louis-Ferdinand: Journey to the End of the Night, 225–26
Celts, 407
Censorship, 154, 354
Centers for Disease Control, 293
Center for Libertarian Studies, 397
Centralization, 370, 373, 468, 470, 472, 474, 476, 482, 594

Cervantes, Miguel de: Don Quixote, 72, 551
Chamberlain, Neville, 548–49
Chamberlin, William Henry: "The Choice before Civilization," 104–18
Chambers, Whittaker, xviii, 13, 15–17; "Foreword in the Form of a Letter to My Children," 119–39
Change, 7, 9, 118, 126, 450, 453, 462
Charlemagne, 199
Chartres Cathedral, 52, 55, 219
Chateaubriand, François-René de, 7, 345
Chaucer, Geoffrey: "The House of Fame," 6
Chautauqua, 546–47
Checks and balances, 36, 176, 269, 377–78, 569
Cheney, Richard, 610
Chesterton, G. K., 18
Chevalier, Michel, 345
Chiang Kai-shek, 560–62
Chicago, Ill., 48, 495, 545, 547
Chicago School, 369
China, xv–xvi, 76, 207, 270, 399, 404, 407, 497–98, 503, 515, 519, 539, 543–44, 560–62, 578
Chinard, Gilbert, 345
Chinese Americans, 296, 438
Chodorov, Frank: "The Most Precious Heirloom," 140–47
Choice, 36, 180, 213–15, 416–18, 420–27, 563
Christianity, xvi, 12, 24–25, 48, 50–51, 91–94, 97, 102, 107, 146–47, 149, 155, 158, 161–62, 245–48, 251–53, 261, 263–66, 269–71, 287, 307, 319, 361, 389, 418, 454, 459, 470, 473–74, 504, 507, 509, 538, 566, 586. See also Catholics; Protestants
Christianity & Crisis, 584

Christian realism, 584–89
Christian Science, 73
Churchill, Winston S., 587, 592, 594, 600–601
Cicero, 6, 89
Citizenship, xix, 157, 244–45, 252, 254–55, 320, 383–84, 432, 519, 565
Civil rights, xvi, 84, 155–56, 158, 188–89, 191, 195–96, 199, 241, 299–302, 369–70
Civil War (American), 72, 110, 168, 189–92, 203, 314, 388, 391, 439, 442, 497, 512, 523, 558, 560, 575, 610
Civil War (English), 6, 29, 111
Civil War (Spanish), 110–11, 546–48
Clark, Kenneth, 296
Class, 105, 197, 206–7, 209, 211, 299–300, 313, 323–25, 390
Classical liberalism, 30–31, 34, 39, 369–70
Clemenceau, Georges, 512, 520
Cleveland, Grover, 523–24
Cobb, Frank I., 59
Cold War, xv, 140, 364–67, 470, 558, 574, 607
Coleridge, Samuel Taylor, 396
Collectivism, 104–10, 114–18, 144–46, 342–43, 346, 373, 425, 594–95
Colombia, 513
Columbia University, xiv–xv, 86
Columbus, Christopher, 50, 249
Commercialism, 363, 499, 538, 543, 553
Committee for a Sane Nuclear Policy, 19
Common law, 158, 200, 407
Communism, xiv–xv, 6, 19, 31, 43, 76–77, 111, 141, 150, 181, 189, 196, 225, 248, 264, 270, 278, 364–66, 378, 390, 395, 403, 468, 549, 551, 579–80, 588–89; anti-communists, 18, 20–22, 183; as dictatorship, 104–10, 112–18, 125, 172–73, 188, 197–99, 372, 566–69, 572–73, 597, 599; as global movement, 35–37, 168, 182, 560–64, 570–71, 577–78, 581–82, 586, 593, 595–96; and Hollywood blacklist, 381–82; legislative response to, 182–84; and Protestant churches, 165–66; Senator McCarthy's attack on, 170–71, 175–79, 186–87; and Whittaker Chambers, 16–17, 119–20, 122–34, 137–38
Communist Manifesto, 127
Communist Party (Britain), 561
Communist Party (Soviet Union), 108, 112, 134
Communist Party (United States), xiv, 112, 119, 129, 197, 342, 366
Communitarianism, 415
Communities, 424–25, 438; loss of, 450–67, 471–74; rural, 481–92
Competition, 78, 83, 342, 353, 372, 437, 451, 469, 471, 474, 542–43, 564
Concentration camps/labor camps, 104, 112, 125, 131, 593
Conflict, 215, 230, 351
Confucius, 404
Congress, U.S., xii, 31–32, 119, 122, 170–71, 176–79, 182, 184, 190–92, 200, 241, 295, 334, 338–39, 412, 500–502, 506, 510, 513, 516, 526–27, 542, 545–49, 595, 598. See also specific legislation
Congressional Record, 501
Congress of Laibach, 509–10
Congress of Troppau, 509
Congress of Verona, 509–10
Congress of Vienna, 508
Conrad, Joseph: Lord Jim, 359
Conscription, 324
Consent, 58, 153–55, 159, 194, 269, 416

Conservatism, defined, 5–11, 28–31
Conservative Party (Britain), 7–8, 548, 551
Constantine the Great, 50
Constitution, U.S., 28, 112, 168, 183–84, 200–201, 203, 253–54, 409, 516; checks and balances in, 377; conflicts in, 190–93; as consensus, 153–54; as conservative document, 6, 35–39; and federalism, 412, 424–25; and national security, 176–79; and original intent, 188, 303; and pluralism, 112; and same-sex marriage, 303–9; and slavery, 191–92; and truth, 60–61, 151; and war, 527. *See also* Bill of Rights, U.S., *and individual amendments*
Constitutionalism, 153–54, 159, 189, 346, 416, 539, 603–4
Consumerism, 278, 423
Contracts, 78
Control-of-Engagements Order, 373–74
Cooley, Thomas, 307
Cooper, James Fenimore: *The American Democrat*, 352
Copernicus, Nicolaus, 50, 126
Cornuelle, Richard C., 42
Corporations, xiv, 116, 392, 474–75, 481, 484
Corruption, 58, 60
Costa Rica, 552
Coughlin, Charles, 170
Council of Europe, 598
Counterculture, 222, 257, 263, 265–67
Country, defined, 316
Cox, Archibald, 298
Creativity, 80, 100
Crèvecoeur, Hector St. John, 257, 272
Crime, 43, 203, 293, 296

Critical legal studies, 476
Croly, Herbert: *The Promise of American Life*, 395–96
Cropsey, Jacob, 385
Crusades, 581
Cuba, 390, 498–99, 501, 503–4, 525, 541, 595
Cultural elites, 261–62, 476
Culture: adversary, 262–64, 267; mass, 265; popular, 261, 263
Czechoslovakia, 595–96

Dachau concentration camp, 593
*Daily Worker*, 16, 119, 380
Daladier, Édouard, 548–49
*Dallas*, 261
Dante Alighieri, 52, 110, 205, 274
Darfur, 606–7
Dark Ages, 105, 141, 199
Darrow, Clarence, 23–24
Darwin, Charles, 68, 247–48, 391
Daudet, Alphonse, 496–97
Davis, Kingsley: *Human Society*, 466–67
Davis, Norman, 544
Dayton Accords, 606
Decembrists, 108–9
Decentralization, 370, 372, 392, 406, 468, 476
Declaration of Independence, 147, 149, 151, 157, 188, 191–96, 199, 203, 253, 276, 304
Declaration of the Rights of Man and of the Citizen, 157
Decolonization, 607
Decorum, 92, 94, 354
Defense spending, 365
Defoe, Daniel: *Robinson Crusoe*, 374–75
Deism, 253
De Jouvenel, Bertrand: *On Power*, 399, 409, 426
Demagogues, 77, 83, 169, 293, 360, 478–79, 611
Demant, V. A., 459

Democracy, 72, 76, 102, 105, 110–12, 115, 117–18, 161, 219, 236, 255, 282, 303, 314, 320, 330, 369, 386, 389, 398, 438, 473–74, 476, 539, 542, 547, 549, 553, 557, 573, 579, 591–94, 596–600, 602, 607; Athenian, 565; defined, 33; egalitarian, 469; and foreign policy, 331–35; and journalism, 58, 60; liberal, 254; life-style in, 222; "make the world safe for democracy," 585; and middle class, 269; and morality, 33, 268; parliamentary, 408; and same-sex marriage, 304; and war, 327, 332–35; and wealth, 116; and working class, 264
Democratic capitalism, 256, 267–68
Democratic Party, 32, 264–65, 294, 299, 342, 449, 506, 524, 546–48, 590, 598
Democratic progress, 598
Democratic socialism, 31, 370
Deneen, Patrick, xviii; "Unsustainable Liberalism," 415–27; Why Liberalism Failed, 415
Derrida, Jacques, 249
Descartes, René, 56, 247
Desegregation, xvi, 299, 477
Determinism, 95, 208, 401–2
Dewey, George, 500
Dewey, John, 94, 420, 457
Dialectical materialism, 15, 125, 134, 248
Dickens, Charles, 73, 95; Martin Chuzzlewit, 345
Dictatorship, 76–77, 79, 81, 111, 161, 181–82, 204, 220, 269, 333, 337, 346, 375, 470, 477, 510, 556, 565, 570, 575, 592–95, 598, 600–601, 603, 611; communist, 104–10, 112–18, 125, 172–73, 188, 197–99, 372,

566–69, 573, 597, 599; fascist, 104–10, 112, 115, 197–99, 344, 372, 468–69, 547, 568; after French Revolution, 150; and intellectuals, 405–7; in Iraq, 606; in Latin America, 542; military, 145
Diderot, Denis, 98
Didion, Joan, xviii; "The Women's Movement," 205–12
Disintegration, 141, 450–51, 453–55, 464, 483
Dissent, 16, 145, 150–51, 161, 381, 384, 393, 396
Distribution of wealth, xvi, 379
Diversity, 10, 230, 235–36, 242, 375, 598
Divine right, 76, 117, 398, 402, 408
Division of labor, 375–76
Djerjinsky, Felix, 112
Djilas, Milovan, 263
Domestic partnership, 228–32, 303
Donizetti, Gaetano: L'Elisir d'amore, 216
Dostoevsky, Feodor, 458
Douglas, Alfred, 280
Douglas, Stephen A., 192–93, 203
Dred Scott v. Sandford, 191
Dreiser, Theodore, 23
Dreyfus, Alfred, 560
Du Bois, W. E. B., 301
Due process of law, 158, 305, 309
Duke, David, 477–78
Dulles, John Foster, 404
Durkheim, Émile, 460
Dynamo, 48–49, 52–53

East Germany, 594, 596
Eastman, Max, 23–25
Eatonville, Fla., 84–86
Economic freedom, 370–74, 414
Economic growth, 396, 423, 593–94
Economic power, 372, 377–78
Edmiston, Susan, 211

Education, 43, 64, 68, 80–81, 83,
    110, 143, 207, 213, 223, 226,
    285, 292, 348, 440, 517; and
    affirmative action, 233–43, 301;
    Catholic universities, 472–73;
    decentralized school systems,
    392; land-grant universities,
    481, 490–91; liberal, 101–2
Edwards, Jonathan, 112, 289–90
Egypt, 504; ancient, 29, 349, 566
Ehrenburg, Ilya, 15
Eighteenth Amendment, 102
Einstein, Albert, 469, 479
Eisenhower, Dwight D., 20, 150,
    166, 404, 406, 485
Election of 1916, 540
Election of 1918 (congressional),
    540
Election of 1920, 540
Election of 1932, 31, 338–39, 343
Election of 1934 (congressional),
    338, 342, 344
Election of 1936, 339, 546–47
Election of 1940, 581
Election of 1952, 84
Election of 1964, 32, 40
Election of 1984, 299
Election of 2008, 609
Election of 2016, xii
Elections, 116–17, 154, 169, 392,
    572
Eliot, T. S., 454, 465
El Salvador, 595–96
Elshtain, Jean Bethke, 426
Emerson, Ralph Waldo, 206
Emerson, Thomas: "Loyalty
    amongst Government
    Employees," 183
Engels, Friedrich, 206, 216, 379
Enlightenment, 78, 154, 157–58,
    161, 250, 252, 281, 452, 456,
    611
Environmental issues, 384, 416,
    424–25, 435–37, 442, 444
Equal Employment Opportunity
    Commission, 235

Equality, 7, 10, 78, 81–82, 172, 192,
    194–95, 204, 215, 236–37, 265,
    384, 389–90, 396, 469
Equal protection of law, 309
Estonia, 579
Ethnic cleansing, 606–7
Euclid, 352
Eugenics, xvi
Euripides, 274
Europeanism, 431, 433–34, 438–40,
    440
Evangelicalism, 253, 307, 470
Evolution, 248, 321
Exceptionalism, xviii, 169, 527,
    554–57
Existentialism, 214, 282
Experts, 398, 402–3
Exposition Universelle, 47, 50, 56
Expression, freedom of, 186, 198,
    270, 308, 579

Fabian Society, 368
Falkland, Viscount (Lucius Cary), 6
Falklands War, 596
Fall, Albert, 541
Family, 206, 228–30, 278, 297–98,
    418, 424–26, 450–51, 454–55,
    471, 484
Farley, James A., 344
Farrakhan, Louis, 294–95
Fascism, xvi, 104, 106, 110–12,
    115–16, 118, 343, 361, 372,
    392, 468–70, 549
Federal Bureau of Investigation,
    178, 293
Federalism, 35–36, 159, 337, 412,
    416, 424–25
Federalist, The, 169, 257, 259, 267,
    272, 309
Femininity, 210
Feminism, 205–12
Feudalism, 77, 109–10, 407–8
Fichte, Johann Gottlieb, 342
Fields, Frederick Vanderbilt, 379
Fifth Amendment, 158, 191–93,
    381–82

Finland, 579
Firestone, Shulamith, 205–7
*Firing Line*, 12
First Amendment, 176, 186, 190, 200–201
*First Things*, 244
Fiscal responsibility, xvii
Fitzhugh, George, 388–89, 469
Florida, 84–85, 584
Flynn, John T.: *The Road Ahead*, 364–68
Follett, Mary, 166
Ford, Henry, 363, 443
Foreign policy, xiii, xviii–xix, 21, 35, 119, 174–75, 315, 328, 331–35, 364, 403–4, 470, 506–57, 574–84, 602–12
Fortescue, John, 153
*Forum, The*, 95
Foucault, Michel, 249
Foundation for Voluntary Welfare, 42
Founding Fathers, 37, 162, 253–54, 259
Fourteenth Amendment, 158, 304–8
Fox News, xii
France, 9, 345–46, 367, 513, 541, 553, 556, 560–61, 595; and American independence, 531; aristocracy in, 117, 214; communism in, 578; education in, 101; Enlightenment in, 157, 452; foreign policy in late 1930s, 226, 546, 548–49, 551; Henry Adams in, 51–55; imperialism of, 523, 544; and League of Nations, 520, 537; Liberal Party, 258; Louis Napoléon's *coup d'état*, 338; loyalty in, 330; in Napoleonic era, 7, 29, 150, 507–12; navy of, 538; religion in, 162; republican government of, 111; in World War I, 529

France, Anatole, 448; "The Gods Are Athirst," 113
Francis of Assisi, 73
Franco, Francisco, 549, 561
Frankfurter, Felix, 308
Franklin, Benjamin, 259, 271
Freedom, xiv, xvii, xix, 7, 9–10, 19, 25, 27, 32, 35, 37, 43, 63, 66, 80–81, 95, 101, 105, 117–18, 120, 133, 153, 156–57, 172–73, 189, 199, 204, 222, 244, 258–59, 267, 276, 283, 303–4, 344, 361, 386–87, 390, 407, 416, 420–21, 423, 426–27, 451–52, 455, 469, 501, 522, 527, 531, 564–70, 573–74, 576–77, 580, 583, 592–96, 599, 601; of assembly, 104, 158, 188; of association, 158, 188; and capitalism, 369–82; economic, 370–74, 414; of expression, 186, 198, 270, 308, 579; of individual initiative, 503; of inquiry, 270; intellectual, 434; from labor, 496; moral, 73; and morality, 156–57; natural, 269, 417; ordered liberty, 254–55, 257, 260, 268–69, 271, 424, 532; personal, 18, 31, 33–34, 36, 38–39, 111, 115, 281, 371, 374, 382, 385, 413–14, 421, 426, 600; political, 371–74, 377–78, 382; of the press, 104, 116, 154, 200–201, 203, 260, 273, 352–53, 414, 597; and progress, 117, 455; of religion, 158, 201–2, 253, 256, 270, 371, 473, 512–13, 575, 579; of speech, 104, 112, 116, 154–55, 158, 176, 182–84, 188, 190, 196–97, 200–201, 203, 327, 414, 579; of thought, 182–83, 186, 195, 198, 201–2; women's, 208
*Freeman*, 32
Freeman, Roger A., 43

Free markets, 26, 30, 36, 38, 270, 369, 372, 374, 376–78, 381–82, 416, 420, 424–25, 475, 478, 481, 593, 604

Free society, 196, 374, 388–89, 394–95, 469

French Revolution, 5–7, 29, 38, 54, 81, 107, 111, 113–14, 150, 152, 157, 256–58, 328, 361, 507, 512

Freud, Sigmund, 96, 217–21, 223–25, 282–84, 286, 290, 463, 469, 479

Friedman, Milton, 16, 394; "Capitalism and Freedom," 369–82

Friendly, Henry, 308

Frierson, William, 440

Fromm, Erich, 462

Frontier, 436, 439, 451, 538

Front Populaire, 226

Fuchs, Klaus, 125

Fugitive slaves, 192

Fukuyama, Francis, 474

Fuller, Margaret, 206–7

Fundamentalism, 253, 307, 470

Fusionism, 28

Gaines, Ernest J.: *A Gathering of Old Men*, 483–84

Galileo Galilei, 50

Gaza, 606

Geertz, Clifford, 482–83

Genocide, 605, 607

Genovese, Eugene: *Roll Jordan, Roll*, 468; *The Southern Tradition*, 468–80

Gentile, Giovanni: *Genesis and Structure of Society*, 470, 480

George, Henry, 20, 140

George III, 448, 591

Georgia, 604

Germany, 7, 76–77, 327, 337, 341, 365, 367, 407, 446, 556, 590–91; Bavarian Soviet Republic, 122; East, 594, 596; education in, 101, 223; foreign policy in late 1930s, 541–42, 546–50; loyalty in, 322, 330; in Napoleonic era, 508–9, 512; navy of, 538–39; Nazi, xiii, 104–10, 112, 117, 199, 342–44, 372, 534, 541–42, 546–50, 552–53, 568, 578, 611; philosophy in, 217, 219, 223, 226–27; post–World War I, 81, 122, 405, 611; post–World War II, 562, 594; Prussia, 330, 436, 508–9, 553; romanticism in, 281; West, 594, 598; in World War I, 528–29, 533; in World War II, 580

Gettysburg, battle of, 558

Gettysburg Address, 188, 192–93

Ghana, 166

Gibbon, Edward, 53–54

Gide, André, 218

Gladstone, William E., 591–92

*Glenn Show, The*, 291

Globalism, 426, 602

Glorious Revolution, 29

Goethe, Johann Wolfgang von, 97, 108, 110, 217; *Faust*, 130

Goetz, Bernhard, 295–96

Goldberg, Bruce, 27

Goldwater, Barry, xviii, 32, 40

Government, defined, 317

Gramsci, Antonio, 264

Grant, Ulysses S., 470, 495, 497–98

Great Depression, xiii, 75, 341, 367, 471, 552–53

Great Seal of the United States, 258

Greece, 561; ancient, 29, 92, 143, 146, 259, 356, 439, 464, 560, 565, 611

Green, Arnold W., 43

Gregory, Dick, 293

Grotius, Hugo, 161

Guam, 543

Guizot, François, 7

Gulf War I, 470

Gulf War II, xiii

Habeas corpus, writ of, 189–91
Haidar, Rustem, 516
Halton, Hugh, 23
Hamilton, Alexander, 82, 272–73, 528, 559
Hamowy, Ronald, 18–19
Hand, Learned, 308
Hannity, Sean, xii
Happiness, 82, 103, 219, 289–90, 451
Harlan, John Marshall, 307
Harlem Renaissance, 84
Harris, Benjamin, 57–59
Harte, Bret, 52
Hartz, Louis, 38; *The Liberal Tradition in America*, xiv
Harvard University, xiv–xv, 50, 62, 72, 128, 358
Hatch Act, 181
Hawaii, 498, 542
Hawthorne, Nathaniel, 458; *The Scarlet Letter*, 214
Hay, John, 538, 544
Hayek, Friedrich, 16, 373, 389–90, 394; *The Constitution of Liberty*, 25, 387–88
Hazlitt, Henry: "The Economics of Freedom," 19, 27
Hedjaz, 515–16, 519
Hegel, G. W. F., 227, 342–44
Heidegger, Martin, 249
Helfeld, David M.: "Loyalty amongst Government Employees," 183
Hemingway, Ernest, 361
Henry, Patrick, 118
Henry of Bracton, 152
Henry of Navarre, 559
Henry VI, 153
Herd behavior, 320–32, 336
Heterosexuality, 210, 219–32, 303, 305–8
Hiroshima, atomic bombing of, 84

Hiss, Alger, 119–22, 125, 132, 137, 171
Hitler, Adolf, 106, 109, 112, 117, 167, 199, 204, 206, 342–44, 346, 352, 542, 546–49, 552, 580–81, 611
Hittites, 566
Hobbes, Thomas, 419; *Leviathan*, 416–17, 422
Hofstadter, Richard: *Anti-Intellectualism in American Life*, xiv
Hohenstaufen dynasty, 559
Hohenzollern dynasty, 404
Hollywood, 354, 381–82
Hollywood Ten, 381–82
Holmes, Oliver Wendell, Jr., 60–61, 199–200, 203, 307–8
Holy Alliance, 508–11, 522
Homer, 71
Homosexuality, 210, 217, 228–32, 303–7, 472, 476
Hook, Sidney, 244–45
Hooker, Richard, 9, 396
Hoopes, Townsend, 405
Hoover, Herbert, 443, 544–45; *American Individualism*, 75–83
Hoover Institution, 233
Horace, 533
Horney, Karen, 462–63
House Committee on Un-American Activities, 119, 122, 178, 378
Housing, 228–29
Huber, Ernst, 405
Hughes, Charles Evans, 544–45
Hughes, H. Stuart, 8, 469
Hugo, Victor: *Les Misérables*, 258
Hukbalahaps, 561
Hull, Cordell, 540, 544–45, 548
Humanism, 31, 92–93, 96, 98–103, 107, 109, 284, 440
Humanitarianism, 34, 92–94, 98–99, 503–4, 607
Human rights, 142, 193, 221, 270
Humility, 92, 94, 96

Humphrey, Hubert, 393–94
Hungary, 511, 596
Hurston, Zora Neale, xviii; "How It Feels to Be Colored Me," 84–88
Hussein, King, 515–16
Hutus, 607
Huxley, Thomas Henry, 26
Hyde, Lewis, 481

Ibn Savond, 515
Iceland, 561
Idealism, 64, 66–68, 70–74, 77, 80–81, 99, 113–14, 116, 195, 207–8, 317–20, 327, 330–35, 342, 362, 384, 531–33, 585–87
Ignatieff, Michael, 607
Illinois, 495
*I'll Take My Stand*, 431
Imagination, 6, 66, 93, 101, 280–81, 286
Immigration, xvi, 516–19, 530, 543, 610
Imperfectability, 10–11
Imperialism, 102, 495–505, 537–44, 556, 565, 571, 584, 586, 589, 598, 603
Incas, 566
Income tax, 20, 140
India, 504, 537, 562, 565, 578, 596
Individualism, xvii, 28, 65, 94–95, 102–3, 143–47, 158, 278, 383, 438, 450–53, 456; anthropological, 416, 420–21; of artists, 279; Herbert Hoover's view of, 75–83; and Protestantism, 160, 458–59, 474; radical, 415; Rousseau on, 154–55; in southern tradition, 471, 474, 477; and suicide, 460; versus herd instinct, 320–21
Industrialism, 116, 324, 349, 436–37, 441–49, 455, 460–61, 468, 499, 540, 560, 567, 581, 587, 592
Industrial Workers of the World, 326

Information technology, 488–89
Inge, William R., 448
Ingersoll, Robert G., 248
Ingraham, Laura, xii
Innocent III, 559
Innovation, 7, 10
Inquiry, freedom of, 270
Integration, 477
Intellectual freedom, 434
Intellectuals, 28, 265, 280, 337; and the state, 397–414; traditions, xii–xviii
Internal Security Program, 178, 187
International Harvester Company, 561
*International Herald Tribune*, 602
Internationalism, 35, 474, 532
Interventionism, xiii, 84, 364, 403, 498–505, 513–14, 534, 537, 539, 544, 574, 602–7
Inuits, 487
Iowa, 444
Iran, 561, 605
Iraq, xiii, 603, 605–7
Ireland, 408
Islam, 328, 608
Islamists, 605
Isolationism, xiii, 403–4, 528, 540, 545, 557, 574–75, 585–86, 602, 608
Israel, 596, 603, 605–6, 612; ancient, 92
Italy, 6, 104–8, 110, 112, 264, 337–38, 342–44, 367, 372, 510, 513, 529, 542, 546–50, 552, 556, 559–61, 578

Jacks, L. P., 318
Jackson, Jesse, 293, 299
Jackson, Maynard, 293
Jackson, Robert H., 186, 308
Jackson, Wes, 481, 485–86
Jacksonville, Fla., 85
*Jacob Abrams v. United States*, 61, 199–200
Jacobin tradition, 7, 149–50, 476

Jacobs, Norman: *The Origins of Modern Capitalism and Eastern Asia*, 399–400

Jaffa, Harry V.: *Crisis of the House Divided*, 192; "On the Nature of Civil and Religious Liberty," 188–204

James, Henry, 361–62; *The Bostonians*, 359; *The Portrait of a Lady*, 207

James, William, 93, 99; *The Varieties of Religious Experience*, 246, 288–89

Japan, xiii, 365, 372, 513, 515–16, 518, 544–45, 547, 549, 552, 561

Jefferson, Thomas, 82, 189, 204, 259–60, 268, 273, 343, 352, 522, 528, 591; First Inaugural Address, 198; *Notes on Virginia*, 201–2; Second Inaugural Address, 202–3. *See also* Declaration of Independence

Jerusalem, 259, 356, 612

Jesus, xvi, 245, 248, 254, 266, 269, 280, 284, 459

Jews, 20, 107, 122, 140, 245, 248, 251, 261, 263, 265, 273, 294–95, 459, 512

Jim Crow laws, 301

John Birch Society, 19, 22

John Paul II, 258, 260, 267–71, 276–77, 479

Johnson, Samuel, 392

Jong, Eric: *Fear of Flying*, 215

Joubert, Joseph, 99

Journalism, 14, 57–61, 348, 351–53, 357–58, 360, 362

Joyce, James, 454

Joyce, Peggy Hopkins, 87

Judaism, 146–47, 248, 275

Judicial review, 409–10

Jung, Carl, 282–85, 287, 359, 459; *Modern Man in Search of a Soul*, 283

Justice, 7, 9, 36, 78–79, 81, 101, 154, 172, 215, 280, 358, 387, 389, 411, 451, 505, 511, 570, 587, 601

Kafka, Franz, 454; *The Castle*, 457; *The Trial*, 457

Kalyaev, Ivan, 124

Kamenev, Lev, 114

Kant, Immanuel, 215, 220, 227

Kaunitz, Wenzel Anton, 507

Kellogg, Frank B., 545

Kellogg-Briand Pact, 540, 544

Kelvin, Baron (William Thomson), 49

Kendall, Willmoore: *The Conservative Affirmation*, 163–87; *Democracy and the American Party System*, 165

Kennan, George F., 404, 602–3, 608

Kennedy, John F., 264, 405

Kennedy, Robert F., 264, 394

Kentucky, 481

Kentucky Resolutions, 200

Keynes, John Maynard, 403

Khmer Rouge, 605

Khrushchev, Nikita, 168

Kierkegaard, Søren, 358, 458–59

King, Coretta Scott, 299

King, Frank, 381

King, Martin Luther, Jr., 264, 299, 301–2; *Where Do We Go from Here*, 302

Kirk, Russell A., xviii, 20, 26, 426; "Conservatism Defined," 5–11

Knox, Philander C., 544

Koestler, Arthur, 360–61

Korean Americans, 261

Korean War, 403, 575–76

Kosovo, 606

Kossuth, Lajos, 511

Kristol, Irving, 265, 273–75; "When Virtue Loses All Her Loveliness: Some Reflections on Capitalism and Free Society," 383–96

Krock, Arthur, 164

Krüdener, Barbara von, 507

Krutch, Joseph Wood: *The Modern Temper*, 285–87, 289–90
Kuehnelt-Leddihn, Erik von, 25
Kuhn, Fritz, 170
Ku Klux Klan, 293

Labor camps (Gulag), 112, 125, 131, 593
Labor Party (United States), 561
Labour Party (Britain), 373–74
*Laissez faire*, 78, 143, 369, 373, 425, 471
Lamb, Charles: *Essays of Elia*, 506
Lamont, Corliss, 379
Land-grant universities, 481, 490–91
Langley, Samuel Pierpont, 47–51
Landon, Gustave, 91
Laos, 605
Lao Tzu, 407
Laplace, Pierre-Simon, 246, 252
Lasch, Christopher, xviii, 426; "The Soul of Man under Secularism," 278–90; *The True and Only Heaven*, 286
Latin America, 270, 408, 510–11, 513, 516, 522, 541–42, 552, 566, 595–96
Lattimore, Owen, 561
Latvia, 579
Lausanne, Stephane, 520–21
Law: common, 158, 200, 407; due process of, 158, 305, 309; equal protection of, 309; moral, 158, 161; of nations, 507; natural, 9, 151–53, 157, 159–62, 193, 419, 476; rule of, xvii, 36, 80, 153, 576, 599–600
Leadership, 10, 80–83, 107, 298–301, 392–94, 423, 559, 563, 567–70, 579–80, 600, 604
League of Nations, 506–33, 537, 576
Leahy, William D., 547
Lebanon, 596, 603
Lee, Robert E., 478
Legitimacy, 153, 386, 391, 409, 411, 416–17

Lend-Lease, 580
Lenin, V. I., 21, 125, 209, 559, 594, 598–99, 611
Leonard, Thomas C.: "Eugenics and Economics in the Progressive Era," xvi
Leopold I, 507
Leviné, Eugen, 122–23
Levy, Leonard W.: *Legacy of Suppression*, 200
Lewis, Sinclair: *It Can't Happen Here*, 115
Lewis, Wyndham, 457
Liberal capitalism, 384–85, 394–96
Liberal democracy, 254
Liberal education, 101–2
Liberalism, xi, xiii–xiv, 8, 13, 15, 40–43, 128, 143, 152, 264, 278, 334, 337, 361, 383, 393, 405, 509, 590; classical, 30–31, 34, 39, 369–70; defined, 5–7, 31; double standard for fascist and communist dictatorships, 111–12; and education, 348; and freedom of speech, 182–84; neo-, 370, 374; and personal freedom, 31, 33–34, 38–39, 374, 421, 426; and progress, 7; and rationalism, 30, 32–34, 38; and same-sex marriage, 228; and science, 420; seen as imprudent, 10; and Senator McCarthy, 167–68, 170; in the South, 434–35, 442–45, 447, 451, 471, 473–74; unsustainable, 415–27; and utilitarianism, 9, 38, 420; and welfare, 369–70
Liberal Party (Britain), 341
Liberal Party (Canada), 607
Liberal Party (France), 258
Liberal Party (United States), 561
Libertarianism, xvi, 26, 28, 37, 39, 140, 156, 198, 313, 337, 397, 400, 407–8, 411–13
Liberty. *See* Freedom

Life-style, 221–22
Liggio, Leonard P.: *Why the Futile
   Crusade?* 404
Limbaugh, Rush, xii
Limited government, xvii, 28, 31,
   35–36, 38, 43, 152, 155, 159,
   177, 257, 412, 452–53
Lincoln, Abraham, 5, 78, 150–51,
   154, 161, 204, 254, 259, 470,
   495, 497–98; Cooper Union
   speech, 203; debates with
   Stephen Douglas, 192–93;
   Gettysburg Address, 188,
   192–93; Message to Congress,
   189–91
Lippmann, Walter, 15, 555–56, 562;
   "Journalism and the Higher
   Law," 57–61; *A Preface to
   Morals*, 95, 97
Lithuania, 579
Locarno Conference, 549
Locke, John, 219–20, 252; *Letter
   Concerning Toleration*, 253;
   *Second Treatise on Government*,
   417–18
Lodge, Henry Cabot, 537, 539–40;
   Speech in Senate on League of
   Nations, 506–33
London, England, 125, 259, 590
London Conference, 545
Long, Huey, 338, 352
Long, John D., 500
Los Angeles, Calif., 229
Louisiana, 338, 477, 483
Loury, Glenn, xviii; "Leadership
   Failure and the Loyalty Trap,"
   291–302
Loyalists, 168, 180
Loyalty, racial, 291–302
Loyalty Order of 1947, 178
Lubyanka Prison, 131
Luckmann, Thomas, 250
Luddites, 488
Ludwig von Mises Institute, 397
Lundberg, Harry, 561
Luther, Martin, 459

Macedonians, 561
MacIntyre, Alasdair, 250–51, 426;
   *Three Rival Versions of Moral
   Enquiry*, 251
Madison, James, 257–59,
   267–68, 272; *Memorial and
   Remonstrance*, 253, 255
Madison, Wis., 229
Madrid, Spain, 546
Magna Carta, 153
Mahan, Alfred Thayer, 537, 539
Maistre, Joseph de, 7, 610
Majority rule, 35, 161, 197
Malaysia, 565, 595
Malinowski, Bronislaw, 462
Malone, Dumas: *Jefferson and the
   Ordeal of Liberty*, 201–2
Manchester School, 8
Manifest Destiny, 584, 608
Mann, Thomas, 225, 454; *Death in
   Venice*, 217–18, 221, 223–24;
   *Tonio Kröger*, 217
Mannheim, Karl, 465; "The
   Democratization of Culture,"
   281–82
Mao Zedong, xv, 561
Marcantonio, Vito, 561
Marconi, Guglielmo, 49
Marion County, Ind., 42
Maritain, Jacques, 459
Marlborough, Duke of (John
   Churchill), 82
Marriage, 228–32, 297–98, 303–9,
   417–18
Marshall, John, 308
Marshall Plan, 578, 580–81
Marx, Karl, 48, 125, 152, 206, 215–
   16, 219, 278, 281, 379, 420,
   450, 452, 594
Marxism, xvi, 15, 28, 109–10, 121,
   172, 202, 206, 208, 215, 225,
   251, 274, 278–79, 281, 404,
   468, 477, 594, 598–99, 611
Masculinity, 210, 495–505
Massachusetts, 307
Mass culture, 265

Masson, P. M., 96–97
Mass organizations, 107, 456–57, 461
Materialism, 70–72, 99, 103, 207, 259, 281, 347, 349, 354, 356–58, 361–63, 371, 396, 401–2, 434, 436–37, 465–66; dialectical, 15, 125, 134, 248
Mather, Cotton, 275
Matteotti, Giacomo, 106
Matthews, J. B., 165
Mayo, Elton, 461
McCarran Internal Security Act, 181
McCarthy, Joseph R., xv, 14, 163–71, 174–79, 181, 185–87, 300, 378, 382
McCarthy, Mary: *The Company She Keeps*, 207; *The Group*, 207
McConnell, Mitch, xii
McWhorter, John, 84
McWilliams, Wilson Carey, 426
Mead, Margaret, 462
Melville, Herman, 458
Mencken, H. L., 23, 248, 400
Metternich, Klemens von, 509–11
Mexican Americans, 438
Mexico, 315, 523, 561, 566
Meyer, Frank S.: "Freedom, Tradition, Conservatism," 39; "The Recrudescent American Conservatism," 28–44
Michelangelo Buonarroti, 136
Middle Ages, 6, 106, 158, 283, 287, 348–49, 406, 452, 499, 581
Middle class (bourgeoisie), 79, 89, 109–10, 217–18, 221–22, 230, 263–64, 269, 280–81, 285, 324–25, 352, 354, 358–60, 362–63, 385–86, 390, 392, 396, 463, 538, 609–10
Militarism, xiii, 76, 107, 145, 313–14, 318, 326, 329–30, 335–36, 364, 611
Mill, John Stuart, 7, 167, 198–99, 420; *On Liberty*, 198

Milton, John, 454; *Areopagitica*, 117–18
Minority rights, 197, 269, 318–19
Mises, Ludwig Von, 16
Missouri Compromise, 191
Mitchell, Juliet, 207
*Modern Age*, 32
Modernity/modernism, xi, 94–95, 262–63, 281, 285–88, 290, 348, 396, 450
Mohammed, 328, 559
Molière (Jean-Baptiste Poquelin), 108
Mommsen, Theodor, 538
Mondale, Walter, 299
Money, 71, 376, 380, 545
Mongols, 566
Monroe, James, 522–23, 528, 551
Monroe Doctrine, 510, 519–24, 582
Montaigne, Michel de, 56
Mooney, Tom, 112
Moral anarchy, 288
Moral choice, 180, 215, 563
Moral ecology, 268, 271
Moral freedom, 73
Moralism, 221–23, 267
Morality, xiv, xvi, 9, 32, 101, 124, 128, 159, 197–98, 208, 218, 254–55, 263, 270, 284, 349, 374, 402, 453, 455, 458, 460, 465, 495, 505, 533, 586–88, 610; in American experience, 64–65, 67, 69–73, 154, 188, 193, 253, 260–61, 474–75, 477–78; and artists, 280; conventional, 280, 451; and democracy, 33, 268; and freedom, 156–57; in international relations, 514, 526, 579–80, 611; liberal double standard about dictatorships, 111–12; political, 362; and race, 295–96; and Rousseau, 89–90, 95, 98; universal law of, 156, 161; and war, 314, 335

Moral leadership, 80, 579–80
Moral nihilism, 287
Moral order, 9, 28, 33, 36, 38–39, 196, 268, 579
Moral progress, 419, 456
Moral relativism, 265, 286, 288, 292, 298
More, Paul Elmer, 388
Morocco, 539
Morris, William, 451
Moscow, Russia, 109, 125, 130, 507, 591
Motion pictures, 354–55, 363, 381–82
Mount Pelerin Society, 26
Moyers, Bill, 297
*Ms.*, 207–8
Murray, Gilbert, 464
Murray, John Courtney: "E Pluribus Unum: The American Consensus," 148–62; *We Hold These Truths*, 185–87
Muskie, Edmund, 393–94
Muslims, 251, 294–95, 328, 504, 581, 605, 608–9
Mussolini, Benito, 106, 112, 338, 342–44, 542, 546–49, 552

Naples, Italy, 510
Napoléon Bonaparte, 7, 29, 150, 246, 507, 560, 610
Napoléon III, 338, 523
Nasser, Gamal Abdel, 31
Nation, defined, 317, 335–36
*Nation, The*, 561
National Association for the Advancement of Colored People, 301
*National Interest, The*, 383
Nationalism, 31, 106, 172, 325, 401, 476, 495, 570, 604
Nationalization, 81
National Recovery Act, 340–41
*National Review*, xv, 12–24, 26, 28, 32, 163, 558
National Security Council, 405

Native Americans. *See* American Indians
Natural freedom, 269, 417
Naturalism, 220–21
Natural law, 9, 151–53, 157, 159–62, 193, 419, 476
Natural rights, 144, 146, 151, 158, 177, 194, 201, 416–17
Nature, xvii, 416, 435–37, 442, 444
Navy, U.S., 353, 499–502, 538–39, 543, 547–48, 553
Nazis, xiii, 31, 104, 106–7, 110, 112, 170, 196–98, 225, 372, 478, 480, 534, 568
Nebraska, 444
Needham, Joseph, 404
Nelson, Horatio, 82
Neoconservatism, xviii, 383, 558
Neoliberalism, 370, 374
Netherlands, 111, 556
Neuhaus, Richard John: "Can Atheists Be Good Citizens?" 244–55
Neustadt, Richard, 405
Neutrality, 332, 521–22, 546, 575, 585–86
Neutrality Act, 548–49
Newark, N.J., 297–98
New Deal, xiii, 31, 84, 364, 411–12, 541, 580
New Humanism, 89
*New Individualism Review*, 27
New Journalism, 205
New Left, xv
Newman, John Henry, 396
*New Masses*, 119
*New Republic*, 57
New Right, 230
New Thought, 73
Newton, Isaac, 352
New York, 561
New York City, 87, 125, 137, 140, 228–29, 294–96, 323, 338, 345, 392
*New York* magazine, 211
*New York Review of Books*, 482

*New York Times*, 216, 228, 296
*New York World*, 59
New Zealand, 519
Nicholas I, 109, 511
Niebuhr, H. Richard, 248
Niebuhr, Reinhold, xviii, 454, 459;
    *The Irony of American History*,
    584–89
Nietzsche, Friedrich, 215, 217–20,
    227, 246–47, 249, 251–52, 323,
    358
Nigeria, 596
Nihilism, 226, 287, 394, 476
Nisbet, Robert A., 425–26; "The Loss
    of Community," 450–67
Nixon, Richard M., 298, 405, 605
Nkrumah, Kwame, 31
NKVD, 562, 572
Nock, Albert Jay, xvii; *Our Enemy,
    The State*, 337–46
Nongovernmental organizations,
    607
Nordlinger, Eric A., 602
Normans, 408
North Atlantic Treaty Organization,
    590, 595, 599, 606
Northcliffe, Viscount (Alfred
    Harmsworth), 59
Nostalgia, 286–87, 434–35
Novak, Michael: *The Catholic Ethic
    and the Spirit of Capitalism*,
    256–77; "The Secular Saint,"
    264; "A Theology for Radical
    Politics," 264
Nuclear weapons, 43, 126, 469, 479,
    563–64, 567, 569, 581, 587,
    590, 593, 599, 611

Obama, Barack, 605, 609
*Obergefell v. Hodges*, 303–9
Objectivism, 15–17
Ochs, Adolph, 59
O'Connor, Flannery, 290
Oedipus, 214
Office of Strategic Services, 558
Ohio, 371

Olmert, Ehud, 612
Olney, Richard, 523–24
Open Door Policy, 543–44
Oppenheimer, Franz, 402, 413
Opportunity, equality of, 78, 81–82,
    235
Optimism, 64–65, 69–70
Order, 9, 27–28, 33, 35–36, 38–39,
    196, 268, 452, 455, 579
Ordered liberty, 254–55, 257, 260,
    268–69, 271, 424, 532
Oregon, 584
O'Reilly, Jane, 209
Original intent, 188, 303
Ortega y Gasset, José, 456
Ostrogorsky, Moisey, 452
Ottoman Empire, 566
Owsley, Frank L., 471–72

Paderewski, Ignacy, 512
Page, Walter Hines: *The
    Autobiography of Nicholas
    Worth*, 359
Pahlavi, Reza, 605
Paine, Thomas, 152
Pakistan, 603, 605–6
Paleoconservatism, 347
Palestine/Palestinians, 603, 605–6,
    612
Panama, 513, 525
Panama Canal, 499
*Panay* incident, 544
Papacy, 559
Paris, France, 47–48, 53, 125, 259,
    590, 602
Parker, Theodore, 388–89
Parliament (British), 168, 408–9,
    510, 590–601
Parrington, Vernon L., 451
Parthenon, 219
Parthia, 566
Participation, 392–94
Pascal, Blaise, 56, 214, 247
Patriotism, 35, 59, 313, 315, 322,
    326, 330, 333, 336, 401
Paul (apostle), 91

Payne, Roger: *Among Whales*, 487
Peace, 76, 142, 324, 326–27,
    332, 442, 469, 479, 506,
    509, 511, 523–28, 531, 533,
    537, 544, 548, 550–51, 554,
    575–76, 578, 581–84, 586,
    599, 601
Peacock, Thomas Love: *Nightmare Abbey*, 466
Pearl Harbor, attack on, xiii, 140,
    534, 579, 581
Peck, Ellen, 211
Peek, George N., 545
Péguy, Charles, 358
Pennsylvania, 371
Performance, 391–92
Pericles, 559
Persia, ancient, 560
Personal freedom, 18, 31, 33–34,
    36, 38–39, 111, 115, 281, 371,
    374, 382, 385, 413–14, 421,
    426, 600
Peru, 8, 521
Petition, right of, 189
Pfaff, William: *The Irony of Manifest Destiny*, 602–12
Philadelphia, Pa., 276
Philippines, 498–504, 528, 537, 539,
    542–43, 560–61
Philistinism, 280–81, 285, 357, 386
Phillips, William Alison, 510–11
Pitt, William (the Younger), 559
Pius XII, 549
Plato, 6, 10, 29, 101, 345,
    349–50, 362, 396; *Epistles*,
    350; *Phaedrus*, 223–24, 350;
    *Protagoras*, 25, 351; *Republic*,
    359–60
Platt Amendment, 541
Plehve, Vyacheslav von, 123
Pluralism, 148–50, 157, 235
Plutarch, 339
Pogrebin, Letty Cottin, 207
Point Four program, 580
Poland, 21, 122, 276, 512, 561,
    591–93, 596–97

Polanyi, Michael: *Personal Knowledge*, 175
Political economy, 258, 260, 267
Political freedom, 371–74, 377–78,
    382
Political opponents, treatment of,
    104–5, 114–15, 118, 131, 611
Political power, 372, 377–78
Political rights, 156
Pollution, 384
Pope, Arthur Upham, 561
Popular culture, 261, 263
Populism, 393, 479, 538–39
*Portable Conservative Reader*, 5
Positive programs, 42–43
Positivism, 38
Postmodernism, 281
Poverty, 172, 257–58, 270, 279, 296,
    299, 339–40, 384, 441, 572, 578
Powell, Adam Clayton, 295
Power, state, 337–46
Preferential treatment, 233–43
Prescription, 9–10
Press, freedom of, 104, 116, 154,
    200–201, 203, 260, 273, 352–
    53, 414, 597
Progress, 56, 76, 78, 83, 127,
    262, 286–87, 355, 357,
    384, 435–36, 438, 450,
    465; by African Americans,
    292; costs of, 451; defined,
    33, 437; democratic, 598;
    economic, 82; and freedom,
    117, 455; and idealism, 80;
    and individualism, 79, 321;
    industrial, 443; intellectual,
    82, 432; material, 7, 396;
    moral, 419, 456; scientific, 199,
    279, 290; social, 82; and state
    power, 343; technological, 47,
    279, 349; and war, 335
Progressive Party, 342
Progressivism, 57, 78, 268, 313, 340,
    419, 432, 434–35, 442–45, 447,
    451, 611. *See also* Liberalism
Prohibition, xvi, 102

Propaganda, 108–9, 128, 203, 251,
    353, 360, 379, 537–40, 556–57,
    571, 598
Property rights, 9–10, 36, 78, 110,
    142, 270, 279, 373, 413–14,
    474–75, 477
Protectionism, 475
Protestants, 102, 160–61, 165–66,
    248, 266, 284, 389–91, 438,
    458–60
Proust, Marcel, 454
Prudence, 10–11, 385
Prussia, 330, 436, 508–9, 553
Psychoanalysis, 96, 82, 284, 462–63
Public Interest, The, 383
Puerto Rico, 498, 503
Puritans, 51, 253, 389
Pushkin, Alexander: "Message to
    Siberia," 108–9
Pyatakov, Georgy, 114

Quakers, 135
Quarterly Review, 7

Racial issues, xvi, 84–88, 104, 172,
    197, 233–43, 291–302, 384,
    477, 479
Racism, 233, 292–96, 298, 300–301,
    473, 608
Radek, Karl, 114
Radicalism, xviii, 7, 9–10, 64, 111–
    12, 378, 383–84, 390, 451, 476,
    479, 558, 604, 608
Radio, 355–56, 363, 565
Rand, Ayn, 15–17, 20; Atlas
    Shrugged, 16; For the New
    Intellectual, 27
Rangel, Charles, 294–95
Ranney, Austin: Democracy and the
    American Party System, 165
Ransom, John Crowe:
    "Reconstructed but
    Unregenerate," 431–49
Raskin, Marcus: "The Megadeath
    Intellectuals," 405–6

Rationalism, 30, 32–34, 38, 90, 100,
    107, 127, 129, 154, 158, 226,
    251–52, 281, 286, 387, 450–53,
    455, 458, 461–62, 464, 587
Ratzinger, Joseph, 256, 260
Rawls, John: A Theory of Justice, 215
Reactionary, 8, 113, 117, 551, 561
Reagan, Ronald, 265, 293, 303;
    Address to Members of
    Parliament, 590–601
Realism, 67, 195, 352, 434, 549,
    602; Christian, 584–89
Reciprocal Trade Act, 545
Reconstruction, 86, 110, 359
Red Cross, 322
Reed, Adolph: The Jesse Jackson
    Phenomenon, 299
Reed, John Shelton, 471
Reformation, 106
Reform Bill (Britain), 591
Reforms, 7, 10–11, 67, 373, 396
Relativism, 225, 249–50, 252, 265,
    286, 288, 292, 298
Relief funds, 338–40
Religion, freedom of, 158, 201–2,
    253, 256, 270, 371, 473, 512–
    13, 575, 579
Religious issues, 23–26, 69, 80,
    260, 280, 348; in America,
    72–73, 148–50; atheism and
    citizenship, 244–55; and Carl
    Jung, 282–85, 287; Catholicism
    and pluralism, 148–51, 157,
    160–62; in China, 399–400;
    communism and God, 126–27,
    130, 132–34; John Paul II's
    challenge to America, 258,
    260, 267–71, 276–77; Jonathan
    Edwards's view of God,
    289–90; Protestantism and
    individualism, 458–59; and
    Rousseau, 89, 91–99, 101–2;
    southern evangelicalism, 470;
    spread of Islam, 328. See also
    individual religions

Renaissance, 97, 106, 419, 456, 482
Republicanism, 111, 154, 198, 254,
    256, 268, 314, 333, 337, 341,
    346, 369–70, 389, 394, 477
Republican Party, xii, 32, 300, 342,
    506, 524, 540, 561, 574, 590,
    598, 609
Revivalism, 73
Revolution, 9, 29–31, 67–68, 75, 91,
    109–10, 113–14, 117, 127, 173,
    205, 207, 251, 367, 416, 418,
    440, 512, 606
Revolutionary War, 6, 111, 152,
    159, 168, 180, 193, 256–57,
    276, 304, 531, 552, 557, 574,
    610
Revolutions of 1848, 7, 511
Richardson, Elliot, 298
Rights: civil, xvi, 84, 155–56, 158,
    188–89, 191, 195–96, 199,
    241, 299–302, 369–70; human,
    142, 193, 221, 270; minority,
    197, 269, 318–19; natural,
    144, 146, 151, 158, 177, 194,
    201, 416–17; political, 156;
    property, 9–10, 36, 78, 110,
    142, 270, 279, 373, 413–14,
    474–75, 477
Rippy, J. Fred, 542
Robespierre, Maximilien, 113
Rolland, Romain, 478
Romanticism, 280–81, 385
Rome, ancient, 105, 117, 141–42,
    259, 338–39, 356, 407, 427,
    438, 555–57, 565–66
Rome, Italy, 125, 590
Roosevelt, Franklin D., 31, 82, 84,
    216, 338–39, 344, 541–50, 579,
    581–82, 590
Roosevelt, Theodore, 524, 535, 537,
    539–41, 543; "The Strenuous
    Life," 495–505
Rorty, Richard, 249–51, 420
Rossiter, Clinton, 15; *Parties and
    Politics in America*, 165; *Seedtime*

*of the Republic*, 151–52, 155,
    159
Rothbard, Murray, xviii, 18–19; *For
    a New Liberty*, 397–414; *Man,
    Economy, and State*, 19
Rougemont, Denis de, 610
Rousseau, Jean-Jacques, 6–7, 89–93,
    95–102, 154, 220, 227, 252,
    420; "Discourse on Inequality,"
    90
Rovere, Richard: *McCarthy*, 164
Rowan, Carl, 297–98
Rule of law, xvii, 36, 80, 153, 576,
    599–600
Rural communities, 481–92
Ruskin, John, 54, 441, 451
Russia (czarist), 108–9, 117, 123,
    141, 328, 372, 507–12
Russia (post–Soviet Union), 270
Russian Revolution, 113–14, 122–
    24, 128, 343
Rwanda, 607
Rykov, Alexei, 114

Sacco, Nicolà, 112
Saddam Hussein, 606
Saint-Exupéry, Antoine de, 361
Saint-Gaudens, Augustus, 53–55
St. Petersburg, Russia, 510
Saint-Pierre, abbé de, 506
Saint-Simon, comte de (Claude-
    Henri de Rouvroy), 345
Salamis, battle of, 558
Same-sex marriage, 228–32, 303–9
Sandburg, Carl, 161
San Francisco, Calif., 229, 296
San Quentin Prison, 112
Santayana, George, 10, 15, 160,
    358; *The Last Puritan*, 62;
    "Materialism and Idealism in
    American Life," 62–74
Sauer, Carl, 487
Savonarola, Girolamo, 15
Saxons, 408
Sazonov, Yegor, 123

Scalia, Antonin: Dissent in *Obergefell v. Hodges*, 303–9
Schiller, Friedrich von, 281
Schlesinger, Arthur M., Jr.: *The Vital Center*, xiv
Schmitt, Carl, 479–80
Schumpeter, Joseph, 260
Science, 49, 97, 118, 161, 175, 199, 219, 262, 279, 287, 290, 419–20, 440, 487, 492, 587
Scientism, 38, 479
Scotland, 447
Sectarianism, 21
Secularism, 150, 278–90, 450, 456, 586, 605
Security, national, 21, 43, 172, 174, 176–79, 398, 402–6, 553, 557, 581–82, 603
Security Council, U.N., 561–62, 606
Sedition, 200, 203
Segregation, xvi, 84, 299
Self-expression, 82
Self-interest, 80–81, 195
Self-trust, 65, 69
Senate Committee on Foreign Relations, 506
Senate Committee on Government Operations, 171, 177
Senate Committee on Internal Security, 178
September 11 terrorist attacks, 602
Serbia/Serbs, 606
Sermon on the Mount, 319
Service, civic, 80–81, 93–94, 436–38
*Sewanee Review*, 440
Sexism, 207
Sexuality, 210–11, 217–21, 223–24, 230, 284, 303, 321, 415, 422, 425
Shaftesbury, Earl of (Anthony Ashley-Cooper), 94
Shakespeare, William, 274; *Hamlet*, 26; *Henry IV*, 534; *King Lear*, 109; *Macbeth*, 136; *Richard III*, 458; *The Tempest*, 109

Shanghai, China, 544
Shangtung Province, China, 515
Sherman, William T., 446, 470, 575
Shlafly, Phyllis, xviii
Shostakovich, Dmitri: *Lady Macbeth of Mtsensk*, 109
Shulman, Alix Kates, 208–9
Siberia, 108, 112, 123, 561
Silone, Ignazio, 361
Simmel, Georg, 467
Simons, Henry, 373
Sinclair, Upton, 23
Singapore, 543
Slavery, 64, 86, 168–69, 189, 191–93, 196, 203, 292, 300, 388, 424, 440, 446, 468–69, 497, 565–66
Smiles, Samuel, 389
Smirnov, A. A.: *Shakespeare: A Marxist Interpretation*, 109–10
Smirnov, Vladimir, 114
Smith, Adam, 385; *Theory of Moral Sentiments*, 386
Smith, Gerald L. K., 20, 22, 170
Smith, J. Allen, 411
Smith Act, 181
Social continuity, 9
Social contract, 253–54, 407
Socialism, xvi, 6, 8, 31, 65, 76, 79, 81, 108, 111, 128, 150, 263–64, 269, 278–81, 326–27, 367–68, 370, 378–81, 390, 395, 474, 573, 580, 584
Socialist Party, 342
Social legislation, 340
Social Security, 18, 43
Socrates, 25, 101, 169, 215–16, 245, 349–50, 358
Sokolnikov, Grigory, 114
Solidarity movement, 592–93
Somalia, 605
Sophists, 29, 101
Sorokin, Pitirim, 454
South, xiv, xvi, 110, 169, 191, 347, 359, 388, 431–33, 438–49, 468–80

South Africa, 270, 295, 462
South Carolina, 469
South Korea, 261
South Sea Bubble, 560
Soviet Union, 76, 81, 119, 130, 220, 337, 352, 371, 594, 598; and American communists, xiv; during Cold War, 22, 124, 365–67, 470, 560–63, 571–73, 578–82, 592–93, 595, 599; as communist dictatorship, 104–10, 112–18, 125, 172–73, 188, 197–99, 372, 566–69, 572–73, 597, 599; containment of, 18; labor camps in, 112, 125, 131, 593; in 1930s, 104–17, 549, 551, 556; and nuclear weapons, 43, 563, 581, 593, 599; U.S. recognition of, 545; in World War II, 579–80
Soviet Writers' Union, 108
Sowell, Thomas, 299–300
Spain, 8, 110–11, 372, 408, 510, 546–49, 552, 556, 561
Spanish-American War, 498–505, 528, 537
Sparta, ancient, 611
Spartacus, 595
Specialization, 375–76
Speech, freedom of, 104, 112, 116, 154–55, 158, 176, 182–84, 188, 190, 196–97, 200–201, 203, 327, 414, 579
Spencer, Herbert, 52, 391, 452
Spengler, Oswald, 102, 358, 438, 454
Spies, 17, 119–20, 137
Spinoza, Baruch, 97
Spiritualism, 73
Sri Lanka (Ceylon), 565
Staël, Anne-Louise-Germaine de, 89
Stalin, Joseph, 109, 112, 114, 168, 199, 204, 207, 579
Standard of living, 36, 111, 115, 577–78, 580
Stanford University, 238

State: defined, 316–17, 335–36; and intellectuals, 397–414; and power, 34, 38, 41–42, 337–46; and war, 313–36
State Department, U.S., 177–78, 540, 545, 549–50
Statism, 17–19, 34, 146–47, 352, 425
Statue of Liberty, 258
Steele, Shelby, xviii; "Affirmative Action: The Price of Preference," 233–43
Stewardship of nature, xvii
Stimson, Henry L., 544–45
Stoics, 97
Stonewall uprising, 230
Story, Joseph, 308
Strachey, John, 104; *The Nature of the Capitalist Crisis*, 112–13
Strasbourg, France, 599
Strategic Arms Reduction Talks, 593
Strenuous life, 495–505
Stuart dynasty, 29
Student loans, 42
Subsidies, 340–42
Suicide, 460
Sukarno, 31
Sulla, Lucius Cornelius, 117
Sullivan, Andrew, xviii; "Here Comes the Groom," 228–32
Sullivan, Harry Stack, 462–63
Sumer, 407–8
Supreme Court, U.S., 61, 151, 179, 191–92, 241, 303–9, 340, 343, 411–12, 599. *See also specific decisions*
Sweden, 561
Switzerland, 111
Syndicalism, 76, 79
Syria, 537

Tacitus, 352
Taft, Robert A., 84, 403; *A Foreign Policy for Americans*, 574–83
Taft, William Howard, 308
Taine, Hippolyte, 114, 451

Taiwan, xvi

Talk radio, xii

Tammany Hall, 81

Taney, Roger B., 191–92

Taxation, 20, 140, 352, 371, 407

Taylor, Jeremy, 6

Teapot Dome scandal, 560

Technocracy, 15, 264, 391

Technology, 47–49, 52–53, 127, 262, 279, 348–49, 360, 363, 391, 396, 415, 465, 470, 482, 492, 562–63, 587

Television, 355

Tennyson, Alfred, 345

Tenth Amendment, 200–201

Terre Haute, Ind., 112

Terrorism, 113–14, 131, 326–27, 338, 596, 602–3

Tertullian, 247

Texas, 584

Thailand (Siam), 519

Thatcher, Margaret, 591

Theism, 33, 250–51

Thermopylae, battle of, 595

Third Plenary Council, 151

Third World, 475

Thirteenth Amendment, 192

Thomson, James: *The City of Dreadful Night*, 466

Thought, freedom of, 182–83, 186, 195, 198, 201–2

Thrace, 566

Thucydides, 352, 611

Thurnwald, Richard, 462

Tillich, Paul, 458

Tillman, Ben, 479

*Time*, 119, 205, 381

Tito (Josip Broz), 129

Tocqueville, Alexis de, 7, 214, 222, 257–59, 268, 272, 275, 345, 385–86, 422–23

Tokyo, Japan, 125

Tolstoy, Leo, 108; *Anna Karenina*, 214–15; "The Death of Ivan Ilyich," 458

Totalitarianism, *See* Dictatorship

Toynbee, Arnold, 29, 456, 465, 568; *A Study of History*, 454, 466

Tradition, xi, xvii, 7, 9–11, 27, 29–33, 37–39, 94–95, 98, 347, 398–99, 451, 458, 462, 473, 475

Trafalgar, battle of, 538

Transcendentalism, 206

Treaties, 506–12, 514, 516–17, 524–25, 544, 604

Treaty of Chaumont, 508

Treaty of Paris, 508–12

Treaty of Tilsit, 507

Treaty of Utrecht, 506

Treaty of Versailles, 110, 533, 540, 555, 557

Treviranus, Gottfried, 106

Tribalism, 407, 461–62, 476

Trieste, Italy, 560–61

Trilling, Lionel, 257, 261–63; *Beyond Culture*, 274; *The Liberal Imagination*, xiv

Trollope, Frances, 345

Trotsky, Leon, 129, 558

Truman, Harry, 178, 582

Trumbo, Dalton, 381; *Johnny Got His Gun*, 381

Trump, Donald, xii

Truth, 59–61, 151, 155, 157, 185–86, 196, 249, 252, 269, 350–52, 358–60, 451

Turks, 566

Turner, James: *Without God, Without Creed*, 247

Tutsis, 607

Twain, Mark (Samuel Clemens): *Adventures of Huckleberry Finn*, 451


Ukraine, 105

Unemployment, 42, 297, 365

Unions, 116

United Nations, 35, 561–62, 576, 581, 596–97, 606–7

United Student Aid Funds, 42

Universal Declaration of Human Rights, 597
University of Berlin, 404
University of Chicago, 213, 347
University of Notre Dame, 415
Urbanism, 461, 487
Urban renewal, 43
Utilitarianism, 7–9, 38, 89, 92–94, 102–3, 409, 420, 422
Utopianism, xvii, 11, 28, 30, 33–34, 114, 116, 127, 279, 412, 435, 449, 470

*Vanishing Black Family, The*, 297–98
Vanzetti, Bartolomeo, 112
Vattel, Emer de, 479
Venice, Italy, 217
Venus, 51–52, 55
Versailles economic summit, 590
Veterans of Foreign Wars, 609
Viereck, Peter, 15
Vietnam, 595
Vietnam War, xiii, xv, 264, 299, 403–4, 468, 604, 608–10
Villard, Oswald Garrison, 362
Virginia Assembly, 258
Virginia Statute for Religious Freedom, 201
Virgin Mary, 51–52, 54–56
Voegelin, Eric: "On Readiness to Rational Discussion," 24–25, 27
*Völkischer Beobachter*, 107–8
Voltaire (François-Marie Arouet), 118, 507
Voluntarism, 416, 418, 420

Wahabis, 515–16
Wallace, Henry, 561
*Wall Street Journal*, 380
War, 111, 114, 145, 313–36, 404, 436–37, 469–70, 479, 507, 511, 526, 529, 546, 549–50, 574–78, 580–83, 587–88, 593–94, 607
Warsaw, Poland, 122, 591, 595
Washington, Booker T., 84

Washington, D.C., 82, 132, 137, 261, 323, 337–39, 353, 440, 443, 448, 500, 541, 543, 591, 599, 605–6
Washington, George, 82, 189, 521–22, 528, 535, 552–53, 575
*Washington Post*, 170, 294
Watson, Thomas E., 479
Wealth, 115–17, 378–79, 464
Weaver, Richard, xvii, 13, 33, 475, 479; "The Great Stereopticon," 347–63; "The South and the Revolution of Nihilism," 468–69
Weber, Max, xi, 221, 281–83; *The Protestant Ethic and the Spirit of Capitalism*, 282
Websites, right-wing, xii
Webster, Daniel, 7
Weeden, Robert B., 487
Welch, Joseph Nye, 169
Welch, Robert, 19–23
Welfare, 369–70, 575, 577–78
Welfare state, 36, 364
Wells, H. G., 435
West Bank, 612
Western civilization, 28–31, 33, 35–37, 40–41, 92, 104–18, 120, 140–47, 264, 286, 315–16, 366, 383–84, 396, 406, 435, 439, 455, 459–61, 522, 527, 531–32, 560, 562–63, 591, 594, 611
West Germany, 594, 598
West Indies, 503, 540–41, 596
Whately, Richard, 59
Wheeling, W.Va., 171, 174
Whitehead, Alfred North, 245
Whitman, Walt, 52
Wilberforce, Samuel, 248
Wilde, Oscar, 281–82, 284, 290, 384; *De Profundis*, 280; *The Soul of Man under Socialism*, 278–80
Wilhelm II, 539
Williams, G. Mennen, 382

Williams, N. P.: "The Ideas of the Fall and Original Sin," 96
Williams, Wayne, 293
Wilson, James Q., 264
Wilson, William Julius: *The Declining Significance of Race*, 299–300
Wilson, Woodrow, 57, 334–35, 506, 520, 538–40, 545, 585
Wittfogel, Karl, 404
Wollstonecraft, Mary, 206
Women's movement, 205–12
Woodward, Bob, 612
Working class (proletariat), 79, 113, 125, 128, 197, 206, 264, 285, 298, 323–24, 326, 390, 538, 609–10
World Court, 545
World Federation of Trade Unions, 561–62
World's Columbian Exposition, 48
World War I, xvi, 57–60, 75–76, 89, 94, 123, 313, 326–27, 332–34, 360, 364, 368, 372, 527–30, 533, 555, 557, 575, 585, 610–11

World War II, xiii–xv, 21, 84, 123–24, 140, 353, 355–56, 364–65, 367–68, 371–73, 483, 534, 557–58, 574–75, 578–81, 586–87, 595–96, 600–601, 610–11
Wright, Ernest Hunter, 90

Yale University, 163
Yan'an, China, 561
Yeats, William Butler, 361; "The Second Coming," 11
Yemen, 605
Yevdokimov, Yefim, 114
Young, Andrew, 299
Young America, 469
Yugoslavia, 21, 518, 560–61, 606
Yupiks, 487

Zen, 250
Zeno, 56
Zhou Enlai, 560
Zhuke, Ukraine, 105
Zinoviev, Grigory, 114

This book is set in 9½ point ITC Stone Serif, designed in 1987 by graphic artist Sumner Stone during his tenure as the director of typography at Adobe Systems. Working with Bob Ishi, Stone developed the ambitious idea of creating an integrated family incorporating different styles in two versions of serif type and two versions of san serif. Coincidentally, *ishi* is a Japanese word for *stone*, which—according to the wording of the release notes—"precluded any squabbling about whose name the font would carry."

The chapter titles and author names are set in Geller Headline, created in 2018 by Ludka Biniek as part of a graduation project at the Academy of Fine Arts in Warsaw, Poland. The san serif display type is Komu, designed in 2010 by Ján Filípek, director of DizajnDesign, a foundry in Bratislava, Slovakia.

The paper is an acid-free Forest Stewardship Council–certified stock that exceeds the requirements for permanence of the American National Standards Institute. The binding material is Arrestox, a cotton-based cloth with an aqueous acrylic coating manufactured by Holliston, Church Hill, Tennessee. Page design and composition by Publishers' Design and Production Services, Sagamore Beach, Massachusetts. Printing and binding by LSC Communications, Crawfordsville, Indiana.